P9-AOK-251

FOREIGN AND COMMONWEALTH OFFICE

DOCUMENTS ON
BRITISH POLICY OVERSEAS

EDITED BY

P. SALMON, PhD,

K.A. HAMILTON, PhD

AND

S.R. TWIGGE, PhD

SERIES III

Volume VII

Routledge
Taylor & Francis Group

LONDON AND NEW YORK

WHITEHALL HISTORIES: FOREIGN AND COMMONWEALTH OFFICE PUBLICATIONS
Series Editors: Keith Hamilton and Patrick Salmon
ISSN: 1471-2083

FCO historians are responsible for editing *Documents on British Policy Overseas (DBPO)* and for overseeing the publication of FCO Internal Histories.

DBPO comprises three series of diplomatic documents, focusing on major themes in foreign policy since 1945, and drawn principally from the records of the Foreign and Commonwealth Office. The latest volumes, published in Series III, are composed almost wholly of documents from within the thirty-year 'closed period', which would otherwise be unavailable to the public.

Since the early 1960s, several Internal Histories have been prepared by former or serving officers, the majority of which concentrated upon international developments and negotiations in which the UK has been directly involved. These were initially intended for use within the FCO, but some of the more substantial among them, studies that offer fresh insights into British diplomacy, are now being declassified for publication.

Published DBPO volumes:

SERIES I: 1945-1950

Volume I: The Conference at Postdam, July-August 1945
    0 11 591682 2
Volume II: Conferences and Conversations, 1945: London, Washington and Moscow
    0 11 591683 0
Volume III: Britain and America: Negotiation of the US Loan, 3 August-7 December 1945
    0 11 591684 9
Volume IV: Britain and America: Atomic Energy, Bases and Food, 12 December 1945-31 July 1946
    0 11 591685 7
Volume V: Germany and Western Europe, 11 August-31 December 1945
    0 11 591686 5
Volume VI: Eastern Europe, August 1945-April 1946
    0 11 591687 3
Volume VII: The UN, Iran and the Cold War, 1946-1947
    0 11 591689 X
Volume VIII: Britain and China, 1945-1950

SERIES II: 1950-1960

Volume I: The Schuman Plan, the Council of Europe and Western European Integration, May 1950-December 1952
    0 11 591692 X
Volume II: The London Conference: Anglo-American Relations and Cold War Strategy, January-June 1950
    0 11 591693 8
Volume III: German Rearmament, September-December 1950
    0 11 591694 6
Volume IV: Korea, June 1950-April 1951
    0 11 591695 4

SERIES III: 1960-

Volume I: Britain and the Soviet Union, 1968-1972
    0 11 591696 2
Volume II: The Conference on Security and Co-operation in Europe, 1972-1975
    0 11 591697 0
Volume III: Détente in Europe, 1972-1976
    0 7146 5116 8
Volume IV: The Year of Europe: America, Europe and the Energy Crisis, 1972-1974
    0 415 39150 4
Volume V: The Southern Flank in Crisis, 1973-1976
    0 7146 5114 1
Volume VI: Berlin in the Cold War, 1948-1990
    978-0-415-45532-9
Volume VII: German Unification, 1989-1990
    978-0-415-55002-4

DOCUMENTS ON BRITISH POLICY OVERSEAS

Series III, Volume VII

German Unification, 1989-1990

First published 2010
by Routledge
2 Park Square, Milton Park, Abingdon, Oxon OX14 4RN

Simultaneously published in the USA and Canada
by Routledge
270 Madison Avenue, New York, NY 10016

Routledge is an imprint of the Taylor & Francis Group, an informa business

© 2010 Crown Copyright

Publisher's note
This book has been prepared from a camera-ready copy
supplied by the editors

Printed and bound in Great Britain by
CPI Antony Rowe, Chippenham, Wiltshire

British Library Cataloguing in Publication Data
A catalogue record for this book is available from the British Library

Library of Congress Cataloging-in-Publication Data
A catalog record has been requested for this book

ISBN10: 0–415–55002–5 (hbk)
ISBN10: 0–203–86663–0 (ebk)
ISBN13: 978–0–415–55002–4 (hbk)
ISBN13: 978–0–203–86663–4 (ebk)

CONTENTS

PREFACE

By 1989 the repercussions of the reforms inaugurated by Mikhail Gorbachev following his appointment as General Secretary of the Soviet Communist Party four years earlier were being felt throughout Europe. The two German states, whose division had formed the bedrock of European security since 1949, were profoundly sensitive to the potential for change that Mr Gorbachev had unleashed. From the British point of view, the most urgent problem posed by Germany in early 1989 had to do with the Federal Republic's role in the Western Alliance. Although their origins could be traced much further back—notably to NATO's controversial 'twin-track' decision on the deployment of intermediate nuclear missiles in December 1979—the growing assertiveness of the West German Government, and the increasing reluctance of its population to accept some aspects of Alliance membership such as the use of low-flying aircraft in NATO exercises, could also be attributed to a diminishing sense of threat from the Soviet Union. By the spring of 1989 a second problem was beginning to emerge as it became clear that the citizens of East Germany were increasingly unwilling to accept the constraints imposed by a visibly moribund regime.

As early as January 1989 the Foreign Secretary, Sir Geoffrey Howe, ordered a study to be made of the implications of a possible removal of the Berlin Wall.[1] In June the Permanent Under-Secretary at the Foreign and Commonwealth Office, Sir Patrick Wright, asked the Joint Intelligence Committee to examine the situation in the German Democratic Republic in the light of the recent repression of dissent by the Chinese leadership at Tiananmen Square. In the course of the summer the massive outflow of East German 'holidaymakers' to Hungary and Czechoslovakia, and their dramatic occupation of FRG embassy buildings, challenged the very existence of the GDR. In doing so they raised a third and still more far-reaching question. Unlike other states of the Soviet bloc such as Poland or Hungary, the GDR was an entirely artificial creation, dependent for its existence on Communist ideology and the maintenance of Soviet power. Its citizens seemed to have little incentive to work for the establishment of a reformist or democratic system when they could see on their doorstep a viable, democratic Germany in the form of the Federal Republic. The events of the summer of 1989 made German reunification (as it was then generally termed) a realistic prospect for the first time since the establishment of two separate German states in 1949.[2]

As one of the victors of the Second World War and as an ally since 1955 of the Federal Republic, the United Kingdom possessed an extensive range of rights and responsibilities in respect of German territory. That territory, defined as the area lying within the borders of the German Reich on 31 December 1937, had been divided in 1945 into four occupation zones, with a separate four-power administration of Berlin and with the area east of the Rivers Oder and Neisse placed under Polish administration. After 1949 the three Western allies, Britain,

---

[1] Series III, Vol. VI, *Berlin in the Cold War, 1948-1990*, No. 350.
[2] 'Reunification' technically implied a return to the Germany of 1937, including the territory east of the Oder-Neisse line placed under Polish administration in 1945 and the city of Königsberg (Kaliningrad), which had been incorporated into the Soviet Union; 'unification' referred only to the FRG and the GDR. Until 1989 British officials and politicians made little distinction between the two terms, and most spoke of 'reunification'. By the beginning of 1990 'unification' had become the preferred term in almost all official communications.

France and the United States, entered into a number of agreements with the Federal Republic aimed at restoring German sovereignty and integrating the FRG into Western institutions, while never losing sight of the ultimate goal of restoring German unity. In October 1954, as part of the process that terminated the occupation regime and brought West Germany into NATO and the Western European Union, they signed the Bonn/Paris Conventions (also known as the Relations Convention and, in Germany, as the *Deutschlandvertrag*). Entering into force in May 1955, these reaffirmed the commitment made in the Bonn Conventions of May 1952 that

> Pending the peace settlement, the signatory states will cooperate to achieve, by peaceful means, their common aim of a reunified Germany enjoying a liberal democratic constitution, like that of the Federal Republic, and integrated within the European community.[3]

The Allied commitment to German unity, along with an insistence on the continued existence of Quadripartite Rights and Responsibilities, was repeated over the ensuing decades, particularly in the era of *Ostpolitik* and *détente*. Both in 1973, when they recognised the GDR and the two German states were admitted to the UN, and in the Helsinki Final Act of August 1975, the Western allies stated unequivocally that Four-Power rights and responsibilities relating to Germany and Berlin remained unaffected. Helsinki confirmed Europe's existing frontiers but was not a treaty and did not rule out the alteration of frontiers by peaceful means. In 1980, on the 25th anniversary of the Relations Convention, the Foreign Secretary, Lord Carrington, reiterated that 'It will remain the policy of my Government to support the efforts of the Federal Republic of Germany to work for a state of peace in Europe in which the German people can recover their unity in free-determination.'[4]

The aspirations embodied in the Bonn/Paris Conventions were important because they did not commit the allies to German unity *per se*, only to a united Germany that was democratic and integrated in Western Europe. By effectively ruling out unification on Soviet terms, or even a neutral Germany between the two blocs of the kind that Marshal Stalin had offered in March 1952, they contained the germ of the solution eventually arrived at in 1990.[5] At the time, however, and for decades afterwards, they looked more like a Western veto. For a united, liberal and democratic Germany was inconceivable as long as Europe itself remained divided by the Cold War. West Germany's allies could therefore proclaim their commitment to German unity without any serious expectation of being called to account. Nor, while never losing sight of German unity as an ultimate goal, did successive West German governments show much inclination to treat it as a matter of practical politics. Indeed the thrust of West Germany's *Ostpolitik*, from Konrad Adenauer's 'reunification through strength' to Willy Brandt's and Egon Bahr's 'change through rapprochement', seemed designed to reinforce the status quo. Normalising relations with the GDR, one of the chief achievements of Herr Brandt's *Ostpolitik* and that of his successor Helmut Schmidt, may have enabled more East German pensioners to visit the West, but it also gave cash subsidies to

---

[3] Cmnd. 9368, *Documents relating to the Termination of the Occupation Régime of the Federal German Republic* (London: HMSO, 1955), p. 5.
[4] Quoted in Nos. 9 and 18.
[5] Cmnd. 8501, *Correspondence between Her Majesty's Government in the United Kingdom and the Soviet Government about the future of Germany, 10th/25th March, 1952* (London: HMSO, 1952).

the East German regime and conferred on it a kind of *de facto* legitimacy. Against expectations, the advent to power of the CDU/CSU-FDP coalition under Helmut Kohl in 1982 marked no break with the policies of its predecessors. Moreover the coalition's determination to maintain dialogue with both the GDR and Soviet Union at a time of deepening East-West tension was matched by its resolute stand in favour of the stationing of intermediate nuclear weapons on West German soil. Thus, while West Germany's allies could detect much that was disturbing in West German politics in the early 1980s including, on the one hand, a greater readiness to address questions of national identity and, on the other, a peace movement several millions strong, German unity seemed to remain no more than an aspiration on the part of the Federal Government.

Britain's commitment to German self-determination had been renewed at a meeting in Oxford in May 1984 between the British Prime Minister, Margaret Thatcher, and the West German Chancellor, Helmut Kohl:

> The Heads of Government reaffirmed the importance of the United Kingdom's rights and responsibilities relating to Berlin and to Germany as a whole. The Prime Minister reaffirmed the conviction of successive British Governments that real and permanent stability in Europe will be difficult to achieve so long as the German nation is divided against its will.[6]

Yet by the end of that year the FCO was persuaded that the German vision was now much closer to the one Britain had maintained for the last thirty years: that freedom was more important than unity, and that any attempt to pursue unity seriously would destabilise Europe: 'Hence a verbal commitment to a goal of self-determination which can only come about in circumstances which cannot at present be foreseen.'[7]

All this changed with Mr Gorbachev. By 1987, while the likelihood of German unification in the foreseeable future still seemed remote, British officials were aware that it had become the subject of lively debate in the Federal Republic—a debate encouraged, it seemed, by Chancellor Kohl himself. Combined with this, and of more immediate concern, were West Germany's renewed self-confidence and heightened assertiveness in bodies such as the European Community and NATO. Officials also recognised that the new mood sweeping through Europe following the advent to power of Mr Gorbachev might have disturbing repercussions in Germany. Popular manifestations of 'Gorbymania' or 'Gorbophoria' were viewed with suspicion, as were the diplomatic manoeuvres of the West German Foreign Minister, Hans-Dietrich Genscher.

Such disquiet, together with 'a less precise feeling in London and elsewhere that something is afoot in Germany and all is not well in the FRG's present relations with her Western allies', led to a paper on 'The German Question and Europe', submitted by the FCO's Planners to the Foreign Secretary in September 1987.[8] On the question of German unification the paper asserted that there was 'no prospect of significant change in the medium term'. Mr Gorbachev was unlikely to repeat Stalin's 1952 offer and, as long as Soviet power in Eastern Europe remained intact, the Germans would not trade unity for neutrality. But in the longer term, the paper argued, change was inevitable. Communism was 'a spent force' and Soviet rule in

---

[6] FRG Embassy press release, 3 May 1984.
[7] Sir G. Howe to Sir J. Bullard (Bonn), 31 Dec 1984 (WRL 020/1).
[8] Minute by D.A. Gore Booth (Head of Policy Planning Staff), 29 September 1987, covering planning paper, 'The German Question and Europe' (RS 21/3/5).

Eastern Europe would come to an end 'probably by the middle of the next century and perhaps much sooner'. The outcome would be the break-up of both the Warsaw Pact and NATO, the withdrawal of US, Soviet and other foreign troops from German soil, and the emergence of a united, neutral Germany. At the centre, therefore, of 'a Europe of free states stretching from the Atlantic to the Black Sea and from the Arctic Circle to the Mediterranean' would be 'a highly developed united Germany of some 70 million people'; and the consequences for British foreign policy would be profound. In order to retain influence with a powerful non-aligned Germany, the paper argued, British diplomacy should already be seeking ways to strengthen relations with the FRG and identifying potential for change in the GDR, as well as engaging in an active policy towards Eastern Europe. The Planning Staff paper impressed the Foreign Secretary and provoked lively discussion within the FCO, but the debate tended to focus on its detailed recommendations rather than its prescient suggestion that change could happen 'much sooner' than most people expected.

Worries about West German foreign policy continued in 1988. There was still no fear that the Germans would 'slide into neutralism in return for reunification'; but, as Sir John Fretwell, the FCO's Political Director, put it in a letter of 14 April to Sir Christopher Mallaby, Britain's new Ambassador at Bonn, there were signs of 'gradually increasing German self-confidence, and perhaps a desire to match their political weight to their economic power—the payer wanting to call more of the tune'.[9] Sir C. Mallaby agreed. In a despatch of 3 June 1988 he recorded his impressions on returning to Germany after a three-year absence (he had served there as Minister between 1982 and 1985).[10] The Federal Republic's Western orientation was not in question, he wrote, but there was an increasing insistence that 'German interests must be given proper weight in the counsels of the West'. He noted a month later that the post-war settlement remained, 'at the psychological and political levels, profoundly unsatisfactory for Germans. That is why they are constantly seeking evolution and movement.'[11] There was a danger that if Western European integration lost momentum Germany would turn eastward. However there was nothing wrong with West Germany's aspiration towards a higher international profile: 'A more active diplomacy by so like-minded a country is in general something to welcome.' There was therefore 'no need for active concern but several things to keep a close eye on'.[12]

The difficulty for British policy—identified in the Planners' paper in 1987 and by Sir C. Mallaby and others in 1988 and 1989—was that the United Kingdom lacked leverage. The Germans liked the British and got on well with them, but did not give full weight to British policies. There was nothing comparable with the close institutional and personal bonds underlying the Franco-German axis within the European Community. And this in turn, many at the FCO felt, was largely the result of the Government's refusal to engage actively with 'Europe', to respond with sufficient vigour to the changes that were taking place in the east of the continent or to show sympathy for German aspirations. By the summer of 1989

---

[9] WRG 020/3.
[10] WRG 020/3.
[11] Letter to Sir J. Fretwell, 8 July 1988, WRG 020/3.
[12] A further Planning Staff paper, 'East/West Relations and the Future of Europe: Or, Genscher Looks for Opportunities and We Think We've Got Problems', circulated on 11 July 1988, called, as its title suggested, for a more positive response to the changes in Eastern Europe and to German aspirations (RS 21/3/7). It did not, however, command as much support as the PPS's 1987 paper.

relations with the Federal Republic did not seem in very good shape. The 'basic problem', as one FCO official put it, remained 'our own rhetoric. So long as that is perceived in continental Europe as being negative and "anti-European" we will make less progress with our policies than, for the most part, they deserve' (No. 7).

Before the Fall of the Wall: Defining British Policy

On 10 September 1989 the Hungarian Government allowed East Germans who had arrived in Hungary over the summer to leave for Austria.[13] The pressure then shifted to Prague where, by the end of September, over 3,500 East Germans were crowded into the West German embassy. On 30 September, in a major propaganda blunder, the veteran Socialist Unity Party (SED) chief Erich Honecker allowed them to leave for the West on a special train that was required to travel through the GDR. The decision was announced by Herr Genscher from the balcony of the embassy; the welcome given to the train and its passengers as they travelled through East German cities indelibly marked the bankruptcy of the regime. The New Forum opposition group had been founded in East Berlin on 11 September. Demonstrations began in Leipzig on 2 October, soon spreading to other cities and raising the prospect of a complete collapse of authority on the part of the SED. Mr Gorbachev visited the GDR on 6-7 October, on the occasion of its 40th anniversary, and issued a famous warning to his hosts: 'Dangers await only those who don't react to life.' By 8 and 9 October the demonstrations in Dresden and Leipzig were taking place on an unprecedented scale—70,000 marched in Leipzig on the evening of 9 October—and the authorities did not attempt to suppress them by force as they had done in several cities only two days earlier, at the end of Gorbachev's visit. On 18 October Herr Honecker was forced to stand down in favour of his former protégé Egon Krenz.

As the GDR's crisis intensified, the first British response was to reiterate the UK's commitment to the principle of self-determination. The remarks of the Foreign Secretary, John Major, in Bonn on 20 September—his first visit to a West European capital since his appointment to the FCO in July—were well received by the West German press. Indeed well into October the UK was perceived by the Federal Government, on the basis of statements by both the Foreign Secretary and the Prime Minister, as being more sympathetic to German aspirations than the FRG's other European allies. But officials at the FCO and at the Embassies in Bonn and East Berlin were alert to suggestions that the accelerating disintegration of the GDR had put the 'German question' back on the international agenda and that this implied the possibility of unification, even if Chancellor Kohl and other West German politicians were reluctant to say so explicitly. By mid-September Sir Patrick Wright had already come to the conclusion that the UK's commitment to self-determination might no longer be sufficient and that 'some public redefinition may now be required' (No. 12).

The task of reformulating Britain's public line fell in the first instance to the FCO's Western European Department (WED), headed by Hilary Synnott, which circulated two papers in draft on 11 October (No. 18). 'Explosion in the GDR' comprised a contingency plan for the sudden and total collapse of the East German regime; 'German Reunification' examined the historical background, the prospects for unification and the implications for British policy. The final version of the

---

[13] Speaking in Frankfurt exactly one year later, Sir G. Howe described the Hungarian decision as 'a decisive event in world history . . . This decision set the German and other central European revolutions in motion' (No. 242, note 5).

latter, completed two weeks later, was more judicious than the original draft but some of the latter's freshness, as well as its positive response to the prospect of German unity, had been lost (No. 25). Influenced by the rapid pace of events in the GDR, WED had sought to strike a balance between the demand for change (but not necessarily for German unity) in the GDR; Britain's long-standing commitment to German unification; the fact that large Soviet forces were stationed in the GDR; and the sensitivities of Germany's neighbours, especially Polish concerns about the Oder-Neisse frontier. The outcome was reaffirmation—not redefinition—of Britain's commitment to self-determination. This approach was endorsed at a meeting between the PUS and the Deputy Under-Secretaries of State on 31 October. It was a policy that maintained Britain's commitment to German unity without prejudging the wishes of the people of the GDR.[14] As such, it was fully in line with the official positions of Britain's allies, including the Federal Republic itself.

All were soon to be caught off guard. Following Erich Honecker's departure on 18 October demonstrations in the GDR grew massively in scale and spread across the country. Further resignations of senior SED functionaries followed in early November. The leading figures remaining at the helm—Egon Krenz and Günter Schabowski, the East Berlin party chief—still imagined they could master the movement for change. They used a major pro-democracy rally in East Berlin on 4 November to announce a programme of reform, but this was now far too modest to satisfy the demonstrators. Nevertheless the demonstration remained peaceful. In early November the authorities started to lift travel and emigration restrictions but these were rejected as too timid by the East German parliament, the *Volkskammer*, and the entire cabinet resigned on 7 November, with the Politburo's resignation following the next day. The reform-minded Dresden party chief Hans Modrow was nominated as prime minister, while Herr Krenz and Herr Schabowski sought to regain the initiative by legalising all private travel abroad. The decision was announced by Herr Schabowski at a press conference on 9 November: probably inadvertently he confirmed, in response to a reporter's question, that the new regulations were in effect 'now'. That evening East Berliners took him at his word and started crossing the Wall. No attempt was made to stop them.[15]

In these circumstances any radical redefinition of Britain's policy of self-determination would have been premature. The East German people had forced the pace and all governments—not just the British—were trying desperately to catch up. It was reasonable to wait until the wishes of the population of the GDR could be determined. But it was not so much the substance as the perception of British policy that mattered. All that was required at this stage was some gesture of support or sympathy for German aspirations. Support for the aspirations of the East German people was soon forthcoming;[16] for Germany as a whole it was another matter.

---

[14] Sir C. Mallaby confirmed in a witness seminar held in October 2000 that at this stage 'British policy was to welcome reform and to look for an act of self-determination in East Germany, rather than assuming automatically at that early stage that we had to aim for unification. There was a preference in London for not moving too fast and for clear certainty about the wishes of the East Germans': Gillian Staerck and Michael D. Kandiah (eds.), *Anglo-German Relations and German Reunification* (London: Institute of Contemporary British History), p. 40.

[15] For reports of these events from the British Embassy in East Berlin, see Series III, Vol. VI, Nos. 401-2.

[16] For the Prime Minister's statement of 10 November see No. 36.

The Attitude of the Prime Minister

The Prime Minister's hostility to the prospect of a united Germany was already a matter of concern to senior officials. As her memoirs make clear, Mrs Thatcher believed that 'the German problem' was inherent in a German national character that derived from Germany's late unification and had led the country to veer 'unpredictably between aggression and self-doubt'.[17] It was a problem that greater European unity would intensify rather than resolve. A reunited Germany would dominate Western Europe, and its inherent economic dynamism would lead it to look east as well as west, thus acting as 'a destabilizing rather than a stabilizing force in Europe'. Only a continuing American presence and close Franco-British relations could contain German power, 'and nothing of the sort would be possible within a European super-state'.[18] These deep-seated convictions were compounded by a difficult personal relationship between Mrs Thatcher and Chancellor Kohl and reinforced by her concern for Mr Gorbachev and the future of the reform movements in the Soviet Union and Eastern Europe. The Prime Minister's public statements in the autumn of 1989 placed greater emphasis on the need to avoid destabilising Gorbachev than on German unification *per se*.[19] Indeed it was only from late January 1990 onwards, when German unity had become inevitable sooner or later, that she publicly gave vent to overtly anti-German sentiments.[20]

Two aspects of the Prime Minister's position on Germany caused officials particular concern. One was its impact on the perceptions of the Bush Administration, carrying the danger that the UK might be marginalised in relations between the United States and Europe. The other was that neither the Prime Minister nor any other member of her Government had yet expressed public support for German aspirations. The United States was beginning to do so, albeit in carefully worded terms: in a speech of 16 October by Secretary of State James Baker III, and in remarks by President George H.W. Bush to the *New York Times* on 24 October. With a more cautious but still positive statement following from President François Mitterrand on 3 November, Britain's official silence on the subject was becoming conspicuous. FCO worries about Mrs Thatcher had been initially expressed to Mr Major. They now became one of the first matters of business to be dealt with by Douglas Hurd, who became Foreign Secretary on 26 October as part of the Government reshuffle that followed the resignation of the Chancellor of the Exchequer, Nigel Lawson. Yet, in the immediate aftermath of the opening of the Berlin Wall on the night of 9-10 November, it was Mr Hurd rather than Mrs Thatcher who contributed most to the impression of British ambivalence. Despite his insistence to the BBC World Service on 10 November that 'it is a matter for self-determination and that we would welcome unification based on free institutions such as there are in the Federal German Republic', Mr Hurd's listeners picked up the remark that immediately followed. The principle of German unity, he said, was not in doubt; 'But the how and when, that is not on the immediate agenda.' Repeated on several further occasions, 'not on the agenda' would resonate almost as much as the Prime Minister's reservations through

---

[17] Margaret Thatcher, *The Downing Street Years* (London: HarperCollins, 1993) p. 791.
[18] *Ibid.*
[19] See for example her Mansion House speech of 13 November: No. 45, note 4.
[20] Privately it was another matter: see George Urban, *Diplomacy and Disillusion at the Court of Margaret Thatcher: An Insider's View* (London: I.B. Tauris, 1996), pp. 99-117 for an account of 'a memorable lunch at No. 10' on 19 December 1989.

British-German relations over the months to come.[21] Indeed Herr Kohl's closest adviser, Horst Teltschik, explicitly contrasted Mr Hurd's 'nicht aktuell' with Mrs Thatcher's helpful reply to Mr Gorbachev's alarmist message to Western leaders on 10 November.[22]

Chancellor Kohl's Ten-Point Programme

On 28 November, in a speech to the *Bundestag*, Chancellor Kohl announced his Government's first formal response to the revolutionary situation created by the fall of the Berlin Wall. Improvised in consultation with a few key advisers, in secrecy from the Federal Republic's allies and even from Herr Genscher, it comprised a ten-point programme. The key fifth point spoke of 'confederative structures . . . with the aim of creating a federation, a federal order in Germany'. Herr Kohl acknowledged that 'Nobody knows how a reunified Germany will look' and he set down no timetable.[23] He nevertheless expressed his conviction that 'unity will come', and declared (in his tenth point) that with 'the attainment of freedom within Europe' the German people would, 'via free self-determination, restore their unity'.

During the eighteen days that separated the fall of the Wall from Herr Kohl's historic speech, the Western powers had tried to hammer out a common position on the German question at a number of high-level meetings. At the meeting of EC heads of government on 18 November Mrs Thatcher felt that her insistence on preserving European borders and keeping NATO and the Warsaw Pact intact had won general acceptance.[24] But her encounter with President Bush at Camp David on 24 November was not reassuring.[25] While the Prime Minister's insistence on maintaining the status quo and not jeopardising Mr Gorbachev's position struck a chord with Brent Scowcroft, President Bush's National Security Advisor, the President himself was unconvinced. He was not impressed by the map of Germany's 1937 borders that she pulled from her handbag and believed that 'we could manage these issues in a way that would obviate most of her concerns'.[26] Further elucidation of American thinking on the German question came a day after Chancellor Kohl's *Bundestag* speech. At a White House press conference on 29 November, Secretary of State Baker announced four principles that the United States believed should guide the unification process. Intended as a reminder of the international and security dimension that Herr Kohl's ten points had largely ignored, as well as a gesture of support, the four principles were to be reiterated by President Bush at the NATO heads of government meeting in Brussels on 4 December.[27] This was the point at which Mrs Thatcher concluded that 'there was nothing I could expect from the Americans as regards slowing down German reunification'.[28]

---

[21] No. 85, note 3.

[22] Horst Teltschik, *329 Tage. Innenansichten der Einigung* (Berlin: Siedler Verlag, 1991), pp. 33-4 (diary entry for 16 November 1989).

[23] Official German translation of speech, communicated to British Embassy on 29 November 1989 (No. 59).

[24] Thatcher, pp. 793-94.

[25] *Ibid.*, pp. 794-5; George Bush and Brent Scowcroft, *A World Transformed* (New York: Alfred A. Knopf, 1998), pp. 192-93.

[26] *Ibid.*, p.193.

[27] *Public Papers of the Presidents of the United States, George Bush: 1989*, Book II (Washington, DC, 1990), p. 1648; Bush and Scowcroft, pp. 196-97.

[28] Thatcher, pp. 795-96.

The next opportunity to define Western policy on Germany came with the Strasbourg meeting of the European Council on 8 December. The responses of European leaders to the FRG's request for a formal endorsement of the right of Germans to self-determination, and thus to unity, were coloured by the accelerating collapse of authority in the GDR. On 3 December the Politburo and the Central Committee of the SED resigned following revelations of widespread corruption among senior officials; on the 5th Herr Kohl's representative Rudolf Seiters reached an agreement with Herr Modrow that made the two parts of Germany a single travel area; the following day Herr Krenz resigned as head of state. There was also a residue of resentment over Herr Kohl's failure to consult before announcing his ten-point programme. Most of all, there was anxiety about what appeared to be a sudden hardening of Soviet attitudes following Mr Gorbachev's relaxed performance at his summit meeting with President Bush in Malta on 2-3 December. After a heated debate the European heads of government agreed on a communiqué that reaffirmed the right of the German people to 'regain its unity through self-determination', while emphasising that the process should respect existing agreements and take place within the contexts of East-West cooperation and European integration. There was no reference to the inviolability of existing frontiers as several leaders, including Mrs Thatcher, had wished. Nevertheless British officials could take comfort from the fact that the Strasbourg declaration, repeated by the North Atlantic Council on 14 December, was fully in accordance with the line that the United Kingdom had been reiterating since September.

Attrition

President Mitterrand had lent his weight to efforts to reach a compromise over the Strasbourg communiqué. In the margins of Strasbourg, however, he initiated two meetings with Mrs Thatcher that seemed to her to amount to an invitation to coordinate joint British-French action to slow, or event halt, the momentum towards German unity.[29] Already concerned at the apparent lack of forward thinking about what might happen if the GDR collapsed completely, the Prime Minister had ordered the FCO and Ministry of Defence to plan possible diplomatic action and contingency measures in the event of violent confrontation or even Soviet intervention in East Germany, as well as looking to more far-reaching scenarios in the longer term. Within the FCO these plans were coordinated by John Weston, who succeeded Sir J. Fretwell as Political Director at the beginning of January 1990, and placed under the supervision of William Waldegrave, Minister of State for Europe. They focused initially on preparations for a wide-ranging seminar scheduled to be held at Chequers towards the end of January. To these were added the need to provide briefing papers for a meeting between the Prime Minister and President Mitterrand, to take place in Paris on 20 January. The planning process became a vehicle for persuading the Prime Minister to bow to the inevitable.

---

[29] No. 71 is the British record of the first of these meetings; it has not proved possible to find a record of the second. See also Thatcher, pp. 796-97. A detailed French record of the first meeting is given in Jacques Attali, *Verbatim*, Vol. 3, *1988-1991* (Paris: Fayard, 1995), pp. 368-70. Neither meeting is mentioned in either of the two more recent accounts based on French official sources, Thilo Schabert, *Wie Weltgeschichte gemacht wird. Frankreich und die deutsche Einheit* (Stuttgart: Klett-Cotta, 2002), pp. 426-29, or Frédéric Bozo, *Mitterrand, la fin de la guerre froide et l'unification allemande. De Yalta à Maastricht* (Paris: Odile Jacob, 2005).

The rate of attrition was slow, lasting at least until early February, and with few clear milestones: there was certainly no point at which Mrs Thatcher explicitly accepted defeat. Indeed the beginning of January was the point at which No. 10 and the Foreign Office came into most direct confrontation. On the eve of the fall of the Wall, Sir C. Mallaby had recommended a public statement on the part of a senior Minister expressing the UK's willingness to accept German unification. Over the following weeks he had repeated the call with increasing urgency. In a telegram of 5 January 1990 he pleaded again for a statement that would counteract the widespread German conviction that Britain was 'perhaps the least positive of the three Western Allies, and the least important' (No. 85). Such a pronouncement would clearly have to go beyond 'self-determination' and could thus imply only the explicit welcome for unification that the Prime Minister still deemed unacceptable. Her sharp response added an extra complication to the planning process. Officials decided that there was little point in mounting a direct challenge before Chequers; but this carried the danger that British-German relations would languish in the continuing absence of a positive statement, particularly in comparison with the United States and France.

Yet it is possible to interpret Mrs Thatcher's conversation with Douglas Hurd on 10 January as an indication that she was already turning her mind to the practical conditions under which unification would take place rather than trying to block it outright. In the process of reluctant and unacknowledged conversion two events, and one non-event, stand out. The non-event can be dealt with first. By late January it was becoming apparent that no serious resistance to the principle of German unification (as opposed to its terms) could be expected from the Soviet Union. There had been stray hints that the Russians might accept German unity as inevitable, if not desirable: one had been picked up by a British diplomat in East Berlin as early as the beginning of November. But for the moment they seemed resolute. In early December the Russians successfully proposed a four-power meeting in Berlin. While the West managed to confine its brief to Berlin-related issues, the meeting, held in the building of the Berlin *Kommandatura* on 11 December, acted as a warning to the Germans against trying to go ahead too fast on their own—something that was not wholly unwelcome to Britain and France. In January Moscow returned to the charge with Mr Shevardnadze's call for four-power discussion of the German question as a whole. German objections and Western prevarication neutralised this initiative, and there seemed little inclination to pursue it vigorously on the part of the Soviet Union. In fact Mr Gorbachev and his advisers were to conclude on 26 January that the problems surrounding German unification should be negotiated in a 'group of six', and on 31 January Mr Gorbachev publicly acknowledged that unification would take place.[30]

Of the two events that may be seen to mark stages in the Prime Minister's reluctant acceptance of German unification, the first was her bilateral meeting with President Mitterrand in Paris on 20 January. M. Mitterrand's position had shifted significantly since their last meeting.[31] 'None of us were going to declare war on

---

[30] Philip Zelikow and Condoleezza Rice, *Germany Unified and Europe Transformed: A study in statecraft* (Cambridge, Mass.: Harvard University Press, 1995), p. 163. Anatoly Chernyaev (compiler), *Mikhail Gorbachev i Germansky Vopros. Sbornik dokumentov 1986-1991*[Mikhail Gorbachev and the German Question 1986-1991. Collected Documents 1986-1991] (Moscow: Ves' Mir, 1996), pp. 307-11.

[31] Herr Kohl and M. Mitterrand had met privately at Latche, the latter's country residence in Gascony, on 4 January. Sir C. Mallaby reported on 19 January: 'The French have made

Germany', he declared, echoing the FCO's advice (No. 103). He agreed to Mrs Thatcher's suggestion of Franco-British talks on the German question and closer defence cooperation between the two countries. Yet by the end of the conversation he had made his position clear enough. Britain and France might not like the idea of German unity but they could do nothing to stop it; and, if they could not stop it, they should remain silent. This, in Lady Thatcher's account, was the point at which Britain and France parted company, with M. Mitterrand making the wrong choice. Rather than following the Gaullist approach of defending French sovereignty and forming alliances to secure French interests, he stuck with the policy of 'moving ahead faster towards a federal Europe in order to tie down the German giant'.[32]

Although the external props of prime ministerial resistance had fallen away—first the United States, now Russia and France—Mrs Thatcher remained defiant. On 25 January the *Wall Street Journal* published a lengthy interview in which, while not overtly hostile to German unity, she dwelt mainly on the practical obstacles that would have to be overcome and threw in a number of gratuitously offensive comments.[33] But the Chequers seminar on 27 January—the second of the two events identified earlier—undermined the Prime Minister's position from within.[34] Long in gestation, its agenda had been transformed by the quickening pace of events in Germany and by the Bush administration's ambition to conclude a treaty in 1990 on conventional forces in Europe. Proposals for a reduction in both American and Soviet troop numbers, broached with Mrs Thatcher and other European leaders on 26-27 January, seemed to threaten a weakening of the US presence in Europe, while revealing a tendency to neglect the implications of German unification for European security structures. The Prime Minister told President Bush that she would be undertaking a thorough review of the situation at Chequers.[35] For her senior advisers, however, what the meeting was really about, in the words of Sir Percy Cradock, 'was getting the Prime Minister over the principle of reunification and on course with the issue of the moment, namely its terms'.[36] Douglas Hurd's diary records the crumbling of resistance:

> Bleary and hard pressed to Chequers. Upstairs meeting on Germany and NATO. Tom King, William Waldegrave (late but good), Archie Hamilton, Alan Clark, P Cradock, Weston etc. Starts gradually but we make progress. Usual diatribe against German selfishness but the hankering to stop unification now comes less often and we are into 'transition' and reducing BAOR.[37]

That evening Mr Hurd consolidated his advantage by ensuring that 'slowing things down' should not be enshrined in a message to be sent by the Prime

contradictory statements and appear to German eyes reserved. But Kohl places reliance on what (Teltschik tells me) Mitterrand has said to him—that if the Germans want unity, the French know they cannot prevent it:' Bonn telegram No. 74 (WRL 020/1).

[32] Thatcher, p. 798.

[33] Text available at http://www.margaretthatcher.org/speeches/displaydocument.asp?docid=107876.

[34] It has not proved possible to find records of the Chequers meeting in either the FCO or the Cabinet Office archives.

[35] Bush and Scowcroft, p. 212.

[36] Percy Cradock, *In Pursuit of British Interests: Reflections on British Foreign Policy under Margaret Thatcher and John Major* (London: John Murray, 1997), p. 112.

[37] Entry for 27 January 1990, reproduced by permission of Lord Hurd. The diary of another participant, Alan Clark, gives a different recollection: 'I argued cogently for accepting, and exploiting, German reunification while they still needed our support. No good. She is determined not to': Alan Clark, *Diaries* (London: Weidenfeld and Nicolson, 1993), pp. 276-77 (entry for 28 January 1990).

Minister to Mr Gorbachev. The term, he wrote, 'puts us in the position of the ineffective brake, which we should avoid as offering the worst of all worlds' (No. 108). The Prime Minister for her part seemed increasingly prepared—despite her indignation at the West German Government's apparent impetuosity and high-handedness—to focus on the practicalities surrounding German unification rather than conduct an isolated and ineffectual rearguard action.

But the injury to British-German relations had already been done. Having had a lengthy and amicable conversation with Sir C. Mallaby on 25 January, Herr Kohl was understandably upset when he heard of Mrs Thatcher's *Wall Street Journal* interview the following day.[38] The Foreign Office and the Bonn Embassy saw Mr Hurd's visit to Bonn on 6 February, and his speech there to the Konrad Adenauer Foundation, as an opportunity to repair the damage. Much effort went into the drafting. Mr Waldegrave made changes because he believed that 'Without more warmth and a little more firmness on the right of a united Germany to be in NATO if it so chooses . . . the speech will be interpreted as an "anti-unification" speech'.[39] Mr Hurd himself admitted on 5 February that the speech now seemed less adventurous than when he had first drafted it, and at the last minute he added an elliptical reference to 'a number of interesting and constructive suggestions' that had recently been made to reconcile German unity with Alliance membership (No. 131). The speech fell flat and the Federal Government was predictably disappointed.[40] Over the next fortnight the atmosphere deteriorated further. By 22 February Sir C. Mallaby was obliged to report that 'Britain's public standing is at its lowest for years' (No. 151).

The Origins of Two plus Four

The 'interesting and constructive suggestions' to which Mr Hurd referred in his speech of 6 February were to lead within a week to the establishment of a definitive framework for the negotiation of German unity. The decision on Two plus Four—the two German states negotiating in parallel with negotiations among the four occupying powers—was reached in the margins of an Open Skies conference in Ottawa on 11-13 February.[41] The need for some kind of framework had been acknowledged with increasing urgency at least since the middle of January. Symbolically, at least, the GDR's fate had been sealed by the ecstatic reception given to Chancellor Kohl's speech before the ruined *Frauenkirche* in Dresden on the evening of 19 December. By mid-January the GDR was in a state of advanced collapse. Emigration was increasing; demonstrations were becoming more aggressive; calls for German unity were becoming more strident. When the Modrow government appeared to be trying to entrench elements of the old regime

---

[38] Teltschik, pp. 115-16; Hanns Jürgen Küsters and Daniel Hoffman (eds.), *Deutsche Einheit. Sonderedition aus den Akten des Bundeskanzkleramtes 1989/90* (Munich: R. Oldenbourg Verlag, 1998), No. 148.

[39] Minute from Mr Asquith (PS to Mr Waldegrave) to Mr Wall, 5 February (Waldegrave Papers, FCO Archive).

[40] In his diary that evening he wrote: 'It's a good speech but British press inevitably damn it as disappointing. It went as far as welcoming German unification as the traffic here [in London] will bear.' Entry for 6 February 1990, reproduced by permission of Lord Hurd.

[41] It is worth noting that the terms 'Two plus Four' and 'Four plus Two' were for a long time used interchangeably by British Ministers and officials, apparently with no suggestion, as some in Germany and elsewhere believed, that the two terms had differing connotations. Only from 22 February onwards was 'Two plus Four' consistently used to designate the negotiating structure agreed at Ottawa on 13 February.

and re-establish the Stasi in the barely disguised form of a new internal security service, demonstrators stormed and ransacked Stasi headquarters in East Berlin. Relations between Herr Modrow and Herr Kohl deteriorated as the former tried to stabilise his government and the latter became convinced that East Germany was beyond saving. To his Western partners, Herr Kohl was still expressing confidence that the GDR could survive until the general elections, scheduled for 6 May, and speaking of a five-year transition to German unity. In fact he had already concluded that the date of the East German elections must be brought forward.[42] But if this were to happen it was imperative that Herr Modrow should not be allowed to seize the initiative. This seemed a possibility when, on 28 January, Herr Modrow declared that elections would now take place on 18 March, and announced at the same time the formation of a non-party Government of National Responsibility. On 1 February, following Mr Gorbachev's green light the previous day, Herr Modrow put forward a four-stage plan intended to lead ultimately to a united, neutral, Germany.

The speed with which the Federal Government now pressed ahead with realising its version of German unity, and its apparent disregard for Four-Power rights, alarmed not only the Federal Republic's European allies but also the more sympathetic United States. By the beginning of February German officials were already speaking of the possibility of using Article 23 of the Basic Law—implying absorption of the GDR into the FRG—rather than the all-German election route envisaged in Article 146, which had governed Western thinking on the question of German unity since the early 1950s. On 7 February Chancellor Kohl submitted a proposal for German economic and monetary union (GEMU) to his cabinet: there was no longer any question of propping up the failing Modrow regime. Equally worrying were indications that the Federal Government did not speak with one voice. In a speech at the Tutzing Academy on 31 January Herr Genscher suggested that, while a united Germany would be a member of NATO, the former GDR would remain outside the organisation's military structures and no NATO forces would be stationed there. Two days later, however, his cabinet colleague Gerhard Stoltenberg, the Minister of Defence, stated that all of the territory of a united Germany would be part of NATO, thus provoking a dispute that was to fester for several weeks. The high point of British alarm was reached following Mr Weston's discussions in Bonn with his opposite number Dieter Kastrup and other German officials on 5 February. Although the idea of a Two plus Four (or Four plus Two) arrangement was already in the air—and indeed Herr Genscher had agreed in principle to the concept in Washington on 2 February—Herr Kastrup was '"adamant" that Four-Power discussions on Germany would not be acceptable' (No. 123). Negotiations on German unity were a matter for the two German states alone, with the Four Powers being consulted only on matters directly governed by the Relations Convention, and in the 'final peace settlement'.

Such truculent signals concealed (and perhaps were designed to conceal) the fact that much progress towards reconciling German aspirations and Four-Power interests had already been made. The key to reconciliation lay in Washington.[43] By mid-January members of the Bush Administration had come to share Kohl's conclusion that the accelerating collapse of the GDR had made a gradualist approach to German unity unworkable, but were divided on the best way to

---

[42] Teltschik, p. 110 (entry for 17 January 1990).
[43] This account of the evolution of US policy is based on Zelikow and Rice, pp. 159-60, 165-72.

proceed. While one strand of American thinking focused on CFE, another focused on Germany. At the White House Robert Blackwill argued that there should be 'a rush toward *de facto* unification along lines worked out between the United States and the Federal Republic', thus presenting both the Soviet Union and the Western allies with a *fait accompli*.[44] His NSC colleague Condoleezza Rice agreed that the pace should be increased but 'preferred to try to achieve rapid reunification through a six-power negotiation that would include the two German states'.[45] She calculated that in the face of such momentum the Soviets would eventually capitulate. By 26 January similar views prevailed among Mr Baker and his advisers at the State Department. At the end of January official opinion in Washington was polarised between the NSC, where Mr Scowcroft, Mr Blackwill, Philip Zelikow and Dr Rice (despite her earlier opinion) all favoured rapid *de facto* unification of the two German states, to be given Four-Power blessing once it had been achieved, and Mr Baker's advisers Dennis Ross and Robert Zoellick who were evolving what they described as a Two plus Four mechanism. This, they suggested, could create a forum in which, on the one hand, the Germans would not be subject to Four-Power tutelage but, on the other, the Soviet Union could play a full part in the negotiating process. Raymond Seitz, head of the State Department's European Bureau and *de facto* Political Director, disagreed, telling Mr Baker on 1 February that what he described as a Four plus Two formula would slow the unification process, alienate the Germans and give the Soviets too much of a voice in the negotiations.

American views were therefore still in flux when Mr Hurd arrived in Washington on 28 January. Little attempt had been made to marry up thinking on CFE—on which consensus had been achieved—and Germany, on which opinion remained sharply divided. The British documents do not support the contention (in circulation as early as mid-February) that the Americans used Mr Hurd's visit to press a Two plus Four solution on a reluctant British Government.[46] The official British record of Mr Hurd's meeting with Mr Baker on 29 January, Mr Hurd's private diary entry for the same date and Mr Baker's memoirs all confirm that, while the two men spoke repeatedly of the need for a 'framework', neither made any explicit suggestion that this should be on a Two plus Four basis.[47] The idea was raised explicitly during a meeting between Mr Zoellick, Mr Blackwill, Sir P. Wright and Andrew Wood at the British Embassy on the evening of 29 January, but in a rather tentative form: 'Zoellick said he, personally, had had the Four plus Two formula at the back of his mind for some time, but that it was not the current

---

[44] *Ibid.*, p. 159.

[45] *Ibid.*, p. 160.

[46] Subsequent claims of British hostility to the Two plus Four concept seem to be based mainly on an article by Thomas L. Friedman and Michael R. Gordon, 'Accord on Europe: Anatomy of a Decision', in the *New York Times* of 16 February 1990, according to which

> The first serious discussion of the idea took place on Jan. 29, when the British Foreign Secretary, Douglas Hurd, met with Mr. Baker in Washington. Mr. Hurd, who had been thinking along similar lines, indicated that his Government's preference would be "four plus zero"—that is, the four Allied powers getting together to discuss the fate of Germany, at first without the Germans. Nevertheless, he gave London's backing to two plus four.

See also Zelikow and Rice, p. 420, note 38, for an authoritative rebuttal of this claim.

[47] Mr Hurd noted in his diary on 29 January: 'To Baker. Brisk, intelligent. 15 minutes alone and we agree on need for a framework for NATO and German unity.' James A. Baker, III, *The Politics of Diplomacy: Revolution, War and Peace 1989-1992* (New York: Putnam, 1995), p. 199: 'Two-plus-Four was in the front of my mind, if not on the tip of my tongue.'

US position also to involve the two Germanies in Berlin Four talks.'[48] On the other hand, there is no indication that the British arrived in Washington with anything resembling a Two plus Four blueprint of their own.[49] It is possible, however, that Mr Hurd's receptive stance helped to crystallise US thinking. It may be significant that the key Ross-Zoellick memorandum on Two plus Four was completed on 30 January, the second day of Mr Hurd's visit; certainly the concept was to be promoted vigorously when Herr Genscher visited Washington only three days later.

Although the Americans were ahead of the game on German unity, they appeared, Mr Hurd felt, to have done much less forward thinking on other aspects, including how a united Germany would fit into NATO, the relationship of the former GDR to the European Community, CSCE, borders and Four-Power rights. Up to a point this was true. Like the German Government, the Americans were convinced that speed was essential because of the GDR's desperate predicament. They also felt that 'we need to get a grip now if we are to exert an influence' (No. 117). Such concerns may have led them to skimp on the details, and the Administration was late in grasping the implications of Herr Genscher's Tutzing formula ('no expansion of NATO territory eastwards').[50] But on some questions American views were firmer than Mr Hurd may have realised. Unlike Britain and France, they thought the CSCE too unwieldy to act as a forum for linking German unity to wider European security concerns.[51] Above all, they felt that forty years of democracy had fitted the German people to make their own choice about their future and that the Four-Power mechanism must be used to facilitate, not to thwart, German aspirations.[52] American diplomacy in early February therefore placed winning assent to the Two plus Four formula above all other considerations. Having got Mr Hurd and Herr Genscher on board, Mr Baker turned to the other key players: first France (meeting the French Foreign Minister Roland Dumas

---

[48] Washington tel. No. 240, 29 January 1990 (PREM: Internal Situation in East Germany). See also Zelikow and Rice, p. 173: 'Zoellick told the British about the Two Plus Four idea. The British displayed interest but made no commitment.'

[49] Elizabeth Pond, *Beyond the Wall: Germany's Road to Unification* (Washington, DC: The Brookings Institution, 1993), p. 318, note 5, refers to 'the compliment paid [by the British] to the success of two plus four in claiming a share in its paternity', and 'the interest of British diplomats in claiming some authorship', but cites no evidence in support of these assertions. The British view of the origins of Two plus Four is perhaps best conveyed in a letter of 20 February in which Mr Tebbit drew Mr Synnott's attention to the *New York Times* article of the 16th (note 46 above). Noting that the article was 'the semi-official version', based on briefings by senior State Department and NSC officials, Mr Tebbit described it as 'a remarkably detailed and accurate piece'. He went on:

> You will however notice that the Americans unsurprisingly come out of it rather better than the rest of us, with Baker portrayed as having arrived at, and advocated, the idea of adding 'the 2' to 'the 4' earlier than anyone else, when the truth of the matter was that several people were coming round to a similar approach at about the same time.
>
> I doubt whether this is much more than the familiar psychological process of believing oneself to have been even wiser after the event than was the case at the time. We would not accuse the Administration's briefers of seeking deliberately to mislead. But it is perhaps unfortunate that in presenting the chronology of events in this way they will have reinforced the old impression that America's policy towards Europe is one of 'Germany first' and that Britain is a reluctant party in the unification process.
>
> We have put the record straight with the journalists concerned, to the effect that the idea of '2 + 4' crystallised on a more collegiate basis, and a bit later, than is suggested in the article. But the article as it stands will remain the definitive account here (WRL 020/1).

[50] Zelikow and Rice, p.184.

[51] *Ibid.*, p. 187.

[52] *Ibid.*, p. 186.

during a brief stopover at Shannon Airport on 6 February) and finally Mr Shevardnadze and Mr Gorbachev on the 8th and 9th. He made enough progress in Moscow to enable President Bush to send a strong message of support to Chancellor Kohl, in advance of the latter's own visit to the Soviet capital on 10 and 11 February. Herr Kohl in turn presented his meeting with Mr Gorbachev as a great success. The Soviet leader would now find it very difficult to retreat from the positive impression that his meetings with Mr Baker and Herr Kohl had created.

With the Americans thus engaged in intensive diplomatic activity, the British concentrated on building bridges with the French and reassuring the Germans that insisting on the need for clarity about the future relationships between a unified Germany and NATO and the EC did not imply any hostility to the principle of German unity. Meanwhile the FCO's Planners began to marshal the detailed arguments that would enable Britain's voice to carry weight in future multilateral negotiations, with papers on a 'Six-Power Forum' and on Germany and NATO. Characteristically shying away from a maximalist position (full NATO membership encompassing the whole of German territory), the Planners recommended (and Mrs Thatcher endorsed) an intermediate solution (NATO membership but no non-German forces in the former GDR) which came close to Herr Genscher's Tutzing formula at precisely the same time as Mr Baker was backing away from that formula in Moscow.[53] Such divergences between allies were inevitable and of little consequence in comparison with the overriding goal of reaching agreement on a framework. That agreement was reached with remarkable speed. 'When I got to Ottawa,' Mr Hurd told the House of Commons on 22 February, 'I found that I was knocking on an open door, because the minds of our allies had moved precisely in the same direction; only the Soviet Union was reticent but, in Ottawa, that reticence was overcome within 24 hours.'[54] On 28 February the FCO was finally able to send a guidance telegram to Britain's representatives overseas emphasising the UK's long-standing commitment to German unification and welcoming the establishment of a framework that would allow the security implications and other external aspects to be properly considered.

Complications

Ottawa released the United Kingdom's German policy from the paralysis in which it had been locked since the opening of the Berlin Wall. Britain now had the opportunity, Mr Hurd told Mrs Thatcher, to 'come forward with some positive ideas of our own' and no longer 'appear to be a brake on everything' (No. 153). It was not quite that straightforward. In one important respect Britain's freedom of manoeuvre remained blocked. The question of how the GDR was to be integrated into the EC was a matter of increasing concern, not least to the Prime Minister. But neither she nor much of her party could accept the argument that the best way to contain German ambitions was to sublimate them in a strengthened European Community. In this area the French were left free to make the running, and M. Mitterrand was able to enhance his pro-unification credentials (though there remained much scope for Franco-German friction and misunderstanding). Nor was there as much mileage as Mrs Thatcher and Mr Hurd hoped in the idea of strengthening the CSCE framework and building links with Eastern Europe and the

---

[53] *Ibid.*, p. 184.
[54] *Parl. Debs., 5th ser., H. of C.*, Vol. 167, col. 1089.

Soviet Union. More importantly, the agreement at Ottawa that the Two plus Four negotiations would start only after the GDR elections on 18 March left more than a month for conflicts and misunderstandings to come to the surface.

Only the bare outlines of a negotiating procedure had been settled at Ottawa. Much of the substance still had to be filled in, and many key issues remained unresolved. An SPD victory in the GDR elections was widely expected. With the Social Democrats in both the FRG and the GDR favouring unity via Article 146 and a non-aligned Germany, Chancellor Kohl's fast-track unification strategy could quickly unravel. Electoral considerations made Herr Kohl unwilling to commit himself on two issues in particular: the permanence of the Polish-German frontier and the relationship between a united Germany and NATO. But any doubts about Germany's commitment to the alliance could be exploited by a Soviet Union still far from accepting that NATO membership was inevitable. Among the Federal Republic's allies only the United States seemed fully alive to German sensitivities, while remaining firmly fixed on the most important issue: that there must be no wavering on the principle of full NATO membership for the whole of German territory. Mrs Thatcher and President Mitterrand, on the other hand, seemed preoccupied with probing Herr Kohl's good faith. For both, Poland was the key test. Fortunately, for Britain's image at least, M. Mitterrand managed to upstage Mrs Thatcher, demanding on 9 March that a Polish-German agreement on the frontier question must be concluded before unification took place. This was despite a *Bundestag* resolution of 8 March reaffirming the inviolability of the Polish-German frontier (itself the outcome of one of the most serious crises within the Federal Government of the entire unification process).

Mrs Thatcher's reservations were expressed mainly *sotto voce*, in dialogue (and disagreement) with the FCO, and only occasionally coming to the surface in conversations with foreign statesmen. Moreover, she won Herr Kohl's gratitude with a warm message of congratulations after the passing of the *Bundestag* resolution, reinforced by a further message following the dramatic success of the CDU and its allies in the East German elections on 18 March. All of this good work was then undone by an interview in the German magazine *Der Spiegel* in which Mrs Thatcher recalled Chancellor Kohl's intransigence on the frontier question, as expressed during a private dinner at the Strasbourg meeting of European heads of government on 8 December. This flurry arose only a few days before the annual Königswinter Conference in Cambridge and the British-German summit on 29-30 March—occasions to which British diplomats had looked forward as an opportunity to mend fences. As they drove from the airport in separate cars, relations between Mrs Thatcher and Herr Kohl were frostier than ever.[55]

It was left to the Americans to bring Chancellor Kohl into line. Characteristically, they did so by persuasion rather than confrontation. The dispute between Herr Genscher and Herr Stoltenberg over the nature and extent of Germany's commitment to NATO had been rumbling for several weeks when Herr Kohl intervened to resolve it. He ordered the two Ministers to make a joint statement, released on 19 February, which made it clear that the Chancellor, whatever his private convictions, had come down on the side of his Foreign Minister. Although the language was slightly less explicit than Herr Genscher's Tutzing formula, it still declared that no NATO forces, including those of the

[55] Teltschik, p. 188.

Bundeswehr, would move on to the territory of the former GDR. Herr Kohl's calculation was easily explicable in terms of both electoral considerations and the need to avoid antagonising the Soviet Union at a critical time, but to the Americans it formed part of a pattern of ambiguity on the NATO question dating back to Herr Kohl's ten-point programme in late November.[56] Although Mrs Thatcher shared the US objective of keeping Germany firmly within NATO, her concern for Mr Gorbachev's position led to another unhelpful intervention. In a telephone conversation with Bush on 24 February she suggested that Soviet troops should be allowed to stay in the former GDR for a transitional period 'without any terminal date' and that a new European security system should be constructed on the basis of the CSCE to prevent Soviet isolation and 'help balance German domination in Europe' (No. 155). The President and his National Security Advisor were not impressed with these suggestions.[57] They hoped that in the informal surroundings of Camp David, where he was to arrive for a short visit later that day, the Chancellor would succumb to the President's friendly but insistent demand for public clarification of the NATO issue. This duly came in a joint press conference on 25 February in which the two leaders declared their shared belief that Germany should remain a full member of NATO, including its military structure, with a 'special military status' for the territory of the former GDR.

The Two plus Four Negotiations

Once a structure for negotiating German unification had been established, with the Two plus Four decision at Ottawa on 13 February, and her remaining concerns about German backsliding had been laid to rest, Mrs Thatcher was content to leave the detailed negotiations to Douglas Hurd and his officials. After the end of February the Prime Minister exerted no noticeable influence over the formulation or execution of Britain's German policy. Intermittently she would continue to fire off public statements that were provocative if not insulting; but she could also show a softer side. Reflecting later on the Königswinter Conference in Cambridge that had started so unpromisingly, Herr Kohl confessed that he had been astonished when Thatcher went out of her way to be friendly.[58] Perhaps she was obeying Charles Powell's injunction, following her seminar with British and American historians of Germany at Chequers on 24 March, to be 'nice to the Germans'.[59] Yet after Königswinter relations between Britain and Germany undoubtedly became less fraught: a corner had perhaps been turned. Herr Kohl's reaction to Nicholas Ridley's *Spectator* interview in July was amused rather than shocked. By that time, of course, he could afford to be relaxed.

Scheduled to begin after the GDR elections on 18 March, the Two plus Four negotiations in fact started a few days earlier, with a meeting of Political Directors in Paris on the 14th. But the process of establishing a Western negotiating position had started earlier still, when the four Allied Political Directors—Bertrand Dufourcq of France, Dieter Kastrup of the FRG, John Weston of the United

---

[56] Robert L. Hutchings, *American Diplomacy and the End of the Cold War: An Insider's Account of U.S. Policy in Europe, 1989-1992* (Washington, D.C.: The Woodrow Wilson Center Press; Baltimore and London: The Johns Hopkins University Press, 1997), p. 120.
[57] Bush and Scowcroft, pp. 247-49.
[58] Helmut Kohl, *Ich wollte Deutschlands Einheit* (Berlin: Propyläen Verlag, 1996), pp. 340-43. The positive impression is confirmed in Teltschik, pp. 188-89. Some British participants still found Mrs Thatcher's speech at the conference distinctly provocative.
[59] Appendix, No. 3.

Kingdom and Raymond Seitz of the United States, along with Robert Zoellick, who had been asked by Mr Baker to lead the American delegation—met in London under Mr Weston's chairmanship on 28 February. It seemed that months, probably more than a year, of detailed negotiation lay ahead: few if any imagined that the unification process would be concluded as rapidly as it was. But detailed negotiation was something British officials felt they were good at, and it was in this respect that the United Kingdom made its distinctive—and, many believed, indispensable—contribution to the final outcome.[60] Britain's greatest contribution, one of the team subsequently argued, was in clarity of thinking. The Americans, Germans and British 'drove the show', with the British playing a vital role as drafters and, they felt, as 'the only ones really thinking through the issues'.[61] They had a further tactical advantage, later in the proceedings, as possessors of the only laptop computer, enabling them to produce 'running updates of the texts in near real time around the table' (No. 238).

The search for a common Western negotiating position was prolonged. In the first phase, leading up to the first meeting of Two plus Four Political Directors in Paris on 14 March, the principal differences concerned the starting date for negotiations, the position of a united Germany within NATO and the question whether unification should form part of a wider 'peace settlement' or even be marked by a formal peace treaty—a demand regarded as humiliating by a democratic Germany forty-five years after the end of the war. On the first and last issues the British and French faced a united American-German front. They were obliged to concede at the outset that, while the Political Directors might meet before the GDR elections on 18 March, the first Ministerial meeting must not take place until afterwards. But it was not until early April that the British and French gave up their demand for a peace settlement—an issue which, in the British view, had revealed 'signs of weakening Western solidarity' in the Paris meeting on 14 March (No. 174). On the other hand, the British and Americans were firm on the need to clarify the details of Germany's NATO membership and worked closely to identify the legal issues that would have to be resolved before the unification process could be completed.

The second phase of inter-Allied discussion, leading up to the first Ministerial meeting of the Two plus Four in Bonn on 5 May, was marked by growing Western solidarity. The decisive victory of the electoral coalition of the CDU and its East German allies, led by Lothar de Maizière, demoralised the Soviet leadership and bolstered Herr Kohl's resolve to accelerate the unification process still further. The election had strengthened his negotiating position in relation to his Western allies and he now hoped that agreement on the external aspects could be completed by the autumn. There were conflicting Soviet messages: while Mr Shevardnadze and President Gorbachev still set their face against NATO membership, there was evidence of greater flexibility on the part of some Soviet officials. But by the beginning of April West German statements on NATO were becoming firmer. The British team, meanwhile, concentrated on clarifying the legal issues and considering the form the final settlement might take. American and German policies remained closely coordinated. At meetings with Mrs Thatcher in Bermuda

---

[60] See Zelikow and Rice, p. 235, and Hutchings, p. 96. Bertrand Dufourcq, '2+4 ou la négociation atypique', *Politique étrangère* 2/2000, pp. 467-84, gives a fuller picture of the French role.

[61] Personal information. The British team possessed considerable legal expertise on German issues. One member was co-author of a definitive study of the status of Berlin in international law: I.D. Hendry and M.C. Wood, *The Legal Status of Berlin* (Cambridge: Grotius Publications Ltd., 1987).

and M. Mitterrand at Key Largo, President Bush secured the agreement of the two leaders to the principle that the Two plus Four negotiations would bring all Four-Power rights to an end and restore full sovereignty to a united Germany. He followed this up with a speech on 4 May outlining an ambitious review of NATO strategy, to be debated at an early NATO summit (later scheduled for 5 July in London).

The first Ministerial meeting of the Two plus Four was conducted in what Mr Hurd called a 'serious and conciliatory atmosphere' (No. 196). Nevertheless Mr Shevardnadze (under pressure from Politburo hardliners) came up with one disconcerting surprise. While accepting German unification as a *fait accompli*, he argued that the internal and external processes should be 'decoupled', and that external unification should occur at some unspecified date after the internal process had been completed. The indefinite prolongation of Four-Power rights was unwelcome to West Germany and its allies alike. The British were less worried than the Americans by Mr Shevardnadze's proposal.[62] They were more alarmed, at least momentarily, by news that the Germans were seeking to accelerate the unification process further by holding all-German, not merely Federal, elections in December. Internal unification, in other words, might be accomplished before the external aspects had been settled, even if the Soviets did not manage to put a spoke in the wheel. Mr Weston did not share this anxiety about German intentions but argued for a robust response to the Soviet decoupling proposal, even to the extent of a unilateral Western renunciation of Four-Power rights—an idea he developed further a few days later when the four Western Political Directors met in Bonn on 22 May.

But a tough line proved unnecessary. 'Decoupling' was not mentioned by Aleksander Bondarenko, the chief Soviet negotiator, when the Two plus Four Political Directors met later that day. Despite the hard line maintained by President Gorbachev, Mr Shevardnadze and Soviet officials in their meetings with Mr Baker and his team in Moscow on 16-19 May, acute economic weakness and the Lithuanian crisis were undermining the Soviet position from within. In Moscow the Soviets had been presented with a nine-point package designed to win their assent to German membership of NATO. Since early May the Soviets had been talking to the Germans about their pressing need for credits: on 22 May Herr Kohl wrote to Mr Gorbachev offering a credit of DM 5 billion, creating a positive atmosphere for the meeting between Herr Genscher and Mr Shevardnadze in Geneva the following day. Both the Americans and the Germans realised that Soviet resistance was weakening— Herr Genscher told Mr Hurd on 28 May that the Russians were 'coming to terms with German membership of NATO' (No. 205)—but that it would be unwise to rush them into accepting an inevitably unpalatable outcome. As Mr Baker remarked, 'It's best to let it happen.'[63] The decisive moment came on 30 May during Mr Gorbachev's visit to Washington when, apparently without consultation and perhaps without prior reflection, he agreed with Mr Bush that Germany had the right to decide which alliance it wished to join.[64] The other Western leaders, even Herr Kohl, did not seem at first to grasp the significance of this concession, though Mrs Thatcher noted, when she met

---

[62] There is an interesting contrast between the relatively positive tone of Mr Hurd's report on the meeting (No. 196) and the much gloomier US assessment presented in Zelikow and Rice, pp. 246-50.

[63] Quoted *ibid.*, p. 266.

[64] *Ibid.*, pp. 276-79.

President Gorbachev in Moscow on 8 June, that he at no point ruled out German NATO membership but 'appeared rather to be reaching round for ways to make this more palatable and explicable to his own people' (No. 209).

For the Americans, making German membership palatable meant pushing through, at the London summit on 5 July, a radical reshaping of NATO strategy that would make the organisation 'more political, less military' and part of a security structure for the whole of Europe that could be presented to the Soviet people as an acceptable price for the loss of eastern Germany to the Western Alliance.[65] The Turnberry meeting of NATO Foreign Ministers on 7 June clearly signalled a more accommodating stance towards the Warsaw Pact, but more was expected from the London summit. The Bush Administration's high-risk strategy, pursued in parallel with the Two plus Four negotiations, involved persuading NATO partners to accept a resolution drafted by the United States and expressing the American vision for the future of the Alliance, rather than one that emerged through the usual channels of NATO bureaucracy.

The Two plus Four Political Directors met twice in East Berlin, on 9 and 20 June. They agreed that the existing borders of the FRG, the GDR and Berlin would no longer be provisional and that Articles 23 and 146 of the Basic Law, designed to leave open the possibility of further territorial additions to the Federal Republic, would be deleted or modified. Other issues remained unresolved, including the question whether a treaty between Germany and Poland should precede or follow the unification settlement. In discussions with their Western partners, the British team remained vigilant for signs of imprecision in the terminology employed in the various draft agreements. They also insisted that sight should not be lost of other issues, such as claims, which were 'not necessarily politically delicate but nonetheless need resolution and hence some solid groundwork' (No. 207). When the Second Ministerial meeting of the Two plus Four took place in East Berlin on 22 June there was a final demonstration of Soviet intransigence. The new Deputy Foreign Minister Yuli Kvitsinsky had belatedly been given the opportunity to establish the kind of negotiating position he wished had been set out at the very beginning of the process, and Mr Shevardnadze duly recited a list of far-reaching demands. It was clear to the West, not least owing to signals from Soviet officials over the preceding weeks, that this hard line amounted to little more than 'window-dressing' (as Herr Genscher put it);[66] the British, too, quickly deduced from informal conversations with Mr Shevardnadze that his 'draft was intended to a great extent for domestic Soviet purposes and was not immutable' (No. 214).

The Breakthrough

The atmosphere at the second Ministerial meeting was 'friendly and workmanlike' (No. 214).[67] Yet East Berlin marked no breakthrough. That had to await the successful conclusion of the London NATO summit, with its concluding proposal to the Warsaw Pact of 'a joint declaration in which we solemnly state that we are no longer adversaries' (No. 215). The stage was now set for Herr Kohl's historic visit to the Soviet Union on 15-16 July and Mr Gorbachev's acceptance, at Stavropol in the Caucasus, of German membership of NATO. The agreement between the two leaders, coming just before the third Ministerial meeting of the

---

[65] *Ibid.*, p. 303.

[66] Hans-Dietrich Genscher, *Erinnerungen* (Berlin: Siedler Verlag, 1995), pp. 824-5.

[67] During a lull in the proceedings Mr Waldegrave led the British team to the Pergamon Museum, where he conversed knowledgeably about the classical antiquities with one of the curators

Two plus Four in Paris on 17 July, had, the FCO reported, 'brought about a sea-change in the negotiations and [put] us firmly in the end game' (No. 219). There was now a good chance that the entire process could be concluded at the next Ministerial meeting in Moscow on 12 September. Polish concerns were assuaged by the presence at the meeting of the Polish Foreign Minister, Krzysztof Skubiszewski, and an agreement that a Polish-German treaty would be signed as soon as possible after unification.

The pace of unification at the inner-German level was also accelerating. Herr Kohl and Herr de Maizière had agreed in April that the two states would enter monetary, economic and social union on 1 July. A state treaty to that effect was concluded on 18 May. There was growing awareness of the costs of bringing about an economic transformation of the GDR. The Federal Government's desire to gain full control of the East German economy was one of the considerations behind its push for all-German elections to be held in early December. It was subsequently agreed that the elections would take place on 2 December—a decision endorsed by the East German CDU on 12 June. But Herr Kohl's political difficulties were also mounting. Electoral setbacks in Lower Saxony led to the formation of a *Land* government by the SPD and the Greens, giving the SPD a majority in the *Bundesrat*, the Federal German upper house, whose approval was needed for any change to the Basic Law. The SPD, under the leadership of Oskar Lafontaine, were not inclined to be cooperative. In the GDR, local elections in early May saw a weakening of support for the CDU and its coalition partners. The solidarity of Herr de Maizière's Government fractured under the impact of GEMU on a fragile economy and accusations of complicity with former Stasi members. Negotiations for a second state treaty, to bring about political union, started on 6 July. The issues raised by the absorption of the GDR into the political, social and legal structures of the FRG were complex and the negotiations, conducted against a background of febrile political activity, proved protracted. In early August Herr de Maizière provoked some alarm with his proposals that the GDR should accede to the FRG on 1 October, and that all-German elections should be brought forward from 2 December to 14 October. In the event, the election date remained unchanged while the *Volkskammer* voted on 23 August for unity on 3 October. Three days earlier, however, Herr de Maizière's coalition had collapsed and he had taken over the foreign affairs portfolio from his erstwhile SPD partner Markus Meckel. 'What has been a long, messy and demoralising period of political infighting over the modalities of unification is now at last coming to an end', reported Sir C. Mallaby (No. 229). The second state treaty was finally concluded on 31 August.

The Endgame

The path to the final Ministerial meeting of the Two plus Four, held in Moscow on 12 September, proved less straightforward than had been hoped. When the Two plus Four Political Directors met in Bonn on 19 July, only two days after the third Ministerial, they divided the outstanding tasks between them with a view to meeting again in early September to resolve the text of the final settlement. Shortly afterwards the British team came up with a creative solution (finally endorsed by Ministers on 12 September) to the danger of a potential legal vacuum: the proposal that Allied rights (QRR) should be 'suspended' upon unification and terminated only upon ratification of the final settlement. Subsequent exchanges took place against the background of the Iraqi invasion of Kuwait at the beginning of August and the negotiations between the FRG and the Soviet Union for a series of treaties to govern political relations between the two countries following unification; financial and other arrangements for the withdrawal of Soviet forces from eastern Germany; and GDR trade obligations to the Soviet Union. With the Soviets raising last-minute demands over the costs and timing of their withdrawal, these talks proved tense: they were not resolved until Herr Kohl and President Gorbachev reached agreement on a figure of DM 15 billion on 10 September.

Controversy among the Western Four arose primarily over the arrangements for a continued Allied military presence in Germany following the expiry, upon unification, of the Presence of Foreign Forces Convention (PFFC) of 1954, and the question whether the Status of Forces Agreement (SOFA) and Supplementary Agreement (SA) should be extended to the whole of Germany. Discussion of the latter issue was conducted in the light of the provision in the Kohl-Gorbachev agreement at Stavropol that NATO 'structures'—meaning non-FRG troops and nuclear weapons—would not be extended into the former GDR until all Soviet forces had been withdrawn. There was ambiguity over whether this meant only that NATO forces could not be stationed permanently in eastern Germany, but could conduct exercises there and over-fly the territory; or whether it implied a blanket prohibition, as the Soviets argued and as the West Germans, at the meeting between Herr Genscher and Mr Shevardnadze in Moscow on 16-17 August, appeared to have conceded.[68] British views on the subject of 'crossing the line' were robust and unequivocal: 'Germany a single legal area. Can't have one rule for soldiers in Düsseldorf and another in Potsdam. It would be as if a diplomat had immunity in Bonn but not in Cologne' (No. 230). There was a further ambiguity, though this ultimately proved easier to resolve, over whether the prohibition of nuclear weapons, which the West was willing to concede, also applied to dual-capable systems: aircraft or artillery which could be adapted to fire or launch nuclear weapons.

By the end of the final meeting of the Two plus Four Political Directors in East Berlin between 4 and 7 September, three substantive questions remained unresolved: dual-capable weapons; the suspension of QRR in the period between unification and their final termination; and the right of NATO forces to move into eastern Germany. The British and Americans were convinced that the Russians were not on strong ground on these three issues and were on the alert for 'signs of vacillation in Bonn' (No. 234).[69] Final resolution now awaited the Ministerial meeting in Moscow. Meeting again on 11 September, shortly before the arrival of their Foreign Ministers, the Two plus Four Political Directors managed to reach agreement on dual-capable weapons, while the suspension of Four-Power rights was agreed without difficulty by Ministers on 12 September. 'Crossing the line' was another matter. The nature of NATO's right to deploy non-German forces in the territory of the former GDR after unification provoked the most serious dispute among the Western allies—specifically between the British on the one hand and the West Germans on the other—of the entire Two plus Four process. Exacerbated by clashes of personality and exploited by the chief Soviet negotiator, Mr Kvitsinsky, when German annoyance allowed Western discord to spill over into the Four-Power forum,[70] the wrangles lasted deep into the night, eventually

---

[68] Zelikow and Rice, p. 356.

[69] For the American position see Schabert, p. 487.

[70] Werner Weidenfeld, *Aussenpolitik für die deutsche Einheit. Die Entscheidungsjahre 1989/90* (Stuttgart: Deutsche Verlags-Anstalt, 1998), p. 851 (note 66).

involving all four Western Foreign Ministers: Mr Genscher, Mr Hurd, Mr Baker and M. Dumas. The question was finally resolved at the Ministerial meeting the following day, when Mr Shevardnadze assented to Mr Baker's suggestion of an agreed minute, to be annexed to the treaty, stating that the interpretation of the word 'deployed' would be a matter for decision by the German Government. The compromise satisfied all parties, while leaving German sovereignty unimpaired.

A number of the participants have given their versions of the affair.[71] Mr Weston's record of the meeting (No. 238) supports the conclusions of the authoritative American and German accounts: that he was not maintaining an isolated British line, still less acting on orders from No. 10.[72] Rather, aware that M. Dufourcq shared his reservations but lacked Ministerial authority before M. Dumas's arrival in Moscow, and with Mr Zoellick's compass, in his view, 'beginning to veer uncertainly', Mr Weston upheld a position that had been agreed by three Western allies and was in the best interests of the fourth. Far from wishing to hold on to the remnants of Four-Power sovereignty, as some German diplomats seem to have believed, Mr Weston insisted, as he had reminded Mr Seitz in July, on 'the over-riding strategic priority of returning sovereignty with unity to the Germans at the earliest possible moment' (No. 221).[73] More confident than the Germans that the Soviets had no option but to sign, he resisted a concession that would have allowed the Soviet Union a residual say in German affairs. It was British stubbornness, in other words, that helped to ensure that Germany was not 'singularised'.[74]

With the signature of the final settlement on 12 September, and a declaration suspending Four-Power rights signed in New York on 1 October, the way was clear for the formal unification of Germany. On 3 October the GDR became part of the FRG in accordance with Article 23 of the Basic Law. Article 23 was then deleted, and Article 146 modified, to make it clear that there would be no further territorial additions to the Federal Republic. The United Kingdom became the second of the Four Powers, following the United States, to ratify the final settlement: the instrument of ratification was delivered to the Federal Government on 16 November. The *Bundestag* election of 2 December was fought almost solely on the single issue of unification. The result was a decisive victory for the Kohl-Genscher coalition. Following ratification by France in January and by the Soviet Union in March, the final settlement entered into force on 15 March 1991.

Conclusion

Looking back on the history of German unification from the vantage point of October 1990, Sir C. Mallaby was able to record the appreciation of German officialdom for the positive and creative role played by the British in the Two plus Four process (No. 242). But there was also, he said, a darker side to the story. This was due almost entirely to the perception that Margaret Thatcher was essentially hostile to unification—a perception so deep-rooted that it distorted Britain's role in the eyes of German politicians and the public at large. Diverted by Mrs Thatcher's

---

[71] Genscher, pp. 865-74; Hutchings, pp. 138-39; Douglas Hurd, *Memoirs* (London: Little, Brown, 2003), pp. 388-89; Frank Elbe and Richard Kiessler, *A Round Table with Sharp Corners. The Diplomatic Path to German Unity* (Baden-Baden: Nomos, 1996), pp. 195-99.
[72] Zelikow and Rice, pp. 359-62; Weidenfeld, pp. 599-602.
[73] For German suspicions see Elbe and Kiessler, p. 198.
[74] See also the testimony of Miss Neville-Jones, Mr Synnott and Mr Wood (interviewed in 1997) in Weidenfeld, p. 851 (note 67).

numerous negative comments, Germans overlooked Britain's positive contribution to the unification process, saw her hand at work even on issues where she was not involved at all, and undervalued the supportive statements made by other members of the British Government. If the United States, not surprisingly, was awarded the 'gold medal' and France, despite President Mitterrand's evident reservations, won the silver, the United Kingdom ended up with the bronze. The implication was not only that Britain had been less helpful than the other allies, but also that it was less important.

In considering the options open to British diplomacy in the winter of 1989-90, one has the impression of a missed opportunity: no major changes were needed, only a little more public expression of support and understanding. Since Britain could do little to influence the pace and direction of unification, the most rational approach would have been an early acknowledgement on the part of the Prime Minister that German unity was going to happen: that the United Kingdom could do nothing to stop it and must therefore accept it with good grace. This would have won the gratitude of Germans—Herr Kohl in particular—at a time when they were feeling exposed and vulnerable as well as elated. No such statement was forthcoming. 'The Prime Minister,' her Foreign Policy Adviser has written, was not alone in thinking and feeling as she did. Other Western leaders shared her concerns. . . . The difference was that her partners composed their features and said very different things in public.'[75] But in the absence of positive signals from No. 10, Britain was bound to appear obstructive and negative.

The Prime Minister's intransigence, by raising doubts about a forty-year-old British commitment to German self-determination, paralysed British policy on Germany for perhaps three to four months. Her subsequent statements, combined with Mr Ridley's *Spectator* interview and the leak of the record of her Chequers seminar, did lasting damage to Britain's image in Germany at precisely the same time as the British team were making their vital contribution to the success of the Two plus Four negotiations—a contribution that, while valued by their German colleagues, did not, of course, make the headlines. They also deprived her of the credit she deserved for helping to bring about the end of the Cold War. German unification, as Sir P. Cradock had reminded her in November 1989, 'was an immense victory for the West and for principles she had been foremost in advocating'.[76]

But it is not obvious that Mrs Thatcher was as misguided in every respect as she appeared at the time or as she has subsequently been portrayed. Her own memoirs have done as much as anything to perpetuate the image of a Prime Minister fixated on the alleged deficiencies of the German national character and determined to thwart German unity. Some of the documents in this volume will reinforce that image. To this extent they do her a disservice. Her welcome for the awakening of democracy in the GDR was unequivocal. There is no evidence that she sought to perpetuate the existence of the East German state in defiance of the wishes of its citizens. As she told her Private Secretary before the Chequers meeting in March 1990, when expressing her belief that in future history would be determined by the character of peoples rather than by the personalities and ambitions of their rulers, 'the lesson of the past two years is that neither character nor pride has been suffocated by oppression'.[77]

[75] Cradock, p. 111.
[76] *Ibid.*, pp. 111-12. See also No. 39, note 6.
[77] Appendix, No. 4.

Moreover, at the core of Mrs Thatcher's misgivings were two considerations, neither lightly to be dismissed. One was the danger that the speed of the unification process might jeopardise Mr Gorbachev's position. The other was the fear that in their drive to unity the Germans and their American champions might destabilise the delicate balance of security arrangements that had preserved European peace since 1945. It was unfortunate that her frankness on Germany undermined her capacity to influence the UK's allies on these important questions. Of course the Germans and Americans would never have been deflected from their conviction that the West had to seize an opportunity that was unlikely to recur; and the achievement of German unity within such a short time and with so little disruption remains a great triumph—perhaps *the* great triumph—of Western post-war diplomacy. Yet within only a few years one American negotiator was moved to reflect:

> First, was Prime Minister Thatcher really so wrong in protesting that the rush to unity was threatening the future of European security? Did the priority we attached to the unification process cause us to neglect other objectives that would have helped 'synchronise' Germany's unification with Europe's?[78]

British diplomacy undoubtedly helped, despite the Prime Minister's interventions, to keep the minds of the United Kingdom's partners focused on such vital issues. It also brought legal experience, expertise and precision to the Two plus Four negotiations. In a sense, therefore, it was altruistic because the most useful role the United Kingdom could play was that of facilitator and guardian of wider Western interests. But it was altruistic by default. Boxed in by the Prime Minister's immovability on Europe, there was no scope for securing specifically British interests: none, in other words, for the kind of bargain that President Mitterrand was able to strike with Herr Kohl.

There remained, finally, a problem in British-German relations: one that had been identified by British diplomats before unification and remained unchanged thereafter. The assessments contained in the 1987 Planners' paper, in Sir C. Mallaby's despatches and letters of early 1989 and in those of late 1990 are almost identical except that the latter are coloured by the realisation that Germany was now a much bigger and more influential power. Britain did not matter to Germans in the way that France did, and British diplomacy still lacked the leverage to convince them that British policies must be taken seriously. It was possible to identify many opportunities for enhancing British influence in the newly united Germany, but these were in danger of being undermined by a further problem: Britain's perceived ambivalence towards the European project. 'The single step which would most enhance our standing in Germany,' Sir C. Mallaby advised, 'would be to make our policies in the Community more positive, in presentation and where possible in content' (No. 244). The unification process demonstrated that hostility to European integration had deprived the United Kingdom of a forum for exerting influence which a more pro-European France could exploit to the full. Moreover, Europe had created divisions at the very heart of Government that were to lead to the Prime Minister's fall from power—ironically during the CSCE summit in Paris in November 1990 that set the seal on German unity. British-German relations quickly recovered from the contretemps and misunderstandings of 1989-90. But British hostility to European integration grew in intensity,

---

[78] Hutchings, pp. 139-40.

undermining Mrs Thatcher's successor and fatally weakening her party. In this context Germany was a symptom of a fundamental dilemma, but one that would have existed whether Germany was united or not.

Acknowledgements

In accordance with the Parliamentary announcement cited in the Introduction to the Series, the Editors have had the customary freedom in the selection and arrangement of documents including full access to all classes of FCO documentation. There have, in the case of the present volume, been no exceptional cases, provided for in the Parliamentary announcement, where it has been necessary on security grounds to restrict the availability of particular documents, editorially selected in accordance with regular practice. The official documents published or cited in this volume are not yet in the public domain and will not be transferred to The National Archives in advance of their due date, but they have been marked for permanent preservation and will be released in the usual way.

The main source of documentation in this volume has been the archives of the FCO held, pending their transfer to The National Archives (TNA), by the Information Management Group (IMG). I should like to thank the present and former Heads of IMG, Jane Darby and Heather Yasamee, and their staff for their help and support. I am also grateful to Michael Kerr and Penny Prior, the present and former heads of the FCO Archive at Hanslope Park, and to members of their team including Margaret Ryan, Rachel Cox, Caroline Puddephat and Elaine King. I would like to offer particular thanks to Sir Peter Ricketts, Permanent Under-Secretary of State and Head of the Diplomatic Service, who has given his encouragement and support to the project at every stage.

This volume draws heavily on the records of the Cabinet Office and the Prime Minister's office, and I am extremely grateful to the former Head of the Cabinet Office Histories, Openness and Records Unit, Tessa Stirling, and to Sally Falk and Chris Grindall for their help. The Cabinet Secretary, Sir Gus O'Donnell, has kindly given permission for the publication and citation of documents from the Cabinet and Prime Minister's collections.

In compiling this volume I have benefited greatly from discussions with former Ministers and with serving and retired officials too numerous to mention individually. I should, however, like to record my gratitude to Lord Hurd of Westwell for permission to reproduce extracts from his private diary, and to Sir Christopher Mallaby, Bob Dixon, Tony Bishop and Jim Daly for their help and advice. Allen Packwood, Andrew Riley, Christopher Collins, David Marsh, Roger Morgan, Mary Sarotte and Svetlana Savranskaya have also offered valuable assistance.

I am grateful to all those current and former members of FCO Historians who have helped on this volume, in particular Gill Bennett, former Chief Historian of the FCO; Christopher Baxter, Alastair Noble and Isabelle Tombs. In addition, valuable technical assistance has been provided by Giles Rose, Grant Hibberd, Hala Bouguerne, Elaine Alahendra, Craig Buchan and Kevin Williams.

PATRICK SALMON

April 2009

ABBREVIATIONS FOR PRINTED SOURCES

Attali	Jacques Attali, *Verbatim*, Vol. 3, *Chronique des années 1988-1991* (Paris: Fayard, 1995).
Bush and Scowcroft	George Bush and Brent Scowcroft, *A World Transformed* (New York: Alfred A. Knopf, 1998).
Cmnd.	Command Paper (London).
Cradock	Percy Cradock, *In Pursuit of British Interests: Reflections on British Foreign Policy under Margaret Thatcher and John Major* (London: John Murray, 1997).
Elbe and Kiessler	Frank Elbe and Richard Kiessler, *A Round Table with Sharp Corners. The Diplomatic Path to German Unity* (Baden-Baden: Nomos, 1996).
Deutsche Einheit	Hanns Jürgen Küsters and Daniel Hoffman (eds.), *Deutsche Einheit. Sonderedition aus den Akten des Bundeskanzkleramtes 1989/90* (Munich: R. Oldenbourg Verlag, 1998).
Genscher	Hans-Dietrich Genscher, *Erinnerungen* (Berlin: Siedler Verlag, 1995).
Hutchings	Robert L. Hutchings, *American Diplomacy and the End of the Cold War: An Insider's Account of U.S. Policy in Europe, 1989-1992* (Washington, D.C.: The Woodrow Wilson Center Press; Baltimore and London: The Johns Hopkins University Press, 1997).
Parl. Debs., 5th ser., H. of C.	*Parliamentary Debates (Hansard), Fifth Series, House of Commons, Official Report* (London, 1909f.).
Public Papers	*Public Papers of the Presidents of the United States, George Bush: 1989*, Book II (Washington, DC, 1990).
Schabert	Thilo Schabert, *Wie Weltgeschichte gemacht wird. Frankreich und die deutsche Einheit* (Stuttgart: Klett-Cotta, 2002).
Series III, Vol. VI	*Documents on British Policy Overseas*, Series III, Volume VI, *Berlin in the Cold War, 1948-1990* (London: Routledge, 2009).
Teltschik	Horst Teltschik, *329 Tage. Innenansichten der Einigung* (Berlin: Siedler Verlag, 1991).
Thatcher	Margaret Thatcher, *The Downing Street Years* (London: HarperCollins, 1993).
Weidenfeld	Werner Weidenfeld, *Aussenpolitik für die deutsche Einheit. Die Entscheidungsjahre 1989/90* (Stuttgart: Deutsche Verlags-Anstalt, 1998).
Zelikow and Rice	Philip Zelikow and Condoleezza Rice, *Germany Unified and Europe Transformed: A study in statecraft* (Cambridge, Mass.: Harvard University Press, 1995).

ABBREVIATED DESIGNATIONS

ACA	Allied Control Authority	COREPER	*Comité des Représentants*
ADIZ	Air Defence Identification Zone	(EC)	*Permanents*/Committee of Permanent Representatives
ADN	*Allgemeiner Deutscher Nachrichtendienst*/German News Agency (GDR state news agency)	CPSU	Communist Party of the Soviet Union
		CSBM(s)	Confidence- and Security-Building Measures
AGF	Anglo-German Foundation	CSCE	Conference on Security and Cooperation in Europe
ALCM	Air-launched Cruise Missile		
APS	Assistant Private Secretary	CSU	*Christlich-Soziale Union in Bayern*/ Christian Social Union of Bavaria (FRG)
ARC	(British Council) Academic Research Collaboration programme		
		DA	*Demokratischer Aufbruch*/ Democratic Awakening (GDR)
ARD	*Arbeitsgemeinschaft der öffentlich-rechtlichen Rundfunkanstalten der Bundesrepublik Deutschland*/ Consortium of public-law broadcasting institutions of the FRG		
		DDR	*Deutsche Demokratische Republik* (GDR)
		DEG	*Deutsch-Englische Gesellschaft*/German-English Society
AUS/AUSS	Assistant Under-Secretary of State	DKP	DKP *Deutsche Kommunistische Partei*/ German Communist Party (FRG)
BAOR	British Army of the Rhine		
BERCON	Berlin Contingency Plans		
BFG	British Forces Germany	DPA	*Deutsche Presse-Agentur*/German Press Agency (FRG)
BK/L	Berlin *Kommandatura* Letter		
BM Berlin	British Mission Berlin		
BMG	British Military Government	DSU	*Deutsche Soziale Union*/German Social Union (GDR)
BRIXMIS	British Commanders'-in-Chief Mission to the Soviet Forces in Germany		
		DTI	Department of Trade and Industry
BW/CW	Biological/Chemical Weapons	DUS/DUSS	Deputy Under-Secretary of State
CAP	Common Agricultural Policy (EC)		
		EBRD	European Bank for Reconstruction and Development
CDU	*Christlich-Demokratische Union*/Christian Democratic Union (FRG)		
		EC	European Community
CFE	Conventional Forces in Europe	EED	Eastern European Department, FCO
CFSP	Common Foreign and Security Policy	EFTA	European Free Trade Area
		ELT	English Language Training
CHOGM	Commonwealth Heads of Government Meeting	EMU	European Monetary Union
		EPC	European Political Cooperation
CINC(G)	Commander-in-Chief (Germany)		
CINC/	Commander-in-Chief, British	ERM	Exchange Rate Mechanism
BAOR	Army of the Rhine	FAC	Foreign Affairs Committee
CINCEUR	Commander-in-Chief Europe	FAZ	*Frankfurter Allgemeine Zeitung*
CITES	Convention on International Trade in Endangered Species of Wild Fauna and Flora		
		FBI	Federal Bureau of Investigation
CMEA	See COMECON	FCO	Foreign and Commonwealth Office
COCOM	Coordinating Committee of the Paris Consultative Group		
		FDP	*Freie Demokratische Partei*/ Free Democratic Party (FRG)
COI	Central Office of Information		
COMECON	Council for Mutual Economic Assistance	FMOD	Federal (German) Ministry of Defence

FOTL	Follow-up to Lance	PFFC	Presence of Foreign Forces Convention
FRG	Federal Republic of Germany		
G-24	Group of 24	POCO	Political Cooperation (in the EC)
G7	Group of Seven		
GA	*General Anzeiger*	PQ	Parliamentary Question
GDP	Gross Domestic Product	PS	Private Secretary
GDR	German Democratic Republic	PUS/PUSS	Permanent Under-Secretary of State
GEMU	German Economic and Monetary Union	QA	Quadripartite Agreement (1971)
HMG	Her Majesty's Government		
IGC	Inter-Governmental Conference	QRR(s)	Quadripartite Rights and Responsibilities
IISS	International Institute for Strategic Studies	S/S	Secretary of State
		SA	Supplementary Agreement (to SOFA)
IMF	International Monetary Fund		
INF	Intermediate-Range Nuclear Forces Treaty	SC	(UN) Security Council
		SDI	Strategic Defense Initiative
IPU	International Parliamentary Union	SDP	*Sozialdemokratische Partei*/ Social Democratic Party (GDR)
JIC	Joint Intelligence Committee		
JPC	Joint Permanent Council (NATO)	SED	*Sozialistische Einheitspartei Deutschlands*/Socialist Unity Party of Germany (GDR)
JSLO	Joint Services Liaison Organisation	SEW	*Sozialistische Einheitspartei Westberlins*/Socialist Unity Party of West Berlin
LDPD	*Liberal-Demokratische Partei Deutschlands*/Liberal Democratic Party of Germany (GDR)	SHAPE	Supreme Headquarters Allied Powers Europe
		SLCM	Sea-launched Cruise Missile
MAFF	Ministry of Agriculture, Fisheries and Food	SNF	Short-Range Nuclear Forces
MBFR	Mutual and Balanced Force Reductions	SOFA	Status of Forces Agreement
		SOXMIS	Soviet Military Liaison Mission Germany
MFA	Ministry of Foreign Affairs		
MIFT/MIPT	My Immediately Following/Preceding Telegram	SPD (FRG)	*Sozialdemokratische Partei Deutschlands*/German Social Democratic Party
MLM	Military Liaison Mission	START	Strategic Arms Reduction Treaty
MOD/ MODUK	Ministry of Defence		
		Stasi	*Ministerium für Staatssicherheit*/Ministry for State Security (GDR)
NAC	North Atlantic Council		
NATO	North Atlantic Treaty Organisation	TASM	Tactical Air to Surface Missile
NBC	Nuclear, Biological and Chemical weapons	TUR	Telegram Under Reference
		UKDEL	United Kingdom Delegation
ND	*Neues Deutschland*	UKMIS	United Kingdom Mission
NPG	Nuclear Planning Group	UKREP	United Kingdom Representative
NSC	National Security Council		
NVA	*Nationale Volksarmee*/GDR National People's Army	UN	United Nations
		VS	Verbatim Series
OD	Overseas and Defence Committee of the Cabinet	WED	Western European Department, FCO
OECD	Organisation for European Economic Co-operation	WEU	Western European Union
		WINTEX	Winter Exercise
PDS	*Partei des Demokratischen Sozialismus*/Party of Democratic Socialism (GDR/FRG)	YEC	Youth Exchange Centre
		YTUR(S)	Your Telegram(s) Under Reference

LIST OF PERSONS

Ackermann, Eduard, Head of Communications and Media Division, FRG Chancellery, 1982-94

Acland, Sir Antony A., British Ambassador, Washington, 1986-91

Adamishin, Anatoly L., Deputy Minister for Foreign Affairs, USSR, 1986-91

Adams, Geoffrey D., Private Secretary to the PUS, FCO, 1987-91

Adenauer, Dr Konrad, Chancellor of the FRG, 1949-63

Alexander, Sir Michael O'D. B., Ambassador and UK Permanent Representative on the North Atlantic Council, 1986-92

Andreotti, Giulio, Prime Minister of Italy, 1989-92

Appleyard, Leonard V., on loan from FCO to Cabinet Office as Deputy Secretary, 1989-91

Bahr, Egon K.-H., FRG Minister without Portfolio 1972-74; Minister for Economic Cooperation, 1974-76

Baker, James A., III, US Secretary of State, 1989-92

Bangemann, Martin, Commissioner for Industrial Affairs and the Internal Market, EC Commission, 1989-95

Bartholomew, Reginald, Under Secretary of State for International Security Affairs, US State Department, 1989-92

Beil, Gerhard, Minister for Foreign Trade, GDR 1986-90 (April)

Bellinghen, Jean-Paul van, Belgian Ambassador, London, 1984-91

Berghofer, Wolfgang, Mayor of Dresden, 1986-90

Berman, Franklin D., Deputy Legal Adviser, FCO, 1988-91

Bertele, Dr Franz, Head of the Permanent Representation of the Federal Republic in the GDR, 1989-90

Bianco, Jean-Louis, Chief of Staff to President Mitterrand, 1982-91

Blackwill, Robert D., Senior Director for European and Soviet Affairs, US National Security Council, 1989-90

Blake-Pauley, Anthony F., Consul-General, Munich, 1988-92

Blüm, Norbert, FRG Minister for Labour and Social Order, 1982-98

Bohley, Bärbel, Co-founder of New Forum, GDR, 1989

Bondarenko, Aleksander P., Head of the Third European Department, Soviet Ministry of Foreign Affairs, 1971-91; Soviet representative in Two plus Four negotiations, 1990

Braithwaite, Sir Rodric Q., British Ambassador, Moscow, 1988-92

Brandt, Willy, Chancellor of the FRG, 1969-74

Brittan, Leon, EC Commissioner for Competition, 1989-93

Broek, Hans van den, Foreign Minister of the Netherlands, 1982-92.

Broomfield, Nigel H.R.A., British Ambassador, East Berlin, 1988-90

Brzezinski, Zbigniew, National Security Adviser to President Jimmy Carter, 1977-81

Büchler, Hans, SPD spokesman on Inner German Relations

Budd, Colin R., Counsellor (Political), British Embassy, Bonn, 1989-92

Bullard, Sir Julian L., British Ambassador, Bonn, 1984-88

Burton, Michael St E., Minister and Deputy Commandant, BMG Berlin, 1985-90

Butler, Sir F.E. Robin, Secretary of the Cabinet and Head of the Home Civil Service, 1988-98

Carrington, Peter A.R.C., 6th Baron Carrington, Secretary of State for Foreign and Commonwealth Affairs, 1979-82

Chalker, Lynda, Minister of State for Foreign and Commonwealth Affairs, 1986-97; Minister for Overseas Development, 1989-97

Charlton, Alan, First Secretary and Deputy Political Adviser, BMG Berlin, 1986-91

Cheney, Richard B., US Secretary of Defense 1989-93

Chernyaev, Anatoly S., Chief Foreign Policy Adviser to Mr Gorbachev

Chevènement, Jean-Pierre, French Minister of Defence, 1988-91

Clark, Alan, Minister of State, Ministry of Defence 1989-92

Cooper, Robert F., Head of Policy Planning Staff, FCO, 1989-93

Cooper, Tommy, Anglo-Welsh comedian; died 1984

Cox, Nigel J., Assistant Head, WED, FCO, 1990-91

Craig, Professor Gordon A., Historian; author of *Germany, 1866-1945* (1978); *The Germans* (1981)

Cradock, Sir Percy, Prime Minister's Foreign Policy Adviser, 1984-92

Dacre, Lord (Hugh Trevor-Roper), Historian; author of *The Last Days of Hitler* (1947)

Dana, Thierry, Assistant to M. Dufourcq the Two plus Four negotiations, 1990

De Michelis, Gianni, Foreign Minister of Italy, 1989-92

Delors, Jacques, President of the EC Commission, 1985-94

Diepgen, Eberhard, Mayor of West Berlin, 1984-89, and of Berlin, 1991-2001

Dinwiddy, Bruce H., Counsellor, British Embassy, Bonn, 1989-91

Dixon, Robert, Research Analyst for Germany and Austria, FCO, 1974-2009

Dobbins, James F., Principal Deputy Assistant Secretary, European Bureau, State Department, 1989-90

Dobiey, Burkhard, Head of German Policy Section in the FRG Ministry for Inner-German Relations, 1986-91

Dregger, Alfred, Chairman of the CDU/CSU Party Fraction in the Bundestag, 1982-91

Dreher, Johann-Georg, Head of NATO Department, FRG Foreign Ministry

Dufourcq, Bertrand, Political Director, French Ministry of Foreign Affairs, 1988-91

Duisberg, Claus-Jürgen, Head of Working Staff 20, FRG Chancellery (dealing with policy on Germany), 1987-90

Eagleburger, Lawrence S., US Deputy Secretary of State, 1989-92

Ehmke, Horst, FRG Minister of Justice, 1969; Head of the Federal Chancellery, 1969-72; Minister of Post and Communications, 1972-74; member of the Directorate of the SPD, 1973-91; Vice-Chairman of SPD Parliamentary Group, 1989

Elbe, Frank, Head of the Ministerial Office, FRG Ministry of Foreign Affairs, 1987-92

Engholm, Björn, Minister-President of Schleswig-Holstein, 1988-93

Eyers, Patrick H.C., British Ambassador, East Berlin, 1990 (February-October)

Falin, Valentin M., Head of International Department of the Central Committee of the CPSU, 1988-91

Fall, Brian J.P., British High Commissioner, Ottawa, 1989-92

Fergusson, Sir Ewen A.J., British Ambassador, Paris, 1987-92

Fischer, Oskar, Member of the Central Committee of the SED, 1971-89; Foreign Minister of the GDR, 1975-90 (April)

Fretwell, Sir M. John E., Political Director and Deputy to the PUS, FCO, 1987-89

Froment Meurice, Henri, French Ambassador, Bonn, 1981-3

Garton Ash, Timothy, Historian, journalist and essayist; author of *The Polish Revolution: Solidarity* (1983); *The Uses of Adversity* (1989)

Gates Robert M., US Deputy National Security Adviser, 1989-91

Gauer, Denis, Deputy Director for Central Europe, French Ministry of Foreign Affairs

Genscher, Hans-Dietrich, FRG Minister for Foreign Affairs and Deputy Chancellor, 1974-92

Gerasimov, Gennadiy I., Head of the Information Section of the Soviet Ministry of Foreign Affairs, 1986-90

Gerlach, Manfred, Deputy Chairman of the GDR Council of State, 1960-89; Chairman of the Council of State (i.e. Head of State), 1989-90 (December-April); Chairman of the LDPD, 1967-90 (February)

Gieve, E. John W., Private Secretary to the Chancellor of the Exchequer, 1989-91

Gillmore, David H., DUS (Americas/Asia), FCO, 1986-89

Giscard d'Estaing, Valéry, President of France, 1974-81

Gorbachev, Mikhail S., General Secretary of the CPSU, 1985-91; President of the USSR, 1990-91

Gore-Booth, David, Head of Policy Planning Staff, FCO, 1987-89

Goulden, P. John, AUS (Defence), FCO, 1988-92

Gozney, Richard H.T., Assistant Private Secretary to the Secretary of State for Foreign Affairs, 1989-90

Greenstock, Jeremy Q., Deputy Political Director, FCO 1990-3

Grinin, Vladimir, Counsellor, Soviet Embassy, East Berlin; member of Soviet negotiating team in Two plus Four negotiations 1990

Guelluy, Philippe, Deputy Director, later Director, Department of Strategic Affairs, French Foreign Ministry, 1983-92

Guigou, Elisabeth, Special Adviser to President Mitterrand, 1988-90

Hamilton, Archibald G., Minister of State, Ministry of Defence 1988-93

Hannay, Sir David H.A., Ambassador and UK Permanent Representative to the European Communities, 1985-90

Harborne, Peter G., Counsellor and Head of Chancery, British Embassy, Budapest, 1988-92

Hartmann, Peter, Head of Group 21, FRG Chancellery (dealing with relations with the FRG Foreign Ministry and Ministry for Economic Cooperation), 1987-91

Haughey, Charles, Taoiseach of Ireland, 1987-92

Haussmann, Helmut, FRG Minister of Economics, 1988-90

Havel, Václav, President of Czechoslovakia, 1989-92

Hemans, Simon N.P., Head of Soviet Department, FCO, 1987-90

Hennekinne, Loïc, Diplomatic Adviser to President Mitterrand, 1989-91

Hennig, Ottfried, Parliamentary Secretary of State, FRG Ministry for Inner-German Relations, 1982-91

Herrhausen, Alfred, Chairman of Deutsche Bank, 1985-89 (assassinated 30 November 1989)

Hill, P. Jeremy O., First Secretary (Legal Adviser), British Embassy, Bonn 1987-90

Honecker, Erich, General Secretary of the Central Committee of the SED, 1971-89; Chairman of the Council of State of the GDR, 1976-1989 (18 October)

Howe, Sir R.E. Geoffrey, Secretary of State for Foreign and Commonwealth Affairs, 1983-89 (24 July); Lord President of the Council, 1989-90

Höynck, Dr Wilhelm, Director for Economic Relations, Director, Eastern Europe and Alternate Political Director, FRG Foreign Ministry, 1986-91

Hurd, Douglas, Home Secretary, 1983-89; Secretary of State for Foreign and Commonwealth Affairs, 1989 (26 October) -1995

Jaruzelski, General Wojciech W., successively Prime Minister, Chairman of the Council of State and President of the People's Republic of Poland 1981-89; President of Poland 1989-90.

Jenkins, Peter, Associate Editor of the *Independent* 1987-92 (d. 1992).

Kastrup, Dieter, Political Director, FRG Foreign Ministry, 1988-91

Keefe, Denis E.P.P., Assistant, WED, FCO, 1990-91

Kerr, John O., AUS (European Community), FCO, 1987-90

King, Tom, Secretary of State for Defence, 1989-92

Kissinger, Dr Henry A., National Security Adviser to President Nixon, 1969-75; US Secretary of State, 1973-77

Klaiber, Dr Klaus-Peter, Minister-Counsellor (Political Affairs), German Embassy, London, 1988-1991

Klein, Hans, FRG Minister without Portfolio and Head of the Federal Press and Information Office, 1989-90

Kochemasov, Vyacheslav I., Soviet Ambassador, East Berlin, 1983-90

Kohl, Dr Helmut, Chancellor of the FRG, 1982-98

Krenz, Egon, Member of Politburo and Secretary of the Central Committee of the SED, 1983-89; General Secretary of the Central Committee of the SED and Chairman of the Council of State of the GDR, 1989 (24 October-6 December)

Kvitsinsky, Yuli A., Soviet Ambassador, Bonn, 1986-90; Deputy Foreign Minister, USSR, 1990-91

Lafontaine, Oskar, Minister-President of the Saarland, 1985-98; SPD Chancellor Candidate, 1990

Lambsdorff, Otto Graf, Chairman of the FRG FDP, 1988-93

Lamont, Donald A., Counsellor and Head of Chancery, BMG Berlin, 1988-90

Latham, Michael, Conservative MP for Rutland and Melton, 1983-92

Lever, Paul J., Head of Security Policy Department, FCO, 1987-90

Llewellyn-Smith, Michael J., Minister, British Embassy, Paris, 1988-91

Logan, David B.C., Minister and Deputy Head of Mission, British Embassy, Moscow, 1989-92.

Luft, Christa, Deputy Chairman of the Council of Ministers of the GDR and Minister of Economics, 1989-90

Lyne, Roderic M.J., Counsellor and Head of Chancery, British Embassy, Moscow, 1987-90

Madel, David, Conservative MP for South-West Bedfordshire, 1970-2001

Magirius, Friedrich, Superintendent of the Leipzig East Church District and Joint Pastor of the *Nikolaikirche* in Leipzig, 1982-95

Maizière, Lothar de, Chairman of the CDU in the GDR October 1989-November 1990; Prime Minister of the GDR April-October 1990; acting Foreign Minister of the GDR, August-October 1990

Major, John, Chief Secretary, Treasury, 1987-89; Secretary of State for Foreign and Commonwealth Affairs, 1989; Chancellor of the Exchequer, 1989-90

Maleuda, Günter, President of the GDR Volkskammer, 1989-90
Mallaby, Sir Christopher L.G., British Ambassador, Bonn, 1988-93
Marsh, David, Chief German Correspondent, *Financial Times*, 1986-91
Maude, Francis A.A., Minister of State for Foreign and Commonwealth Affairs, 1989-90
Maximychev, Igor F., Deputy Head of Mission, Soviet Embassy, East Berlin
Mazowiecki, Tadeusz, Prime Minister of Poland, 1989-91
Meckel, Markus, Co-founder of the SDP (later SPD) of the GDR, October 1989; Foreign Minister of the GDR 1990 (April-August)
Medvedev, Vadim, Member of the Politburo of the Central Committee of the CPSU and Chairman of the Central Committee's Ideological Commission, 1988-91
Meisner, Joachim, Bishop of Berlin, 1980-88 (Cardinal 1983); Archbishop of Cologne
Mischnick, Wolfgang, Chairman of the FDP Party Fraction in the Bundestag, 1968-91
Mittag, Günter, SED Politburo member, 1966-89; Secretary for Economics, SED Central Committee, GDR, 1976-89
Mitterrand, François M.A.M., President of the French Republic, 1981-95
Modrow, Hans, SED Central Committee member and First Secretary of the Dresden regional leadership, 1973-89; Chairman of the Council of Ministers of the GDR, 1989-90
Momper, Walter, Governing Mayor of Berlin, 1989-91
Mottram, Richard C., DUS (Policy), MOD, 1989-92
Munro, Colin A., Counsellor, British Embassy, East Berlin, 1987-90
Nanteuil, Luc de la Barre de, French Ambassador in London, 1986-90
Neuer, Walter, Head of the Chancellor's Office in the FRG Chancellery, 1987-94
Neville-Jones, L. Pauline, Minister, British Embassy, Bonn, 1988-91
Nickel, Uta, Minister of Finance and Prices, GDR, 1989-90
O'Brien, Dr Conor Cruise, Minister for Posts and Telegraphs, Irish Republic, 1974-77
Phippard, Sonia S., Private Secretary to Secretary of the Cabinet, 1989-92
Pöhl, Karl-Otto, President of the Bundesbank, 1980-91
Poincaré, Raymond, Prime Minister of France, 1912-13, 1922-4, 1926-9; President of France, 1913-20
Pollock, Richard, Professor of Russian, University of Bradford, and Russian translator for the Prime Minister
Powell, Charles D., Private Secretary for Foreign Affairs to the Prime Minister, 1983-91
Powell, Jonathan N., Assistant Head, Policy Planning Staff, FCO, 1989-91
Ralph, Richard P., Head of Chancery and Congressional Counsellor, British Embassy, Washington, 1989-93.
Ramsden, Sir John C.S., Bt, First Secretary, FCO, 1988; Assistant, WED, 1989-90, Counsellor, British Embassy, East Berlin, 1990
Ratford, David J.E., Assistant Under-Secretary of State (Europe), FCO, 1986-90
Rau, Johannes, Minister-President of North Rhine-Westphalia 1978-98
Reagan, Ronald W., President of the United States, 1981-89
Reich, Jens, Co-founder of New Forum, GDR, 1989
Reinhold, Professor Otto, President of the GDR Academy of Sciences

Richthofen, Hermann, Freiherr von, Ambassador of Federal Republic, London, 1988-93

Ricketts, Peter, First Secretary, Security Policy Department, FCO, 1989-91

Ridley, Nicholas, Secretary of State for Trade and Industry, 1989-90

Rocard, Michel, Prime Minister of France, 1988-91

Rogozhin, V.S., Head of section dealing with external German affairs, Soviet Ministry of Foreign Affairs

Rühe, Volker, Secretary General, CDU, 1989-91

Salvesen, C. Hugh, First Secretary, WED, FCO, 1988-93

Sands, Richard M., First Secretary and Head of Chancery, British Embassy, East Berlin 1989-90, and British Embassy, Berlin Office, 1990-92

Schabowski, Günter, First Secretary of the SED in East Berlin, 1986-89

Schäfer, Norbert, Minister of State, FRG Ministry of Foreign Affairs

Schäuble, Dr Wolfgang, FRG Minister of the Interior, 1989-91

Scheer, François, Secretary-General, French Foreign Ministry, 1988-91

Schmidt, Helmut, Chancellor of the FRG, 1974-82

Schnur, Wolfgang, Chairman of Democratic Awakening, GDR, 1989-90

Scowcroft, Brent, National Security Adviser to President Bush, 1989-93

Seiters, Rudolf, FRG Minister without Portfolio and Head of the Federal Chancellery, 1989-91

Seitz, Raymond G.H., Assistant Secretary for European and Canadian Affairs, State Department, 1989-91

Shevardnadze, Eduard A., Minister of Foreign Affairs of the USSR, 1985-91.

Skubiszewski, Krzysztof J., Foreign Minister of Poland, 1989-93

Sonnenfeldt, Helmut, Senior Staff Member, US National Security Council, 1969-74

Späth, Lothar, Minister-President of Baden-Württemberg, 1978-91

Stern, Professor Fritz R., Historian; author of *The Politics of Cultural Despair* (1963); *Dreams and Delusions* (1987)

Stolpe, Manfred, Consistorial President of the Evangelical Churches of Berlin-Brandenburg, 1982-89

Stoltenberg, Gerhard, FRG Minister of Defence, 1989-92

Stone, Professor Norman, Historian; author of *The Eastern Front, 1914-1917* (1975); *Hitler* (1980)

Stoph, Willi, Prime Minister of the GDR, 1976-13 November 1989

Strauss, Dr Franz Josef, Minister-President of Bavaria, 1978-88 (d. 1988)

Sudhoff, Jürgen, State Secretary, FRG Foreign Ministry, 1987-91

Synnott, Hilary N.H., Head of Western European Department, FCO, 1989-91

Tebbit, Kevin R., Counsellor (Politico-Military), British Embassy, Washington, 1988-91

Teltschik, Horst, Chief Adviser to Chancellor Kohl on Foreign Policy and Inner-German Relations, 1982-91

Thatcher, Margaret H., Prime Minister, 1979-90

Thomas, Sir Derek, British Ambassador, Rome, 1987-89

Thornton, Neil R., PS to Secretary of State for Trade and Industry, 1988-90

Trevor-Roper, Hugh (see Dacre, Lord)

Urban, George, Broadcaster and author of books on Eastern Europe and East-West relations; Director of Radio Free Europe, 1983-86

Védrine, Hubert, Official Spokesman for President Mitterrand, 1988-91

Vogel, Hans-Jochen, Chairman of SPD Party Fraction in the Bundestag, 1983-91; Chairman of the SPD, 1987-93.

Vogel, Wolfgang, Representative of the Government of the GDR for the Regulation of Humanitarian Questions, 1965-90

Voigt, Karsten, SPD foreign affairs spokesman, 1983-98

Waigel, Theodor, FRG Minister of Finance, 1989-98

Waldegrave, William A., Minister of State for Foreign and Commonwealth Affairs, 1988-90

Walker, Peter, Secretary of State for Wales, 1987-90

Wall, J. Stephen, Private Secretary to the Secretary of State for Foreign and Commonwealth Affairs, 1988-91

Wallis, Peter G., Head of British Liaison Office, later Acting High Commissioner, Windhoek, 1989

Walters, Lieutenant-General Vernon A., US Ambassador, Bonn 1989-91

Watts, Sir Arthur D., Legal Adviser, FCO, 1987-91

Weizsäcker, Richard Freiherr von, President of the FRG, 1984-94

Weston, P. John, DUS (Defence), FCO 1989-90; Political Director and DUS (Europe), FCO, 1990-91

Wilms, Dorothee, FRG Minister for Inner-German Relations, 1987-91

Wörner, Manfred, Secretary General of NATO, 1988-94

Wood, Andrew M., Minister, British Embassy, Washington, 1989-92

Wood, Michael C., Legal Counsellor, FCO, 1986-91

Wordsworth, Stephen J., First Secretary, WED, FCO, 1988-90

Wright, Sir Patrick, Permanent Under-Secretary of State, FCO, and Head of British Diplomatic Service, 1986-91.

Yakovlev, Aleksandr N., Secretary of the Politburo, USSR, 1986-90; Member of the Politburo, 1987-90; Chairman of the Commission for International Policy of the Central Committee of the CPSU, 1988-90

Zamyatin, Leonid M., Soviet Ambassador, London, 1986-91

Zhivkov Todor, General Secretary of the Bulgarian Communist Party 1954-89; Head of State 1971-89

CHAPTER SUMMARIES

CHAPTER I

10 April – 9 November 1989

CHAPTER II

10 November 1989 – 13 February 1990

1

CHAPTER III

14 February – 30 November 1990

CHAPTER I

10 April – 9 November 1989

No. 1

Sir C. Mallaby (Bonn) to Sir G. Howe

[*WRG 020/3*]

Confidential   BONN, *10 April 1989*

Summary . . . [1]

Sir,

The Federal Republic of Germany: How Reliable an Ally?

1. There is another burst of doubt in NATO capitals about the reliability of the Federal Republic. This despatch considers which doubts are justified.

2. It would be hard to find any responsible observer in the Federal Republic, German or foreign, who sees any prospect of the Federal Republic leaving the Alliance or of an early move to achieve reunification. But there is debate about how far there is a danger that the lure of detente or a prospect of reunification could one day weaken Federal German alignment in the West. And there are concerns about present attitudes in the Federal Republic. Two worrying trends have recently grown. The first is uncritical enthusiasm for Gorbachev and a willingness to believe that the Soviet threat has gone. The second trend, related to the first, is growing public impatience with defence activities in Germany, above all low flying and other military training. The question is whether the causes for concern will grow, and the Federal Republic become an increasingly difficult partner.

A Special Psychology

3. The history and psychology of the Federal Republic are different in important ways from those of our other Allies. German history is full of uncertainties and late political development. Until the founding of the Federal Republic there was little experience of democracy: only the heavily authoritarian version left by Bismarck and the feebly unstable one of the Weimar Republic from 1919 to 1933. Stability has been unusual in German history, and was not present in this century until after 1945. Even the extent of Germany has never been decided. Unity came only in 1871 and lasted but 74 years. Today, the Eastern part of the Germany of 1871-1945 is lost and the remainder is divided. So the Federal Republic is less than half

_____
[1] Not printed.

1

the size of Bismarck's unified Germany. The appalling crimes of Nazism, which many still remember, cause a lack of self-confidence and a tendency to guilt. Germany has a history of looking East as well as West. For centuries Germans colonised areas stretching eastwards to places which are today within the Soviet Union. More recently, the Nazi-Soviet pact was the worst but not the only example of the Eastern connection prevailing for a time over the Western.

4. One of the effects today of this combination of past factors is that the West Germans are prone to emotional surges of hope whenever things seem to be improving in East-West relations. One reason is the division of Germany and the aspiration to reunification and of course the position of Berlin. Another is Angst about another war, caused by memories of the last one and by the Federal Republic's geographical position as the West's frontline state, bound to suffer terrible destruction in any East-West conflict. Another factor in the wish for reconciliation with the East is guilt, because of Nazi aggression and atrocities. Guilt is strong in the Federal Republic's view of Poland and an element in its view of the Soviet Union. Even West Germans who are agnostic about reunification want to help the East Germans, who are seen as suffering much more for Hitler's wrongs than the free and prosperous Federal Germans.

5. Adenauer's contribution was to establish the principle that the Federal Republic's integration into the West must take priority over efforts to achieve reunification. The aim of reunification was written into the Federal Republic's constitutional law, but the implication was that it was a long term objective. Freedom was to be the condition of reunification not the price. A strong Federal Republic, profiting from the Western connection, would be better able to influence the question of Germany's future. That has remained the general view. Today opinion polls show that a majority, even among the young, still think of the Germans as one people. No-one questions in any serious way the heavy subsidies that are essential to Berlin's viability. But in 1987, 72% of West Germans were found not to expect reunification in the foreseeable future. In 1986, less than half of people in their twenties thought it worth continuing to state the long term goal of reunification. Polls are only indications. But it is safe to conclude that, for most West Germans, the European status quo is a matter for questioning discussion, and for a considerable number it is unsatisfactory as a lasting arrangement. Reunification is still an aspiration of many people, but definitely not a worked out policy.

The Federal Republic's Achievements

6. This 40th anniversary year is a time to recall the impressive achievements of the Federal Republic. It is the one successful democracy in German history, and has already lasted 3 times as long as Weimar. The Federal Republic has achieved security and peace for a period longer than the tragic stretch from 1914 to 1945. It has achieved great prosperity, building Europe's largest and the world's third largest economy. It has gained considerable international respect and self-respect. For many years people spoke of the Federal Republic, with its economic miracle, as an economic giant but a political dwarf. Today the voice of the Federal Republic in the West and its role in East-West relations have brought the dwarf to normal height, though there still are limitations deriving from the war—for instance the FRG is not a Permanent Member of the Security Council and still has serious inhibitions about military activities or exports outside NATO. The Federal Republic's successes have helped to prevent reunification becoming a major issue

in this country. The successful development of contacts of many kinds with East Germany in the past 20 years has contributed to that effect.

7. After 40 years, democracy, stability and prosperity are taken for granted. The great successes of the Federal Republic are often left unsung. As the head of the Deutsche Bank put it to me: 'Man doth not live by bread alone, especially when he hath plenty of it'.[2] People seem to focus on further wishes for the future. The West Germans are always yearning for something and will, I think, continue thus. Sometimes this restlessness is expressed in bouts of emotion about particular issues. The focus seems to change once or twice a year. Sometimes it is an environmental question, such as acid rain. Low flying by military aircraft is a current example. The latest is intense concern about pressure on housing and jobs from the wave of immigrants of German stock from Eastern Europe. But it is possible that the West German need to yearn will focus in due course on something of far greater international importance. Intense pressure for progress in relations with Gorbachev's Soviet Union is a likely candidate. Reunification could theoretically be one in the longer term.

Federal German Interests

8. The Soviet threat was the biggest factor in causing the Federal Germans to bind themselves to the West. But even if it was lastingly reduced, freedom and prosperity ought to provide reason enough for not tampering with the Western connection that has brought such successes. Public opinion polls show high support, around 75%, for NATO. Support for the *Bundeswehr* is even higher. But attitudes are muddled: one frequent result of opinion polls is to show a majority for deterrence and a majority against nuclear weapons. And the support for NATO co-exists with the new intolerance of aircraft noise and of other corollaries of credible military preparedness. A threat to freedom or security would bring public opinion back firmly to support of NATO, defence and the American connection. In safer times opinion is uncertain and inconsistent, and in a prolonged period of East-West calm it could become more so.

9. The absence of the nation as a focus of identity, a major element in the West German need to yearn, caused the Federal Republic in its early years to seek success in other things. Prosperity was one. The European Community was another. In the fifties and sixties, the European cause caught the imagination. Today it is still a popular theme, though somewhat dulled by familiarity and by years of press reports about the daily grind in Brussels. While enthusiasm has diminished, German integration into the Community has of course advanced, and today permeates innumerable aspects of every day life from the German passion for tourism via measures to reduce pollution to day to day foreign policy. Another popular cause was and is the new friendship with France, referred to in speech after speech here as a cornerstone in the construction of European Union. The West German public are grateful that the hereditary enemy, which Germany invaded three times in a century, offered unqualified reconciliation. Almost no-one here would question that the Community and Franco-German reconciliation are precious achievements which must be preserved because they are essential to the interests, indeed the very nature, of the Federal Republic.

10. On the economic side, things are clear. The Federal Republic's prosperity depends on exports. Of these 86% go to the Western world, 54% to the Community. Exports to CMEA countries, at 3.5%, are small by comparison. The

---

[2] Alfred Herrhausen (assassinated 30 November 1989).

rate of growth of exports to the Western world is also higher. Indeed the amount by which they grew in 1988 was double the total of Federal German exports to the CMEA countries in that year. As described in my despatch of 27 January, there is great interest in increasing trade with the CMEA countries. But there is no way that the Federal Republic can afford a foreign policy that would jeopardise its economic integration in the Western system, and no voice in the Federal Republic is arguing that there is.

Other Important Factors

11. America is still seen here as the home of democracy and prosperity. The usual German view, since Vietnam, has ceased to be uncritical but still is a generally admiring one. Anti-Americanism exists in certain sections of opinion and was at a high point in the early Reagan years. It could grow again. A separate factor in Federal German attitudes to East-West relations is the perception that America's interest is shifting away from the Atlantic and towards the Pacific. The Federal Chancellor is a strong believer in this view. Most people expect some withdrawals of American forces from the Federal Republic within a matter of years. Kohl's reaction is that everything should be done to hold on to the Americans while efforts are made at strengthening the European pillar of the Alliance. The left is not greatly concerned. All believe that the prospects of a greater German contribution to defence in the Alliance are slight and that it will be hard enough to maintain the present strength and effectiveness of the *Bundeswehr*.

12. Another significant and growing trend is insistence that Federal German interests be given full weight, in the policies of the West as well as the Federal Republic's own policies. Voices on left and right, including some prominent members of the CDU, say that, so long after the war, the Germans should not have their role in the world prescribed by others. The SPD is trying to launch a debate, which may or may not become important, about whether the Federal Republic's rights as a state are limited, because of the reserved rights of the Allies in relation to Berlin and the German question and also the unequal nature, so the SPD would wrongly argue, of the treaties under which Allied forces are stationed in this country. Sometimes the call to assert German interests can get mixed up with aspects of German psychology, so that Germans seem to be saying in one breath that Allies should not discriminate against them because of the now distant Nazi past and that we should discriminate in favour of them because of their special interests, such as the division of Germany.

13. Germans of nearly all persuasions call constantly for major progress in East-West relations, to remove barriers, increase cooperation and eventually attain a European Peace Order. Much weight is placed on CSCE as a framework for progress.[3] The vision of a European Peace Order is undefined but the hope is that one day, in a Europe without divisions, reunification might become possible and natural. The leading German nationalist in the SPD, Egon Bahr, who was the architect of Brandt's *Ostpolitik* and is a major figure in this debate, sees conventional force reductions and nuclear weapon free zones in central Europe as a part of a policy for producing a state of peace where the two Germanies would cooperate closely over all types of policy. He might put German interests in this, as he interprets them, above loyalty to the Alliance. He sees a special responsibility of both Germanies, because of the Nazi past, for peace; and he wants them to make a

---

[3] For the Conference on Security and Cooperation in Europe (CSCE), held in Helsinki in 1975, see Series III, Vol. II, *The Conference on Security and Cooperation in Europe 1972-1975* (London: The Stationery Office, 1997).

special joint contribution to progress. He says he does not favour reunification as such. And there are some others, in the SPD and elsewhere, who realise that a big Germany would disturb the balance in Europe and say that a Europe without barriers would enable the two Germanies to cooperate so well that reunification would be superfluous.

14. The metamorphosis taking place in Eastern Europe adds to the excitement in the Federal Republic caused by Gorbachev. There is hope that a better deal for Poles and others would reduce some of the remaining effects of the war; that would be good in itself, contribute to removal of East-West barriers and reduce German feelings of guilt. At the same time there is concern that stability in Eastern Europe could be endangered. West Germans want to develop the successful policy of building close contacts with the GDR, but not to a point where this could provoke a crisis in that country. Indeed, there is a fear that change will set in before long in East Germany, and could reach a point where even Gorbachev might clamp down, so that East-West and inner-German relations could face another crisis. This contradictory concern for Eastern Europe—gratification at the change but fear of instability—is likely to be a major factor in Federal German attitudes so long as the process of change continues in Eastern Europe.

Party Attitudes

15. German leaders insist, as Genscher did to you in Frankfurt in February, that integration in the West is essential to the Federal Republic and permanent.[4] That is undoubtedly Kohl's firm position and that of the CDU/CSU. He led the government steadily and firmly to the stationing of Cruise and Pershing missiles in the early eighties.[5] He has told me that his wish to make progress towards European Union 'irreversible' is caused partly by a concern that some other political force in the FRG might give the Western connection less priority. When he affirms the aspiration to reunification, he does it because he believes in the aspiration and in order to deny this theme to the left and the far right in politics; not because he expects soon to make actual progress towards reunification. Yet the fact is that Kohl can cause difficulty in the Alliance. He wavers about modernising short range nuclear forces. I attribute that partly to the current resistance in this country to matters military and the aversion to nuclear weapons which was left behind in parts of public opinion by the INF controversy, and partly to Kohl's weakness as a leader, these elements combining to make him put domestic party interest above the case in terms of security. Kohl's government's concern to ease conditions for the population of the GDR, and to keep inner-German relations on the move, push him towards conceding more to the GDR than other Allies may think safe, particularly in financial matters. The CDU Defence Minister, rather than standing up to popular sentiment against low flying by military aircraft, puts pressure on the Allies to make cuts in flying that in our judgement would be harmful to military effectiveness. On the other hand the decision to lengthen national service from 15 to 18 months was recently reaffirmed despite pressures

---

[4] The annual British-German summit had taken place in Frankfurt from 20 to 21 February.

[5] In December 1979, responding to West German concern about the SS-20 intermediate-range nuclear weapons that the Soviet Union had begun to deploy in 1977, NATO had taken a 'twin-track' decision to deploy Pershing intermediate-range and Cruise missiles in Europe from 1983, and to initiate negotiations with the Soviet Union for the limitation, or elimination, of intermediate-range nuclear weapons (INF). The subsequent failure of arms control negotiations to materialise alarmed a substantial body of European opinion, especially in the Federal Republic, who feared that Central Europe could become a nuclear battleground in a future war between the superpowers. Herr Kohl's decision to go ahead with deployment was taken against this background.

for postponement. One could also imagine Kohl and the CDU bowing to public concerns on some matters concerning the Community, such as pressures against further curbs on subsidies for agriculture or outdated industries.

16. The FDP too is pro-Western in its principles. But Genscher is a tactician, driven by domestic political interest. He is liable for the sake of popularity to urge speed rather than careful reflection in seeking East-West progress. That also accords with his own views about East-West relations; his origins in East Germany are among his reasons for championing detente. He is not aiming at a German position separate from NATO's—rather at being seen as the one who leads NATO's positions forward towards East-West cooperation. There is a danger that he will urge concessions to the East which are unnecessary or premature. There is a danger that he will make Western decisions on defence matters very difficult so long as East-West relations are progressing, as he has done recently with his pressure on Kohl against a decision this year on SNF modernisation.[6] So long as Genscher is Foreign Minister, we must expect this kind of difficulty to arise.

17. The SPD under Brandt and Schmidt caused the Alliance some concerns. Brandt sometimes seemed to be going very fast on *Ostpolitik*. Schmidt's reaction to Soviet misdeeds, such as the invasion of Afghanistan, was liable to be weak. But fundamentally the SPD in those days supported the Alliance and the Federal Republic's integration into the Western system. After leaving government in 1982, it abandoned Schmidt's support for modernising NATO's medium range nuclear forces and moved sharply to the left on security policy. The party experimented with East-West arms control and defence policies far from those of the Alliance. Since then it has moved back some distance towards the centre. The party is formally committed to the Alliance. But it is for a third zero in short range nuclear forces, and large sections reject nuclear deterrence altogether. It favours nuclear and chemical weapon free zones in central Europe and a demilitarised strip between the two blocs. Some prominent SPD figures have advocated a citizen's defence in the form of local militias. Lafontaine, who may be the SPD's candidate for Chancellor in the 1990 Federal elections, has been an advocate of German withdrawal from NATO's integrated military structure, but his present position is unclear. The party is attracted by Gorbachev's slogan about a common European house:[7] it tends to view the Soviet Union as a fellow European state which could and should be successfully meshed into a joint European Peace Order. The SPD, if it returned to office, might drop some of its more way-out ideas, but it would remain different from the SPD of Schmidt and would be far more uncomfortable as an ally than the present Federal government.

18. The Greens are an inchoate movement. Their policies are imprecise and changeable. Insofar as they have a foreign and security policy, it is founded on the primacy of non-violence and the furtherance of peace. They favour the dissolution of NATO and the Warsaw Pact, want the Federal Republic to be neutral, and insist

---

[6] Following the 1987 INF Treaty, the United States had demanded the modernisation of the short-range Lance missiles (SNF) stationed in the Federal Republic. Since such a move was unpopular with West German opinion, a decision was delayed by Herr Kohl and the demand was subsequently dropped by President Bush at the NATO summit in Brussels in May 1989.

[7] A concept first publicly outlined by Mr Gorbachev in his speech to British parliamentarians on 18 December 1984 (while still Second Secretary of the CPSU) and developed in more detail in a speech given in Prague in April 1987. It was intended to signify a European identity transcending, but not replacing, the existing military-political alliances. Over time, however, NATO and the Warsaw Pact would be gradually transformed, 'their relations shifting away from tension towards eventual stability' (Mikhail Gorbachev, *Memoirs* (London: Doubleday, 1996), pp. 161, 427-33).

that the Federal armed forces should be unable to threaten other states. While on that basis they might be expected to treat the superpowers evenhandedly, in fact the United States receive a greater share of criticism. One reason is that there are many Communist sympathisers among the Greens. Another is that the Greens see the United States as the greater obstacle to unilateral disarmament and withdrawal from NATO by the Federal Republic. That said, some important voices among the Greens have begun to argue for more traditional positions on defence, including support of NATO, as part of the adjustment needed to increase the prospects of entering Government. If the Greens did join a Federal coalition, it would be as junior partner of the SPD. They might not have great influence on foreign affairs and defence. But such influence as they had would encourage the least welcome trends in the SPD, and such a coalition would cause many problems in the Alliance.

Electoral Politics

19. Adenauer used to win elections with the slogan 'no experiments'. There are still many in this country who are shy of change. But the eighties have seen the reappearance of irresponsibility in politics, with the electoral successes of the Greens. While up to 10% of the electorate were voting Green, the majority seemed to be wary of the idea of having them in office. Just recently, however, that fear has seemed to wane. We shall see whether the behaviour of the new SPD/Green governments in Berlin and Frankfurt will frighten the voters back into their accustomed wariness of Greens in office. The Berlin election at the end of January also threw up another new phenomenon, this one on the right-hand edge of democratic politics—the Republican party. All this flux, as I have argued in reports to your Department, means that the Federal election in December 1990 is wide open. The present coalition of CDU/CSU and FDP may have the best chance of winning, but that bet is no longer reliable. The other horses in the race are a grand coalition of CDU/CSU and SPD, a coalition of SPD and FDP and even, possibly, a coalition of SPD and Greens.

British Policy

20. There is an important question about the Federal Republic's reliability. It is not whether this country will cease to be an ally or will adopt a policy of seeking reunification in the foreseeable future. The question is how willing our German ally will be to take difficult decisions on defence matters and how precipitate it will be in seeking progress in East-West relations: in other words, how difficult an ally and partner the Federal Republic will be. I do not see the present difficulties getting easier. There is risk, even with the present government, of their becoming rather worse. Much depends on the general election in December 1990. I believe that the present Federal government, which through lack of will presents certain problems for us, presents distinctly fewer than would any alternative coalition that might then be formed.

21. The Federal Republic matters greatly to the United Kingdom—to our security and our prosperity. So we have a major interest in a steady pro-Western foreign policy in Bonn. We should do all we can to encourage that, by showing the Federal Republic, in every way possible, the value of its Western connection. Suggesting how this can be done is a major continuing function of this Embassy; I will note some major areas. We should foster our close bilateral relationship with Bonn, notably on defence matters. We should continue to ensure that the

consultation processes of European Political Cooperation[8] and in NATO are in active working order, and to encourage the Germans to make full use of them. We should encourage the Americans to act similarly; and also the French, who are prone to worry about German reliability.

22. We should show understanding where we can of German preoccupations. For instance, if we can adjust our military training here in ways which reduce side-effects on the population but maintain military effectiveness, we should do so. Progress in the European Community is a major tool for maintaining the Federal Republic's interest in integration in the West, and that should be a consideration in our European policies. We should warn of the uncertainties that are inherent in East-West relations even when things are going well. We should cooperate as much as we can with Germany on East-West matters, seeking common ground whenever possible and adjusting our policies where we can in order to achieve this. This is one reason for being seen to seize the opportunity to advance Western interests through East-West negotiations, by setting a demanding Western agenda reaching out to such ambitious goals as the dismantling of the Berlin Wall. We should consult closely on the changes in Eastern European countries, looking actively for joint policies, for this is an area where Bonn and London could diverge.

23. To increase the chance that the Federal Republic will not become actively discontented with Germany's division or actively impatient with the Allies' continued rights in relation to the German question, we should continue to give verbal support from time to time to the aspiration to reunification and more frequently to Bonn's policy of increasing contacts with the GDR. We should maintain our role in Berlin, adapting where necessary as time goes on and public attitudes there change.

24. And, if I may conclude with a wider point, we should remember that the Federal Republic's economic and political weight in Western Europe, coupled with the uncertainties about its steadiness, form an additional reason—on top of the dominant reason, namely the sheer size of the Soviet Union—for working to preserve the United States' commitment to Europe.

25. I am sending copies of this despatch to HM Representatives in NATO and EC posts, Moscow, Warsaw, East Berlin, Vienna and the United Nations in New York; to the British Commandant in Berlin and our Consuls-General in the Federal Republic.

> I am, Sir,
> Yours faithfully,
> CHRISTOPHER MALLABY

---

[8] European Political Cooperation (EPC) had been initiated informally in 1970, following the recommendations of the Davignon Report, with the intention of coordinating the foreign policies of EC member countries. It was superseded by the Common Foreign and Security Policy (CFSP) following the conclusion of the Maastricht Treaty in November 1993.

No. 2

Mr Broomfield (East Berlin) to Sir G. Howe

[*WRL 020/2*]

Confidential   EAST BERLIN, *20 April 1989*

Summary . . . [1]

Sir,

Inner German Relations: Where Will It All End?

1. In answer to Mr Madel in the House recently you reiterated the view that 'real and permanent stability in Europe will be difficult to achieve so long as the German nation is divided against its will'.[2]

2. On 7 October this year the GDR will celebrate the 40th anniversary of its existence as a separate German state. In the run up to what promises to be the major event of the year in East Berlin, I think it might be useful to look once again at the relationship between the two German states from the point of view of the smaller and more insecure of the two. I hope this despatch will be read as complementary to the passages on reunification in Sir Christopher Mallaby's recent despatch of 10 April.

3. The existence of the FRG (and West Berlin) is the single biggest problem which has confronted the SED leadership in the GDR in the 40 years of its existence. The fact that another German state exists, that it is successful, democratic and committed to upholding the goal of unity through free self-determination and that anyone from the GDR reaching its territory or that of West Berlin is entitled to the full privileges of a Federal German citizen, has added a unique dimension to the difficulties faced by the SED.

4. In this despatch I describe the internal and external pressures for change working within and upon the GDR. The pressures within are similar to those experienced by other East European countries whose centrally planned economies and one-party political systems have failed. The pressures without, principally from the FRG and West Berlin, magnify these internal strains.

5. Unlike other countries in Eastern Europe the GDR cannot look to nationalism as a binding force. It was only in its 1974 version that the Constitution dropped all references to reunification and to the GDR as 'a socialist state of the German nation'. The GDR is now officially a 'socialist state of workers and farmers'. In the SED's eyes the GDR's legitimacy rests on its political system which in turn is based on the old communist ideology. It is not possible to modify this fundamentally as the Hungarians and Poles are doing. Take away ideology and you are left with Germany. It was not therefore surprising that when confronted during his visit to Bonn in 1987 by Chancellor Kohl's reassertion of the national unity of Germany, Honecker defended himself by referring to the systemic difference between the two German states—it is as easy for socialism to mix with capitalism as fire with water.

---

[1] Not printed.
[2] *Parl. Debs., 5th ser., H. of C.*, vol. 146, cols. 978-9, 8 February 1989.

Internal Pressures

6. First the internal pressures which are both political and economic. Notwithstanding the Prussian tradition of obedience and industry, the efficiency of the state security, massive propaganda campaigns against the FRG and ability to export troublesome dissidents to the West, I judge that the mood of the country is changing. There is unlikely to be a major confrontation between a strong protest movement and the authorities of the sort we have seen in various forms in other East European countries. There is hardly a 'dissident' movement in any real numerical sense in the GDR. But in another sense there is a growing resistance movement. The young are increasingly answering back and questioning decisions and orders from above. They are well-informed and even if sometimes they are not prepared to voice their doubts publicly, privately they no longer believe what they are told. Interdependence between East and West in Europe has not yet arrived, but interconnection has. The flow of information which has always been high through television and radio in the GDR is now supplemented by 1.4 million younger visitors out of a total of some 7 million visits to West Berlin and the FRG last year. This is a development of the greatest significance. For the first time since 1961[3] younger people are able to see for themselves the sort of life they could lead under a different system.

7. Not only is the desire for change growing, it is in my view, consistent in its direction. People want to express their views more freely, to judge matters for themselves, to travel more widely. It is getting more like a prison one of my acquaintances remarked. Poland is a mess. Hungary is too expensive. The Soviet Union is too difficult and uncomfortable. And now even Czechoslovakia is putting up customs barriers. People here feel penned in. They want the same freedoms as others in Eastern Europe. Lenin's dictum that post-revolutionary man would be as different from pre-revolutionary man as a man is now from an ape, has been proved wrong in the GDR as well. The desire for individual expression and individual development has not been educated out of the population, however much they may appreciate the social security of the system in which they live.

8. Schizophrenia is a condition of life in the GDR. From an early age people become accustomed to living at many levels and presenting a variety of faces to the world. Some of my acquaintances already lead double lives. When they visit their relations in the FRG they slip into their Western selves, pick up their FRG passports and visit France, Italy or the UK before returning on their GDR passes which record none of their wider travels. Tourism in Italy in a two-stroke Wartburg on an FRG passport is a truly all European experience, commented one of them.

9. At a less subjective level the other source of pressure for change within the GDR is the economy. The present SED leadership consistently reaffirm the unity of economic and social policy which is shorthand for state allocation of resources and rewards. They claim, and rightly, that the economy already contains a substantial private sector and that new systems like 'self-financing' for the larger industrial enterprises are being tried out. But central planning dominates. Subsidies on rent, basic food and medical care amount to at least 18.5% of the gross national income. *Neues Deutschland*[4] has had to admit that within the Party there is a lively debate on the whole question of subsidies and price policy. But no-one believes

---

[3] i.e. since the building of the Berlin Wall.
[4] The principal organ of the Socialist Unity Party (SED).

that change will come under the present leadership and that could be a matter of years not months.

10. The leadership's answer is to invest in micro-technology. But this will increase their problems. East European experiments in the 1970s showed that Western technology, designed to assist de-centralised decision-making, was not easily compatible with a slow-moving centrally planned system. By East European standards, however, the GDR's economy is still relatively efficient and in the short term I do not expect the sort of economic pressures which exist in Poland or the Soviet Union to become the catalyst for political change in the GDR. In the medium-term, however, pressure will certainly grow and the technological remedies the GDR are now seeking are likely to exacerbate their problems.

External Pressure from the FRG

11. The already difficult internal situation is made infinitely worse from the SED leadership's point of view by the force of attraction of the FRG. This is felt in every sphere of life and at every level in the GDR. Obsession is not too strong a word to describe both the official and unofficial attitude towards the FRG.

12. At a popular level the knowledge of all aspects of life in the FRG is remarkable. Firm views about politicians are held. President von Weizsäcker is popular. He is considered 'a real representative of Germany'. The late Franz Josef Strauss was even more popular. He stood up to the SED leadership and called things by their real names. These feelings are never far below the surface. The emotion which burst through the police cordon in Erfurt in 1970 when Willy Brandt made his first official visit to the GDR manifested itself again last year in a standing ovation for Helmut Schmidt in Rostock Cathedral and more recently in spontaneous applause for Eberhard Diepgen at St Hedwig's Cathedral in East Berlin at Cardinal Meisner's farewell mass.

13. Since my arrival I have conducted a one-man survey on attitudes towards reunification. My sample is tiny and unrepresentative. But the unanimous view expressed was for unity with the FRG. Closer questioning revealed that the desire for unity was mainly based on a profound distrust of their leaders and the system they represent. If a change of system and leaders could be guaranteed would reunification still be essential? The answers then become more equivocal. Most people have a strong attachment to the area where they live even though they refuse to regard the GDR as their homeland (*Heimat*) or 'Socialist Fatherland' as the ideologues would prefer. Many have pride in what they have achieved against all the odds. Some have bitter memories of being patronised by West Germans in other East European countries (and being treated as second-class Germans in those countries by their socialist allies). It is never easy to be the eternally grateful receiver. To be treated to an after-dinner cognac by a 'loads of money' West German in Budapest or Prague is not the surest way to a GDR heart. But this sort of envy and irritation exists in many places (North East versus South East in the UK) and in the end I have been left with the strong impression of a quarrel within a family and not rivalry between two separate states.

14. Since Honecker's visit to Bonn in 1987 the FRG Government has pressed ahead with implementing the various agreements signed then. Cultural exchanges have multiplied. Over 50 town twinning agreements have been concluded. The first exchanges of students have taken place. In every area that it can the FRG has sought to build up a network of contacts. The then Minister at the Federal Chancellery, Schäuble, told me last year that a greater level of contact between the FRG and GDR now exists than before 1961 when the Wall was built. And

although the GDR's State Security Service does its best to contain the effects, it cannot supervise every meeting and listen to every conversation.

15. Underpinning the political and personal attractions of the FRG and West Berlin is the enormous economic impact of West Germany. Half of all the GDR's trade with the West is with the FRG and it is on their Western trade that the GDR relies for essential technological inputs. Analysts differ over the size of the official and unofficial transfers to the GDR. But the most conservative estimate from the Institute of Economic Research in West Berlin recently put the figure at DM 3 billion in 1988. When every source is counted including private gifts and church donations, the figure is probably higher. Over 140 West German companies have licensing or buy-back agreements with GDR combines. Within the GDR the Deutschemark is an alternative and a more valued currency. Without Deutschemarks or Forum (hard currency) cheques most essential services and repairs are hard to come by. Deutschemarks buy access to Western goods in the Intershops which exist in every town. The 12 year waiting period for a car can be cut to a week through payment by a relative in the West. The three class society is a constant theme of conversation—the bosses, those with Western connections and the rest. The divisions and envy this engenders cannot be good for the future stability of this society.

16. One effect of the West German economic lifeline has been to shield the leadership from the full effects of the failure of their policies. Without it I am convinced that more radical economic reforms would have had to have been introduced. But the option of using direct economic leverage to secure political benefits has never appealed to West German politicians. West Berlin is a potential hostage and the desire to improve the lot of fellow Germans, in many cases relatives, has been strong. Nevertheless, the effect of the policy of 'change through rapprochement' originally devised by Egon Bahr and put into effect by Willy Brandt in the 1970s (and taken over almost completely by the CDU) has been to open up the GDR to FRG influence over the years. The GDR could not now easily reverse this process.

The Medium-Term Future

17. How will this strange, basically unstable relationship work itself out in the years ahead? My speculations are necessarily tentative and I apologise at the outset for straying outside my field. The main arbiters of the GDR's fate will continue to be the Soviet Union and the FRG. The GDR leadership and any that might follow will continue to try to obtain the economic advantages of close association with the FRG while minimising the political effects. I do not think they can succeed.

18. If the conventional security talks in Vienna are successful and if the reform programmes now under way in the Soviet Union, Poland and Hungary are maintained (two big but not impossible 'ifs'), then the next generation of GDR leaders will, by the middle of the 1990s, face a much more difficult problem than the present septuagenarians. A resumption of political reform in Czechoslovakia would complete a ring of change and liberalisation around the GDR. In a Europe in which military confrontation has been substantially reduced and in which political divisions between 'socialism' and 'capitalism' have become blurred, possibly beyond recognition in the cases of Hungary and Poland, the Berlin Wall and the border wire will stand out in sharper and ever less excusable relief.

19. Given the uncertainties over developments in the next few years it would be foolish to make firm predictions about the course of inner-German relations during that time. The most likely direction in my view, however, lies in a continuation and

deepening of the trends of cooperation and contact which will correspond to popular wishes here as well as to economic need. The outward form is likely to be maintained. Survival of the SED will be an important factor. Continued membership of the Warsaw Pact and support for 'socialism' will remain strategic necessities not only for the SED but presumably also for the Russians. But beneath that outwardly correct exterior I would expect the reality of nationalist aspirations fed by the attraction (and assistance) of the FRG to grow.

The Distant Future

20. There are those who argue that although history will prevail over a bankrupt system it will not necessarily lead to a single unified German state. They point out that the coincidence of the majority of German people living within a single state has been very much the exception—just 74 years from 1871-1945—rather than the rule. Two German states would, from a historical point of view, be perfectly acceptable. These two states might exist in the same relationship as Austria now does with the FRG—open borders, similar economic systems and international agreement banning union. Such a solution might indeed be the highest common factor of agreement between, on the one hand, Soviet, Polish (and French) security needs and on the other German aspirations to freedom and self-determination. The decisive voice in any such solution would, in my view, be the Russians. They would have to decide, taking into account wider developments in Europe, that their national security interests were adequately served by such an arrangement. They might alternatively conclude that the cost of maintaining their present relationship with the GDR was no longer commensurate with the benefits, perhaps because the GDR had become economically or politically unstable.

21. Any such solution would also have to take account of the third element in the 'German question'—Berlin. There would seem to be three main possibilities. In a situation where the borders between the two German states were open including presumably those between East and West Berlin, the city could become united as the capital of the GDR. Such a capital would of course be disproportionate in size to the State, but then so is Vienna to Austria. This solution seems to me most unlikely given the history of West Berlin, the commitments of successive Federal Governments and the three Western Allies. The city could alternatively remain divided with free circulation between the two parts but with Soviet and GDR recognition that West Berlin was in fact a *Land* of the Federal Republic and an integral part of West Germany. Allied post-war rights and responsibilities together with their guarantees might be replaced by contractual rights between the two German states. Finally, the city could be reunited as part of a process of reunifying the two German states, and become again the capital of 'Germany'.

22. My own guess, for what it is worth, is that although an 'Austrian solution' with a divided Berlin might be an intermediate step, the symbolism of Berlin may prevent it from being a final one. I admit that my judgement may be distorted by the fact that I have had regular exposure to this city over a period of some 26 years. Perhaps I see the Brandenburg Gate, the Reichstag and Unter den Linden from too romantic a point of view. Maybe Berlin has become a provincial bore and an expense to the average West German. But to me it is the only city which has the feel of a world capital in either part of Germany and if the Wall were one day to disappear or become freely permeable then the urge to reunite the city and with it Germany might once again flow strongly. The national aspirations which found their expression in the establishment of Hungary, Poland, Czechoslovakia, etc,

after the first world war in the Treaties, were suppressed by the Soviet Union after the second world war. Over forty years later they are again stirring to a greater or lesser extent in all the countries of Eastern Europe. Although unique in its circumstances I see no reason why such aspirations should not find expression one day in Germany.

23. All I can say now is that the feeling of belonging to a single nation and not to a separate German socialist state remains as strong here as it was when I first travelled around the GDR as a member of the British Military Liaison Mission attached to the Group of Soviet Forces in Germany in 1963. I do not think it will diminish in the years ahead or be supplanted by loyalty to the sort of socialist state which now exists. Your answer to Mr Madel therefore represents an accurate picture of the aspirations of the majority in this part of Germany.

24. I am sending copies of this despatch to Her Majesty's representatives at Bonn, Paris, Washington, Warsaw Pact Belgrade, to the UK Representative NATO, the Commandant of the British Sector in Berlin, and the Commanders in Chief BAOR and RAF Germany.

I am, Sir,
Yours faithfully,
NIGEL BROOMFIELD

No. 3

Letter from Sir J. Fretwell to Sir C. Mallaby (Bonn)

[*WRG 061/1*]

Confidential   FCO, *18 May 1989*

My dear Christopher,

The FRG: How Reliable an Ally?

1. Thank you for your despatch of 10 April which has been sent for printing and given a general distribution.[1] The Secretary of State commended it to the Prime Minister in the approach to the Deidesheim meeting.[2] Thank you also for your letter of 21 March on Federal German politics which warned that a period of turbulence and weak government was in prospect.[3] Quite how much turbulence, and how soon it would hit us, we had not foreseen.[4]

---

[1] No. 1.

[2] See note 4 below.

[3] In this letter Sir C. Mallaby warned that 'Kohl's government is in greater difficulty than ever before', and that 'The prospects for the election in December 1990 are wide open' (WRG 020/3).

[4] On 14 April, following setbacks in municipal elections, Herr Kohl reconstructed his Government. Herr Stoltenberg became Minister of Defence, Herr Waigel Minister of Finance and Herr Schäuble Minister of the Interior, with Herr Seiters becoming Head of the Chancellery. On 28 April Herr Kohl announced a new security policy, postponing a decision on modernising Lance missiles until 1992 and linking it to progress in negotiations for the reduction of nuclear and conventional arms in Europe. Herr Kohl's emphasis on disarmament was aimed at winning domestic political support, but threatened a collision with NATO allies, especially the United States and the United Kingdom, in advance of NATO's 40th anniversary summit in Brussels on 29-30 May. Mrs Thatcher and Herr Kohl forcefully reaffirmed their differing positions when they met at the Chancellor's home town of Deidesheim on 30 April. For Lady Thatcher's account of the meeting see Thatcher, p. 746-48.

2. I agree that the FRG will continue to profess wholehearted commitment to NATO, but what we face, as you say, is an increasingly difficult partner. There seems to be a sense of satisfaction, right across the political spectrum in Germany, at the greater assertiveness we have seen from Bonn in recent months. We shall have to be careful not to react against the mere fact of German assertiveness (a reaction which, I fear, still tends to come naturally unless curbed). It is encouraging to see that, in some quarters at least, the Germans themselves seem to be reacting against some of the more populist remarks we have heard recently, e.g. by Dregger.

3. Events in East Europe may yet take a turn for the worse and it is possible that the Germans would then scuttle back into the shelter of NATO orthodoxy. But it would hardly be good enough to rely on this sort of outcome. The present wobble in Germany is partly a product of NATO's very success. The problem is to convince the Germans of that and to carry forward the success while overcoming, or at least containing, the wobble.

4. This is going to be easier said than done. My first worry is the poor quality of German political leadership. As you say in your letter, lack of leadership and bad presentation were the root causes of the Coalition's recent set-backs in Berlin and Frankfurt. Since then the retreat has been headlong. We must hope that Kohl has now found a position, following his re-shuffle and wholesale policy review, from which he can re-establish some sort of control over the political agenda. But the decision to abandon the extension of the conscription period is not a good omen. My second worry is the sheer lack of logic in the German position (and in the broader public debate on security issues in the FRG). This may be partly due to poor leadership in Bonn. But it seems to go deeper than that. Absence of leadership and imperviousness to logic in the FRG promise to make the debate there on security issues a particularly difficult one for outsiders to intervene in successfully. Yet Germany's NATO Allies could hardly have a more legitimate or vital concern in the outcome.

5. As to personalities, you say in your despatch that Kohl is basically putting party above security interests, and thus imply that his own instincts on security matters are sound. I hope this will remain the case. Yet we were struck, for example, by the force of his remarks about Wintex.[5] And he has looked pretty comfortable, for instance in recent remarks on TV, with his latest public posture on SNF (although in private, at least, he seems to be aware that his position on SNF is not as compatible with past NATO decisions as he pretends). Genscher certainly seems driven by domestic and tactical concerns. But he looks to be increasingly the dominant voice on security issues. As for the SPD leadership, your despatch makes pretty grim reading. We shall be focussing our attention particularly on the evolution of SPD policies and in this connection we are interested in your account of your recent call on Vogel.[6] If there is even an outside chance of men like Lafontaine coming out on top in 1990, it will be as well for us to be prepared.

[5] Under pressure from German public opinion, Herr Kohl had described as 'completely insane' the outcome (in itself nothing new) of the NATO exercise WINTEX in February-March 1989. This had shown that a Warsaw Pact invasion of Western Europe could be halted by the use of short-range nuclear missiles over the territory of Germany and other European states, while sparing the territories of the two superpowers.

[6] In a minute of 3 May Sir C. Mallaby reported a 'relaxed and friendly' meeting with Herr Vogel in which the latter had expressed concern about the recent WINTEX exercise (to which Sir C. Mallaby had replied that 'there was no thought to moving to a war-fighting strategy') and had given 'an impression of great confidence about the federal political scene' (WRG 020/3).

6. It may be, as you suggest, that some other subject, such as the environment, will take over as the primary focus of German 'yearning'. But so long as the weather is fair on the Eastern Front, I doubt if we shall get more than partial relief from this sort of quarter. Another problem is that German views on nuclear matters, in particular, are finding quite an echo with others on the continent. (The French are one of the few who look relatively sound, yet you will have seen Ewen Fergusson's letter of 3 May arguing very cogently that it would be fruitless to expose French strategic thinking to a 'head-on application of logical argument'. I must say it is worrying when, for very different reasons admittedly, neither of our two principal European Allies seems amenable to logic in such a vital field.)

7. So what can we do? Your despatch looked beyond the current debate over SNF to longer-term issues. So does this letter. There will be little substitute for the hard slog of engaging the FRG, through all the available bilateral and multilateral channels, in an effort to arrive at common analyses and to accentuate the very large number of positives in our relationship. David Ratford will be replying separately to some of the points in your letter to him of 28 March.[7] The talks at Chevening last week concentrated on handling the security relationship (the papers prepared for Chevening raised some important questions which we shall need to continue to work on. The record of Chevening is being circulated separately).[8] Meetings in London over the coming weeks with Schäuble, Stoltenberg and Waigel will enable us to get off first base with some of the key men in Kohl's new Cabinet. The recommendations in your paragraphs 21 and 22 make obvious good sense. I also agree that we must try to engage the Americans, the French, and indeed others as fully as possible. However we are already doing our best in many of the directions you list. The formula continues to look broadly right, but as things are going it is hard not to feel the lack of a 'Miracle ingredient X'. Perhaps the problem, as David Ratford has noted, is that the source of difficulty lies not so much between the UK and FRG, but in the FRG itself.

8. I was particularly interested in your analysis of the ambivalent attitude in the FRG towards change in East Europe, and especially the GDR: 'gratification at the change but fear of instability.' On present trends (and indeed almost whatever happens) the instability in East Europe can only grow. There could hardly be a worse time to loosen the stability of NATO. Time is perhaps the one variable we can use to our advantage with the Germans. Although we shall engage them in vigorous debate on every point of specifics, it will be difficult to dispute their 'yearnings' head on. But we should be able to persuade them that these yearnings could more safely and certainly be assuaged over a considerably longer time-frame. Our difficulties stem in good measure from the urge for rapid results. One other strength we should be able to play on is the need for Alliance unity. Just at

---

[7] In his letter of 28 March Sir C. Mallaby analysed the current state of British-German relations, arguing that, while the Germans did not see the UK as an alternative to France, 'It was important that we should do everything possible to maximise the weight given here to our views.' There remained 'considerable potential for occasional friction over the year ahead', especially over defence (low flying) and European Community questions; but the recent Frankfurt summit had seen agreement over a wide range of issues, and there was now 'something of a lull in Franco-German relations'. Herr Kohl's current political difficulties called for 'a nicely judged approach, combining sympathy for his predicament . . . with firm advocacy of our positions'. An opportunity would be offered by Mrs Thatcher's visit to Deidesheim at the end of April (see note 4 above), and it was desirable that further meetings between the two leaders should take place over the coming year (WRG 020/3).
[8] Not found.

the moment, over SNF, this seems to be cutting both ways. But in the longer term the centre of gravity in NATO should help pull Bonn back from too enthusiastic 'yearning'. 16 have to tango in the Alliance: we may have to get used to Bonn stepping on our toes rather more often, but Bonn will run into political problems of its own if it appears to be too badly out of step with the rest.

9. I am copying this letter to recipients of your despatch

Yours ever,
JOHN FRETWELL.

No. 4

Minute from Mr Adams to Mr Synnott

[*WRE 014/2*]

Confidential   FCO, *12 June 1989*

East Germany

1. Reading the telegrams over the weekend, the PUS[1] was very struck by the dramatically differing reactions in Soviet bloc countries to recent events in China. To take the two extremes: the official reaction in Hungary (Budapest telno 291) has been strongly critical of the Chinese leadership's handling of the crisis; in East Germany, by contrast (East Berlin telno 169), no deviation from the official Chinese line is being permitted. [2]

2. The PUS thinks that it would be interesting to see an assessment of the impact of events in China on the Communist world generally—there have been a number of press stories on this theme over the weekend. But he thinks that we should focus in particular on the situation in East Germany, described by Teltschik to HM Embassy in Bonn (their telno 616) on 9 June as 'potentially explosive'.[3]

---

[1] Sir Patrick Wright.

[2] Between 3 and 5 June student demonstrations in Tiananmen Square, Beijing, were forcibly suppressed by the People's Liberation Army. On 5 June Solidarity won a landslide victory in Poland's first free elections. In Budapest telegram No. 291 of 9 June, Mr Harborne reported official Government and Party statements condemning the violence in China and calling for a peaceful solution (WRE 021/2). In East Berlin telegram No. 169 of 9 June, Mr Broomfield, reporting media coverage of events in Poland and China, commented that the GDR leadership's 'inability to adjust their view of the world as it ought to be to the world as it is demonstrates how slow moving and inflexible the system here has become. The result is a further loss of credibility among their own people who have followed both events on Western television with the closest attention' (WRE 014/2).

[3] In this telegram Sir C. Mallaby reported comments by Herr Teltschik to the US, French and British Ambassadors on the current situations in Poland, Hungary and the GDR: 'Teltschik's personal view was that the GDR was potentially the most explosive country. The economic and supply situation was worsening. Nobody in the Politburo wanted to suggest himself as a successor to Honecker. He agreed with me that there was no unrest at present, but said it could suddenly break out' (WRG 021/1).

3. The PUS thinks that the reaction (or non-reaction) of the East German leadership to events in China will have dealt a further heavy blow to their credibility with the GDR population—who will have been, of course, exposed to the very different treatment of China by the Western media. In the light of this, he thinks the time may have come for the JIC to look at East Germany in some detail.

G. D. ADAMS

No. 5

Minute from Mr Synnott to Mr Adams

[*WRE/014/2*]

Confidential   FCO, *14 June 1989*

East Germany

1. The PUS has asked us to set action in hand on East Germany (your minute of 12 June).[1] Having consulted other departments and the Cabinet Office, we have agreed a programme of work as follows:

(*a*) *Impact of events in China on the Communist World.* EED will coordinate a paper, already commissioned from Research Dept, which should be ready in draft next week. It will also cover reactions to the elections in Poland;

(*b*) *JIC paper on the GDR.* Assessment Staff have scheduled a meeting for 6 July to discuss a paper which they will draft in the meantime, consulting ourselves and the post in East Berlin.[2]

2. We have also been given a paper on the GDR by the *Auswärtiges Amt* (in the margins of the NATO Summit)[3] and will be taking discussion forward on this over the coming weeks. Its tone is less dramatic than Teltschik's view in Bonn telno 616.[4] Nevertheless this paper, and a despatch from Mr Broomfield recently submitted,[5] paint a picture of deepening economic problems and a depressing political logjam.

3. The PUS may recall the intervention of one of the German participants at the Chatham House Conference on the FRG last week to the effect that the GDR has been insulated to some extent from the pressures for reform which have affected other East European countries. There is much truth in this. Economic support from the FRG has eased the economic pressure on the GDR regime while emigration to the FRG has eliminated many potential dissident leaders. The prospect of a Party Congress in 1990 has aroused some speculation that Honecker (now 76) and the others in the old guard might step down in favour of younger leaders. But Honecker shows no sign of wanting to retire and no potential alternatives have yet revealed themselves.

4. The GDR leadership meanwhile are showing a blithe disregard for the changes going on around them. Shevardnadze visited the GDR on 9 June with a

---

[1] No. 4.
[2] Not printed.
[3] Not printed.
[4] No. 4, note 3.
[5] Probably No. 2, submitted to Mr Ratford by Mr Synnott on 5 June (WRE 014/2). See also No. 6.

reassuring message of support for the GDR's right to choose its own path and the need for others to respect it.

5. Mr Waldegrave may wish to explore these issues further if his projected visit to Bonn goes ahead next week.[6]

H.N.H. SYNNOTT

[6] Sir P. Wright minuted to Mr Waldegrave, the Minister of State for Europe, on 14 June: 'I discussed some of this briefly with the Secretary of State on 12 June. The action in hand should be useful.' Mr Waldegrave minuted on 14 June: 'Yes. I hope I can go to Bonn—it would be timely.' During his visit to Bonn on 22 June Mr Waldegrave discussed with senior officials, Ministers and CDU and SPD foreign affairs spokesmen his suggestion that 'the UK and FRG should consider concretely and at senior levels, what would be the contents of a common policy towards Eastern Europe, especially Poland and Hungary, in the new phase of East-West relations' (Bonn telegram No. 664 of 25 June). Sir C. Mallaby commented that 'Cooperation of the kind proposed would help us to influence German policy at a time when temptations to irresponsibility exist'. Talks on Eastern Europe and the Soviet Union between an FCO team led by Mr Ratford and a German Foreign Ministry team led by Dr Höynck were held in London on 25 October. They were judged useful but no definite plans were made to repeat them (minute from Mr Synnott to Mr Ratford, 2 November, WRG 021/1). See also No. 7, note 6, and No. 77, note 2.

No. 6

Letter from Mr Synnott to Mr Broomfield (East Berlin)[1]

[*WRE 014/2*]

Confidential   FCO, *10 July 1989*

Dear Nigel,

Inner-German Relations: Where Will It All End?

1. We have now received a number of comments on your despatch, which we gave a wide distribution.[2] It has been well received in the Office and has proved to be most timely. Mr Waldegrave found it most interesting, and Mrs Chalker described it as 'an excellent despatch'.

2. The conclusion we draw from it is that there is at present something of an uneasy balance of forces. Four principal factors have so far combined to hold up progress. The first is the ideological factor, the fact that the regime cannot question its own socialist foundations without questioning its very existence. The second is the economic support it receives from the FRG, which has perhaps helped to stave off the crisis that has proved the catalyst for change elsewhere. The third is the reluctance of the Russians to push the East Germans into reform, when the consequences must be so uncertain. The fourth is the longevity of Honecker.

3. Set against these elements, there are the factors for change. These are principally the faltering economy, the changing public mood (which is itself a reaction to the economic situation, as well as to the new wind blowing from the East), and the 'pull' of the FRG. It is difficult to see quite how the resolution of

[1] Copied to Sir C. Mallaby, Bonn; Mr Burton, BMG Berlin; Mrs Dean, Assessments Staff, Cabinet Office.
[2] No. 2.

forces will work out in the future. The leadership may have to change once, and possibly twice, before we can expect major reforms.

4. Looking further ahead, it seems likely that the German question will be one of the last pieces of the new European jigsaw to fall into place. Sir John Fretwell was much attracted to your speculation about the long-term future, and found the 'Austrian parallel' thought-provoking. To go beyond this, and consider the possibility of eventual reunification, is of course to raise a great many important questions.

Mr Waldegrave wondered whether the Russians might not find, paradoxically, that the popularity Gorbachev is now enjoying in the FRG will itself re-kindle pan-German feeling. Any significant drift of the popular mood in this direction in either the FRG or—especially—the GDR would be profoundly worrying for the Russians; it is clearly something that we shall need to watch very closely in the months and years ahead.

Yours ever,
H.N.H. SYNNOTT

No. 7

Letter from Sir C. Mallaby (Bonn) to Sir J. Fretwell[1]

[*WRG 020/3*]

Confidential   BONN, *27 July 1989*

Dear John,

British-German Relations

1. In my despatch of 10 April about the Federal Republic's reliability, I discussed the trends in this country, notably euphoria about Gorbachev, which are likely to make the Germans more difficult as Allies. One of those trends—a new assertiveness in foreign affairs—has intensified this summer. The strong German line about short-range nuclear forces (SNF) before the NATO summit was the biggest example. But German interests and the need to insist on them are now a constant theme of public and political debate on foreign policy. This is particularly important at a time when fundamental changes are taking place in Europe; and notably with regard to the East-West changes, for the Federal Republic has many reasons, described in my despatch, for wanting rapid progress in East-West relations and a build up of contacts with the Eastern Europeans.

2. The recent visits here by Bush and then Gorbachev showed that both superpowers are taking the Germans very seriously. Bush called the Germans 'partners in leadership'. His initiative, at the NATO summit, about conventional force reductions in Europe ensured that the argument between the Germans and the Americans about SNF left no ill-will here. German-American relations are widely expected to grow in importance. France, for its part, has a very close relationship with the Federal Republic, deriving from many years of careful development of cooperation. In this country, the success of Franco-German relations is popular, as a centrepiece in the construction of Europe and a demonstration that the historical

---

[1] Copied to UKDEL NATO, UKREP Brussels, Paris, Washington and Minister, BMG Berlin.

enmity between the two countries is gone. Politicians want to achieve new successes with France, because that enhances their public standing. During the French Presidency of the EC, German Ministers will be particularly keen to cooperate closely with France.

3. The Federal Republic's relations with Britain, however, as viewed by many in Bonn, are not in good shape. We were seen as pursuing an even harder line than the Americans in the argument about SNF, and some ill-feelings have remained. Moreover, in NATO and the EC, there are important subjects where there are British-German differences which soon may become more active. Perhaps more serious, there is, after the NATO summit and the Madrid European Council, a perception here that Britain's views matter less than they used to.[2] The prevailing German view of the NATO summit is that we took an extreme position and failed to get our way. And the agreement at Madrid that there should in due course be an intergovernmental conference about European Monetary Union is seen (despite the other things that happened at the European Council) as having resulted from a concession forced on us by the majority. Current economic difficulties and the conservative performance in the European elections make lesser contributions to the impression here that Britain's weight has recently diminished somewhat.

The Components of our Influence

4. Britain's political influence in the FRG depends mainly on how the Germans see us in four key areas:

(*a*) *Defence*: has traditionally been the especially strong suit in our bilateral relationship. With a third of the peacetime British army and half of our frontline air force stationed in the FRG (the largest force here after the US), we make a major contribution to the security of the FRG. Though often taken for granted by media and public, this has been appreciated by many important people and has given us influence. But it may now in political terms be a diminishing asset. With the advent of Gorbachev, the threat is thought to have receded and many Germans consider that defence is becoming less important to ensuring security than political and economic policies. Public concern about the nuisance of low flying and ground exercises by our forces and others is no longer counter-balanced by consciousness of a clear threat, so that political pressures on armed forces here have intensified.

(*b*) *European Community*: most Germans are keen on European integration, both as a substitute for national loyalty (because Germany is divided) and for the sake of economic and political progress towards European Union, a goal which has political appeal in the FRG. The dominant German perception at present is that Britain is acting as a brake on progress beyond the Single Market, namely on monetary cooperation and the social dimension, and does not have allies of any significance in this.

(*c*) *Berlin and the German Question*: As one of the four powers responsible for Berlin and Germany as a whole we have a major and continuing role. This is a plus. Our role in Berlin particularly gives us influence, and we are generally seen to perform the role effectively and with sensitivity. The task, as time goes by, is increasingly to make adjustments in order to avoid any accusation that we

---

[2] At the NATO summit on 29-30 May Mrs Thatcher was isolated in her insistence that there should be no negotiations with the Soviet Union over the modernisation of short-range nuclear forces (SNF). At the Madrid meeting of the European Council on 26-27 June Mrs Thatcher committed the UK to joining the Exchange Rate Mechanism (ERM) of the EMU without, however, setting a date for entry.

are maintaining 'anachronistic' Allied rights.

(*d*) *Ostpolitik*: 'The Federal Republic of Germany lies in the heart of Europe, on the demarcation line which separates East and West. Is it then not the most natural thing in the world that we Germans, as a divided people, follow with particular attention the developments in Central, East and South-East Europe?' (Chancellor Kohl on 30 May, during President Bush's visit.) German links with Eastern Europe are deeper-rooted than ours and more substantial in economic terms; and they have now overcome a lag in top-level contacts with the Soviet Union. The Germans feel a strong inclination to upgrade their relations with Eastern Europe. They would not take kindly to any signs of British suspicion of the FRG's enthusiasm in this area.

Rocks Ahead

5. In the Alliance, the German perception that the threat has receded is likely to cause further arguments. The next could concern the Vienna CFE talks.[3] As we pass late this year the 6-month point after the Bush initiative on conventional arms control and approach the 12-month point, and as the Federal election in December 1990 increasingly influences Ministers here, the latter, notably Genscher, are likely to want to accelerate the negotiations. They will see two kinds of electoral advantage in this: to show results, at German urging, in CFE and to come nearer to SNF negotiations. They might press early in 1990 for Western concessions to achieve progress; or they might suggest that we split the Western proposal in order to go for a rapid first agreement. Further ahead, the question of a successor to Lance[4] may come back in 1992, and the prospects of any German government agreeing to modernisation are slight. Airborne stand off nuclear weapons (TASM)[5] could cause argument: the FDP are probably not sound and the SPD, who could return to government after the Federal election, are against. In the short term there is another kind of problem looming: the SPD is trying to launch a political debate about Allied rights in Germany, particularly in respect of stationed forces.

6. On the Community side the French Presidency is going to present us with a number of challenges, particularly as regards EMU and the social dimension, where we differ from the Germans. Kohl will be prepared to resist the French where he judges major FRG interests to be at stake, but he will want neither to be seen to be braking European construction nor to be spoiling Mitterrand's European Council. And on the social dimension he will feel an increasingly pressing need, as the Federal election in 1990 comes into sight, to protect his left flank against the SPD.

[3] Negotiations for a treaty to limit conventional forces in Europe (CFE) had begun in Vienna in March 1989, in succession to the negotiations for Mutual and Balanced Force Reduction (MBFR) that had been held in Vienna since 1973. At the NATO summit on 29-30 May President Bush announced the goal of more far-reaching cuts in NATO and Warsaw Pact forces, and accelerated progress in the Vienna negotiations, combining this with the shelving of the controversial issue of Lance modernisation until agreement on cutting conventional forces had been reached. The CFE Treaty was ultimately signed on 19 November 1990.

[4] See No. 1, note 6.

[5] Tactical air to surface missiles (TASM) formed part of the Bush Administration's proposals for the modernisation of short-range nuclear weapons. It was hoped that they would prove less politically controversial in the FRG because the planes on which they were carried would be based in a number of West European countries, unlike land-based missiles, which would be based exclusively in the FRG.

What is to be done?

7. We must as far as possible ensure that the Germans take full account of our views. As we formulate our policies, we should think through their effects on the FRG, and allow time to explain our ideas at first hand to German Ministers and officials. I set out in a separate letter some suggestions designed to help us to maximise our influence here.[6] But I want to stress now one important general point about East-West relations. The German public believe, with the advent of Gorbachev, that they have security and that progress in East-West relations is what is now needed. Our view, I take it, is that NATO continues to need adequate defences and that, on this basis, we should seek progress through hard-headed negotiation and intensified East-West contacts. If we give the impression of advocating caution and adequate defences, without advocating and pursuing enthusiastically dialogue and contacts, that will undermine our influence and credibility here. I suggest that the UK should be advocate of sound defence and active dialogue. That approach should stand to win us friends in all camps in NATO. Stress on negotiations would strengthen our hand in stressing continued defence. I realise that Ministers' speeches have sought to take account of this point, but more emphasis is needed on opportunities for progress if we are to be influential in the FRG.

Yours ever,
C.L.G. MALLABY

[6] Among the actions suggested in this letter of 27 July were (*a*) building up the bilateral politico-military relationship, (*b*) finding common ground on European Community issues, (*c*) pre-empting accusations that the Allies were maintaining 'anachronistic' regulations or prerogatives on Berlin and the German question and (*d*) building on Mr Waldegrave's initiative for a British-German study of *Ostpolitik* (No. 4, note 6) as a basis for a more coordinated Western policy. He recommended, finally, 'that there should in the near future be a major British Ministerial speech in Germany on East-West relations', preferably by the Secretary of State. The Konrad Adenauer Foundation would be 'a prestigious and effective forum'. 'The purpose, I suggest, would be to show that the United Kingdom is keen to seize all opportunities to make progress in East-West relations . . . but also to show that there are many uncertainties and that the process of change in the enormous area from the Elbe to the Pacific will last at least a generation and involve setbacks and crises (and perhaps counter-reformation) and have results that cannot be foreseen, so that adequate Western defences will remain essential. A major speech like this would be a further steadying influence on the Germans.' A minute by Mr Ramsden of 28 July detailed proposals for follow-up actions. Mr Ratford minuted on 29 July: '(1) Sir C. Mallaby's approach is clearly right, and I endorse Mr Ramsden's proposals for follow-up. (2) That said, the basic problem remains our own rhetoric. So long as that is perceived in continental Europe as being negative and "anti-European" we will make less progress with our policies than, for the most part, they deserve.' Sir J. Fretwell minuted on 8 August: '. . . Both diagnosis and proposed remedies have the soothingly professional ring of a good professional G.P., far removed from the P.M.'s gut feeling that something has gone wrong in the FRG. May we at some stage need surgery rather than syrup?' (WRG 020/3).

No. 8

Letter from Mr Synnott to Miss Neville-Jones (Bonn)[1]

[*WRL 020/4*]

Confidential   FCO, *5 September 1989*

Dear Pauline,

The German Question

1. The recent exodus of GDR refugees to the Federal Republic via Hungary has inevitably led to increased interest in the 'German Question'.[2] Kohl's comment (your tel 810)[3] that this question is now back on the international agenda has been echoed by the press here. Recent articles have suggested that the exodus confirms the GDR's long-term unviability. The *Sunday Telegraph* on 3 September concluded that 'German reunification now looks like an idea whose time has come'.

2. I see from your press summary of 4 September[4] that the German press is also considering what recent events mean for inner-German relations and the 'German Question'. The report of a piece by Loewenstern in *Die Welt* particularly caught our eye, with its reference to a 'Bertele Report' and its suggestion that the FRG had been wrong all along to try to avoid destabilising the GDR. The *Financial Times* of 1 September picked up a report in the *F[rankfurter]A[llgemeine]Z[eitung]* that a senior FRG Government member had proposed an international conference on reunification (but was blocked by Kohl).

3. Sir Christopher Mallaby considered the reunification issue in his despatch of 10 April on 'How Reliable an Ally?',[5] noting that while reunification remained an aspiration for many, young people in particular thought it too distant a prospect to be worth thinking about. May I ask you to bear in mind, in considering whether or not there is reason to update that assessment, that we have a hearty appetite for signs of developments in popular mood and in official thinking on inner-German relations and the reunification question. We shall need to be ready to offer comment at short notice. I would also welcome your views on the significance of Kohl's reference (your TUR) to the Allies' continuing 'special responsibility' (I

---

[1] Copied to Mr Munro, East Berlin, Mr Lamont, BMG Berlin, and Paris, Washington and Moscow Chanceries.

[2] Since the opening of the border between Hungary and Austria in May 1989, thousands of East Germans—initially mainly holiday-makers, later people seeking to leave permanently—had attempted to cross the border although this was still illegal for those without valid GDR exit stamps in their passports. Many of those turned back had sought refuge in West German embassies in Budapest and other Eastern bloc capitals. On 10 September the Hungarian Government repudiated its agreement with the GDR and allowed East Germans to leave for the West (reported in Budapest telegram No. 431 of 11 September (WRE 350/1).

[3] In this telegram of 23 August Miss Neville-Jones reported a public statement by Herr Kohl on 22 August in which he placed responsibility for the emigration crisis on the GDR's unwillingness to embrace the reform process taking place elsewhere in Eastern Europe and 'linked the developments of recent weeks to the German question which, he said, was now back on the international agenda'. Miss Neville-Jones commented: 'The new, but not unexpected, element in the Federal Government's public rhetoric is the connection made with the German question. We can expect to hear a lot more of this' (WRE 350/1).

[4] Not printed.

[5] No. 1.

assume that he has in mind not only the Berlin angle but also the question of Allied 'rights relating to Germany as a whole' and in the context of the Bonn/Paris Conventions).

4. Nigel Broomfield's despatch of 20 April[6] looked at reunification from the East German point of view. I imagine that the mood in the GDR will be harder to divine. Nevertheless, any comments from Colin Munro would be very welcome.[7]

Yours ever,
H.N.H. SYNNOTT

---

[6] No. 2.

[7] In addition to writing to Miss Neville-Jones, Mr Synnott asked Mr Robert Dixon, the FCO's Research Analyst for Germany and Austria, for information on Allied 'rights and responsibilities relating specifically to Germany as a whole (as opposed to Berlin) and to the question of reunification (as opposed to a peace settlement)'. In a minute of 5 September Mr Dixon emphasised that the Allied commitment to a united Germany, as laid down in the Bonn/Paris Conventions of May 1955 (see enclosure in No. 15), was not to 'German reunification *per se*, but only to a form of it acceptable (as it then seemed) to the West, namely one peaceably achieved and resulting in a Germany that would be (*a*) a Western-style democracy, (*b*) linked to the West if not part of the West.' Among other things this would, he thought, rule out the possibility of a neutral Germany outside NATO (WRL 020/4).

No. 9

Teleletter from Sir C. Mallaby (Bonn) to Mr Ratford

[WRL 020/4]

Confidential   BONN, *11 September 1989, 12.15 p.m.*

The German Question

1. When Kohl said in the *Bundestag* on 5 September (my telno 853)[1] that the German question was on the agenda of world affairs, he was thinking, as he told me in a long social conversation on 7 September, of the German question in a wide sense. He did not mean only the question of reunification. He, like participants generally in the widespread discussion here, meant also the questions of the condition and prospects of the GDR and the predicament and mood of the East Germans and the question of Federal German and Allied policy towards the GDR.

2. The wave of emigrants from the GDR to the Federal Republic—the number may exceed 100,000 in 1989—and the drama of the escapes through Hungary are the major reason why discussion of the German question has welled up in this country in recent weeks. The exodus is seen here as demonstrating the frustration of the people of the GDR. Marxism-Leninism has lost all credibility. There is change to the east, freedom and prosperity to the west. Kohl said to me 'patience one day has an end'. Change in the USSR, Poland and Hungary is also a direct reason for the renewed debate here: West Germans ask themselves whether all this rapid change could bring reform in the GDR; whether it could even make reunification or some kind of federation possible one day. Reunification, one could

---

[1] This telegram of 6 September reported Herr Kohl's budget speech, much of which was devoted to recent developments in the GDR. These, it stated, 'had clearly shown that the German question remained firmly on the world agenda' (WRL 020/4).

say, is still only a hope but there is suddenly more interest in it than before and people are beginning to wonder whether it could become more than a hope. Politicians and experts do not expect it to become a goal of active policy in the foreseeable future. The usual line remains the vague one that the German question can be solved in due course through the development of a European peace order.

3. Kohl's main reason for speaking out on the German question is a domestic political one. The official in charge of this subject in Kohl's office, Duisberg, admitted as much to me (my telno 859).[2] Kohl's purpose is to prevent other parties, especially but not only the extreme right wing Republicans, becoming the main players on a subject of great public interest. Kohl also wanted, as he said in my conversation with him, to alert the three Allies to the Federal Republic's wish for support from them with regard to the German question. He said to me that this question (defined widely as at the start of this letter) was the most interesting one around at present. I think that most politicians here and the media would agree. He said: 'so long as I'm around, we shall try to handle that question with the Allies.' By that he meant that the Federal Republic would not act alone or with a risk of undermining its anchoring into the West or against the will of the Allies: but he was also implying that some future Chancellor might try to go it alone on the German question. I asked Kohl what specific policy or actions he wanted from us, and he gave no answer. That chimes with Duisberg's admission in reply to the same question, that there was little specific that we could do in the way of new policies towards the GDR. On a wider point, I have found that it is generally recognised here that talk of reunification as a German aim would cause anxiety in Poland, and indeed in the USSR and elsewhere, and could strengthen opponents of reform.

4. Duisberg's, and the official Federal German, view of the situation in the GDR was summarised in my telno 859. They see growing public frustration but the course set against reform and they see little chance of change in that position, or of major disruption of public order, for several years. But Teltschik is still peddling the line that the GDR is in a highly precarious state and that explosions are possible any time. Egon Bahr, the SPD's top expert on the German Question, gave me the same opinion last week. There is also disagreement here about the wishes of the GDR population for the future. Everyone here regards the current exodus as proof that the East Germans want to live like the West Germans. Many extrapolate that the East Germans obviously want reunification. Others here say that the East Germans would prefer a system retaining some characteristics, e.g. no giant private firms, of their present system and for the foreseeable future a separate East German state. Weizsäcker talks in the latter sense. No-one here nowadays sees any chance that reunification, if it did come one day, would be on any basis other than Western pluralism.

5. At a private seminar about East/West relations here last week, Larry Eagleburger and I referred in traditional terms to our Governments' support for German self-determination.[3] We were challenged (by Jonathan Carr, the *Economist* correspondent here) to say whether, after years of supporting reunification as an idea, we would really support it if it became a possibility. Eagleburger replied that ordinary Americans, believing that reunification would be in democracy, were not worried by the thought. I said that there would be important questions to consider

---

[2] Telegram of 8 September, recording a conversation with Herr Duisberg on 7 September (WRE 350/1). Not printed.

[3] A meeting of the *Bergedorfer Gesprächskreis* on 6 September. See also No. 11, note 1.

at the time, if reunification became an active issue: such as the effects on the EC and economic patterns in Europe as a whole and (a possibility raised by Carr) the fundamental change that would be involved if neutralism were introduced across today's two Germanies.

6. I shall continue to report the debate here on the various aspects of the German question. I personally see no need, and no scope, for major change in our policy toward the GDR. The USSR, Poland, and Hungary are more important. But a public expression of solidarity with the Federal Government on the problem of refugees would go down well here, and might be given by the Secretary of State when he is in Bonn on 20 September.[4] We also need to think about our public line on reunification—for domestic use, e.g. in parliament, and for use in Germany. We cannot renege on the established line that we support the principles of self-determination and of reunification in freedom. A classic example was Lord Carrington's letter to Genscher in 1980: 'It will remain the policy of my Government to support the efforts of the Federal Republic of Germany to work for a state of peace in Europe in which the German people can recover their unity in free self-determination.' At the same time I for one do not think that reunification is likely, in the foreseeable future, to be in British interests. Two pluralist Germanies with the FRG still in NATO, would certainly be preferable to a single, neutral Germany. That is why, in my talk to the seminar last week, enclosed in a separate letter to you, I stressed the Germans' right to self-determination and spoke of reunification only as an option, not as the certain result of self-determination.[5] My immediate suggestion is that we should

(*a*) put the stress on self-determination

(*b*) repeat the established line on reunification (e.g. Carrington) when that is necessary

(*c*) refer if necessary to the important implications of the subject and the impossibility of judging the specific arrangements unless and until reunification becomes a possibility and the circumstances at the time can be seen.

7. Point (*a*) is justified by the less than complete certainty as to whether East Germans want reunification as such, as well as by the differing views in West Germany on the desirability of reunification. One alternative view, held by many left-of-centre people, is that the myriad contacts between the FRG and the GDR, as between all other European countries, that would develop as part of a 'European peace order' would make reunification superfluous in addition to its being unwelcome to countries all around. We shall continue to reflect on this subject as a whole and on the public line in particular.

8. I am repeating this teleletter direct to Munro in East Berlin and copying it by bag to Ambassadors at Washington, UKDEL NATO, UKREP Brussels, Paris, Moscow, Warsaw, Budapest, Vienna, Prague, and Sofia and to Burton at BMG Berlin.[6]

SIR C. MALLABY

---

[4] Mr Major was paying his first visit to Bonn following his appointment as Foreign Secretary in July.

[5] Not printed. See No. 11, note 1.

[6] Mr Ratford minuted to Mr Synnott: 'These are extremely important issues. My snap reaction is that the Ambassador's line (to Carr) [on?] reunification was over-cautious, because over-specific in taking up the question of neutralism. 6(*a*) and (*b*) are surely right. For the rest, should we not simply state the assumption that, when reunification comes, it will be on Western terms (i.e., effectively, the GDR merging in the FRG). The question of 'neutralism' would by then have been overtaken. P[lea]se arrange appropriate distribution and follow-up action in my absence.'

No. 10

Teleletter from Mr Munro (East Berlin) to Mr Ratford[1]

[*WRL 020/4*]

Confidential   EAST BERLIN, *15 September 1989, 7 a.m.*

The German Question

1. In view of the Secretary of State's visit to Bonn on 20 September, I should like to comment on the (East Berlin and) GDR aspects of Sir Christopher Mallaby's teleletter to you of 11 September.[2] The Secretary of State's visit would be the opportunity for discussion of the GDR's future, a question which has seen brought into sharp focus by the exodus from Hungary.

2. On the question of our policy towards the GDR (para 6 of Sir Christopher's teleletter), although the USSR, Poland and Hungary are in many respects more important, because of the GDR's status as part of a divided country and the obsession of each German state with the other (the obsession is greatest in the SED Politburo), we do need, in formulating our policy on East/West (and West/West) relations to attach as much importance to events here as we do to those in these other countries. I would welcome a public expression of solidarity with the Federal Government on the problem of the refugees and repetition in public of our line on reunification. GDR officials and much of the diplomatic community here claim that the three Western powers (above all the French) are hypocrites when they refer to their commitment to reunification under the Bonn/Paris Conventions (Article 7 para 2).[3] GDR officials argue that because the UK is in favour of the division of Germany it must logically support the strengthening of the socialist order in the GDR because as Professor Otto Reinhold (President of the GDR Academy of Sciences and chief academic ideologue) has put it, a capitalist GDR would have no *raison d'être* alongside a capitalist FRG. The GDR is only conceivable as an ideology-based state. The line which we take here (together with the French and the Americans) is that the immediate question is one of self-determination. People living in East Berlin and the GDR have not exercised it. Why, especially at a time when the Poles, Hungarians and the peoples of the Soviet Union are exercising self-determination should people here be denied this right? Poles and Hungarians here agree with us on this point, but the Soviet Embassy say they agree with Reinhold.

3. I agree, not only with Sir Christopher's advice that we should put the stress on self-determination, but also that we should repeat the established line on reunification. I also suggest using again a formula which has been used in Parliament (and by the then Secretary of State with Genscher in 1984) that the British Government considers that there can be no lasting peace and stability in Europe so long as the German people remain divided against their will. Sir Christopher's third point (the impossibility of judging specific arrangements unless

---

[1] Copied by bag to Ambassadors at Washington, UKDEL NATO, UKREP Brussels, Paris, Moscow, Warsaw, Budapest, Vienna, Prague and Sofia, and to Mr Burton, BMG Berlin.
[2] No. 9.
[3] See enclosure in No. 15.

and until reunification becomes a possibility) strikes me as exactly right. I would comment that as seen from here the West German concept of overturning the division of Germany looks less futuristic than it used to.

4. We are reporting developments here connected with the emigration crisis as they occur. You might find it helpful to have [a] snap shot view of the reasons for it and possible developments (bearing in mind that things could have moved on again in unexpected directions by the time the Secretary of State arrives in Bonn). I agree with most of the points about the GDR made to Sir Christopher by his West German interlocutors. The exodus does indeed demonstrate popular frustration. I consider the proposition that Marxism/Leninism has lost all credibility to be no more than a statement of fact as far as the population here are concerned. In my view, the exodus has not been larger still because Germans are especially attached to their 'Heimat'. It is a tremendous wrench for these people to leave possessions, friends and familiar surroundings.

5. Given that the exodus is still only likely to amount to about one-fifth of the numbers who will have left for the West legally by the end of 1989, why have the SED leadership treated it as such a big crisis, a plot staged by the FRG to threaten the viability of the GDR as a state? The answer in my view is in two parts. Firstly, the steady legal exodus takes place unobtrusively. Emigrants do not appear in front of the cameras with instant comments on the reasons for their departure. West German TV programmes about the GDR can be dismissed by the SED faithful as hostile propaganda. But it has been different this time. The population here have seen well-qualified, happy young people arriving in the West expressing delight at having reached freedom and disgust at the oppressive state bureaucracy that they have left behind. The exodus has thus had something of the characteristics, if not of an election, at least of a very public opinion poll among just the people (young, educated) on whom the future of the GDR depends. The second reason has to do with the question of travel. It is a widely held view here that if there is one thing that could provoke an explosion it would be a ban (or severe restrictions) on travel to Czechoslovakia and Hungary. By opening their frontier, the Hungarians have created a situation for the GDR authorities where permission to travel to Hungary is the same as permission to travel to West Germany. This explains why rumours are now circulating that the authorities will soon allow travel (which they could control) to West Germany for people without relatives there. Although the present situation is one of lack of leadership and drift, the authorities cannot allow a situation to develop where people feel they must at all costs get out before the gates are closed. Teltschik and Bahr (para 4 of Sir Christopher's letter) could be proved right if the SED leadership fail to come up with something which at least preserves the present position on travel possibilities.

6. The Western press are making much of the possible emergence of an opposition (the New Forum). It may be that conditions here are at last producing a reform movement, with leaders. But I doubt it. I understand that New Forum leader Reich (who has been interviewed by the BBC) is on sick leave from university at home but he has not yet been threatened with the usual alternatives of imprisonment or deportation. I think it likely however that the authorities will continue to prevent the emergence of effective opposition by forcing this choice on its potential leaders. And although the Protestant Church is now calling more strongly on the authorities to introduce reform, there is still no sign of leading churchmen acting effectively in a political sense.

7. As in the Soviet Union before Gorbachev, there is now incessant speculation about Honecker's health and possible successors. For the present Honecker's indisposition has greatly added to the impression of drift and indecision. It is unlikely that he and his associates will be able to take charge of the Party conference in May 1990, and there is speculation about whether he will recover in time for the 40th anniversary on 7 October. It is possible therefore that there will soon be a new leader. Whatever his background and credentials a new leader will be less able than Honecker to resist pressure for change particularly in the management of the economy. Once the economic system (starting I predict with reduction of the enormous subsidies of basic necessities) begins to change, the second pillar (the first is ideology) on which the GDR rests, will begin to crumble. The question then will be, can the GDR be preserved as a separate German state but with Western political, economic and social conditions or is reunification unavoidable.

C. A. MUNRO

No. 11

Minute from Mr Adams to Mr Synnott

[WRL 020/4]

Confidential   FCO, *18 September 1989*

German Reunification

1. The PUS read over the weekend the two recent reports from Sir Christopher Mallaby on 'Prospects for a common Western *Ostpolitik*' and 'The German Question', which you submitted to PS/Mr Maude with your minute of 14 September entitled 'UK/FRG Inter-Party Meeting at Lake Como'.[1]

2. He commented that these reports were very interesting and important. He would like to see a further submission soon on our public line on reunification: he agrees with Sir Christopher Mallaby that some public redefinition may now be required.

G.D. ADAMS

[1] This meeting, to be attended by Mr Maude and Mr Waldegrave, was to take place at Cadenabbia, Italy, from 16 to 19 September. The two reports submitted by Mr Synnott were a letter from Sir C. Mallaby to Mr Ratford of 11 September enclosing a copy of a speech he had given at the *Bergedorfer Gesprächskreis* on 6 September (see No. 9, note 5), and No. 9. For comments on the discussion of the German question at this meeting see No. 9, para. 5.

No. 12

Letter from Sir M. Alexander (UKDEL NATO) to Sir P. Wright

[*Wright Papers*][1]

Personal and Confidential   BRUSSELS, *18 September 1989*

Dear Patrick,

US/UK Relations

1. I have just returned from the annual meeting of the IISS held, this year, in Oslo. It was an interesting occasion. Len Appleyard will no doubt have given you a general impression of what transpired. This letter is to record one part of one conversation which I had.

2. Bob Blackwill of the NSC is, you may recall, a close personal friend (my letter to you of 13 February).[2] He arranged, rather formally, a lengthy *tête à tête* to seek my views on, *inter alia*, a matter affecting the President's relations with the Prime Minister. Without saying as much, he left the impression that he was raising a problem preoccupying those even nearer the summit of the US hierarchy than he is himself.

3. The burden of the message was that President Bush is increasingly concerned about 'how to manage the Germans'. To this end, as his speeches and statements e.g. at and before the NATO Summit show, he wishes to see European cooperation developed—including in the defence/security field. A sound European framework and the active involvement of the Federal Republic's main partners will be necessary in the years ahead. The President knows that the Prime Minister has and will continue to have a critical influence on what happens.

4. The White House (it was not at every point clear whether Blackwill was talking about President Bush personally but the implication was that there were few differences of view in the inner circle on the issue) fears that the positions taken up of late by the Prime Minister—as evidenced in public statements and at inter-governmental meetings—have not advanced matters. Leaving aside the public pronouncements Blackwill particularly highlighted the personal aspect of the problem. He said (you will no doubt have confirmatory or contradictory testimony from other sources) that Chancellor Kohl refers to the Prime Minister in conversation with the President as 'that woman'. President Mitterrand—with whom Mr Bush now apparently has an excellent understanding—has told the President of his great irritation over what happened on and immediately before Bastille Day and of his puzzlement as to how to deal with the Prime Minister.[3] President Bush is accustomed to, but uncomfortable with, the Prime Minister's

---

[1] These papers will eventually be transferred to The National Archives in Class FCO 73 (Private Office Papers).

[2] Not printed.

[3] On the eve of the bicentenary of the French Revolution on 14 July 1989, Mrs Thatcher gave an interview to *Le Monde* in which she declared, *inter alia*, 'Human rights did not begin with the French Revolution'. She later recalled that on her arrival in Paris the following day she gave President Mitterrand 'a first edition of Charles Dickens's *A Tale of Two Cities*, which he, a connoisseur of such things, loved, but which made somewhat more elegantly the same point as my interview' (Thatcher, p. 753).

dismissive references to the Germans, and more particularly to Genscher, in their private conversations.

5. Blackwill is now asking himself whether there is any way in which the President could convey his concern to the Prime Minister e.g. during a *tête à tête* in the course of the visit which the Prime Minister is due, I understand, to pay to Washington/Camp David in November. He is conscious that Mrs Thatcher when pressed on these matters tends to argue that the Americans would not like it if the UK became more enthusiastically committed to European cooperation in all its various aspects. Was there, therefore, any way that the President could say to the Prime Minister 'please don't cut yourself out of the game' without causing offense [*sic*]? Blackwill stressed that the President disliked giving awkward messages and would probably not do so if he thought the outcome would be an argument. Even though Mr Bush's attitude to the Prime Minister was not quite the same as that of Mr Reagan, he greatly respected her.

6. I reminded Blackwill that it was some time since I could have legitimately claimed any special insight into how best to persuade the Prime Minister. I had been making the case about Europe and Germany to her in writing and orally for several years and had clearly failed to find a convincing way of putting it across! I could only make the obvious comments. There was no point in asking the Prime Minister to change her basic views and reactions. What the President could do (and what I personally very much hoped he would do) would be to speak to her frankly and personally about his concern and about the need to contain and manage the German problem in the period ahead e.g. by strengthening the European structures within which this might be done. He could underline, again, his government's— and more particularly his own—commitment to the development of European cooperation. In that general context the President could stress his confidence that the Prime Minister would play an active and positive role, and would help in carrying the Germans along. Without her involvement, nothing could be achieved. The consequences of failure might be considerable.

7. Blackwill listened carefully and indicated his intention of taking things further. He repeated that the President would, in his judgement, only pursue the matter if a non-confrontational way of raising it could be found.

8. In response to my query, Blackwill confirmed the President's personal commitment to the development of 'Europe'. The White House was ahead of the State Department in this regard. Blackwill commented that he had recently intervened with the State Department who were embroiled in an argument about whether the French nameplate for the forthcoming CSCE conference on the environment in Sofia should also refer to the Community.[4] He had reminded Seitz vigorously of the President's views and told him to stop resisting the Europeans.

9. One element in overall US concern about the German question is, incidentally, Genscher's health. His last heart attack seems to have been much more severe than has been publicly acknowledged. Chancellor Kohl has told Vernon Walters of his concern that Genscher may well die before the next election. This would, of course, have serious implications for the present coalition's prospects. Great efforts have been made, according to Blackwill, to get Genscher to slow down. Success has been limited. (I am sure Len Appleyard will have told you that the German question, in its several manifestations, was the subject of

---

[4] This conference took place from 16 October to 3 November 1989.

much attention in Oslo. It has risen up the international agenda with startling speed in recent weeks.)

10. I asked Blackwill whether he had discussed all this with any other British official. He said that he had touched on it with Robin Butler but with no-one else.

11. I cannot, of course, judge precisely with what authority Blackwill spoke. However it seems clear that he has a position of real influence and access. I did not ask him whether I could report the conversation. But he is enough of a professional to know that I would probably pass it on unless requested not to do so. I would be grateful, for very obvious reasons, if this letter could be given an extremely limited distribution.[5]

Yours ever,
M. ALEXANDER

[5] Sir P. Wright minuted to Mr Major on 21 September: 'You might like to glance at this before you see Sir M. Alexander tomorrow. I would welcome a word about it (e.g. the end of para 4) when you have a moment.'

No. 13

Sir C. Mallaby (Bonn) to Mr Major[1]

No. 904 Telegraphic [WRG 026/9]

BONN, *21 September 1989, 1.43 p.m.*

Your Visit to the FRG 20 September: Media Coverage

Summary

1. Wide coverage, including main national TV news. Useful editorial comment in the influential *Frankfurter Allgemeine Zeitung.*

Detail

2. Your visit has been extensively and positively reported in the FRG media. The main evening TV news carried film of your morning meeting with Herr Genscher and commented that your talks had been friendly and useful. The same report said that you had discussed the reunification issue, and quoted you as saying that the UK maintains the position it has held for over thirty years on the desirability of self-determination for the German people, but that there is likely to be some way to go before reunification can become a practical proposition.

3. Four of the major newspapers carried photographs: the Bonn-based *General Anzeiger* (GA) and the *Kölner Stadt-Anzeiger* on their front pages. Under the front page headline 'London emphasises Bonn's role', the GA picked out the main areas of discussion, with emphasis also on the friendly nature of the talks, the large measure of agreement, and your choice of the FRG for your first European visit.

4. The *Frankfurter Allgemeine Zeitung* (conservative) has an editorial by its foreign editor, Nonnenmacher, which comments that it would be unwise, 'to put it mildly', for the FRG to neglect relations with the UK: 'both in the EC and in

[1] Repeated for information to Routine Paris, Washington, UKDEL NATO, UKREP Brussels, Moscow, Warsaw, Budapest, and to Saving other NATO and East European Posts.

NATO London is one of Bonn's important partners. 60,000 BAOR soldiers are involved in the forward defence of the Federal Republic.'

5. The Berlin newspaper, *Tages[s]piegel*, had a story on the visit, mentioning the UK's continued support for the German wish for reunification and your impression that support in the GDR for reform is gathering momentum.

6. Most reports covered the UK's support for the reformers in Eastern Europe, especially in Poland and Hungary. A three minute report, in English, will go out on *Deutsche Welle*, the FRG equivalent of the BBC external service, this afternoon. This is primarily aimed at audiences further afield than Europe, but can be picked up on s[hort]w[ave] in Eastern Europe.

No. 14

Mr Broomfield (East Berlin) to Mr Major[1]

No. 291 Telegraphic [WRE 014/2]

Confidential   EAST BERLIN, *5 October 1989, 10 a.m.*

GDR: Internal Situation

Summary
1. Tension is mounting as the anniversary and Gorbachev's visit approach. US Embassy problem resolved. Serious disturbances at Dresden reported.
Detail
2. The mood of the country on the eve of the 40th anniversary is tense. While at one level the build-up to the celebrations proceeds unperturbed with veteran resistance-fighter rallies, parades, messages of solidarity, etc, at another, scenes eerily reminiscent of the last war with sealed trains of refugees travelling through the south of the country to freedom and another life are followed avidly by the GDR population on Western television.

3. We are getting reports of serious disturbances in Dresden last night with police and would-be emigrants in violent clashes involving water-cannon and stone-throwing to prevent people from boarding the refugee trains to Prague.[2] It seems likely that the trains avoided Dresden on their return journey which would account for their long delay in reaching Hof.

4. The eighteen sitting in the US Embassy (para 5 of my telno 290)[3] were persuaded to leave later yesterday on the basis of a double assurance conveyed to them by Lawyer Vogel: no prosecution and a rapid and 'favourable' consideration,

[1] Repeated for information Priority to Prague, Warsaw, Bonn; Routine to Moscow, UKDEL NATO, Washington, BMG Berlin; Saving to Paris, UKREP Brussels, East European posts.
[2] In the course of September over 5,000 would-be East German emigrants, refused permission to leave Czechoslovakia, had occupied the West German embassy in Prague. On 30 September the East German leadership gave way to international pressure and allowed those occupying the embassy to emigrate, on condition that they travelled to the West through the GDR in special sealed trains. This was a miscalculation: many East German citizens expressed their solidarity with the emigrants as the trains passed, and some tried to board the trains themselves.
[3] This telegram of 4 October reported an increase in the number of would-be refugees attempting to enter Western diplomatic establishments, following the GDR Government's 'temporary' closure of the border with Czechoslovakia, the only country with which the GDR had visa-free travel (RS 021/17).

within two months, of their applications to emigrate. Before they left, however, a crowd of between 100 and 200 tried to force their way into the US Embassy and had to be forcibly restrained by the police.

5. An EC meeting has been called this afternoon in the FRG permanent representation where we will presumably be informed of the situation there.

Comment

6. GDR propaganda continues to blame the FRG for the present difficulties. Members of the Politburo are reported as meeting the workers in various parts of the country to congratulate them on their achievements during the last forty years. Beneath that, however, as far as I can judge, tension is running high as people desperately look for a way out or of joining their friends and relatives in the West before the door closes on 8 October. While the security forces are on full alert and probably capable of dealing with local disturbances, the margin for miscalculation is narrow, particularly in relation to Gorbachev's visit.

No. 15

Submission from Mr Synnott to Mr Waldegrave, with minute by Mr Ratford

[*WRL 020/4*]

Confidential   FCO, *6 October 1989*

The German Question: Line to Take

1. I understand that the Secretary of State requires advice today on a line to take on the German Question.

2. I *submit* a range of points which can be drawn on freely. News Department concur.

3. These points are essentially modernised variations on a longstanding theme: the concept of self-determination; the reiteration of CSCE principles; and our acceptance of the principle of reunification on a liberal-democratic basis. They take into account the desirability of avoiding speculation about the nature of reunification, if and when the German people were to choose such a step.

4. As Bonn telno 947[1] indicates, the line used by the Secretary of State in Bonn on 20 September has gone down well in Germany: this is not only because of the words which the Secretary of State used, but also what he did not say. The Germans themselves are aware of the risks of laying too much emphasis on reunification and of frightening their Allies and their East European neighbours: hence the desirability of stressing the need for reform in the GDR.

5. I realise that there is an enormous appetite domestically for speculation on this subject, but it is best not to gratify this.

6. The Department have in hand a more considered paper on this question which provides a detailed rationale for the thrust of the line proposed. We shall submit

---

[1] In this telegram, dated 5 October 1989, Sir C. Mallaby reported a statement by Herr Kohl in the newspaper *Bild* and a conversation in which Herr Teltschik expressed appreciation for Mr Major's call for reform and human rights in the GDR at his press conference on 20 September (No. 13) (WRL 020/4).

this very soon, as soon as consultation with Posts is completed.[2] We also have near completion a contingency plan for possible instability in the GDR and East Berlin.[3]

7. Meanwhile, BMG Berlin have made contingency arrangements in the event of trouble at the Berlin sector boundary during Gorbachev's visit tonight and tomorrow.

H.N.H. SYNNOTT

ENCLOSURE IN NO. 15

GDR

Line to Take

What we have seen in the GDR shows the desperate need for reform there. The GDR must become a place where people *want* to live, without being *forced* to. They must move with the times. And give people freedom.

—CSCE commitments entered into by the GDR only *this January* are quite plain:

- Participating States 'will respect fully the right of everyone . . . to leave any country, including his own, and to return to his country'.
- Incredible that women and children should have to camp out in the cold and mud in order to win the exercise of this right.

—CSCE also commits all signatories to bring their laws, practices and policies into line with their international obligations:

- Could not be plainer that GDR is massively in breach.
- Call for reform in the GDR is but another way of calling on it to respect the obligations it has freely entered into.

Poland, Hungary and, to a great extent, the Soviet Union are showing the way.

We warmly endorse Chancellor Kohl's call (on 5 October in *Bild*) on the GDR leadership to respond to the demands of their people.

We have no wish to see the GDR destabilised. Nor does Chancellor Kohl. He has made that clear. It is the stubborn refusal of the GDR leaders to listen to their own people which is making the GDR less stable. People in the GDR want their aspirations met. They want the opportunity to determine their own future. Clear that such a future would include far greater democracy and freedom than the GDR currently enjoys.

FRG/GDR

Some progress had been made in developing links and overcoming the Cold War divisions between the 2 States in Germany. We welcome this. But the Wall still stands. There is a long way to go.

'The Prime Minister reaffirmed the conviction of successive British Governments that real and permanent stability in Europe will be difficult to achieve so long as the German nation is divided against its will.' (Thatcher/Kohl Joint Declaration, May 1984.)

Self-determination is the key. Freedom comes first. It follows that we will respect the free choice of the German people. This has always been our position. Chancellor Kohl clearly recognises the implications of this issue for the FRG's

---

[2] See Nos. 18 and 25.
[3] See No. 18, note 3.

friends and neighbours. The German Government has always shared its thinking with us. We shall continue to work closely together, as we have for 40 years.

Supplementaries (if pressed)

Allied Rights and Responsibilities

The policy of the Three Western Allies has been to ensure that the German Question is held open for eventual resolution.

This is illustrated by continuance of Four Power responsibilities for Germany as a whole.

And it is illustrated by the continued presence of Allied Powers in Berlin as protecting powers.

1937 Frontiers (if raised)

Herr Genscher has said (at the UN on 27 September) that the right of the Polish people to secure borders will not be called into question by the FRG.

Membership of Warsaw Pact (if raised)

Under CSCE (Helsinki Final Act) all signatory states have the right to belong, or not to belong, to alliances.

Key Texts

(1) Article 7 of the Convention on Relations in the Bonn/Paris Conventions, ratified in 1955, states: 'Pending the Peace Settlement the signatory states will cooperate to achieve, by peaceful means, their common aim of a reunified Germany enjoying a liberal-democratic constitution, like that of the Federal Republic, and integrated within the European community.'

(2) The Helsinki Final Act (1975) provides that participating States 'consider that their frontiers can be changed, in accordance with international law, by peaceful means and by agreement. They also have the right to belong or not to belong to international organisations, to be or not to be a party to bilateral or multilateral treaties including the right to be or not to be a party to treaties of alliance; they also have the right to neutrality'.

CSCE signatory States agreed in Vienna in January 1989 that 'they will respect each other's right freely to choose and develop their political, social, economic and cultural systems . . . they will ensure that their laws, regulations, practices and policies conform with their obligations under international law and are brought into harmony with the provisions of the Declaration on Principles and other CSCE commitments.'

They also agreed that 'by virtue of the principle of equal rights and self-determination of peoples and in conformity with the relevant provisions of the Final Act, all peoples always have the right, in full freedom, to determine, when and as they wish, their internal and external political status, without external interference, and to pursue as they wish their political, economic, social and cultural development.'

Minute by Mr Ratford

Confidential   FCO, *6 October 1989*

1. We have two shared interests with the Germans (and with our other Western partners):

(*a*) To emphasise that the door to reunification remains open (otherwise, there will be a temptation for the Germans to turn against the West); and

(*b*) To avoid being drawn into wholly premature speculation about the manner and circumstances in which reunification might eventually take place.

2. I believe the latter to be of primordial importance. Reunification, if and when it takes place, will raise fundamental questions about NATO and, even more so, about the EC. To take a few obvious examples, could the EC of Twelve tolerate a much larger and more powerful German member? If not, would we need enlargement to 'dilute' the German effect? What would be the institutional knock-on effect? and so on—Pandora's box with a vengeance.

3. In a nutshell, therefore our line should continue to be positive but unspecific.

D. J. E. RATFORD

No. 16

Letter from Miss Neville-Jones (Bonn) to Mr Synnott[1]

[WRL 020/4]

Confidential   BONN, *6 October 1989*

Dear Hilary,

Deutschland Politik

1. West Germans who watch their television sets each evening and who have met some of the 45,000 East Germans who have come across the borders since mid August know that they are witnessing a turning point in modern German history. They do not know where it will lead, nor at what speed or cost. But they feel very self aware, rather excited, and somewhat apprehensive. Across the inner German border they see the humiliation and crisis of a regime—and possibly of a state, taking place. The government's earlier assessments about the GDR regime's life expectancy no longer command confidence. The policy of 'small steps' in inner German relations no longer has a context to fit into. Moreover its gradualism and [the] marginal nature of the changes it brought about now seem too little, too slow. So what to do? There has been much debating and speculation here about the significance of what is happening in the GDR; about the right policy for the FRG to pursue towards the GDR; about the possible longer term consequences of change in the GDR for relations between the two Germanies; the connection between developments in inner German relations and relations with countries in Eastern [Europe] and, finally, the significance of all this for the wider European and Western scene. Discussion has been about both ends and means. A convincing

---

[1] Reply to No. 8. Copied to Mr Broomfield, East Berlin, Mr Burton, BMG Berlin, and to Moscow, Warsaw, Prague, Budapest and Washington Chanceries.

inner German policy is not yet in sight, nor is there yet consensus on the goal of a revised policy. The swirling over the future of the two Germanies has produced old ideas and new twists. Some shapes are emerging which could influence policy in important ways. I shall attempt to distinguish these.

Inner German Relations

2. There is cross party consensus in Bonn that the self imposed isolation of the GDR is dangerous. I detect no serious stream of opinion in the Federal Republic that thinks that allowing the GDR to stew in its own juice is a good idea. Whatever may be long term West German ambitions for the GDR, in the short term they do not want it to explode. Quite apart from the suffering that would be inflicted on East Germans, the effects would repercuss in the rest of Eastern Europe, almost certainly setting back the cause of reform. So there is also consensus that greater stability must be restored in the GDR.

3. Greater stability in the GDR will not, however, come without a reform programme and that Honecker has set his face against. This will not deter the Federal Government. They will continue to press their attentions after the 40th Birthday Party is over in Berlin. There is evidence that Genscher already has quite evolved thoughts about ways in which financial help for economic restructuring and reform could be provided. In yesterday's popular newspaper *Bild*, Kohl made clear in precise language that if the GDR undertook fundamental political and economic reform, then the Federal Government would support this with comprehensive cooperation, both of a general economic kind, and also in such fields as science and technology, transport and environment. (Bonn telno 947 to FCO.)[2] The Chancellery however is trying to minimise the inevitable impression this gives of buying reform—as much for the unhelpful effect this will have on Honecker.

4. The Federal Government knows that pressure from other quarters will be needed to get the process of reform going. They are hoping against hope that the Russians—especially Gorbachev—will talk hard and exert pressure while in East Berlin. Kohl's statement in *Bild* was timed with this in mind. The central issue of how to get reform going was discussed on 26 September at a meeting of CDU/CSU leaders called by Cabinet Minister Seiters who is in charge of inner German relations in the Federal Chancellery. Volker Rühe (now Secretary General of the CDU) told the Ambassador two days later that two ways of exerting outside pressure on the GDR had been canvassed. The FRG should pursue the development of relations with Poland and Hungary energetically so as to increase the pressure on the GDR to reform. Secondly, an idea urged by Dregger, the Chairman of the Parliamentary CDU/CSU Party, was that the allies should use their *locus standi* in *Deutschlandpolitik* to deliver a message. Asked to be more specific, Rühe referred to Article 7 of the Relations Convention of 1955.[3] The Ambassador reminded Rühe that the Secretary of State, in his press conference here on 20 September, had said that HMG stood by the commitment of the Allies (in the Convention) [to] cooperate to achieve their common aim of a reunified Germany with a democratic system like that of the Federal Republic.[4] The Ambassador added that the British line was also to stress self-determination, which logically came before the choice of what would be the future shape of Germany. He also recalled that Mr Major had made the obvious point which Rühe accepted

---

[2] See No. 15, note 1.
[3] See No. 15.
[4] No. 13.

that time would have to pass before reunification could become an active question. He went on that one idea discussed at the meeting on 26 September, viz whether to propose a Summit meeting of NATO to discuss the German Question, was unlikely to be followed up. Instead, the Chancellor would seek to use his bilateral summits with close allies to give public articulation to its importance. Rühe answered affirmatively the Ambassador's question whether Kohl would be seeking from friendly heads of government the kind of line taken by Mr Major in Bonn. According to Teltschik, Kohl thinks the more often statements are made which carry the message that the GDR must liberalise, the better.

5. The SPD have not managed to make capital out of the government's inability to get inner German dialogue going again. This is partly because they agree about the need anyway—their fox has been shot—and partly because they are caught in an uncomfortable situation. The SED's recent disinvitation to Ehmke, because he wanted to talk to reformers in the GDR, has been an embarrassment.[5] It looked like a vindication of Volker Rühe's accusation that a hard-line Communist party responsible for the current situation in the GDR were hardly appropriate interlocutors. The SPD are now in a bind: for the present it is not respectable to talk only to the SED. But while they continue to declare their intention of talking to opposition groups as well they may not get into the GDR at all. Büchler, in his guise as SPD spokesman on inner German relations, is setting up an all party parliamentary group to develop and coordinate policy towards the GDR. This looks distinctly like an attempt to clothe the SPD's present nakedness, though in the longer run it could perhaps help in the development of consensus once there is a policy around which to coalesce.

The German Question

6. Reunification suddenly seems much less theoretical and hypothetical. The Ambassador has asked me to add a gloss to the end of para 7(*a*) of Bonn telno 947 where we said that, while reunification used to be seen as remaining a hypothetical hope indefinitely, it now seemed a less distant prospect.[6] What this means is that, whereas until now one could not foresee any circumstances in which reunification could become a real issue, it is now possible, given the crisis in the GDR to imagine such circumstances emerging in time. This perception has led to a lively debate about the necessary and sufficient conditions for reunification. Voices like that of Waigel (CSU Finance Minister), who still insists that the question of the borders of Germany must remain open, suddenly seem old hat and counter-productive.

According to Teltschik, Kohl is very alive to the danger of excited talk about reunification standing in the way of its attainment, which is one reason why he talks more broadly of 'the German Question'. Secondly, an increasing number of Germans understand that reunification, if it comes, will only comprise the territory of the present FRG and GDR. Two separate ideas are beginning to run together here. The first is Adenauer's old dictum about freedom before unity. This implies two things: that a reunited Germany would be like the FRG and not some mid-way

---

[5] On 16 September Horst Sindermann, President of the GDR *Volkskammer*, informed Horst Ehmke, Deputy Chairman of the West German SPD Parliamentary Group, that a planned visit by an SPD parliamentary delegation could no longer take place owing to recent comments by Herr Ehmke and SPD Chairman Hans-Jochen Vogel which represented unwarranted interference in the internal affairs of the GDR.

[6] See No. 15, note 1. In this part of the telegram Sir C. Mallaby summed up the 'voluble and voluminous debate here about the state of the GDR and its implications' (WRL 020/4).

house and, secondly, that the only valid reunification would be the result of an authentic act of self determination. This can only take place if genuine freedom is extended to the GDR. This underlines the long, as well as short term, importance of reform. The second idea is the view associated with von Weizsäcker and Genscher that acceptance by the FRG of the continuing existence of two German states for the foreseeable future is the precondition of ever making the 'coming together' (as Genscher would put it) of two German states (others would say reunification) acceptable to other Europeans and thus possible. Kohl, in *Bild*, added as a further precondition the maintenance of the security interests of those involved. (One can perhaps detect assumptions here which are different from those being made by Genscher (see the Ambassador's letter of today's date to John Kerr).)[7] Genscher sweetens the pill for Germans of this long drawn out process by talk of 'overcoming the divisions' in Europe caused by boundaries. This is not new. But reforms in Poland and Hungary have lent new credibility to this formula as a way forward. Practical politicians like Volker Rühe see the development of close relations with Hungary and Poland as important in their own right and as a way of putting pressure on the GDR to reform. Beyond that, ideas float in peoples' minds about some vast future European omnium gatherum in which a reunified Germany is simultaneously made possible and acceptable. These days the German Question has come to mean something larger than reunification, with a tendency in some quarters (not Genscher) to regard European policy as the servant rather than the context of *Deutschland-politik*.

Conclusion

7. The SPD do not have much of an inner German policy at present and the Government is having difficulty getting one off the ground. They need the cooperation of the GDR in pursuing a course which Bonn knows it will be very difficult indeed, and possibly impossible, for Honecker, to accept. They do not expect anything to happen quickly. It is not yet a question therefore of when a possible policy of supporting reform in the GDR will work, but whether it will work. The Federal Government is apprehensive about the policy vacuum and wants help from among [*sic*] others, including the allies, in creating the right climate. All the other ideas about the longer term hang on getting a reform process going in the GDR.

8. The interesting thing about the debate on the longer term—which will sober up as the formidable nature of the task ahead becomes clear to more people—is the preoccupation which is now being shown with making inner German rapprochement and eventual reunification acceptable to their allies and other Europeans. West Germans understand, by and large, that they cannot dispense with this. They also know that there is nothing inevitable about reunification and that getting there, if they do, will take a long time.

Yours ever,
P. NEVILLE-JONES

---

[7] This letter discussed Herr Genscher's attitude to change in Eastern Europe in the light of his vigorous support for Austrian membership of the EC (as expressed in a speech in Austria on 14 September). Sir C. Mallaby concluded: 'Genscher, the most powerful advocate to European integration, is also the great activist in *Ostpolitik*. German thinking about the accession of Austria may increasingly be influenced by this Eastern dimension. My guess is that, when the time comes, the Germans will campaign actively for Austrian membership' (WRA 022/1).

No. 17

Mr Broomfield (East Berlin) to Mr Major[1]

No. 295 Telegraphic [END 020/4]

Confidential   EAST BERLIN, *8 October 1989*

GDR 40th Anniversary and Gorbachev's Visit

Summary

1. Old thinking and new thinking graphically counter-posed in the speeches and appearance of Honecker and Gorbachev. No discernible give on reform by Honecker. Notwithstanding massive security precautions, a major anti-regime demonstration in East Berlin on 7 October. A watershed.

Detail

2. My following telegrams summarise Honecker's and Gorbachev's speeches on 6 October (saving to most).[2]

3. Honecker's performance throughout was typical and traditional, as was the programme (speeches, huge youth torchlight procession, and military parade). Although Honecker carried out a gruelling programme his voice cracked quite frequently and overall his physical bearing could not have inspired confidence in his followers.

4. Gorbachev was his energetic self. Although his speech was carefully worded his message was clear. By emphasising his commitment to the reform process in the Soviet Union he pointed up starkly the lack of perspective in the GDR. World leaders—Bush, Thatcher, Mitterrand and Kohl—were mentioned. Honecker's name was not. Responsibility for the Berlin Wall was placed firmly on the GDR.

5. His impromptu response to a few people crying 'Gorby, help' on Unter den Linden on 6 October was that 'dangers await only those who don't react to life'. This has been interpreted by the Western press as his most 'direct advice' to the GDR's leaders. Whatever advice he gave Honecker at their meeting on 7 October, the official GDR agency report quotes Honecker as emphasising that the SED would continue to follow 'its proven course of the unity of economic and social policy, of continuity and renewal . . . Hopes of bourgeois politicians and ideologues that are based on reforms in the direction of bourgeois democracy through to capitalism are however built on sand. The GDR will hold firmly to the basic values of socialism.'

6. During the past week security in East Berlin has been intense. Large areas of the centre of the city have been cordoned off. Around the embassy area in Unter den Linden a number of people have been detained, presumably because they were suspected of trying to enter diplomatic premises to obtain an exit visa from the GDR for the West. Visits from West Berlin were selectively restricted. After the large peaceful demonstrations in Leipzig at the beginning of the week, and the violent clashes in Dresden on 4/5 October, the authorities clearly intended to prevent any public demonstration of opposition in East Berlin on 6/7 October. They were unsuccessful.

---

[1] Repeated for information to Immediate Bonn, BMG Berlin; Priority Moscow, Washington, UKDEL NATO, Paris; Routine East European Posts, UKREP Brussels, and Saving Peking.
[2] Nos. 296 and 297 (WRE 014/2). Not printed.

7. In the early evening of 7 October a group of young people, many from the Gethsemane and Erlöse churches, gathered in Alexanderplatz on the fringes of an official people's fair (*Volksfest*). Their number grew to between two and three thousand and the column moved off to demonstrate outside the palace of the Republic where Honecker was entertaining his foreign guests, including Gorbachev, as well as the diplomatic corps and a number of senior members of the party

8. The procession which was chanting Gorbachev's name was halted by the police some distance from the building and then moved back up Schönhauser Allee towards the Gethsemane church. It was joined as it moved by considerable numbers of other young people before it was finally halted and dispersed by the police with the assistance of the plain clothes Stasi (security police) and uniformed civilian *Kampfgruppen* (factory-based auxiliary police). Sporadic running clashes went on through most of the night, observed by the Western press (see separate telegram on the arrest of Peter Millar, *Sunday Times*).[3] I and two members of Chancery separately observed parts of the police preparations and the demonstration and subsequent clashes. There are also reports of other demonstrations in Potsdam, Plauen and Leipzig on 7 October.

9. I recommend that our public line should be a strong condemnation of the GDR authorities' use of force to suppress public expression of views together with the warning that things will certainly get worse if they continue to deny large sections of their population any genuine way of expressing their views and wishes and of exercising the human rights set out in the CSCE agreements. (The official GDR line is that 'rowdies' accompanied by Western journalists tried to disrupt the peoples' festivities on Alexanderplatz and were prevented 'with restraint' by the police.)

10. The events of the last few weeks both inside and outside the GDR have been traumatic and will have a major impact on future developments here. While hitherto the police have been able to head off, expel or suppress dissidents they have been powerless in the face of the large scale 'demonstrations' in Budapest, Prague, and Warsaw, by the GDR refugees. These examples, which are followed here on Western television, have encouraged others inside the GDR by showing that they are not alone. Belief in police/security invincibility has been considerably undermined.

11. The demonstrations in Dresden and East Berlin had a specific focus (the refugee trains, and Gorbachev). The test now for the new reform groups will be to maintain these protests without such specific events to focus on. But they have increasingly been joined by voices from within the establishment (the writers' union, members of the 'CDU' and even non-protest minded churchmen).

12. I am commenting, in a separate despatch, why I think a watershed has been reached in the development of this country.[4] Whether events will move slowly or rapidly is open. It will depend on a number of incalculable factors *inter alia* the performance [. . .][5] of the reform groups, [whether?][6] the authorities try a crackdown, the progress of reform in Eastern Europe and the attitudes of the Soviet Union and the FRG. But I agree with Sir C. Mallaby (his teleletter of 19 September

---

[3] Not found.
[4] No. 19.
[5] The text here is indecipherable.
[6] The text here is uncertain.

to Mr Ratford)[7] that we should now look urgently at the broader and longer term implications of 'the German Question'.

13. In preparation for Teltschik's visit on 11 October (Bonn telno 947)[8] I am telegraphing to Bonn and the Department a summary of the recommendations in my despatch.[9]

---

[7] Presumably No. 9 of 11 September 1989.

[8] Not printed. See No. 15, note 1. Although this telegram refers to a conversation between Sir C. Mallaby and Herr Teltschik on 5 October, it makes no mention of a visit by Herr Teltschik to the GDR.

[9] Mr Gozney minuted to Mr Synnott on 16 October: 'The Secretary of State has seen East Berlin Telno 295. He agrees strongly with Mr Broomfield and Sir Christopher Mallaby that we should now look urgently at "The German Question". The sooner we do so the better' (WRL 020/4).

No. 18

Letter from Mr Ramsden to Mr Budd (Bonn)[1]

[WRL 02/4]

Confidential covering Secret   FCO, *11 October 1989*

Dear Colin,

'German Reunification' and 'Explosion in the GDR?'

1. You, and other recipients of this letter, will already have seen Hilary Synnott's submission of 6 October to Mr Waldegrave, putting forward a 'line to take' on the German Question.[2]

2. I now enclose two papers we have prepared in the Department.[3] These look at the question of German reunification, and our options for reacting to an explosion in the GDR. The paper on reunification is intended to provide the analytical underpinning for the 'line' (which Ministers have now approved). The contingency plan is intended primarily as an illustrative work, outlining the sort of measures open to us and looking at the pros and cons. The aim at this stage is to get a broad agreement within the FCO on the sort of things we might need to do in the event of a crisis in the GDR. We would then be that much further down the road if and when we had to act quickly.

3. Inevitably, some [of] the ground in both papers has been covered in previous works, but we hope that they may nevertheless be useful. They are not, of course, intended in any way to pre-empt the work which you, or other recipients, are already doing or planning, particularly on reunification.

4. We should very much welcome comments from all concerned on both papers. We would hope in due course to be able to submit them to Ministers. I should perhaps make clear that this is at this stage a purely in-house operation. We are not

---

[1] Copied (with papers) to Mr Munro, East Berlin; Mr Lamont, BMG Berlin; Mr Gowan, Soviet Department; Ms Lewis, EED; Mr J. Powell, Policy Planning Staff; Mr Dixon, Research Department; Mr Lance, Research Dept.

[2] No. 15.

[3] 'German Reunification' printed as enclosure; 'Explosion in the GDR' not printed.

yet consulting other Departments e.g. we have deliberately not approached the MOD about the military aspects (e.g. Live Oak)[4] in order not to set hares running.

5. In view of the many enquiries we are receiving from within the office for our views on these questions (particularly on Reunification) it would be helpful to have early comments. Could I ask you and other recipients to let me have your views, by teleletter if need be, by Thursday 19 October?[5]

Yours ever,
J. C. J. RAMSDEN

ENCLOSURE IN NO. 18

DRAFT PAPER ON GERMAN REUNIFICATION

[*WRL 020/4*]

Confidential   FCO, *11 October 1989*

INTRODUCTION

1. Recent events have led to renewed speculation about the German Question. Some press reports have tended to portray reunification as inevitable, and even imminent. Chancellor Kohl's remark that the 'German Question' is now back on the international agenda has been widely portrayed as German pressure for reunification, although Kohl has stressed its broader connotation. This Paper examines the causes of, and prospects for, change; whether change inevitably means reunification; and the implications for British policy.

BACKGROUND

2. Much of the existing literature remains relevant, including despatches by successive Ambassadors in Bonn and East Berlin, formal replies to these, and Planning Staff Papers in 1987 and 1988.[6] But much has changed since the last

---

[4] LIVE OAK was a tripartite planning staff established under the command of CINCEUR in April 1959 by the US, UK, and France, in order to make military preparations to deal with possible interference with Allied access to Berlin. In the event of these plans proving unsuccessful, further plans were developed in a NATO context which envisaged broadening the conflict. Known as BERCON (Berlin Contingency Plans), they involved a quadripartite planning group comprising the US, UK, France and the FRG.

[5] Replies printed as Nos. 20-22. A teleletter of 19 October from Mr Lamont (BMG Berlin), dealing only with Berlin issues, and comments in other replies on 'Explosion in the GDR', are not printed. Mr Munro's reply, in East Berlin telegram No. 332 of 24 October, read, in part: 'I agree with Bruce Dinwiddy (his letter of 19 October to you [No. 21]) that more attention to the Soviet position is needed. As far as our own position is concerned, I recommend deleting references (such as that in para 8a on the possibility of an explosion in the GDR) to our 'limited influence'. As a power with responsibility for Berlin and Germany as a whole, we have a major role to play, even though, as the papers argue, we need to gear our response to the behaviour of others and to coordinate very closely with the Americans, the French, the Germans (FRG and West Berlin), and as the Ambassador has recommended, under certain circumstances, the Russians. . . . I think it important that we in Britain should be clear about our position with regard to the 'German question'; have a clearly worked out policy to deal with possible developments; and be clear about the consultation/coordination mechanisms that we are employing. It is always important in dealing with the Germans to have a clear conceptual approach to guide specific actions.'

[6] For the Planning Staff papers see Preface, pp. xi-xii.

FCO paper a year ago. Poland has a non-Communist Government. Hungary is heading the same way. Nationalist movements in the Soviet Union are posing previously unthinkable challenges to Moscow's authority. The perceived politico-military threat has greatly diminished. The FRG is becoming more self-assertive in the political field. Many in Germany, and elsewhere, feel that the post-war framework has lost its previous immutability. We no longer know for certain either where the limits of Moscow's tolerance are; or whether the Russians still have the will to prevent that which they consider intolerable. Since 1990 sees four sets of *Land* elections and the Federal elections, emotions in the FRG may run high.

REUNIFICATION: THE HISTORY

3. Formally, the UK, US and France have long been committed to supporting German reunification, with certain qualifications. Article 7 of the Relations Convention of the Bonn/Paris Conventions of 1955 states:

> Pending the peace settlement, the Signatory States will cooperate to achieve, by peaceful means, their common aim of a reunified Germany enjoying a liberal-democratic constitution, like that of the Federal Republic, and integrated within the European community.

4. But even before this, the Federal German Basic Law (agreed by the Allies) envisaged the FRG in its present form as a temporary state, with Bonn as its temporary capital. The Basic Law is not a Constitution, and provides that it shall cease to be in force 'on the day on which a Constitution adopted by a free decision of the German people comes into force'. The division of Germany remains a highly emotive issue for many Germans. Successive Federal Governments have committed themselves to the ultimate goal of reunification.

5. In practice, however, reunification has not been an immediate policy goal for over 35 years. The FRG's post-war history has been characterised by committed membership of the EC and NATO. Successive FRG Governments have understood very well the doubts which exist about the economic and political implications of German reunification if it were likely to come about. These doubts have in some cases (e.g. France, Poland and others) been about the principle, and in others have related to questions of time and conditions. Their aim has always been to carry their Western allies with them on the 'German Question'—which in their eyes covers the whole issue of the nature of the GDR as a state and the West's relations with it, as well as the issue of reunification—and to avoid any charges of 'going it alone'.

RECENT ATTITUDES

6. In 1980, Lord Carrington, then Foreign Secretary, wrote to Genscher:

> It will remain the policy of my Government to support the efforts of the Federal Republic of Germany to work for a state of peace in Europe in which the German people can recover their unity in free self-determination.

In May 1984, the Prime Minister and Chancellor Kohl issued a joint statement which included the words:

> It is the belief of successive British Governments that real and permanent stability in Europe will be difficult to achieve so long as the German nation is divided against its will.

In February 1989 Sir Geoffrey Howe used a similar phrase in the House of Commons.[7]

7. These statements are entirely consistent with our 1955 commitments. But, by their references to self-determination, they leave open the possibility that the final result of a settlement of the German Question might be something other than full reunification.

8. The Germans remain somewhat indistinct about their long term vision. They are firm in rejecting fears that they might ever be tempted to trade reunification for neutrality. Speaking on 14 September, Genscher affirmed that one German nation was 'a reality which must be accepted when building the European House'. But the aim of the Federal Government too was 'to strive for the right of self-determination of the German people'. The FRG should not de-Europeanise its foreign policy and 'Deutschlandpolitik'. Steering a neutralist course single-handed would be 'a retrograde step', creating new instabilities and damaging the national interests of the Germans. Elsewhere, the Germans speak deliberately vaguely of the importance of nation states declining as European cooperation increases, and the issue of reunification finally being resolved in the context of a new 'European Peace Order'.

Eastern Views

9. German reunification is a neuralgic issue for many of the East Europeans. The Poles are particularly wary, and are alarmed when some right-wing German politicians refer to Germany's 1937 borders and appear to question whether the Oder-Neisse line is really the final border between 'Germany' (currently the GDR) and Poland. References by Federal Government Ministers to the 'German Question' being resolved within the framework of a new 'European Peace Order' are intended to calm some of these fears. The West Germans recognise that direct talk of reunification could endanger the process of reform in Poland, and even in the Soviet Union. Genscher publicly reaffirmed at the UN on 27 September that the FRG had no territorial claims on Poland.

10. The Soviet position recently has been to say that the 'German Question' is one for the Germans to resolve. [Update on Gorbachev's views.][8] Their current policy elsewhere in Eastern Europe seems to be genuinely to leave the countries concerned to make their own decisions. They would probably now welcome some kind of reform in the GDR, since its present immobilism is itself becoming a cause of instability. But there seems little doubt that they regard GDR membership of the Warsaw Pact as a matter of great importance for their own security. They currently have nearly 400,000 troops in the GDR (although these are currently being reduced in numbers). In an apparent reference to the Oder/Neisse line question, Shevardnadze indicated in his speech to the UN in September that the Soviet Union is still concerned about 'German revanchism'. The Russians would be sure to criticise sharply any moves towards reunification on the basis of the integration of the present GDR into an expanded Federal Republic which would retain its membership of the EC and NATO.

Other Views

11. Several of the FRG allies have similar concerns about the prospect of reunification, inside or outside the EC. These were expressed trenchantly in recent talks with the PUS by the Secretary General of the *Quai d'Orsay* and the French

---

[7] See No. 2, note 2.
[8] Parentheses in original.

Ambassador in London, and by the Belgian Ambassador. Many Dutch, Danes and Norwegians share these sentiments.

12. The prospect of reunification also has wide-ranging implications for the possible future political shape of Europe, relevant to possible enlargement of the EC and not excluding the development of Mitteleuropa. These are only now first being considered.

THE GDR: DEVELOPMENTS AND PROSPECTS

13. Until very recently, observers generally agreed that the GDR and the 'German Question' would be the last parts of the Eastern European reform jigsaw to fall into place. But events have now upset this assumption. The increasing level of emigration from the GDR shows that the regime has failed to win the hearts and minds of its people. Those staying behind are less afraid to express dissatisfaction with the GDR's failure to adopt reforms and with the worsening supply situation. For the first time since 1953, thousands are taking to the streets in protest. Umbrella opposition groups are forming. The Church, including at last the Catholics, is lending its weight also to calls for reform.

14. Honecker seems likely to continue to oppose reform. Despite his recent illness, he may after all be able carry on up to and beyond next May's Party Congress. Even if he stepped down, his successor might be reluctant to depart very far from the present rigid 'socialist' course. The GDR's very existence is justified in ideological terms.

15. But events could force the leadership's hand. Although they will probably not hesitate to use force against individuals and gatherings that they see as subversive, they may be compelled to look for ways of satisfying popular demands for change if the protest movement gathers strength.

16. We cannot predict when reforms might first be introduced, or how far they will go. The regime will probably be as grudging as possible. They will not, in particular, want to do anything which could put in doubt the Party's dominant role. When they can resist no longer, however, reforms might take the following line:

(*a*) The economy could be liberalised; releasing the grip of the state apparatus. This could lead to short-term hardships, and benefits might take some time to emerge.

(*b*) At the political level, the authorities could allow the existing 'independent' parties to become genuinely independent and to stand against the Socialist Unity Party in a national election, and also allow greater freedom to other groups to engage in political activity.

(*c*) We can know little about the possible outcome of such changes. The regime might at first try to limit the opposition's share of power (as in Poland). But it seems likely that any genuine extension of democracy would lead, sooner or later, to the Socialist Unity Party losing its present monopoly on power.

(*d*) This might lead to a situation where the GDR evolved into a democratic socialist state, separate from the FRG but with greatly expanded contacts (this seems to be what some of the new dissident groups want). The change in the social structure would suggest much greater freedom for GDR citizens to travel to the West.

17. The problem for any reforming GDR would be how to avoid losing their best-qualified people. Rapid economic development in the GDR would be the best way to reduce the 'pull' of life in the West. The Federal Government would certainly help, as Kohl has recently indicated, in order to try to stem the westward

flow, and would look to its EC partners to do the same. FRG (and some other Western) companies would be likely to see cost advantages in trying to locate some of their production facilities in the GDR, despite manpower shortages there. West Berlin would be a powerful pole of attraction for new economic activity. In time a reformed GDR could even become eligible for EC membership (as the CDU Secretary General apparently envisages), if further expansion of the EC were then considered.

PROSPECTS FOR REUNIFICATION

18. We cannot say whether, in this scenario, the two German states would ultimately reunify. Although the present Communist leaders say they can see no scope for the GDR to exist separately if it moves away from dogmatic adherence to orthodox 'socialism', there is no objective reason why a more modern and liberal GDR should not continue to exist alongside the FRG, as Austria does. Some form of confederation might be set up. German unity was only a comparatively brief phenomenon in the life of the German-speaking peoples. With freedom of expression and travel, there would in some ways be less need for the final step of formally dissolving the GDR. There is in any case no firm evidence as to whether GDR citizens would actually vote for full reunification (a recent poll, of unknown validity, referred to 64% support in the GDR). At least one of the new political groupings advocates retention of a separate socialist state.

19. The two countries' membership of opposing military blocs provides a further obstacle to full reunification. If future West German governments stick to the line that they will not accept reunification at the cost of neutrality, unity would involve bringing the GDR into NATO. The Russians clearly would be hostile, and could threaten difficulties over the withdrawal of their forces. On present form at least, the West Germans would be reluctant to provoke a crisis of this sort. In this scenario, reunification therefore seems still a distant prospect, since it would require the prior or simultaneous dissolution of the two military blocs.

20. But we cannot rule out the question arising more suddenly, if events in the GDR take a dramatic turn. A number of senior West German politicians, including Genscher, have spoken of their fear that an 'explosion' could take place in the GDR. An uprising which led to dramatic changes in the GDR could trigger an emotional surge amongst the West German public in favour of rapid moves towards reunification. The Federal Government could be forced to react, virtually regardless of their Western partners' views or reactions elsewhere. The federal nature of the FRG could facilitate the process in practice.

IMPLICATIONS FOR THE UK

(*a*) *UK Policy*

21. German official thinking is currently running on the right lines. Our aim should be to encourage the West Germans to continue to exercise caution, and to take the Allies fully into their confidence as their thinking develops. We for our part should recognise the pressure the Federal authorities are under from public opinion, particularly when any dramatic events take place in the GDR. We should continue to do what we can to ensure that the FRG remains bound into the West and does not, for any reason, feel cause to question, for example, the benefits of its membership of the EC and NATO.

22. Under the 'gradual reform' scenario, our task would initially be fairly easy. We would not need to face the question of reunification for some time. We

probably would, however, have to consider the nature of an economic assistance package to secure reform in the GDR, and eventually possibly even the question of EC membership. Decisions cannot be taken now. But granting EC assistance to a reforming GDR would be fully in keeping with our current approach to Poland, and showing an open mind on the question of GDR EC membership would reduce the risk of extremist politicians in the FRG one day arguing that 'Germany' must seek its destiny alone.

23. We should note in passing that, in resolving the German Question, the rationale for a continued Allied presence in Berlin would presumably lapse.

24. Although we, with others, can exert some influence, we cannot block reunification, if that is indeed the direction in which events lead. The possibility of it is inherent in the concept of self-determination. But a reunited Germany could present various disadvantages to our interests:

(i) commercial/economic; an expanded FRG with greater productive capacity would dominate the West's trade with Eastern Europe more than ever, and increase the FRG's existing economic dominance of the EC;

(ii) political; the FRG is already growing more assertive in the political field. On past and present form, FRG leaders seem likely to be reluctant to assume the role of the leading European power. But future leaders of a united Germany could, conceivably, argue for a political role for Germany commensurate with its overwhelming economic strength;

(iii) security; what would be the impact for NATO? It is impossible to answer this now, since we cannot know how far ahead we are looking. But reunification might trigger French resentment and fears of German domination amongst the Benelux countries.

25. But these aspects should not be exaggerated. They can be largely averted by good management of any evolution towards reunification. The advantages which could flow from reunification are considerable. It would be a victory for Western values, and would bring an improvement in Western security. It might increase in [sic] the European Community's overall economic strength, to general advantage. Much of the FRG's surplus capital would be absorbed by the infrastructural projects that would be needed to bring the East up to West German standards, putting an end to the FRG's chronic capital surplus and holding out the prospect of more balanced trade flows in the EC. UK industry should also benefit from the opportunities offered (the FRG is already our second largest export market).

26. The UK's best approach, therefore, is not to seek discourage reunification, but rather to exert influence over the speed and timing of any moves in that direction. Close contacts with the Germans at all levels, including the highest, will be a crucial element in this process. They will be particularly important if events in the GDR take a dramatic turn.

27. Finally, if the current process of reform in Eastern Europe were to fail, the prospects of reunification could similarly disappear. It would be in the nature of the German psyche for deep depression to follow the current euphoria. We should maintain the position of wise and moderate counsellors throughout.

(*b*) *Public Presentation*

28. The West should continue to call for greater political freedom for the citizens of the GDR. This fits in well with our approach bilaterally elsewhere in Eastern Europe, and in the CSCE.

29. We should also continue to say that the German people should be allowed free self-determination. We support self-determination for other national groups.

Support for self-determination for the Germans is consistent with (but more flexible than) our 1955 commitments; it is likely to be less objectionable to the Russians than simple calls for reunification; and it is in line with what the Germans themselves are saying. The Secretary of State used this line in Bonn on 20 September.[9] It was much appreciated, and generally judged by the Germans to have been exactly right.

30. Where necessary, we should reaffirm that we stand by our 1955 undertakings. We should not however let ourselves be drawn on detail until it is clear whether, and in what circumstances, reunification is likely to become a reality. As illustrated above, there are fundamental questions about NATO, the EC and enlargement.

31. We should nevertheless perhaps be clear in our own minds whether we are thinking ultimately of a single act of self-determination by all the German people together, or of separate acts by the populations of the two German states. Since the former option could imply the annexation of the GDR regardless of the views of its inhabitants, we should probably be thinking of the latter.

[9] No. 13.

No. 19

Mr Broomfield (East Berlin) to Mr Major

[WRE 227/1]

Confidential   EAST BERLIN, *12 October 1989*

Summary . . .[1]

Sir,
Party and People at the GDR's 40th Anniversary: Immovable Object or Irresistible Force

1. On 7 October the GDR leadership treated itself to an extravagant old-style Communist birthday party. Intended to mark the climax of a life's work by General Secretary Honecker and his like-minded septuagenarians and octogenarians in the Politburo, it in fact turned out to be a profoundly depressing occasion. The events leading up to the anniversary and the anti-regime demonstrations on the day itself in East Berlin and elsewhere in the GDR were intensely embarrassing for the leadership and in my view mark a watershed in the development of this country.

2. The roots of the trouble the SED now face can be traced back to the circumstances surrounding the establishment of the GDR forty years ago when its inhabitants were denied the free choice about their future envisaged in the Potsdam Agreements. The current unravelling, however, began in earnest with the reform movements in the Soviet Union, Poland and in Hungary. Although the SED leadership has desperately maintained that theirs is the only true path to socialism which takes account of the special circumstances of the GDR, growing numbers of East Germans have sought alternative paths either in the reform policies of Gorbachev or in the material success of pluralist democracy in the Federal

[1] Not printed.

Republic. Their convictions have been reinforced by such recent events as the GDR's massive official support for the Chinese authorities' actions in Tiananmen Square and the refusal by the SED to answer an avalanche of letters from ordinary people about reports from eye-witnesses that officials had rigged the local elections in May. Many found the chance to express their view of the SED's policies when Hungary decided to dismantle its defences on its Austrian border thereby creating a gap in the SED's fence around its population.

3. This external crisis was compounded by an internal crisis in the leadership here following Honecker's early return from the Warsaw Pact Summit in Bucharest on 8 July with a gall bladder infection. After allegedly two operations, he did not return to play a full and visible part in running the country until the end of September. The growing exodus in July and August took place therefore in something of a leadership vacuum on the GDR side.

4. The crisis came to a head in the immediate run-up to the 7 October celebrations with the dramatic sit-ins in FRG Embassies in Budapest, Prague and Warsaw. In every case these were resolved by last minute climb-downs by an increasingly humiliated GDR leadership. Their priority was evident—to clear the decks before the arrival of Gorbachev and the world's press in East Berlin.

5. It is difficult to describe the atmosphere of tension, fear, expectation and at times near hysteria which seemed to grip the country in the week before 7 October. A large peaceful demonstration in Leipzig was followed by widespread and bloody confrontations on 3/4 October in Dresden between the police and would-be emigrants trying to board the refugee trains bound for Prague. (Sealed trains have powerful and disturbing echoes in the German consciousness.) There appeared to be only one topic of conversation, whether to go or to stay, or for older people, whether their children would go or stay. Our German maid twice arrived for work in tears because she was terrified her son had 'taken the Prague exit'. The owner of the shop where my wife has her hair done gestured to the empty chairs. His three assistants had gone. And so on in numerous families, shops and factories throughout the country.

6. It was also becoming clear that as in the 1950s it was overwhelmingly the young and qualified who were going. The message they left, as in their thousands they abandoned safe jobs, flats and cars, for which they had waited for up to twelve years, was unmistakable. For all its many good points, the society which had been created in the GDR over the last forty years was deeply unsatisfying for them. Not by bread alone . . . State Secretary Bertele, who travelled on the trains from Warsaw and negotiated with the GDR refugees in the FRG Embassy in Prague, told me that the main reason given by the young was deep frustration at their inability to have any real control over their lives in the GDR and over those who took decisions affecting them.

7. This message will continue to be played back into the GDR. Family ties are very close here. Contacts between those who have left and those who remain will be maintained. In fairly short order a further generation of family reunification problems will confront the GDR authorities. The impact of the exodus was (and will continue to be) far greater than the numbers involved, significant though these have become. Taken together, authorised and unauthorised emigration from the GDR will reach about 130-140,000 by the end of the year. This is nearly the rate of emigration before the wall was built in 1961 and already represents an enormous economic setback. If it continues at this rate economic collapse (implosion) will become a greater worry for the leadership than political explosion.

8. The second conclusion drawn by those remaining in the GDR and observing the exodus on their televisions was that collective action against their authorities can be successful. There is now a much better understanding by the population throughout the country about the real level of discontent. It is this that led to public expressions of protest in so many cities in the GDR on 7 October, and which has been influential in getting between 50 and 70,000 people onto the streets in Leipzig on 9 October. Each time they come onto the streets the young are becoming more experienced and less intimidated by the authorities. And by making it clear that they want to stay rather than obtain a quick ticket to the West, the protesters have considerably increased their appeal to ordinary East Germans.

9. Notwithstanding the exodus and the demonstrations the SED leadership has remained unyieldingly opposed to political reform. Again and again, from Honecker downwards, the Politburo has reaffirmed the basic values of (their version of) socialism and the policies they have hitherto pursued. Those hoping for change in the direction of capitalism were building their hopes on sand, Honecker told Gorbachev.

10. It is this completely wooden response, coupled with deeply unpopular moves such as the 'temporary' suspension of visa-free travel to Czechoslovakia (visa-free travel to Poland has remained 'temporarily' suspended since 1980), which has in large measure precipitated the rash of new reform groups and even open criticism among some normally considered to be part of the establishment, like Hermann Kant, head of the Writers' Union, and others among the usually tame front parties like the liberals and the CDU. Even if the leadership has not grasped the point, those directly concerned with security are almost certainly aware that it is impossible to seal completely not only the border with the FRG and West Berlin, but also the borders with Czechoslovakia and Poland. Even if the Czechoslovaks decide to cooperate with the GDR in turning back 'illegal' emigrants, it is by no means certain that the Poles will. Reform has now reached at least one Eastern frontier of the GDR.

11. I believe the convergence of events and the focussing of emotion at the 7 October commemorations have brought the country to a watershed. The comfortable assumptions (in East and West) about acceptance of this regime, on the basis of a reasonable standard of living and no real prospect of escape, have been stripped away. Given a chance, the young have rejected the SED leadership's claims and policies in the most emphatic way possible. The most disillusioned (and ambitious) have left. Increasing numbers are, however, declaring their intention of staying and of pressing for reform from within. The new reform groups, New Forum, Democratic Awakening, the Social Democratic Party, etc, are embryonic. Their leaders have yet to show whether they are any more than courageous idealists. But the numbers on the streets are growing, united at least in their opposition to the present system and their desire for political reform in a more democratic direction. For the time being the Evangelical church is providing a focus for the opposition groups and has given a lead in calling for a non-violent approach. Unless, however, the first very limited steps towards dialogue in Leipzig and Dresden are built upon there is a likelihood of further violent clashes.

12. It is not possible to make confident predictions about the future course of events. The authorities are by no means powerless and the old men in the Politburo are far from admitting their mistakes or being near to any form of real power sharing. In the short term I believe that direct outside intervention will have relatively little effect. Even if Gorbachev is now convinced that stability in the

GDR may be threatened by Honecker's continuation in power there is little he can do directly to influence his departure which would not be likely to precipitate the crisis he obviously wishes to avoid.[2]

13. The FRG could probably bring the crisis to a head if it chose to exploit to the full its economic leverage on the GDR. But the FRG also has no interest in destabilisation of the GDR. Chancellor Kohl has instead offered a carrot—economic assistance for political reform. I assume his objectives are longer term. It is not likely that Honecker or his contemporaries will rise directly to this. They are, in my view, too ideological, too power-conscious and too old in their memories of Nazi gaols and Stalin to sell what they regard as their birthright for a mess of capitalist pottage. But therein lies the irony. The more they insist on remaining true to their present course, the more inevitably they will ensure its eventual rejection. (I am commenting in a separate letter to Mr Ratford on the line, as seen from the GDR, which the FRG might most usefully take.)[3]

14. Three major questions remain. How rapidly will events develop? Where are they likely to end? What should HMG do about it?

15. As I have indicated above, the first is impossible to answer at this stage. Any one of a number of factors, such as Honecker's physical or Gorbachev's political collapse, could change the picture substantially. So could patent insincerity by the authorities in their discussions with the reformers or official mishandling of a major 'peaceful' demonstration. The only prediction I would make is that the process of demanding political reform now underway cannot be completely suppressed.

16. I addressed the question of where relations with the FRG and GDR might end in my despatch of 20 April.[4] All I would repeat here is that those who automatically assume political reform in the GDR must inevitably end in full political union with the FRG have ignored the lessons of German history and the very strong regional attachments felt by most Germans, whether that be for Prussia, Saxony, the Rhineland or Bavaria. A number of solutions short of simple 'reunification' are possible. Germans have lived for most of their history in political configurations that seem bizarre to us. When, in the 18th century, Britain and France were well-developed nation-states, most Germans lived in the Holy Roman Empire of the German nation—abolished by Napoleon. If the need were to arise, the Germans should be able to devise a constitutional framework, short of reunification, that fulfils their goal of freedom and self-determination.

17. On the twin assumptions that the forces now loose in the GDR will sooner or later prevail, and that our overall national interest lies in trying to avoid serious

---

[2] In fact Herr Honecker was to resign as General Secretary of the SED on 18 October. Herr Egon Krenz, Party Secretary for Security, Youth and Sport, was elected General Secretary of the SED and Chairman of the Council of State of the GDR on 24 October.

[3] In this letter of 12 October Mr Broomfield commented on No. 16 and suggested ways in which the FRG might best respond to developments in the GDR, bearing in mind 'that what might be a counsel of perfection from the point of view of influencing the various players in the GDR may well not be practical politics in Bonn'. 'My first comment is that over-activity by FRG politicians is likely to be counter-productive.' Mr Broomfield went on to say that the FRG Government was right (*a*) not to refer to 'reunification', (*b*) to continue to say that the FRG accepted the existence of the GDR, (*c*) to continue to condemn human rights violations and support reform and (*d*) to stand by its offer of economic assistance in return for reform. He saw no 'advantage in the FRG terminating any of its existing economic arrangements with the GDR' but suggested that the FRG might consider putting on ice projects such as the high-speed rail link to West Berlin, which would deprive the GDR of 'very large sums of hard currency', or terminating the Leipzig air links (WRL 020/4).

[4] No. 2.

instability in this critical area in central Europe, I offer the following recommendations for our policy.

18. Recommendations.

Internal

(*a*) We should try to establish which of the options in any eventual relationship between the FRG and GDR, lying between the present one and reunification, i.e., association, Federation, separate State but with a liberal democratic constitution (the Austrian solution) etc., would suit long-term British security (NATO) and economic (EC) interests best. Our long-term policy should be guided by this assessment.

With the GDR

(*b*) We should thicken up our political dialogue to enable us to put our views on reform directly to the present leaders, as well as to identify and influence the next generation, both in the ruling Party (SED) and outside it.

(*c*) We should increase our programmes for management training, academic exchanges for younger East Germans and English language teaching to help prepare future managers and decision takers for a transition to a pluralist political system and decentralised economy. We should, to the greatest possible extent channel these resources through organisations which enable the British side to decide who is invited.

(*d*) We should maintain the level of our present information effort, including the BBC German Language Service.

(*e*) We should cultivate our contacts with the potential leaders of the new opposition groups and with those in the church and the present Party/Government establishment who show interest in democratic reform, and offer them what assistance we can (visits to the UK, introduction to Western politicians, etc).

(*f*) In our public statements about the future relationship between the FRG and the GDR we should avoid as far as possible references to 'reunification' and speak more about self-determination, reform, openness and human rights, on the basis of the CSCE.

With the FRG

(*g*) The FRG is the only Western country with major influence on the GDR. Whether because they do not know or because they have instructions to be 'economic with their information' FRG representatives in East Berlin are often backward in sharing their information and assessments. This underlines the need for as close as possible an exchange on both *Ost-politik* and *Deutschland-politik* (relations between the FRG and GDR) with the FRG in Bonn and London.

(*h*) We might consider with the FRG (and with the Americans and French) what might be done on a contingency basis in terms of talking to the Russians should the GDR look to be on course for violent internal disorder on a major scale. The aim would be to seek and give assurances that wider strategic destabilisation should not take place and to establish that all were agreed that reforms on the lines of those in the Soviet Union, Hungary and Poland were the only way to restore stability in the GDR.

In the EC

(*i*) The GDR should feature as a normal subject for discussion in the Eastern European Working Group and other fora of EPC. This will help coordinate and compare policies and to ensure that the importance of developments in other Eastern European countries (whether for or against reform) is taken into account in assessing likely future developments in the GDR.

(*j*) We should examine what scope exists for assisting economic and political reform in the GDR through its growing relationship with the Community institutions (mandate for EC/GDR agreement, contacts with the European Parliament, etc).

19. I am sending copies of this despatch to Her Majesty's Representatives at Bonn, Paris, Washington, Warsaw Pact posts, Belgrade, to the UK Representatives NATO and UKRep Brussels, the Commandant of the British Sector in Berlin, and the Commanders in Chief BAOR and RAF Germany.[5]

> I am, Sir,
> Yours faithfully,
> N.H.R.A. BROOMFIELD

---

[5] Mr Synnott wrote on 3 November to thank Mr Broomfield for this despatch, noting that it had 'served as indispensable background to some brainstorming here'. He also thanked Mr Broomfield for his reports on recent events in the GDR, 'most of which we have copied to No. 10'. Mr Synnott concluded: 'Your comments on reunification, and planning for the contingency of a crisis, are well taken . . . There is full agreement here that our line on the German Question should be to stress the importance of self-determination and go no further. This is evidently very welcome to the Federal German government. The FRG will obviously be the main mover on the German Question and we have in mind to develop our contacts on it with the West Germans. The Embassy in Bonn are monitoring statements closely. But we shall not neglect the East German angle' (WRE 227/1).

No. 20

Minute from Mr J.N. Powell (Policy Planning Staff) to Mr Ramsden

[*WRL 020/4*]

Confidential   FCO, *16 October 1989*

German Reunification

1. Thank you for copying your papers on German reunification to us.[1] The main gap we see is the absence of any analysis of the different ways in which reunification could take place. This seems the key to us. The Stalin offer of a reunited neutral Germany no longer seems a runner. At the other extreme is a solution along the lines of the West German Government's 'European Peace Order', whereby as a result of EC integration and expansion Eastwards, the border between Saxony and Prussia and the other *Lände*[*r*] becomes less important. Between the two are a wide variety of possibilities to which the paper ought at least to allude, in the section beginning with paragraph 18.

2. We also have the following specific comments:

Para 4/5: The first sentence of para 5 might better come at the end of para 4. We think it is wrong to put the FRG's commitment to the EC and NATO purely in the context of reunification. Para 5 therefore begins better with its current second sentence.

Para 9: Omit the second last sentence. First we are not sure if it is true that

---

[1] No. 18.

'direct' talk would endanger the process of reform in Eastern Europe. Secondly it does not seem to stop the Germans or others talking about it.

Para 10: You might perhaps mention Stalin's offer and say why it is unlikely to be repeated. We are not sure whether you are right about the reasons for the Soviet Union's probable welcome for reform in the GDR. It is notable that until recently the Soviet Union has done very little to urge reform in the GDR. We suspect that reform would lead to more rather than less instability, at least in the short run (which is all that politicians usually care about). If the Soviet Union does welcome reform in the GDR it may be:

(*a*) because of the benefits in broad East-West relations;

(*b*) because it reinforces the legitimacy of Gorbachev's reform programme if others are doing the same in the Socialist Bloc (and correspondingly undermines it if they are not).

Shevardnadze's reference to German revanchism was surely about reunification generally and not just a reference to the Oder/Neisse line.

Para 12: We think you are right not to try and tackle this subject at length in this paper, and this sort of brief mention is probably the right approach. But what is meant by 'the development of *Mitteleuropa*'? Is this meant to be an organisation like the EC or what? If it is just a geographical name then we have it already.

Para 15 made us wonder exactly who was going to compel the GDR authorities to do anything. One can imagine the Soviet Union exercising some pressure but if change comes from within it would be as a result of a loss of self-confidence by the regime rather than compulsion from public disorder.

Para 16: There are of course all sorts of possibilities. It might therefore be better to introduce your four sub-paragraphs by saying something like 'one version of reform might be'.

Para 17: We were interested to see that you thought a reforming GDR would lose their best qualified people. This seems to be true of an unreforming GDR as well. Surely the main problem for a reforming GDR would be a crisis of legitimacy. What justification would there be for a separate German state without Communism? (as you observe in the following paragraph).

Para 19: We think that German reunification is still one issue that would put the Russian tanks on the streets and perhaps even bring down Gorbachev. In the light of that your third sentence seems rather mild. With respect to your last sentence we can (with a little effort) imagine a confederation which did not involve either the dissolution of two military blocs or neutralisation of Germany—one country two foreign policies: although this is not the most likely possibility.

Para 20: We would expect an uprising to be put down; and that the Soviets would help (that is why the FRG is concerned about the possibility of an explosion—they are not worried about reunification they are worried about detente). The scenario you describe in para 20 seems to suggest that the Russians have opted out altogether. If this was the case then perhaps the FRG government might indeed react regardless of Soviet views. But on the whole we found this paragraph rather difficult to believe.

Para 21: Omit first sentence.

Para 23: You might wish to flag up the need for a proper look at Allied powers and responsibilities, not least because of SPD pressure.

Para 24:
(i) A larger and more prosperous Germany would not necessarily imply a reduction in the UK's prosperity.
(ii) Replace end of last sentence by '. . . try to turn this economic strength into political power'.
(iii) I think the only thing you can say on this is that reunification would take place in the context of a Europe, and a Soviet Union, very different from today's. Personally I am not sure that a big Germany in the middle of Europe (i.e. between us and the Russians) is necessarily to our disadvantage in security terms.
Para 25: I did not understand how 'good management' was going to have any impact on the disadvantages you mentioned. I also found the advantages you listed rather unconvincing. Will there be such a thing as 'western security'? It seems funny that security should be both an advantage and disadvantage. And I would rate it a disadvantage if reunification led to the FRG investing in the GDR rather than in the UK.
Para 26: This seemed rather weak, and did not seem to follow from what came before. Surely you should say rather that we have a moral, political and legal commitment to reunification in the terms explained earlier, that this is an important element in our relations with the FRG which are important to us and to NATO, that what the UK government says is unlikely to make much difference any way, that this is a sensitive issue for others as well as the Germans and that it would hardly improve stability in Europe for us either to make vigorous calls for reunification or change our line and start saying that it was a thoroughly bad thing, that it remains important to us that reunification should be reunification westwards and our policies should be directed to ensuring a high degree of integration in the Community and NATO (not just binding the Germans in but binding ourselves in too) .
Para 27: Omit.

J.N. POWELL

No. 21

Letter from Mr Dinwiddy (Bonn) to Mr Ramsden

[*WRL 020/4*]

Confidential   BONN, *19 October 1989*

'*German Reunification' and 'Explosion in the GDR'*

1. Thank you for your letter of 11 October[1] to Colin Budd, in whose absence I am replying. We were glad of the opportunity to comment on these two papers, which stimulated some useful discussion here. I set out below some general comments. Attached in two annexes are some more detailed suggested amendments.

---

[1] No. 18.

'German Reunification'

2. We suggest that this paper would benefit from some significant restructuring (and a more general title!). Our main criticism of the paper as it stands is that it tends to examine only one line of development: reunification. While change in Central Europe leading to reunification cannot be ruled out, the paper should present a more thorough analysis of the various options for an eventual close relationship between the two German states and, above all, of their implications (political, economic and defence) for the UK and what policy we should adopt towards them. Most FRG politicians discussing developments in the GDR now consciously avoid the term 'reunification', preferring instead 'unity' or 'overcoming of division'. The reasons are two fold: presentational and, more important, substantive. First, talk of 'reunification' upsets Germany's eastern neighbours, with its implications of an overturning of the post-War order and of a possible revived claim to the former German territories east of the Oder-Neisse line (i.e. reunification of Germany to its 1937 borders). The Federal Government is aware that such talk can strengthen the position of the Communist regimes in Eastern Europe which can present themselves as guarantors of stability and the territorial status quo. It sees the FRG's first interest as lying in promoting reform and the forces of gradual change in these countries. Secondly, while reunification is a goal which cannot and should not be renounced, the Federal Government, and indeed the opposition, recognises that it may never happen and that it would be unwise to hitch everything to it. Moreover, if it does come about the process will be a long one.

3. We further suggest that there should be more analysis of the position and role of the USSR. While Gorbachev now appears to believe that some reform in the GDR is necessary to maintain stability, the evidence equally suggests that the Soviet Union remains firmly opposed to German reunification, at any rate on terms acceptable to the West (and almost certainly to the West Germans themselves). FRG politicians have recently stressed the old formulae: 'freedom before unity' and 'no going it alone'. Nowadays Soviet officials are permitted to talk more freely about the subject but the motive for this is to play on the well-known sensitivities in the FRG and NATO as a whole, rather than any serious intention to permit a move towards German unity. The strategic and economic importance of the GDR to the USSR should not be underestimated.

4. We need to distinguish private thoughts and public presentation. As you suggest, we would probably be against a modality of self-determination which appeared to predestine the outcome, and the West Germans might disagree with us. But that issue is a long way down the road and should not affect our firm public commitment to self-determination expressed in general language.

5. There are two notions that we would, in passing, like to dispel from future analysis. First, that Germany's short experience of unity diminishes its importance as a goal. This is wrong: the will for and commitment to unity, expressed not least in the preamble to the Basic Law, continues, generational change notwithstanding. No German politician can ignore this. Secondly, that the FRG would react to an explosion in the GDR by trying somehow to go it alone towards reunification. We think this most unlikely. Such action would be contrary to the interests of the FRG and to the policy of successive Federal Governments. It is, moreover, not clear

how they would go about it. We consider it far more likely that they would look to their Western Allies and partners for support . . . [2]

Yours ever,
B.H. DINWIDDY

ANNEX

'German Reunification'

Title: change to 'The German Question'.

Paras 1-8. We agree that some introduction and background is needed. But as it stands this is a cursory account of a complicated subject. There is too much black and white and not enough of the shades of grey that exist in current West German thinking. Paras 3-4 (particularly the legal background) could usefully be expanded, and moved to an Annex.

Para 8 might better begin 'The West Germans remain somewhat differing . . .' It would be worth adding at the end that it is the view of many in the SPD and others that a great burgeoning of inner-German contacts could make reunification superfluous.

Paras 13-15 need more analysis. The last sentence of para 14 is too compressed, and needs to be explained.

Paras 16-17 are mainly for East Berlin, but at present the paper postulates just one possibility. The last sentence of para 17 should spell out in whose eyes a reformed GDR could ever become eligible for EC membership, and the reference to the CDU Secretary General, while topical, might be omitted.

Paras 18-20. Under our suggested title these paras would not remain in their present form or position. At this point the paper should set out the various forms that German unity might take and analyse the advantages and disadvantages for the UK:

(*a*) Association: the burgeoning of links between the two States, the development of common institutions and infrastructures, free movement of labour, massive FRG investment in the GDR. This would be a gradual evolution, and could take place within the present system of Alliances.

(*b*) Federation: the two German states, while retaining separate governments in Bonn and Berlin, share common political structures and consult closely on issues to develop a common German policy. This is a considerable step beyond Association, and would be scarcely conceivable without fundamental reform in the GDR and withdrawal of Soviet influence.

(*c*) The Austrian solution: real reforms in the GDR lead to a democratically elected government which continues to exist as a separate state, perhaps neutral, but enjoying the same close relationship with the FRG as Austria does.

Para 30, last sentence. In order properly to define the UK's long-term aims and short-term policies fundamental questions about NATO, the EC and enlargement need to be thought through now.

---

[2] Paras 6-7 and Annex on 'Explosion in the GDR' not printed.

No. 22

Minute from Mr Dixon (Research Department) to Mr Ramsden

[*WRL 020/4*]

Confidential   FCO, *19 October 1989*

1. I found your paper[1] an excellent review of the present position and developments and extremely level-headed in its conclusions. My main general observation would probably be that whilst you set the scene well, emphasising the uncertainties attending the present pace of developments, you concentrate on a 'gradual reform scenario' in which (as I understand it) the European political landscape remains essentially intact. The result seems to me somewhat unfocussed. There is no objection to the gradualist approach. This is the way forward we should all prefer. But in your version, German reunification would seem to be confined to an isolated pocket of change. It is more realistic, indeed, in my view, essential, to take account of the changing nature of the European political environment as a whole. You speak of a certain vagueness in the FRG vision of the future. This is in fair measure because Federal Germans prefer a contextual approach. Change in Germany cannot and should not occur outside the wider framework of antecedent European change: a 'Federal [reunified][2] Germany within a Federal Europe' as Genscher recently expressed it. He has the weight of German orthodox opinion since Adenauer on behind him. It may sound vague. But it is their version of practical politics, and I think it makes good sense. However that may be, German opinion is important; and partly for that reason and partly to give the paper a sharper focus, I would recommend extending this exercise to take a hard look at current German thinking on the German question, official and unofficial, and within the different parties, using that as a starting point for listing all the different sets of circumstances, likely and less so, that might lead to German reunification and considering our policy options on each permutation in turn.

2. My more detailed comments are as follows:

Para 5: Sentence 1: I would prefer 'active policy issue' to 'immediate policy goal'. The Berlin Wall brought the East-West traffic in reunification plans to an effective end. Kohl put the German Question back on the international agenda in 1982/3.

Final sentence: The FRG traditionally distinguishes between '*Deutschland-politik*' and the '*deutsche Frage*'. The latter is the issue of reunification, the former relates to GDR matters, including inner German relations. But I am inclined to agree that in current FRG (and foreign) usage the distinction has become rather blurred.

Para 8: why 'But' in sentence 3? To West Germans (and formerly to the Western Allies) German self-determination and German unity have always seemed to mean one and the same thing. I am not entirely sure whether this is so today. But it is language sanctioned by long usage and has its basis in the preamble to the Basic Law which calls upon 'the entire German people . . . to achieve in free self-determination the unity and freedom of Germany'; and I

---

[1] No. 18.
[2] Parentheses in original.

would reckon that Genscher's reference was quite probably to this source.

Final sentence: see my prefatory remarks. There are essentially two standard Federal German views on reunification. The one sets the solution within the post-war and present European political order (i.e. a reunified Germany within Nato); the other envisages reunification within the framework of a transformed Europe (i.e. a united Germany within a united Europe encompassing East and West). They are complementary strands of thought. But confusion arises when they are intertwined and the Federal Germans are not infrequently capable of this. The latter, incidentally, has of recent years been the preferred FRG model, although with the present speed of developments and everyone having to think on their feet, things may well have moved on. However, it is as well to remember (*pace* sentence 3) that the FRG believes in the concept of one German nation whether or not it is split into two states.

Para 12: The French view may be changing or more flexible than we have long believed. Ex-French ambassador to the FRG, Froment Meurice, was given a big spread in the *F[rankfurter]A[llgemeine]Z[eitung]* last week for saying that German reunification was inevitable and that France should do nothing to stop it.

Para 13ff: Some revision necessary here of course! But most of what you say still holds good in my view. Greater flexibility from the GDR authorities must, however, be expected under the new leadership, despite the hard-line tone of its initial statements.

Para 18: Which 'scenario' exactly? I think there is a lot of sense in what you say in this paragraph. I only wish I could agree with it. My own view, however, is that the GDR's sole rationale is ideological, and that in the longer term, the two Germanies are bound to come together as a federation once that rationale is removed. Confederation could well intervene. But it is difficult to see it being more than a step along the way. The economic pull of West Germany is likely to prove irresistible, for one thing. But everything else seems to me against it as well, and that means geography, history, culture and family ties. The GDR is a purely artificial creation of the post-war political circumstances. The GDR has developed no individual national identity in that time (or at none that has visibly emerged) and East and West remain a cultural unity. None of this applies to Austria, and your analogy therefore seems to me misplaced. It is of course correct to say that Germany has only a relatively short history as a unified state. But this is somewhat misleading: German aspirations to unity have a much longer history; and as I noted above West Germany insists that Germany remains one nation.

Para 19: See my introductory paragraph.

Par. 20: The FRG will be doing its utmost to put the brakes on and keep them on. Its hand might be forced but the idea of going it alone without the consent and approval of its Western Allies is, I judge, unthinkable to the Federal authorities. We have more reason to fear our collective hand being forced (i.e. could we really say no to reunification if it came to the point?).

Para 21ff: I agree subject to the strictures in my first paragraph, and I particularly agree with paras. 25-26. I am not at all sure however about your reading of the likely German response to a disappointment over reunification prospects. West Germans at least have been conditioned to regard it as a distant goal; and the issue is nothing like as emotive amongst the younger generation as the older, and even there it is a right wing issue rather than evenly spread throughout the population. It was after all no coincidence that it was a CDU-led government in 1982/3 which put the subject back on the international agenda after years of SPD benevolent neglect, and at a time when the international community had given it no serious thought for years and so [there was] no reason to start doing so.

Par. 31: I agree we should be clear about this. It is an important distinction. But it is a new one and it is prudent to tread carefully here. All Western reunification proposals (as far as I recall) foresaw self-determination as a single act and the FRG might feel we were not honouring our commitments if we changed our ground now. I think there is an overriding case for not being bound by earlier policy and I also think the FRG is likely to accept this as wise, even necessary perhaps, in today's changed circumstances. But I am not sure that official West German thinking has yet reached that stage.

R. Dixon

No. 23

Minute from Sir J. Fretwell to Mr Synnott

[WRL 020/4]

Confidential   FCO, *20 October 1989*

The German Question

1. I have not yet seen the paper you are preparing on the German Question, referred to in your minute of 17 October, which is to respond in part to the concern expressed by the Secretary of State.[1] Having therefore a mind uncluttered by too much contact with the details of the subject, I would like to offer some general reflections which might find a place in further work.

2. The German Question will be, from now on, the dominant issue in Europe. It is clear that the post-war order, which seemed immutable, is now cracking up. The future relationship between the FRG and the GDR is at the heart of the problem. This change has come about in the short-term because the Gorbachev reform process has permitted and stimulated political evolution in Eastern Europe of a type until very recently quite unthinkable. But these changes take place against a background of events of much greater sweep:

(*a*) the crumbling of Marxism as a theory and of Soviet communism as a system of government. In my view the Soviet Union is now in irremediable decline. Gorbachev probably understands the nature of the problems; and his attempts to recreate a political process are courageous and far-sighted; but sixty years of totalitarian dictatorship, falsehood and brutality make it impossible to regenerate the country in a matter of years or even decades. Whether Gorbachev

---

[1] Mr Synnott's minute of 17 October to Mr Ratford and Mr Wall, responding to Mr Gozney's minute of 16 October (No. 17, note 9), outlined the work on the German question currently being undertaken by WED, including the circulation of a draft paper on the subject (No. 18) and the submission of Mr Broomfield's despatch of 12 October (No. 19). Mr Synnott noted that there was to be 'a teach-in for the Secretary of State on 27 October on East/West affairs generally', including the German question, and that the subject was also to be considered at a meeting of DUSs on 31 October (No. 30) (WRL 020/4).

stays in office or not will be important politically (e.g. in providing an alternative to Tiananmen Square) but will not radically affect the economic prospects, which are grim;

(*b*) the economic strength of the FRG becomes ever more formidable. It provides a model which the East Germans must now regard as the one to which they should ultimately aspire. (Japanese experience would be too remote for them.) We talk rightly of the European Community as a model and a magnet for Eastern Europe, but for most of them that really means the FRG, not Portugal, the Netherlands or even France or the UK. Moreover the FRG has the resources and the political will to play a role in Eastern Europe above and beyond that exercised by its Community partners;

(*c*) these factors are bringing about a new shift in the age-old cycle of competition and conflict between Russians and Germans for predominance in Eastern Europe. (The older generation will recall the filmed epic of Alexander Nevsky crushing the Teutonic Knights; it is a saga without beginning or end.) 1945 appeared to have resolved the issue decisively in Russian favour. But if events continue on their present course, that era will soon come to a close.

3. The German Question seems likely to arise in three main forms, closely related but which may need to be looked at separately:

(*a*) the direct FRG/GDR relationship. I see little prospect of a reversion to the old idea attributed to Stalin and later to Khrushchev that the GDR would be handed over to the FRG in exchange for German neutralisation. The prospect is rather that of a jerky political evolution in the GDR, influenced by the Soviet example as well as by that of Poland and Hungary, leading to the gradual abandonment of the Marxist doctrines and practices which have been held so far to justify the existence of a separate East German state This may well be accompanied by the relaxation of travel rules as a new balance is found between the (declining) repulsiveness of the State and the (growing) porousness of the borders. At some point the barbed wire and the Wall could come down. The economy, media and ideology of the GDR would become subject to ever greater FRG influence, even if the appearance of a separate state was maintained for a long time. In the end it would not matter all that much if one had formal reunification, confederation, or separate membership of the European Community for the two German states. Nor would it matter if the GDR followed the Austrian example by being formally committed to neutrality. I think this is how the FRG is beginning to envisage the future.

(*b*) this has to be fitted into a wider vision of the future of Eastern Europe. Barring catastrophes, we can look for the growth of genuine independence on the model of Hungary and Poland. The Warsaw Pact will remain in existence for the foreseeable future and would be invoked if Gorbachev or an alternative Soviet regime attempted a renewed crackdown. But barring that eventuality, the Pact will gradually be deprived of substance as independent governments assume greater authority over their armed forces and determine their size, shape, role and command structure. It could finish as no more than a convenient fig-leaf for those in the Soviet Union who need to maintain that nothing has changed. At the same time the influence of the FRG will grow as the East European economies become more closely tied to that of the FRG in trade and investment, and the economic role of the Soviet Union declines. The remnants of the old German communities in these countries will assume greater significance as the FRG assumes the role of protecting power for their interests. (This has long created difficulty in FRG relations with Poland but the question seems now to have been resolved to FRG satisfaction.)

(*c*) this new role in the East will exercise growing influence on FRG policy on a whole range of other subjects, including the European Community and the Alliance. It is a vast field which will merit much thought but we already have certain pointers:

(i) in the Community the Germans are already giving much weight to the requirements of their East European policy. They have abandoned the idea that the Twelve should assume ultimately a role in matters of defence. This clears the way for the admission of Austria, which will certainly be an objective of the FRG and thereby opens the door for closer association and ultimate membership for Hungary, Poland and—I believe—the GDR. The Germans will continue to mouth support for European Union, but will accept whatever price has to be paid in terms of reduced cohesion on foreign policy if that is necessary for further enlargement. I would expect their views of the desirable institutional structure of 'European Union' to follow suit. I am not sure whether they have yet begun to think through the relationship between EMU and the expansion of the Community's interests Eastwards. If at some stage a conflict *appears* between the two objectives, I have little doubt in present circumstances that EMU would be slowed down or possibly even abandoned. In general the FRG's objective will be to discourage any steps in the Community which would tend to rule out eventual closer association with Eastern Europe.

(ii) within the Alliance we have already seen German resistance to certain forms of SNF. We must now expect them to give growing priority to getting all ground-based nuclear arms out of Central Europe; and to the extent that the CFE talks succeed and the sense of military confrontation in Europe recedes, I think the FRG will move in favour of complete denuclearisation of Europe. In the 'New Peace Order' of which they speak, confrontation along the old dividing line will be replaced by cooperative relationships between East and West. They will want this reflected in facts on the ground, starting with nuclear weapons.

4. This all raises many complex policy problems for the UK. The prospects in Eastern Europe are uncertain and possibly dangerous. One regime or another may take the route of Tiananmen Square. Gorbachev could be replaced by a hardline militarist regime which would try to turn the clock back, or he might eventually see no alternative to going that way himself. For many in the UK it would be more reassuring to try to keep things as they are, than move into uncharted waters. Memories of the Second World War are still fresh; and the prospect of changing the 1945 dividing lines and accepting some form of unity for the 80 million Germans is for many people a very alarming one. But whether we like it or not, events are on the move and I do not think it is in our power to stop them, even if we could bring ourselves to oppose greater freedom and democracy for the countries of Eastern Europe. If we tried to stand against this tide, we should enter into fundamental political conflict with the FRG and with many of our allies, including the United States. Mr Baker's formula in his speech of 17 October was carefully chosen: he foresaw the reconciliation of the German people through self-determination 'with the end result being a people integrated into the Community of democratic European nations'. We cannot oppose to that vision a policy of maintaining the status quo in Central Europe.

5. We can however influence the process. We can attempt to foresee and to avert actions by the East Europeans which could lead to early catastrophe. We can seek to steer Soviet thinking in sensible directions. We can encourage political and economic change in selected countries such as Poland and Hungary. We can ensure that the Alliance safeguards its essential interests throughout the negotiations on arms control. We can influence Community thinking about the acceptance or rejection of the neutrals. We can work closely with other governments, particularly with France, in moderating and channelling German ambitions. We therefore have a very full policy agenda. The one point I would like to stress, arising from these reflections, is that we have to start putting the German Question at the centre of it.

J. FRETWELL

No. 24

Letter from Sir C. Mallaby (Bonn) to Mr Ratford

[*WRL 020/4C*]

Restricted   BONN, *23 October 1989*

Dear David,

The UK and the German Question

1. I called on Ackermann, a senior political adviser in the Federal Chancellery and longstanding confidant of Kohl, on 19 October. Ackermann began by conveying to me formally, on Kohl's instructions, the Federal Government's thanks for the public position taken recently by HMG on developments in Eastern Europe and on the German Question. Ackermann particularly mentioned the Prime Minister's speech at the Conservative Party Conference, where she had demonstrated 'in exemplary fashion' the importance of the movement towards freedom in parts of Eastern Europe and had pressed for change in East Germany. Ackermann said that we were right to stress self-determination, more than reunification as such, in our comments on the German Question, as the Secretary of State had done here on 20 September.[1] The British media had also taken, in general, a responsible attitude towards recent developments involving Germany.

2. Ackermann contrasted the British position with that of Andreotti who, when asked about reunification at his joint press conference with Kohl on 18 October, had avoided giving any answer.

3. Ackermann said that the main operational message to get across in commenting publicly on the GDR was the need for reform and for full observance of human rights and the freedoms set out in CSCE documents.

4. Ackermann's compliments stem, I think, from two considerations. First, satisfaction at the line we have taken. The French line, as well as the Italian, is considered less helpful, while American statements are in general considered helpful. The Germans are always grateful for supportive statements and political solidarity when they face a difficult problem having associations with Nazism and the War. The second reason for Ackermann's bouquet, I believe, is that Kohl

[1] No. 13.

intends to emphasise the theme of freedom in the Federal election campaign in 1990, much in the way the Prime Minister presented it at Blackpool. [2]

Yours ever,
C.L.G. MALLABY

[2] Mr Ratford minuted to Mr Synnott on 25 October: 'This is very important. It should be conveyed to No. 10—p[lea]se consult the Private Office over mechanics.' A copy was sent to No. 10 on 26 October with a covering letter from Mr Gozney to Mr Powell: 'Ackermann's congratulations about HMG's public position on the German Question chime in well with other West German reactions. The leadership are sensitive to the fact that the prospect of reunification can cause alarm both in Eastern Europe and among the FRG's friends and allies.'

No. 25

Submission from Mr Synnott to Mr Ratford

[*WRL O20/4*]

Confidential   FCO, *25 October 1989*

The German Question

1. I *submit* a paper on the German Question for consideration before the DUSS's meeting on 31 October. It takes account of comments from Bonn, BMG Berlin, East Berlin and some Departments, although it may not reflect them entirely. It also draws on Sir J Fretwell's minute of 20 October.[1] Depending upon the conclusions of the DUSS's meeting and the Secretary of State's meeting on 27 October,[2] it might form the basis of a submission to Ministers.

2. The German Question remains, as the PUS minuted last year, a sensitive, complex and fascinating subject on which it is difficult to reach clear conclusions. The paper is necessarily tentative in places. Its message is that the German Question, in its wider sense, is indeed firmly back on the international agenda. The paper explores various attitudes towards the question; the situation in the GDR; possible 'answers'; and policy implications.

3. A *public line* ('self-determination is the key') is attached as an annex. This has already been considered by Ministers and the thrust of it has been used with apparent success. The paper seeks to set out the rationale behind this line, and recommends no change.

4. The possible ramifications of the German Question are vast. As Genscher has been saying recently, it has implications both for EC integration and EC enlargement. It is relevant also to security arrangements in Europe. The paper does not attempt to do more than flag up these issues. But we should recognise, as do many of our partners, the interrelationship between them. I entirely agree with Sir J. Fretwell that the German Question should be at the centre of a policy agenda.

5. Another more general conclusion drawn in the paper is that our influence on the German Question will depend critically on our influence in Bonn. Dialogue

[1] No. 23.
[2] See No. 23, note 1.

and mutual confidence between London and Bonn will be essential. We need to maintain this as a highest priority.

H.N.H. SYNNOTT

ENCLOSURE IN NO. 25

Confidential   FCO, *25 October 1989*

GERMAN REUNIFICATION

I INTRODUCTION

1. As Chancellor Kohl has put it, the German Question is now back on the international agenda, although he has been careful to stress that the phrase covers a much broader range of ideas than reunification alone. This Paper examines the causes of, and prospects for, change in the relationship between the two Germanies; what options exist in addition to 'full' reunification; and the implications for British policy. In doing so it largely assumes that current positive trends in Eastern Europe will continue.

2. Much of the existing literature remains relevant, including despatches by successive Ambassadors in Bonn and East Berlin, replies to these, Planning Staff Papers in 1987 and 1988, and subsequent minuting.[3] But much has changed since the last FCO paper a year ago. Poland and Hungary have undergone radical reform in the direction of democracy. The challenges facing the Soviet Union seem ever more intractable. There is much less fear of the politico-military threat from the East. The FRG's prosperity, its influence in both East and West Europe, and its assertiveness, continue to grow. Partly in consequence of the changing scene around the GDR, the leadership in the GDR has changed, and the GDR itself is at a watershed. Many in Germany, and elsewhere, feel that the post-war framework is no longer immutable. We are no longer certain about the extent to which the Russians still have the will or the means to prevent developments in the GDR which might be unwelcome to them.

3. Meanwhile, traditional fears about the darker aide of the German character retain a powerful political force. In the minds of many, especially in Europe, memories of the Nazi period, the Franco-German wars, and of Rapallo, are still very much alive.[4] Although changed immeasurably since the War, and patently cured of militaristic ambitions, Germany arouses mixed feelings in most of her neighbours.

II THE HISTORY (SEE ALSO ANNEX A)

4. It was never the intention to divide Germany into two separate states after the War. The Potsdam Agreements of 1945 envisaged a peace treaty with a unified Germany after a period of occupation. Pending this, the Germany of 1937 (see map in Annex)[5] was divided into six: East Prussia was shared between the Soviet Union

---

[3] For the Planning Staff papers see Preface, pp. xi-xii.

[4] The Treaty of Rapallo, concluded between Germany and the Soviet Union on 16 April 1922, ended the diplomatic isolation of both countries following the First World War and the Bolshevik Revolution, and laid the foundation for secret military and economic cooperation between the two countries during the Weimar era.

[5] Not printed.

and Poland, Silesia and Pomerania went to Poland, and the remaining territory west of the Oder-Neisse line was divided into the US, UK, French and Soviet zones of occupation. In practice, the areas ceded to Poland and the USSR can be considered as lost for good. But their fate remains an emotional subject for some older West Germans and legally, so far as the West is concerned, they remain part of Germany until a peace treaty is signed.

5. The current division of Germany gradually crystallised over a period of four years, until the founding of the FRG and GDR in 1949. To begin with, both states saw themselves as the true stem onto which the other would sooner or later be grafted (the GDR subsequently reversed its position as it became clear that reunification would actually mean the end of the Communist experiment). The Federal German Basic Law, drawn up with the full agreement of the Allies, envisages the FRG as a temporary state with Bonn as its temporary capital. The Basic Law is not a constitution, and provides that it shall cease to be in force 'on the day on which a Constitution adopted by a free decision of the German people comes into force'.

6. In the early years of the FRG reunification remained a burning political topic. For instance the SPD opposed the FRG's rearmament and entry into NATO on the grounds that it would put an end to hopes of reunification. Bonn was faced with a stark choice: either to seek reunification as a neutral country outside either military bloc; or to join NATO, the EC and the West at the price of the continued division of Germany. For Adenauer, the decision was clear. Offers of reunification in exchange for neutrality made by Stalin in 1952 and Khrushchev in 1955 were ignored.

7. By joining NATO and the EC, the FRG committed itself wholeheartedly to a Western anchorage. But reunification remained a goal: the FRG and the three Western Allies were committed, in the Bonn/Paris Conventions of 1955, to achieve the 'aim of a reunified Germany enjoying a liberal democratic constitution, like that of the Federal Republic, and integrated within the European community' (NATO endorsed this line in 1972). The question gradually sank from the forefront of the political agenda. In the Eastern Treaties of 1970 the FRG renounced its claims to the areas ceded to Poland and the Soviet Union, without prejudice to an eventual settlement in a Peace Treaty. The Helsinki Final Act of 1975 carefully allows for changes of frontiers by peaceful means and thus maintains the prospect of an eventual answer to the German Question.

8. Thereafter, a number of broad trends have continued to operate more or less continuously:

—the FRG has grown stronger, both economically and in political appeal, relative to the GDR;

—the FRG's influence elsewhere in East Europe has increased;

—the FRG's integration into the EC and the West has deepened, as the War years receded; and

—attitudes to reunification within the FRG have evolved over the years, as acceptance of Germany's wider Western ties became common across the political spectrum. The German Question has come to be thought of less as a 'go it alone' option between the two German states, and more as part of a wider process of healing the divisions of Europe as a whole (in Genscher's phrase, the 'Europeanisation of *Deutschlandpolitik*').

III ATTITUDES

(i) *British*

9. The UK has stuck closely to the formal position set out in the 1955 Bonn-Paris Conventions. In practice, we have come to put less emphasis on reunification and more on self-determination. Democracy, a free choice and, a prerequisite, change in the GDR must clearly come first.

10. In 1980, Lord Carrington, the Foreign Secretary, wrote to Genscher:

'It will remain the policy of my Government to support the efforts of the Federal Republic of Germany to work for a state of peace in Europe in which the German people can recover their unity in free self-determination.'

In May 1984, the Prime Minister and Chancellor Kohl issued a joint statement which included the words:

'It is the belief of successive British Governments that real and permanent stability in Europe will be difficult to achieve so long as the German nation is divided against its will.'

In February 1989 Sir Geoffrey Howe used a similar phrase in the House of Commons.[6]

11. These statements are entirely consistent with our 1955 commitments. But, by their references to self-determination, they leave open the possibility that the final result of a settlement of the German Question might be something other than full reunification.

(ii) *West German*

12. The West Germans remain somewhat indistinct about their long-term vision. They are firm in rejecting fears that they might ever be tempted to trade reunification for neutrality. Speaking on 14 September, Genscher affirmed that the aim of the Federal Government too was 'to strive for the right of self-determination of the German people'. The FRG should not 'de-Europeanise' its foreign policy and inner-German policy. Steering a neutralist course single-handed would be 'a retrograde step', creating new instabilities and damaging the national interests of the Germans. Elsewhere, the Germans speak deliberately vaguely of the importance of nation states declining as European cooperation increases, and the issue of reunification finally being resolved in the context of a new 'European Peace Order'.

13. Most FRG politicians now consciously avoid the term 'reunification', preferring instead 'unity' or 'overcoming of division'. In recent months they have shown greater consciousness of sensitivities both among the FRG's other EC partners and in Eastern Europe (although this does not always prevent jarred nerves). The FRG has an obvious interest in playing reunification long: premature talk of it could hinder the very reforms the FRG is trying to promote.

14. The FRG's policy towards the GDR may well, paradoxically, have helped sustain the old regime by reinforcing the economy and allowing the departure of potential new leaders. West German thinking is now having to evolve quite rapidly. Both major political parties recognise that their previous inner-German policies must be modified to take account of the changes in the GDR. 'Buying out' political prisoners, for example, could become more politically controversial. So far there are few, if any, fundamental differences between the major parties, although the prospect of Federal elections and four *Land* elections next year may lead to some mud-slinging. In the short term, all parties advocate real reform in the

[6] See No. 2, note 3.

GDR. As for the longer term, Kohl and Genscher seem determined to put the further strengthening of the EC at the centre of their foreign policy, but in such a way as to allow, ultimately, the objective of a closer association between the EC and the GDR and other reformers in Eastern Europe. Kohl said on 16 October that the EC must remain open to all free peoples. Various kites have been flown: e.g. the 'concentric circles' model of Europe with EC integration in the inner ring and outer rings for EFTA, the East Europeans etc. There is a debate as to whether EC integration should now be slowed down in the interests of *Ostpolitik*.

(iii) *Soviet and East European Views*

15. German reunification is a neuralgic issue for many of the East Europeans. The Poles are particularly wary, and can be alarmed by right-wing German questioning of the Oder-Neisse line as the final border between Germany and Poland. References by Federal Government Ministers to the German Question being resolved within the framework of a new 'European Peace Order' are intended to calm some of these fears. Genscher publicly reaffirmed at the UN on 27 September that the FRG had no territorial claims on Poland (as indeed it should not, given the 1970 treaty between the FRG and Poland).

16. The Soviet bottom line appears to be the continued existence of the GDR as a separate state and its membership of the Warsaw Pact. Subject to that, the Russians have been maintaining that relations between the two Germanies are a matter for them. They seem to have no problem with improved FRG/GDR ties as such. Gorbachev has clearly indicated that he would welcome reform in the GDR, and appears to consider reform less risky in the longer term than maintaining Honecker's form of Stalinism. GDR membership of the Warsaw Pact is of great importance for Russian security. They currently have nearly 400,000 troops in the GDR (some have been withdrawn unilaterally and more would go as part of a CFE agreement). Soviet memories of the War are of course still vivid. In an apparent reference to the Oder-Neisse line question and to reunification generally, Shevardnadze expressed concern in his speech to the UN in September about 'German revanchism'.

(iv) *Other Views*

17. The concern of several of the FRG's allies about the prospect of reunification has led them to focus particularly on this rather than on any more short-term, and perhaps more probable, development. French views have been expressed trenchantly, recently by the French Defence Minister, by the Secretary General of the *Quai d'Orsay* and the French Ambassador in London.[7] Mitterrand has spoken publicly in more measured terms: reunification was 'in the logic of history but would take time and must be peaceful and democratic. We must be careful of destabilisation. Meanwhile there might be new agreements between the two Germanies: the time ahead should be used to reinforce the EC, a pole of attraction for the peoples of Europe drawn towards democracy'.

18. The Belgian Ambassador has voiced fears of eventual German preponderance.[8] Many Dutch, Danes and Norwegians share such sentiments. Old memories die hard in these neighbours of Germany.

19. The Americans, like the French and ourselves, are publicly committed to the principle of reunification but, choosing words carefully, Baker said on 17 October that he foresaw the reconciliation of the German people through self-determination

---

[7] Respectively, Jean-Pierre Chevènement, François Scheer and Luc de la Barre de Nanteuil.

[8] Jean-Paul van Bellinghen.

'with the end result being a people integrated into the community of democratic European nations'.

IV PROSPECTS WITHIN THE GDR

20. The GDR is at a watershed. The young in particular have grown fed up with the rigidity of the system, the lack of control over their own lives and the absence of political change. The regime has lost the hearts and minds of many of its people. Many have left this year (perhaps 150,000 by the year's end). Those staying behind are less afraid to express their dissatisfaction. For the first time since 1953, they are taking to the streets to protest in their tens of thousands. Umbrella opposition groups are forming. The Church, including at last the Catholics, is lending its weight in favour of reform.

21. Honecker's replacement by Krenz may have been intended to suggest that changes are on the way.[9] He has opened an early dialogue with the Church, and has promised some improvements in travel arrangements to 'socialist' countries. There are a few, limited, signs of openness in the GDR press. But Krenz's past career suggests little propensity for change. He will probably share the view frequently expressed by Party leaders that, without socialism, the GDR would have no basis for its existence separately from the FRG: hence he will want any change in the GDR's present 'socialist' course to be minimal.

22. But events could force the leadership's hand. If the protest movement gathers strength, they may feel compelled to introduce some changes, in the hope of satisfying some of the protesters and so dividing the opposition. We cannot rule out the possibility of force; but the consequences of this for the regime would be unpredictable, and the international cost is rising by the day.

23. When the regime can resist no longer, reforms might take the following line:

(*a*) The easing of travel restrictions. This could be slight or wholesale. Either way, the drain from the skilled workforce would continue, with damaging economic effects. If anything, the exodus has increased since Honecker's departure.

(*b*) The introduction of more openness. Again, there is scope for graduated change. This might encourage some people who are now disaffected to stay in the hope of further reforms.

(*c*) The economy could be liberalised, releasing the grip of the state apparatus. This could lead to short-term hardships, and benefits might take some time to emerge. But the FRG would help considerably.

(*d*) At the political level, the authorities could allow the existing 'independent' parties to become more genuinely independent and perhaps even to stand against the Socialist Unity Party in a national election (but they will bear in mind the result this produced in Poland).

(*e*) Other groups might also be given greater freedom to engage in political activity. This would be even further down the track.

24. The process of change, once begun, would be very hard to manage:

—*expectations* will be formed by reference not to Poland or Hungary but to the FRG;

—the *economy* is relatively well placed to benefit from reform. This could result in a rapid *de facto* meshing in with the FRG economy, and particularly that of West Berlin;

---

[9] See No. 19, note 2.

—the leadership have to face the *frustrations* of a well-educated population.

25. We can know little about the possible outcome of a reform process. It seems likely that any genuine extension of democracy would lead, sooner or later, to the Socialist Unity Party losing its present monopoly on power. And the economy (with generous help from the FRG, as promised by Kohl) could start to slip through the Party's fingers.

26. The attraction of the FRG, as a partner and a model, would in these circumstances be inexorable. The possible consequences of this are explored further below.

27. Of course there are other possibilities, including a crisis of the GDR's legitimacy and, at worst, a repeat of Tiananmen Square. But these are outside the scope of this paper and are considered in a separate Contingency Plan for a crisis in the GDR.[10]

V POSSIBLE OPTIONS FOR THE TWO GERMANIES

28. Assuming that current trends in East Europe continue, these are, broadly:

(*a*) Association: the burgeoning of links between the two states, the development of common institutions and infrastructures, free movement of labour, massive FRG investment in the GDR. This would be a gradual evolution, and could take place within the present system of Alliances.

(*b*) 'The Austrian solution': perhaps a development of (*a*). Real reforms in the GDR lead to a democratically elected government which continues to exist as a separate state, perhaps neutral, but enjoying the same close relationship with the FRG as Austria does.

(*c*) Confederation: the two German states, while retaining separate governments in Bonn and East Berlin, share common political structures and consult closely on issues to develop a common German policy. This is a considerable step beyond Association, and would be scarcely conceivable without fundamental reform in the GDR and withdrawal of Soviet influence.

(*d*) Federation: East Germany is subsumed with West Germany as a single broadly homogenous unit, with some central institutions and some responsibilities devolved to *Länder*, as in the FRG. This amounts to full reunification.

29. Although the present Communist leaders say they can see no scope for the GDR to exist separately if it moves away from 'socialism', there is no objective reason why a more modern and liberal GDR should not continue to exist alongside the FRG. With freedom of expression and travel, there would be less need for the final step of formally dissolving the GDR. There is no firm evidence as to whether GDR citizens would actually vote for full reunification (a recent poll, of unknown validity, referred to 64% support in the GDR). At least one of the new political groupings advocates retention of a separate socialist state.

30. The two countries' membership of opposing military blocs provides a considerable obstacle to federation because of the views of their respective allies as described above. Reunification at the cost of neutrality does not look a serious option for any foreseeable Federal Government. The Russians do not want it. Nor do any of Germany's NATO partners. The Germans are more likely to work within NATO to minimise the number of nuclear weapons on their soil and negotiate down each Alliance's military strength as far as possible, consistent with the demands of their own security (which they may interpret rather differently to ours).

---

[10] Not printed.

If neutrality is not an option, the Russians would also obviously not countenance the GDR's entry to NATO and would refuse to withdraw their troops. The FRG would not wish to provoke such a crisis.

31. The question of reunification could nonetheless become more urgent, especially if events in the GDR were to take a dramatic turn or if, notwithstanding the massive GDR security apparatus, they were to progress as quickly as in Hungary. Such events could trigger emotional surges amongst the West German public which would require great steadiness on the part of the leadership in the FRG and elsewhere. They could also provoke considerable strains in the two alliances.

VI POLICY IMPLICATIONS

32. The prospect of possible reunification has wide-ranging implications for the possible future political shape of Europe, relevant both to Germany's commitment to further EC integration and to the shape of further EC enlargement. Revival of the concept of 'Mitteleuropa' as an additional power bloc could not be ruled out. These are only now first being considered and are not addressed in this paper.

33. Our aim should be to encourage the West Germans to continue to exercise caution, and to take the Allies fully into their confidence as their thinking develops. We should recognise the pressure of public opinion in the FRG, particularly when dramatic events take place in the GDR. We should not appear to stand in the way of German aspirations, but should encourage freedom and democracy in the GDR as essential prerequisites. We should encourage the Germans not to 'go it alone'. It follows that we must be sympathetic about their efforts to Europeanise the problem and hence play our full part within the EC and NATO in responding to German concerns and needs: for a Western anchorage, for a sense of momentum in Western Europe, and for security arrangements which reconcile defence and developments in East Europe.

34. In order to forestall the development, in isolation, of divergent views and of potential misunderstandings and suspicions, we should promote a close dialogue with the FRG (as the Federal Chancellery have suggested), with France (as the Secretary General at the *Quai* has suggested) and with the US, severally and, if appropriate, collectively.

35. We should bear in mind our position and role in Berlin. Reunification would presumably entail a change in Berlin's status. The rationale for Allied rights and responsibilities, and therefore the Allied presence, could lapse. As a protecting power, the UK would be directly affected. It would be important to show that we were not seeking to cling on to our position in Berlin come what may.

On the other hand we should need, in conjunction with the *Senat* and Federal government, to maintain calm and confidence in the city's future during the intervening period, and demonstrate that we would not leave the city until satisfactory alternative arrangements were in place. Our interests should coincide with the French, and probably also with the Americans (although they might be more reluctant to surrender their military facilities when the time came). We could earn lasting credit with the Germans by handling the situation in a sensitive, forward-looking way.

36. We should develop relations with the GDR as and when circumstances allow. We should, without in any way diluting our message on the need for reform:

(*a*) consider thickening up our political dialogue with the ruling party (taking care not to get out of step with the FRG);

(*b*) establish such a dialogue with dissidents and opposition groups;

(*c*) as circumstances permit, increase training and exchange programmes;

(*d*) maintain our information effort;

(*e*) cultivate leaders of opposition groups.

37. We should consider with our main Allies possible contacts with the Russians aimed at securing mutual assurances in the event of crisis in the GDR.

38. In the Twelve, we should foster regular exchanges of information about the situation in the GDR. In the EC we should examine the scope for assistance to the GDR so as to promote reform, including the possibility of an EC/GDR Agreement on industrial products.

39. In general, we should not seek to discourage reunification (our power to do so is anyway limited). But we are potentially a major force of influence and we should exert this over the speed and timing of any moves in that direction. At some point, probably not now, the balance of advantage to our interests of the different forms of closer association between the two Germanies outlined in para 28 above should become apparent, be carefully assessed, and used as a guide for our long-term policy.

VII PUBLIC PRESENTATION (SEE ALSO ANNEX B)

40. The West should continue to call for greater political freedom for the citizens of the GDR. This fits in well with our approach elsewhere in Eastern Europe, and in the CSCE.

41. We should also continue to say that the German people should be allowed free self-determination. We support self-determination for other national groups. Support for self-determination for the Germans is consistent with (but more flexible than) our 1955 commitments; it is likely to be less objectionable to the Russians than simple calls for reunification; and it is in line with what the Germans themselves are saying. The Secretary of State used it in Bonn on 20 September. It was much appreciated, and generally judged by the Germans to have been exactly right.

42. Where necessary, we should reaffirm that we stand by our 1955 undertakings. We should not however let ourselves be drawn on detail until it is clear whether, and in what circumstances, reunification is likely to become a reality. Speculation about implications for NATO and the EC could be destabilising and become self-fulfilling prophecies.

43. We should nevertheless be clear in our own minds that we are thinking ultimately of separate acts of self-determination by the populations of the two German states.

ANNEX A

HISTORICAL BACKGROUND

1. In 1871, following the German victory in the Franco-Prussian War, Bismarck succeeded in uniting the smaller German states, which had been fragmented for centuries, into the German Empire (Reich) under an Emperor from the Prussian ruling house. This was neither a stable nor a democratic creation, and its subsequent history was turbulent, leading through World War I and Weimar to the Nazi period.

2. Since World War II the focus has been on the geographical area which lay inside the borders of the German Empire as it existed on 31 December 1937. This area has still not been the subject of a Peace Treaty. Substantial parts of it were subsumed into the Soviet Union and Poland immediately after the War. What remains is the GDR (which was formerly under Soviet occupation), and the FRG (which was under American, French and British occupation).

3. Deriving from the unconditional surrender of Germany in 1945, and pending a peace settlement, the Four Powers of Britain, France, the United States and the Soviet Union still retain certain 'rights and responsibilities' for 'Germany as a whole'. These relate directly to the question of reunification and have their most visible manifestation in the Allied presence in Berlin. It was never the intention of the three Western Powers permanently to divide Germany, and the Potsdam Conference in 1945 made clear that: 'during the period of occupation Germany shall be treated as a single economic unit'. But difficulties with the Soviet Union culminating in the Blockade of Berlin and the final collapse of 4-power control made the fulfilment of the Potsdam commitments, and reunification, impossible at that time.

4. The Federal Republic of Germany was created in 1949. The FRG's Basic Law, or temporary constitution, which was endorsed by the Western Allies, calls for the FRG 'to achieve in free self-determination the unity and freedom of Germany'. The Bonn/Paris Conventions agreed between the three Western Allies and the FRG which came into force in May 1955 terminated the occupation regime in the Federal Republic. Article 7 of the Relations Conventions included the following undertaking:

> Pending the peace settlement, the signatory states will cooperate to achieve, by peaceful means, their common aim of a reunified Germany enjoying a liberal democratic constitution, like that of the Federal Republic, and integrated within the European community.

This means that we are not committed to German reunification *per se* but only to a form of it acceptable to the West, namely one peaceably achieved and resulting in a Germany that would be both a Western-style democracy and linked to the West if not part of the West.

5. Up to 1959 the Western Allies regularly made specific proposals with the direct aim of securing a reunified Germany on the terms described above. The last UK proposal of 14 May 1959 (like its predecessors) envisaged, *inter alia*, democratic elections in the FRG and the GDR leading to the election of an all-German Assembly with the task of producing an all-German constitution. This would give rise to an all-German government with full freedom of decision which could then negotiate a peace treaty and decide on whether or not the new entity wished to be a member of either of the Pacts.

6. Stalin in 1952 made an offer to the FRG of reunification in exchange for neutrality. But Adenauer, with the support of the majority in the FRG, gave Western integration precedence over reunification. Stalin's offer was rejected. The FRG joined NATO in 1955.

7. The SPD came to see an active reunification policy as incompatible with reconciliation with the East and, under Willy Brandt's leadership, the Federal government renounced its claims to the Eastern territories annexed by the Soviet Union and Poland, by means of the Moscow and Warsaw Treaties of 1970. These do not, however, affect the rights of the Four Powers, which still relate to the entire

area within the 1937 borders of Germany. Despite the 1970 Treaties, the western border of Poland remains controversial for some in the FRG, e.g. the CSU.

8. Through the 1972 NATO Communiqué, the entire NATO Alliance became associated with the objective of unity for Germany through self-determination. In 1982/3 Kohl put the German Question back on the Western political agenda, but remained committed to the *Ostpolitik* of previous Federal governments.

ANNEX B

GDR

Line to Take

What we have seen in the GDR shows the desperate need for reform there. The GDR must become a place where people want to live, without being forced to. They must move with the times. And give people freedom.

—CSCE commitments entered into by the GDR only this January are quite plain:

- Participating States 'will respect fully the right of everyone . . . to leave any country, including his own, and to return to his country'.
- Incredible that women and children should have to camp out in the cold and mud in order to win the exercise of this right.

—CSCE also commits all signatories to bring their laws, practices and policies into line with their international obligations:

- Could not be plainer that GDR is massively in breach.
- Call for reform in the GDR is but another way of calling on it to respect the obligations it has freely entered into.

Poland, Hungary and, to a great extent, the Soviet Union are showing the way.

We warmly endorse Chancellor Kohl's call (on 5 October in *Bild*) on the GDR leadership to respond to the demands of their people.

We have no wish to see the GDR destabilised. Nor does Chancellor Kohl. He has made that clear. It is the stubborn refusal of the GDR leaders to listen to their own people which is making the GDR less stable. People in the GDR want their aspirations met. They want the opportunity to determine their own future. Clear that such a future would include far greater democracy and freedom than the GDR currently enjoys.

FRG/GDR

Some progress had been made in developing links and overcoming the Cold War divisions between the 2 states in Germany. We welcome this. But the Wall still stands. There is a long way to go.

> The Prime Minister reaffirmed the conviction of successive British Governments that real and permanent stability in Europe will be difficult to achieve so long as the German nation is divided against its will. (Thatcher/Kohl Joint Declaration, May 1984.)

Self-determination is the key. Freedom comes first. It follows that we will respect the free choice of the German people. This has always been our position. Chancellor Kohl clearly recognises the implications of this issue for the FRG's friends and neighbours. The German Government has always shared its thinking with us. We shall continue to work closely together, as we have for 40 years.

Supplementaries (if pressed)
Allied Rights and Responsibilities
  The policy of the Three Western Allies has been to ensure that the German Question is held open for eventual resolution.
  This is illustrated by continuance of Four Power responsibilities for Germany as a whole.
  And it is illustrated by the continued presence of Allied Powers in Berlin as protecting powers.
1937 Frontiers (if raised)
  Herr Genscher has said (at the UN on 27 September) that the right of the Polish people to secure borders will not be called into question by the FRG.
Membership of Warsaw Pact (if raised)
  Under CSCE (Helsinki Final Act) all signatory states have the right to belong, or not to belong, to alliances.
Key Texts
  (1) Article 7 of the Convention on Relations in the Bonn/Paris Conventions, ratified in 1955, states: 'Pending the Peace Settlement the signatory states will cooperate to achieve, by peaceful means, their common aim of a reunified Germany enjoying a liberal-democratic constitution, like that of the Federal Republic, and integrated within the European community.'
  (2) The Helsinki Final Act (1975) provides that participating States 'consider that their frontiers can be changed, in accordance with international law, by peaceful means and by agreement. They also have the right to belong or not to belong to international organisations, to be or not to be a party to bilateral or multilateral treaties including the right to be or not to be a party to treaties of alliance; they also have the right to neutrality.'
  CSCE signatory States agreed in Vienna in January 1989 that 'they will respect each other's right freely to choose and develop their political, social, economic and cultural systems . . . they will ensure that their laws, regulations, practices and policies conform with their obligations under international law and are brought into harmony with the provisions of the Declaration on Principles and other CSCE commitments.'
  They also agreed that 'by virtue of the principle of equal rights and self-determination of peoples and in conformity with the relevant provisions of the Final Act, all peoples always have the right, in full freedom, to determine, when and as they wish, their internal and external political status, without external interference, and to pursue as they wish their political, economic, social and cultural development.'

No. 26

Minute from Sir P. Wright to Mr Wall

[*Wright Papers*]

Top Secret and Strictly Personal   FCO, *30 October 1989*

The German Question
  1. Events in East Germany over the last few weeks have ensured that the so-called 'German Question' is now very high on the West's political agenda. The

'Question' has, of course, been put in various forms: is Germany on the way to becoming one State? Will East Germany remain a separate State, but join the European Community? Or will East Germany simply strengthen its existing special relationship with the Community? The Department have prepared a paper exploring these themes,[1] which I will be discussing with DUSs tomorrow afternoon; and which I hope to submit to the Secretary of State soon.[2]

2. Meanwhile, the Secretary of State will wish to be aware that on at least three occasions recently, the Prime Minister has aired her misgivings about German reunification in very stark terms:

—first with *President Mitterrand* on 1 September, when she discussed the subject at some length (I attach Mr Powell's record of the conversation);[3]

—and then with *President Gorbachev* in Moscow (Mr Powell's letter of 24 September, also attached).[4]

---

[1] No. 25.

[2] No. 30.

[3] The three letters from Mr Powell to Mr Wall of 1 September found in the FCO and Cabinet Office files record the general tenor of the meeting and discussions of European Community affairs and international political issues, but make no mention of the German question (WRF 020/12; PREM: Visits of President Mitterrand). According to Lord Powell's subsequent testimony it was M. Mitterrand who, at this Chequers meeting, first 'alarmed' Mrs Thatcher about developments in Germany (interview of 3 June 1997, cited in Weidenfeld, p. 694, note 29). This is plausible in the light of subsequent meetings between the two leaders: see Nos. 71 and 103. However, according to Elisabeth Guigou, the French note-taker at the meeting (reconstructing Mrs Thatcher's words from memory), it was the Prime Minister who first raised the German question, telling President Mitterrand that she had read much on the history of Germany during her vacation and was very disturbed. It would be intolerable, she said, if there was a single currency and Germany reunified as well. President Mitterrand responded that he was less alarmed than she was, not least because a single currency would act as a restraint on a unified Germany (Elisabeth Guigou, *Une femme au cœur de l'État. Entretiens avec Pierre Favier et Michel Martin-Roland* (Paris: Fayard, 2000), pp. 75-77). The account given in Attali, p. 297, confirms Mrs Thatcher's hostility to a united Germany, but records President Mitterrand as reassuring her that Gorbachev would never accept a united Germany as a member of NATO, while the United States would never accept the Federal Republic's leaving the Alliance: 'Alors, ne nous inquiétons pas: disons qu'elle se fera quand les Allemands le décideront, mais en sachant que les deux Grands nous en protégeront.' The anti-German thrust of the conversation is recalled by John Major (*The Autobiography* (London: HarperCollins, 1999), pp. 121-22.

[4] This letter has not been found in the FCO files, but there is a copy in PREM: Prime Minister's Visits to the Soviet Union. It records a part of the talks on 23 September for which it was agreed between the two leaders that no notes should be taken. The relevant section reads: 'The Prime Minister then asked Mr Gorbachev's assessment of the prospects in the GDR. Surely there would be changes in the direction of greater democracy there as well. That would awaken fears in some quarters of German reunification. Although NATO traditionally made statements supporting Germany's aspiration to be reunited, in practice we would not welcome it at all. She was not speaking for herself alone. She had discussed the matter with at least one other western leader. She would welcome some reassurance about Mr Gorbachev's attitude. Mr Gorbachev said that he could see what the Prime Minister was driving at. The Soviet Union understood the problem very well and she could be reassured. They did not want German reunification any more than Britain did. It was useful that the matter had been raised and that he and the Prime Minister knew each other's mind on this delicate subject.' This corresponds closely with the notes made by A.S. Chernyaev, Mr Gorbachev's chief foreign policy adviser, according to which Mrs Thatcher declared: 'Britain and Western Europe are not interested in the unification of Germany. The words written in the NATO communiqué may sound different, but disregard them. We do not want the reunification of Germany. It would lead to changes in the post-war borders, and we cannot allow that because such a development would undermine the stability of the entire international situation, and could lead to threats to our security' (printed in Svetlana Savranskaya, Thomas Blanton and Vlad Zubok (eds.), *Masterpieces of History: The Soviet Peaceful Withdrawal from Eastern Europe, 1989* (Budapest:

Needless to say, the fact of these conversations has been held very tightly indeed: because there is no doubt that the Prime Minister's views, if they became known, would raise eyebrows (at least) both in Germany and in the United States.[5] They form a particularly stark contrast with President Bush's remarks to the *New York Times* on 24 October: 'I do not share the concern that some European countries have about a reunified Germany, because I think Germany's commitment to, and recognition of, the importance of the Alliance is unshakeable.'

3. The third occasion on which the Prime Minister has made clear her views on this subject was:

—at CHOGM earlier this month. The Secretary of State may wish to glance at my minute of 26 October.[6]

As I say in my minute, in consultation with Mr Powell we arranged for her remarks on this subject to be removed from the record produced by the Commonwealth Secretariat: and as far as I know, neither this nor the remarks themselves have attracted any attention. But it cannot be long before it becomes more widely known what the Prime Minister's views on this subject are.[7]

P. WRIGHT

Central European University Press, 2009)). For Lady Thatcher's account of the discussion see Thatcher, p. 792. See also Rodric Braithwaite, *Across the Moscow River: The World Turned Upside Down* (New Haven and London: Yale University Press, 2002), pp. 135-36.

[5] In fact the content of the Prime Minister's conversation with Mr Gorbachev was already known to the FRG Government: see minute by Ministerial Director Hartmann of 13 October citing a report from the West German Embassy in Moscow, in *Deutsche Einheit*, No. 61.

[6] In this minute Sir P. Wright noted that during her remarks at the first Executive Session of the Commonwealth Heads of Government Meeting, held at Kuala Lumpur from 18 to 24 October, Mrs Thatcher had 'referred to the prospect of greater freedom throughout Eastern Europe. She went on to describe the upsurge of nationalist groupings, whether Serbs, Croatians or Macedonians, and then said that there was a risk of German Reunification raising its head again. Great uncertainty could lead to great insecurity, and there was a need to watch this' (Wright Papers).

[7] On 30 October Mr Hurd minuted: 'Thanks.' On 31 October Mr Wall minuted: 'I have retained Flags A & B [Mr Powell's letters of 1 and 24 September] here.'

No. 27

Minute from Sir P. Wright to Mr Wall[1]

[Wright Papers]

Confidential and Strictly Personal   FCO, *30 October 1989*

The UK and Europe: US Views

1. There has been some correspondence over the past six months about the attitude of the Bush Administration to Europe in general, and to British attitudes towards Europe in particular.

2. In his recent despatch on Bush's foreign policy (paragraphs 30 and ff.),[2] Sir Antony Acland drew attention to this question; and in his own valedictory despatch

[1] Copied to Sir J. Fretwell, Mr Gillmore and Mr Kerr.

[2] Paragraph 30 of Sir A. Acland's despatch of 5 September read, in part: 'The necessary leverage . . . may not always be easy to find; and it will I believe increasingly require us to work in close concert with our European partners and allies if we are to be successful. The Americans respect strength;

from Rome (especially paragraph 8), Sir Derek Thomas pursues a similar theme.[3] The point made by both can be (fairly crudely) summarised in a couple of sentences from the brief on the US/UK relationship which the Secretary of State saw over the weekend: 'There is a risk that the Americans may harbour the suspicion . . . that we may be playing a spoiling rather than a constructive role (in Europe) . . . it is vital that the United States sees the UK as a key player, and that we are not 'marginalised'.

3. Against this background, the Secretary of State might like to see a personal letter which I received last month from Sir Michael Alexander at UKDEL NATO, in which he records a conversation with Blackwill, an influential adviser to the Bush White House.[4] As you know, I showed the letter to Mr Major; and discussed with him whether (and if so when) the points Blackwill made should be drawn to the attention of the Prime Minister.[5] (I should add that I gave a copy of Sir Michael's letter, on a strictly personal basis, to Sir Percy Cradock; and Sir Antony Acland's despatch was, of course, copied to No 10).

4. Mr Major decided at the time not to pursue Sir Michael Alexander's letter with No 10 immediately, and instead to take a suitable opportunity to feed in this thinking. In the light of this, I thought that the Secretary of State should be aware of the subject before his first bilateral with the Prime Minister this week; not least in the context of the Prime Minister's visit to Camp David to see President Bush next month.[6]

P. WRIGHT

---

they will listen more to Western Europe as a whole than to its constituent parts; and [Secretary of State James] Baker with his instinct for deal-making, will be unsentimentally looking for who is best placed to "deliver". It will help us to promote our own interests here if we are seen to be in the vanguard of European activity on the security and economic fronts; and we should be more inclined than we have been—or have needed to be—in the past to concert positions in Brussels and with key European capitals before taking action in Washington' (Wright Papers).

[3] In paragraph 8 of his valedictory despatch of 16 October (WRS 014/1) Sir D. Thomas endorsed the views expressed by Sir A. Acland. In paragraph 9 he wrote: 'What depresses me, if I may speak candidly in my last despatch from Rome, is that during the past decade when so much had been done by the present Government to restore Britain's economic position and while our national leadership has enjoyed such unparalleled authority in the outside world, we have once again missed an opportunity to put ourselves in the lead in Europe.'

[4] No. 12.

[5] See No. 12, note 5.

[6] Mr Hurd minuted: 'Grateful if the PUS c[oul]d. discuss.'

No. 28

Teleletter from Mr Broomfield (East Berlin) to Sir J. Fretwell[1]

[*WRE 014/2*]

Confidential   EAST BERLIN, *31 October 1989, 1.35 p.m.*

GDR: Internal Developments: Overview

Summary

1. The SED's policy of renewal under great time pressure. People in the GDR have to be persuaded to stay. The signs to look for.

Detail

2. In the last three weeks, events have moved much faster than expected. The underlying reason is that the SED leadership can no longer deprive the people of the choice of going or staying.

3. One of the last (instinctive) reactions of Honecker's regime on 3 October was to ban visa-free tourism into Czechoslovakia. But, with a reform-minded Poland on their eastern frontier and a largely unprotected border with Czechoslovakia to the south, this could not be a long term policy. Recognition came with the announcement on 27 October that visa-free travel to Czechoslovakia was being restored on 1 November. A new policy on freedom of movement is likely to be confirmed in a draft law on foreign travel to be published next week. If that is both liberal in principle as well as application, then a fundamental change in the relationship between rulers and ruled in the GDR will have taken place. (If it is not, then the demonstrations will redouble their force and Krenz's position will be in doubt.)

4. Krenz has signalled his concern on this score in every public statement since he became General Secretary and Head of State. He stressed the underlying twin problems of nationality (the concept of one common German citizenship which entitles everyone here to a FRG passport) and finance most recently in his telephone conversation with Kohl on 27 October. I do not think he expects the FRG to move on nationality but he will hope for some financial help. He is also trying to signal, without losing too much face, that this problem is one for the FRG too.

5. In my view Krenz started by believing that 'dialogue' was a way of letting off steam. It could be controlled within the existing framework of tame block parties, official trades union, churches, etc. He wanted to focus it on the mainly economic agenda proposed by the Politburo on 11 October. But the strength and depth of feeling released by 'dialogue' surprised him. He is, in my view[,] an opportunist and has adjusted. There is now a genuine dialogue going on and it is being reported in the media. The realisation of their collective power has dawned on the population. 'We are the people' they chant in increasing numbers as they confront the 'people's police' and 'the people's representatives'. Their demands are for fundamental political rights as well as for economic and social improvement.

6. Confronted by this, Krenz has stated the SED's bottom line as a policy of renewal (no longer continuity and renewal) of a socialist society based on the

---

[1] Repeated as Teleletter Bonn, BMG Berlin; copied to Mr Synnott (FCO), Sir C. Mallaby (Bonn), Mr Burton (BMG Berlin).

constitution. The underlying principles of socialism in the GDR may not be called in question. He means (like Gorbachev) the leading role of the Party, but the rest is a matter of definition. He has given ground on a number of points such as an amnesty 'for illegal emigrants', an enquiry into police behaviour on 7/8 October, acknowledgement (if not formal recognition) of New Forum. He has, however, put off until May 1991, the *Volkskammer* elections (which were at one stage to be held in June 1990) in order to buy time on this critical issue while saying that all proposals and experience in previous elections will be taken into account. (This is dangerous ground for Krenz whom the population hold responsible for the local election fraud on 7.5.89.)

7. Behind all this Krenz must know that he is operating under intense time pressure. The economy (and social services such as hospitals) are feeling the effects of the summer exodus (around 500 a day continue to leave via Hungary) and the mass demonstrations since then. (The exodus has in fact been running at levels approaching the pre 13.8.61 rate. At that time the SED leadership concluded that if it was not stopped the country would no longer be a viable concern.) If travel is to be liberalised by the end of the year, Krenz must by then have convinced the people that they should stay in the GDR because there is a real prospect of renewing the society. If not they will leave. And if thousands more were to do this, a vicious circle of economic decline leading to increasingly vocal, and possibly physical protests would be likely. The country could start to run out of control.

8. In the next two to three weeks, Krenz will be judged on the following:

(*a*) his reception by Gorbachev in Moscow,

(*b*) the changes he makes in the Politburo (and Council of Ministers) at the central Committee meeting on 8-10 November,

(*c*) the proposals the Central Committee makes on a range of important economic and possibly also political matters,

(*d*) the draft of the new travel law,

(*e*) the report into police brutality at the demonstrations on 7/8 October,

(*f*) the leadership's attitude to new groups outside the official structure.

If on these points Krenz shows real acceptance of the unavoidability of reform, then I believe a second mass exodus can be avoided.

9. The FRG will have a number of difficult decisions to take. What they decide will also affect the situation particularly as regards travel. I imagine Minister Seiters will be in East Berlin as soon as possible after the Central Committee meeting on 8-10 November.

10. I made recommendations for our policy in my despatch of 12 October.[2] I believe our public line should be to continue to call for reform in the GDR without which instability would increase. I suggest we should focus on the rule of law. We might say that many of the GDR's present problems would fall away if they brought their internal legislation into line with their external commitments (e.g., on the UN Charter for Political and Civil Liberties, CSCE, etc). This would have the double advantage of not attacking the political system head-on and of reinforcing the demands for legally guaranteed rights (a *Rechtstaat*) made by lawyers and others here (see separate report) and acknowledged by Krenz.

11. I have painted a challenging scenario. How it will actually turn out is uncertain but I thought it right to focus on the immediate problems. To end on a

---

[2] No. 19.

more positive note, the distance moved in the last three weeks over freedom of expression (*glasnost*) has been remarkable. If it were to continue and be supplemented by economic decentralization and political reform then the GDR is probably the best placed of all East European countries to be able to take advantage of these new opportunities. It has an embryonic multi-party system, capable industrial managers who know about a market economy, a well-trained work-force, etc. It could, in short, make reform work.

12. Grateful if WED could send copies by bag to HM Ambassadors at Washington, Paris, Moscow, UKDEL NATO, UKREP Brussels, Eastern European Posts, Peking.[3]

N.H.R.A. BROOMFIELD

[3] Replying on 3 November, Sir J. Fretwell complimented Mr Broomfield and his staff on their reporting, adding that 'you will have the satisfaction of knowing that you are dealing with events of epoch-making importance' (WRE 014/2).

No. 29

Letter from Mr Powell (No. 10) to Mr Wall

[*PREM: Internal situation in FRG, Part 3*]

Secret and Personal   10 DOWNING STREET, *2 November 1989*

[No salutation on this copy]

Germany

The Prime Minister had a talk yesterday afternoon with Sir Christopher Mallaby about Germany.

Sir Christopher judged the prospects for the CDU/FD[P] coalition to be quite good. They stood at some 50 per cent in the opinion polls. The economy was performing outstandingly well. Chancellor Kohl was trying to strike a cautious and balanced attitude towards developments in East Germany and elsewhere in Eastern Europe, and he had deliberately avoided talk of German reunification. He had acted responsibly in his handling of President Gorbachev's visit in the summer. There was no doubt that the alternatives to Chancellor Kohl—a coalition involving the SPD and the Greens—would be much worse from the point of view of Britain's interests.

The Prime Minister accepted without question that it was very much in our interests that Chancellor Kohl should continue in office and that the Federal Republic should remain a steady and reliable partner. But there were nonetheless aspects which caused her concern. At the risk of over-simplifying, she saw a tendency for official thinking to spend too much time speculating on Germany's geopolitical position and how it might develop. Of course this was important. But it was clear that—whatever their formal position—Britain, France and the Soviet Union were fundamentally opposed to German reunification. It was Germany's role in Western Europe rather than Central Europe which should be the more pressing concern. The massive and persistent trade surplus—the sum of bilateral surpluses with every other EC member state—based on an under-valued DM and subsidies to German industry was leading to increasing German economic dominance of Western Europe. The special arrangements for imports from East Germany strengthened this tendency.

The Prime Minister continued that this dominance was reflected in Germany's determination to get its own way on Community issues, for instance the desire to reduce the competitiveness of other European countries evident in support for the Social Charter. Other European Governments seemed disinclined to challenge Germany on its permanent trade surplus: there was a contrast here with the robust way in which the United States was tackling Japan about its proportionately smaller trade surplus. She would like to see the focus of our diplomacy turn more single-mindedly towards tackling these problems by:

—enlisting German support against a restrictive and anti-competitive Social Charter;

—bringing home to the German government and German industry the dangers inherent in the Delors Stages 2 and 3 for the sound money policies of the *Bundesbank*;[1]

—pressing for a revaluation of the German mark (although this would need to be handled very discreetly to avoid repercussions in the exchange markets);

—and urge [*sic*] the importance of reducing State Aids and other subsidies.

She would be ready to send a message to Chancellor Kohl (or, as she subsequently told the Foreign Secretary, to see him ahead of the Strasbourg European Council) to make some of these points. They were crucial to our own economic prospects and to securing the sort of Europe we want. None of this was to belittle the importance of developments in Central Europe and Germany's role in them. They would need the most careful handling. But the problems with Germany in Western Europe—including Germany's attitude to SNF and other defence issues—were of even greater concern and the weight of our effort should go into dealing with them.

I should be grateful if this letter could be given *a very limited circulation only*.

I am copying this letter to John Gieve (H.M. Treasury).

C.D. POWELL

[1] In April 1989 the report of a committee headed by Jacques Delors, President of the European Commission, proposed that European Monetary Union (EMU) should be achieved in three stages. By adopting the first stage, the liberalisation of all capital movements within the Community from 1 July 1990, the EC would be committed irrevocably to the completion of stages 2 and 3, culminating in the adoption of a single European currency.

No. 30

Submission from Sir P. Wright to Mr Wall

[*Wright Papers*]

Confidential   FCO, *3 November 1989*

Enlargement of the EC and the German Question

1. As I have already mentioned to the Secretary of State, my monthly meeting with DUSs on 31 October was largely devoted to the inter-connected subjects of

Enlargement and the German Question. You may like to have a note of the discussion, and of the (tentative) conclusions reached.

Enlargement

2. We agreed that for the immediate future the *tactical approach* in the draft OD paper,[1] which you have already seen and which Mr Maude has agreed, was right. We should not commit ourselves on the Austrian application to join the Community while events in Eastern Europe were moving so rapidly. Whatever the Community decided on Austria would be taken as a long term signal in Hungary, and possibly in the GDR too. More immediately, a decision to open negotiations with Austria would provoke rethinking in other EFTA countries, not to mention Turkey. There would be little difficulty in postponing a firm position on Austria until after 1992.

3. We felt, however, that while this was the right approach for the short term, there was also a place in our thinking (as the Planners had argued in their own contributions to the debate) for a *longer-term vision* (or strategy, to use a more hard-nosed expression). If we wished to influence developments in Europe, we needed now to be seen to be thinking *beyond* 1992. But it would be a mistake to be explicit at this stage on the precise form which links between Eastern Europe and the European Community would take: 'variable and extensive geometry' might be the solution.

4. In this context we also discussed the possible *security dimension*, a critical question as we looked at the application from a neutral Austria. On the one hand, to admit another neutral would probably mean abandoning our current objective of building a security dimension (in the sense of defence rather than counter-terrorist cooperation etc) to European political co-operation. On the other hand, this objective—though reflected in the Single European Act—has been long deferred, and there was some doubt whether it would ever come to fruition: we might one day need a Community flexible enough to accommodate two German states, one of them neutral. For the moment, we could do no more than keep our policy in this area under review, ensuring in particular that it retains sufficient flexibility to allow an imaginative response to circumstances which might change rapidly.

The German Question

5. We discussed this on the basis of a number of papers, including Sir John Fretwell's minute of 20 October and Mr Synnott's paper of 25 October.[2] The Secretary of State will wish to look at both these papers; I particularly draw his attention to paragraphs 28 to 43 of the latter.

6. We agreed that:

—Developments were likely to be fast and disorderly. The weight of people on the streets in the GDR meant that the dialogue Krenz proposes might not be enough; the policy of a return to repression might not work either.

—This did not mean that Reunification was round the corner; but some degree of self-determination might come sooner than we had expected. The pace of developments elsewhere in Eastern Europe (e.g. Poland and Hungary) had far outstripped our expectations.

—The Soviet attitude remained uncertain, though it was easier to believe that they could accept self-determination than reunification. (Some doubt had been

---

[1] This was a paper on 'Britain and Europe' for the Overseas and Defence Committee of the Cabinet (OD), the first draft of which had been circulated by the Policy Planning Staff on 18 July (not printed) (WRG 021/1).
[2] Nos. 23 and 25.

cast on Soviet spokesmen's apparent readiness to contemplate Hungarian departure from the Warsaw Pact.)

7. In the light of this, we *concluded* that:

—We need to consider internally whether we have *strong preferences between the options* set out in paragraph 28 of Mr Synnott's paper, as well as other options not included, such as a unitary state. But we need to bear in mind that the choice will not necessarily, or even primarily, be ours.

—We should begin to *talk carefully and privately* to the *Americans* and the *French* about possible patterns of development. Above all we need to explore their own thinking with the *Germans*. We can begin by discussing with them how possible changes might impact on Berlin and on the Community.

—We need ourselves to look again at our position and responsibilities in *Berlin* in the light of possible future developments.

8. We agreed that, for the moment, our *public position* of support for self-determination was the right one, not least because it is welcomed strongly by the Germans. We should *avoid* revealing any public trace of anxiety about developments in Germany.

9. In the light of this, the Secretary of State may wish to consider a *major speech* on East/West relations, covering the future development of Europe as a whole. A number of areas will require delicate drafting: but there is a case for an authoritative statement on how *we* would like to see Europe develop. There would be much to be said for making such a speech somewhere in Germany, but the Secretary of State will need to take into account the Prime Minister's reservations about the advisability of a major speech in (and on) Germany next year, on which Sir Christopher Mallaby's advice is being sought (your minute of 2 November)[3].

P. WRIGHT

[3] Covering No. 29.

No. 31

Minute from Mr Munro (East Berlin) to Mr Broomfield[1]

[*WRL 020/4*]

Confidential   EAST BERLIN, *3 November 1989*

The German Question

We discussed my call on V. Grinin, Counsellor at the Soviet Embassy on 2 November and agreed that I should record [the] main points in a minute copied in the bag on 3 November to those immediately concerned with our policy towards Germany. I shall record in slower time in more detail Grinin's many observations about Krenz's performance in Moscow on his first visit as Honecker's successor, and on prospects for political developments here.[2] Our conversation (in German)

[1] Copied to Sir C. Mallaby, Bonn; Sir R. Braithwaite, Moscow; Sir E. Fergusson, Paris; Sir A. Acland, Washington; Sir J. Fretwell, FCO; Sir M. Alexander, UKDEL NATO; Mr Burton, BMG Berlin; Mr Synnott, WED.

[2] In a letter to Mr Ramsden of 15 November Mr Munro commented: 'In the light of what has happened since 2 November it seems to me that Krenz accepted the message he received from

lasted for nearly two hours. I had asked for a call originally after Gorbachev's visit to East Berlin for the GDR's 40th anniversary on 6-7 October. Unusually there was delay in fixing it up, but on 30 November [*sic*] Grinin asked me, at a social function, if a call after Krenz's visit to Moscow on 2 November would be convenient. I have got to know Grinin quite well over the last 2½ years. He is less genial than Maximychev but seems to me to be a better conceptual thinker. He is also under less pressure than Maximychev who has a huge task running the Embassy. Ambassador Kochemasov is detached from this work.

2. We began by evaluating Krenz's performance in Moscow. Grinin said that unlike most new leaders, including Gorbachev, Krenz would have no period of grace. He had made great strides in two weeks notably on freedom of expression and assembly. He had promised a radical change in travel. But the decisive moment for the SED would occur on 8 November at the meeting of the Central Committee. This would deal with personnel, and with policy including the democratisation of political life in the GDR. If the population received a transparently honest account of proceedings; many new and convincing personalities were introduced into the Politburo, the Central Committee and the Council of Ministers; and new policies were announced then the SED could continue to exercise its leading role. If on the other hand Krenz failed to bring about this transformation the SED and indeed the GDR would be overtaken by events. Krenz had introduced *glasnost* already. He had but one chance to put the SED in charge of *perestroika*. Grinin agreed with me that the demonstrations (latest prediction is of 1 million people) in (East) Berlin on 4 November would be a barometer of the public mood.

3. Grinin had prefaced these remarks by asking about the British analysis of Krenz's position and our view of the future of the 'German region'. Were we not 'under pressure from the FRG over reunification'? I said I regarded the present period as one in which the possibility of a third way between old style socialism in the colours of the GDR and reunification was being explored. We were not under pressure from the FRG over reunification. The FRG welcomed our stand on self-determination. In response to Grinin's question about the possibility of the mass exodus continuing I said it all depended on Krenz. He had opened his account with three serious debits—electoral fraud, praise of the Tiananmen Square massacre, and responsibility for security in the Politburo. On the credit side he had now added, the more open media and dialogue. Travel would be a credit if it came up to popular expectations. Meanwhile the perceived continuing lack of real democracy and Krenz's insistence on the leading role of the SED were major debits. Asked to predict the future course of events, I said that in the light of recent events any timescale I predicted was likely to be too leisurely. We lived in a period of ever shortening timescales.

4. Grinin asked what was the decisive issue for the UK in the German question. I repeated that it was self-determination. The people here had not exercised their rights in this respect. We would accept their choice freely exercised. If they chose reunification the UK was bound by treaty to accept that choice. Grinin made no attempt to claim that the people here had exercised self-determination. He said that elections to the *Volkskammer* would be held in 1991. If they were genuinely free

Gorbachev but has not grasped its implications. He has only acted under further pressure from the streets, the opposition groups, the bloc parties and from within the SED itself. . . . Modrow on the other hand has shown that he can not only follow but can also understand Gorbachev' (WRL 020/4).

and fair, would the UK consider that the population (*Bevölkerung* not *Volk*) had exercised self-determination, or would the UK think it necessary to 'hold a referendum on the unity of the German Nation'? I said that I would not wish my answer to be regarded as a definitive statement of British policy. But, if it was clear after such elections that the people were content with the result we might well regard the German Question as essentially solved. Ministers had said repeatedly that it was a question of the will of the German people. If they opted to live in two states we would be content. But we could not then just wash our hands of the matter, because of Berlin. The four powers (UK, US, France, Soviet Union) would have to resolve this aspect of the German question. I asked Grinin to comment on recent statements by Soviet spokesmen to the effect that 'in principle' the Soviet Union could accept reunification.

5. Grinin said that there were two particular problems for the Soviet Union—the speed of events in the GDR, and the relationship between these events and developments in arms control affecting the Soviet view of European security. The Soviet Union could now envisage a world in which NATO and the Warsaw Pact had outlived their usefulness. They had been established and Germany had been divided in circumstances completely different from those which prevailed today. There had been a great change in political relations between east and west. But the military reality was still that of two powerful, mistrustful alliances. The difficulty over developments in the GDR was that the movement to reunification could gather unstoppable momentum before sufficient east/west trust under-pinned by disarmament had been achieved to make reunification, German confederation or whatever, an acceptable development to all concerned in the Soviet Union. Grinin said that there were still a lot of influential people in Moscow who were very nervous about developments in Central Europe. Triumphalist statements in the west about Germany and the victory of capitalism did not help, adding some power if not decisive power, to their elbow. Grinin added however that while the Soviet Union would give Krenz every possible support and held to the view that post war reality included two German states, other peaceful developments would have to be accepted. He said he agreed with me absolutely that events were moving at great speed and that even in a week's time we might have to meet to discuss if not a different agenda, at least a different shorter timescale. Grinin said that it was in this spirit that Gorbachev had encouraged Krenz to seize his chance and move fast.

6. I then went over this ground again to be sure I had understood Grinin's thinking correctly. It became clear (to me at least) that the Russians now think reunification is possible although not at all desirable. If it occurs they will not (or at least Gorbachev will not) physically seek to prevent it. I deduce that the Russians might have planned to make a move on the German question later when they were much closer than they are now to their goal of the dissolution of alliances. They are unhappy (but resigned) about the real risk of their policy being overtaken by events. The logic of this situation is that the Russians will themselves follow the advice they gave Krenz in Moscow to get out in front of events and control them. This would mean in their case making a reunification offer (a referendum on German unity as mentioned by Grinin) contingent on dramatic steps in disarmament to meet their security requirements and calm the nervous suspicious squad in Moscow. Perhaps (and this is speculation on my part)

Gorbachev will have something up his sleeve for his Mediterranean summit with President Bush.[3]

7. At the end of the conversation I said I was sure we should stay in touch. Mr Broomfield hoped to pay a farewell call on Ambassador Kochemasov. Grinin said he agreed but there was a problem. If representatives of the four powers met, there would be suspicions in Bonn and indeed among those in Moscow who had not understood the pace of developments in the GDR. Nonetheless the situation was such that dialogue and cooperation between us were indispensable.

Comment

8. I wish to comment only on Grinin's repeated references to the speed of events. We dwelt at length on the reasons for the exodus from this country. Grinin accepted that it would continue unless Krenz moved very fast to transform the situation. I think the Russians reckon he really does have one chance only—at the Central Committee meeting beginning on 8 November. If he blows it then the exodus will gather pace and reunification will force its way to the top of the agenda.[4]

C. A. MUNRO

[3] The two leaders were to meet at Valletta, Malta, on 2-3 December.

[4] Sir J. Fretwell noted: 'A very valuable report from E. Berlin. The GDR is sliding out of control' (WRL 020/4). The conversation was also brought to the attention of the FRG Government, where Herr Hartmann noted that it was 'Sehr wichtig!': *Deutsche Einheit*, No. 80, note 2.

No. 32

Mr Broomfield (East Berlin) to Mr Hurd[1]

No. 354 Telegraphic [*WRE 014/2*]

Confidential   EAST BERLIN, *5 November 1989, 4 p.m.*

Following for Secretary of State['s] Party.
My teleletter of 31 October to Sir J. Fretwell.[2]

GDR: A Country in Crisis

Summary

1. Krenz's appeal on 3 November, on the eve of a massive demonstration, fails to halt a second exodus via Czechoslovakia. The 'action programme', to be published at the Central Committee meeting on 8/10 November, promises much. But it may well be too late to save the SED, without a move on its 'leading role'.

Detail

2. In the evening of 3 November Krenz went on GDR television with an appeal to the citizens of the GDR to stand firm and to do all they could for their common homeland. 'I appeal again to those citizens who are thinking of leaving the GDR: have faith in our policy of renewal.'

[1] Repeated for Information Immediate to UKREP Brussels, Bonn, BMG Berlin, UKDEL NATO, Prague, Moscow, Washington; Priority to Paris, East European Posts; Routine to Peking, CICC(G).

[2] No. 28.

3. Details of the far reaching reforms promised by Krenz together with a further round of dismissals of the old guard from the Politburo are set out in MIFT. My 2 IFT covers the demonstration. (Both Saving to some.)[3]

4. Krenz has so far received two answers, neither satisfactory from his point of view. The most immediate came from the continuing stream of people leaving the GDR for the FRG via Czechoslovakia. The second and most damaging in my view, came from a record crowd of about a million demonstrators in the Alexanderplatz in East Berlin on 4 November (carried live on GDR television). The most tangible feeling was of antipathy to the ruling SED and the most insistent demand was for an end to its monopoly of power.

5. On 4 November a new GDR arrangement agreed with the Czechoslovak government came into effect 'temporarily until the entry into force of the (new) GDR travel law' under which people living in the GDR can leave on their ID cards and cross Czechoslovakia without a visa. All would be allowed to return to the GDR. The latest West German estimate today, 5 November, is that about 10,000 people have taken advantage of this to emigrate. Queues of cars are reported to be cutting across the small slice of Czechoslovakia which lies between the south west border of the GDR and Bavaria.

6. The draft of the new travel law is due to be published on 6 November for open discussion followed by ratification by the *Volkskammer*. It is not yet clear when it might come into effect. But it looks as if the Czechoslovak exit may remain open for a few more weeks at least. Party contacts have told us that the new travel law will enable people to travel freely to the West for 30 days with their families. We will see if this line is maintained in the light of the Czechoslovak experience.

Comment

7. Events are snowballing out of the SED's control. Every attempt to take the initiative has been overtaken by events. Offered a year ago, Krenz's package would have seemed revolutionary and could have gained the party the trust which it so critically lacks now. But Krenz's present concessions are seen as being exacted under duress. This together with the strong personal distrust of Krenz has undermined the effect of what has been done so far and promised for the future.

8. The struggle between the Party and the people has now focussed on power sharing—the leading role of the Party. Krenz has so far been unyielding on this while the demonstrators have become more insistent. I spoke on 3 November to Gerlach (head of the Liberal Democratic Party) who has called for the Government to resign. I reminded him that he had previously acknowledged the leading role of the Party. But only if the party had the confidence of the people, was his reply— and that is a widely held view.

9. The next few days will be critical for the SED. If their 'action programme' and new draft travel law fail to halt the exodus, the country will be on course for political and economic collapse. Krenz's gamble is that by allowing people to go and return and by offering a perspective of real political and economic reform, they will agree to stay. But so far his package lacks the critical ingredient of legally guaranteed power sharing. And that together with 40 years of accumulated dislike and distrust is likely to tilt the balance against him.

10. In the middle of a revolution, albeit a peaceful one, it is hard to predict the exact course of events. I believe very many East Germans would prefer to stay here

---

[3] Telegrams Nos. 355 and 356 of 5 November (WRE 014/2). Not printed.

but change the system. I also think that the changes on offer have made an impression on people and the *'wir bleiben hier'* (we remain here) element has become stronger. There are nevertheless many people who will continue to vote with their feet until the SED agree to move on the leading role of the party and put into effect the promises they are now making. If only 50 to 60 thousand more were to go then I think the economy could start on a downward, spiral which in a relatively short time scale would give rise to a second crisis. (Unless they get help from somewhere. Bertele has told me that he expects Minister Seiters here on 30 November.)

11. Honecker was dismissed at the same time as the earthquake hit San Francisco.[4] The after-shocks on the political St Andreas fault line in Europe are gathering rather than diminishing in intensity.

---

[4] On 17 October an earthquake measuring 7.1 on the Richter Scale hit the San Francisco Bay Area, killing 67 people.

No. 33

Minute from Mr Wall to Mr Adams

[WRL 020/4]

Confidential   FCO, *7 November 1989*

Enlargement of the EC and the German Question

The Secretary of State has seen the PUS's submission of 3 November and accompanying papers.[1] In addition to reading the new paper circulated by Mr Synnott,[2] he saw Sir J. Fretwell's minute of 20 October[3] and Mr Cooper's minute of 23 October,[4] both of which he found well worth reading. He would like to discuss these papers at the seminar on 15 November.[5]

At his bilateral with the Prime Minister last week, the Secretary of State suggested that she might hold a private seminar on the subject once we had assembled our own thoughts.

The Secretary of State wants to have a proper talk with Herr Genscher before long. At yesterday's Foreign Affairs Council, Herr Genscher invited the Secretary of State to visit Bonn. We are looking for dates.

J.S. WALL

---

[1] No. 30.
[2] No. 25.
[3] No. 23.
[4] Not found.
[5] No record of this seminar has been found.

No. 34

Letter from Sir C. Mallaby (Bonn) to Sir J Fretwell[1]

[*RS 021/17*]

Confidential   BONN, *8 November 1989*

Dear John,

The German Question

1. This letter pulls together some broader thoughts about the debate on the Federal Republic on the German Question, the prospects and our policy. It is intended partly as background thinking to our ad hoc reports in this fast-moving situation.

2. The big changes in the German question have so far been in the GDR. The one change in the Federal Republic is that reunification, which until recently was a distant, hypothetical aspiration, has now become much more. The Basic Law of the Federal Republic calls on the entire German people 'to achieve in free self-determination the unity and freedom of Germany'. That has been a long term aspiration which successive Federal governments have rather ritualistically supported. People now see the possibility of sufficient change in the GDR to allow significant change in the structure of the relationship between the two Germanies. Opinion polls show that 80% of the Federal German population is in favour of reunification. That has not changed in recent years. The novelty is that a majority—64% in one recent poll—now regards it as a real possibility.

3. West Germans now expect real reform in the GDR, but as I write still doubt that it will be enough to stop the demonstrations and the exodus. There is concern that there could be not only instability in GDR but even a breakdown in public order. There is a strong feeling that evolution in the GDR, not rapid change, would suit West German interests but does not at present look likely. West Germans realise that Soviet policy will remain of critical importance. The view here is that Gorbachev has evidently decided that reform in the GDR is less dangerous to that country's stability than no reform. But there is also a feeling that the Russians, because the GDR is their frontline state, will be more reluctant about a political transformation there than in Poland or Hungary and will seek to insist on maintaining the 'statehood' of the GDR. There is an impression here, but no confidence, that the Soviet Army in East Germany (which at 380,000 is larger than United States Forces in Europe) would not be used to halt political change.

Federal German Policy

4. The general conviction in the Federal Republic is that its future lies firmly in the West. People know that the Federal Republic has benefitted immensely, in freedom, security, peace and prosperity, from the Western connection. Kohl never stops stressing this when speaking of the German Question. Another example of the Federal Government's care on this subject has been its avoidance of the theme

---

[1] Copied to HM Representatives: NATO Posts, UKRep Brussels, Dublin, East Berlin, Moscow, Warsaw, Budapest, Vienna, British Commandant, Berlin, Consuls-General in the FRG, Commanders-in-Chief of BAOR and RAF (Germany).

of reunification per se, maintained today by Kohl in the *Bundestag* (my telno 1064).[2]

5. In relations with the GDR itself, there has long been a dilemma. Cooperating with the regime can give it legitimacy in the short term even when the aim is to undermine its viability as an autocracy in the longer term. Today, the abject unpopularity of the GDR regime makes cooperation with it especially questionable. The keynote of Kohl's and Genscher's policy towards the GDR is to call for reform and self-determination and the observance of human rights and CSCE obligations. As a stimulus Kohl has spoken of a comprehensive and far-reaching programme of support and cooperation, principally economic but also in science, technology, transport and environmental protection, if the GDR undertakes fundamental political and economic reforms. One openly declared motive in calling for reform is that it might cause the exodus to abate (see again my telno 1064).[2] The FRG has such a strong interest in this that cooperation with the old regime in East Germany on measures designed to persuade people to stay must be on the cards.

6. Another element in the Federal German attitude is Kohl's and Genscher's stress on the importance of not separating the future of Germany from the future of Europe. That is not only intended to reassure neighbours that the Germans will not seek some special destiny of their own. It reflects a view widely held for many years in the Federal Republic that improvement in East-West relations can solve the German Question. The proliferation over years of cooperation and contacts between the European states, East and West, in a so-called 'European Peace Order' (mooted in the Harmel Report) would take place in particular between the two Germanies; so that one day the two could be so close that reunification would be a purely formal act or might even be considered superfluous. We shall see whether the pace of events leaves this rather long term vision behind.

7. Kohl and Genscher see the European Community as having the role of magnet, stimulating reform in Eastern Europe and drawing Eastern Europe, economically and politically, towards the West. They want to drive ahead with West European integration, to increase this magnetic force and to head off suspicion of their own motives in the West. Their view will, I think, prevail over a minority view that favours deceleration in the Community to make it easier one day for East European countries, if they became democratic and achieved economic progress, to associate with the Community or even join it. But I expect the theme of the Community's relations with Eastern European countries, and the question of possible membership for the latter, to be important in Federal German attitudes to the Community in the coming years. One question for the future is whether Germany's pressure for further integration in the EC would relax if the GDR was included in it and was not in a position to go as fast as the FRG has wanted.

8. The SPD is not saying much about its policies on the German Question but most of its leading figures seem to agree generally with the Federal Government. The Greens see the German Question as an historical anachronism, and the wish for reunification as a reversion to dangerous precedents. They want close Inner-German relations. At the other extreme, the *Republikaner* claim to be the only party unequivocally supporting the injunction of the Basic Law to achieve German

---

[2] This telegram of 8 November reported that Herr Kohl continued to put all the emphasis on the need for reform in the GDR and 'again played down the theme of reunification, not even mentioning the word itself' (RS 021/17).

unity, and they want it to embrace the old German territories east of [the] Oder-Neisse line.

Possible Forms of German Unity

9. This aspect has not been much discussed in the Federal Republic, because it has so far been seen as hypothetical as well as difficult. If the two states do one day come together, it will not be in a centralised state like Bismarck's—'a fourth Reich'—since the FRG itself is a decentralised federation. Also, it is inconceivable nowadays that a reunified Germany might have some kind of mixed political system with elements of the East European communist model. That model is discredited in the eyes of the people of the GDR as well as the people of the Federal Republic.

10. As this Embassy has suggested in correspondence with the Department, a major change in the structural relationship between the two Germanies, if it became possible, might take various forms:

(*a*) Association: the proliferation of links and cooperation between the two states, some common infra-structure, free movement of labour and massive West German investment in the GDR. This would require considerable reform in the GDR.

(*b*) The 'Austrian solution': this would require pluralism in the GDR, which would continue to exist as a separate democratic state but would have relations with the Federal Republic as close as those of Austria today, or indeed closer because the GDR might be in the Community or at least would retain close links with it.

(*c*) Confederation: the Federal Republic and the GDR would retain separate governments in Bonn and East Berlin, but would share citizenship and many common structures, and would consult closely to develop as much common German policy as possible.

(*d*) Federation, which might follow after (*c*), would involve a single Federal German government and a state divided into *Länder* without any intermediate level of government.

11. One fundamental factor is the future alignment of Germany and its parts. For the foreseeable future it remains critical to the West that the Federal Republic should be in NATO and that Allied forces, including American, be stationed there (even if in reduced numbers). The Federal Government and the great majority of West Germans in responsible positions affirm that this country will stay firmly aligned to the West and that neutrality is not an option. But a public debate about neutrality could occur in due course. The possible outcomes at 10 (*a*) and (*b*) above would not require the abolition of existing security arrangements in Europe, though the GDR's relationship to the Warsaw Pact might become tenuous. But what if the Soviet Union offered reunification (10 (*c*) or (*d*)) in return for neutrality? I can see some West Germans being tempted. But if, as might be the case, the Soviet Union were acting from a position of weakness, in the face of the loss through change in the GDR of its security glacis in Europe, I can imagine the West Germans finding such an offer as resistible as in 1952, this time in the knowledge that things were anyway going their way. Less easy to foresee would be West German reactions in a situation where neutrality was not a Soviet ploy but an apparently logical response to a Soviet withdrawal from Eastern Europe. It is widely assumed that the outcome in 10 (*c*) above, and certainly 10 (*d*)—a federal reunited Germany, must require neutrality, since this would be the condition demanded by the Soviet Union. But if the Soviet position in Eastern Europe were

to collapse, the Russians might not be able to insist. The scope for keeping West Germany in NATO and/or Allied forces in West Germany should be a major subject for the studies recommended at the end of this letter.

12. Resolution of the German question would require a new deal for Berlin. West Berliners will feel a mixture of hope and anxiety if structural change in the relationship between the two Germanies comes into sight. Theoretically, reform and economic progress in the GDR could in the long term make the disadvantages for West Berlin of incorporation into the GDR seem less than the disadvantages and complications of remaining a political island. In the near term the Allies should think about the possible risk that unrest in East Berlin might cause major incidents at the Wall. More generally, we should maintain our guarantee of West Berlin's security while responding sensitively to public concerns there about aspects of our presence which may come to seem anachronistic.

13. The pace of change on the German Question will depend critically on what reform takes place in the GDR and whether it is punctuated by setbacks and crises, and on the policy of the Soviet Union. Assuming some continuing change in the GDR, we are likely during the 1990s to see, at a minimum, much greater cooperation between the two Germanies. The Federal Republic will probably become even more preoccupied with relations with East Germany and points East. The Federal Republic's ties with the West are likely to be maintained in the Alliance and developed in the Community, but their proportionate importance in Federal foreign policy may diminish with the rise of Eastern preoccupations. The prediction in my despatch of 10 April 1989 about the Federal Republic's reliability as an ally—that this country would remain an ally but become a much more difficult one—is reinforced by this analysis.[3]

14. If there is serious reform in the GDR, we are also likely to see structural change in the relationship between the two Germanies. Many people in the Federal Republic profess to expect one of the first two arrangements in paragraph 10 to be the answer to the German Question. That is indeed possible. But there are also reasons for expecting (*d*), i.e. reunification, to be the final outcome, possibly coming after one or more of the others. If, during a process of reform in the GDR, there were major setbacks or a crisis, might reform movements call for reunification as a means of guaranteeing freedom? In such circumstances, would a political party or charismatic leader in the Federal Republic issue a ringing appeal for a drive for reunification? West German opinion might then be swept by a wave of emotion supporting that appeal. And would the people of East Germany feel confident that a reformed system, once achieved there, would last if the country remained separate? Another reason for wondering whether a democratic East Germany would remain separate is that its raison d'être would be primarily external—the wishes of other countries especially neighbours and the Soviet Union—since the appeal to nationalism as a source of legitimacy is not available when another, bigger German state flourishes next door. Yet another reason is that German nationalism is one element in the psychology of West Germany today and seems unlikely to disappear. As to the timescale of structural change between the two Germanies, it is of course quite unpredictable. It depends on the pace of change in the GDR. Rapid collapse of the old regime there could bring early change between the two Germanies.

[3] No. 1.

15. We need to do all we can to maximise the chance that the Federal Republic will remain a reliable member of the West. That includes helping to point up the advantages that the Federal Republic gains from the Western connection. We should work hard at ministerial and official contacts. We should persist in our efforts, bilaterally and multilaterally, to coordinate policy in East-West relations. We should continue to show the Federal Republic that we understand its concerns about East Germany. We should consult closely and privately with France and the United States on subjects concerning Germany, especially those which can affect the Federal Republic's relations with its Western friends.

16. The German question is relevant to our policy on further integration in the Community. Germans determined to keep Germany in the West are always urging us to cooperate in further steps forward in the Community as a means of strengthening the Western ties of the Federal Republic. The Permanent Secretary in the *Auswärtiges Amt* has described this to me as a two-way life insurance policy: the Federal Republic gets embedded more deeply in the West and thus should be less tempted by any eastern option and we get greater confidence that the Federal Republic will not drift eastwards. I argued in my despatch of 10 April[4] that trade with the Community was a major and irreplaceable feature of Federal German interests. The Community, whether or not integration goes further beyond the Single Market, is essential to the Federal Republic. But it is also true that lack of progress in further developing the Community could give the impression here that western links could not produce further benefits; and as a result the attractions of devoting more attention to Eastern Europe, especially the GDR, could seem stronger. So I suggest that the importance of maintaining Germany's reliability be taken into account in forming our policy on further integration in the Community.

17. The German Question is also relevant to possible future enlargement of the Community. The Community's effectiveness as an instrument for maintaining the Federal Republic's strong connections to the West will be greater if the EC remains a Western organisation and could diminish in so far as members neutral between East and West were added.

18. I agree with Nigel Broomfield (his despatch of 12 October)[5] that we should try in the near future to develop a dialogue with the Soviet Union about the GDR. There are signs that the Russians might be willing. Such a dialogue could be useful were there to be a real crisis in the GDR.

19. Also like Nigel Broomfield, I believe that we need to do some serious private thinking about the future. We should consider, in the light of possible political, security and economic developments in East and West Europe, what future structures of the two Germanies are feasible and desirable. The existence of two democratic Germanies, as well as being an improvement on the status quo, could suit us well if the Federal Republic remained in NATO and the GDR was at most nominally in the Warsaw Pact. If it came to reunification, what conditions would make it as tolerable as possible for us? What would be the implications for our economic interests and for the Community and above all for NATO? We should make a plan to do what we can, if possible with the United States and France, to influence events so that the arrangement that suits us best can be promoted and the worst effects of other arrangements can be avoided or contained. As one of the four powers responsible for Berlin and Germany as a whole, we shall

---

[4] No. 1.
[5] No. 19.

have a hand in the eventual settlement, and we should exploit the influence we can derive from that.

Yours ever,

C.L.G. MALLABY

No. 35

Sir C. Mallaby (Bonn) to Mr Hurd[1]

No. 1077 Telegraphic [WRL 020/4]

Priority. Confidential   BONN, *9 November 1989, 6.47 p.m.*

My Telno 1073: UK Position on the German Question[2]

Summary

1. A recommendation about our public line on the German question, in the context of your visit to Bonn on 15 November.

Detail

2. The absence of any statement by a senior member of HMG on the German question comparable to those made recently by Mitterrand (my telno 1049)[3] and by Bush and Baker (Washington telnos 2794 and 2912)[4] has been commented on here. The German press, while noting News Department's statement on the resignation of the GDR Government, have begun to make comparisons (my TUR).[5] Hartmann (Teltschik's deputy in the Federal Chancellery) this morning remarked to my Minister that he hoped HMG, which had always been supportive, would say something in the near future. Hartmann emphasised that he was neither speaking on instructions, nor complaining, but we can take it that he reflects a general view in Kohl's entourage.

3. I recommend you make a public statement on the German question in connection with your visit here on 15 November—while you are here, if the programme permits, or before you come, if it does not. This could build on the statement made here by Mr Major on 20 September, the main point of which was the right of the German people to self-determination.[6] This remains the central point, but in the light of the movement of opinion in the FRG (my telno 1064)[7] I

---

[1] Repeated for information Priority to East Berlin, BMG Berlin.

[2] This telegram of 9 November reported that the FRG press had reported prominently the positive comments made by Leon Brittan (EC Commissioner for Competition) on the prospect of German unification, contrasting them with the absence of comparable statements from the Prime Minister or her colleagues (WRL 020/4).

[3] This telegram reported comments made by M Mitterrand during a press conference on 3 November following a Franco-German summit, including: 'I am not afraid of reunification . . . I see the German wish for reunification as legitimate. If they want it and can achieve it, then France will adapt its policy so as to be able to act in the best interests of Europe and of France' (WRG 021/6).

[4] Washington telegram No. 2794 of 26 October reported an interview with President Bush in the *New York Times* of 24 October, in which he expressed confidence in the FRG Government's handling of the German question (WRL 020/4). Washington telegram No 2912 not found.

[5] The East German Cabinet resigned on 7 November; the Politburo resigned the following day.

[6] No. 13.

[7] See No. 34, note 2. The telegram reported that 'Although the Federal Government is reticent about it, reunification is beginning to be a theme of the debate about the German question'.

judge that you will now need to say something about reunification. Article 7 of the 1955 Relations Convention, which specifies reunification with a democratic constitution, is the best starting point. It will be important to convey the impression that we express our firm current conviction. You will not want to follow the words that the Americans and French have used, but we must reckon that your statement will be subjected to textual analysis. In our own interests, it should not be thought to fall short in two respects: willingness to accept reunification, if that is the way things go, and confidence in the Federal Government to conduct FRG policy in ways which are consonant with Western interests.

CHAPTER II

10 November 1989 – 13 February 1990

No. 36

Letter from Mr Wall to Mr Powell (No. 10)

[*WRL 020/4*]

Confidential   FCO, *10 November 1989*

Dear Charles,

East Germany: Telephone Call by Chancellor Kohl

The Prime Minister's statement this morning will be welcome to the Germans.[1] The FRG Ambassador has said he was very pleased to hear it. When Chancellor Kohl telephones this evening, the Prime Minister may wish to take the line that recent developments in East Germany represent a triumph of freedom. The priority must now be the establishment of a genuinely democratic form of government. We shall give whatever practical help we can in coping with the refugees. The Prime Minister might also say to Chancellor Kohl that heads of government will clearly want to discuss developments in Eastern Europe at Strasbourg, and she hopes he will give a lead to that discussion.

Sir Christopher Mallaby had a meeting this morning with Seiters, Minister in charge of the Federal Chancellery, in company with the American and French Ambassadors.[2] Seiters stressed the historic nature of current developments. He referred to the need for help in Berlin, especially over accommodation. We have already been very helpful in Berlin (providing land, tents and blankets) and the

---

[1] Following a press conference on 9 November at which Herr Schabowski, probably inadvertently, confirmed that the GDR's new relaxed travel regulations would come into immediate effect, East Berliners started crossing the Wall and East German border guards made no attempt to stop them. First-hand accounts of the dramatic events of the night of 9-10 November are given in Series III, Vol. VI, Nos. 401-2. Mrs Thatcher's statement read:

I very much welcome the decision to lift travel restrictions on the people of East Germany, so that they can travel freely to the West. We all hope this is only a prelude to the dismantling of the Berlin Wall. Events are unfolding very rapidly and we must take them a step at a time. The priority must be to see a genuinely democratic form of government in East Germany. We fully support the demand of the East German people for free elections and a multi-party system.

. . . The response of the West German Government and people in providing refuge and jobs for those leaving East Germany—some 200,000 already this year—commands great admiration in this country. We have agreed to provide any practical help we can in coping with refugees at our military installations in West Berlin and in the Federal Republic' (WRL 020/4).

[2] German record of meeting in *Deutsche Einheit*, No. 78.

Berlin Mayor and *Senat* have pronounced themselves well satisfied. But further, more urgent help may be needed if the numbers swell: there is already an acute housing shortage there. MOD are able to make available some more land, in the FRG itself. We shall let you have details separately.

Chancellor Kohl is reaffirming the FRG's offer of economic help to the GDR provided that free elections and the end of one-party rule are bindingly declared.

Chancellor Kohl will be speaking later today also to Gorbachev, Krenz, Bush and Mitterrand.

Chancellor Kohl is to visit Berlin tonight for a large public meeting outside the *Rathaus* (City Hall), intended to mirror a similar event in 1961 when the Wall was erected.

The Federal authorities believe that the new liberal travel arrangements leave the East German authorities with no alternative but to hold free elections since, without them, there will be no holding back the exodus. The only question that remains is one of timing.

I am copying this letter to Brian Hawtin (MOD) and Trevor Woolley (Cabinet Office).

Yours,
J.S. WALL

No. 37

Letter from Mr Powell (No. 10) to Mr Wall

[WRL 020/4]

Confidential   10 DOWNING STREET, *10 November 1989*

Dear Stephen,

East Germany

Chancellor Kohl telephoned the Prime Minister this evening to discuss developments in East Germany.[1]

The conversation opened with the Prime Minister remarking that it was a great day for freedom. Chancellor Kohl said he wanted to give the Prime Minister his impressions following his visit to Berlin. But he would start by making a few remarks about Poland where he was returning tomorrow. The situation there was very difficult and the Poles needed support. The new government was not very practised in the art of politics but had great idealism. He would be writing to the Prime Minister and other colleagues at the end of his visit to give fuller impressions and make some suggestions. But there was one urgent point. The Poles were in negotiation with the IMF and he had urged them to get things straight as rapidly as possible. It is no less important that the IMF itself should act rapidly. He hoped that the British representative could be instructed to encourage the IMF to get through the negotiations with Poland as soon as possible, so that they could be completed by the end of November or early December at the latest. That would give the Polish Government a clear basis on which to pursue their economic policies. The Prime Minister said that she would discuss this with the Chancellor of the Exchequer. We certainly wanted to see the negotiations with the

---

[1] German record of conversation printed in *Deutsche Einheit*, No. 81.

101

IMF completed as soon as possible. She asked Chancellor Kohl to give the new Polish government and General Jaruzelski her warm regards.

The Prime Minister said that she had been watching the scenes in Berlin on television both last night and this morning. They were some of the most historic which she had ever seen. She was anxious to hear Chancellor Kohl's impressions. It seemed to her that the most important task now was to establish a genuine democratic government in East Germany. Chancellor Kohl said that the scene in Berlin was incredible. There were hundreds of thousands of people in the streets. He had attended a rally organised by the *Senat*, at which there had been a lot of left wing rowdies. Following that, the CDU had organised a rally with between 120-200,000 participants, at least half of whom were from East Berlin and elsewhere in the GDR. Enormous numbers of people had passed through the wall into West Berlin during the day, mostly just to have a drink, look around the shops and wander about. The most noticeable thing was that they were all happy. The Chancellor continued that he had visited Checkpoint Charlie and spoken to the young British soldiers there. They had never experienced anything like the scenes in their lives, with thousands of people going in both directions.

Chancellor Kohl said that one could not avoid the conclusion that the political system in East Germany had been mortally wounded. He was not sure what would happen next. A new government would probably be formed next week. But there still seemed to be two groups fighting for leadership of the Party. One group continued to believe that the GDR could do without pluralism. The other group was ready to follow the example of Poland and Hungary, but at least for the time being they were in a minority. Without real change, he did not think the situation would calm down. More and more people would leave and the economic situation would rapidly become disastrous. The next six weeks would be crucial. One thing that had struck him about the demonstrations in East Germany was the enormous discipline. He hoped that would remain the case. The West Germans would do everything possible to avoid anything provocative which could lead to conflicts or upheavals. He would like to keep in touch with the Prime Minister as the situation developed and contact her immediately if there was anything dramatic.

The Prime Minister asked whether the East Germans would take advice from anyone about the political situation. Chancellor Kohl did not think they would, for the time being at least. The Prime Minister continued that it would be a great mistake for them to do too little now. The demand for political change was so great that they must move towards genuine democracy. Chancellor Kohl said that Krenz had told him that he did not want to follow the Polish and Hungarian example. He had replied that he was very sceptical whether Krenz could succeed without doing so—and he had been proved right. The Prime Minister asked whether Chancellor Kohl was keeping in touch with President Gorbachev, who would be anxious about the turn which events had taken. Chancellor Kohl said that Gorbachev was indeed extremely concerned. He intended to speak to him within the next day or two and would say that without pluralism the situation in East Germany could not be resolved.

The Prime Minister thanked Chancellor Kohl for telephoning. It was important they should keep in touch. If he would like her to come over for half a day before the European Council in Strasbourg she would be delighted to do so. Alternatively he might like to come over here. Either way they must remain in contact. Chancellor Kohl said he thought this was a good idea and he would telephone the Prime Minister again on his return from Poland.

The Prime Minister referred to the help our Forces in Germany were providing for refugees from East Germany. Chancellor Kohl expressed gratitude for this.

I am copying this letter to Brian Hawtin (Ministry of Defence), John Gieve (HM Treasury) and to Trevor Woolley (Cabinet Office).

Yours sincerely,
C. POWELL

No. 38

Letter from Mr Powell (No. 10) to Mr Wall

[*WRE 014/2*]

Confidential   10 DOWNING STREET, *10 November 1989*

Dear Stephen,

East Germany

The Soviet Ambassador came to see the Prime Minister at 2200 hours tonight with what he described as an urgent personal message from Mr Gorbachev. I enclose the text which he handed over.[1]

After reading the note, the Prime Minister said that she had spoken to Chancellor Kohl earlier in the evening. The impression she had received was that the situation in Berlin was cheerful but orderly and that the West German Government was determined that it should not get out of hand. In her own public statement she had been at pains to emphasise that matters should develop step by step and that the most urgent task was to establish a genuinely democratic government in East Germany. Her main concern was that the present leadership in East Germany had not sufficiently appreciated the need for political reform. Only if they could hold out hope for the future to their people would they be able to stop the exodus from East Germany. Her own view was that people should be encouraged to stay in East Germany, and build a better life there. But it all depended on the willingness of East Germany's political leaders to carry through the necessary reforms.

The Soviet Ambassador said that what worried Mr Gorbachev most was that emotions might run high, leading to demonstrations and calls for reunification. There seemed to be some in West Germany who were keen to whip up such feelings. The Prime Minister said there had not been the slightest evidence of this in her talk with Chancellor Kohl. He had been at pains to emphasise the sober and cautious approach of the West German authorities. She thought he appreciated very well the sensitivities on the Soviet side. She had clearly understood Mr Gorbachev's insistence during their talks in Moscow that, while the countries of Eastern Europe could choose their own course in their domestic affairs, the borders of the Warsaw Pact must remain intact.

The Prime Minister continued that it would certainly be right for the Berlin Powers to keep in close touch. The Soviet Ambassador said that the key phrase in

---

[1] Not printed. An English translation of this message, also sent to President Mitterrand and President Bush, was published in *Cold War International History Bulletin* 12/13 (Fall/Winter 2001), p. 159.

Mr Gorbachev's message was the reference to the post-war realities, the co-existence of two German States. The Prime Minister repeated that her purpose had been to urge the need for a measured approach, with priority for establishing a genuine democracy in East Germany. She assumed that the Ambassador had reported the text of her various interviews earlier in the day. The Soviet Ambassador said that he had indeed done so and they had been noted with satisfaction. There were nonetheless worries in Moscow about public statements about reunification made by some of the other Western leaders.

I have subsequently spoken to General Scowcroft in the White House and given him an account of this exchange. He confirmed that the Americans had received a similar approach and had responded in very similar terms. They were not disposed to take at all an alarmist view of the Soviet approach, and were impressed more by its positive features. That said, there was certainly a risk that the situation would get out of hand. I said that I assumed that the Americans were making clear to the Russians that there was no intention of exploiting the present situation to the detriment of the Soviet Union's security. General Scowcroft confirmed that this was so.

I subsequently also informed Herr Neuer in the Federal Chancellery in Bonn.

You will no doubt want to take more formal action to draw this demarche to the attention of the Americans, French and Germans, and consider whether any further instructions are needed to our Mission in Berlin. The Prime Minister would also like the Foreign Secretary's advice on whether it would be appropriate for her to send messages to President Bush and President Gorbachev about the situation in the next few days.

I am copying this letter and enclosure to Brian Hawtin (Ministry of Defence) and to Trevor Woolley (Cabinet Office).

Yours sincerely,
C.D. POWELL

No. 39

Minute from Sir P. Wright to Mr Wall

[Wright Papers]

Secret and Personal   FCO, *10 November 1989*

The UK and Europe: US views

1. Following my talk with the Secretary of State on 8 November, you asked me, in your minute of that date:[1]

(*a*) to ask Sir Michael Alexander to write to No. 10 (copied to us) about his conversation with Blackwill, in effect repeating the points in his letter of 18 September[2] in a form which could be shown to the Prime Minister; and

(*b*) to let you have a speaking note on the handling of these questions for the Secretary of State's use at his bilateral with the Prime Minister on 14 November.

[1] Not printed.
[2] No. 12.

2. I duly discussed the first point with Sir Michael Alexander: who revealed to me that, in line with an arrangement of which Sir Geoffrey Howe was aware (and on which he had intended to brief the Secretary of State at the first convenient opportunity) he had in fact sent a personal letter to the Prime Minister last week. I attach a copy, together with his covering letter to Mr Powell.[3]

3. Sir Michael's letter to the Prime Minister did, of course, pre-date the Secretary of State's suggestion that he write to No 10 about the Blackwill conversation. He explained to me (with some embarrassment) that he would frankly find it very difficult now to write a further letter: the Prime Minister would find it incomprehensible why he had not covered the point earlier. I should add that he also made clear to me that it would cause him considerable difficulties if the Secretary of State, in talking to the Prime Minister, were to reveal any knowledge of his private exchanges with her.

4. I have, therefore, drafted the attached speaking note for the Secretary of State's use *without* any reference to the Alexander/Blackwill conversation, or indeed to any other of the pieces of evidence about US views which we have picked up.[4] In talking to the Prime Minister, however, the Secretary of State should bear in mind that she may perhaps feel somewhat 'under siege' from her advisers, private and otherwise, all of whom are currently urging her to take a much more forthcoming line on German reunification than her instincts would dictate. (On that, incidentally, I understand that the Prime Minister was frankly horrified by the sight of the *Bundestag* rising to sing *Deutschland über alles* when the news of developments on the Berlin Wall came in.)[5] Sir Percy Cradock has told me privately that he is putting to the Prime Minister today a note concentrating chiefly on analysis (on which he is, of course, well qualified, as a former Ambassador in East Berlin, to comment); but drawing the policy conclusion that the Prime Minister should above all aim to keep very close to Chancellor Kohl, and to ensure that her public statements on Germany will be seen there as supportive of him.[6]

5. I am submitting these papers today to give the Secretary of State time to consider them carefully over the weekend: but the speaking note might need some

---

[3] Sir M. Alexander's letter to Mrs Thatcher of 3 November, printed in Michael Alexander, *Managing the Cold War: a View from the Front Line* (London: RUSI, 2005, pp. 185-89), urged her to 'make a major statement on European issues', since it was 'vital that the German problem be acknowledged by HMG as being of crucial importance and that we make plain our determination to be involved, sympathetically, in the search for solutions' An extract from his covering letter to Mr Powell is quoted *ibid.*, p. 184. He told Mr Powell: 'the plain fact is that history is being made around us. As viewed from Brussels, HMG's silence and apparent non-involvement is becoming uncomfortably obvious.'

[4] Not printed. For the final version see Enclosure in No. 45.

[5] Mr Hurd minuted: 'Have not the words changed? I'd better know!' Sir P. Wright minuted to Mr. Wall on 15 November: 'to retain in your safe? (we must answer the S. of S's query).' On 15 November Mr Adams sent Mr Wall a copy of the score of the German national anthem (words by von Fallersleben, music by Haydn), which contained a note that in 1952 the third verse of von Fallersleben's poem (*'Einigkeit und Recht und Freiheit . . .'*) was substituted for the first (*'Deutschland, Deutschland über alles . . .'*).

[6] Sir Percy Cradock had been Ambassador in East Berlin 1976-78. His note to Mrs Thatcher of 9 November is paraphrased in Cradock, pp. 111-12. Sir P. Cradock argued that, whatever the Prime Minister's private reservations, 'we should hasten to embrace publicly what we cannot prevent. From the wider standpoint, what was happening was an immense victory for the West and for principles she had been foremost in advocating. It might not be an unalloyed pleasure for her. But it would be tragic if, because of this private qualification, we failed to be given the credit due and allowed ourselves to be edged away from the centre of influence in the new Europe that was emerging.'

adjustment on 13 November in the light of fast-moving events on the ground; any refinements in the public line taken by the Prime Minister and other Ministers (on which I see the Secretary of State had a very useful discussion with van den Broek in The Hague yesterday); and the telephonic contacts today between the Prime Minister and Kohl and the Secretary of State and Genscher. We shall also need to consider, in the light of the Secretary of State's bilateral with the Prime Minister on 14 November, how our advice on handling this subject with the President might best be incorporated into written briefing for her visit to Camp David.

6. I should mention, finally, that the draft speaking note incorporates the comments of Mr Gillmore, Mr Kerr and Mr Ratford (in Sir John Fretwell's absence at a POCO meeting in Paris today). In showing them the draft, therefore, I have had to let all of them know of the existence, but not the contents, of the Prime Minister's recent exchange of messages with Gorbachev.[7]

P. WRIGHT

[7] Mr. Hurd minuted on 11 November: 'Noted'.

No. 40

Sir R. Braithwaite (Moscow) to Mr Hurd[1]

No. 1883 Telegraphic [WRE 014/2]

Confidential   MOSCOW, *11 November 1989, 1.22 p.m.*

Soviet Attitude to Change in East Germany and Eastern Europe

Summary

1. Gorbachev's policy in Eastern Europe is being overrun by events. This has implications for his domestic position as well as his foreign policy. It is in the Western interest to help him through this critical period: he kept his silence in public, but presumably sees joint crisis management as preferable to other options. I doubt if the West can wait until his Summit with Bush.

2. This telegram comments on the Soviet view of events. My 2 IPTs [*sic*: IFTs][2] contain recommendations: essentially that the Prime Minister should write to Gorbachev before she sees President Bush.

Detail

3. Despite the spectacular events of recent weeks, Soviet policy in Germany is what it was before Honecker fell (my telegram 1702 of 6 October):[3] out-of-date, incoherent, and shot through with potentially dangerous internal contradictions. But Gorbachev's underlying dilemma of four weeks ago has now become a pressing crisis. It cruelly highlights the contrast between his requirement to maintain the stable post-war order in Central Europe (not least as a framework for

[1] Repeated for information Immediate to Washington, Paris, Bonn, East Berlin, BMG Berlin and UKDEL NATO.
[2] Nos. 41 and 42.
[3] This telegram, entitled 'Germany = Gorbachev's dilemma', summarised his predicament as follows: 'Gorbachev goes to the GDR without a coherent policy. His overriding need for stability there conflicts with forces he himself has generated. While he shuts his eyes and hopes that the German question will go away, events on the ground are overtaking him' (WRL 020/4).

the Soviet armies there until these can be reduced or withdrawn following an orderly east-west negotiation), and the forces of change which he has unleashed within the Soviet Union and its empire. This is becoming a major test to [*sic*] Gorbachev's capacity to make policy in a crisis, of his ability to hold his government together, and perhaps of his personal authority. We have no direct evidence of divisions within the leadership on this issue—but in the eyes of many Russians it must sharpen an image of Gorbachev as a leader presiding over simultaneous internal and external disintegration. The stilted and old-fashioned language of his message to the Prime Minister,[4] a desperate appeal rather than a constructive proposal, shows how far he has to go towards constructing a coherent new policy.

4. In public the leadership have offered virtually no guidance this week. The only public comment has been through routine press briefing by MFA press spokesman Gerasimov, trying as best he can to adhere to the existing line (reported by separate telegram).[5] Not much even of Gerasimov's line has filtered through to the Soviet press.

5. Meanwhile the gap between events on the ground and Soviet strategy is widening. The strategy runs roughly as follows:

(*a*) Over the past years the Soviet Union has proclaimed the 'de-ideologisation' of internal relations and an end—if the West will comply—to the Cold War.

(*b*) What has failed in Eastern Europe, according to Soviet strategists, is not socialism but Stalinism. Stalinism has given socialism a bad name, helped to provoke the Cold War, had become untenable internationally, and was imposing burdens which the USSR could no longer support.

(*c*) It has therefore been in Soviet interests actively to promote Destalinisation in Eastern Europe and an end to monolithic regimes based on a single concept of socialism (Zhivkov is the latest victim).[6] But they should be replaced by forms of government which were still 'socialist', though popularly supported and adapted to local circumstances. (Gerasimov's 'Sinatra doctrine': they can go their own way).

(*d*) While these changes are taking place, stability and the essential framework of the post-war order must be preserved. This means that in the medium term (say the next ten years):

— there should be no question of changing post-war boundaries. Now is not/not, in the Soviet view, the time to address 'the German Question':

—Warsaw Pact membership should not be changed, though the Warsaw Treaty Organisation should progressively adapt its structures and evolve from a 'military/political' into a 'political/military' alliance:

—the balance between the Warsaw Pact and NATO should be sustained, while force levels are reduced through negotiation.

(*e*) The fundamental relationship between East and West in Europe should change only after and through negotiations to remove military confrontation. It

---

[4] See No. 38, note 1.

[5] No. 1881 of 11 November, reporting a press briefing on 10 November. Mr Gerasimov stated, *inter alia*: 'The new leadership of the GDR is carrying out a package of measures to renew socialism, stabilise the political system and democratise social life, these are not piecemeal measures. They are full-scale transformations affecting all spheres of life in the Republic and its contacts with the outer world' (WRE 014/2).

[6] Todor Zhivkov had been replaced as General Secretary of the Bulgarian Communist Party on 10 November after a 35-year rule.

should not be precipitated by internal changes in Eastern countries. Military barriers should be dismantled before political barriers, not vice versa. Otherwise military forces (notably the Soviet forces in East Germany), will be left stranded, and instability will ensue.

(*f*) In the long term, this will lead to 'the parallel and symmetrical merger of blocs in the common European home, with unnecessary walls disappearing' (to quote one Soviet commentator). At that distant point the German Question may answer itself.

6. The pace of events in the GDR threatens steps (*d*) and (*e*) in this strategy. The Soviets must fear that Krenz will not have time to establish a distinctive form of East German socialism, and that East Germany will not wait for the orderly processes of multilateral East/West negotiation. And the popular movement, which has so far claimed Gorbachev as an ally, may well turn against the Russians who stand as a visible barrier to reunification. What then happens to the Soviet troops there?

7. Gorbachev's problem is now to control the forces he has unleashed. I do not think the Russians know how to do this. Hence their public silence. Hence their increasingly unrealistic attempts to avoid addressing the question of Germany's future, and to try to persuade others that this question should not be addressed for the time being (the criticism of Western statements by Zamyatin in YTURS: Yakovlev's remarks to Brzezinski in my telno 1865).[7] Hence also the tone of Gorbachev's message to the Prime Minister. It is very difficult to discuss this problem with Soviet officials, for obvious reasons: but when we get near to it, their automatic response is that it is as much our problem as theirs.

8. Given the Soviet military and political stake in East Germany, it would be almost impossible for any Soviet leadership simply to let events take their course there. We must assume they are looking at a number of policy options, including (as Zamyatin's demarche shows) crisis management with the west. In MIFT[8] I look at ways we might respond to their immediate concerns.

[7] In this telegram of 6 November Sir R. Braithwaite commented that Mr Yakovlev's remarks reinforced his impression, and that of his US and West German colleagues, that 'Soviet thinking about the future of Eastern and Central Europe, and especially Germany, is at a very embryonic stage. Theory, and even day to day policy making, are unable to keep up with the pace of events' (WRL 020/4).
[8] No. 41.

No. 41

Sir R. Braithwaite (Moscow) to Mr Hurd[1]

No. 1884 Telegraphic [WRE 014/2]

Confidential   MOSCOW, *11 November 1989, 1.42 p.m.*

MIPT: East Germany—Possible Response to Gorbachev[2]

1. I note that you may be sending me instructions.

[1] Repeated for information Immediate to Washington, Paris, Bonn, East Berlin, BMG Berlin and UKDEL NATO.
[2] No. 40

2. I recommend that the Prime Minister should respond as quickly as possible—in writing and with as much substance as possible in the time available—to Gorbachev's message.[3] Joint crisis management with the West is only one of a number of options which we must assume the Russians are debating. Gorbachev may be under pressure—perhaps from his colleagues, or even the General Staff, who may be increasingly worried about the role and security of their force in East Germany in the event of an uncontrollable crisis there—to act unilaterally, or bilaterally with the East German apparatus. To head this off, the West should consider ways of drawing the Russians into dialogue. In particular, some means needs to be found of filling in the three week gap between now and Gorbachev's summit with Bush. That will help Gorbachev to show his domestic critics that he has a viable policy, and that the West is supporting it rather than exploiting his troubles.

3. In MIFT,[4] I suggest elements for a written reply by the Prime Minister to Gorbachev's message. I recommend that I should be instructed to deliver this message by the most direct available means. I have suggested that the emphasis should be on proposals for practical action. This is intended to defuse immediate Soviet concern about the destabilisation of Europe and the risk of a headlong rush towards German reunification.

4. Aside from private messages and a measure of practical co-operation, you will also be considering what further line we should take in public. The Russians will have been reassured by the emphasis given in British statements over the past 24 hours to maintaining the present framework of NATO and the Warsaw Pact. But they will have been alarmed by triumphalist statements by leading West Germans on both left and right. I cannot judge from here what chance we have of cooling rhetoric in the FRG or the United States. I am acutely aware of the—legitimate—popular pressures building up in both Germanies. But I hope that we can make the obvious points to the Western Allies that every statement about German reunification strengthens the hand of those Russians who must be advocating measures to protect the post-war settlement.

---

[3] No. 38, note 1.
[4] No. 42

No. 42

Sir R. Braithwaite (Moscow) to Mr Hurd[1]

No. 1884 Telegraphic[2] *[RS 021/17]*

Confidential   MOSCOW, *11 November 1989, 2.03 p.m.*

My 2 IPTs: Possible Message to Gorbachev[3]

1. Elements for a reply from the Prime Minister to Gorbachev's message might include:

---

[1] Repeated for information Immediate to Washington, Paris, Bonn, East Berlin, BMG Berlin and UKDEL NATO.
[2] This should evidently have been telegram No. 1885.
[3] Nos. 40 and 41.

(*a*) Analysis of the situation based on the Prime Minister's interview with the press on 10 November, emphasising our agreement that it needs to be managed within the framework of the Quadripartite Agreements, while looking forward to a longer term settlement which would take account of a CFE agreement. This section of the message would emphasise that there was no prospect of stability unless the GDR leadership responded to popular demands for reform and introduced a political system which reflected these (i.e. this point would be made as an analytical proposition rather than a Western political slogan):

(*b*) Re-emphasis that the Western Allies have no wish or intention to interfere in developments in the GDR: we have made this point publicly and will continue to do so:

(*c*) At the same time reassurance that, while the West has a limited role to play and it is up to the people of the GDR to determine their future, we believe that it is in all our interests that current developments should be managed cooperatively between East and West.

(*d*) Mention of the fact that the Prime Minister would be having talks with President Bush on 14 November, and that she would be glad to convey to Bush personally any points which Gorbachev might like to make in response.

2. Moscow is not the best vantage point from which to make recommendations on how to pursue the point in para 1 (*c*) above. But seen from here it will be important to try to lock the Russians into Quadripartite discussion of how to proceed as a means of reducing the risk of hasty unilateral action taken in response to Soviet domestic or Warsaw Pact pressures and of calming Soviet nerves. This could perhaps be achieved in a framework of a Quadripartite combined with inner German talks on the model of the negotiations which led to the Quadripartite and related agreements. But of course a response to Gorbachev's message will not wait for agreement among the Four on modalities such as this, let alone the agenda for such talks, even if this suggestion is not legally impossible, practically unmanageable, or simply too complicated to put together in the face of fast moving developments.

No. 43

Mr Broomfield (East Berlin) to Mr Hurd[1]

No. 381 Telegraphic [*WRE 014/2*]

Confidential   EAST BERLIN, *13 November 1989, 9.10 a.m.*

My Telno 377: Future Developments in the GDR[2]

Summary
1. A new chapter in Germany's post war history.

---

[1] Repeated for information Immediate to Bonn, BMG Berlin, Washington, Moscow, Paris, UKDEL NATO; Routine to Eastern European Posts; Saving to EC Posts, UKREP Brussels, Peking.

[2] In this telegram of 11 November Mr Broomfield commented on the reformist 'action programme' produced by the SED Central Committee. It was, in his view, an uneasy compromise between real and tactical reformers: 'I would put Modrow in the first category and Krenz in the second' (WRE 014/2).

Detail

2. It is not for me to comment on the effect on West Berlin and the FRG of the influx of some three million East Germans over the past four days. But viewed from East Berlin the last four days mark a decisive change in the political life of the GDR.

3. Even though 4.2 million visas were issued since 9 November, only 10,144 were for emigration according to GDR figures. This is an encouraging ratio for the leadership, and indeed there are reports of people returning. But the situation remains fluid, the exodus could begin again at any time if the leadership started to resile on the numerous promises they have given in the last few days about new policies. The Politburo will have to learn to live under this sword of Damocles.

4. The breaching of the Berlin Wall, the opening of a new crossing at Potsdamer Platz, the scene of the 1953 uprising and the heart of old Berlin, by the Mayors of East and West Berlin, are deeply symbolic acts. The millions who crossed into West Berlin and the FRG since 9 November are fundamental political facts for the future of this country.

5. The tears and euphoria will die down and no doubt aggravations and resentments will surface in some areas but first hand knowledge of the other German state and of their friendly reception there over this weekend has spread very widely among the population here and not just as before, among the privileged few with relatives in the West. This cannot be taken away again without risking an overwhelming political reaction.

6. Krenz may claim as he did on GDR television on 11 November after talking to Kohl and agreeing to meet 'soon', that what had happened were sovereign decisions by the GDR and that for him reunification was not on the agenda. But power has passed in substantial measure to the people and it is they who from now on will increasingly decide the future of this country. How they will decide is not yet clear.

7. Unless a cataclysm occurs in the Soviet Union and sets back with it the reforms in Poland and Hungary I can not see how a rapid process of growing together of the two German states can be avoided. Krenz may be replaced by Modrow, who may succeed for a time in making the Party popular again. There is wide support among the bloc parties as well as the protest groups for the principles of socialism variously defined. But the present system of planning the economy based on widespread public ownership can not satisfy the people's demands, sharpened as they will be by increasing familiarity with West Berlin and the FRG.

8. Whether in a dramatic move to stave off economic collapse in the next few months or in a more gradual process, the strength of the FRG economy acting on the structural and systemic weaknesses of the GDR is bound to have a profound effect. (I think it impossible that the structural alterations to the GDR's economy can take place by the time Kohl and Krenz have their first meeting in November/December. And without these alterations Kohl has said, quite sensibly in my view, investment from the FRG will not be attracted to the GDR. The threat of imminent economic collapse looks to be a more likely trigger for West German assistance than slow structural change.)

9. I do not think it fanciful to see something of the same process happening on the political front with existing links between parties in East and West Germany. The CDU (West) has just begun to have contact with the CDU (East). The same is true for the SPD (West) and the SDP (East, still unofficial) whose membership of

the Socialist International the former will support.[3] The FDP (West) has long had links with the LDPD (East, 'liberal'). The SED will derive little benefit from its close contacts with DKP (West) and the SEW (West Berlin).

10. There will no doubt be many twists and surprises in the way events actually work out between the two German states. But from the point of view of our policy towards the GDR we should take note of underlying realities which the events of the last few days and weeks have exposed so clearly.

---

[3] The *Sozialdemokratische Partei* (SDP) had been founded in October 1989 as a counterpart to the West German *Sozialdemokratische Partei Deutschlands* (SPD). It was renamed SPD in January 1990 and was united with the West German SPD in September 1990.

No. 44

Sir C. Mallaby (Bonn) to Mr Hurd[1]

No. 1098 Telegraphic [WRG 026/11]

Confidential   BONN, *13 November 1989, 7.34 p.m.*

Your Visit to Bonn 15 November: Scene Setter

Summary

1. Turning point in post war German history seems in sight. Domestic debate beginning on new basis for relations with the GDR. Federal Government wants to consult close allies. Genscher riding high. German question, Eastern Europe, European integration and arms control at the top of his agenda. Will want a good discussion of these. Opportunity to get your views across and lay basis for close contact in months ahead. Recommended press line.

Detail

2. West Germans feel increasingly that a turning point in the post war history of Germany and Europe is coming into sight. The great satisfaction of recent days with people witnessing the dramatic events in Berlin via television, is giving way to debate about relations with the GDR (my telno 1096).[2] There is greater confidence that some serious reform will come. Fears of a breakdown in public order in the GDR have receded for the moment. The pressure of new immigration on resources here has eased as the great majority of visitors from the GDR are not (not) staying in the FRG. The Government needs a strategy and does not have one. Part of being master of events will be to be seen to consult, especially with the 3 Berlin Powers, over issues affecting the Alliance as a whole. They will want to keep in step over handling the Soviet Union.

---

[1] Repeated for information Immediate to BMG Berlin; information Priority to Paris, Washington, Moscow, East Berlin, Warsaw, Budapest, UKREP Brussels and UKDEL NATO.

[2] Reporting on 'the mood in the Federal Republic' in this telegram of 13 November, Sir C. Mallaby commented: 'The political statements are deliberately restrained. One purpose is to discourage emotions among the people, another to avoid causing concern among neighbours, especially reforming states in Eastern Europe. The press mostly echoes the sobriety of the politicians. The tone is certainly not triumphalist. The element of surprise at the dramatic developments is still strong' (WRG 021/1).

Genscher's Position

3. Genscher seems in reasonably good health and politically is riding high. He is currently the most popular politician in the FRG. He feels that his forecasts about East West relations and reform in the Warsaw Pact have been borne out.

4. He can be irritating, sometimes devious, and some of his themes—notably full speed ahead to European Union—are against our interests. But he is being responsible about the German question. He does not use the word reunification. He insists that Federal policy should continue to be based full square on the Community and NATO. He has been moved by recent events in the GDR, where he grew up and stayed until 1952 (aged 25). He makes regular visits to his home town there. A few months ago, he said to the *Bundestag* that in his oath of office as Foreign Minister he had undertaken to represent the interests of all Germans.

5. At the top of Genscher's agenda are:
—breaking down the barriers between the German people:
—the emancipation of Eastern and the rapid integration of Western Europe, and the interpenetration of the two halves of the continent:
—early progress in arms control.

Inner German Relations

6. Genscher will have a lot to say when you meet. I think he will be cautious on substance and will not suggest that the time has come for a major change in the role of the Allies in Berlin. But it will be right to show that, while discharging our responsibilities in Berlin with understanding and efficiency, we are willing to move with the times, adjusting our practices in cooperation with the Berlin and Federal authorities. I suggest you welcome Genscher's proposal for thorough discussion of the German question among the four Foreign Ministers on 13 December.

7. Our good relations with Moscow enhance our standing in Genscher's eyes and our influence with the *Auswärtiges Amt*. He will want to know your views on handling the Russians. He agrees that they should be reassured about events concerning Berlin and the GDR.

8. Genscher will probably thank you for UK help with accommodation of resettlers in Berlin and the FRG. It would be helpful to state our readiness to consider more assistance if needed.

Eastern Europe

9. Genscher attaches great importance to the process of revivifying Eastern Europe. He would be interested to hear at first hand about our 'know how' programmes for Poland and Hungary.[3] Our readiness over the last few months to work together with the Germans over *Ostpolitik* has met with a consistently warm response from the *Auswärtiges Amt* (as well as from the Federal Chancellery). This is an area where the French have tended to hang back, and where we can gain from getting close. It would be useful if you and Genscher were to agree that, in the wake of the talks between officials in London on 24 October, we and the Germans should take forward our bilateral cooperation in this field.

Arms Control

10. In Berlin on 10 November Genscher repeated his call for early progress in arms control negotiations in step with political developments and improvements in human rights. The CSCE process, which integrates all three, is at the heart of his

---

[3] The Know-How Fund for Poland had been launched in June 1989. In October 1989 it was announced that the Fund would be extended to Hungary with effect from 1990.

policy. Even before the latest developments, he and other Germans saw CFE and the parallel negotiations on further confidence and security building measures as means towards the larger goal of overcoming the division of Europe. He will now press harder than ever for a CFE agreement during 1990. As that comes into sight, we can expect him to press for NATO to start preparing for SNF arms control negotiations, so that he can face the electorate in December 1990 with a CFE agreement in the bag and SNF negotiations on the way.

Press Line

11. The Federal Government has welcomed the statements by the Prime Minister and yourself since the GDR opened its borders. You will be expected in Bonn and Berlin to comment on the German question. The keynote, I suggest, should be to welcome the new freedom of movement and call for democratic reform in the GDR including free elections involving different parties competing on an equal basis (i.e. without the leading role of the SED guaranteed). If asked about reunification, I suggest that you repeat the formula ('we would welcome unification based on free institutions such as those . . . in the FRG') in your interview on BBC World Service on 10 November.

12. See separate telegram on EC issues.[4]

---

[4] Not found.

No. 45

Minute from Mr Adams to Sir J. Fretwell, with Minute by Sir J. Fretwell

[*Wright Papers*]

Secret and Personal   FCO, *14 November 1989*

The Prime Minister's visit to Camp David

1. The PUS had a word with you yesterday about the speaking note on Germany for the Secretary of State's use with the Prime Minister later today. You saw a draft at the end of last week, of course.[1]

2. I now attach a copy of the note, in the form in which it was submitted on 10 November.[2] The PUS would be very grateful if you would have a quick look at it, and let the Private Secretary have any amendments or updatings in the course of this morning. Subject to your views, the PUS thinks that the general thrust of the note remains valid, but that somewhere we should aim to fit in references to:

—the Prime Minister's telephone conversation with Kohl on 10 November;[3]

—her speech in the City last night;[4]

—the EC meeting in Paris on 18 November;[5] and

---

[1] See No. 39.
[2] Not printed. Final version printed as enclosure in this document.
[3] No. 37.
[4] No. 46, note 5.
[5] In his capacity as Chairman of the European Council, President Mitterrand had called a special meeting of EC Heads of Government to discuss developments in Central and Eastern Europe.

—the Secretary of State's prospective visit to Berlin on 16 November.[6]

G. D. ADAMS

Secret and Personal   FCO, *14 November 1989*

1. I have incorporated these additions in a slightly revised draft, attached.

2. I am convinced that if we were to adopt a policy of opposing German re-unification either publicly or privately, we should soon find we were standing alone, with grievous damage to our relations with the FRG and serious harm to our relations with the US. When the tide of history is bringing a chance of freedom and democracy in Eastern Europe, with the prospect of reducing or even eliminating the Soviet presence, the Americans would have no sympathy with a policy which put all that at risk in order to maintain the division of Germany. The French would not stand against that tide either, whatever they may say in private. It will soon become apparent, if it is not already, if our tone is markedly colder than that of other Western governments. We can work constructively to help manage change, taking account of existing alliance structures and of a possibly greatly expanded European Community role in relation to Eastern Europe. Our role in Berlin will give us an important handle on events. But we cannot try to maintain the artificial division of Germany as an end in itself.

J. FRETWELL

ENCLOSURE IN NO. 45

SPEAKING NOTE FOR USE WITH THE PRIME MINISTER ON 14 NOVEMBER

The Prime Minister's Visit to Camp David[7]

Events moving in Germany very fast. Not necessary for us to respond publicly at every juncture. Your statement on 10 November is acceptable to the Federal German Government, and adequate for the time being. As I have told you, I have called an in-house meeting this week to review the position. Much common ground with the Dutch (I saw van den Broek last week); I shall see Genscher in Bonn tomorrow and visit Berlin on Thursday morning.

Our primary objective should be to sustain Kohl. As Sir Christopher Mallaby has pointed out, his re-election as Chancellor offers the best prospect of binding Germany to the Alliance and the Community. *Need to consider, therefore, how best to support him, both privately and publicly.* Your telephone conversation with him on 10 November established useful common ground.

You will have seen his speech to the *Bundestag* on 8 November,[8] when he appeared to go out of his way to thank Bush and Mitterrand for their supportive statements (Mitterrand's statement attached).[9]

Your Guildhall speech set out our priorities:[10] we do not want a beauty contest over who can appeal most to German public opinion but nor do we want to appear markedly cooler than the others. A common line emerging from the 18 November

---

[6] No. 52.

[7] Mrs Thatcher was to meet President Bush at Camp David on 24 November.

[8] No. 34, note 2.

[9] Not printed. See No. 35, note 3.

[10] See No. 46, note 5.

Paris meeting would be useful in this regard. *The US/Germany link may be the key.* The Americans have devoted considerable effort to their links with the French and (particularly) the Germans. We know that they attach particular importance to the London/Bonn relationship, and to your relationship with Kohl personally. In this context, noted that *Bush said publicly recently that he 'did not share the concerns expressed by some Europeans over German reunification'.*

When you speak to Bush at Camp David, therefore, think it important that your central theme be *support for Kohl.*

We all have our worries about the future: and I am conscious that others (e.g. Mitterrand to you at the beginning of September—although for reasons of policy he would *never* allow them to become public) share those anxieties.[11] *May* be possible to share some of this thinking very privately with President Bush.

But there must be a real *danger that concerns expressed by us, however privately, may eventually reach the ears of Kohl and his advisers.* For example, Zamyatin tackled me on this subject at the Soviet National Day last week—with explicit reference to your exchange of letters with Gorbachev—in circumstances which were by no means private.[12] Furthermore, although it has been very tightly held on our side, we know that at least the fact—and possibly the substance—of your exchanges with Mitterrand in September has got back to the Germans. *The French may be with us in their hearts, but we must expect them to play a very canny game in talking to the Germans.*

All the signs are that the Americans and the Germans are co-ordinating very closely over all this. There are also signs of a much closer link between Bush and Mitterrand since the Mitterrands visited Kennebunkport in the summer.[13] I conclude that *we must make it clear to Bush that we are prepared fully to join in, and that we accept that a sound political and security framework for Europe, in which we, the French and the Germans are cooperating closely, is the best way to lock West Germany into the Alliance and the Community.*

[11] See No. 26, note 3.
[12] Nos. 38 and 50.
[13] Walker's Point in Kennebunkport, Maine, the Bush family's summer residence.

No. 46

Mr Broomfield (East Berlin) to Mr Hurd[1]

No. 387 Telegraphic [WRE O14/2]

Confidential   EAST BERLIN, *14 November 1989, 3 p.m.*

My Telno 386: GDR Internal Developments: Policy[2]

Summary

1. Some suggestions for our policy on the GDR. We should concentrate on political reform.

[1] Repeated for information to Desk by 5.30 p.m., Bonn and Moscow; information Immediate Washington, Paris, UKDEL NATO, BMG Berlin and UKREP Brussels; information Routine to Warsaw, Prague, Budapest and Sofia; and information Saving to other East European Posts.
[2] This telegram of 14 November reported the GDR's new frontier crossing arrangements, including the opening of new crossing points and the ending of border guards' orders to shoot (WRE 014/2).

Detail

2. On the assumption that our immediate objectives in relation to the GDR are:

(*a*) that the people of the GDR should be given a genuine opportunity to decide their future (including their relationship with the FRG) without having their options foreclosed through overwhelming political or economic pressures,

(*b*) to ensure that nothing occurs that would put at risk Gorbachev's position in the Soviet Union,

I offer the following thoughts which are based on the underlying realities here.

3. The exodus to the FRG has slowed down considerably because people here are, for the time being, prepared to see whether the system can be changed from within. It will start again if either the political process breaks down or there is an economic collapse. It is possible to make political changes more quickly than economic reforms and that is what in fact what the majority of the people here want at the moment. The popular slogans are for free elections and an abolition of the leading role of the Party.

4. The final guarantee of political reform is free, fair and democratic elections. The key instrument in securing such elections is a properly drafted electoral law. I therefore recommend that in calling for free elections, both in public and in any private contacts with the GDR, Western Ministers should combine references to elections with a reference to the need for very rapid agreement on a democratically-based electoral law.

5. Although the opposition groups are not well equipped to fight a general election (my telno 378),[3] they may in practice find it impossible to withstand pressure from the streets for this. They would face the prospect of losing rank and file support if they urged delay and there is also the danger that the whole political process might be brought to a halt by an economic crisis. This is a question which is relatively impervious to external influence, and indeed most Western leaders have already called for free elections. Provided they took place on the basis of a satisfactory electoral law (allowing for new political parties), I have no doubt that the increasingly untame bloc parties together with any others that might by then have been permitted (e.g., the SDP) would constitute a large majority of parliament even if opposed by a reforming SED led by Modrow. And although not ideal, this would at least break the mould of the SED monopoly of power.

6. Western public statements should not refer to reunification, to the GDR's role in the Warsaw Pact, still less to Germany's 1937 frontiers. Apart from causing acute concern in Moscow, such references are unpopular among the general public here.

7. An economic crisis may be unavoidable. But a senior member of the FRG permanent representation told me today that to avoid another exodus, and for general political reasons, the FRG would be bound to offer help (excluding long term structural funds) to stave this off.

8. If we are to have some influence on the FRG's policy in this area, then it can only come through a UK contribution to a wider programme of assistance on the lines of our approach to Poland and Hungary.[4]

---

[3] In this telegram of 11 November Mr Broomfield reported that Frau Bärbel Bohley, a leader of New Forum, had 'told a member of Chancery on 11 November that free elections held too soon would not be a good thing. The opposition groups were too small and needed to organize themselves first' (WRE 014/2).

[4] See No. 44, note 3.

Comment

9. I do not believe opinion polls which claim to reflect the 'views of the GDR population' on reunification with the FRG (see report in *The Times* on 13 November). The attitude of people here to that question is changeable. It is affected by the political conduct of their own Government and the economic conditions in which they live. Most of the leaders of the unofficial parties have opposed reunification. The bloc parties have hitherto also opposed it and will almost certainly continue to do so. How far they reflect the views of the people is not clear. But the fact that so many have returned to the GDR after visiting the west is significant.

10. I judge there to be at least a possibility of delaying 'reunification' for some time (even though in my despatches I have stated my belief that in the longer term it is likely principally because of the role of Berlin). And if the question can be prevented from becoming actual for the next two/three years then that would at least allow the main Soviet concerns to diminish as a result of success in the conventional arms negotiations in Vienna. We would have got the German question and arms control back in the right order.

11. It is for this reason, and because political reform is now increasingly equated here with free elections, that I recommend we should put our weight behind pressure for political reform on the lines taken by the Prime Minister's references to the GDR in her Mansion House speech on 13 November.[5] As far as the GDR is concerned it is the best hope of convincing people that they should stay here and build its future (and not vote with their feet for de facto reunification with the FRG) still less of starting to see it as a conscious political goal.

12. On the economic front, the FRG will clearly play the leading role. The only question is whether we wish to have some influence in this area. If so, I see no option except for us to offer a contribution should that be necessary either to meet a short term crisis (on the lines of Poland's food shortages) or in offering funds for longer term structural assistance (e.g. Know-How Funds, etc).

---

[5] In her Mansion House speech Mrs Thatcher had declared that the objective in East Germany 'must be to see genuine democracy, with free elections and more than one party'. But this must be attained 'in an orderly way which preserves stability in Europe'.

No. 47

Mr Hurd to HM Representatives Overseas[1]

Guidance No. 67 Telegraphic [WRE 014/2]

Restricted   FCO, *14 November 1989, 6 p.m.*

Developments in the GDR

Introduction (unclassified)

1. The opening up of the Berlin Wall is an event of major significance.

---

[1] A copy of this telegram also appears in Series III, Vol. VI, No. 411. It is printed here for its bearing on wider German as well as Berlin issues.

2. You may use the line to take (para 3 below) freely. Beyond a warm welcome for developments in the GDR there is no need to be drawn into discussion of the German problem. If necessary, you may draw on paras 4-12 with trusted contacts.

Line to Take (unclassified)

3. We wholeheartedly welcome the opening up of the Berlin Wall. But freedom of travel is not enough. The GDR must honour all its CSCE commitments. Above all people in the GDR want free elections which permit genuine political choice.

Additional Points (unclassified—unattributable)

4. The first priority, as the FRG authorities have emphasised, is for people in the GDR to be able to decide their own future in freedom. We are by no means there yet.

5. We agree with the statement by Federal President von Weizsäcker on 10 November in which he called for responsibility and proportion in achieving step by step conditions in which the people in both parts of Germany can live together in freedom and dignity.

6. We admire the response of the West German government and people in providing help for those leaving East Germany. We have agreed to provide practical help to cope with refugees at our military installations in West Berlin and in the Federal Republic.

Background (paras 7-12 unclassified—for use with trusted contacts; para 13 restricted—for your own information)

7. On 7 October the GDR, still led by Honecker, celebrated its 40th anniversary. However the exodus through Hungary was by then under way. President Gorbachev brought with him the message that 'dangers await only those who don't react to life'. In the days that followed huge peaceful demonstrations in Leipzig, Dresden and elsewhere called for reform in the GDR. The initiative passed to the people.

8. On 18 October Honecker was replaced by Krenz. On 4 November a million people demonstrated in East Berlin. On 7 November the Government resigned and the *Volkskammer* (parliament) threw out a new and slightly more liberal draft travel law as 'unacceptable'. On 8 November the Politburo resigned en bloc and was replaced by a new one, still under Krenz (since then one full and two candidate members of the new politburo have resigned). On 9 November the opening up of the Berlin Wall was announced. A congress of the ruling SED (Socialist Unity Party) has been convened for 14/15 December. It may then become clearer how far the party is prepared to go in meeting the key demand—for free elections allowing a genuine expression of political choice.

9. The Soviet Union has endorsed the reforms in the GDR, making it clear that these are a matter for the GDR alone. But it has also emphasised the importance of the GDR's continued existence as a separate state, and its adherence to the Warsaw Pact.

10. Chancellor Kohl told the *Bundestag* on 8 November that thoroughgoing reform in the GDR, including free elections, was essential. If it was introduced the FRG would offer 'a new dimension' of economic help. Freedom and self-determination for the GDR were the key points. The FRG was firmly rooted in the Atlantic Alliance and the community of free nations in the West. This was irrevocable.

11. The UK, along with other key Western Allies, has expressed a warm welcome for developments in the GDR and full confidence in the FRG's handling

of the issue (see the Prime Minister's Guildhall speech of 13 November—VS 095/89).[2]

12. The UK stands fully by its long-standing commitments as regards Germany. Under the 1955 Bonn/Paris convention the allies are committed to the:

'Aim of a reunified Germany enjoying a liberal democratic constitution, like that of the Federal Republic, and integrated within the European community'.

In 1984 the Prime Minister and Chancellor Kohl issued a joint statement including the words:

'It is the belief of successive British governments that real and permanent stability in Europe will be difficult to achieve so long as the German nation is divided against its will.'

(Restricted—for your own information)

13. We are in close touch with the FRG (and our Western Allies). Our approaches are fully in step. The first priority is thoroughgoing political and economic reform in the GDR. This in itself would be an achievement of historic proportions. The FRG authorities have been careful to play down the question of reunification. Speculation about it at this early stage is unlikely to be helpful.

---

[2] See No. 46, note 5.

No. 48

Letter from Mr Powell (No. 10) to Mr Wall

[WRL 020/4]

Secret   10 DOWNING STREET, *14 November 1989*

Dear Stephen,

East/West Relations

The Prime Minister and the Foreign Secretary had a talk this evening about the present state of East/West relations and the action required by the Government over the next week or so.

The following points were agreed:

—the Prime Minister should reply as soon as possible to Mr Gorbachev's message conveyed to her by the Soviet Ambassador on 10 November. The reply ought to issue on the evening of 15 November.[1]

—the Prime Minister will send a message to President Bush setting out her views on the way ahead in East/West relations, and telling him of the general line she proposes to take at the meeting of EC Heads of Government in Paris on 18 November (for which see below).[2]

—this message would be the prelude to a telephone call to the President, probably on the evening of 17 November, to underline our intentions to consult and keep in close touch with the United States at every stage. The message will therefore need to issue in time for the President to have read it before the telephone call.[3]

---

[1] See No. 50.
[2] See Nos. 45, note 5, and 51, note 1.
[3] See No. 51.

—the Foreign Secretary will let the Prime Minister have his reflections on the handling of the Paris meeting in a minute following his own visits to Bonn and Berlin on 15/16 November.[4]

—the Prime Minister will want a discussion with the Foreign Secretary and Defence Secretary before she goes to Washington on 23 November about the general line she should follow in her talks with the President.[5] We will be in touch to set a time for this on 21 or 22 November.

—we should plan to circulate a paper at Strasbourg with proposals on how the Community might in future manage its relations with Eastern Europe.[6] This would draw on the ideas in the Prime Minister's speech at the Lord Mayor's Banquet and answers in the House of Commons this afternoon, and make clear recommendations about the future structure of these relations and the form they should assume (e.g. Association Agreements, Co-operation Agreements or something new). The options should cover not only association with the Community but also membership of the Council of Europe. The paper would not be discussed in advance with our other partners but launched as a United Kingdom initiative at Strasbourg.

As regards the handling of the Paris meeting, we obviously need the best assessment we can make of President Mitterrand's intentions and no doubt the Embassy will be letting us have that. The Prime Minister suspects that the meeting will be used to try to clear East/West relations from the agenda of the Strasbourg European Council, in order to leave that meeting free to concentrate on EMU and the Social Charter. The Prime Minister would not regard that as satisfactory. She sees the Paris meeting as only a preliminary to a full discussion of East/West relations at Strasbourg. This argues against any agreed conclusions or text at the Paris meeting or any mandate to President Mitterrand to meet President Bush or President Gorbachev on behalf of the Twelve (should that be in his mind).

The Prime Minister's own remarks at the Paris meeting should be based on what she said at the Lord Mayor's Banquet, in her various statements to the press and in the House.[7] She would say that our twin priorities should be to see democracy securely established in East Germany and elsewhere in Eastern Europe, while managing the situation in such a way that it does not undermine or put at risk Mr Gorbachev. This will require the West Europeans to show the same degree of restraint and discipline as have the East Europeans, bearing in mind that the risks and penalties for them if the present situation were to be reversed would be far greater than for Western Europe. We should make clear that it is not Western Europe's intention to exploit the current situation in the GDR against the Soviet Union or in ways which would damage its perceived security interests. Our public statements should be based on the assumption that the existing Alliances will continue, and acknowledge that reunification is not for now on the agenda. While others of us understand the strong emotions which recent developments arouse in West Germany, we hope they will equally show understanding for the emotions of others. We are all playing for very high stakes, and the crucial element is Gorbachev's survival. If we undermine his position and there is a reversion to a much more hard-line approach by the Soviet Union which extinguishes the new freedom enjoyed in Eastern Europe, we should all be culpable. We must therefore

---

[4] See No. 52.
[5] See No. 53.
[6] The European Council was to meet at Strasbourg on 8-9 December.
[7] See No. 46, note 5.

proceed with the maximum prudence and restraint, concentrating on building up democracy in Eastern Europe. We should co-ordinate our position very closely with the United States at every point. And we should have a further and more considered discussion at Strasbourg.

Yours sincerely,
C.D. POWELL

No. 49

Extract from Conclusions of a Meeting of the Cabinet held at 10 Downing Street on 15 November 1989 at 9.30 a.m.[1]

[CC (89)34]

Secret

Foreign Affairs: German Democratic Republic
3. *The Foreign and Commonwealth Secretary* said that events in East Germany had moved very rapidly, particularly following the measures taken to introduce freer travel between East and West Berlin. The key question now was whether the East German government would agree to hold free elections. Their intentions were still obscure. The new Prime Minister, Herr Hans Modrow, the former Party Secretary in Dresden, had been elected on 13 November. He had the reputation of a reformer. The Party Congress had been brought forward to 15/17 December. This was bound to be a crucially important occasion. The opposition groups were pressing for free elections, but did not want these to take place immediately since they were not yet ready. There had been intensive diplomatic activity as events in East Germany unfolded. The Prime Minister had been in close touch with other allied leaders. Despite excessive press speculation, allied governments had reacted steadily and with caution. This had emerged clearly at the Western European Union Ministerial meeting on 13/14 November. The French President, M. Francois Mitterrand, had organised a meeting of European Community (EC) leaders on 18 November. It was to be hoped that EC leaders would express their support and welcome for the changes taking place in Eastern Europe while agreeing on the need for a careful and steadfast approach, based on existing well-tried institutions. Account had to be taken of the position of the Soviet President, Mr Mikhail Gorbachev. He faced a difficult situation but it was very much in the interests of Western governments that he should remain in power. The question of German reunification was extremely sensitive. Given the German Constitution and political

[1] Present at this meeting were: Mrs Thatcher, Sir G. Howe, Lord Mackay (Lord Chancellor), Mr Hurd, Mr Major, Mr D. Waddington (Secretary of State for the Home Department), Mr Walker, Mr N. Fowler (Secretary of State for Employment), Mr King, Mr Ridley, Mr K. Baker (Chancellor of the Duchy of Lancaster), Mr K. Clarke (Secretary of State for Health), Mr J. MacGregor (Secretary of State for Education and Science), Mr M. Rifkind (Secretary of State for Scotland), Mr C. Parkinson (Secretary of State for Transport), Mr J. Wakeham (Secretary of State for Energy), Lord Belstead (Lord Privy Seal), Mr A. Newton (Secretary of State for Social Security), Mr C. Patten (Secretary of State for the Environment), Mr P. Brooke (Secretary of State for Northern Ireland), Mr J. Selwyn Gummer (Minister of Agriculture, Fisheries and Food) and Mr N. Lamont (Chief Secretary, Treasury).

life in West Germany, it was inevitable that there should be some discussion of reunification. All the allied governments had been committed to this general principle for many years. At the same time no-one in a position of influence in the West or East believed that reunification was likely to happen rapidly, or that this would be desirable in the near future. This view was also shared by reformers inside East Germany. President Mitterrand's purpose in organising the meeting on 18 November was probably to try to dispose of developments in Eastern Europe before the European Council meeting in Strasbourg on 8/9 December. This was unrealistic. Much was likely to happen in the intervening period before the European Council. Moreover, these issues were so important for the future of the EC that they would need to be discussed again in depth at the European Council. Nevertheless, on the whole the allied response in Eastern Europe had been sensible and prudent.

In discussion, the following points were made:

(*a*) A clear framework for dealing with the changes in Eastern Europe had been laid down, most recently in the Prime Minister's speech at the Lord Mayor's Banquet on 13 November. It was essential to maintain existing institutions, especially the North Atlantic Treaty Organisation. Ministers should not raise the issue of German reunification, which was not an immediate issue. Progress had already been achieved on strengthening the EC's economic relations with East European countries. The EC had signed trade agreements with Poland and Hungary, and an association agreement with Yugoslavia. In due course Poland and Hungary might want to negotiate association agreements. Such a development was unlikely to cause major problems for the Soviet leadership. If events moved too quickly or Western governments did not continue to take a measured and prudent attitude, there was a risk that President Gorbachev might be swept away. This would cause grave damage to the broader Western objective of promoting democracy throughout both parts of Europe, and ultimately from the Atlantic through the Soviet Union to the borders of China. The EC could not ignore these crucially important processes of historic change which would have a profound effect on developments within the Community.

(*b*) The West German Finance Minister, Herr Waigel, had made clear both in the formal and informal meetings of the Economic and Finance Council on 13 November that West Germany saw its future as remaining an integral member of the EC and Western Europe. Herr Waigel had emphasised that West Germany was not seeking reunification at the present time. The same line had been taken by the West German Foreign Minister, Herr Genscher, and the Defence Minister, Herr Stoltenberg, at the Western European Union Ministerial meeting. Nevertheless, these statements contrasted with the greater attention paid to the theme of reunification by Chancellor Kohl in recent speeches, though it should be remembered that he had always been one of the foremost advocates of reunification among German political leaders.

(*c*) Against this background, the West German government was likely to show an increasing tendency to examine new proposals for greater integration within the EC in the light of the implications for closer relations between East and West Germany and eventual reunification. In certain cases this tendency might be helpful to Britain's own interests.

(*d*) In reality there were already close links between East and West Germany. West German companies were able to take advantage of cheap labour in East Germany in their manufacturing processes. Goods from East Germany were admitted to West Germany, and hence into the EC, without tariffs or quotas. Hitherto West German companies had been deterred from major investment in East Germany because of the political situation there. The recent changes were likely to stimulate a significant flow of new West German investment in East Germany. The Polish and Hungarian governments had stressed recently that they attached importance to securing increased investment from Britain and other EC countries to maintain the preponderant weight of West German trade and investment flows. On the other hand, East Germany and the other reforming East European countries would have great difficulty in practice in implementing the structural changes necessary to create genuine market economies based on private enterprise. This was likely to be a long process.

(*e*) West Germany had a trade surplus of £35 billion with the rest of the EC in 1988. Closer economic links between East and West Germany would present a formidable challenge to the other members of the EC. With a combined population of nearly 80 million people this economic entity would have a major distorting effect on EC projects for closer economic and financial unity and the concept of a Single Market. The EC could not afford to ignore the EC's relations with the European Free Trade Area (EFTA). The EC's import standards would need to be maintained both in relation to East Germany and EFTA.

The Prime Minister, summing up the discussion, said that it was of cardinal importance for Western governments that all these complex questions should be handled carefully and prudently. Allied governments should remain in close touch, especially Britain, France and the United States who had Four Power rights and obligations. Although Western governments had taken a formal position since 1955 in favour of East German self-determination, German reunification should not be treated as an immediate issue. Governments should take due account of the implications of the present turn of events for President Gorbachev's position. A change in the Soviet leadership would inflict major damage on the prospects for the further spread of democracy in the Soviet Union and Eastern Europe. The EC would need to discuss these issues in depth both at President Mitterrand's dinner and at the European Council in Strasbourg. EC member states could not simply concentrate on internal developments within the Community without taking account of trends in Europe as a whole. A single European currency was no answer to these wider changes. Although events were moving in a favourable direction, Europe faced a difficult decade ahead.

No. 50

Mr Hurd to Sir R Braithwaite (Moscow)[1]

No. 1549 Telegraphic [WRE 014/2]

Confidential   FCO, *15 November 1989, 8 p.m.*

Bonn for Private Secretary

MIPT: Message from the Prime Minister to Gorbachev[2]
Message begins
Thank you for your message conveyed to me on 10 November by Ambassador Zamyatin.[3] Historic events are taking place and I share your view that developments in East Germany are encouraging. The lifting of travel restrictions for GDR citizens is most particularly welcome.

The events in Berlin over the weekend have made a great impression on public opinion in Britain and in other Western countries. I have been struck by the good sense of all concerned and their readiness to work together. Very great credit is due to your policies of glasnost and democratisation, and I have paid sincere tribute to your role in my public statements.

I agree with you that the speed with which these changes are taking place carries its own risks of instability. I have publicly underlined the need to proceed in an orderly way which preserves stability and to take a measured view of the way ahead. As I told your Ambassador the firmest basis for stability in the longer-term is thorough-going reform in East Germany—including free elections with a multi-party system and complete freedom of movement, so that there is genuine democracy and an economic system which can support it.

There is no repeat no intention on the part of any Western country to intervene in the GDR or to act in a way which might damage GDR or Soviet security interests. I am confident that Britain's allies and partners share this view. West Germany's leaders have been at pains to stress the importance of a step-by-step approach to change in the GDR and the need to avoid destabilising the wider European situation: and Chancellor Kohl has assured me of this personally when we spoke on the telephone.

We are very ready to enter into contacts with representatives of the Soviet Union in Berlin, as you suggest. The contacts which have already taken place between British officials in Berlin and the Soviet Embassy have proved useful and I hope that they will continue. Our Ambassador in Bonn is ready to meet the Soviet Ambassador to the GDR at any time. In this connection, the British Government remain committed to the Quadripartite Agreement on Berlin of 1971 and attach importance to the provision by which the four governments concerned will strive to promote the elimination of tension and the prevention of complications.

I very much hope that you and I can remain in regular contact about these issues.   Message ends

---

[1] Repeated to Desk by 5.30 a.m., 16 November, Bonn; and to Immediate Paris and Washington; and for information Immediate to East Berlin, UKDEL NATO and BMG Berlin.
[2] FCO telegram No. 1548 to Moscow contained instructions for the delivery of the Prime Minister's message (WRE 014/2).
[3] See No. 38.

No. 51

Letter from Mr Powell (No. 10) to Mr Wall

[*RS 021/17*]

Secret   10 DOWNING STREET, *17 November 1989*

Dear Stephen,

Eastern Europe: Prime Minister's Talk with President Bush

The Prime Minister had a talk on the telephone this evening with President Bush about the situation in Eastern Europe and the forthcoming meeting of European Community heads of government in Paris.

The President said that he had read in detail the Prime Minister's 'marvellous message'.[1] He was looking forward to the two of them putting their feet up at Camp David for a really good talk.[2] The Prime Minister said there was a great deal to discuss. She had thought it useful to put her views in writing before the Paris meeting, so the President could see what she intended to say there. Her impression was that they were thinking in very much the same way. The President said they were indeed very, very close: really eye to eye. A lot of people wanted the United States to posture more, but he was not keen on that.

The President asked what the Prime Minister expected to come out of the Paris meeting. The Prime Minister said that there was unlikely to be anything very concrete. There might be some sort of communiqué but even that was uncertain. Her view was that we should concentrate on supporting economic reform and the introduction of genuine democracy in Eastern Europe. That in itself was a considerable task and would take several years. It would only succeed in conditions of stability, and that meant that we must be very careful not to undermine Mr. Gorbachev. His main concern was to maintain the present borders in Europe and keep the Warsaw Pact intact. This meant that we should avoid talking about German reunification, which still aroused strong emotions in the Soviet Union and in Europe. No one could foresee what would happen in a few years' time. The Prime Minister continued that her impression was that the situation in Europe had steadied after a bumpy few days. She thought most

---

[1] This message, sent by Mr Powell to General Scowcroft on 16 November (WRE 014/2), read, in part:

> It seems to me that our Western response to the events in East Germany and more widely in Eastern Europe needs to be a measured one. There is every reason for celebration: democracy in Eastern Europe is something we always wanted to see. Nothing should dim our success. At the same time, those with most at stake are the people of Eastern Europe. Their restraint and discipline has been remarkable. We should be culpable if a false step or injudicious action on the part of the West resulted in their newly won freedom being once more extinguished. We must in particular be careful to do nothing which might undermine Mr Gorbachev's position, given his crucial role in these events.
>
> Our priority must be to see genuine democracy established in the GDR and the rest of Eastern Europe (as well as, eventually, in the Soviet Union), and other issues should take second place to that. We must demonstrate that we do not intend to exploit the situation to the detriment of the Soviet Union's security interests. This will involve continuing to make plain our view that the future of the Warsaw Pact, like that of NATO, is a matter for its members to decide without interference from outside; and that German reunification is not a matter to be addressed at present.

[2] See No. 45, note 7.

governments understood the need for a measured approach. She knew that Chancellor Kohl had problems with the right wing of his own party: but talk of reunification would be seriously destabilising and would interfere with other positive developments such as arms control negotiations. Finally, we needed to re-affirm the importance of NATO and the conclusions reached at its May Summit, and try to tone down public euphoria. President Bush said that he wholeheartedly agreed with the Prime Minister's approach.

President Bush said that the Prime Minister's visit to Camp David would be very timely and he would want to discuss with her the handling of his meeting with President Gorbachev.[3] Two particular points which concerned him were first to spot in advance any surprises which Gorbachev might try to spring; and second to think about initiatives which he might take which would capture people's imagination. He was not thinking of anything specific, for instance in the arms control field, but some more general gesture. He would very much welcome the Prime Minister's views. He was determined to avoid another Reykjavik.[4] The Prime Minister said that she would give some thought to this before she met the President next week.

The Prime Minister mentioned that our Ambassador in Moscow had seen Mr. Gorbachev this morning and had found him in excellent form. That in itself was interesting considering the scale of the problems he faced. The President agreed that it was interesting and a preview of what he would encounter when they met in Malta.

The President said that Dr Wörner had suggested that he might stop over in Brussels after his meeting with Gorbachev to brief NATO heads of government. He would be very ready to do so. The Prime Minister said that this would be an excellent idea and an occasion to re-affirm NATO policies. This would help steady the ship. President Bush agreed that it was very important in the present situation to stress NATO's role.

I should be grateful if the Foreign and Commonwealth Office and the Ministry of Defence could give consideration to the two points mentioned by President Bush and take account of them in the briefing which you are preparing for the Prime Minister's meeting with the President on 24 November.

I am copying this letter to Brian Hawtin (Ministry of Defence), John Gieve (HM Treasury), Neil Thornton (Department of Trade and Industry) and Trevor Woolley (Cabinet Office).

Yours sincerely,
C.D. POWELL

[3] See No. 31, note 3.
[4] At the Reykjavik summit in October 1986 Mr Gorbachev had taken President Reagan's delegation by surprise with a far-reaching offer to cut the nuclear arsenals of both the Soviet Union and the United States by 50 per cent. See also No. 209, note 4.

No. 52

Minute from Mr Hurd to Mrs Thatcher

[*WRL 026/2*]

Confidential   FCO, *17 November 1989*

Eastern Europe

1. I had talks with Genscher in Bonn on 15 November and visited Berlin yesterday. The German analysis of developments in the GDR is very close to our own. They want to encourage free elections, avoid talk of reunification and reassure the Soviet Union. Only the right-wing of the CDU are making much of reunification. The reformers in the GDR are deliberately avoiding the topic. Genscher thought the new government in the GDR would want free elections. These might well come a month or two before the elections in West Germany and the FRG political parties are already thinking about what role they might play. Whatever happens, it is clear that developments in the GDR will be a major election issue in the FRG over the next year. So far the government parties are benefiting but the SPD claim that what is happening was started by Willy Brandt, and that the credit belongs to them.

2. The Germans think the time has come for the Commission to open negotiations on a Community trade agreement with the GDR. If democracy takes hold, we shall need to look at other forms of cooperation. Genscher agreed with me that we should look at all the models, including EFTA and the Council of Europe. But he doubted if EFTA would turn out to be the right model and thought that different agreements would be needed with each emerging Eastern European democracy, tailored to their requirements. The Association Agreement which we have with Turkey looks forward to eventual membership of the EC, which may not be realistic for the East Europeans for a long time to come. As agreed at our talk this week, we are working on a paper on all this for Strasbourg.

3. We agree with the Germans that the Community has been a pole of attraction to the countries of Eastern Europe. The Germans think we will give the wrong signal if we do not now proceed apace with further integration. I suspect the French may try and point up differences with us on this in Paris at the weekend. I said to Genscher that we too wanted to see progress in Europe. The best signal we could give to Eastern Europe was to show that the Community was implementing its existing undertakings, notably completion of the single market. The argument about EMU was less about the pace than about whether we should have a liberal free market approach or a more bureaucratic centralist one.

4. The French have proposed in the Monetary Committee the establishment of an investment bank for Eastern Europe. It would have a capital of 10 billion ecu, 20% up front. It would be financed primarily by EC countries but participation by other OECD members is envisaged. Mitterrand will mention this on Saturday. We shall want to look in detail, but I think we should welcome it as an interesting idea.

5. Genscher agreed that the kind of message which should emerge from Paris would be:

—an enthusiastic welcome for developments in Eastern Europe;

—reaffirmation of NATO and EC policies which have helped to make these developments possible;

—recognition both of Gorbachev's role and his concerns.

Mitterrand will obviously want to talk to Bush after the weekend meeting. I see no point in trying to prevent him from conveying the sort of message outlined above.

6. There are a number of other issues which you will want to discuss with President Bush and which we can talk about with Tom King next Wednesday.[1] I shall send you a note on these before our meeting but some of them may come up on Saturday night, notably what kind of initiative Gorbachev may produce at Malta. It would be surprising if he does not produce a trump card. This might be:

—some dramatic proposal on nuclear weapons so as to get SNF talks underway straight away;

—a proposal to give Berlin back to the Germans: East Berlin to the GDR and West Berlin to the FRG;

—a proposed peace treaty to end the Second World War.

I hope Bush would resist being bounced. But he should be prepared.

7. The press were suggesting a few days ago that NATO was now redundant. People have sobered up since then. It was very obvious to me that the role of the Allies continues to give a tremendous sense of stability to West Berlin and is one reason why they have been able to react with such controlled enthusiasm to developments in the East: they know they still have the underpinning of Allied support. The British garrison in Berlin has responded to recent developments with everything from accommodation to soup kitchens. We shall have to adapt to changing circumstances and the Commandant and his team are giving thought to this. But our presence remains a necessary insurance policy for the democratic reforms that are now taking place.

8. I am copying this minute to the Chancellor of the Exchequer, the Defence Secretary and the Cabinet Secretary.

DOUGLAS HURD

[1] Mr King was Secretary of State for Defence.

No. 53

Minute from Mr Hurd to Mrs Thatcher

[WRE 014/2]

Confidential   FCO, *21 November 1989*

East/West Relations

1. Tom King and I will be discussing East/West relations with you before you go to Washington.[1] It may be useful to set out in advance some of the main issues.

Support for Gorbachev

2. Gorbachev has real difficulties which could endanger his survival: political turmoil, strikes, shortages, and concealed hyper-inflation in the economy, and the nationality issue. Without Gorbachev, progress in democratising Eastern Europe and in arms control negotiations would certainly be slower and might come to a halt. Nothing we do can provide a quick solution to any of Gorbachev's problems

[1] See No. 45, note 7.

but I believe we should look for a way of making a substantial gesture of Western commitment to *perestroika*. When he saw you, Gorbachev stressed the need for Western help with management training. Given the scale of the Soviet Union and its problems, a UK project along the lines of our Polish or Hungarian know-how funds would not go far. But there might be scope for a UK initiative to launch a multilateral effort. One element of this might be an international institute of management in Moscow. All OECD countries could contribute to this institute, which could organise management training inside and outside the Soviet Union as well as providing a pool of first-class management skills on which the Soviet Union could draw when it wished to look at specific industrial problems. If you think this worth pursuing, you might mention it to the President.

Gorbachev's line at Valletta

3. Some new initiatives might come from Mr Gorbachev at Valletta.[2] The Americans believe that his margin for manoeuvre on this occasion is limited; and that he will not wish to give Mr Bush the appearance of being irresponsible. The Americans are expecting something on naval arms control (either a call for a nuclear free Mediterranean or a call for naval arms control in general). He may call for an accelerated reduction (conceivably, though less likely, even a complete withdrawal) of US and Soviet forces in the two Germanies; and/or a commitment to a CSCE Summit next year to sign a CFE Treaty. The Americans see no attraction for themselves in naval arms control (though there are some in Washington who might be disposed to go along with a few limited naval confidence building measures). They have assured us that they will not enter into any new CFE-related commitments without consulting their Allies, though Cheney's comments at the weekend tend to undermine the value of that assurance.[3]

4. Other possibilities for Gorbachev at Valletta include a proposal for a conference of the four powers plus the two Germanies to negotiate a treaty settling European borders; or a proposal for the Soviet Union to join, or to participate in a meeting of the Summit seven. None of these is attractive. An attempt to turn the inner German border into an international boundary would be unacceptable in the FRG.

The Western Agenda

(a) General

5. The challenge on the Western side is to maintain the coherence of the security arrangements which have served us so well over the last 40 years and which are now bearing such remarkable political fruit in Eastern Europe; while taking account of popular expectations that some of the ways in which our security requirements are translated into force levels may evolve. The domestic political and economic pressures on the US defence budget and in relation to burden-sharing within the Alliance are a further complicating factor.

6. The general message you might seek to impress upon President Bush before he sees Gorbachev is:

—Decisions about Western security arrangements must be security led, not driven by budgetary/domestic considerations.

---

[2] See No. 31, note 3.

[3] In the *New York Times* of 20 November US Defence Secretary Dick Cheney was reported to have said that the Bush Administration was considering 'proposals for troop reductions in Europe that would go well beyond the cuts now being negotiated in Vienna by NATO and the Warsaw Pact' and that the 'conceptual outlines' for such reductions could be presented to Mr Gorbachev at the Valletta Summit in early December.

—The Soviet Union still enjoys massive military advantages in Europe. Now is not the time to encourage a belief that sound Western defence is no longer needed.

—NATO, in its present form and membership, will remain the foundation of Western security for the foreseeable future. Though it is not for us to prescribe to the members of the Warsaw Pact about the future of their alliance, we should do nothing to imply that we are encouraging or expecting its dissolution.

—As, but not before, the military threat declines, there can be changes in Western force structures, both nuclear and conventional. But flexible response, based on nuclear deterrence, and a substantial (i.e. not merely symbolic) presence of US forces in Europe remains the best security recipe.

—US force levels in Europe are not immutable and can be reduced. But this should happen in the context of a negotiated CFE Treaty, not through unilateral action. It will be helpful to have an early indication of how large a share of the prospective CFE cuts the United States would wish to take.

(*b*) *At Valletta*

7. You have already made clear to President Bush our view that we should re-assure Gorbachev that we do not wish to undermine his security, including by not pushing Baltic independence. Beyond this we shall not want the Valletta meeting to focus too exclusively on Eastern Europe. That would be reminiscent of Yalta. The Americans' suggestion that they should seek more co-operation on regional issues seems right. President Bush might also try to reach a private understanding with Gorbachev that nuclear weapons and US forces in Europe, albeit perhaps in smaller numbers in both cases than at present, are stabilising factors for security in Europe; and should be regarded as durable elements of the scene throughout the potentially turbulent 1990s.

Eastern Europe

8. The cumulative volume of assistance for Poland is now substantial. In addition to economic assistance, the access which the Community will give to Polish industrial and agricultural products from the beginning of next year is potentially of great importance. There may nevertheless be a crisis in Poland this winter and further crises beyond that; in addition to the colossal economic problems of that country, the coalition government is operated by inexperienced politicians. But it remains of enormous importance that this venture should not fail. I shall be sending you separate recommendations.

9. Less attention and resources have so far been devoted to Hungary. It is, however, of no less importance that we should help the Hungarians. There is a real chance that the Hungarians might succeed in the transition to a Western-style economy in the long run. If they did so, this would give others a model to follow. In many ways their chances of success are greater than those for Poland. It will be of critical importance to find ways of relieving Hungary of its burden of debt, after an IMF programme is in place.

GDR

10. The line we have taken on the GDR has, I believe, been generally welcomed. We shall continue to emphasise the need for genuinely free elections there. Democracy and freedom of travel are at the top of the East German people's agenda; and Gorbachev has made clear that German unification is not on his agenda. I do not think that the question of assistance for the GDR arises at this stage. Even if the regime there introduces genuine measures of reform there will still be a case for caution since the GDR is much the richest of the COMECON

countries. It is certainly not a poor country (not as poor, for example, as Portugal). If a need arises, we should make clear that the idea of a four-power meeting on Germany (with or without representatives of the two Germanies) is unwise at this stage. Such a meeting could only have as its purpose to re-examine the question of German borders. This is certainly not the moment to embark on such an exercise.

11. I am copying this minute to the Defence Secretary and the Cabinet Secretary.

DOUGLAS HURD

No. 54

Teleletter from Mr Synnott to Mr Munro (East Berlin)[1]

[*WRE 014/2*]

Confidential   FCO, *22 November 1989, 7.31 p.m.*

Developments in the GDR

1. Many thanks for your teleletter of 20 November about the debate following Modrow's government statement.[2]

2. I was struck by the references to the restoration of historic provinces and to a possible confederation with the FRG. It need hardly be said that we would be most interested in any development of this sort of theme. So far, references in the GDR to the concept of national unity have been conspicuous by their absence. But it is hard to imagine that this silence will continue. The possible proximity of elections in the FRG and the GDR will surely lead to a chattering in the dovecotes.

3. I was also grateful for your telno 402 on the economic crisis.[3] As I mentioned on the telephone, I have asked economic advisers to set in hand an analysis of the current economic situation, what needs to happen to turn the economy round, and what is likely to happen. I expect an initial contribution from them soon, to help to get all our minds working, with a more considered piece in slower time.

H.N.H. SYNNOTT

[1] Repeated to BMG, Berlin and Bonn. Copied to Mr Lamont, BMG Berlin, and Mr Budd, Bonn.
[2] Not printed.
[3] Not printed.

No. 55

Minute from Mr J.N. Powell (Policy Planning Staff) to Mr Cooper

[*WRL 020/4*]

Unclassified   FCO, *22 November 1989*

Berlin: The German Question

1. I attended a conference in Berlin from 15-17 November. BMG kindly also arranged for me to call on a number of academics. Not surprisingly discussion at

the Conference centred on the German question as well, I have recorded the main points on more general East/West issues separately.[1]

2. The *main points* on Germany were:

(*a*) Krenz and Modrow are both figureheads. The real reformer in the SED is Schabowski. All the mistakes of the past would be blamed on Honecker and Mittag. If there were free elections the SED would score very badly. New Forum was over-estimated by the Western press. The most likely party to win was the SDP which had not been compromised in the same way that the CDU etc had been.

(*b*) The people of the GDR were not yet asking for reunification but in their hearts they all demand it. The key factor would be economic. The third way would not work. People in the GDR wanted to live like the people of the FRG, and not to be second class Germans.

(*c*) The drift towards economic confederation was irresistible. The rate of the *ostmark* against the *deutschmark* was falling constantly as people from the GDR bought consumer goods in the West. If this carried on unchecked it would lead to hyper-inflation by Christmas. The two governments would need to move quickly to a common currency. Boards would need to be set up to administer railways, the post etc.

(*d*) No-one I talked to believed the Russians were seriously concerned by the prospect of confederation. Gorbachev had said nothing in public and Falin and others had indicated that reunification was acceptable. Gorbachev was preoccupied with his internal problems.

(*e*) No-one seriously addressed the practicalities of how there could be confederation with the FRG remaining in NATO and the GDR remaining in the Warsaw Pact. Some suggested that the alliances might change in nature in the direction of cooperative security. Others suggested a zone of neutrality might be established right down the middle of Europe from Scandinavia to Germany.

(*f*) The Four powers should do nothing until the Germans had decided what they wanted to do. Voigt (SPD foreign affairs spokesman) said it was important that the allies did not appear to forbid reunification. Such a move would give the Republicans 30% in the forthcoming elections. Of course consultation with the three western allies should go on behind closed doors but the allies should not appear to dictate to the Germans. Reunification was certain to be an election issue.

(*g*) An Italian suggested that Germany should be reunified and become neutral but that the 4 power troops should be maintained by bilateral treaty. A German professor suggested that the existing zones should be disbanded and instead the 4 power troops should be scattered around Germany e.g. a British garrison in Rostock and a Soviet garrison in Munich.

(*h*) One German academic told me that he opposed recognition of the Oder-Neisse line until the Germans had been given the right to go back to Silesia and to re-possess their property. Germany should not surrender its leverage until it had secured these points.

(*i*) Another German professor told me that we should not look for a rational explanation of what was going on. It was an emotional response rather than a question of interests.

3. The *conclusions* I draw from the discussion are:

[1] Not printed.

(*a*) Whatever West German politicians say everyone I talked to in Berlin had already decided that the answer to the German question was one (one state, one people, one capital). The only questions remaining were how to get there and how long the transition would take. The general view seemed to be that it could happen very fast.

(*b*) The most likely course is that gradual economic integration of East and West Germany will lead to the establishment of joint political bodies (railway boards etc) and thereby gradually to political confederation. Confederation will raise problems for the European Community (can a member of the Warsaw Pact join the EC?) and for NATO: either a German confederation would be in the Warsaw Pact (unacceptable to us) or in NATO (unacceptable to the Russians) or neutral (thereby destroying NATO) or the two halves could be in different alliances (defying logic but possibly allowing a growing together of the two military blocs).

(*c*) Unless the Russians speak up we will be unable to convince the Germans that it is they who are stopping reunification. They are convinced that Gorbachev has enough on his plate in the Soviet Union and will not interfere to prevent German reunification.

(*d*) On four power rights we will need to conduct a difficult balancing act. We should avoid a 4 power conference like the plague. Any suggestion that the 4 powers are preventing reunification could lead to a massive swing to the Republicans in the FRG. We should therefore try to downplay the role of the 4 and dismantle those of our rights that are most anachronistic, e.g. allow Lufthansa to fly to Berlin (if the Russians will let us). At the same time we need to use 4 power meetings in Berlin to reassure the Russians that nothing can happen without their say so (e.g. a lunch of the 4 Ambassadors or discussion of the Berlin initiative).

(*e*) Gorbachev could well render our plodding policy academic with a headline catching initiative on Germany at Valletta.

J.N. POWELL

No. 56

Teleletter from Mr Wordsworth to Mr Sands (East Berlin)[1]

[*WRE 014/2*]

Confidential   FCO, *24 November 1989, 1.30 p.m.*

Opposition in the GDR

1. There have been UK press reports that demonstrators are now increasingly often calling for reunification. One report in particular reported that many ordinary people are beginning to lose patience with the intellectual opposition leaders who talk about introducing a reformed variant of socialism, and are coming to think that reunification offers the best chance of improving their standard of living ('The Independent' of 23 November).

---

[1] Repeated for information as Teleletter Bonn and BMG Berlin; copied to Mr Dinwiddy, Bonn, and Mr Charlton, BMG Berlin.

2. Grateful for your own assessment of these reports.[2]

S.J. WORDSWORTH

[2] No specific reply to this teleletter appears to have been received. However, several subsequent reports referred to calls for unification at demonstrations, e.g. Nos. 58 and 82.

No. 57

Sir C. Mallaby (Bonn) to Mr Hurd[1]

No. 1151 Telegraphic [WRL 020/4]

Confidential   BONN, *27 November 1989, 7.56 p.m.*

The German Question

Summary

1. Federal Ministers, especially Genscher, continue to take a responsible line. Government not managing to give appearance of being master of events. Bickering between and within parties growing, especially about conditions to be attached to new aid to GDR. Reunification and confederation featuring more in the debate.

Detail

2. The dominant public feeling in the FRG about events in the GDR is still strong satisfaction. The Government has generally maintained its responsible line. Genscher, whom you will see again on 29 November, is particularly careful. He is the most popular politician in the FRG and his restraint is influential in the political debate. He continues to avoid the word reunification and always couples the idea of German unity with that of a free, united and stable Europe.

3. There is a feeling in the air that the Federal Government, especially Kohl is not rising to this historic moment and looking like the master of events. One reason is that the Government is obliged to refrain from clear statements on various matters by its line that the people of the GDR should be allowed to decide their own future and the West Germans should not tell them what to think. There is also increasing argument about aspects of the German question within and between the political parties.

4. One major subject of controversy is the conditions to be attached to new aid to the GDR. The SPD argues that intrusive preconditions amount to tutelage. Even Genscher and the FDP are now arguing against conditions for new aid. The CDU today has said there will be no financial injections to save socialism and that major new help will depend on laws being introduced in the GDR to abolish the leading role of the Communist Party and to ensure free elections.

The Government has already modified its insistence on conditions for aid by stating that humanitarian and infrastructure support can take place before reform. There is a risk that economic conditions in the GDR could deteriorate before reform, posing acute dilemmas, as well as a threat of a new wave of immigrants, for the Bonn Government.

[1] Repeated for information Immediate to East Berlin and BMG Berlin; and for information Priority to Moscow, Paris, Washington, UKDEL NATO, Warsaw, Budapest, Vienna and Prague.

5. The flow of permanent emigrants from the GDR to the FRG has fallen from 10,000 a day before the frontier was opened to about 3000. That is a great improvement but the figure is still high. And it would probably rise again if people in the GDR become more dissatisfied for political or economic reasons. That would further intensify the housing problem and could cause a political backlash. An opinion poll in the FRG has indicated that 67 per cent of West Germans no longer see a valid reason for permanent emigration from the GDR. There are also the beginnings of a public feeling that West Germans ought to gain something from the changes on the inner German border. Hence the increasing stress on [*sic*: ?of] the CDU on the demand for easier visa arrangements for West Germans visiting the GDR and the abolition of the minimum exchange requirement. One motive in the Federal Government's interest in a fund to replace welcome money for GDR visitors is that the latter would make a payment in East Marks and thus would not be getting something for absolutely nothing, which annoys a proportion of West Germans.

6. Lafontaine, left-wing Minister-President of the Saarland and a candidate to lead the party in the Federal election in December 1990, has argued that, because of the prospective pressures on the FRG's social security system, it is no longer sensible to maintain open access to, and automatic citizenship of, the FRG for all Germans. Automatic citizenship is a hallowed principle, and Lafontaine has been sharply criticised by people within as well as outside his own party. But he has a sharp nose for what the public wants to hear, and his remarks suggest that he believes that ordinary people are getting worried about the money spent on East Germans in the FRG.

7. The theme of reunification, though still shunned by Kohl and Genscher, is gradually becoming more prominent in political debate. Belief in the likelihood of reunification within 10 years is growing: one poll suggests that it doubled from 24 per cent to 48 per cent in the past four weeks. It has been widely reported that Krenz mentioned the idea of confederation in his interview with the *Financial Times* on 25 November and the *Frankfurter Allgemeine Zeitung* has said it should not be dismissed out of hand. It has also been widely reported that reunification has begun to appear on placards in demonstrations in the GDR. Labour Minister Blüm, on the left of the CDU, now agrees with Dregger on the party's extreme right that reunification must be the aim of CDU policy, and plans to include it in his platform as CDU candidate for Minister-President in North-Rhine Westphalia's *Land* election in May. On the other hand the executive committee of the CDU decided today not to make an unequivocal commitment to reunification. It said that it did not expect there to be two German democracies but that it would respect a vote by the people of the GDR to maintain their own state.

No. 58

Mr Broomfield (East Berlin) to Mr Hurd[1]

No. 417 Telegraphic [WRE 014/2]

Confidential   EAST BERLIN, *28 November 1989, 8.50 a.m.*

My Telno 413: GDR Internal Developments[2]

Summary

1. Renewed calls at Leipzig demonstrations for unity/reunification. No party now rules this out entirely but time scales vary greatly.

Detail

2. Over 200,000 people turned out on 27 November to press demands for reform. Similar demonstrations took place in Dresden, Halle, Cottbus, Neu-Brandenburg and Schwerin.

3. As at last week's demonstration (para 2 of my telno 405)[3] there were again calls for reunification. According to *Neues Deutschland* (ND) such calls were rejected by the majority—'one people—two states, that is the reality' was the SED's reply. Two members of Chancery were in Leipzig last night and have, however, reported that in addition to attacks on the old regime the theme of unity/reunification was pressed strongly. A sizeable proportion of the crowd appeared to be in favour and a considerable number of the banners carried messages such as—Don't be afraid, reunification now.

4. There have been a series of statements about the possibility of unity/reunification in the last few days. On 25 November Krenz, in an interview with the *Financial Times* said that German unity was not on the agenda. In the longer term, however, he thought that the question could not be ruled out depending on the 'framework' of the common European home. According to *Neues Deutschland's* account of that interview Krenz did not exclude the possibility that 'the GDR and the FRG could move in the direction of a confederation if, in the coming years, NATO and the Warsaw Pact were disbanded'.

5. I asked Gerlach yesterday, in his capacity as Deputy Chairman of the Council of State, what interpretation to put on Krenz's word[s]. Gerlach said that for the present two realities existed in the GDR. It was a socialist state and a sovereign state. What might happen in the future would depend on developments in Europe. He did not personally rule out a more closely structured relationship such as confederation or federation.

---

[1] Repeated for information Immediate to Bonn and BMG Berlin; information Priority Moscow, UKDEL NATO, Paris and Washington; information Routine Prague, Warsaw, Budapest, Sofia, CICC(G) and UKREP Brussels; and information Saving Belgrade, Peking.

[2] In this telegram of 24 November Mr Broomfield reported that the SED had initiated an investigation into Honecker's conduct when in power, and that the Council of Ministers had introduced a number of emergency economic measures to prevent speculation in currency and goods. 'Although sensible in themselves', he wrote, 'I do not think they can prove an effective and lasting answer by themselves to a fundamental problem' (WRE 014/2).

[3] In this telegram of 21 November Mr Broomfield reported a demonstration of over 100,000 people in Leipzig on 20 November. The main demands were for the abolition of the leading role of the Party, free elections and the trial of SED leaders who had committed offences; but 'West German TV reporting also drew attention to calls for reunification' (WRE 014/2).

Comment

6. The question of unity/reunification has in the last week or so become much more prominent in the GDR. Official attitudes towards it have moved considerably in a fairly short time. From Honecker's position of the inseparability [*sic*: ?incompatibility] of socialism and capitalism (fire and water), none of the official parties now rule out the possibility of a much closer relationship with the FRG involving structural change although this is referred to as a possibility for the distant future.

7. I judge this to be an acknowledgement of pressure from the streets. While the intellectual and cultural leaders of the reform groups in Berlin remain cautious, if not hostile to the idea of unity/reunification, the perceptions of the people, particularly in the industrial towns of the south, has [*sic*] definitely been affected by what they have been able to see of the FRG and West Berlin since 9 November. They are becoming conscious of the deception practised upon them by the previous leadership about life in the West, and are increasingly aware of the enormous gap in the living standards as well as political freedoms between the two countries. The editor of ND, to whom I put this question yesterday, acknowledged that there was the beginnings [sic] of a new mood on the streets. The SED would have to face this and win the people back to their version of socialism by becoming a thoroughly reformed party, adopting coherent reforming policies.

8. I will send a further round up on political and economic developments here before the NATO Ministerial Meeting on 4 December.

No. 59

Sir C. Mallaby (Bonn) to Mr Hurd[1]

No. 1156 Telegraphic [*WRL 020/4*]

Confidential   BONN, *28 November 1989, 5.28 p.m.*

My Telno 1154: Kohl's Speech on the German Question[2]

Summary

1. Teltschik, briefing US and French Ambassadors and me, presents Kohl's speech as an attempt to put German unity at the end of a lengthy process and thus to head off calls for early unity. It is true that the major innovation in Kohl's 10-point programme—the suggestion of confederative structures—need not alter present alliances and in itself may not be harmful. But Kohl's decision to set out a programme culminating in unity, without agreement of coalition partners or prior consultation with allies, is a sign of the speed with which the debate is moving. And Teltschik volunteered that Kohl's vision of a lengthy process before unity could be overtaken by other views before long.

---

[1] Repeated for information Immediate to East Berlin, BMG Berlin, Moscow, Paris, Washington and UKDEL NATO; information Priority to UKREP Brussels, Warsaw, Budapest, Vienna and Prague.
[2] This telegram of 28 November reported the details of the ten-point programme outlined in Herr Kohl's speech to the *Bundestag* on 28 November.

Detail

2. Teltschik, Kohl's diplomatic adviser, briefed the US and French Ambassadors and me about Kohl's speech two hours after the Chancellor had spoken. He said that the 10-point programme in the speech[3] had been advanced on Kohl's own authority, without agreement with coalition partners or allies. But it had taken account of numerous telephone calls between Kohl and Bush, contacts between Kohl and Mitterrand, the EC summit on 18 November and contacts at many levels with the GDR.

3. The Chancellor's ten points had also taken account of his contacts with Gorbachev around 9 November. There had also been important contacts with advisers to Gorbachev. They had suggested that the Federal Chancellor should not visit the GDR before the Communist Party congress there on 14/15 December, thus implying that the present leadership might no longer be in place after the congress. Teltschik said that the earliest the Chancellor could visit East Germany was 19 December. He would not go to East Berlin and hoped to go to Leipzig. His decision would depend on the policy decisions taken at the Party congress. Returning to what Gorbachev's advisers had said, Teltschik said they had revealed that the Russians were reflecting about far-reaching possibilities including a Four-Power conference, a peace treaty, and a united, neutral Germany. But the Soviet position still insisted on two basic points: no departures from the Warsaw Pact and maintenance of the separate statehood of the GDR. It was interesting, however, that Gorbachev's advisers were limiting this statement about the Soviet bottom line to present circumstances and no longer implying that the bottom line could never change. Gorbachev's advisers had asked Teltschik whether the Federal Chancellor wanted a peace treaty or a Four-Power conference and what form of unity would in due course be preferred.

4. Teltschik continued that these Soviet remarks among other factors had made the Chancellor decide that it was time to present a way forward on the German question. The Federal Republic's allies should carefully note that Kohl's speech, before setting out the 10 points, drew attention to the factors which had produced positive change in Europe. These factors began with the FRG's membership of the community of democracies and the firmness of NATO over INF. It also included West European integration, Gorbachev's policy of reform, the reform in Poland and Hungary, CSCE, the frequency of East-West summits, the Federal Republic's *Ostpolitik* and the Federal Republic's insistence that the German nation remained one. Teltschik said that these points, especially the one about NATO, should be seen as belonging inseparably with the 10 points themselves. As we knew, the

---

[3] A fax of the official translation stated that the programme comprised: (1) immediate practical help to deal with problems arising from the events of recent weeks; (2) increased cooperation with the GDR in the economic, cultural, technological and environmental fields; (3) an extensive increase in help to the GDR if fundamental and irreversible changes were made in its political and economic system; (4) joint treaty-based commissions in such areas as the economy, transport, health and culture; (5) taking 'a further decisive step, namely to develop confederative structures between the two States in Germany with the aim of creating a federation, a federal order in Germany', for which a democratic GDR would be 'an absolute pre-requisite'; (6) anchoring the development of inner-German relations in the pan-European process and in East-West relations; (7) the conclusion of a trade and cooperation between the EC and the GDR; (8) advancing East-West cooperation through the CSCE process; (9) accelerating progress on disarmament and arms control; (10) 'working towards a state of peace in Europe in which the German people can regain its unity in free self-determination. Reunification, that is the regaining of the national unity of Germany, remains the political objective of the Federal Republic' (WRL 020/4).

Federal Government stood firmly by its membership of the Alliance. Teltschik continued that the 10 points should be seen as a single package. The major novelty was point 5, about confederative structures. These were presented as opening up the aim of a federation in due course in Germany. (My TUR described this mistakenly in paragraph 2(5) as a confederation.) Teltschik continued that the Chancellor had deliberately not spoken of a confederation since that required a treaty between two separate states and therefore would confirm the existence of two states in Germany. A further advantage of proposing confederative structures but not a confederation was that the former did not call the two Germanies' membership of alliances into question. Teltschik pointed out that Kohl's point 9 about arms control referred to nuclear reductions only by the superpowers.

5. I asked Teltschik why the Chancellor had made this major move on the German question at this time. Teltschik said that the Chancellor had felt a need to set out clear German views, to influence the thinking that was evidently taking place in Moscow. Secondly Kohl had wanted to lead the debate in the FRG, which had been floundering recently (my telno 1151).[4] He had also wanted, by setting German unity at the end of a lengthy process also involving a European settlement, to influence people in the GDR who increasingly were calling for German unity and might start saying that it should happen soon. The Chancellor also hoped that a clear programme culminating in German unity would instil patience into the people of the GDR and thus reduce the likelihood that the flood of emigrants might begin again. Finally, the Chancellor wanted to pre-empt calls for reunification in neutrality, which might come from the left in the Federal Republic before long. Teltschik admitted, however, that Kohl's attempt to be a rock in the storm and to set reunification way down the road could be overtaken by other views.

Comment

6. Teltschik was at pains to stress that Federal German membership of NATO was not in question and that the reference to it in Kohl's speech should be taken as part of the 10 points. I am sure that Kohl and Teltschik are sincere about the Alliance. But it is a pity that the 10 points themselves do not mention the Alliance and do mention other matters covered in the preliminary part of the speech. I find generally convincing Teltschik's explanation of Kohl's reasons for speaking up now. And it is true that confederative structures, at least in the examples given in Kohl's speech, may not in themselves be harmful. But some of them, notably 'a common parliamentary body' could acquire major significance over time. The key point is that the pressures have reached a level where Kohl has felt obliged to make a high profile statement of a policy expressly intended to lead in time to German unity. And he has done so on his own authority, not on behalf of the whole coalition, and without prior consultation with the Allies having responsibility for the German question. It shows how fast the German question is moving.

[4] No. 57.

No. 60

Mr Broomfield (East Berlin) to Mr Hurd[1]

No. 422 Telegraphic [*WRL 020/4*]

Confidential   EAST BERLIN, *29 November 1989, 3.40 p.m.*

MIPT: GDR Reaction to Kohl's Ten Points[2]

Comment

1. The official GDR reaction to Kohl's ten points has been predictable, but also revealing. The 'irritation' referred to in the spokesman's statement (para 4, TUR) was visible today when I asked the *Volkskammer* President, Maleuda, for his reaction. He said with some force that it verged on direct interference, but then added hastily that, everything would of course be discussed during the forthcoming visits of Seiters and Chancellor Kohl.

2. The economic realities mean that the GDR cannot reject Kohl's statement outright. They will try to dine 'a la carte', taking the economic offers while firmly rejecting the political conclusion put forward by the Chancellor. In many points, however, they should be able to satisfy the Chancellor's political conditions, i.e. freedom to travel, a liberal electoral law, etc. Whether Kohl will be able to maintain the linkage between economic assistance and political progress in the GDR over a period of months remains to be seen. An economic collapse during this winter caused by a continuing high rate of emigration (my telno 420)[3] and the effects of past economic mismanagement is [a?] distinct possibility.

3. My Counsellor and another member of Chancery have today returned from a two day visit to Leipzig and Jena where they have talked to a wide cross-section of political activists and others. The views reported in my telno 417[4] about the strength of feeling outside Berlin on the unity/reunification theme were strongly reconfirmed. Confronted by the economic facts of life most people saw no way forward except through FRG assistance, and seemed to take it for granted that this would entail in a very short time scale a much closer political relationship with the FRG.

4. Kohl's intention may have been to stand like a rock in the storm and set reunification way down the road (para 5 of Bonn telno 1156).[5] I think it more likely, however, that his statement will act as a catalyst for discussion in the GDR

[1] Repeated for information Immediate to Bonn and BMG Berlin; information Priority to Paris, Moscow and Washington; information Routine to UKDEL NATO, UKREP Brussels, Warsaw, Prague and Budapest; and information Saving to CICC(G), other East European Posts, Peking and UKDEL Strasbourg.

[2] East Berlin telegram No. 421 of 29 November reported official rejection of the idea of confederation contained in Herr Kohl's statement, but a positive reaction to his specific proposals for cooperation with the GDR (WRG 021/8).

[3] This telegram of 29 November reported that an average of over 4,000 people a day had left the GDR since 3 November. Mr Broomfield commented: 'While there was a sharp reduction in the very high level of emigration following the introduction of free travel on 9 November, the flow is clearly still continuing at a damagingly high rate for the GDR. Contacts here tell us that people are more inclined to take their time and look for a job and a flat in the West before deciding to go. But the effect on the GDR economy is the same' (WRE 350/1).

[4] No. 58.

[5] No. 59.

and probably accelerate the process of bringing the future relationship with the FRG to the top of the political agenda here. Anyone wishing to achieve political influence, whether among the established parties or unofficial groups, will now have to respond to Kohl's ten points if they are to retain any credibility with the people at large, whatever the intellectuals in Berlin and the Party spokesman may have to say.

No. 61

Sir C. Mallaby (Bonn) to Mr Hurd[1]

No. 1166 Telegraphic [WRL 020/4]

Confidential   BONN, 29 *November 1989, 3.46 p.m.*

My Telno 1156: Kohl and the German Question[2]

Summary

1. Further comments on Kohl's landmark speech. Reunification in the form of a German federation is now clearly an aim of policy, though without a timescale. Subject to reform in the GDR, an organic process of the two Germanies coming together through cooperation agreements and 'confederative structures' may now begin. Kohl's programme could be overtaken by events, as elections in both Germanies approach.

Detail

2. Kohl's 10-point plan has gone down well with Genscher and the opposition, and very well with the media. He has managed to satisfy the domestic constituencies he was addressing, and will be awaiting with anticipation the reactions of the external ones—the GDR leadership, the Western Allies and the USSR.

3. I see Kohl's speech as a major event. For the first time, it takes reunification out of the realms of aspiration and makes it the culmination and aim of a staged programme. He has made clear, however, that unity is subject to the Germans wanting it, and this shields him from the accusation of telling the East Germans what they should want.

4. Many of the 10 points are familiar, but they gain in impact by being assembled in a programme. The key novelty is 'confederative structures'. As I argued in TUR, these may not be harmful in themselves but they could develop into the elements of a future German federation, and Kohl said explicitly that this was the aim. Another novelty is that it is now the Federal Government's explicit position that a united Germany should be federal in structure.

5. Assuming the GDR falls in with major parts of the plan, the two Germanies look like embarking on a process of coming together through intensified cooperation and far reaching bilateral agreements as well as 'confederative structures'.

---

[1] Repeated for information Immediate East Berlin, BMG Berlin, Moscow, Paris, Washington and UKDEL NATO; information Priority to UKREP Brussels, Warsaw, Budapest, Vienna and Prague.
[2] No. 59.

6. Kohl no doubt hopes that his new position will hold the ring for quite a time and provide a basis for the CDU's election platform. But his 10 points may well be taken increasingly for granted, as the debate on the German question moves forward. It is helpful that Kohl has set no timescales and has linked his programme to wider European developments which will take considerable time. But in an election year in both Germanies, his new position could be overtaken by events.[3]

---

[3] Mrs Thatcher noted on her copy of this telegram: 'Christopher Mallaby seems to *welcome* reunification' (PREM: Internal situation in East Germany).

No. 62

Minute from Sir J. Fretwell to Mr Wall

[*WRG 026/11*]

Secret   FCO, *29 November 1989*

Genscher Visit: Handling of Kohl's Programme for German Unity

1. Kohl's ten-point programme for German unity marks an important new step in the development of the German Question. For the first time it puts on the table a coherent, if sketchy, programme which offers a serious prospect of leading to reunification. (The Allied proposals of the '50s offered no such prospect.) Despite the initial negative reaction in East Berlin, debate in both parts of Germany and elsewhere will now focus on this plan. It may have been Kohl's intention simply to take control of the debate and to impose a lengthy timetable. But I think that in practice the effect of the programme will be to focus attention much more directly on reunification and on the steps leading towards it, bringing it to the forefront of political interest in the FRG and perhaps also the GDR, and thereby to increase pressures for early moves in this direction. The fact that high-level exchanges have already taken place with the Soviet Union (para 3 of Bonn telegram No 1156),[1] touching on the question of a peace treaty and the form of unity the FRG would in due course prefer, indicates that the door is not closed on the Eastern side.

2. In responding to these developments, we can for the time being stick to our existing public line: briefing has already been submitted by WED.[2] But we have to be very careful about what we say to the Germans, starting with today's meetings with Genscher.[3] They will be alert for evidence that we are more hostile to German unity and more interested in maintaining the status quo in Europe than our principal allies. They probably suppose this already: it is striking that in briefing Sir C. Mallaby and his US and French colleagues, Teltschik referred to previous consultation with Bush, Mitterrand, Gorbachev and 'contacts at many levels with the GDR'.[4] There was apparently no time to consult the UK, except to the extent that our views were conveyed at the EC Summit on 18 November. This implies that the Germans see our position as being outside the mainstream. So, I think, do the Americans. The account of the Prime Minister's meeting with President Bush

---

[1] No. 59.
[2] No. 25.
[3] Herr Genscher was visiting London on 29 November. See also No. 69, note 6.
[4] No. 59. Sir J. Fretwell's supposition is confirmed by Herr Teltschik's memorandum of 17 November, printed in *Deutsche Einheit*, No. 94B.

in Mr Powell's letter of 25 November[5] shows the President taking his distance from us on the Warsaw Pact and on German reunification: 'The President said he was also troubled about supporting continuation of the Warsaw Pact . . . The West could not assign countries to stay in the Warsaw Pact against their will.' In response to the Prime Minister's statement of her position on German reunification, 'the President asked whether this line gave rise to difficulties with Chancellor Kohl. The Prime Minister said that Chancellor Kohl was being very sensible on the issue.'

3. There are of course countless good arguments for moving cautiously on the question of German unity and the future of the Warsaw Pact. The central one is the necessity to avoid creating further threats to Gorbachev's position, which we have assumed would be jeopardised by the loss of control over the Soviet Union's empire in Eastern Europe and, above all, by the emerging possibility of a reunified Germany. But this argument loses some of its conviction, particularly in German eyes, if it begins to appear that we are being *plus royaliste que le roi*. Gorbachev is not intervening to stop Communism being swept away in Eastern Europe. The Soviet line of twelve months ago insisting on two absolute requirements—membership of the Warsaw Pact and maintenance of the leading role of the Party—has already been partly abandoned. The Warsaw Pact itself may now be evolving towards a political, rather than a defence, structure. The Germans are getting their own read-out of Gorbachev's intentions. It would be all too easy to give the FRG the impression that we want stability, the maintenance of the two Alliances, a cautious approach to arms control etc. because we rather like Europe the way it is and do not share the vision of a Europe 'whole and free' (in the words of President Bush).

4. The impression we create on this arises from the nuances rather than from the basic statement of our position. It is all right to insist on the need for prudence in handling the present dramatic developments in Europe, but we need to convey to the Germans that we too have a positive vision of what should emerge at the end of the day and what we are prepared to work for. Now that Kohl has put a programme on the table, we need to be able to say that we too are looking for progress towards a Europe in which the division imposed by Stalinist tyranny will fade into history and in which the German people will have freely exercised their right to come together if that is their choice. If we do not start conveying this impression to the Germans soon, starting with Genscher today, they will conclude that we are fundamentally hostile to that sort of vision. They will be tempted increasingly to move ahead without us on these fundamental issues of European policy. We could ultimately impose a block, based on our position as one of the four Powers responsible for Germany and Berlin. But we should not count on carrying anyone else with us.

J. FRETWELL

[5] Not printed. Mrs Thatcher met President Bush at Camp David on 24 November. For accounts of the meeting see Thatcher, pp. 794-5; Bush and Scowcroft, pp. 192-3.

No. 63

Sir C. Mallaby (Bonn) to Mr Hurd[1]

No. 1171 Telegraphic [WRL 020/4]

Confidential   BONN, *30 November 1989, 2.45 p.m.*

*Washington Telno 3105 and Paris Telno 1581: The German Question:
Public Line*[2]

Summary
1. I recommend an early statement by you on Kohl's ten point plan.
Detail
2. Compared with the statements by Baker and Dumas reported in TURs, our reticence so far in response to Kohl's ten point plan (my telno 1154)[3] is conspicuous here.

3. I recommend that you make an early statement,[4] designed to emphasise the need for stability in Europe and the undesirability of speed, to overlap with what allies are saying and not to alienate the FRG unnecessarily. It might include the following points:

(*a*) The British, who have shared difficult times with the Berliners, now share the joy of all Germans at the opening of the Wall and the inner German border and the increased freedom of travel.

(*b*) The fundamental principle in the German question is that the German people should have the opportunity for self-determination, without prejudice to the outcome. We look forward to free and democratic elections in the GDR. That is the current question.

(*c*) Welcome the Chancellor's stress on the need to maintain security in Europe. The Federal Republic plays a crucial role in the Western Alliance. We acknowledge the Federal Government's repeated reaffirmation of full commitment to NATO.

(*d*) If democratic reform is to succeed in the GDR and elsewhere, stable conditions in Europe will be needed. That argues for avoiding speed on the German question.

(*e*) Glad that the Chancellor set no timetable and linked his approach on the German question to progress in Europe as a whole.

4. A reference to frontiers and the Final Act could be added. But suggest not, because we have made the point several times and there is currently an argument between CDU and SPD on an aspect of it (my telno 1169) such that we could appear to be siding with the SPD.[5]

---

[1] Repeated for information Immediate to East Berlin, BMG Berlin, Moscow, Paris, Washington.

[2] Washington telegram No. 3105 of 30 November reported Mr Baker's 'Four Principles' on German unification (see No. 76, note 3) (WRG 021/8). Paris telegram No. 1581 of 29 November reported comments by M. Dumas (French Foreign Minister 1988-93) in the National Assembly repeating the French view that the German desire for unity was fundamentally legitimate but underlining that the German problem had an international dimension (WRF 021/2).

[3] No. 59, note 2.

[4] Mrs Thatcher minuted on her copy of this telegram: 'Most inadvisable' (PREM: Internal situation in East Germany).

[5] Telegram No 1169 of 30 November reported that the SPD's unqualified support for Herr Kohl's plan had proved short-lived. Negotiations with the Coalition parties for a *Bundestag* resolution in

support of the Chancellor's statement had broken down over SPD demands to add to the resolution statements on Poland's western frontier and SNF modernisation (WRG 021/8). Mr. Gozney minuted on 1 December on telegram No 1171: 'The Secretary of State thinks that the suggested elements are valid points for him to make. He thinks he should probably try to work them into interviews he gives after the NATO summit on Monday.'

No. 64

Minute from Mr Weston to Mr Synnott

[*WRL 020/4*]

FCO, *4 December 1989*

Ditchley Park Conference on Germany 1-3 December

1. As you know I attended this conference over the weekend, in the company of David Ratford and Frank Berman. The Minister of State, Mr Maude, attended for the final two plenary sessions on the Sunday. The full list of participants is attached. I was most grateful for the department's briefing.

2. Mr Ratford and Mr Berman may have their own comments, on what I found a very interesting though necessarily inconclusive weekend. The following are among the points I drew from discussions.

(*a*) A strong feeling on the part of Germans present that, with free movement and a single passport, de facto reunification of the German people was already well underway: 'as inevitable as the laws of physics'. The process could prove messy to handle, and might well outrun the best attempts of officials and governments to organise and control.

(*b*) Much interest centring on Kohl's 28 November speech to the *Bundestag*— the 10 points. Failure to consult Allies strongly registered. Regret at omission of any real reference to NATO in the 10 points. A general view that, particularly after FDP rejection, this part of the Kohl speech could hardly be read as a ringing endorsement of deeper EC integration going hand in hand with opening toward the East. Kohl's accent was heavily on the looser, more open, pan-European approach. There was therefore some tension in German policy on this score.

(*c*) The steps set out in Kohl's 10 points could be read as a careful attempt to slow up the process. But the more likely effect would be to accelerate interest, particularly since the decisive step to confederative structures was made dependent only on the appearance of a legitimate democratic government in the GDR, which could happen by the end of 1990. It was argued strongly by Sir C. Mallaby that the model which might best suit both East and West (e.g. on continuing troop presences, Soviet tolerance, EC assimilation and 'self respect' for East Germans) was a true confederation, i.e. an evolution retaining an underlying binary structure: whereas this was in fact the only variation apparently excluded from the Kohl speech.

(*d*) Continuing uncertainty over how the GDR people would in fact express themselves when it came to self-determination; and what the Soviet bottom line was on statehood of the GDR. But some feeling that the latter could well be a moving line, particularly if suitable political/security/economic incentives were offered to Moscow.

(*e*) The Western interest in not allowing NATO and the Warsaw Pact to be equated in the rhetoric (some criticism of the Prime Minister e.g. by Sonnenfeldt on this). Even if the Warsaw Pact were to collapse and dissolve completely NATO would continue to have a viable and necessary function in maintaining the US troop connection and an overall balance in Europe. The West European peninsula would otherwise be dominated by the Eurasian land mass to the East.

(*f*) Caution over Gorbachev's proposal for a Helsinki 2 summit meeting. This was seen primarily as an attempt to underscore the Soviet claim in effect to have reached a final peace settlement at Helsinki 1 and to legitimise and fireproof Soviet territorial acquisitions dating from the Hitler period.

(*g*) On Berlin a sense that status was eroding and that great skill would be needed by the Allies in not over-egging the pudding. Need for attention to voting rights for Berlin representatives in the *Bundestag* and air traffic (Sir C. Mallaby agreed with Duisberg and the German Ambassador that these should be considered at a higher level than the Bonn Group).[1]

3. In an attempt to harness some of the weekend's headier discussions around a more sober median point I suggested (and Mr Maude endorsed) the main elements of the British position were as follows:

(*a*)Points of reference:

—the Thatcher/Kohl statement of 1985.[2]

—the latest public opinion poll showing 61% in UK in favour of German unity.

(*b*)Need for a measured tread:

(i) cement democracy in Eastern Europe;

(ii) allow self-determination, including in GDR, to take place;

(iii) remember four power rights and responsibilities retain an inevitable place in any outcome;

(iv) avoid saying or doing anything to provoke Gorbachev or unnecessarily complicate his fragile position.

(*c*) Elements also in our mind:

(i) the EC had an active agenda and would continue to develop, but recent events were unlikely to leave the nature of the EC integration process wholly unchanged;

(ii) NATO has a lasting function. We should not alter prematurely a winning recipe, though changes of emphasis would no doubt be needed;

(iii) the need for caution was underlined by the lack of consensus on many key factors, e.g. the Soviet bottom line on the GDR, and the outcome of East German self-determination;

(iv) this reinforced the need for very close consultation between close allies including UK/FRG. The UK remained ready to help support and encourage the FRG in confronting fast moving events on the basis of sound Allied positions (we might even be somewhat more generous in recognising the German need for Allied support at this time);

(v) we needed to be alert to the possible emergence of new kinds of threat to

---

[1] The Bonn Group, comprising representatives of the three Western Allied embassies in Bonn and the Federal German Foreign Ministry, was a forum for discussion of issues relating to Germany as a whole, including Berlin and the GDR.

[2] In fact of 1984: see enclosure in No. 15.

security and stability in Europe. This might require creative thinking about new mechanisms and procedures. One point of departure could be the CSCE process. But keeping an open mind for the future did not mean relinquishing our strategic points of reference (NATO, EC) which remain valid and had brought us to the present success.

P.J. WESTON

No. 65

Letter from Sir C. Mallaby (Bonn) to Sir J. Fretwell[1]

[*WRL 020/4*]

Confidential   BONN, *5 December 1989*

Dear John,

The German Question and Some Implications for Security in Europe

1. This letter offers some further reflections on future policy regarding the German Question, taking into account the Ditchley Conference last weekend and developing some of the ideas discussed there.[2] Much of what follows is intended as a contribution to the thinking process in the FCO about what political and security system we want in the new era in Europe.

2. In my letter of 8 November I wrote that rapid collapse of the old regime in the GDR could bring early change in the structure of the relationship between the two Germanies.[3] Events since then have made early progress towards German unity seem more likely. Kohl said at NATO on 4 December that reunification was not on the agenda today.[4] That statement sits uncomfortably with the last of his ten points of 28 November and would not be endorsed by many people here. The major uncertainties include the Soviet bottom line and the wishes of the people of the GDR. Both seem to be shifting in the direction of possible reunification. Kohl's ten points may now be taken for granted in the debate in the FRG. The debate may continue to quest forwards, focussing not only on the question of the finality of Germany's Eastern frontier but before long perhaps on timetables for movement towards reunification. Egon Bahr of the SPD said to me today that the two main parties in the FRG would compete, in the run-up to the General Election here on 2 December 1990, in their support for German unity. The GDR election, at present expected in 1990 (not the timescale of 2-3 years attributed to Kohl in UKDEL NATO telno 375),[5] is the trigger set by the Chancellor for introducing the 'confederative structures' between the two Germanies and is likely to accelerate

---

[1] Copied to Ambassadors in East Berlin, Moscow, Washington, Paris, UKDEL NATO, Mr Burton, BMG Berlin, and Mr. Cooper, Policy Planning Staff.

[2] See No. 64.

[3] No. 34.

[4] A NATO Summit/Ministerial meeting was held in Brussels on 4 December.

[5] This telegram recorded the afternoon session of the meeting of NATO Heads of State and Government on 4 December. Herr Kohl was reported to have stated that there was no timetable for German unification: 'Unless there was a change in world politics there would be free elections in the GDR in two or three years' time. After that joint bodies would be set up . . . Then one must think of confederative structures (not, he underlined, confederation)' (WRL 020/4).

change in the inner-German relationship, if that has not happened before then through collapse of the regime or economic problems in the GDR.

3. For reasons of stability among other things, our interest at present is to argue for gradual change, stressing for the time being that genuine self-determination is the big item on the agenda and not giving the impression that we assume that unity will be the outcome. We should have in mind the possibility of suggesting a lengthy period for the complicated and ramified process of implementing reunification if self-determination opts for it. One argument for that would be that Kohl and everyone else wants German unity and a comprehensive settlement in Europe to proceed in parallel, and the latter will take some years. But we should also prepare ourselves to cope with the eventuality of fast movement, in case events, notably on the streets of the GDR, produce it. This reinforces the point I have made several times that we should think what possible answers to the German Question would suit us best and aim to steer events, insofar as we can, towards those answers.

4. The change in Eastern Europe, where several new democracies seem likely to emerge, is greatly in our interest. But because of the sheer size of the Soviet Union, the expansionist history of Russia, the risk that a truculent and reactionary leadership could one day have its finger on the Soviet nuclear button and also the prospect of years of uncertainty in Eastern Europe, we still need a Western security system including a lasting United States military presence in Europe. That requires on political grounds alone a continuing albeit reduced level of American forces in Germany. I hope that British forces would also stay—a subject for a separate study involving role specialisation in Western defence among many other things. I guess that the Soviet Union, fearing that a strong, united Germany could one day threaten its interests, would want American forces to remain in Germany and that this and other motives would cause the Russians to want to keep some forces of their own in Germany.

5. Agreement on continued stationing of some forces in Germany and elsewhere could be incorporated in the instruments approved by the future Peace Conference to agree the eventual answer to the German Question. But that could be a conspicuous way of doing it, with a risk of the Germans feeling singularised because more forces were to be stationed on their territory than elsewhere. Another approach, perhaps preferable, might be to embed agreement about stationed forces among the many elements of a new pan-European system.

6. Before discussing that, I want to deal with a question concerning the structure of a possible united Germany. It would be easier to justify keeping forces in Germany if Germany was a confederation—that is a binary arrangement in which the old FRG and GDR would be two distinct elements each consisting of *Länder*— than if Germany was a federation of some 16 *Länder* and a Federal government but no level of government between these two. I think that the Soviet Union, insofar as it can continue to insist on maintaining the statehood of the GDR, might find confederation easier to stomach because the GDR would not completely disappear. I suppose that a confederation would also make it easier to manage an adjustment period if the GDR joined the Community.

7. Kohl's ten points were notable for avoiding the option of confederation. He spoke of 'confederative structures . . . with the aim of creating a federation, a federal order in Germany'. That omission was deliberate. Kohl feared that, if he spoke of confederation, he would be accused by the right in Federal politics of foreseeing the continued existence of the bankrupt GDR. Another important

objection to confederation is that it is a contrivance to have a confederal government, two governments responsible for the old FRG and GDR and some 16 *Land* governments. The natural arrangement would omit the middle tier. Contrivance can be hard to preserve.

8. Duisberg of the Federal Chancellery said at the Ditchley Conference that confederation might be what in fact developed in Germany. Egon Bahr told me today that he favoured it but thought it unlikely to emerge. My feeling is that we should have the idea in mind as an answer to the German Question which might suit us, but should be prepared for a situation where the difficulties inherent in it would make it unattainable.

9. We must also think about wider arrangements to preserve Western security in the future. I hope that NATO will be adapted, not replaced. That is a major aim, and we should not lose sight of the possibility of a united Germany belonging to the Alliance. But the point about the Russians at the end of paragraph 4 and other considerations may make NATO and German unity difficult to reconcile. We may anyway need some new system for settling disputes in Eastern Europe and limiting instability there, and the Warsaw Pact (which we should treat neither to resuscitation nor euthanasia) is likely to prove unpopular and ineffective over time. That brings me back to consideration of some kind of pan-European security system. In other words, to the question of what the long-touted proposition of a European peace order ought in our interests to mean.

10. One way of approaching this is to consider a Helsinki Final Act with teeth. Another is to devise a kind of United Nations for Europe. Since CSCE exists and involves the Americans, and also has made headway on human rights, I prefer it as a starting point. The new Final Act would be a treaty, legally and not just politically binding. It would incorporate much (or all) of what is in the Helsinki Act as well as provisions to make pluralism and the rule of law and open frontiers etc as irreversible as possible. It would build on Basket II in order to foster market reforms in Eastern Europe. There would have to be some enforcement arrangement. It might be a standing commission, to which suspected violations could be referred. There might be a corps of inspectors to investigate complaints and even a peace keeping force. All this, needless to say, needs a great deal of thought. One of the biggest difficulties is how the correction of violations and the deployment of any peace keeping force would be decided. The United States would need to be involved in these matters. A kind of European Security Council, on the lines of the UN SC, raises the question of permanent membership and of vetoes; we cannot give the Soviet Union a veto over Western European matters and thus arguably more power over us than now. The idea of weighted voting ought to be investigated.

11. The new arrangement could provide for stationing of one member's forces in the territory of another, by mutual agreement. This would render illegal any unilateral reoccupation of an Eastern European country by the Soviet Union under different leadership. The agreement of the two states could be registered with the coordinating organisation of the European security system. Certain stationing arrangements agreed before signature, notably for forces in Germany, could be recorded in the new agreement itself, possibly with a requirement for renewed registration of consent by the sending and receiving states after a stated period of years.

12. One big question in all this is whether the Germans, East and West, would tolerate stationing of foreign forces. In the context we are discussing, they would

be achieving the goal of unity. They would know that this achievement was altering the system that has kept the peace in Europe for 40 years. They would be getting major reductions in the forces currently present in Germany. I think that there should be a worthwhile chance of pulling it off provided the superpowers were clearly for it. Our standing in relation to the German Question, and the need for our signature on the treaty embodying the answer to it, give us some leverage. We should consult the Americans and French about this and many other aspects, and then try to establish in the public mind in Europe the position that a new security system is going to be needed if there is German unity and that stationing of some foreign forces in Germany must be part of it.[6]

Yours ever,
C.L.G. MALLABY

[6] Mr Powell minuted on 12 December on Mrs Thatcher's copy of this letter: 'A useful contribution to thinking about the future. At least we've got him off reunification!' (PREM: Internal Situation in East Germany).

No. 66

Mr Broomfield (East Berlin) to Mr Hurd

[*WRE 014/2*]

Confidential   EAST BERLIN, *6 December 1989*

Sir,

GDR 1989: From 'Continuity and Renewal' to 'Revolutionary Renewal'

1. It is difficult to write a valedictory despatch about a revolution which is still in progress.[1] I propose therefore to try to identify some of the factors underlying recent developments and to draw some conclusions about the likely future course of events and their significance for our interests.

2. There are some striking resemblances between the GDR today and Germany immediately after the War. The country is living through a profound identity crisis. The old idols have fallen. The former leaders have been disgraced and political certainties based on scientific socialism have failed. If nature abhors a vacuum, then the German people above all abhor a political and philosophical vacuum. The future of this country and indeed post-war Germany will be decided by who, and on what platform, manages to fill the gap created by the passing of the old order. As yet no clear rallying point for the people has emerged. The question posed earlier this year by the Head of the Academy for Social Science, Dr Reinhold—'If this country is not socialist, on what basis can it continue to exist'? hangs in the air. (Reinhold's answer was that a non-socialist GDR could not exist alongside the FRG.)

[1] Mr Broomfield retired as Ambassador to East Germany in December 1989 but stayed on in East Berlin until 24 January because his successor, Mr Patrick Eyers, was not to take over until the beginning of February. See also No. 107, note 4.

3. Before looking more closely at the contenders for power, it is important to understand that what is now happening in the GDR is essentially a German development. Non-German outsiders have almost no influence. As Sir Rodric Braithwaite has observed, Gorbachev, having lit the blue-touch paper of reform in Eastern Europe, has stood back.[2] The Russians clearly panicked on the night of 9 November when the borders were opened, but by appealing to the three Western Allied Heads of Government, Gorbachev signalled his effective impotence. The US Secretary of State can lay down conditions for reunification but they carry almost no weight with the people of the GDR. And it is they, we have all agreed, who should be the final arbiters on that question. Whether we like it or not the pace and direction of the revolution in the GDR will be dictated by the people of the GDR, influenced, if at all, by the FRG. I realise that this brings an (unwelcome) element of uncertainty into one of the key issues affecting European strategic, political and economic development. But I fear we will all have to learn to live with it.

4. If the GDR is to survive as an independent sovereign country then it can only do so on the basis of a popularly elected government, pursuing political and economic policies which convince the majority here that it is a better place to live in than the FRG. Such a government could count on the strong regional attachment, felt by most East Germans for the provinces where they live. It could also count on widespread acceptance of a broadly socialist ethos, deriving originally from Prussian paternalism and now supported by the Evangelical Church. Against that has to be set a range of specific problems which I will touch on briefly, as well as a fundamental one. Although at the local level there is a strong feeling of belonging, at the (German, not GDR) national level there is an equally strong feeling of belonging to a single nation—'*Wir sind ein Volk*' (We are one people) is now one of the Leipzig chants. There is, however, no feeling of belonging to the GDR as such. Its policies, leaders and record, even its sporting achievements, have not succeeded in forging a bond between the people and this particular German State.

5. Against that background the current GDR contenders for power do not look all that convincing. The Socialist Unity Party (SED) is shattered by failure and corruption. Prime Minister Modrow is the Party's best hope of salvaging something from the wreckage. He has integrity and seems genuine about reform. But to expect that in the five days between the Politburo and Central Committee's resignation and the Party Congress now brought forward to 8 December, a new reformed Party can rise from the ashes of the old is unrealistic. The Committee of Investigation will continue to uncover corruption which will reinforce popular anger and alienation from anything to do with the old SED. A new name for the Party will have to be found. Before the scandal broke Modrow thought that the old SED might win 20% in an election. It would certainly win less now.

6. Even if, and it is a big if, Modrow succeeded in establishing a new social democratic party prepared to accept the verdict of the polls, there is no sign that such a reformed Party would follow economic policies capable of dealing with the current acute economic crises or of producing a second German economic miracle in the longer term.

7. At present the aim is a 'socialist planned market economy', which is all things to all men. The reformers insist that the accent will be firmly on the market.

---

[2] In Moscow telegram No. 1950 of 22 November (WRL 020/4).

But most of the large concerns (*Kombinate*) will remain in State hands and be subject to a State plan. No new definition has yet been suggested for 'people's property' in a revised constitution. One of the Government's leading advisers told me earlier this week that there was no way the GDR, even with reformed policies, could approach living standards in the FRG for the foreseeable future. People would have to be convinced of the counter balancing virtues of this society, such as social security, no unemployment, etc. This is a fine aim, but I very much doubt if it will persuade those who do not live in privileged Berlin but in the grimy depressing industrial towns in the south of the GDR. If, as seems unavoidable, reform leads to temporary unemployment, the attractions of the GDR will be further diminished.

8. The other authorised Parties and as yet unauthorised groups are frankly unimpressive. Some leaders like Gerlach (Liberal Democrats) have some political skill, some like the new CDU leader, de Maizière, have integrity, but none have much experience of governing and all lack an understanding of the economy. There is now increasing pressure for early elections, possibly May 1990. It is hard to see convincing leaders with coherent alternative policies emerging in that time scale, even though I do not doubt that if the elections are held in May the majority of votes will be cast for the opposition parties and groups. A further period of uncertainty seems inevitable during which the stability and predictability of the FRG will appear even more attractive to people in the GDR. The leader of one of the groups remarked to me bitterly that the gravest charge against the SED was not that they had bankrupted the country and their own Party, but that they had wrecked political life as a whole by their insistence that 'opposition' was a criminal and not a political word.

9. The people remain the great imponderable. They showed great fortitude, discipline and humour in bringing down the old regime without violence. But increasing exposure to the West and revelations of widespread corruption in the SED has given their latest demonstrations in Leipzig and elsewhere a harder and more aggressive edge. Minor acts of violence have occurred and more general violence cannot be ruled out. Faced with a political vacuum, the number of people openly demonstrating for unity with the FRG has grown considerably. The young particularly seem to have no ideological aversion to West Germany, indeed quite the opposite.

10. The absence of legitimate authority in the GDR together with the publication of Chancellor Kohl's ten points, will I think force the question of this country's future relationship with the FRG into the centre of next year's elections. Although initially opposed to any talk of unity with the FRG, the intellectuals and opposition groups in Berlin have been forced to recognise the strength of feeling among workers and others in the demonstrations on the streets. Shades of opinion are beginning to emerge with 'Democratic Awakening', positively supporting Kohl's ten points, while Modrow's official line is not to rule out confederation or, as he puts it, a 'treaty partnership' with the FRG, provided that this acknowledges the reality of two sovereign independent German States. My guess is that the people's impatience may cut through the niceties of expression and demand that the benefits of the FRG be made available in the GDR now and not after a further forty years of endeavour. And if that is not possible under the present system the workers are likely either to emigrate to the FRG or to look for some way of forcing the political parties to take note of their demands. Overall I am sure that the majority would prefer to remain here and change the system.

11. The driving force for political change is likely to be the economy. The full extent of mismanagement and false statistics under the recently arrested Gunther Mittag is now becoming apparent. Although hunger as a result of acute food shortages is not likely, industrial and financial collapse during this winter is a possibility. Emigration during November averaged between 2 and 3,000 a day. In December it is still running at over a thousand a day. And the army cannot cover all the gaps. Modrow recently told Bertele, the FRG Permanent Representative, that the country had only one and a half days of lignite reserves available for power supplies. This is not enough to cope with a prolonged cold spell. If an economic collapse occurred, the FRG would be obliged to step in and stabilise the situation. But the result would almost certainly be a considerable increase in internal pressure in the GDR for unity.

12. I have, myself, no doubt that the two German States will one day be politically united. From 1 January East and West Germany, including Berlin will become a single travel free area. Berlin, about whose political and symbolic importance to Germans in both countries I have commented before, is leading the way. Mr Bush has proposed that the 2004 Olympics should be held in Berlin as evidence of a Europe 'whole and free'. I am sure that the city will be whole and free before that. The question is how will German unity be achieved and when.

13. On the 'how' the tide, even in the GDR, is beginning to run in the direction of 'confederation'. But the fate of confederations (cf Switzerland) is to end up as unitary states. The model of a German federation suggested by Kohl as the final step in the process of unification would fit with the strong local traditions here, particularly if, as seems likely, the old provincial entities like Saxony, Thuringia and Brandenburg replace the present 14 districts.

14. The 'when' is more difficult. So far every observer (myself included) has seriously underestimated the speed of change in the GDR. We saw the strength but did not pay sufficient attention to the brittleness of a Government not based on consent nor the emotional charge which lies at the heart of inner German relations. Telescoping time scales have been about the only consistent factor in recent developments. As I write the atmosphere in the GDR has become highly charged as a result of the sensational revelations of corruption at the highest levels of the Party. A witch-hunt is in progress and it is not possible to say how fast and how far it will go. Central authority has been weakened to the point where there is a danger that some minor incident could get out of control. The odds are therefore that events are likely to move faster than most people had originally thought possible.

15. The basic reasons are not far to seek. The opening of the borders for East to West travel on 9 November acted like the release of a massive tourniquet. Life has been pumping down the long disused arteries ever since. West Berlin buses advertising MacDonald's hamburgers have appeared in East Berlin and Potsdam. The first East Berlin handicapped child has been admitted on a daily basis to a West Berlin school. Governing Mayor Momper has proposed to the GDR authorities a joint commission to regulate Berlin matters and has met his East Berlin opposite number to start the process. The first West German doctors and nurses are due soon in East German hospitals. Interflug and Lufthansa are connecting more cities in both countries. Volkswagen and the Springer publishing house are already trying to set up joint ventures in the GDR. And whenever it happens, the first GDR/FRG joint venture in this country will act as a magnet for young East German industrial talent.

16. The abolition of restrictions for West to East travel, which will enter into force on 1 January is another enormous step in the direction of bringing the two Germanies together. For the first time since the borders became established after the last War both parts of Germany, including Berlin, will become a free travel zone. The surge of West Berlin purchasing power which this will release into the countryside around Berlin could have a dramatic effect. And the build up will be emotional. There are already plans for enormous numbers of intra-Berlin and cross border parties and religious services in the run up to Christmas and the New Year.

17. My conclusion is that the question of German unity is now actual. It could become operational at any time over this winter if there is a breakdown in law and order or an economic collapse. It could again become operational if, as I believe, next year's elections in the GDR focus on the question. Or it might take place progressively after that, as the natural process of growing together becomes stronger and stronger. Already there has been a rapid build up in contacts between the political parties in the two countries. Herr Genscher told you that he would like to campaign in next year's elections in the GDR, but didn't know if it would be permitted. Permitted or not, I am sure that the elections in both countries separated by only a few months will reinforce the tendency to see the political processes as linked to one another. Television coverage will see to that.

18. If this analysis is correct, what should we do about it? I hope you will excuse me if I go outside my local remit to make some suggestions which draw on involvement not only in the present wave of change in the Soviet Union and Eastern Europe, but also on our (collectively) unsuccessful attempts to exert economic influence in Eastern Europe in the late 70s and early 80s. The subsequent string of debt rescheduling meetings with various East European countries in Warsaw, Paris and Berne were the measure of our failure. I hope on this occasion we are giving primacy to selectivity, coordination and the allocation of adequate human as well as material resources. Because

(*a*) if the resources we allocate to various countries are not matched by adequate staff to apply them selectively, they are likely to be ineffective. And because

(*b*) given the wide range of questions with which we will be dealing (food aid, management training, know-how, English-language training, joint ventures, access to the EC market, parliamentary and political contacts, etc) overview and coordination within national administrations and similarly within the Twelve/Twenty-four will be essential. Our policies should at least be complementary.

19. Specifically with regard to the GDR, I recommend:

(*a*) that we should make the most of our unique asset—the English language. It is likely soon to replace Russian as the first foreign language taught in schools and universities. We have been told that up to 500 new English language teachers may be needed. It is in our political and long-term commercial interests, to help this germano-centric country to widen its interests;

(*b*) we already have management training programmes in place, they would be fully subscribed if we could expand them;

(*c*) our parliamentary contacts are rudimentary. I hope they can be expanded, particularly after the elections. Parliamentary traditions have not existed here since the Nazis took over in 1933;

(*d*) we have had almost no political contacts at ministerial level during the last 18 months. I welcome Mr Waldegrave's intention to visit East Berlin in February. I hope that you will also find time to do so after the elections next year.

20. Following the recent string of successes for reform movements in East Berlin, Prague and Sofia, to match those in Moscow, Budapest and Warsaw, we now have a real chance to redraw the political map of Europe. Forty-four years ago, with the critical exception of West Berlin and the subsequent exception of Austria, the lines were drawn where the allied armies met. We have now won the much longer battle of political and economic values and ideas. With patience and skill I hope that we will be able to capitalise on this. If we succeed it will be the crowning achievement of European history in this century. It would enable Europe, and the UK within a developing EC, to play an important part in tackling the global problems of the next century: population, poverty and pollution. If we do not we will experience these problems on our own doorstep here in Europe. Over the last few months I have observed the weekly invasion of East and West Berlin by Poles trading almost anything for West Marks. I have also seen hundreds of thousands of East Germans leaving for West Germany. Economic migration will not be the least of our problems if the East European economies fail.

21. My final thanks on leaving go to the staff of this Embassy and their spouses. We were lucky that the crisis did not come a year ago when we were understaffed and under-trained. As it is, the recent long hours, the ancient cypher machines, etc, have been overcome with a high level of professional ability and commitment. I drew great vicarious satisfaction from the fact that as a result of contacts built up over a long period by junior members of Chancery, often in oppressive and sometimes in hostile circumstances, the British Embassy became the focal point for enquiries after 9 November from our EC colleagues about the unofficial 'opposition'. I leave Berlin, therefore, for the third time in my military and diplomatic career grateful to the people with whom I have worked, conscious of my good fortune in having been in Berlin at this time and optimistic about the future.

22. I am sending copies of this despatch to Heads of Mission at CSCE posts, the Permanent Representative at NATO, the Permanent Representative to the European Communities, the Commandant of the British Sector in Berlin and the Commanders in Chief, Germany.

I am, Sir,
Yours faithfully,
N.H.R.A. BROOMFIELD

No. 67

Sir C. Mallaby (Bonn) to Mr Wall[1]

No. 1202 Telegraphic [WRG 021/8]

Confidential   BONN, *7 December 1989, 3 p.m.*

Strasbourg Personal for Wall—No Distribution

German Question: Assessment of the Position in the FRG

Summary
1. The view in FRG political circles is that the GDR regime is collapsing and the GDR people are calling increasingly for unity. Main political parties in FRG likely to start competing in support for goal of unity. SPD leaders talking of a German confederation allowing FRG and GDR to stay in their alliances. SPD talk of a long transition period from a decision on unity to its implementation.

Detail
2. I have discussed the position and prospects of the GDR in recent days with Seiters (CDU), Lambsdorff and Mischnick (FDP) and Vogel, Brandt and Bahr (SPD). I have set out our case that self-determination without prejudice to the result is the subject now on the agenda, that reunification is not a current issue, that a measured tread and preservation of stability are essential, and that nothing should be done to complicate things for Gorbachev. I have said that the Allies attach importance to their rights and have stressed the importance of NATO for the future. These points are not contested. But the way these leading politicians talked about the future showed that they in fact expect rapid developments. Most of my discussions are reported by bag. But Seiters, as the responsible Cabinet Minister, and Vogel, as leader of the opposition, are worth reporting here.

Seiters
3. Briefing the US and French Ambassadors and myself today, Seiters said that the SED was collapsing. The Party Congress tomorrow could produce no credible leadership and might wind up the Party or its major institutions. The GDR could become a country where the Government (not the Party) did the governing. But even that might not be possible: all authority could fade away within weeks. It was more a question of the death of institutions than of chaos in the sense of public order breaking down. Seiters made clear that this prediction was not the only possible one. Things might not collapse fast, but the major lesson of recent events was that the pace of change had accelerated. It was still accelerating. A depressing novelty in recent days was the aggressive mood of the demonstrators in the GDR. The Federal Government hoped that the new agreement on travel by West Germans to the GDR (my telno 1136)[2] and the Federal Chancellor's visit to Dresden on 19 December (my telno 1193)[3] might calm the East German

---

[1] Repeated for information Immediate to Moscow, East Berlin, BMG Berlin; information Priority to Paris, Washington, UKDEL NATO, Strasbourg. Mr Wall was accompanying the Foreign Secretary at a meeting of the European Council in Strasbourg from 8 to 9 December.
[2] Not found.
[3] Not found.

population, but this was only an uncertain possibility. It was probable that 60-80 per cent of the people of the GDR were now for unity, and the main reason was that they had become convinced that their own leaders could not cope and that reform could not be achieved in a separate GDR. Elections in the GDR were now likely before autumn 1992: they might be even sooner or might be overtaken by events. If things get worse in the GDR, the rush of emigration would resume. Seiters agreed that the East Mark was extremely weak but thought that it would not be completely swamped by the DMark in the very near future.

Vogel

4. Vogel, on whom I called today, said the SED was in ruins and even the Government was weak. Modrow was the only figure on the scene but he would prove transitional. Public calls for unity were multiplying in the GDR. It was possible that, within a matter of weeks or months, it would become clear and certain that the people of the GDR in great majority wanted German unity. All the West German political parties except the Greens would support unity in those circumstances. Vogel wondered whether there would be a referendum on unity in the GDR in 1990 and whether that might be followed by one in the FRG. He said that a transition period of years would be needed between a decision for unity and the completion of its implementation. Like Brandt and Bahr in conversations with me, and Brandt in public, Vogel spoke of confederation as a desirable structure of German unity, where the two Germanies would retain their identity within a new arrangement and thus could stay in their alliances. Such a confederation might last until a pan-European settlement was achieved and the German question thus lost its separate importance. He said that the German question would be the biggest issue in the Federal election campaign next year. The SPD would claim that the changes in Eastern Europe were the fruit of the *Ostpolitik* of Brandt and Schmidt. The SPD supported Kohl's ten points because they had invented most of them. One issue that might be sensitive in the run-up to the Federal election would be how living standards in the FRG would be affected if the latter undertook a vast economic rescue operation for the GDR.

Comment

5. On top of the unity of nation, language and culture which has continued to exist in Germany, the new freedom of travel in both directions is a big event. A proliferation of cooperation agreements between the two Governments and a burst of joint venture activity by FRG industry in the GDR are likely to be the next stages. The Federal Chancellor's visit and the other ministerial meetings planned this month (my telno 1193)[4] are likely to set the scene for that stage.

6. The general view in the FRG now is that the SED can no longer play a serious role and could disappear at any moment, and that the only leadership in the GDR will be a very weak Government. Almost no one but the Greens is talking any longer about the answer to the German question being two German democracies. A united and unmistakable call for German unity in the GDR is considered possible within weeks, since that is seen as the only way the people of the GDR can be confident of democracy and prosperity. Politicians increasingly assume that 1990 will be the year when unification becomes a certainty, though the means by which that would happen remain unclear. The methods discussed are the GDR election, referenda in the GDR and then the FRG, overwhelming demonstrations, or a new wave of emigration.

[4] Not printed.

7. The political parties of the FRG, except the Greens, are coming out for reunification as the goal. If there was a clear call for unity in the GDR, I am sure they would all support it. I expect that Kohl, again fearing being left behind by the debate, would make another major speech moving the Federal Government's position forward. At present the SPD is ahead of the Government in playing up a particular form of unification, namely confederation. Other subjects that I think may appear soon in the public debate in the FRG are a timetable for moving towards unity, including the idea of a long transition period between the decision and the act of unity, and the possible need for a vast package of West German economic help for the GDR this winter. Some politicians may start saying that, with the GDR weak and without leadership, the FRG would need to take the lead in moving towards unity.

8. Our line can hold at present. But we need to prepare to cope with faster movement on the German question in case we are faced with it.

No. 68

Minute from Sir J. Fretwell to Mr Adams

[*WRL 020/4*]

Confidential   FCO, *7 December 1989*

Planning Staff Paper on Germany[1]

1. I have had a quick look at the paper. It seems to me to cover the main points.

2. At the present time I have no idea whether Chancellor Kohl's orderly progression through three Stages will prove possible. It seems to me perhaps more likely that authority in the GDR will gradually decompose, and that the country will slide imperceptibly into some sort of union with the FRG. If such a process occurs—and it may already be in train—it will not go smoothly. There will be efforts to reconstitute a Government in the GDR, deriving from the SED, or emerging from an electoral process. There will be pressures on Gorbachev to put his foot down before the GDR finally disintegrates. But the prestige, authority and economic resources of the FRG will constitute a magnet to which Parties, economic groupings and individuals in the GDR will increasingly want to attach themselves. Total freedom of movement between the two parts of Germany will accelerate this process. So will ideas for new transport links and telecommunications systems. The initiative of Momper in settling practical questions with his opposite number in East Berlin is a pointer to the way things may go. I think our paper should make some reference to this sort of scenario.

3. One other area I should like to see covered is the possibility—I have no idea how realistic it might be—of the GDR becoming a demilitarised zone (I suppose it would be seen as two demilitarised *Länder*) forming part of a united Germany in which the original FRG stayed within NATO and of course within the European Community. There must be several historical precedents for such an arrangement. The Treaty of Versailles arrangements for the Saarland might appear discouraging

[1] Planning Staff Paper, 'Implications of Chancellor Kohl's Proposals', 6 December 1989 (WRL 020/4). Not printed. This paper had been commissioned at the PUS's meeting with DUSs on 29 November.

as a precedent, but the circumstances would be totally different. It is worth looking at this if only to have some alternative to the rather stark conclusion in paragraph 5 of the paper that the Soviet Union would not agree to a unified Germany in NATO, with the implication that we must plan on the withdrawal of the FRG from the Alliance. It may be objected that the Soviet Union would similarly reject a demilitarised zone, knowing that there could be no guarantee of its permanence. But the future presence of Soviet forces in Eastern Europe is now becoming questionable. Pressures against them may well mount rapidly in Hungary, Czechoslovakia and Poland. They will in any event be reduced drastically in the GDR under the CFE (and its likely successor even if we refuse to admit that). A cordon sanitaire of neutral, Finland-style countries running from the Arctic to the Mediterranean (I would happily throw in Greece!) might not be such a bad idea for the Soviet Union once it finally renounced its Imperial pretensions in Europe. So why not a partially demilitarised zone?

J. FRETWELL

No. 69

Sir R. Braithwaite (Moscow) to Mr Hurd[1]

No. 2055 Telegraphic [WRL 020/4]

Confidential   MOSCOW, *8 December 1989, 8.20 a.m.*

MIPT: Soviet View on Germany: Comment[2]

1. I do not know Falin's mood (the German Ambassador, who knows him well, says he is temperamentally apocalyptic). But he had the depressed air of a man whose life's work was crumbling.

2. Falin, like Sir C. Mallaby (Bonn tel. no 1191)[3] sees Kohl as playing for high stakes. But as far as Falin is concerned, Kohl is overplaying his hand, and has

---

[1] Repeated to desk by 8.09 a.m., UKDEL Strasbourg; information Immediate to Bonn, East Berlin, BMG Berlin, Paris, Washington, UKDEL NATO; information Routine to Warsaw, Prague, Budapest, UKREP Brussels.

[2] Moscow telegram No. 2054 reported a conversation between Sir R. Braithwaite and Mr Falin, a former Ambassador to Bonn and Gorbachev's senior adviser on German affairs, who was 'exhausted and lugubrious'. He expressed 'deep concern at scale and tempo of events' and warned of 'possible dramatic consequences'. Soviet bitterness about Kohl's ten-point programme was due to the fact that 'Literally two days before he announced his plan, Kohl had told Gorbachev that the FRG would not launch any pan-German initiative: and promised to consult him on any important developments, in the spirit of their talks this year in Bonn'. Asked about the Soviet attitude to Four Power talks, 'Falin said the Russians did not yet have the latter in mind: but that he did not exclude the possibility. For political reasons it would probably have to come as a Western initiative. He agreed that we should keep in touch through different channels, though the value of this depended on the degree of frankness and constructiveness' (WRL 020/4). In fact the Soviet Union itself proposed a Four Power meeting on 8 December: see Nos. 72, 73. When Moscow telegrams No. 2054 and 2055 were shown to Mrs Thatcher before the Strasbourg meeting, Mr Powell minuted: 'This underlines the seriousness of developments. You should *NOT* refer to these exchanges openly, but will want to have *them in mind*, as you *pursue your discussions*' (PREM: Internal situation in East Germany).

[3] In this telegram of 6 December Sir C. Mallaby reflected on Herr Kohl's preoccupations as he approached the forthcoming Strasbourg meeting of the European Council. He wrote: 'Kohl is on the highest wire of his life. If he handles the German question well he should win the general election

---

reopened the breach which was closed with difficulty when Gorbachev visited Bonn. Falin was openly worried that events in the GDR were about to take a violent turn, and that the tempo of disorder plus reunification pressures seriously threatened stability.

3. Falin is only part of the Moscow picture, and has no executive responsibility. He was bewailing the situation, rather than suggesting ways of mastering it. He is one of Gorbachev's close advisers on the subject of Germany, but Gorbachev has taken the more statesmanlike approach of toning down the rhetoric, playing for time, and leaving options open (including reunification).

4. Nevertheless the collapse of political authority in East Germany is bound to worry the Russians intensely. It probably is sufficient explanation for the distinct sharpening of the tone of public comment on 5 December, which is no doubt intended to convey to the Federal Government that this is definitely not the moment to say or do anything which could bring nearer a real crisis, including a violent breakdown of order in East Germany.

5. It would not be surprising if Kohl's own performance in the last week or so had aroused wide Soviet suspicions of the Federal Government, which are always just below the surface. Falin was strikingly bitter about Kohl's alleged failure to warn Gorbachev about the 10 points (despite the numerous contacts between Kohl's and Gorbachev's advisers referred to by Teltschik: Bonn telegram 1156).[4] As seen from here, one major step Kohl could make to repair the damage would be to state firmly, publicly and unequivocally that he agrees with Genscher that the post-war boundaries of Germany (i.e. the Oder-Neisse Line, not the Elbe, which is a qualitatively different matter) are definitive, and that there is no question of them being challenged by the Federal Government, or even discussed, at an eventual peace conference or anywhere else. This would go very far to allay Soviet (and Polish: see Warsaw telegram 745)[5] fears of revanchism. I know that it would upset the susceptibilities of German international lawyers: and that it would complicate Kohl's electoral calculations (as Genscher indicated to you: FCO tel 694 to Bonn).[6] But now that things are going so much his way, he can surely afford this gesture of international statesmanship.

6. With the Russians in a suspicious and emotional mood, it is desirable to maximise exchanges with them about Germany at all levels. Falin favoured bilateral exchanges between the Allied Ambassadors in Berlin, and said he would pass to Shevardnadze the thought that his Ministry should intensify their contacts

---

in one year's time. That would give him the chance of going down in history as the man who ensured German unity. But putting a foot wrong on the German question could lose him the election. The next few months—or possibly weeks—could make or break his prospects. He knows it. The international limelight is gratifying yet somewhat alarming. The Federal Republic is not accustomed to acting on its own in pursuit of goals not shared by others, and the handling of Kohl's ten points showed the lack of deftness and experience. Kohl wants two things that may not be entirely compatible: to be the one to map the route to unity and also to retain the support and comfort at all stages of his allies and partners. The Bush Administration has been assiduous in its public support. But the European neighbours, not excluding France, are trickier for Kohl to handle' (MWF 100/22/89).

[4] No. 59.

[5] Not found.

[6] This telegram of 29 November recorded the discussions between Mr Hurd and Herr Genscher in London on the evening of that day. The relevant paragraph read: 'The constraints on the Chancellor were not always the same as the considerations which Genscher had in mind. For example he had wanted to repeat what had recently been said about the permanence of Poland's borders but this could have created domestic political problems for Kohl' (WRE 014/2).

with me and my colleagues. The proposed dinner for Shevardnadze and the European Ambassadors on 19 December will provide a good occasion, though at the present speed of events it looks rather a long way away.

No. 70

Letter from Mr Powell (Strasbourg) to Mr Wall[1]

[*RS 020/2/3*]

Secret and Strictly Personal   STRASBOURG, *8 December 1989*

Dear Stephen,

East/West Relations

We are finding that we are almost daily being taken by surprise by the pace of developments in the Soviet Union and Eastern Europe. The Prime Minister would like to be confident that we are properly prepared for some of the things that might happen.

Taking first current developments in East Germany. Several of the telegrams from Bonn and Moscow which the Prime Minister has seen imply that we *could* face a breakdown of the system of government, the disappearance of authority and economic collapse, with rapidly rising pressure for German unity—an appeal which could prove irresistible on the West German side. This could be accompanied by:

—widespread disorder

—a renewal of mass emigration to West Germany

—some West German involvement in East Germany (either popular in the form of West Germans joining demonstrations in the East, or official in the form of despatch of West German police to help maintain order)

—accelerated progress towards German reunification

—attacks on Soviet forces and their families

—some reassertion of authority by the East German armed forces and/or security police

—Soviet intervention.

I do not suppose that the list is complete but it is a start. Similar developments could occur in other Eastern European countries, most notably Czechoslovakia: and perhaps also in some parts of the Soviet Union, such as the Baltic republics.

I wrote to you this morning about possible *diplomatic action* in the face of these eventualities.[2] The Prime Minister's thought was that we might take the initiative

---

[1] Mr Powell was accompanying the Prime Minister at a meeting of the European Council in Strasbourg from 8 to 9 December.

[2] This letter summarised conversations between the Prime Minister, Mr Lubbers and Signor Andreotti, and between Mr Hurd and Herr Genscher. Mrs Thatcher and Mr Lubbers, it stated, 'took the view that it would be useful for a meeting of the four Berlin powers plus Germany [to take place] reasonably soon, to anchor all the main participants and classify their intentions. The Prime Minister recalled that she had floated the idea of a Berlin Four meeting at the time of the NATO Summit but the United States had thought it risked being divisive. However the situation had moved on since then. Mr Lubbers thought that such a meeting would be useful but suggested it might be best to persuade the Germans to ask for it, so it did not look as though it was imposed upon them. It was agreed that the Foreign Secretary would mention this to Herr Genscher.' The letter went on:

to convoke a quadripartite meeting of the US, UK, France and Germany, which might be followed rapidly by a meeting involving the Soviet Union as well. These could be at the level either of Ambassadors in Berlin, Political Directors, Foreign Ministers or even Heads of Government. The Department are looking urgently at the options. Support for some such action is gathering among our European Allies. M. Dumas has expressed interest and President Mitterrand told the Prime Minister at lunch that Mr. Gorbachev was very concerned at the pace of developments over Germany. (He has now asked to see her for a fuller discussion.) We need soon to involve the Americans in discussion. It is a pity in retrospect that our proposal for a quadripartite Heads of Government meeting in the margins of the NATO Summit was not taken up.

The Prime Minister's view is that the immediate need is to try to assert a greater degree of Allied influence over the actions of the West German government and to reassure the Russians that we are doing so. The risk is, of course, such meetings would provoke a sense of crisis. But the Prime Minister feels that at the moment we are constantly lagging behind developments and there is no sense of direction in the West. We do not want to wake up one morning and find that events have moved entirely beyond our control and that German reunification is to all intents and purposes on us. Her inclination is therefore to initiate the process of quadripartite meetings soon at an appropriate level. But they are not the only possibility. Should we be seeking a meeting between the Foreign Secretary and Shevardnadze? A message from the Prime Minister to Gorbachev? A Ministerial visit to East Germany?

But convoking a meeting presupposes that we have marked out some sort of plan as to what we would seek at it. The fact of consultation could itself be stabilizing. But presumably we would want to go beyond that and bind the West Germans more tightly into common positions as well as a commitment to consult before acting. What exactly would we propose?

I assume some thought is also being given in MOD and FCO to contingency action in relation to our forces in Berlin and in the FRG, in the event of violence in East Germany and a possible crack-down by the East German forces or Soviet intervention, however unlikely these may at present seem. I am not of course suggesting that we would intervene. But there might be steps which we should take—reinforcement of Berlin, higher states of readiness for BFG. I think that the Prime Minister would want to know what plans we have and how they would be implemented.

Looking now into the more distant future, and wondering what we might in certain circumstances have to confront over a period of a few years, the Prime Minister hopes that thought is being given to the consequences for BFG of moves towards a confederation of the two parts of Germany or towards reunification. This would probably follow a CFE I and perhaps a CFE II agreement. There would presumably be a major reduction of BFG. What legal steps would we have to take

'The Prime Minister subsequently mentioned the idea to Signor Andreotti who expressed support, *provided* that it was clear that the technical grounds for summoning the meeting was [*sic*] the responsibility of the powers concerned for Berlin (so as to avoid the appearance of a *directoire*) and that broader matters continued to be considered within NATO. Herr Genscher's reaction when the Foreign Secretary raised it with him was more cautious. He confirmed that the Russians were worried about developments in East Germany, particularly the risk to the families of Soviet soldiers. But he thought that summoning such a meeting could increase the sense of crisis. It was something which should be kept in reserve. The Prime Minister intends to take an early opportunity to discuss this further with President Mitterrand, possibly at lunch-time. . . .' (WRL 020/4).

in relation to the Brussels Treaty? What could be the consequences for NATO's strategy (assuming NATO continued to exist—and presumably at least one scenario ought to assume a dissolution of NATO)? What would be the implications for the structure of our forces and their deployment, if some of these developments were to take place? We ought to be speculating similarly on the diplomatic front: a new *entente cordiale*? an Anglo-American alliance? an Anglo-Russian Reinsurance Treaty?

I realise this is rapidly entering the realm of science fiction. But with the unthinkable happening with alarming regularity, the Prime Minister would like to feel that we are doing some serious thinking on these points and on the shape of the new world which could confront us really quite rapidly. Perhaps some of the work is already being done: I rather hope it is. If not, perhaps a study could be set in hand in FCO and MOD, consulting the Assessments Staff and the Cabinet Office as well.

I am copying this letter to Brian Hawtin (Ministry of Defence) and Sir Robin Butler.

Yours sincerely,
C.D. POWELL

No. 71

Letter from Mr Powell (Strasbourg) to Mr Wall

[*PREM: Internal Situation in East Germany*]

Secret and Strictly Personal   STRASBOURG, *8 December 1989*

Dear Stephen,

Germany

President Mitterrand asked to see the Prime Minister immediately following the session of the European Council this afternoon. He got down to business without delay. There were other problems of much greater importance than the Social Charter, which had just been discussed in the Council, which he and the Prime Minister needed to talk about. He was very worried about Germany. Gorbachev had spoken to him very harshly on the subject and the time had come for action. He and the Prime Minister needed to consider what role might be played by the Four Powers.

The Prime Minister said her reaction had been much the same. She felt the Four Powers ought to meet soon and she had already mentioned this idea to one or two other Heads of Government. All reports from East Germany were indicating that there could be a total collapse of the system with increasing demands for reunification. If we were not careful, reunification would just come about. If that were to happen all the fixed points in Europe would collapse: the NATO front-line; the structure of NATO and the Warsaw Pact; Mr. Gorbachev's hopes for reform. No doubt Britain and France and other European countries would try to resist. But we would probably face a *fait accompli*. This was why she thought we must have a structure to stop this happening and the only one available was the Four Power arrangement. The Four Powers still had certain responsibilities for Germany and Berlin. President Mitterrand interjected that the Germans seemed completely to have forgotten this. The Prime Minister said that Chancellor Kohl had no conception of the sensitivities of others in Europe, and seemed to have forgotten that the division of Germany was the result of a war which Germany had started. Before taking a decision on summoning a Four Power meeting we would all need to consult the United States. It was also possible that we would be pre-empted by the Soviet Union. She had just heard that a message was on the way from Mr. Shevardnadze proposing a meeting.

President Mitterrand repeated that he had found Mr. Gorbachev much harsher on the subject of Germany than he had expected. He was particularly worried about his troops in East Germany and their families. But in practice there was not much Gorbachev could do. If his forces were attacked, they would no doubt open fire. But he could hardly move his divisions forward. The Germans had probably analysed this which was why they were pressing towards reunification. President Mitterrand said that he was very critical of Chancellor Kohl's ten point plan and speech. At least Brandt's statements were much more thoughtful. He acknowledged the need for two German states. But Kohl was speculating on the national adrenalin of the German people and it seemed that nothing could stop him. Indeed it was very difficult to withstand the drive of a people. In history Germany had never found its true frontiers: they were a people in constant movement and flux. At this, the Prime Minister produced her map showing various configurations of Germany from her handbag to underline President Mitterrand's point. President Mitterrand continued that the German people were in a process of motion and we did not have many cards to stop them. Nor could the Russians do much. It seemed that the United States did not have the will. All that was left was Britain and France. He was fearful that he and the Prime Minister would find themselves in the situation of their predecessors in the 1930s who had failed to react in the face of constant pressing forward by the Germans. For the moment he agreed with the Prime Minister that all that could be done was to have a Four Power meeting. This might reassure Gorbachev.

The Prime Minister said it would also be important to have a strong communiqué from the European Council referring to the Helsinki Agreement and the need to maintain the structure of NATO and the Warsaw Pact. President Mitterrand said that he had given Herr Genscher a piece of his mind on the matter, warning him that Germany's behaviour was a lesson which others in Europe would not forget. It might be a case of Britain, France, the Soviet Union and Italy coming together to contain Germany. Indeed he had even put this thought to Mr. Gorbachev. German reunification depended on many elements, most of them beyond our control. It might happen. It would happen. But if it did so simply as a result of German *diktat* which took no notice of the Allies it would be disastrous.

The Prime Minister said that the meeting of EC Heads of Government in Paris had come up with the right answer and the aim ought to be to reaffirm that now. President Mitterrand agreed but noted that Chancellor Kohl had already strayed well beyond the conclusions of the Paris meeting. He felt we were on the threshold of momentous events. We might find ourselves in a position where we had to say no to the Germans. At moments of great danger in the past France had always established special relations with Britain. He felt that such a time had come again. We must draw together and stay in touch. If the Russians were indeed proposing a meeting, we should co-ordinate our response. He would be happy to come across to the UK at any time to see the Prime Minister and continue their discussion. He hoped there would be discussions between the Foreign Secretary and M. Dumas.

He and the Prime Minister should meet again tomorrow before she left Strasbourg. The Prime Minister said that she agreed it was very important for the two of them and their governments to keep in touch, although knowledge of their discussions should be very tightly restricted. She would brief only the Foreign Secretary.

The Prime Minister noted that President Mitterrand was shortly going to East Germany. President Mitterrand said that Chancellor Kohl had been panicked by this and brought forward his own visit to be sure that he got there first.

My record may sound rather breathless but this actually reflects President Mitterrand's manner and approach. The subject matter is clearly sensitive and should be held very tight.

I am copying this letter to Brian Hawtin (Ministry of Defence) and Sir Robin Butler.

Yours sincerely,
C.D. POWELL

No. 72

Sir C. Mallaby (Bonn) to UK Delegation, Strasbourg[1]

Telegraphic No. Flash 001 [WRL 020/4]

Confidential   BONN, *9 December 1989, 11.04 a.m.*

For Wall.

Soviet Proposals for Four Power Talks[2]

Summary

1. Federal Republic will need careful handling. Germans should be told the truth about the Soviet demarche, but the public line, agreed in substance with them, should be low key and focussed on the Allies' Berlin initiative. The US is already consulting them in Bonn.

Detail

2. The West Germans will be sensitive about the Soviet approach. The Federal Government have made clear in private and in public that they do not consider Four Power talks opportune. If it were to appear that the Four Powers were getting together to consider the future of Germany over Germans' heads, this would cause anxiety, hostility and nationalism in the country at large. To preempt mistrust

---

[1] Repeated for information to Desk by 12.45 p.m., Paris, Washington, FCO, BMG Berlin; and for information Immediate to Moscow, UKDEL NATO, East Berlin.

[2] On 8 December the Soviet Union proposed, in the light of 'the emerging, extremely acute situation in the GDR and around it', that the Ambassadors of the Four Powers should hold a meeting in Berlin at the earliest opportunity. 'The subject of the meeting could be any, because under existing conditions it is considered very important to demonstrate by the very fact of such a meeting the continuing responsibility of the Four Powers in German affairs.' While the Soviets favoured an exchange of views on the German situation as a whole, they suggested that, if the Western powers preferred, the declared subject of the meeting could be confined to a discussion of Berlin questions, in particular the Allied 'Berlin initiative'(see Series III, Volume VI, pp. 102, 106). The proposed venue was the building of the former Allied Control Council, the *Kommandatura* (text of Soviet proposal in BMG Berlin telegram No. 220 to Flash Bonn and Flash FCO, 8 December, WRL 020/4). Despite considerable reservations on the part of the FRG Government, the three Western powers agreed that the meeting should take place on 11 December (see No. 73).

between ourselves and the Federal Government and since it will become known that the Russians really wanted to discuss German affairs, it will be important to tell them the truth about the Soviet approach. At the same time we should agree with them the main points for a public presentation of our acceptance of the Soviet proposal designed to reassure German public opinion and avoid as far as possible an impression of drama. Seen from here, the Americans are right to want to go for the 'narrow' Soviet option (Washington telno 1 to UKDEL Strasbourg)[3] without preventing the Russians from raising other matters of common interest, which we cannot do anyway.

3. Against this background, I recommend that:

(*a*) The Germans are brought in early:

(*b*) They are told the truth about the Soviet proposal and our proposed response to it: *viz* that the Soviets want meetings to exchange views on German affairs (FCO telno 93 to Strasbourg)[4] notably the GDR and that they have made it clear that they define this as including the Allied initiative. The Allies welcome this belated response to the initiative and will agree to the Soviet proposals for talks on this basis while accepting that the Russians cannot be prevented from raising other matters. In that event, the Allies would intend in the first instance to listen and take note.

(*c*) The Allies will keep the Germans very closely in the picture and consult.

4. Timing, place and level of talks. According to the US Embassy here, the Americans want to avoid talks coinciding with Baker's visit to Berlin on 12 December and would like talks either on 11 or 13 December. As for place, the Allied Control Authority building was used for the negotiation of the Quadripartite Agreement and is appropriate for talks on the Allied initiative: but it may be less so for talks on wider German matters since it was a seat of Four Power authority for Germany and its use could fuel an impression of resurrection of Allied control of Germany. We could start at the ACA and consider later whether to rotate among missions in Berlin. As for level of representation, Washington is proposing one level down from Ambassadors i.e. Ministers in Berlin. But the US Embassy here agree that it would be natural to start negotiation on the Allied initiative at Ambassadorial level. The French Ambassador believes that Paris will want talks among the 4 Ministers in Berlin but seems personally inclined that the first meeting should involve Ambassadors.

5. Since the above was drafted the US Embassy have told us that their Ambassador is now seeing Sudhoff at the *Auswärtiges Amt*. We have remonstrated about failure to consult.

---

[3] Not found.

[4] This telegram of 8 December reported the Soviet proposal (WRL 020/4).

No. 73

Sir C. Mallaby (Bonn) to Mr Hurd[1]

No. 1216 Telegraphic [ESC 020/36]

Confidential   BONN, *10 December 1989, 2.07 p.m.*

Your Telno 717: Berlin Meeting[2]

Summary

1. The three Allied Ambassadors agree on arrangements and line for meeting with Kochemasov. Line will be to advocate Berlin initiative and on other matters to take a position designed to reassure without entering into specifics.

Detail

2. The US and French Ambassadors and I agreed this morning that the Americans would inform the Russians in Berlin as soon as possible today that we agree to a meeting with Kochemasov at 11 a.m. on Monday 11 December in the Allied Control Authority building in Berlin. We agreed on a short draft statement for issue this evening: see separate telegram. The French are informing the *Auswärtiges Amt* and the *Senat*.

3. The delay since yesterday evening in finalising the arrangements was caused by US insistence, now withdrawn, that we should all first agree that there be no (no) advance press statement.

4. We agreed to advocate to Kochemasov the contents of, and arguments for, the various elements in the Berlin initiative. Detailed points for this will be prepared in the Bonn group this afternoon.

5. We agreed that, when the Russians raised wider matters, one purpose would be to respond reassuringly but to avoid entering into specifics. We would undertake to report any suggestions made by Kochemasov, including e.g. any suggestion for a substantive joint statement on Berlin and/or Germany by the four Ambassadors. We would stress repeatedly the importance of stability, drawing especially on the European Council's Strasbourg declaration (UKDEL Strasbourg telno 89)[3] including its references to responsibility and no unilateral advantages. The US Ambassador thought this declaration admirable. We would stress the principle of self-determination, and note that the Soviet Union is committed to it in international documents. If Kochemasov blamed Kohl's ten points for the situation in the GDR, we would say that Kohl had set no timetable for movement on the German question and that what was happening in East Germany was an expression of the feelings and hopes of people there. If the Russians proposed revival of the Quadripartite system and regular Ambassadorial meetings, we would agree to

---

[1] Repeated for information to Desk by 3 p.m., BMG Berlin, and for information Immediate to Washington, Paris, Moscow.

[2] This telegram of 9 December informed Bonn that the American, French and British Governments were content for the four Ambassadors to meet in Berlin, provided that, as the West Germans had requested, there was proper preparation in the Bonn Group beforehand (WRL 020/4).

[3] Telegram not printed. The Strasbourg declaration read: 'We seek the strengthening of the state of peace in Europe in which the German people will regain its unity through free self-determination. This process should take place peacefully and democratically, in full respect of the relevant agreements and treaties and of all the principles defined by the Helsinki Final Act, in a context of dialogue and East-West co-operation. It also has to be placed in the context of European integration.'

'further meetings at appropriate levels' and reiterate our wish to discuss the Berlin initiative.

6. The defensive material in paragraph 5 is designed to steer a path between the important aim of reassuring the Russians and the need to consult the Federal Government on any new Soviet proposals.[4]

---

[4] The Ambassadors of the Four Powers met in Berlin on 11 December. Their discussion was amicable but inconclusive. The US Ambassador, General Walters, proposed future talks on Berlin-related issues, while the Soviet Ambassador, Mr Kochemasov, proposed the establishment of a new standing work group, again dealing only with Berlin. Sir C. Mallaby commented: 'The Soviet purpose in proposing this meeting was obviously to remind the Germans of the rights and interest of the Four Powers in the German question. The fact of the meeting will have achieved that aim. This is also in our interests. At the same time, we have taken care not to alienate the Federal Government' (Bonn telegram No. 1223, 11 December, ESC 020/36). The photograph of the four Ambassadors outside the *Kommandatura* building caused considerable resentment in Germany and was described by General Walters as 'the worst picture of the year' (Zelikow and Rice, p. 141). For the subsequent Soviet proposal for Four-Power discussions see No. 96.

No. 74

Letter from Mr Wall to Mr Powell (No. 10)

[*RS 020/2/3*]

Secret and Strictly Personal   FCO, *12 December 1989*

Dear Charles,

East/West Relations

Thank you for your letter of 8 December about possible developments in Central and Eastern Europe.[1]

You list a number of requirements. This interim reply is to tell you what is already in hand and what further work we now plan. It does not seek to take full account of yesterday's meeting in Berlin of the Ambassadors of the Four Protecting Powers or of the discussions in London with Secretary Baker, both of which are, however, clearly relevant. What follows should be read against the background of the objectives which we conveyed to you while the Prime Minister was still at the European Council in Strasbourg last week, namely:

—to discuss how the process of change in the GDR might be steadied and made less risk-prone;

—to pre-empt excessive Soviet reaction to current developments;

—to remind the FRG of Allied responsibilities over Berlin and of Four-Power responsibilities for Germany as a whole, and hence to impress upon the FRG the need to consult;

—to secure and demonstrate a unified Western approach;

—to secure agreement that the Allies should indicate, notwithstanding the formal legal position, that they have no designs over the territory to the east of the Oder-Neisse line (the GDR/Polish border). (Although domestically sensitive for Kohl, this would involve no more than restating the Federal Government's position in the 1970 Polish Treaty.)

---

[1] No. 70.

—on Berlin, to secure agreement in principle, particularly from France and the US, that, notwithstanding their legal position and with due regard to military preparedness, the three Western Berlin Allies should look favourably upon early far-reaching adaptation (e.g. over air services and minor status points);

—to pursue the possibility of a conference of the Four Berlin Powers plus, for some or all of the meeting, representatives of the two Germanys.

Taking your points seriatim:

(*a*) *Consultative process* over East Germany and other possible East European or Soviet hot spots. As you know intensive diplomacy is now underway, the main features of which are

12 December—Secretary Baker's visit to the Federal Republic

13 December—Meetings in Brussels at Political Director and Foreign Minister level

14/15 December—North Atlantic Council at Ministerial level

18 December—Shevardnadze's meeting in Brussels with the Foreign Ministers of the EC Twelve.

This should hold and stabilise matters for the coming week, as well as reassure the Russians. The Foreign Secretary believes that a message from the Prime Minister to President Gorbachev could well be timely: we shall prepare a draft in the light of discussions in Brussels on 13 December. The Foreign Secretary also plans to have a meeting with Shevardnadze in the margins of the Brussels meeting on 18 December (as Shevardnadze has himself suggested in an oral message delivered by the Russians yesterday). A Ministerial visit to East Germany should perhaps await the emergence of a more stable authority there. But the Prime Minister may wish to consider pursuing her own idea of some further contact with President Mitterrand, who visits East Germany on 20 December and is also due to see President Bush in the Caribbean this weekend.

(*b*) *A 'stabilising' plan*, as a basis for the UK input to this intensive consultation process. The UK has already proposed in the regular secret consultations among close allies that contingency planning could usefully be undertaken to focus on how Western policy should cope with the risk of sudden over-heating of any hot spots in East Europe or the Soviet Union leading to widespread disorder or violence (we have given thought to this within the FCO *vis-à-vis* the Baltic Republics and have indeed, as you suggest, drawn up a wider list of possible scenarios to be covered). We shall press for acceleration of this process in Brussels later this week and report on progress. But the existence of such work on wider contingencies needs to be closely held, since although the participants are the same, it is not strictly relevant to the work on Berlin among the Four, which is openly avowed.

As for the West Germans themselves, again we have been giving a good deal of thought over recent weeks to the implications of the reappearance of the German question on the agenda and also to the consequences for Western policy of Chancellor Kohl's speech to the *Bundestag* on 28 November. On 'binding in' and on consultation, apart from maximising the use of the EC and NATO frameworks for this purpose, the Foreign Secretary considers that the attitude and tone of our bilateral diplomacy toward the FRG remain the key, rather than specific blueprints which risk being overtaken by events. The aim should be to envelop and contain the West Germans with activity which we would present as assiduous 'help and support on the basis of firm Allied positions'. This will make it very difficult for them to move again without clearing their lines first as

Kohl did on 28 November. We should, so to speak, smother them with diplomacy. There is too the formal and legal status we enjoy for Berlin and Germany as a whole, as yesterday's meeting of the four Ambassadors in Berlin will have reminded the Germans.

(*c*) *Contingency planning in relation to British Forces in Berlin and BAOR*. We have been in touch with MOD over the weekend. I understand that they will be reporting to you, in consultation with the FCO, on the state of current contingency plans; though it occurs to us that much of the traditional work that we have exercised so fully over previous years (Live Oak) was designed to respond to somewhat different circumstances.

(*d*) *Consequences for BFG of German moves toward confederation or unity*. Sir Christopher Mallaby's preliminary view, which we share, is that the time frame may well be shorter than you imply by your reference to after 'a CFE 2 agreement'; and that some kind of confederation may well prove to be the least (and perhaps the best) that we can reasonably hope for. Clearly this needs further analysis and the Foreign Secretary has put this work in hand. The implications for British and other Allied troop levels in the FRG of a rapid evolution of events toward German unity are not self-evident, and Russian views would also be relevant.

There is a separate question [of] at what level of further Allied force reductions in Europe, whether stemming from German unity or from a continuation of the CFE process, NATO strategy would become unworkable, and the implications for structure and deployment of our forces. The MOD take the lead in the follow-up work on this flowing from the Prime Minister's seminar at Chequers.[2] They will no doubt report on where it now stands and progress on analogous work at SHAPE and in Washington. It would be valuable if, notwithstanding the complexities, this work could be accelerated, at least to draw provisional conclusions.

(*e*) *Long term speculation on the diplomatic front*. Here too we have given early thought within the FCO to the perspectives opened up by President Bush's references at the NATO Summit to the need for a new European 'architecture'. We shall continue to flesh out this work urgently, as an input to Allied consultations. We have taken on board your own suggestions. The Foreign Secretary's aim is to have a coherent plan in place to guide our approach to bilateral consultations before the Bush/Gorbachev summit, the Prime Minister's visit to the Soviet Union and the Summit of the Seven during 1990.

The Foreign Secretary believes that some collective Ministerial discussion of these issues soon would be valuable. Unless the Prime Minister favours OD for this, a further informal session, e.g. at Chequers, might be a good way to take stock. Mr Hurd has asked Mr Waldegrave within the FCO to oversee this complex of work identified above. John Weston will coordinate work here at official level, since as Political Director (from 2 January) he will be the main UK official involved in the various Allied consultative fora. We shall, of course, continue to make a full input to the work of the JIC, whose assessments of events in Eastern Europe continue to provide the essential point of departure, and will keep closely in touch with Sir Robin Butler and his staff in the Cabinet Office, as work progresses.

---

[2] This seminar, scheduled at this stage for late January or early February, eventually took place on 27 January: see No. 80 and No. 108, note 2.

I am copying this letter to Brian Hawtin (MOD) and Sonia Phippard (Cabinet Office).

Yours,
J.S. WALL

No. 75

Mr Hurd to Sir C. Mallaby (Bonn)[1]

No. 722 Telegraphic [WRL 021/4]

Confidential   FCO, *14 December 1989, 4.20 p.m.*

Berlin Meeting, Brussels, 13 December

Summary

1. Foreign Ministers agreed a passage on Berlin/Germany for the NAC communiqué which repeats Strasbourg formula on German unity. Bonn Group to look urgently at question of direct elections. Short exchange on situation in GDR.

Detail

2. Genscher said the situation in the GDR was fragile. The FRG was not interested in any sort of emotional developments. He was using speeches and interviews to urge calm on the people there. He was grateful for the reference in the G-24 communiqué to the possibility of help for the GDR. The FRG needed to convince the public in the GDR that political reform was bound to lead to economic improvement. Much could be done without any change in the status of the two states. There could be a dense web of economic links. Above all, the people needed confidence that their standard of living would improve.

3. I asked if some authority was beginning to reassert itself in the GDR. Genscher said Modrow (and perhaps Berghofer) were the only representatives of authority who commanded enough confidence to be able to help stabilise the situation. The SED was finished. The other parties were not in a position to fill the vacuum. The problem was to get through the gap between now and the election in May.

4. Baker said he had gone to Potsdam to lend Modrow legitimacy. As the church leaders had told him in Potsdam, the more Modrow was in charge the better the chance of peaceful and stable elections on 6 May. Both Modrow and the church leaders had underlined the GDR's dire economic problems. It had been right to mention the GDR in the G-24 communiqué. People seemed more driven by economic concerns than nationalist feelings. The church leaders seemed to think unity might solve the country's economic problems. But there would be economic integration whatever happened.

5. Genscher explained the case for the direct election of Berlin members of the *Bundestag* once there were free elections in the GDR. It was agreed to study this urgently in the Bonn Group.

6. At the insistence of US officials the Bonn Group had laboriously put together a paraphrase of the Strasbourg formula on German unity for Ministers to approve.

[1] Repeated for information Priority to Paris, Washington, UKDEL NATO, BMG Berlin, East Berlin, Moscow, UKREP Brussels.

Baker said he preferred the original Strasbourg formula and had no hang-ups about using EC language in a NATO communiqué. It was therefore agreed to use the Strasbourg formula as it stood.[2] If other NATO allies had offered comments in the JPC the French did not pass them on.

[2] See No. 73, note 4.

No. 76

Letter from Mr Tebbit (Washington) to Mr Synnott

[*WRL 020/4*]

Confidential   WASHINGTON, *14 December 1989*

Dear Hilary,
The German Question
1. Many thanks for your letter of 3 November to Richard Ralph, with the paper on the German question and request for views.[1] The speed of events has undermined successive attempts here to complete a comprehensive assessment—so too has the Bush Administration's tendency on this subject, as with others, to decide policy moves with only minimal involvement of the 'experts' in the bureaucracy.

2. To some extent, our task has now been eased by the decision—rushed through in the wake of Kohl's Ten Points, but based on work over the past couple of months—to articulate the Administration's own Four Principles. The criteria were first put forward by Baker and later, with slightly strengthened conditionality, became one of the mainstays of the President's interventions in NATO on 4 December and central element in Baker's own speech in Berlin on 12 December.[2]

3. That in itself gets us somewhere—most obviously in underlining the American readiness to continue to talk openly in support of unification as the objective, (the 're' is now carefully dropped). But it leaves many questions to be answered: notably whether the conditionality, drawn as tightly as it is, signifies an American attempt to put a firm brake on the process without flying too directly in the face of German attitudes; or whether the terms sketched out (continued commitment to NATO, for example) are seen here as serious and realisable objectives.

[1] Letter not printed; paper on the German question printed as Enclosure in No. 25.
[2] At a White House press conference on 29 November, Secretary of State Baker announced four principles that the United States believed should guide the unification process: (1) it should be based on self-determination without prejudice to the eventual form that unity might take, (2) it should 'occur in the context of Germany's continued alignment with NATO and an increasingly integrated European Community', (3) the process should be peaceful, gradual and step-by-step (4) while respecting the principle of the inviolability of European frontiers enshrined in the Helsinki Final Act of 1975, there should be scope for those borders to be changed by peaceful means. These principles were reiterated by President Bush at the NATO Heads of Government meeting on 4 December: *Public Papers*, p. 1648. Mr Baker's speech to the Berlin Press Club on 12 December advocated the creation of a new European security structure to overcome the division of Berlin and of Germany, while keeping US and European security linked.

4. There is certainly evidence of an evolution in American attitudes towards more caution of late. The Administration no longer talks with quite the bland equanimity that it did only a few months ago [about?] being able to contemplate reunification more readily than many Europeans. Events have had a sobering effect, notably the growing evidence of Soviet alarm, rapid deterioration in the GDR and, indeed, the concerns raised by Kohl's decision to surface his own formula without adequate consultation. These have also obliged the Administration to recognise the need for them to play a more active role in managing the problem (to the extent that non-Germans can) rather than talk, as they did, of this being primarily a matter for Europe. Baker's visit to Potsdam to see Modrow is interpreted by the German research cell in State Department as signifying two things in this context:

(*a*) an interest in at least shoring up the GDR sufficiently to give it a temporary lease of life, with the Administration considering its own small steps to develop stronger US/GDR relations;

(*b*) a deliberate signal to the FRG leadership (and by implication one of reassurance to Moscow) that they are not the only players with the GDR and that the Allies are involved in all aspects of the German question. It is worth noting in this context that the reference to 'due regard for the legal role and responsibilities of the Allied powers' was not included in the Four Principles as enunciated originally by State Department and were added on instructions from the White House.

5. That said, we would still judge that although the game plan has become more complicated, the Americans continue to see unification as being the inevitable (and probably desirable) result, and one occurring sooner rather than later despite a US policy of hasten slowly. The enclosed minuting by Andrew Wood reinforces that assessment.[3]

6. There is one major potential stumbling block still conjured up by the American approach. Their advocacy of reunification on US or Western terms (the alternative of a neutralised Germany is basically rejected) implies that a number of changes would have to be achieved in the architecture which they advocate for the future of Europe. These pose varying degrees of difficulty: EC integration (into which a united Germany would fit) poses its own set of problems, in the broader/deeper context; a CSCE structure with sufficient teeth to provide the wider 'commonwealth of free nations' raises others; above all there is perpetuation of a NATO Alliance—albeit with a stronger emphasis on the political rather than military aspect—which the GDR would, in effect be joining. The US formula seeks to avoid posing this last problem so starkly by deliberately not specifying any particular vision of unity. But a united Germany in NATO would nevertheless be the logical conclusion. It is by no means clear that the Administration has calculated that Gorbachev's view of the contracting nature of Soviet power and ambition extends so far that he could contemplate such an outcome. It seems equally likely from my own discussions with officials here that they have not faced up to the full implication of their approach to this area (as indeed Andrew Wood implies in 2(*b*) of his minute).

7. To a large degree American policy has been spared rigorous analysis by the prudent circumspection that is being shown on all sides. It has been possible to argue that Kohl's Ten Points and the Four Principles amount to broadly the same

---

[3] Not printed.

thing. Equally to the point, the Soviet reaction so far has not been so drastic as to oblige the concept of a united Germany in NATO to be put under the microscope. By emerging as the demandeur in calling for Allied Consultations in Berlin, Gorbachev is seen by some in State Department as making it easier to proceed in the shorter term without (and while the Soviet armies remain in Germany) facing the impalatable [*sic*] alternative of a Soviet crackdown in the GDR or the appearance of an humiliating Soviet sell out.

8. Perhaps the main achievement from the American perspective is that there is now the prospect of more intensive consultations involving the Germans and, indeed, the Russians. I doubt that they would pretend to have a perfect blueprint which strikes the right balance between the various competing objectives: supporting the Germans in general and Kohl in particular; influencing the pressure for unification in the hope of controlling the speed and achieving it on Western/US terms; while not antagonising the Soviet Union and enabling the evolution of Eastern Europe generally to continue. In some ways there is slight embarrassment here that Ministers have had to walk back from their earlier more gung-ho positions. But they will hope that there is at least a reasonable basis for discussions in the various fora, on both Germany and Berlin, that will keep the balls in the air and enable the changes to be coped with, if not fully controlled. Having done a good deal of talking publicly 'at' the Germans with the Four Principles (an exercise which may now be becoming counter-productive) they may hope to do some more useful work 'with' them. In terms of German/German relations the US concept (as conceived by the policy planners) would build up gradually on confederal lines rather than moving immediately to the incorporation of the GDR as such. The wild card which might of course undermine all that is the attitude of the GDR population. It is seen here as the main uncontrollable element in the process which could force the pace and nature of unification despite the new US effort to move it in a slower and more controlled way.

Yours ever,
K.R. Tebbit

No. 77

Submission from Mr Synnott to Mr Ratford

[*WRE 014/2*]

Confidential   FCO, *14 December 1989*

GDR: Valedictory Despatch

1. I submit Mr Broomfield's valedictory despatch, dated 6 December.[1]

2. Owing to the present crisis in the GDR, Mr Broomfield's tour has been extended by some six weeks: he will now leave in mid-January. I aim to reply, subject to others' comments, before he leaves. Meanwhile I have acknowledged the despatch.

3. Mr Broomfield does not mince his words and sets out clear judgements:

—non-German outsiders have almost no influence on events in the GDR

---

[1] No. 66.

—potential leaders lack experience and understanding of the economy, which will be the driving force for change

—events will continue to move fast, pressed on by popular impatience

—the two sets of German elections next year will be linked

—the two German States will be politically united 'one day'

—we should devote more human and material resources to further our interests and exert influence so far as is possible.

I would not disagree with any of this.

4. Looking back, Mr Broomfield notes that every observer, including himself, seriously underestimated the speed of change in the GDR (para 14). This is true: while conventional wisdom had long been that change would occur quickly once started, very few observers were not surprised by its pace in the event. Although events moved with similar rapidity in Czechoslovakia, this pace of change might in part be explained by the specifically German dimension to it all: the same philosophy which lay behind the FRG's policy of 'change through rapprochement' obliged the FRG actively to assist in the process of change once it started. FRG diplomacy in Hungary, especially, helped open the floodgates. The affluence, common language, kinship and generosity in the FRG maintained the flow.

5. Despite the general surprise, it must be recognised that the FRG were less wrong about their predictions than we were. Teltschik and Ehmke were right when they told Mr Waldegrave in June that the situation in the GDR was potentially explosive (although the *Auswärtiges Amt* were more sanguine).[2] Our own Assessment at that time does not look too good with hindsight. We should recognise that the resources available to the FRG to make truly informed judgements are of a different order of magnitude to our own: it is all too easy to dismiss the Germans as being emotionally involved and hence unsound. Our own infiltration of the GDR, at present and historically, is tiny in comparison.

6. Mr Broomfield refers to resources allocated to dealing with these issues (para 18). As suggested in a departmental paper on Relations with the GDR (being submitted separately),[3] I share his view that we should now do much more. The pan-German dimension calls for a special approach to the GDR: it should not be regarded as a more affluent part of East Europe which merits correspondingly less effort; it could also be a means of influencing the FRG.

7. On the same theme, I would entirely endorse the reference (para 21) to the value of the contacts built up by junior members of Chancery in East Berlin. The main point of contact with the churches and with New Forum was a Grade 9 in Chancery with excellent German. As I saw for myself when I visited in July, he knew them well and to great effect. Given the slim resources available to the Post, the Embassy have done a remarkable job.

H.N.H. SYNNOTT

[2] See No. 5, note 6, for Mr Waldegrave's visit to Bonn in June 1989.
[3] Not found.

No. 78

Mr Hurd to Sir C. Mallaby (Bonn)[1]

No. 723 Telegraphic [WRL 020/4]

Secret   FCO, *15 December 1989, 6.10 p.m.*

The German Question: Consultations with the FRG

1. The background to Kohl's speech to the *Bundestag* on 28 November and the subsequent Russian initiative to hold a meeting of Four Power Ambassadors in Berlin demonstrate the continuing need for consultation with the FRG and the desirability of binding the Germans closely into developments. In addition to making the best possible use of the EC and NATO frameworks for this purpose, we aim to envelop and contain the Germans with activity which we would present as assiduous help and support for them on the basis of firm Allied positions. One objective in this would be to make it much more difficult for them to move again without clearing their lines first, as Kohl did on 28 November. It would also help ensure that they are aware of the development of our own thinking, so that neither side is surprised by subsequent turns of events.

2. We should be grateful for your views on how best to proceed with this. Several mechanisms spring to mind. There could be more contact at Ministerial level (Genscher has said that he would be willing to have talks at short notice if necessary). Apart from the Berlin-related grouping, we could make further, more frequent and regular use of the Höynck/Ratford talks[2] supplemented, if appropriate, by Head of Department-level contacts. Political Director-level contacts would also be useful, but the pressure on diaries is already considerable.

3. But there are of course considerable complications arising, on the German side, from the division of responsibilities and differing attitudes as between the Chancellor's Office, the *Auswärtiges Amt*, and the Inner German Ministry. Visits from London to Bonn would allow greater flexibility and ranges of conversations than vice versa. You will no doubt wish to take these factors into account.

---

[1] Repeated for information to Desk by 4.09 p.m. BMG Berlin, East Berlin, Moscow, Paris, Washington, UKDEL NATO, UKREP Brussels.

[2] See No. 5, note 6.

No. 79

Letter from Mr Broomfield (East Berlin) to Sir J. Fretwell

[*WRL 020/4*]

Confidential   EAST BERLIN, *15 December 1989*

Dear John,

The German Question and Some Implications for Security in Europe

1. I have now read with interest Christopher Mallaby's letter of 5 December to you.[1] The question he tackles is daunting since any structure we might try to put in place would rest on a potentially volatile foundation. I offer the following thoughts from the perspective of East Berlin.

2. I do not know what work has been put in hand in London, but I assume, for the purposes of this letter, that the outcome which would best suit British interests, at least for the medium term, would be a German confederation embracing the present two German states and with those two states remaining, if at all possible, in their respective security alliances.

In my despatch of 6 December I explained why I think this is unlikely to be a lasting solution, but it could exist for some time.[2]

3. It is possible that any plan we make will be made redundant by the short-term collapse of the GDR. This state continues to walk gingerly across very thin ice. There are two potential short-term threats. The first would entail a breakdown of law and order, possibly sparked by disagreement over the question of unification on the lines of the opposed chanting crowds we have seen recently in Leipzig. Notwithstanding official disapproval, the idea of a plebiscite on unity with the FRG is gaining ground, and I am more than ever convinced that this question will dominate the elections in the GDR in May next year.

4. The other main threat is an economic collapse. It is the one that worries Modrow and the Government most (and he made no secret of it when he spoke recently to Mr Baker in Potsdam). I agree that this is a serious threat. Emigration continues at a high rate. The loss of skilled workers, mainly in the industrial towns of the south, is very damaging. While for the time being the distribution of food and essential supplies seems unaffected, the outlook for industrial production is gloomy. One can only hope that the official package of assistance which Kohl will bring with him on 19 November and private assistance from West German industry thereafter will help to stabilise things.

5. In the short-term, therefore, I see no alternative to gestures of public support for Modrow, who is the only figure commanding respect on a sufficiently wide scale in the present coalition government to prevent a complete breakdown. In anything we might say publicly we should, I think, also refer to the Round Table process which, curiously enough, is about the only legitimate institution commanding widespread public support in the GDR. We should also, in line with the decisions taken at the Group of 24 Ministerial Meeting on 13 December, be

[1] No. 65.
[2] No. 66.

prepared to offer economic assistance as well as confirming, as rapidly as possible, the EC's willingness to negotiate a cooperation agreement.

6. The reason for all this is that Modrow is strongly in favour of a confederation between the two Germanies based on two sovereign independent states.

7. I do not know what the landscape here will look like after the May elections. I suspect they will result in a confusing allocation of votes among a number of parties. But, as of now, the present coalition Government is in favour of everything that defines its political separateness from the FRG. This includes membership of the Warsaw Pact, and an almost positive attitude to Quadripartite Rights and Responsibilities to judge by their reporting of the recent quadripartite Ambassadorial meeting. There is no particular hostility to Soviet forces stationed here at present and, if there have been incidents of violence against Soviet installations or troops, the stories have not gone the rounds in East Berlin. The only one retailed by the Soviet Embassy is about a party of officers' wives bundled out of a shop because they refused to show their ID cards as foreigners are now obliged to do when shopping in the GDR. While from an economic point of view the GDR would like less Soviet soldiers in this country, for the time being there is no move, popular or official, to question their right to be here at all.

8. Against that background, and assuming that the process of 'belonging together' can be slowed down into a process of 'growing together' over some years, I think that there is some chance of constructing the sort of security arrangements which might meet our needs.

9. Some time next year we should be signing a CFE agreement, together possibly with another round of confidence-building measures on the CSCE Stockholm model. The result might be to achieve in effect the sort of security committee for Europe which Christopher refers to in paragraph 10 of his letter, in that the Warsaw Pact and NATO would become a monitoring organisation to supervise the implementation of the CFE withdrawals, and the 35 CSCE states would be involved in monitoring and checking military activities throughout Europe to the Urals. Political activities of a security destabilising nature could also be discussed.

10. While I can see a number of drawbacks to Gorbachev's proposal for Helsinki II, there might also be some advantages. It would reconfirm the post-war status quo with frontiers that can only be changed by agreement of those concerned. It is clear from recent telegrams from Moscow and from our own conversations with the Soviet Embassy here that Gorbachev is very worried about the example which a change in borders between the two German states might have for internal developments in the Soviet Union (the Baltic States, Armenia/Azerbaijan, etc). Helsinki II won't prevent a change or even abolition of the inner-German border if both states want it, but it could slow down the process, and it might be an occasion for the FRG at last to say something definite about the Western Polish frontier (even though it would be in the run-up to the Federal German elections). Helsinki II would be supported by the present GDR coalition.

11. Basically, what I am suggesting is no more than a further role for NATO and the Warsaw Pact, which could enable Soviet and American forces to continue to be stationed in Europe for some time ahead. At the moment this is an outcome which I believe all the political groups and parties currently active in the GDR could either live with or would actively support.

12. I realise that this is not a particularly visionary approach but in the circumstances of rapid change and unpredictability a policy of 'small steps' may be sensible.

13. I should also say on a personal basis that I think we make the problem a lot more difficult if we approach it in an antagonistic frame of mind. I have seen no convincing economic reason why we should object to a reunified Germany within the EC. Indeed, if one of our objectives is to prevent further enlargement of the EC, while developing a series of relationships with aspirant and other countries, then admitting the GDR while keeping the core membership to twelve, i.e. by unification, might actually be an advantage in that precedents would be avoided.

14. Our security interests would of course be affected in a major way if over-rapid political unification were to lead to Gorbachev's fall or the FRG leaving NATO for a unified but neutral place in the centre of Europe. Gorbachev's fall on German grounds should begin to recede from the signature of the CFE onwards. Until then there is not much he or we can do about the minds of the people in the GDR or their economy other than the measures the EC/24 collectively are taking, but most of all the FRG. The maintenance of the two alliances, or at least NATO with the FRG in it thereafter seems to me to be more likely on the basis of confederation, of the Germanies for as long as possible, and for as long as NATO is seen actively to be engaged in arms control.

Yours,
N.H.R.A. BROOMFIELD

No. 80

Minute from Mr Weston to Mr Waldegrave

[*RS 021/2/3*]

Secret and Personal   FCO, *15 December 1989*

East-West and Germany

1. As I reported to you orally last night, I held a meeting yesterday to carry forward the work referred to in the Private Secretary's letter of 12 December to Mr Powell.[1] As you know the Prime Minister has said she wishes to chair a meeting at Chequers toward the end of January or early February: papers must be with No 10 by 20 January. My meeting was also attended by Mr Mottram (MOD) and Mr Appleyard (Cabinet Office).

2. I attach at annex a summary of the existing work programme, including decisions taken yesterday on further work. Exactly which papers go to No 10 as a basis for discussion at Chequers will be for Ministers to decide, on the recommendation of the PUS. But speaking personally, I am inclined to think the seminar will need to concentrate on the papers about moves towards German unity, the longer term perspectives for a 'Europe whole and free' and the future of the CFE process.

3. On the follow-up to more immediate points arising from our recent correspondence with No 10, I have asked Mr Ratford to look at next steps on high

---

[1] No. 74.

level diplomatic contacts between HMG and the Russians, President Mitterrand and the Germans respectively (including the possibility of a visit soon to the FRG by yourself); and to make proposals. We may need to follow-up with a further letter to No 10.

4. My group will meet again to take stock of progress at 3.30 p.m. on Thursday 21 December.

P.J. WESTON

ENCLOSURE IN NO. 80

Work Programme

1. *Background*
(*a*) General paper on German Question (WED).[2]
(*b*) Broomfield Valedictory on the GDR.[3]
(*c*) Historical note on Berlin (COI, November 1987).[4]

2. *Check lists for on-going use*
(*a*) Crisis over the GDR: contingency plan (WED).[5]
(*b*) Berlin: becoming an open city (WED).[4]
(*c*) UK/GDR relations: the next steps (WED).[4] These papers may need to be the subject of further submission to Ministers as events unfold. WED will also ask Mr Mottram for any MOD contributions on (*b*).

3. *The move toward German unity*
(*a*) Mallaby letter of 5 December.[6]
(*b*) Paper on Kohl 10 point plan (Planners).[5]
These components will now form the basis of a new paper on German unity by WED/Planners, which will set out the main conceptual models, analyse them in relation to the overall British interest, and review the diplomatic means by which British influence can be brought to bear on the process.

4. *Instability in Eastern Europe*
Paper on the Baltics, with annex on possible types of instability in Eastern Europe (Planners).[4]
This paper will now be reviewed and possibly expanded with the aim of using it to compare notes more actively on possible contingency planning, at the restricted meeting of Political Directors in January.

---

[2] No. 25.
[3] No. 66.
[4] Not found.
[5] Not printed.
[6] No. 65.

5. *The CFE process after CFE 1*

Mr Goulden, with help from Planners, will take the lead in drafting a new paper. This will work up options for use if HMG is to be able to steer the Alliance toward a tolerable CFE 2, and will explore wider issues raised by continuing reductions in Allied force levels in Europe. The first draft will be passed to Mr Mottram, with a view to the paper becoming a joint FCO/MOD product.

6. *Longer term perspectives for a 'Europe whole and free'*

(*a*) Euro Architecture paper (Planners)—for consideration at DUSs' meeting on 20 December.

(*b*) Baker's speech in Berlin on 13 December.[7] Subject to discussion at the PUS's meeting on 20 December, it is proposed that the Planning Staff paper suitably adapted be the basis for examining the future relationship between the Alliance, European Community and the CSCE process, taking account inter alia of Baker's proposals for new ways of consolidating the US commitment to Europe and other possibilities mentioned in Charles Powell's letter of 8 December.

Pour mémoire

7. *Other MOD contributions*

(*a*) Mr Mottram will ensure that the question of the alert status of British forces in Berlin and BAOR is covered soon in an MOD letter to No 10. He will also contribute to 2(*b*) above from the viewpoint of British forces in Berlin.

(*b*) A further piece of work, stemming from the September Chequers seminar, is proceeding somewhat autonomously. This is an examination by the Minister for Defence Procurement of alternative models of British defence posture.

8. *Coordination of assistance to Eastern Europe*

This work does not fall to the Weston group, but will obviously be relevant to any discussion at Chequers of broader aspects of British policy.

9. *Guidance for Posts abroad and Whitehall*

At some point consideration should be given to reflecting some of the above work in general guidance to Posts. There may also be a case for briefing Permanent Secretaries in other Whitehall Departments.

[7] In fact of 12 December: see No. 76, note 2.

No. 81

Sir C. Mallaby (Bonn) to Mr Hurd[1]

No. 1251 Telegraphic [WRL 020/4]

Secret   BONN, 18 December 1989, 10.04 a.m.

Your Telno 723: Consultations with the FRG on German Question[2]

1. Kohl took a deliberate decision not to consult Allies (or his coalition partners) in advance about the ten points speech on 28 November. He wanted to avoid argument about the contents, which could have caused delay and prior leaks and thus endangered his aim of personally becoming master of the debate here on the German question. He has paid a price: not only the Allies and the FDP but also the opposition and the German media have repeatedly criticised the lack of consultation. This, and more particularly the Four Ambassadors' meeting in Berlin, have given the Federal Republic in general a salutary reminder of Four Power rights.

2. The Federal Chancellery are well aware of the need to consult properly. The three Ambassadors have had two meetings so far this month with Seiters, where Kohl's forthcoming visit to Dresden has been discussed.[3] Another is scheduled for 21 December, to brief us after the visit. The three Allied Ministers are seeing Duisberg, the responsible Under Secretary in the Federal Chancellery, on 18 December for a final briefing before Kohl's visit.

3. Nevertheless it is possible that Kohl will again see a balance of advantage in not consulting the Allies about a new step on the German question. In trying to reduce that risk, we should intensify bilateral consultation but also bear in mind that involvement of all three Allies can have a stronger Gulliver effect than bilateral contact.

4. The Federal Chancellery was the department at fault last time. I shall continue my campaign for more contact with Seiters and Duisberg. When you are next in Bonn, we should seek a call on Kohl, citing Genscher's recent one on the Prime Minister. You should also see Seiters. We should seek calls on him and on Teltschik for Ministers of State and senior FCO officials visiting Bonn. I would welcome a visit by Sir Percy Cradock, who could call on Seiters and Teltschik as well as the intelligence community.

5. As for the Auswärtiges Amt, we should make full use of NATO, EPC and especially the Berlin-related forum. On the bilateral aspect, frequent meetings between you and Genscher will be the most important element. I hope Mr Waldegrave will come in early January. Sudhoff is to visit London for talks with the PUS on 9 February. I hope Weston will visit Bonn in January, to get to know Kastrup and experience the atmosphere on the German question.[4] I agree that

---

[1] Repeated for information Priority to BMG Berlin, East Berlin, Moscow, Paris, Washington, UKDEL NATO, UKREP Brussels.
[2] No. 78.
[3] Herr Kohl was to visit Dresden on 19-20 December.
[4] Mr Weston met Herr Kastrup on 5 February: see No. 123.

Ratford's talks with Höynck, who plays a significant role here, should be used to the full.

6. The Inner German Ministry is much less important in policy making. But it can be a useful source of information. Visiting Ministers and senior officials should call on Frau Wilms, the Minister, or Dobiey, the very competent Deputy Secretary.

No. 82

Mr Broomfield (East Berlin) to Mr Hurd[1]

No. 482 Telegraphic [WRE 014/2]

Confidential   EAST BERLIN, *19 December 1989, 3.35 p.m.*

GDR Internal Developments: Demonstrations

Summary

1. Demonstrations in Leipzig and elsewhere on 18 December pass off peacefully. But unity issue has not gone away.

Detail

2. Head of Chancery[2] observed the last Monday demonstration in Leipzig on 18 December, and confirms the press reports of a quiet and well-disciplined, static crowd of some 150,000 silently carrying lighted candles instead of placards. A small group defied the general rule by displaying Weimar flags of red, black and gold and placards calling for 'One Germany one Fatherland'. Discussions on the edge of the group were often heated, but never showed signs of getting out of hand.

3. Demonstrations in other GDR cities and in East Berlin passed off similarly quietly. (Some demonstrations in Dresden were in favour of German unity.) One of the two organisers of the Leipzig demonstration, Father Magirius (St Nicholas Church) told the Head of Chancery later that he was pleased with the outcome. He could not, however, be sure that the same calm would be evident when the demonstrations resume on 8 January (he feared an influx of extremists from the FRG to swell the re-unification elements).

Comment

4. The fact that in Leipzig and in a number of other major cities the demonstrations passed off quietly will be a relief to the GDR authorities. The issue of German unity has not, however, gone away, notwithstanding that and the Round Table appeal (my telno 481).[3] Together with the economy, and law and order, it remains one of the three critical factors in the GDR.

---

[1] Repeated for information Priority to Bonn, BMG Berlin; Routine to Washington, Paris, UKDEL NATO, Moscow; Saving to East European Posts, CICC(G), Peking.

[2] Mr Sands.

[3] Not found.

No. 83

Submission from Sir P. Wright to Mr Waldegrave and Assistant Private Secretary

[*RS 020/2/3*]

Confidential   FCO, *20 December 1989*

East/West Relations and Germany: The Prime Minister's Chequers Seminar

1. Papers for the Prime Minister's Chequers Seminar (for which no date has yet been set, but which is likely to take place at the end of January) are being prepared under the supervision of Mr John Weston, who has set up a committee to supervise this work, reporting to Mr Waldegrave. Current plans are to put the following three papers to No 10 by 20 January:

(*a*) German Reunification.[1]

(*b*) The Future of the CFE process.[2]

(*c*) Longer term perspectives for 'European Architecture'.[2]

2. I hope that there will be an opportunity for the Secretary of State to hold a meeting to discuss this range of subjects before papers are submitted to No 10. There is a seminar fixed for 11 January on Arms Control, and some of that discussion (e.g. on CFE) will be relevant. But a separate meeting on East/West and Germany early in the New Year would be useful, if that can be arranged.

3. Meanwhile, Ministers may like, over the holiday period, to look at the precursors to papers (*a*) and (*c*), together with:

(*d*) Sir John Fretwell's and Sir Arthur Watts' comments on the first paper;[3]

(*e*) Sir Christopher Mallaby's letter of 5 December;[4]

(*f*) Mr Broomfield's valedictory despatch from East Berlin;[5]

(*g*) Mr Goulden's comment on the Policy Planning Staff paper on European architecture (*c*) above).[2]

Other papers have been prepared on Berlin and on Contingency Planning for instability in the GDR and the Baltic States; but I am not submitting these for the time being.

4. I discussed these subjects, with particular reference to the papers on German reunification and European architecture, at my monthly meeting of DUSs on 19 December. The following were the main themes to emerge:

Germany

—German reunification was already under way, and moving faster than predicted. After next May's elections in the GDR, the referendum on the new constitution would in effect be a plebiscite on reunification. Meanwhile, from 1 January the free travel area would begin to grow into a single economic area.

—A German Confederation would be easier to handle than a Federation. But in Kohl's speech of 28 November 'confederate structures' are seen as no more

---

[1] Final version printed as No. 99.
[2] Not printed.
[3] Sir J. Fretwell's comments printed as No. 23. Sir A. Watts's comments not printed.
[4] No. 65.
[5] No. 66.

than a transitional stage to federation, and transition might not last long. So far all observers have consistently underestimated the speed of events.

—The paper on German reunification should cover the need to settle the question of Germany's eastern frontier (the Oder-Neisse line). At the moment Kohl was systematically avoiding this problem for electoral reasons. This was dangerous for European stability.

—The paper might also say more about Soviet, French and American attitudes. The Soviet aim seemed to be to use Four Power arrangements, and possibly the CSCE process, as a way of slowing down or preventing unity. We should not let ourselves be implicated in such motivation. It was important that we should not be seen to use our residual powers as a barrier to reunification. To do so would not only damage relations with Germany (and perhaps provoke even greater pressure in both parts of Germany for reunification), it could also create a very damaging split with the United States.

—A final peace settlement need not be in the form of a Four Power agreement. It might be sufficient, and perhaps more fitting 40 years from the end of the war, for the Four Powers to say that they regarded a wider European Treaty, perhaps emerging from the CSCE process, as a peace settlement. In reality events had already passed the point where the Four Powers could determine the shape of Europe.

European Architecture

—The Policy Planning Staff paper placed too much emphasis on the desirability of the Warsaw Pact surviving. There could be no question of our attempting (or appearing) to prop the Warsaw Pact up. Whether it remained in place or fell apart was in other hands. Of the two, collapse was the more likely outcome, and we should be prepared to adapt to that reality.

—The paper rightly focussed on the same tripod of institutions (Alliance, Community, CSCE) as Baker had in his Berlin speech. But it gave too much weight to widening (as opposed to deepening) the European Community. The model of integrative security described was valid, but more perhaps as a terminal goal for Europe. Meanwhile, the paper was right to suggest that we were moving into a world of co-operative security, in which a reinforced CSCE would have an important role to play. Although the European Community had performed an important role in Franco-German reconciliation and in creating shared interests among the Member States, it had not been the main instrument of maintaining stability in Europe since the war. This has been the result of the cohesion of the Alliance in the West and Soviet domination of the East.

—Security issues would need further examination: we would need to look at a greater range of security options, in which Germany might play a greater or lesser part. Sustaining US presence and nuclear guarantees was important, but in the long term the idea of large numbers of foreign forces based in Germany was not plausible. We would have to look again at the position of France and the role that it might play in European security.

PATRICK WRIGHT

No. 84

Paper by the FCO Legal Adviser[1]

[*MRA 184/623/1*]

Confidential   FCO, *22 December 1989*

Germany: Legal and Procedural Considerations

1. This paper considers the main legal and procedural considerations which are relevant to any major developments in the position of Germany. It suggests that there are certain legally essential minima for participants (which include the UK) and procedures involved in any new settlement of German questions, but that beyond that minimum there is a lot of flexibility.

2. While the details are intricate, the post-war legal position of Germany is based on three fundamental elements:

(i) the assumption in 1945 by the USA, USSR, UK and France of 'Supreme Authority' over Germany;

(ii) the 1952-1954 Convention on Relations between the FRG and the USA, UK and France, which preserved certain residual Allied rights regarding Germany whole;

(iii) as regards Berlin, the Quadripartite (i.e. USSR, USA, UK and France) Agreement of 1971. A fuller summary of the major legal landmarks in the post-war history of Germany is at Annex A.[2]

3. All the main elements involve the UK. The underlying Four Power rights in relation to various aspects of the post-War German situation give us an undoubted right to participate as a main player in the settlement end-game. This is, of course, quite separate from whether, as a player, we wish to slow the game down or speed it up, or see it move in one direction rather than another. While our ability to influence events may be limited, and most of the running may well be made by the Germans themselves, nevertheless our Four Power rights and responsibilities give us a firm foundation for whatever role it is that we wish to play.

4. Any final settlement involving German reunification would need to bring the three main elements to an end; even a more limited and transitional re-arrangement of German affairs would be likely to involve one or more of those basic elements. Any such settlement or re-arrangement would presumably also need to address the question whether any new arrangements consistent with the present status of Germany are to be agreed.

5. A preliminary point is that since the war was with Germany, a 'peace settlement' ought also to be with Germany as a whole. The traditional Western view is that a notional State of 'Germany' continues in law to exist, and that effective reunification (presumably of the FRG, GDR and Berlin) must precede a peace settlement. At least in recent times the Soviet view has been that a peace settlement could be reached with the FRG and GDR, who between them represent 'Germany'. The Soviet Union has tended to treat the CSCE process as a kind of

---

[1] Sent by Sir A. Watts to Mr Weston with a covering minute: 'I attach a first shot at a paper of the kind you asked me to prepare at the meeting yesterday afternoon. . . . '

[2] Not printed.

substitute for a peace settlement; the Western position was made clear on signing the Helsinki Final Act.

6. The tidy way to proceed would be to conclude a formal Peace Treaty with Germany, just as Peace Treaties were concluded with the other enemy States in Europe in the late 1940s.

7. However, the conclusion of such a Peace Treaty in the 1990s, some 50 years after the end of the war, would probably not be a realistic exercise. The role of the Four Powers as the major participants (with Germany) in a Peace Treaty is less clear today than it would have been in the 1950s. Furthermore, it would not be altogether easy to arrange suitable representation of 'Germany' as the other negotiating party to a Peace Treaty. Finally, the scope of any peace settlement would seem very likely to affect quite a number of other States who might feel entitled to participate in the settlement and indeed whom it might be in our interest to see associated with it (not over-looking possible claims by some non-European, non-Atlantic States which actively participated in the war e.g. Australia, New Zealand, India).

8. There are alternative legal structures. They are less tidy, but probably politically more realistic and can be just as effective. They involve wrapping up legally necessary post-war accommodations in a much wider legal framework— wider both as regards the parties to it and the kind of matters dealt with in it. Legally there is quite a lot of room for flexibility. To take the three main elements identified in paragraph 2 above, the basic legal requirements could be met as follows.

9. As to *the Four Powers' supreme authority over Germany*, steps to renounce that authority could be taken in a number of ways, e.g. a Treaty between themselves, or the same sort of joint declaration as that by which they proclaimed their supreme authority in the first place. Such a renunciation of the Four Powers' authority could be incorporated in, or associated with, a Treaty to which other States were also parties, so long as somehow the Four Powers could each be said to have agreed that their supreme authority over Germany had come to an end.

10. As to *Allied rights in respect of Germany as a whole* (which is matched by an equivalent Soviet right), any renunciation (or variation) would on the Allied side presumably need to involve some kind of treaty instrument amending the relevant provisions of the 'Relations' Convention; there might be, on the Soviet Union's side, a similar need for treaty amendment *vis-à-vis* the GDR. The necessary renunciation of rights over Germany as a whole could be embodied in a Treaty specifically prepared for that sole purpose, and limited to those few States. But this is not essential. The necessary provisions could be included in some much wider Treaty instrument. What matters is that everyone must be able to point to some specific Treaty provisions which would clearly stipulate that rights as regards Germany as a whole had come to an end (or been varied).

11. Much the same goes for the *status of Berlin*. While specific amendments to, or total termination of, the 1971 Quadripartite Agreement by agreement between the Four Powers alone would be one way of proceeding, it would be possible, legally to wrap up the necessary treaty agreement between the Four Powers in a much wider settlement instrument.

12. Any settlement document would need to provide something to replace the various Four Power rights which were being renounced—otherwise one would risk leaving a legal vacuum. The 'something' would presumably involve conferring the equivalent rights on German authorities. In particular, there would need to be some

provisions regarding frontiers (since otherwise it could be argued that the animal which was being let loose by the renunciation of Four Power rights was Germany as constituted within its pre-War boundaries) and some provision regarding the successor German State(s) and the future status of Berlin. The provisions included in the Peace Treaties with Italy, Hungary, Bulgaria, Romania and Finland, indicate additional ground it might be appropriate to cover. Although the three western Allies might reasonably take the view that much of that ground was in practice covered quite adequately in the various 1952-1954 Agreements with the FRG, they do not have any similar agreement with the GDR, nor does the Soviet Union with the FRG. There could also be a wide range of other matters which, in a broad contemporary European context, might be covered, such as democratic institutions, human rights, and settlement of disputes procedures.

13. Excluding a bare Peace Treaty between the Four Powers, and presumably, the FRG and GDR, broad options for putting together a settlement deal might include:

(i) a wide-ranging CSCE settlement agreement, to which all 35 States would be parties, incorporating (perhaps as annexes) the terms which are necessary to put the War finally to bed. As between the Four Powers and Germany this agreement would constitute a formal end of the War's aftermath while the other parties would be merely subscribing to that event; for all parties, they would be agreeing as equals to whatever new arrangements for the future were being agreed.

(ii) a set of agreements and declarations each of which might be self-contained but which need not have the same parties or status, dealing separately with each of the various matters needing to be covered, but together forming a package held together by a common negotiating history and perhaps concluded within the framework of some general umbrella agreement.

(iii) a limited party 'core' agreement (Four Powers, FRG/GDR) to which other interested States could subscribe/accede, as associated parties.

14. Finally, we should not under-estimate inherent German legalism. If the Germans want to move ahead in particular directions, they would be likely to attach importance to it being done with the proper observance of the necessary legal requirements. If they do not do that, they will be leaving themselves open to serious challenge, both internally and internationally, on the constitutionality and general legality of what has been achieved by way of a settlement. The Federal German Constitutional Court, for example, gave everyone a fairly anxious time several years ago in trying to find ways to prevent the FRG/GDR Relations Agreement being struck down as unconstitutional. The Germans will presumably not want to run similar risks over a much more far-reaching settlement which would be likely to set the foundation for Germany for the next century.

A. D. WATTS

No. 85

Sir C. Mallaby (Bonn) to Mr Hurd[1]

No. 12 Telegraphic [WRE 026/1]

Confidential   BONN, *5 January 1990, 4.41 p.m.*

The German Question: Our Public Line

Summary

1. Despite our supportive line on the German wish to achieve unity through self-determination, the UK is perceived here as perhaps the least positive of the three Western Allies, and the least important. Need to present our policy in the most positive light we can. Your visit to East Berlin and the GDR an opportunity.

Detail

2. I remain concerned that despite our consistent support for the principle of German unity through self-determination, the UK is perceived here as opposing, or at least wishing to brake, reunification. The French, on the other hand, whose doubts seem if anything stronger than ours, manage to maintain a more positive public image (Mitterrand's remarks in Kiev notwithstanding).[2] The US are perceived as the most supportive of German aspirations even while laying down conditions for German unity.

3. Two recent British statements have stuck in German minds and coloured their perception of our policy. The first was your comment in Berlin on 16 November that German unity was not on the agenda.[3] This was true at the time. But Kohl's ten point statement on 28 November put it on the agenda, even if without a timetable. The second was the Prime Minister's statement in Brussels on 1 December that reunification should not take place for ten to fifteen years.[4] The latter continues to be quoted by German commentators as evidence of a negative and mistrustful British attitude.

4. As against the background of Bush's policy of a 'Europe whole and free', Baker's four conditions for German reunification have been well-received here, because of the spirit that is thought to lie behind them and because they are seen as designed to facilitate, rather than prevent, German unity.[5] The same cannot be said of Mitterrand's contributions. In Bonn on 3 November he said he had no fear of German reunification, which posed no problems for France.[6] Three days later in Kiev he said reunification 'is not a question for now' and that the question of frontiers should not be raised again. The fact is that as the FRG's best friend and

---

[1] Repeated for information Priority to East Berlin; Routine BMG Berlin, Washington, Moscow, Paris, UKDEL NATO.

[2] President Mitterrand had met President Gorbachev in Kiev on 6 December. At a joint news conference he had stated: 'None of our countries, and especially one whose weight is so great and whose geographical position is such, can act without taking into account the balance of Europe.'

[3] In fact Mr Hurd had used this formula on at least three previous occasions: in a press conference in The Hague on 9 November, a BBC World Service interview on 10 November and a BBC Radio interview in Bonn on 15 November.

[4] In fact at the NATO Heads of Government meeting on 4 December.

[5] See No. 76, note 2.

[6] See No. 35, note 3.

most important European partner, France can get away with a great deal. It is characteristic that Kohl should have visited Mitterrand in south-west France on 4 January to mend fences.[7] The UK by contrast is at present seen as neither especially important nor as well disposed. Both aspects can reduce our influence on the FRG at this critical time.

5. Your visit to East Berlin and the GDR which is likely to be widely reported here, provides an important opportunity to try to put a more positive spin on our presentation.[8] You could use the Strasbourg/NATO formulae (East Berlin telnos 003 and 007)[9] but present them as a statement of British policy. You could also draw on other elements in the public line recently produced by the Department in consultation with this Embassy.

[7] Herr Kohl had visited President Mitterrand's private residence at Latche in Gascony .
[8] Mr Hurd's visit was to take place on 22-24 January.
[9] Telegrams not printed. For the Strasbourg declaration see No. 73, note 3. The Strasbourg formula was repeated in the communiqué issued at the end of the NAC Ministerial meeting on 14-15 December.

No. 86

Submission from Mr Weston to Mr Waldegrave[1]

[*WRL 020/1*]

Confidential   FCO, *8 January 1990*

Chequers Seminar: East-West Relations and Germany

1. I submit four papers on the lines agreed earlier with you, together with a covering draft minute from the Secretary of State to the Prime Minister, which are intended to form the basis for discussion at Chequers on 27 January.[2] As agreed with the Private Secretary, it will be helpful if these papers could be seen by the Secretary of State, together with your own views, before the Secretary of State's office meeting on Arms Control on 11 January.[3] Thereafter I shall try to take account of any further Ministerial views on the papers before re-submitting them formally to the Secretary of State on 16 January, so that they may go to No 10 to meet Charles Powell's deadline of 20 January.

2. The papers in their present form represent a broad consensus within my working group, which included Mr Appleyard (Cabinet Office) and Mr Mottram (MOD). Mr Mottram has so far provided his advice on a personal and informal basis only. He hopes to obtain formal MOD endorsement by 16 January. You told me this morning that you were concerned that the papers going to No. 10 should not leave any doubt that German unification is likely to take place sooner rather than later, whatever our own private preferences might be; and that events are also likely to force a major change of strategy upon NATO in the near future. Both

[1] Mr Weston had taken up the post of Political Director on 2 January.
[2] Covering draft minute ('East-West Relations and Germany') and three papers ('German Unification', 'Conventional Defence and Control in Europe' and 'European Architecture') not printed. Fourth paper printed as No. 84. Earlier drafts had been submitted under cover of Sir P. Wright's submission of 20 December (No. 83).
[3] For this meeting see No. 97, note 4.

these aspects were discussed at considerable length at the meetings of my working group.[4] I hope you will feel that the end product now reflects a better balance on these points than the earlier drafts you saw. In my personal view the fact that events have repeatedly out-stripped our expectations or predictions in recent months, and may do so again, does not mean we should not continue to try to influence them in pursuit of our major objectives, if we can.

P.J. WESTON

[4] These took place on 29 December and 5 January (see minutes by Mr Synnott of 4 and 8 January, WRL 020/1).

No. 87

Minute from Mr Waldegrave to Mr Weston

[*WRL 020/1*]

Secret   FCO, *8 January 1990*

East-West, Germany etc

1. I am very impressed by the quality of the papers submitted under the PUS's minute of 20 December, especially the paper called 'Implications of Chancellor Kohl's Proposals'.[1] The analysis seems to me clear, and the realities to be recognised.

2. I am not so happy with the clearly tactical considerations which have converted this analysis into the draft minute to the PM submitted under cover of your minute of 2nd January.[2] I am not against sensible tactics in relation to No 10, but if ever there was a time when the Office should present the stark truth about what is likely to happen, and should avoid feeding illusions, that time is surely now. In my view the draft minute has made too many concessions to the views we expect to be held in No 10.

3. Particular examples are (I have numbered the paragraphs):

(1) Para 5. We should not over-emphasise fears of the addition to German economic preponderance reunification would bring. The figures the Department has already produced show that the change is not very great. The economic preponderance is there already.

(2) Para 6. I think we talk up the 'confederal', binary outcome far too high, as a result of wishful thinking. I *don't* think the key to German politics is a fear by Kohl of 'exposing too much flank to the SPD' on this: the boot is on the other foot. The SPD will damage itself by getting sucked into support for a two state solution. No 'confederal' solution has ever, or will ever, work for long. Most important of all, in view of what I believe to be the unstoppable desire for full reunification in the GDR, an attempt to delay it like this will make the GDR ungovernable. I think we will find GDR voters not going for some leftist, neutral half way home; they will vote for reunification; many of them will probably join the right of German politics.

[1] See No. 83.
[2] Minute of 2 January not found, but seems to have been superseded by No. 86.

(3) Paragraph 7 gives the misleading impression that it would be seen in Germany as a positive and friendly step on our part to work for the binary solution. Particularly starting from the position we are in now, it won't. We are already distrusted, and the ploy will be seen for what it is. The 'diplomatic initiative' suggested would be seen as hostile and I doubt whether the US would support it. And all this is *not* going to wait until after the German elections.

(4) Paragraph 8, with the main point of which (recognise the reality of CFE 2, 3 etc) I agree, gives the misleading idea (from which MOD must soon wake up) that CFE 2 etc will be compatible with 'the retention of NATO's existing strategy'. Actually, I doubt if CFE 1 really will be.

(5) The last sentence of 11 shirks the challenge: we have to *find* a strategy for keeping a reunified Germany attached to western defence. I do not believe it is impossible.

(6) We must plainly say in the covering minute what is said in paragraph 7 of the underlying paper, 'the prospects of agreement to FOTL[3] seem negligible'. (I would delete 'seem' and replace by 'are'). We must make suggestions as to how to avert the repeated isolation of the UK on this front, and recognise the fact that already the changes in Poland, Czechoslovakia and the GDR have converted the Warsaw Pact from an alliance which could launch a co-ordinated surprise attack into one where any Soviet move west would probably have to contend with a major insurrection from its 'allies'. A defensive strategy on our part which involves retaliation against the territory of those 'allies' (*only* those allies according to the last WINTEX) is indefensible.[4]

4. I think the form of the minute should be changed, to start with our beliefs about what is likely to happen; to be followed by our objectives (which I do not think are quite complete in the draft—we must mention *freedom*, or self-determination); and ending with proposals for reconciling the two. I attach an Aunt Sally framework, as an aid to argument.[5]

THE RT HON WILLIAM WALDEGRAVE

ENCLOSURE IN NO. 87

ALTERNATIVE FRAMEWORK FOR MINUTE TO PM

A. *What do we think is likely to happen?*

(1) Pressure for German reunification will be unstoppable: events, as they have in the last twelve months will move faster than commentators predict;

(2) The Warsaw Pact will disintegrate, or may already have disintegrated, as an alliance capable of united and co-ordinated aggressive action; members may actually leave it;

(3) FOTL will not be deployed; no German politician of weight believes the question still to be open;

(4) CFE 1 will be followed by CFE 2 etc which will involve further deep cuts and the end of a plausible forward defence strategy (there will in any case be no

---

[3] Follow-up to Lance: see No. 1, note 6.

[4] See No. 3, note 5.

[5] On 16 January Mr Weston sent this minute to WED with the note: '(No further action) . . . (Discussed at S/S meeting on 12/1)'.

conventional surprise attack capability on the other side);

(5) The USSR itself may break up; at any event it will be increasingly dominated by internal concerns.

B. *Objectives*

(1) To maintain our long term security against continental Russia by maintaining the defence alliance with the US/Canada;

(2) To achieve (1) without damaging the commitment to self-determination which underlines our whole political and moral position;

(3) To recognise that (2) must apply to Germany, but to discuss with Germany the development of collective western positions on the safest route to inevitable reunification.

Proposals for the reconciliation of A with B

(1) Can we envisage a NATO without FOTL? Yes. Can we envisage a security doctrine involving the US which has residual deterrence deployed behind a low level conventional 'picket line' defensive deployment? Yes. We should be putting our resources into analysis of how to achieve this against the real danger, not of a threat to our security in the next 18 months from the east, but of NATO breaking up if it is not flexible enough. So, proposal (1) is: work up the successor doctrines to forward defence and flexible response.

(2) Can we envisage a reunified Germany in NATO? That is what the self-determination of Germans will choose if they are allowed. Can we offer security guarantees acceptable to the USSR which would allow it? Yes—since the exercise of force by the USSR to stop reunification would involve perhaps terminal strains on the USSR's system itself. So, proposal (2) is: work up a NATO strategy probably along the lines of no forward deployment in present F.R. Germany (and perhaps Norway) in exchange for no deployment in a reunified present GDR—probably with joint monitoring posts a la Sinai but with Germany in NATO.

(3) Proposal 3—work up CSCE institutions, as in paper.

(4) Proposal 4—develop Anglo-French nuclear co-operation, as in paper.

(5) Proposal 5—make a reality of the Bruges speech by firmly accepting that Europe one day will include Eastern Europe, but emphasising not only the economic and political conditionality, but also that Europe will not be disarmed, and will remain part of the liberal-democratic alliance of NATO or its successor.[6] Make it clear that the USSR is not part of Europe, though is welcome to join the wider liberal community (some hope).

---

[6] The relevant part of Mrs Thatcher's speech to the College of Europe in Bruges on 20 September 1988 read: 'The European Community is *one* manifestation of that European identity, but it is not the only one. We must never forget that east of the Iron Curtain, people who once enjoyed a full share of European culture, freedom and identity have been cut off from their roots. We shall always look on Warsaw, Prague and Budapest as great European cities.'

No. 88

Letter from Mr Powell (No. 10) to Mr Wall

[WRL 020/1]

Confidential and Personal   10 DOWNING STREET, *9 January 1990*

Dear Stephen,

The German Question: Our Public Line

The Prime Minister has seen Bonn telegram number 12 commenting on our public line on the German question.[1] She thought it showed a lack of understanding of our policy which she finds alarming. She would like to see any reply before it is sent.[2]

Yours sincerely,
C. POWELL

---

[1] No. 85.

[2] On 8 January Mr Synnott had sent a submission to Mr Weston outlining forthcoming opportunities to act on Sir C. Mallaby's recommendation to present British policy in the most positive possible light, including Mr Waldegrave's visit to Bonn (17 January), Mr Hurd's visit to East Berlin and the GDR (22-24 January), Mrs Thatcher's meeting with President Mitterrand (20 January) and Mr Hurd's speech to the Konrad Adenauer Foundation (6 February). On 9 January Mr Weston minuted: 'Until I saw Mr Powell's letter of today [No. 88], I was thinking of briefing the S/S to raise this with the PM tomorrow. Having discussed with the PS and the PUS I have decided it would be better to leave things until Chequers. I will raise it there if no-one else does!' (WRL 020/1).

No. 89

Minute from Mr Weston to Mr Wall

[WRL 020/1]

Confidential covering Secret and Strictly Personal   FCO, *9 January 1990*

Secretary of State's Bilateral with the Prime Minister

1. The Secretary of State will no doubt wish to discuss with the Prime Minister tomorrow the line she will take with President Mitterrand on 20 January over Germany. Sir Christopher Mallaby has recently sent advice about HMG's public line on this question, which the Prime Minister has questioned on the grounds that it shows a misunderstanding of our policy.[1]

2. It would be helpful to the Department if the Secretary of State could clarify this with the Prime Minister. The public line to which HMG subscribed at

---

[1] Nos. 85 and 88.

Strasbourg and NATO Summits (text attached)[2] must presumably be one element in our policy, however much we may entertain private reservations over too rapid a rush toward German unity. Sir Christopher Mallaby was in a sense only asking that HMG should use this collectively agreed formula a little more often in Ministerial statements.

3. It is important for all concerned to be re-assured about this, since otherwise officials risk having to operate without any clear sense of policy direction.

4. A UK restatement of this formula at or around the time of the Prime Minister's visit to Paris would be useful in off-setting what may otherwise be damaging speculation about the meeting.[3]

P.J. WESTON

[2] For the Strasbourg/NATO declarations see Nos. 73, note 3, and 85, note 9.
[3] Mr Gozney minuted on 11 January: 'Thank you. The Secretary of State might need this pack again next week if the Prime Minister holds a meeting on Germany before going to Paris.'

No. 90

Minute from Mr Synnott to Mr Weston

[*WRL 020/1*]

Personal and Confidential   FCO, *9 January 1990*

Prime Minister's Meeting with President Mitterrand, 20 January
1. We are required to get a brief to No 10 for this meeting by 17 January. In the absence of the Secretary of State in Hong Kong, I am working to submit it through you and through Mr Waldegrave on 15 or in the course of 16 January (Mr Waldegrave leaves for Bonn that evening). But Mr Waldegrave's minute of 8 January and Mr Powell's letter of 9 January[1] reveal differences of underlying approach which may be difficult to reconcile before the Paris meeting.

2. Without trying to tackle the subject head on, I have tried my hand at a brief for the meeting with Mitterrand which attempts to be consistent with the sentiment of your Group and yet does not require the Prime Minister fully to accept the Waldegrave thesis before the issues are thoroughly argued through at Chequers.[2] Nonetheless, as we discussed yesterday, I envisage and Private Office have agreed that your Group's papers should be regarded as part of the Prime Minister's background for her meeting with Mitterrand. The remainder of the brief is therefore in the form of 'bull points' rather than a précis.

3. I should be grateful for your preliminary views on my draft extract as it stands at present.[3]

H.N.H. SYNNOTT

[1] Nos. 87 and 88.
[2] Not printed. Final version printed as No. 99.
[3] Mr Synnott minuted to Mr Ramsden on 12 January: 'Now overtaken. But language may be of value.'

No. 91

Letter from Sir C. Mallaby (Bonn) to Mr Weston[1]

[*WRL 020/1*]

Confidential   BONN, *9 January 1990*

Dear John,

The German Question and Its Repercussions

1. I wrote on 5 December about policy on the German Question and future European architecture.[2] This letter offers further reflections.

2. I still think that a binary German confederation would be the best form of German unity from our point of view. Since I wrote on 5 December, the SPD has espoused the idea. A significant minority in the SPD regards confederation as the permanent answer to the German Question. But there was a majority at the recent SPD Congress for seeing confederation as a stage before the final arrangement of a German federation. It is a pity that it is the opposition here that nailed its colours to this mast, while Kohl is known to dislike confederation on the grounds that it would perpetuate the GDR in some form. Hence his deliberate avoidance of it in his Ten Point speech on 28 November. And Genscher told me today (see separate telegram) that the idea of a confederation was artificial and had no future.

3. As argued in my letter of 5 December, we must recognise that a confederation would be a complicated contrivance. There would be three levels of government—the confederative government, the two governments of the areas which now comprise the FRG and the GDR, and the (presumably 16) *Länder* governments. Moreover, the traditional idea of a confederation gives foreign policy and defence to the highest level of government, whereas we would want them to be at the middle level, so as to enable the territory of the Federal Republic to remain in NATO and to facilitate continued stationing of American forces there.

4. My feeling is that confederation remains unlikely to be the final answer to the German Question. There might possibly be a chance that it would stick, if espoused by the Three or Four Powers, as a transitional stage lasting a number of years. (One could argue, for instance, that it should last until achievement of a new European system or 'European Peace Order', in line with the Federal Government's position that German and European unity should be achieved together.) But we must allow for the possibility that confederation will not run even as a transitional stage. So we need another idea in our quiver.

5. One possibility might be an agreed transition period from the moment when German unity becomes certain until the completion of its implementation. Such a period might last 5 years, perhaps a bit longer. This is an idea which so far has not surfaced in the debate here on the German Question. But it presumably will before long. If you ask top Germans whether a transition period would be necessary, they say that it obviously will be. The purpose of establishing a transition period before German unity was completed would be to provide a stable framework not least for

---

[1] Copied to Ambassadors in East Berlin, Moscow, Washington, Paris, UKDEL NATO, Mr Burton, BMG Berlin, Mr Cooper, Policy Planning Staff.
[2] No. 65.

the negotiation of all the other complex matters that would need to be settled; and to fend off pressures for rapid, unstable movement towards unity.

6. The suggestions in this paragraph are designed to stimulate discussion, not as a blueprint. We could consider going, once the Germans had made clear in free self-determination that unity was their wish, for an early agreement or declaration where the 35 CSCE countries would agree, for example, on the following elements:

(*a*) They support the wish of the Germans for unity and will cooperate in a stable process aimed at implementing this, which should be completed by such and such a date (i.e. this would avoid a definitive undertaking that unity would be completed on a certain date, so as to give the Germans a motive to cooperate in achieving the other elements in the declaration).

(*b*) The Four Powers declare their intention that their rights and responsibilities in relation to Berlin and Germany as a whole will cease to exist when German unity is complete, and the other signatories take note of this.

(*c*) The signatories agree that the Oder-Neisse frontier could only be changed by mutual agreement in line with the Helsinki Final Act and acknowledge that such change is not acceptable to Poland; they take note of the intention of the Four Powers to fix this frontier definitively in law at the moment when German unity is completed. (This element would present domestic political difficulty for Kohl, who would prefer on present form to confine it to repetition of the Helsinki provision. But other states would want the rest and the FDP and SPD would share this view.)

(*d*) The signatories agree that levels of national and stationed forces in Europe during the transition period until completion of German unity will be determined by the CFE process and (if this must be conceded) by national decisions of stationing states.

(*e*) The signatories agree that arrangements for a permanent European security system ('European peace order') will be incorporated in a new CSCE Final Act in legally binding form, which will enter into force at the moment when German unity is completed. This will cover stationing of forces, procedures for peaceful settlement of disputes etc.

7. Such an agreement would buy some time to see how the USSR develops. If, during the transition period, the Soviet Union was seen again to become dangerous or unpredictable, progress in CFE would presumably be set back and force levels, under the above suggestion, would not fall as much as might today be expected. The prospect, as well as the need, for US forces staying in Western Europe including West Germany would in those circumstances be enhanced. We should try to preserve NATO until and beyond the completion of German unity, irrespective of whether the Warsaw Pact withered away. One might even hope that, during a transition period, independence and democracy in Eastern Europe could progress to the point where those countries would see and state their interest in including the stationing of US troops in Europe in the permanent arrangements to be agreed under (*e*).

8. All that said, however, there would be a risk that, if East-West relations happily were still making progress at the end of the transition period, we would be unable to negotiate a European security system for the further future which provided lasting deterrence against the possibility of the Soviet threat one day reappearing.

9. I also have a more current point about the Oder-Neisse frontier. The debate continues to rage here about whether it should be definitively recognised. Kohl is under pressure to concede this. I think that it would be less difficult for him, for political as well as legal reasons, to make a political statement about the finality of the frontier than to call on the Allies to declare it finally fixed in law. There is no certainty that Kohl will decide to make any concession; but were he to move that way, I think our interest would be to encourage a political declaration and discourage a move on the legal front. The reason is that I am sure that we should retain our legal rights and responsibilities in relation to Germany as a whole and Berlin, and the leverage they afford, as long as possible—indeed, as suggested above, until German unity was complete. Yet to amend the Convention on Relations in respect of the frontier point, would, on the Pandora principle, invite proposals to change other elements among our rights and responsibilities.[3]

Yours ever,
C.L.G. MALLABY

[3] Mr Weston minuted on 10 January: 'The basic idea of a 'transitional period' is a fertile one which we should find ways of building into our paper for Chequers.'

No. 92

Letter from Mr Powell (No. 10) to Mr Wall

[*WRL 020/1*]

Secret and Personal   10 DOWNING STREET, *10 January 1990*

Dear Stephen,

German Reunification

The Prime Minister told the Foreign Secretary this morning that she would need to have some specific proposals to put to President Mitterrand on 20 January on how Britain and France could work together more closely. This pre-supposed that we had first worked out our own ideas in rather more detail in relation to German reunification. We should not simply regard this as inevitable and wait for events to overtake us. The statement made at the Strasbourg European Council was useful so far as it went but was hardly operational. We needed to think through much more carefully the implications of reunification and the conditions which would have to be fulfilled if it were to proceed with the full support of Germany's allies. She cited as an analogy our position on membership of the ERM, which was cast in terms of: 'we shall join when . . .' The view which she had articulated from the beginning was that priority must go to establishing democracy, freedom and the rule of law throughout Eastern Europe, and this remained her view. We also had to be clear about the implications for NATO and how our common security needs could be met in circumstances where Germany was reunified. We had to consider the question of borders, of East Germany's relationship with the European Community and of the wider application of the principle of self-determination. We also had to think through the consequences for Gorbachev: we did not want to lose the greater good of seeing his reforms succeed throughout the Soviet Union and

Eastern Europe in order to satisfy a German wish for faster progress with reunification.

The Foreign Secretary said that work was already being done on these points. He would let the Prime Minister have the results before her meeting with President Mitterrand, together with some specific proposals which she could make at that meeting. What we could not produce was a blue print for stopping German reunification. The Prime Minister accepted this, while stressing that equally we should not approach work on the German question in the spirit that reunification was inevitable and all we had to do was adjust to it.

Yours sincerely,
C.D. POWELL

No. 93

Minute from Mr Wall to Mr Weston

[WRL 020/1]

Secret and Personal   FCO, *10 January 1990*

German Reunification

I attach a letter from No 10 recording the Secretary of State's conversation with the Prime Minister on this subject this morning.[1] An additional point which the Secretary of State made to us orally after the meeting was that the Prime Minister hoped to have a discussion with him on the issue of German reunification before her visit to France on 20 January. The Prime Minister remained very wary of German reunification but recognised that it would be difficult to stop and the question therefore was the sort of language and steps that could be used to hedge it around;

The Secretary of State said that among the cards we held were:

—the definition of frontiers: the Germans appeared to accept their 1937 frontiers (the Prime Minister was rather more doubtful about this);

—the European Community: it was difficult to imagine the GDR able to fit into the Community, at least in the near future;

—NATO.

The Secretary of State told the Prime Minister that he thought we should also engage the US in discussion about a CFE2. The alternative was to face unilateral US cuts. The Secretary of State thought that the Prime Minister was not yet persuaded of this point.

J.S. WALL

[1] No. 92.

No. 94

Letter from Sir C. Mallaby (Bonn) to Mr Weston[1]

[*WRL 020/1*]

Confidential   BONN, *10 January 1990*

Dear John,

The German Question: Teltschik on the Wider Aspects, 9 January

1. My conversation with Teltschik, reported in my telno 20,[2] also touched on wider policy issues concerning the German Question.

2. Teltschik told me that the Federal Chancellor was very conscious that the question of Gorbachev's survival and the question of how cleverly Kohl handled German issues were in part the same. Kohl was determined to achieve a steady course of events, if this was possible. The current behaviour of the GDR government and the SED was making the task much harder.

3. Teltschik pooh-poohed the idea of a German confederation. He said that the question how to reconcile German unity with NATO was too difficult to answer at present. (Kastrup made the same remark to me on 9 January.) With time, a way forward might be found. It was obvious that time would be needed for the process of achieving German unity, during which negotiations on future architecture for European security could be held.

4. Teltschik did not refer to Genscher's idea, reported in my telno 18,[3] that the territory of the FRG might remain in NATO after creation of a German federation. This confirms my view that Genscher's remarks did not represent settled federal policy. Teltschik did not specify a fixed or agreed transition period from the moment when German unity becomes certain until its completion, such as I sketched out in my letter of 9 January about 'The German Question and its Repercussions'.[4] But what he said comes close to that idea.

5. I will continue to seek and report indications of Federal thinking about future architecture in Europe, which clearly is now beginning to take place intensively.

Yours ever,
C.L.G. MALLABY

---

[1] Copied to Ambassadors in East Berlin, Moscow, Washington, Paris, UKDEL NATO; Mr Burton, BMG Berlin; Mr Cooper, Policy Planning Staff.
[2] This telegram of 9 January reported Herr Teltschik as having stated that Herr Kohl would not announce any new policy at his press conference on 10 January, but would express the Federal Government's concern that, while the GDR Government and the SED were intending to exploit their unlimited funds and media monopoly unfairly in the run-up to the elections on 6 May, they were not doing enough to tackle the GDR's economic problems: they 'seemed to be more interested in re-establishing a security and intelligence service than in economic reform' (WRL 020/1).
[3] In this telegram of 9 January Sir C. Mallaby reported a conversation in which Herr Genscher had expressed the view that 'it was too much to ask Gorbachev to contemplate the GDR's absorption into NATO'. He could, however, 'envisage a German federation in which the Länder now comprising the FRG would remain in NATO but the former territory of the GDR would not join it and might stay in the Warsaw Pact if that survived.' When Sir C. Mallaby queried whether such an arrangement could last, 'Genscher acknowledged that this could be a problem, and said that a great deal would depend on what progress was made in arms control' (WRL 020/1).
[4] No. 91.

No. 95

Minute from Mr Synnott to Mr Weston

[*WRL 020/1*]

Confidential   FCO, *10 January 1990*

The German Question: FRG Views on the British Line

1. The attached fax of an extract from a minute by Sir Christopher Mallaby records that, according to Teltschik, the impression in the Federal Chancellery was that the British were the most negative of the three Allies on the German Question.[1] This is by way of a supplement to Sir C. Mallaby's telegram of 8 January[2] suggesting that we modify our public line.

2. Since Bonn have been pressing for a response to this telegram, on which I submitted on 8 January, I have told the Head of Chancery there that it had been decided not to pursue Sir Christopher's advice for the time being, pending further discussions later this month.[3] Mr Budd subsequently telephoned me to say that Sir C. Mallaby was of the view that something more should be said on the subject in public in the context of the Secretary of State's visit to the GDR. Waiting until the end of the month would not allow this. He therefore proposed to discuss the matter further with Mr Waldegrave during his visit next Wednesday.

3. You may wish to pass this on to Mr Waldegrave so that he is forewarned.

H.N.H. SYNNOTT

---

[1] Not printed.
[2] *Sic*: presumably No. 85 of 5 January.
[3] See No. 88, note 2.

No. 96

Sir C. Mallaby (Bonn) to Mr Hurd[1]

No. 42 Telegraphic [*WRL 020/1*]

Confidential   BONN, *12 January 1990, 5.48 p.m.*

Call on Genscher: The Four Powers and the German Question

Summary

1. Genscher emphasises risk of negative reactions in West German public opinion if Four Powers discuss German question as distinct from Berlin. Describes latest thinking on the proposed 'contractual community' between the two German states, including that the FRG might seek after the GDR elections a treaty which inter alia would indicate what stages would follow after 'contractual community'.

---

[1] Repeated for information Immediate to Paris, Washington; Priority to BMG Berlin, UKDEL NATO, UKREP Brussels, Moscow.

Detail

2. When I called on Genscher today, I gave him (in line with your telno 024)[2] the outline of the Soviet Ambassador's approach to you on 10 January and of your oral comments on that occasion. I pointed out that the operative paragraph of Shevardnadze's message, with the suggestion of a new Four Power exchange, was tentative in style. I said that (despite Genscher's earlier impression) the Soviet approach to us and the Americans had proposed an exchange of views at the level of 'special envoys or the four Ambassadors' and Foreign Ministers had not been mentioned.

3. Genscher said that, as he had told you in Brussels last month, the Federal Government had no objection to Four Power talks about the Berlin initiative, which might be at a level lower than Ambassadors. He was grateful for the care with which you had reacted initially to the Soviet Ambassador. He agreed that the talks now proposed by the Russians would be different from those on 11 December, since the German question would now be the subject.[3] Genscher said that, if the impression arose in the Federal Republic that others were negotiating about affairs of the Germans, that could bring a wave of nationalism here, a phenomenon that was virtually absent at present. He returned to this point several times. Genscher said he hoped that there would be consultation between the three Western Allies and the Federal Republic about the reply to be given to the Soviet approach.

4. I said that we were aware that there could be negative reactions in the Federal Republic to Four Power discussions about the German question as a whole. At the same time, we had an interest in handling the Russians in a way which would not increase the likelihood of their becoming greatly concerned about developments concerning the GDR. The three Western Allies could maintain a dialogue with the Russians about the Berlin initiative, while considering how to reply to the Soviet approach. Genscher said that bilateral contacts between individual Western Allies and the Soviet Union did not cause problems.

5. I asked Genscher about the latest thinking in the Federal Government concerning the framework treaty that would be the basis of the 'contractual community' (Vertragsgemeinschaft) between the two German states, since that was the particular matter which the Russians had singled out for proposed Four Power exchanges. Genscher said that the Federal Government's thinking on this

---

[2] This telegram of 10 January reported a message from Mr Shevardnadze, delivered by the Soviet Ambassador on the evening of 10 January, proposing an exchange of views among the Four Powers on German affairs (WRL 020/1). In conversation with Mr Zamyatin, Mr Hurd had observed that, while the UK had been glad to take up the Soviet suggestion of Four-Power discussions on Berlin-related matters, the current proposal would substantially extend the basis of such meetings: 'We understood and appreciated the Soviet motivation. But we would need to consider the question carefully and how it would fit into our relationships and friendships. A reply would be sent after further reflection.' Similar messages had been delivered to the French and US Governments and the latter had informed the Government of the FRG. On 11 January the German Ambassador in London, Herr von Richthofen, delivered a message from Herr Genscher asking for the closest possible consultation with the FRG before any response was given to the Soviet proposal (FCO telegrams No. 27 and 28 to Bonn, WRL 020/1). Subsequent consultations among the four Governments resulted in a reply along the lines suggested by the US Government. This confined the proposed discussions to relatively low-level contacts on Berlin matters, but was softened, at British suggestion, by the concession that 'Four Power diplomats stationed in Berlin could coordinate with the FRG and GDR on traditional Berlin issues such as the status of Berlin and public safety in the city': Zelikow and Rice, pp. 155-6.
[3] For the previous Soviet initiative for Four-Power discussions see Nos. 72 and 73.

had advanced in recent days. Kohl's and his latest idea (which both had today referred to in public) was that there might be two documents to form the basis for the 'contractual community'. The first might be 'a pragmatic bringing together' of the various intended fields of cooperation, notably economic but also the environment. Such a document would simply say that cooperation in these fields would be developed rapidly. Its status would be such that it did not require ratification, and thus need not be considered by the present undemocratically appointed East German Parliament. After the GDR elections there could be a second document, this time a proper treaty requiring ratification. This document might set the aims for the relationship between the two Germanies after the stage of 'contractual community'. I asked Genscher whether he meant that such a treaty might mention confederal structures or a federation as the future aim. Genscher said that this would be for consideration. The present GDR Government would not agree to setting the future direction in this way, and much would depend on the composition of the GDR Government after the elections. There was much thinking to do in Bonn and I would be kept closely informed.

Comment

6. It is clear that the Germans will try to dissuade us from agreeing to the new Soviet proposal for Four Power discussions. I believe Genscher is right that such talks would cause negative reactions in German public opinion. At the same time we have a clear interest in upholding Four Power rights in relation to Germany as a whole, as well as Berlin. As seen from here, the balance of advantage at present lies in avoiding damage to our public standing here, since that would severely reduce our ability to influence the Germans and a nationalistic mood here would make events even more unpredictable. For the time being, given especially the tentative wording of the Soviet proposal, it should be possible to hold it at arm's length, while using Four Power contacts about Berlin matters and bilateral contact with the Soviet Ambassador in East Berlin (whom I am trying to see again) to maintain dialogue with the Russians. But we might in due course want Four Power contacts about wider German matters. That aside, the new idea of a treaty between the two German states foreseeing a future federation could accord with our position on the German question (set out in the NATO and EC statements last month) only if the Germans had meanwhile opted in free self-determination for unity.

No. 97

Submission from Mr Weston to Mr Wall

[*RS 020/1*]

Secret   FCO, *12 January 1990*

East-West Relations and Germany: Papers for the Prime Minister

1. I submit herewith three draft minutes from the Secretary of State to the Prime Minister covering:

(*a*) Western Security in the 1990s;[1]

(*b*) the Anglo-French defence relationship;[2] and,

(*c*) Germany.[3]

These are on the lines discussed at the Secretary of State's meeting yesterday; but have been produced at speed in order to be with you before departure for Hong Kong.

2. Could I high-light the practical handling difficulties which may arise next week. Mr Goulden and Mr Lever will be in Moscow on 16-18 January inclusive (for long-standing Pol-Mil talks with the Russians). I myself will be in Dublin on 17 and 18 January for the Political Committee which is preparing the Informal Foreign Ministers meeting on 20 January. If the minutes are to reach the Prime Minister in good time, any re-working that the Secretary of State may require will in effect have to be done on Monday, 15 January.

3. The specific proposals for the Prime Minister to put to President Mitterrand on how Britain and France could work together more closely are covered in each of the draft minutes. Briefly they are:

(i) to return to the charge on the Anglo-French Defence Cooperation Initiative.

(ii) bilateral Anglo-French talks with them over adaptation of the NATO Alliance and France's possible contribution to that.

(iii) bilateral talks on the implications of German unification and how to manage the transition toward it.

4. It was implicit in yesterday's meeting[4] that the draft minute from the Secretary of State to the Prime Minister covering the papers on German Unity, Conventional Defence and Arms Control in Europe, European Architecture and First Thoughts on a Final Peace Settlement, has now been overtaken by events. This, together with the four associated papers, also submitted to you via Mr Waldegrave on 8 January,[5] were the product of the work commissioned by No 10, in which both No 10 and Sir Robin Butler were anxious that the MOD and Cabinet Office should be involved; and which therefore represents tripartitely agreed work. (In the time available we have not been able to clear the new draft minutes with them.) I rather hope that in respect of at least three of the four papers which I submitted to you on 8 January, the Secretary of State will agree that these should be annexed to the new draft minutes. They represent quite a lot of work over the past month, covering ground discussed at the Secretary of State's meeting yesterday; and there will I think be the expectation in the MOD and Cabinet Office, as well as in No 10, that something of the sort will emerge. On previous such occasions, the Prime Minister has shown no reluctance to devour paper. But if they are to be sent across, it would be preferable to meet Mr Powell's deadline of 20 January, thus providing a week for digestion. The paper on German Unification (and perhaps the Legal Adviser's Note on Legal and Procedural Considerations) would annex logically to the draft minute on Germany. The papers on Conventional Defence and Arms Control in Europe and on European Architecture would fit naturally behind the draft minute on the Alliance.

5. As you know, I also recommend that the two papers on NATO's Nuclear Stockpile in the Nineties and Nuclear deterrence and Negotiations on SNF, which

---

[1] Not printed.

[2] Not printed.

[3] No. 99.

[4] Mr Hurd's office meeting on Arms Control: see No. 86, note 3.

[5] No. 86.

were commissioned by the Chequers meeting last September, should be forwarded to No 10, perhaps under cover of a draft Private Secretary letter rather than a joint minute from the Foreign and Defence Secretaries, if the latter is thought too high profile. It really is important in my view to show the Prime Minister that these issues have been thought about hard both in MOD and in the FCO over the past months and to give her an accurate assessment of where matters now stand. It is very relevant to some of the ground we are trying to cover in our separate thoughts on the need to adapt the Alliance.

P.J. WESTON

No. 98

Minute from Sir C. Mallaby (Bonn) to Mr Waldegrave[1]

[WRL 020/1]

Confidential   BONN, *16 January 1990*

Our Public Line on the German Question

1. At your press conference in Bonn on 17 January, you are bound to be asked about the British attitude to German unity.

Background

2. Despite our consistent support for the principle of German unity through self determination, we are perceived in the Federal Republic as opposing, or wishing to brake, reunification. Teltschik told me recently that the impression in Kohl's entourage was that the Americans were more favourable towards German unity than the French or the British. French statements were contradictory but Mitterrand had told Kohl that the French were realistic enough to know that, if the Germans wanted unity, the French could not prevent it. The British seemed to be the most negative of the three Allies.

A number of normally pro-British politicians and media editors have asked me with incomprehension why we were giving the impression that unity would be over our dead body.

3. Sir A. Acland has reported American urging that we should find a way of working more effectively with the Germans and has suggested that this would help our standing in Washington: 'We are well placed to exercise real influence [on the Americans] provided we can find the right formula and provided our policies carry weight in Bonn and Paris.'[2]

4. Our purpose, in deciding our public line, must be to preserve and enhance our influence here, so that we can apply it in British interests. That means devising a

---

[1] Mr Waldegrave was to visit Bonn on 17 January.

[2] Parentheses added by Sir C. Mallaby. In Washington telegram No. 84 of 11 January (Waldegrave Papers: see No. 12, note 1) Sir A. Acland also referred to the suggestion made in his Annual Review that 'we might try privately to increase our contacts with the Administration on the US/EC relationship'. Conversations between Mr A. Wood and Mr Zoellick on 8 January and Mr Blackwill on 9 January had 'made it plain the Americans would very much like us to play a central part, though with two provisos. First, that we would find some way of working more effectively with the Germans (and to a lesser degree the French) especially in the EC context. Secondly, that we should not act too often as an anchor to windward.'

line which helps to retrieve our standing by not sounding unnecessarily negative. Sir M. Alexander's Annual Review put well a point I have made several times: if a single Germany is inevitable, there is little point in bewailing it, and a risk of real danger if one consequence of appearing to do so is to contribute to suspicion and resentment between the Federal Republic and the Allies.[3]

5. I have attached an excerpt of Mr Maude's speech to the Anglo German Association in London on 15 January.[4] He preceded his quotation of the Strasbourg formula about German unity with a couple of remarks designed to sound good to Germans—that the eventual structure for the Germanies is a matter for the Germans and that for decades we have stood by the right of Germans to decide their own future.

Recommendation

6. I suggest that we should stick to the substance of the Strasbourg formula but present it as a British position and in a form designed to sound friendly to Germans. The line might be:

(*a*) We are willing to support German unity if the Germans decide for that in free self determination.

(*b*) The process should enhance peace, stability and democracy in Europe and be in accordance with relevant agreements, just as the Federal Government always says.

Additional points for use if necessary:

(*c*) The first priority is democratic reform and free and fair elections in East Germany. Self determination requires democratic means for its expression.

(*d*) Britain of course, like many other countries, has a major interest in the arrangements in Europe that would accompany German unity. We also have a right to be consulted as one of the Four Powers. That right, incidentally, was set out in the Relations Convention of 1952,[5] which of course was ratified by the *Bundestag*.

C.L.G. MALLABY

---

[3] In his despatch of 9 January, 'The Revolution of 1989: How Should the Alliance respond?', Sir M. Alexander argued that German unity was probably inevitable and that there was 'little point in bewailing it': 'An outcome acceptable to the Alliance is more likely if the Allies display, at least in public, confidence in the Germans and a desire to help them than if we emphasise our doubts and desire to constrain' (DZN 014/1).

[4] Not printed.

[5] See Preface, p. viii.

No. 99

Minute from Mr Hurd to Mrs Thatcher

[*WRL 020/1*]

Secret   FCO, *16 January 1990*

The German Question

1. Your meeting with President Mitterrand on 20 January will be an important opportunity to discuss the concerns which we share with the French about German unification.

2. If the people of the FRG and the GDR decide freely and democratically in favour of unity, there is no way of stopping that, short of military action. Residual rights and responsibilities of the Four Powers provide a locus standi in the process. The same is true of the texts of the Helsinki Final Act, the European Community treaties and North Atlantic Treaty. These rights can legitimately be used to influence the pace and nature of events provided the governments concerned act in unison; but they do not amount to a veto.

3. If the process leading to unification gets under way the question therefore becomes how best to influence the process of achieving it so as to maximise the British and Western interest and to minimise adverse repercussions elsewhere, particularly in the Soviet Union. The point of departure is the European position jointly and publicly agreed at Strasbourg that German unity should take place 'peacefully and democratically in full respect of the relevant agreements and treaties and of all the principles defined by the Helsinki Act in a context of dialogue and East-West cooperation' and 'in the perspective of European integration'. The US position complements this, with its emphasis on the need for Germany's continued commitment to NATO and an increasingly integrated European Community; with due regard for Four Power rights and responsibilities; as part of a gradual and step by step process in the interests of genuine European stability; and respecting the Helsinki Final Act on the question of borders.

4. As you observed, these general principles have yet to be translated into operational terms. You could explore with President Mitterrand how far this can be done. One important idea, which has not yet been given full play and which you might well air with President Mitterrand, is the notion of a transitional period. German unity carries practical implications of great political, legal, economic and institutional complexity. It follows that there is bound to be a transition of significant duration between the point at which the two German states decide freely and unambiguously in favour of the *principle* of unification and the point at which a single and unified German state is finally brought into existence and recognised as such. This intervening period would be of great political and psychological importance. It should be used to provide a suitable framework for the negotiation of the various complex matters which will come up, including implications for the Alliance and any future European security structures, for the European Community and for the future of the CSCE process, among many others. We would have to concentrate with other key Allies on bringing our views and our weight to bear during this period. Despite Chancellor Kohl's vagueness, many in the FRG who are wholly committed to a peaceful, democratic and united Germany,

very well understand the desirability of such a transitional process. We need to acquire a position which allows us to work with the grain in the Federal Republic over this. I am sure you will find President Mitterrand responsive. His own undertaking that France would recognise and respect the reality of the desire of the Germans for unity earned a special word of thanks in Chancellor Kohl's first major public comments of the New Year. The concept of a sizeable transition period could help him to reconcile these words with the French anxieties of which he has told you.

5. The French should be just as concerned as we are about the further growth of German economic power in the longer term which German unity would be likely to bring, and the increased political clout which this would imply. There are different views about how far what is already the most dynamic economy in Europe will be changed by the absorption of the GDR. But in the longer term the combined strength of the two economies, once they reflect higher and more efficient investment in the East combined with successful economic restructuring, will be considerable. Britain will not be alone in facing this challenge and great efforts will need to be made to avoid German predominance in the wider European market.

6. On the political front our best way of guaranteeing that a larger and more powerful Germany remains closely tied to Western standards and values will be the collective grip provided by the European Community and the North Atlantic Alliance. That is why all our partners, including the Americans, attach so much importance to the continuing strength, vigour and development of both organisations. In the future new mutual CSCE obligations and commitments, building on the Helsinki Final Act, may also have a role to play. Alternatives such as a neutral Germany perhaps more closely aligned with Central European countries at less advanced stages of political and democratic development would be worse for our interests and for general security and stability in Europe.

7. I deal more fully with Alliance aspects in a separate minute.[1] But in terms of influencing the process of German unification through a transitional period, the European Community dimension, important in its own right for the reason just mentioned, may also have some tactical relevance. The unique political circumstances of a divided Germany and the degree of *de facto* economic integration make GDR accession to the Community as part of a process of German unification before 1992 a possibility. Nevertheless reunification from the Community point of view could not take place purely by osmosis. The Germans could not simply appear at the Council of Ministers one day and say that they were now united. The process of negotiating the terms of accession would require the agreement of all present Community members and a negotiation with GDR representatives, e.g. to extend the Community's external frontier to include the present territory of the GDR. There would have to be transitional arrangements on such matters as GDR state aids or the improvement of GDR environmental standards. The Community angle therefore constrains the pace of *de jure* German integration and reunification. But provided the GDR met basic conditions on the establishment of genuine democracy and the mechanisms of a market economy, the process could not in practice be extended indefinitely without creating a dangerous antagonism between the FRG and her EC partners.

[1] Not printed.

8. The Four Powers would also of course have a stake in the transitional period. They would be monitoring the process. The UK, the US and France are obliged under Article 7 of the 1955 Convention on Relations to 'consult with the FRG on all matters involving the exercise of their rights relating to Germany as a whole'. Under war-time and post-war agreements the three Western powers (UK, US and France), together with the Soviet Union, retain rights and responsibilities for Berlin which are recognised and accepted by the FRG and Berlin authorities. The four-power status of Berlin means that we, the US, France and the USSR are responsible for the security of the territory. The rights of the Four Powers in Berlin could hardly in practice be used to prevent the city becoming the capital of a united Germany as a result of a free choice of the people of the two Germanies. But we should maintain our rights and responsibilities until agreed alternative arrangements, satisfactory to us, are in place. Meanwhile, the Allied presence would help us, with the Berlin Senate and the Federal Government, to maintain calm and confidence in the city. We and the other powers may need to be ready to adapt our presence, while maintaining our legal position, so that our involvement in the city continues to be welcome, and seen as a positive symbol of the outside Western guarantors, to the people of Berlin.

9. Contacts between the Four Powers would also have an important role to play, along with bilateral contacts with the Soviet Union, in ensuring that the Russians did not nourish unjustified anxieties or concerns and that the transition towards German unity was carried out in a way which did not prejudice the process of reform in the Soviet Union and Eastern Europe generally. Finally, the Four Powers would have an important role in relation to borders which bears on the geographical scope of a united Germany. You have rightly emphasised the importance of the fact that under Helsinki, frontiers in Europe are inviolable and can only be changed by agreement. We should be well placed to ensure that German unity could only take place on the basis that the Four Powers (as well as Germany) would fix the Oder/Neisse frontier definitively in law at the moment when unity occurred. In short, while we cannot veto German self-determination we can confine it to the peoples of the FRG and GDR. In the interim the FRG would need to make a further political statement about the finality of that frontier. This should not be a problem for Chancellor Kohl once he is through his elections.

10. German unity need not imply that the territory of the GDR is included within NATO (which appears to be the attitude of some Americans). There are a number of precedents (including the Eden Plan and other ideas to which HMG subscribed in the Fifties) for dealing with this aspect in terms of de-militarised zones. This would need to be looked at further. One could conceive, like Dr Kissinger, of a united Germany within NATO but with the territory of the old GDR completely demilitarised by treaty.[2]

11. In airing these and other issues with President Mitterrand on 20 January, you might like to propose that British and French officials do some further work on how best the transition to German unity (if the Germans decide for it) can be managed, stabilised and influenced. There might then be further discussion with the Americans with a view to the three of us talking this over with the FRG.

---

[2] Dr Kissinger had recently visited London, meeting Mr Hurd on 9 January and Mrs Thatcher on the 10th. In his conversation with Mr Hurd he had 'thought that for most purposes there would be a unitary German state, but there needed to be a confederation for military purposes with a demilitarised East Germany': letter from Mr Wall to Mr Powell (No. 10), 9 January 1990 (AMU 027/4).

12. I am sending copies of this minute to the Secretary of State for Defence, the Chancellor of the Exchequer and Sir Robin Butler.

DOUGLAS HURD

No. 100

Sir C. Mallaby (Bonn) to Mr Hurd[1]

No. 56 Telegraphic [*WRL 020/1*]

Confidential   BONN, *17 January 1990, 6.52 p.m.*

Mr Waldegrave's Visit to Bonn 17 January: The German Question

Summary

1. Mr Waldegrave's discussions confirmed that the Federal Government intend to build up practical cooperation with the GDR as quickly as possible but not to sign ratifiable agreements until there is a democratically elected government in the GDR. Concern at continued emigration and fear that widespread demonstrations demanding immediate unity could break out at any time in GDR.

Detail

2. Mr Waldegrave had talks with Rühe, Secretary General of the CDU: Minister of State Schäfer, *Auswärtiges Amt*: Teltschik and other officials in Kohl's entourage: and over lunch a range of politicians from Government and opposition.

3. The talks showed that those concerned with policy on the German question acknowledged that Modrow has made some useful concessions, notably postponement of the question of reconstituting the state security service and on economic policy. But these might not suffice to give the people of the GDR the feeling that life would soon get better. The hope here was that the GDR might remain more or less stable, despite the muddle it was in, until the elections on 6 May. They would produce a coalition government in favour of German unity. Then would come the question of arranging a transition period until completion of unity. But a number of Mr Waldegrave's interlocutors saw a risk of the GDR population losing patience and calling through widespread demonstrations for early unity. That could happen at any time. Teltschik wondered whether the GDR elections should be held sooner than May. There was widespread concern at continued emigration, at 25,000 so far this month.

4. Rühe and others urged that the three Western Allies should present their position on the German question in a way that showed sympathy and understanding for the German wish for unity. If that was done, the Allies' ability to influence the Germans by calling for stability etc would be greatly enhanced. Rühe saw a risk that the SPD would play up opposition to Allied rights in the Federal election campaign, unless the Allies managed to project a sympathetic image. Mr Waldegrave's interlocutors were satisfied with the way the three allies have played the matter of Four-Power talks. Teltschik said that he could envisage circumstances in future, for instance a crisis of public order in the GDR, where it might be necessary to agree to a Soviet wish for a 4-Power meeting.

---

[1] Repeated for information Priority to East Berlin, Washington, Paris; information routine to BMG Berlin, UKREP Brussels, UKDEL NATO.

5. Teltschik and Rühe stressed that the pressure for movement towards German unity was coming from the GDR and not the Federal Government. Teltschik thought that the transition from a decision for unity until its completion might last 5-10 years. Duisberg (Federal Chancellery) said that the treaty on establishment of a 'contractual community' to be concluded after the GDR elections might not only point towards future stages of development, such as confederal structures or even a federation, but might also set a time period to allow for gradual change and ample opportunity for discussion of European repercussions of German unity. He accepted Mr Waldegrave's point that any mention of federation in an inner German treaty would immediately call the question of Allied rights into play. He said that there would be very close consultations with us about any such step. He thought that the most likely means for the exercise of self-determination would be the election in the GDR of a majority consisting of groups favouring unity, although he said that some people in Bonn thought that some further act of self-determination might be needed in the FRG. He spoke as though he expected Allied rights to remain in being until transition to German unity was complete. Hartmann (Teltschik's deputy) agreed with us that the question of reconciling German unity with NATO was extremely difficult and must be answered.

6. There was much satisfaction at Delors' view that moves concerning GDR association with the EC or an application for membership should be possible before 1993.

7. Hennig, Acting Minister for Inner German Affairs, said that Kohl would speak in the *Bundestag* on 18 January on the German question and would not announce any new policy.

No. 101

Mr Broomfield (East Berlin) to Mr Hurd[1]

No. 63 Telegraphic [*WRE 014/1*]

Confidential   EAST BERLIN, *18 January 1990, 6.50 p.m.*

GDR Internal Situation

Summary

1. A report on the GDR before the Prime Minister's talks with M Mitterrand and your visit to East Berlin.

2. The situation is fragile and volatile. The governability of this country is in question.

Detail

3. Developments in the first half of January have been characterised by deterioration in both the political and economic stability of the GDR.

4. The cause has been a backlash against an attempt by the old guard in the SED-PDS to slow down or reverse the reform process. The central issue in this political struggle was Modrow's proposal to re-establish an internal security

---

[1] Repeated for information Priority to Bonn, BMG Berlin, Paris; information Routine to Moscow, Washington, UKDEL NATO; information Saving to CSCE posts, CICC(G).

service before the elections in May, allegedly to protect the country against neo-fascism (daubings on Soviet war memorials, entry by FRG *Republikaner*, etc).

5. Modrow has had to confirm that no new security service will be set up before the elections. The SED-PDS has been forced to give up a number of its party buildings and printing presses.

A range of other improvements for the opposition groups and parties has been instituted (but still does not go far enough). Economic reform plans have been given a sharp shove forward.

6. But the cost to the stability of the GDR has been considerable.

—Modrow's standing has been diminished (and it is on his credibility that to a great extent the GDR's survival rests, even though after the elections he and his party will be voted out of power).

—Disillusion has boosted emigration. About 1500 a day, mostly qualified workers who have no difficulty in finding jobs in West Germany.

—Strikes are beginning to be used as a political weapon.

—Demonstrations have become more aggressive.

—More people are calling more stridently for unity with the FRG.

—More parties are ruling out a coalition with the SED-PDS after the election (thus ensuring a politically and economically inexperienced successor government).

As a leading Church figure put it to me recently either people will resolve the question individually by going there (FRG) or they will resolve it collectively by bringing them here (unification).

7. The future of the present coalition Government looks uncertain. The CDU (East) will decide on 19 January whether to remain in the coalition. If they decide to leave others may follow (even though most say that the highest priority is to maintain government and order until elections on 6 May). Whether the unravelling of the present coalition starts on 19 January, or after the new electoral law is passed in about a month, the general direction looks fairly clear.

8. The broad coalition (excluding the SED-PDS) which is likely to be formed after the election on 6 May, (or earlier if the coalition breaks up) will contain mainly parties (CDU, LDPD, SPD) who are in favour of a free market economy and eventual unity (undefined) with the FRG. The issues on which such a government would be likely to move most rapidly are, in my view, currency union and economic integration with the FRG. I believe that a revised constitution will form the basis of a national plebiscite later this year on what will in effect be the question of German unity.

9. The most striking feature of recent political developments here has been the close inter-action between West and East German political parties. The SPD (West) is giving full political and practical support to the SPD (East).[2] Given the SPD's historical popularity in this part of Germany and the possible transfer to them from the SED of Berghofer, the popular Mayor of Dresden, they should get considerable support at the polls. Once the CDU (East) breaks its coalition with the 'Communists' (SED) I would expect it to receive similar backing from the CDU (West). (The head of Democratic Awakening said on 17 January he was confident the CDU would leave the coalition soon and that a right of centre coalition of the CDU (East), Democratic Awakening and CSDP (backed by the CSU) with support from the CDU (West) could get 50% of the vote.) Comment: the takeover of

[2] See No. 43, note 3.

political parties is happening faster than the takeover of the economy (particularly if, as is likely the FDP backs the LDPD).

10. In general both the new political leaders and the people are coming to realise that for all its imperfections the FRG already offers 'a third way' between state socialism and 'unrestrained capitalism'. They are beginning to see through the SED's propaganda about 'capitalism' and unemployment and to understand instead the generous social security terms available in West Germany.

11. The overriding priority now is to get people to stay in the GDR and work. The FRG government is doing all it can to help economic regeneration (Kohl offered some DM 12 billion in Dresden). There are also increasing signs that the GDR Government is now prepared to move more rapidly towards a market economy and conditions attractive to Western investors. But the system can not change overnight. and, as GDR Finance Minister Nickel told FRG Finance Minister Waigel last week, apart from any question of principle, the GDR simply does not have the bureaucratic skills, experience or people to make a rapid revision of tax, currency and other fiscal laws. Waigel offered full FRG 'know-how' support.

12. You will find this an introspective country. The intensity of exchanges at all levels and in all fields with West Germany and West Berlin coupled with the drama of internal political developments, almost wholly occupies interest here. Although close attention is paid to the position of the 4 powers in German unity, foreigners, (including Mitterrand or Baker) have not made a deep impression. There have been rumours of an impending visit by Gorbachev but otherwise the Russians are keeping a low profile.

13. From the perspective of East Berlin I recommend that the main objectives for your visit should be to:
(*a*) press Modrow and others to continue the political and economic reform process[es] which are essential if people are to be persuaded to stay in the GDR,
(*b*) stress the need for fair elections in which all the participants will have an equal chance,
(*c*) make clear our interest in peace and stability in the GDR and our willingness to assist in various ways (know-how, English language teaching, Parliamentary exchanges, etc).
14. Please advance to Head of WED.

No. 102

Minute from Mr Cooper (Policy Planning Staff) to Mr Weston

[*WRL 020/1*]

Confidential   FCO, *18 January 1990*

Germany
1. Over the next few weeks, and leading up to the Secretary of State's speech in Bonn on 6 February, we should keep firmly in mind that Germany is now the most important country in Europe. It will become even more important if unification is completed. In the long run it may even become more important to us than the United States.

2. The Soviet Union is withdrawing from Europe into its own domestic chaos. It will be less interested in foreign affairs, less willing and able to exert influence. The only card they hold is the probably unusable military one. The extremely tentative nature of Shevardnadze's proposal for a Four Power meeting on Germany illustrates the extent to which they will be prepared to back down when the West takes a firm line.

3. As the Soviet Union declines Germany's position is enhanced:

—the opportunity of unification has been opened up, increasing the long-run potential of the German economy and its political weight;

—the liberation of Eastern Europe from Soviet domination returns its economic hinterland to Germany;

—as military power becomes less important and economic power more important it will matter less that Germany has no nuclear weapons.

4. The UK is in the curious position that our relations with the declining power have never been better while those with the rising power are mixed. We need not only to anchor Germany in the West (probably not that difficult) but also to anchor ourselves firmly to Germany. Closer relations with France is no substitute.

—we have many shared interests and attitudes with the Germans. If we work together effectively we can have a major influence on the Community and the Alliance.

—as they incline more to independent action we shall want them to consult us more (c.f. our relations with the US).

—it always makes sense to have good relations with powerful actors.

5. Our number one foreign policy priority should be better and closer relations with Germany. This should not just be a matter of more visits, more exchanges, more teaching of German in schools, important as all those things are. We should in the future take particular account of the German position in framing our policies on the Community and on NATO. Above all we should recognise that Germany is now at a historical turning point. What we say and do towards Germany in the next few months will leave a lasting impression. This should be a long term policy but the current hiccups in Franco/German relations[1] give us an excellent and immediate opportunity.[2]

R.F. COOPER

[1] Undated marginal note by Mr Weston: 'They are actually getting on *very* well together.'

[2] Mr Weston minuted on 19 January 1990 to Mr Ramsden and Mr Wordsworth: 'I think this point of view is largely *acquis* in the FCO. The problem lies in No 10.'

No. 103

Letter from Mr Powell (No. 10) to Mr Wall

[*WRL 020/1*]

Secret and Personal   10 DOWNING STREET, *20 January 1990*

Dear Stephen,
Prime Minister's Meeting with President Mitterrand
The Prime Minister had lunch with President Mitterrand at the Elysée Palace in Paris today. The President's Diplomatic Adviser, M. Hennekinne, was also

present. The President was at his most affable and courtly. Virtually the whole discussion was about German reunification and European security, with a broad measure of agreement, in particular on how the talks should be followed up. It was agreed that neither side would say anything to the press about the substance of the discussion.

The Prime Minister opened by saying that events were moving very fast in Germany and throughout Eastern Europe and the Soviet Union. She was concerned that the Western powers were cloaking their response to these developments in rather vague and general declarations and failing to get to grips with the full implications of them. West Germany was constantly pressing forward towards reunification, and the sort of linkages which Chancellor Kohl typically made between reunification and the ending of the division of Europe were not very convincing. Moreover the Germans seemed just to assume that they could bring East Germany into the European Community. It had been most unhelpful of M. Delors to appear to endorse that.

The Prime Minister continued that East Germany for its part seemed to be close to collapse. It was by no means impossible that we would be confronted in the course of this year with a decision in principle in favour of reunification of the two Germanies. This would confront us all with a major problem and could cause particular difficulties for Mr. Gorbachev, perhaps threatening his position and reforms. It was very important for Britain and France to work out jointly how to handle these developments. Beyond that, no two countries in Europe were more staunch than Britain and France on defence. We needed to sort out our thinking on the implementation of a CFE Agreement and our attitude to the inevitable pressure for further reductions thereafter. What she was really saying was that the time had come to turn the rather vague remarks in the conclusions of the Strasbourg European Council into firm policies.

President Mitterrand agreed that German reunification was a central theme for both Britain and France. The sudden prospect of reunification had delivered a sort of mental shock to the Germans. Its effect had been to turn them once again into the 'bad' Germans they used to be. They were behaving with a certain brutality and concentrating on reunification to the exclusion of everything else. It was difficult to maintain good relations with them in this sort of mood. Of course the Germans had the right to self-determination. But they did not have the right to upset the political realities of Europe. He did not think Europe was yet ready for German reunification: and he certainly could not accept that it had to take priority over everything else.

The President continued that he thought West Germany was pushing for reunification harder than East Germany. At least this was the conclusion which he had reached from his visit to East Germany before Christmas. East Germany was far behind the West and people there did not like the idea of being 'bought' by West Germany. Even when meeting students in Leipzig, he had not detected any great enthusiasm for reunification. He was convinced that some of the demonstrations in East Germany in favour of reunification had been encouraged by West German 'agents', who had provided the banners and other material calling for reunification, although he was not saying they were necessarily sent by the West German government. But we had to recognise that the East German government was losing authority and there was a danger of disorder as well as economic breakdown. This could lead people to the conclusion that there was no alternative to reunification.

The President continued that we had to accept that there was a logic to reunification. But everything depended on the how and when, and on the reactions of the Soviet Union. Britain and France were arguing for caution. The trouble was that the West Germans did not want to hear this. They treated any talk of caution as criticism of themselves. Unless you were wholeheartedly for reunification, you were an enemy of Germany. Because the Prime Minister was such a close friend and they had a tradition of working together, he would tell her in strict confidence some things which he had said to Chancellor Kohl and to Herr Genscher. He had been very blunt with them. He had said to them that no doubt Germany could if it wished achieve reunification, bring Austria into the European Community and even regain other territories which it had lost as a result of the war. They might make even more ground than had Hitler. But they would have to bear in mind the implications. He would take a bet that in such circumstances the Soviet Union would send an envoy to London to propose a Re-insurance Treaty and the United Kingdom would agree. The envoy would go on to Paris with the same proposal and France would agree. And then we would all be back in 1913. He was not asking the Germans to give up the idea of reunification. But they must understand that the consequences of reunification would not just stop at the borders of Germany. The attitude of Italy, Belgium, the Netherlands, Britain and France in the discussions at the Strasbourg European Council should have been a warning to the Germans. Was it really in Germany's interest to ignore all this?

The President said that he drew the conclusion that it would be stupid to say no to reunification. In reality there was no force in Europe which could stop it happening. None of us were going to declare war on Germany. Nor judging by his statements was Mr. Gorbachev. There were the Four Power agreements and they served a useful purpose. But at the end of the day they could not prevent reunification. In short he agreed with the Prime Minister's analysis and shared her wish to talk all these issues through very carefully. Indeed she was the only person to whom he could talk frankly about them. But he was honestly at a loss what we could do.

The Prime Minister said she did not necessarily agree there was nothing to be done. If other countries all made their views felt together, then we could influence Germany. Indeed there were some signs that this was happening already. The instruments available to us were the obligation in the Bonn/Paris Convention to consult about the future of Germany, the Four Power Agreements, the Helsinki Final Act, the need for negotiation on East Germany's membership of the European Community and the inevitable requirement for a substantial transition period between a decision in principle on reunification and its realisation in practice. We should make use of all of these to slow down reunification. The Germans could not simply ignore these agreements or ride rough-shod over them. The trouble was that other governments were not ready to speak up openly. We should say to the Germans that reunification would come one day, but we were not ready for it yet. We should insist that agreements must be observed and that East Germany must take its place in the queue for membership of the Community. If we all spoke up, then the Germans would have to take some notice. German policy was to test how far they could go with the rest of us, and at the moment they were getting away with too much. She accepted that in the end reunification would come about. But we must find some way to slow it down.

President Mitterrand said that he agreed. But he came back once more to his main preoccupation: what means did we have? There would be nothing worse than to remind the Germans of their obligations but then find we had no means to enforce them. If we spoke harshly, we would not carry conviction. The Prime Minister said that we would if we acted together. For instance we could remind the Germans that they were constantly saying that reunification would only come about as part of ending the division of Europe. Yet we were a long way from that. We must turn the Germans' own statements against them. The decision over the East German membership of the European Community gave us some leverage. President Mitterrand said that French experience over the Schengen Agreement had been instructive. Chancellor Kohl had telephoned him to complain that the French were dragging their feet and must sign the agreement. He had given the necessary instructions to the French Interior Minister, only to find the next day that the Germans were insisting on expanding the agreement automatically to include East Germany. The Germans could not be allowed to throw their weight around like this. He had subsequently discovered incidentally that the East Germans had known nothing about it. The Prime Minister commented that this illustrated the importance of retaining the ability to block certain decisions. This was precisely the sort of approach we needed to adopt to slow down German reunification. Once France and Britain had worked out a common position, we should try to bring others such as the Italians and the Dutch to our point of view.

The Prime Minister continued that she thought that we had a stronger hand on German reunification than President Mitterrand believed. We must try to tie the Germans down on a substantial transitional period as well as on the aspect of East German membership of the Community. President Mitterrand commented that he was surprised by M. Delors statement on East Germany.[1] He would also like the Prime Minister to know that he had declined to attend Chancellor Kohl's recent speech in Paris or to meet him.[2] This was the first time for years that they had not met on such an occasion. He had wanted to make clear that what Kohl said in no way reflected France's views. He was much criticised in the French press for trying to stop the inevitable thrust of history and failing to understand the Germans. The Prime Minister said that she and President Mitterrand should stand together on this. The 1990s ought to be a decade of hope. We must not let it become a decade of fear. We must insist the Germans stand by agreements. President Mitterrand added that we should perhaps try to persuade the Soviet Union to stiffen East German resistance to reunification.

President Mitterrand said that he shared the Prime Minister's concerns about the Germans' so-called mission in central Europe. The Germans seemed determined to use their influence to dominate Czechoslovakia, Poland and Hungary. That left only Rumania and Bulgaria for the rest of us. The Poles would never come to like the Germans while the Oder-Neisse Line remained in question. Nor would the others want to be under Germany's exclusive influence. But they would need

---

[1] Probably M. Delors' address to the European Parliament on 17 January, introducing the European Commission's programme for 1990, in which he declared that there was 'a place for East Germany in the Community should it so wish, provided, as the Strasbourg European Council made quite clear, the German nation regains its unity through free self-determination, peacefully and democratically, in accordance with the principles of the Helsinki Final Act, in the context of an East-West dialogue and with an eye to European integration. But the form that it will take is, I repeat, a matter for the Germans themselves.' (*Bulletin of the European Communities, Supplement 1/90* (Luxembourg, 1990), p. 9.)

[2] Herr Kohl had delivered a speech in Paris on 18 January in which he sought to reassure French opinion by insisting that 'the German house must be built under a European roof' and that German unity would mean no change to Poland's borders.

German aid and investment. The Prime Minister said that we should not just accept the Germans had a particular hold over the countries of Eastern Europe but do everything possible to expand our own links.

The Prime Minister added that Britain and France should also look at the position on the defence of Europe, which was no less worrying. There seemed to be growing opposition in West Germany to the presence of foreign troops. It was also clear that the West Germans and the Americans were determined to press ahead with further reductions in conventional forces after a first CFE agreement. She was absolutely determined to maintain adequate defence and believed the President thought in similar terms. We must also ensure that the Americans continued to keep forces and nuclear weapons in Europe.

The Prime Minister continued that she would like to suggest that our Foreign and Defence Ministers should each get together privately to talk over the issues of German reunification and the scope for closer defence cooperation between Britain and France, and report to the President and to her at the next bilateral summit or possibly earlier. President Mitterrand readily agreed. He enquired when the Summit would take place and, on being told, asked M. Hennekinne how this related to the date of the next Franco-German Summit. It might be better for him and the Prime Minister to meet before that. In any event, he would try to speak to M. Dumas in Dublin this evening and give him the necessary instructions to talk to the Foreign Secretary.

As you will be aware, I conveyed the gist of this to the Foreign Secretary this afternoon before his departure for Dublin. The sense of the meeting was clearly that Defence Ministers should also meet very soon. The Prime Minister did not hand over any speaking note to the President or offer to write to him in more detail about either German reunification or defence cooperation. But it would be in order for the Foreign and Defence Secretaries to draw on the more detailed material in the Foreign Secretary's papers on these subjects in talking to their French opposite numbers.

This letter contains extremely sensitive information and I should be grateful if it could be given a very limited distribution only. But Sir Ewen Fergusson in Paris should receive a copy since the Prime Minister mentioned it orally to him.

I am copying this letter, on a strictly personal basis to Simon Webb (Ministry of Defence).

Yours sincerely,
C.D. POWELL

No. 104

Letter from Sir C. Mallaby (Bonn) to Mr Weston

[*WRL 020/1*]

Confidential   BONN, *24 January 1990*

Dear John,

The German Question and its Repercussions

1. This letter summarises some current issues, as a contribution to thinking in London as Ministers approach decisions on policy.

The opportunity to influence events

2. If we can present an image of goodwill here, at this time of major decisions for the Germans, we can have considerable influence, with the USA and France, on the speed of events and the new arrangements that are likely to be needed in Europe. Since the Four Power meeting in December, the German public has realised that the Allies still have rights in relation to Germany. We should retain these rights all through the process of change, and should make use of them to exert influence and advance British interests. I believe we can exert some influence, if the Allies project the right image, without exciting nationalist sentiment here. Now is the time, while German minds are not made up on many issues.

3. Especially since Kohl's Ten Point speech on 28 November, I have led the Ambassadors of the three Western Allies here in insisting that we be informed of the plans for Kohl's and Seiters's discussions with the East German government and in warning that close and timely consultation would be needed if steps that would affect Allied rights were to be considered for incorporation in an inner-German agreement. Seiters said in the *Bundestag* on 18 January that in the context of confederal structures (i.e. well short of an actual federation) basic questions would need to be settled in agreement with the Powers having responsibility for Berlin and Germany. I have taken every opportunity to remind German Ministers and officials that a decision of the Germans, in free self determination, is needed before assumptions are made as to what will be the answer to the German Question.

4. A Kohl government remains the most likely result of next December's election. But this is far from certain. Any impression here that Allies were seeking to hinder unity would help the *Republikaners*, and if they get above 5% the present coalition will not have a majority. The successful rebirth of the SPD in East Germany, combined with the difficulties of the Federal CDU in promoting a sister party in the GDR, may mean that the East German SPD will be a leading element in the GDR government after the May elections. That in turn could help the SPD here in the Federal elections in December. An SPD-led government in Bonn, probably with the opportunistic and unpredictable Lafontaine as Chancellor, who is unsound to say the least on defence, would be far more difficult for us to handle on the critical questions about the future of NATO and European security than a government led by Kohl. (It is true that Lafontaine is ambiguous about German unity, but that is not likely to help us, since his policy will go where the votes are to be won and his party declared in December for unity.) These points underline the need for us to cooperate with Kohl in 1990: and also the need to make as much progress about future European architecture as we can with him this year.

Aspects of German unity

5. The practical difficulties involved in uniting the two Germanies are gradually dawning here. One big example is the difficulty of creating a single social security system, where the existing one in the FRG is very generous and in the GDR is rudimentary. Although the idea of an organised transition process lasting some years has not yet begun to feature in the public debate, it is increasingly considered by people directly concerned to be an obvious necessity. If this could be agreed, there should be time to negotiate about the international repercussions.

6. The biggest conundrum, and the one where we have major interests and undeniable locus, is how to reconcile German unity with NATO. Kohl and Genscher know it's difficult and want if possible to find a way of preserving the

Alliance after unity. Kohl's lack of public clarity on the point is explained by his staff as reflecting the wish to avoid antagonising Gorbachev by saying that the GDR must move across to NATO. People here see no difficulty about maintaining the Alliance during a period of 'confederative structures'. They hope that by the end of that, the NATO/German unity conundrum might have become a bit easier. We must insist that West Germany remains in NATO. Beyond that, our first aim should be to secure the lasting presence of some American forces in West Germany, to deter the Soviet Union in the future and also to eliminate any risk, at present not foreseeable, that Germany might again fall under dangerous leadership at some future time. In the context of the Germans getting unity and also a major reduction in stationed forces, I believe this to be a reasonable and realistic aim. It is also highly desirable, and may be possible, to keep some British forces in Germany. All this would be easier in the context of an international force, integrated at corps level and perhaps below, with command rotating among the participants including Germany.

7. A united Germany would of course be the biggest economic force in Europe, though considerably smaller than the United States or Japan. Adding the two Germanies together now would produce (on a tentative assumption about the GDR's current GDP) joint GDP of £854 billion, compared with the Federal Republic's GDP, already the largest in Europe, of £757 billion. Calculations about the future economic weight of a united Germany are hazardous. If the GDR had been liberalised ten years ago and had already achieved the same rate of per capita GDP as the FRG, the two together would represent approximately 30% of the European Community's GDP. It has so far been estimated that the joint population of the two Germanies in 2020 might be 67 [*sic*] million, compared with the current joint total of 78 million. Whatever the utility of such projections, the key point is that Germany's neighbours will not advance their interests by adducing economic weight as an argument against unity. It will be better to seek a sensible arrangement on the GDR's relationship with the EC: to go for a share of GDR imports as the economy there is boosted by West German investment; and to seek to exploit opportunities in third countries from which the West Germans are diverted by their East German priority.

8. It will be far easier to address the wider issues if change is orderly on the German Question. That is far from certain. If there was a break down in East Germany or an avalanche of emigration, a rapid initiative to steady things will be needed—perhaps a call for a referendum in the GDR and an organised transition if that chose unity.

9. I should be grateful if you could pass a copy of this letter to Percy Cradock, with whom I have been in telephone contact this week because of the postponement of his visit to Bonn and Munich.

Yours ever,
C.L.G. MALLABY

No. 105

Sir C. Mallaby (Bonn) to Mr Hurd[1]

No. 92 Telegraphic [WRL 020/1]

Confidential   BONN, *25 January 1990, 6.04 p.m.*

My Telno 31: Call on Kohl: German Question[2]

Summary

1. Kohl describes to me his concern about the present juncture in the GDR and the difficulty of promoting there a partner for the CDU. But he expresses optimism about early moves to give the GDR population a feeling of light at the end of the tunnel. Therefore believes that GDR should reach elections on 6 May without collapse.

2. Kohl expects after that an East German coalition favouring unity. He is thinking in terms of trying then to arrange an organised process until the completion of German unity, in line with his ten points. He let fall the date of 1 January 1995 as a possible time for transition from confederative structures to a German federation. That would be conditional on discussion with others, though not their explicit approval. Frontiers to be settled then. Also continued stationing of US forces in Germany. Kohl unable to answer question how to reconcile German unity and NATO. Stresses his wish to work closely with the three Western Allies and promises very close contact about the proposed treaty on a contractual community with the GDR, to be concluded after the elections there.

Detail

3. Kohl received me for an hour today, at his suggestion. I began by describing your visit to the GDR, your talk with Modrow, and what you had said in public. Kohl agreed that the East German government was weak. He dismissed Modrow's estimate that the Republikaners party might have 15-20 per cent support in the GDR as emotional guessing. He forecast that the SED would fall below 10 per cent in the GDR elections. The East German SPD had got off to a good start and was not burdened by past association with the Communist regime. The Federal CDU was having difficulty in promoting a partner in GDR politics. But an alliance of opposition groups with views similar to those of the CDU would be formed in 2-3 weeks. Kohl would visit the GDR to speak to this new alliance, thus demonstrating that those in the GDR who supported him and the attitudes of the Federal CDU should vote for the new alliance. Kohl remarked that the two most popular politicians in the GDR were himself and Willy Brandt.

4. I asked how a breakdown before the elections in the GDR could be prevented. Kohl said it was tragic that Modrow had made three serious mistakes: the attempt to resuscitate the secret police, the delay and hesitation about economic reform, and the delay over the electoral law. But Kohl was confident that a range of steps would now be taken to give the East German population confidence that

---

[1] Repeated for information Immediate to East Berlin, BMG Berlin, Washington, Paris; Priority to Moscow, UKDEL NATO, UKREP Brussels.

[2] In this telegram of 11 January Sir C. Mallaby listed calls he was due to make on FRG leaders: 'my general purpose will be to probe expectations and policy regarding the German question' (WRG 400/2).

there was light at the end of the tunnel, so that the rate of emigration should decline. Kohl believed that Seiters, visiting East Berlin today, would be told that thorough-going economic reform had been decided, including the concession that foreign participation in joint venture companies might exceed 50 per cent. Kohl said that he was in contact with about 50 major West German companies which were interested in joint ventures. He would persuade them to take immediate steps to demonstrate that those joint ventures would come soon. As soon as the three point star of Mercedes was shining above the planned site of a Mercedes car factory in the GDR, people would see that life was going to get better. Kohl also believed that 400-500 small businesses would be established with West German participation in the coming months. One example, of which he knew, would be a small firm producing windows for sale to the booming construction industry in West Germany. Another development which would give early hope to East Germans would be the installation with West German help in the coming months of several hundred thousand modern telephones with international direct dialling.

5. I said that self-determination required some clear act of choice. Kohl said that the new Government in the GDR after the elections would declare for German unity. I said that there would still be a need for an orderly process for change thereafter. Kohl agreed, and said the critical need would be time. Many things would need to be arranged within Germany. For instance, the extremely different social security systems would need to be amalgamated. Meanwhile, West European integration should go ahead as fast as possible. The more German sovereignty was fused in the European Community, the less there should be articles about a supposed Fourth Reich in London newspapers. I interjected that the article in question, by Conor Cruise O'Brien in *The Times*, had been written by a former Irish Minister.[3] Kohl continued that a united Germany, although the capital would be Berlin in the east, would have its economic weight in the west and south-west. The south-west was where economic growth had recently been strongest, that would continue and an economic miracle in the GDR would never make as important economically as the southern FRG. The west of Germany was the hinterland towards the Community, in which Germany's economy would remain embedded.

6. Kohl let fall, as a possible example, that the date of 1 January 1995 might be when Germany would move from confederative structures to federation. He would want the real, not the nominal, agreement of Germany's neighbours and also the United States and the Soviet Union. The transition to federation would be conditional on discussion with other countries, but not their express approval since such a condition would not be tolerable politically in Germany. The legal instrument establishing German unity would perhaps not be a peace treaty, since that concept hardly fitted present circumstances, but it would cover frontiers and the continued stationing of American forces and other matters. Kohl remarked that his recent move on the Oder-Neisse frontier had gone down reasonably well in the Federal Republic but that he could not go further on frontiers at present. I asked how one could reconcile German unity with NATO. Kohl frowned and paused and said that he could not answer this question now. But this did not give him headaches, for the question would get easier over time to answer. For example, all

---

[3] Mr O'Brien had served as Minister for Posts and Telegraphs in the Government of the Irish Republic between 1974 and 1977. His article 'Beware, the Reich is reviving' had appeared in *The Times* on 31 October. Its concluding sentence read: 'But I fear that the Fourth Reich, if it comes, will have a natural tendency to resemble its predecessor.'

armed forces in the Warsaw Pact except Soviet forces had in 1989 become irrelevant to East/West security. Kohl said that the Soviet Union had begun to see reality in relation to Germany, i.e. that unity would come. He remarked in passing that he had had several telephone conversations with Gorbachev.

7. In conclusion Kohl asked me to report this message: he wanted to work with the United States, the United Kingdom and France, in close communication and information. It had been politically impossible for him to consult us in advance about his ten point design. But he promised me that Germany would fulfil its duty of consulting the Western Allies closely on the proposed treaty about the contractual community with the GDR. His request to us was that we should not misunderstand the psychology of the Germans: they were not over the top nationalists, but were happy, as any normal people would be, at the prospect of unity. I said that full consultation was critically important. For instance, any idea of mentioning federation in an inner German treaty would immediately bring Allied rights into play.

Comment

8. Kohl was confident, energetic and loquacious. He answered at length my questions about his thinking. He did not ask about British views, but I gave him our main points. He made clear that his remarks about possible developments after the GDR elections represented thinking still in progress, not settled views.

9. This conversation reinforces my recommendation that we should put British views to the Germans soon, while their ideas are still in gestation. Kohl's hesitation about NATO and his illustrative mention of 1 Jan 1995 for the birth of a German federation (on both of which I made clear my surprise) alone demonstrate the need for us to exert influence.[4]

---

[4] Mr Powell minuted on Mrs Thatcher's copy of this telegram: 'A very clear and direct statement of Kohl's *ambitions*: reunification by *1 Jan. 1995*. Wants US forces to *remain* in *Germany*, but no mention of British or French' (PREM: Internal Situation in East Germany).

No. 106

Minute from Mr Hurd to Mrs Thatcher

[*PREM: Internal Situation in East Germany*]

Confidential and Personal   FCO, *25 January 1990*

Visit to the GDR: 22-24 January

1. The main concern in the GDR is whether they will get safely through the free elections on 6 May. Modrow spoke to me very freely—a decent, tired man near the end of his tether. His own party and the others now in government have seen their authority ebb away to the point where it is no longer sufficient to sustain a government. Emigration is doing great harm; 1,500 people are leaving each day. Students have to run the Leipzig University Hospital and soldiers try to keep factories going. Modrow has appealed to the Round Table groups to join and share responsibility. They are suspicious that too many of the old Communists still hold key positions, but the ones I spoke to accept that they ought to help if Modrow will make it clear that there is an emergency. The students who discussed this with me at Leipzig agreed. On balance, I think the GDR will just manage it to 6 May.

2. The noise off the streets is different. The Monday demonstrations in Leipzig have changed character. The majority in the crowd no longer presses for reform and democracy but for unification, and is rough with the minority who dissent. All the Ministers and groups I spoke to believe that unification will come, but the Ministers worry about the activities of the Republikaners in the south of the GDR and the dangers of resurgent nationalism. No-one I spoke to had thought through the implications of unification for NATO and the EC and for the moment it was therefore rather easier to hold the Strasbourg line than I had expected.

3. But practical unification is occurring day by day. Lufthansa has moved in to dominate the GDR airline. Volkswagen has announced a huge car factory. Germany is already one television audience. The best-known politicians in the GDR are Brandt, Weizsäcker, Genscher and Kohl. The GDR parties and groups are jostling for financial support from the wealthy FRG parties. The FRG election campaign has in effect started, in the GDR. We must thicken up our trade and educational links; but neither we nor anyone else can match the German thrust. The GDR has no real identity now that Communist rule, which created it, is crumbling.

4. One further thought which may be important in the spring. The groups and parties in the GDR, reacting strongly against single-party domination, are hard at work trying to devise a perfectly democratic Parliament—proportional with no threshold. The SPD boast they will get a clear majority and are probably the best placed. But a kaleidoscopic parliament is more likely, and they have hardly begun to think how a government would be formed. There may be a gap of several weeks between the elections (assuming they get that far) and the emergence of a government with a working majority.

DOUGLAS HURD

No. 107

Mr Munro (East Berlin) to Mr Hurd

[*WRE 026/1*]

Confidential   EAST BERLIN, *26 January 1990*

Summary . . . [1]

Sir,
Your Visit to East Berlin and the German Democratic Republic:
22-24 January 1990

1. Your visit, the second by a British Secretary of State for Foreign and Commonwealth Affairs, took place in circumstances vastly different from those prevailing at the time of Sir Geoffrey Howe's visit in April 1985 at the beginning of the Gorbachev era. However, if Sir Geoffrey had come here as planned at the beginning of July 1989 (the visit had to be postponed at short notice because of the repercussions in Hong Kong of the Peking massacre) he would have found, at least

---

[1] Not printed.

on the surface, little change after 4 years. He would have met the same people in the Politburo—Honecker, Stoph and Mittag—the same Ministers, a divided, oppressed and weak opposition, dignified and influential churchmen. Talks would have involved remonstrating with the GDR over their failure to honour their human rights commitments, over stagnating and unbalanced trade, over complaints about obstacles to access for the Embassy to local contacts.

2. In the event, only Foreign Minister Fischer and Foreign Trade Minister Beil are still members of the cast. And you found both acting in a completely new play now that the SED Politburo script writers are in retirement or prison. Indeed the SED, while claiming to have become a party of democratic socialism, was teetering on the brink of dissolution at the time of your visit. Modrow (as reported by the Private Secretary in East Berlin telno)[2] left you with the overall impression that the GDR could easily tip over the edge into chaos. He left me also with the impression of a man who could succumb to the pressure of events—and exhaustion—at any time.

3. Fischer and particularly Beil relish their new script; they welcomed all your proposals for putting bilateral relations on a completely new basis. The announcement of extension of our Eastern European know how fund to the GDR on 22 January provided exactly the right backdrop, removing the concern of this Embassy that the short notice for your visit would not allow time to prepare a package of cooperation and assistance sufficient to back up our interest in reform and stable progress to the first free, fair and democratic elections in this part of Germany since before Hitler came to power in January 1933. Your discussions with Fischer and Beil revealed complete agreement on what we should try and do together to transform bilateral relations. The choice of guests assembled by Fischer at his dinner to welcome you on 22 January was intended as evidence of this transformation. He invited not only representatives of the government, and what might still be described as the establishment, but also Evangelical Church Consistorial President Stolpe, who was until 9 October 1989 the subject of vituperative editorials in the SED Organ *Neues Deutschland*. Fischer accepted your invitation to visit Britain again.

4. You heard from all your interlocutors that the government (which Modrow wants to function as a coalition) wish to work together with the opposition and churches, primarily through the Round Table but also through the Parliament to bring the country to genuinely free and fair elections on 6 May. The agreed aim thereafter is to form a real coalition government responsible to a legitimately elected Parliament. Thus the objectives of reform here and the means of achieving them, are little different from those being pursued in countries such as Poland, Hungary and Czechoslovakia. But the prospects of preserving an East German State are unclear. Overhanging everything is the question as to whether the GDR has any future at all as a State.

5. From 1949-71 we regarded this country as the Soviet zone of occupation in Germany. After conclusion of the Quadripartite Agreement on Berlin in 1971, in the context of the relaxation of tension which provided the basis for the CSCE Final Act, we accepted the GDR as a State and opened an Embassy in East Berlin. The events of the last six months have destroyed this foundation. In a country such as Hungary, the removal of communist ideology strengthens national identity. In the same way the defeat of ideology in the GDR has strengthened German national

---

[2] Of 23 January (WRE 026/1). Not printed.

feelings. The SED ideologues were never under any illusions about this and used to argue in defence of communism that a capitalist GDR would have no justification for separate existence as a state alongside a capitalist FRG. Your visit took place at a time when the Germans themselves and all other participants in the CSCE, in particular the Four Powers with rights and responsibilities for Berlin and Germany as a whole, are wrestling with the implications for European security of the prospect of the early achievement by the German people of the goal of unity through free self-determination, set out in the Basic Law of the FRG and supported as a treaty commitment by the UK, France and the United States. The German question has been placed at the top of the international agenda by Gorbachev (the Sinatra doctrine for Eastern Europe) and specifically in the GDR's case by the Hungarian decision to dismantle their part of the iron curtain at the beginning of September 1989. The people voted with their feet for Western values. Six weeks later Honecker had been forced out of power. Three weeks after that the Wall was opened. Your visit took place at a time of intensive negotiations between the two German states about a 'contractual community' between them which nearly all concerned expect to lead to German unification.

6. You sought to sustain our objective that this process should develop in ways that are compatible with the UK's national security and prosperity in NATO and the European Community. This means, in the GDR domestic context, support for Modrow's effort to bring the country to free elections on 6 May. If properly prepared elections are not held there is a possibility of unity by incorporation without people here exercising their right to self-determination. Enormous responsibility thus rests on the shoulders of those with authority in the two German states trying to cope with the pent-up frustration, anger and impatience of people trying to catch the first train to freedom and prosperity for nearly 60 years.

7. Will they manage it? You gained the impression that things are on a knife edge. I said in my telno 74[3] that the opposition idea of accepting Modrow's invitation to join his coalition if he declares a state of emergency is a high risk strategy which could precipitate collapse. I also said that you could not have done more to assert the British interest in stability and equality of opportunity in the run up to the 6 May elections. An editorial in *Neues Deutschland* of 25 January indicated that the GDR government (*Neues Deutschland* is still the SED's paper) took the same view of your achievement here. The writer considered that you had handled tactfully matters which went to the heart of the future existence of another sovereign state. Your performance was compared favourably with other conservative visitors including those from the 'other German Republic', so prone to patronise the GDR as the 'poor relation'. The editorial went on to praise your sensitive handling of the 'German question', the role of the Four Powers, and the vital importance of 'self-determination for the population of the two German states'. Finally, *Neues Deutschland* appreciated the fact that your advice, from the 'cradle of parliamentary democracy', had been combined with news of plans to develop contacts with the GDR particularly in trade, and culture. This editorial reflects the substance of your talks with Acting Head of State Gerlach, Prime Minister Modrow, Foreign Minister Fischer, Foreign Trade Minister Beil, and the Leipzig District Council Chairman.

8. Your visit to Leipzig, the home of the GDR's peaceful revolution, was also an opportunity to meet representatives of the opposition under church auspices,

---

[3] Of 24 January (WRE 026/1). Not printed.

and English language students. You saw something of the shabbiness of this city, although a strong wind had dispersed air pollution on the day. You did not witness a demonstration, but you did hear about the continuing pressure from the streets for unity, as the means of achieving prosperity. And of course you heard about the continuing exodus to West Germany, in particular its serious economic effects on cities such as Leipzig. These themes were echoed at the Ambassador's informal buffet for opposition and church personalities back in Berlin. The disarray of the opposition was illustrated by the performance of Böhme, the leader of the SPD (East). He arrived late (he had lost the map attached to his invitation) and then left early for another meeting. Nonetheless, he told you that he was confident of 50% at the elections on 6 May. Böhme's confidence was based on support from the SPD in West Germany.

This reflects reality in this country. The political personalities in the GDR are von Weizsäcker, Brandt, Schmidt, Bahr, Genscher and Kohl (since his visit to Dresden on 19 December). Among the local leaders, Modrow commands respect but is a transitional figure. His Dresden ally, Mayor Berghofer, has resigned from the SED and is waiting in the wings for a call after 6 May to serve the country in the SPD interest. Berghofer is the only other politician of substance with a future in the GDR.

9. Your visit was thus an opportunity to assert British interests, and announce commitments to a substantial development of bilateral links. If followed up the initiatives which you announced would increase out of all recognition our involvement in this country whatever its future political configuration. Follow-up will be vital. Baker's visit to Potsdam for a meeting with Modrow before Christmas was much appreciated at the time. But there has been no follow-up (apart from 51 members of both Houses of Congress in six weeks, anxious to be photographed with GDR reformers and churchmen). We need to press ahead in all the areas that you mentioned: a cultural agreement involving the opening of cultural centres and a greatly expanded role for the British Council; a democracy seminar in March under IPU/Great Britain East Europe Centre auspices; contacts and cooperation in trade (Beil said he would quote you as his principal witness in the case for a majority shareholding for foreign investors here), banking and finance; relaxation of travel restrictions through a simplified visa regime (the GDR would welcome abolition).

10. I was therefore dismayed to learn on 25 January that a decision was taken in London in the week preceding your visit to postpone until 1991 the refurbishment of the Chancery building which is essential to accommodate additional staff who are needed to implement the new programmes of cooperation which you have announced. The refurbishment is also highly desirable in terms of the morale and motivation of staff who put up with cramped, shabby (and in summer suffocating) conditions. The refurbishment is also essential if we are to continue to follow the instructions issued by Security Department after an inspection in March 1989. But this is not just a question of the priorities and resources of an overstretched Overseas Estate Department. In recent months, and particularly as we prepared your visit, we have told the MFA (in writing) and virtually all our contacts, that the Chancery building, which we purchased in 1988, would be developed as an Embassy commensurate with Britain's position as one of the Four Powers with rights and responsibilities for Berlin and Germany as a whole, determined to raise its profile and influence here. Postponing refurbishment until 1991 will lead many people here to suppose that after your visit the UK believes that the GDR has no

future and that representation here can be left on a care and maintenance (with precious little maintenance) basis until greater Berlin becomes once again the capital of a united Germany.

11. I am sending copies of this Despatch to Her Majesty's Representatives at Bonn, Warsaw Pact posts, Belgrade, Washington and Paris, to the Permanent Representatives at NATO and to the European Communities, the Commandant of the British Sector in Berlin and the Commanders in Chief BAOR and RAF Germany.[4]

I am Sir,
Yours faithfully
C. A. MUNRO

[4] Mr Munro was Chargé d'Affaires between Mr Broomfield's departure on 24 January and the arrival of the new Ambassador, Mr Eyers, a few days later. Submitting his despatch to Mr Ratford and Mr Waldegrave on 6 February, Mr Synnott wrote that it was 'more than simply a full account of the Secretary of State's activities during his visit. It provides a useful resumé of the recent transformation of the GDR (paragraph 5).' Mr Ratford minuted on 7 February: '1. Such is the headlong acceleration of events that the two weeks that have elapsed since Mr Munro wrote the despatch make it look already somewhat dated. In the interval the possibility that the GDR will collapse altogether has increased considerably and, however much we hope to see an orderly and measured transition, its continuation as a separate state for any length of time must be open to question. 2. Short term one can sympathise with Mr Munro's disappointment about the Embassy building. But it could turn out by 1991 to have been the right decision' (WRE 026/1).

No. 108

Minute by Mr Hurd[1]

[*ESB 020/2*]

Secret   FCO, *27 January 1990*

As I told the PM yesterday[2] I am not in favour of using (and thus tying the PM to) the phrase 'slowing down'.[3] I know it appeared in the Wall St. Journal,[4] but it

[1] This minute was written in response to a submission of 25 January by Mr Hemans covering a draft reply to a letter from Mr Powell of 23 January asking for comments on a proposed oral message from the Prime Minister to Mr Gorbachev, to be conveyed by the Soviet Ambassador who would be returning to Moscow for a meeting of the Central Committee of the CPSU on 5-6 February.
[2] The Prime Minister's seminar on East-West relations and Germany, in preparation since mid-December (see Nos. 83, 86 and 87), had been held at Chequers on Saturday 27 January. This suggests that Mr Hurd's minute was written at home either late on the 27th or in the early hours of the 28th.
[3] The relevant paragraph of Mr Powell's letter read: 'The Prime Minister's views on the German question remain as she described them to Mr Gorbachev in Moscow in September [see No. 26, note 4]. The priority is to establish democracy throughout Eastern Europe. Any movement in the direction of reunification should be governed by the provisions of the Helsinki Final Act, take account of Four Power responsibilities and be part of wider progress towards removing the divisions of Europe. We are doing our best to counsel caution and slow things down. We assume that the Soviet Union is encouraging caution on the part of East Germany (where our influence is very limited).'
[4] The *Wall Street Journal* had published an interview with the Prime Minister on 25 January. The text is available at http://www.margaretthatcher.org/speeches/displaydocument.asp?docid= 107876. For discussion of its impact on the West German Government see No. 116.

puts us in the position of the ineffective brake, which we should avoid as offering the worst of all worlds. In my view, the transition is needed in its own right, not as a delaying tactic. Following the discussion at Chequers, the line with the Russians sh[oul]d be

(*a*) the Strasbourg communiqué on Germany was satisfactory, but vague. Our public line will be based on it. In practice it means:

(*b*) a clear expression of view by peoples of FRG and GDR. This has not occurred. Important that Modrow sh[oul]d continue till May 6,[5] and that street opinion sh[oul]d not prevail over free orderly elections. (This was my advice to GDR groups) then

(*c*) a substantial transition, during which all those with legitimate interests, inc[luding] the USSR, work out the right context and conditions, e.g. Berlin, e.g. frontiers.[6]

DOUGLAS HURD

[5] On 28 January Herr Modrow announced that the elections scheduled for 6 May would be brought forward to 18 March.

[6] Mr Gozney's reply to Mr Powell of 29 January suggested that the paragraph quoted in note 3 above should be replaced by the following: 'The Strasbourg Communiqué on Germany was satisfactory, but vague. Our public line will be based on it. In practice it means a clear expression of view by the peoples of the FRG and GDR. This has not occurred. It is important that Herr Modrow should continue until 18 March and that street opinion should not prevail over free orderly elections. Subsequently, there should be a substantial transition, during which all those with legitimate interests, including the Soviet Union, work out the right framework and conditions, for example over Berlin and frontiers.'

No. 109

Sir A. Acland (Washington) to FCO[1]

No. 231 Telegraphic [*WRL 020/1*]

Secret   WASHINGTON, *30 January 1990, 1.45 a.m.*

From Private Secretary.[2]

My Telno 229: Secretary of State's Meeting with President Bush: Germany[3]

1. Bush said that everyone was worried about Germany. What was our mood? The Secretary of State said we realised that, if there was a democratic vote in both Germanies in favour of unification, then unification would happen, but a great deal would need to be sorted out between the decision of principle being taken and reunification actually happening. The questions which needed to be addressed included how a unified Germany could be kept as part of NATO, membership of the European Community (the Germans could not simply announce that the GDR was now part of Germany and therefore a member), and the Russian aspect, i.e. how to reassure the Russians and how to handle 4-Power responsibilities. He had

[1] Repeated for information Immediate to Bonn, Paris, UKDEL NATO, Moscow
[2] Mr. Wall.
[3] Telegrams No. 229, 230 and 231 of 30 January reported Mr Hurd's 40-minute meeting with President Bush. No. 229 (AMU 026/1) covered China and Hong Kong; No. 230 (DZM 084/4) covered CFE (for discussion of this issue see No. 114).

found on his visit to the GDR the previous week that people were not addressing these issues at all. We needed to find a framework within which to work out our own approach.

The President asked whether the Prime Minister and President Mitterrand saw eye-to-eye on this issue. The Secretary of State said that the British and French analysis was very close, though France's commitment to the Bonn axis made it difficult for the President to express a view. Bush said that meanwhile the reunification issue was good politics for Kohl. The Secretary of State said that Kohl was trying to keep ahead of the game. He would be worried by the results in the Saarland elections the previous day. He was trying to keep the Republikaner party from gaining ground. It was difficult to press him on any of these difficult issues at present. Bush asked whether there was [*sic*] any differences between Genscher and Kohl on reunification. Baker said the only difference he could detect was that, for political reasons, Genscher was more willing to say clearly that Germany would stand by its post-war frontiers.

3. Baker said he had discussed with the Secretary of State the need for a framework to discuss the implications of a united Germany and in particular the implications for NATO.[4] Bush asked what line Kohl took about membership of NATO by a united Germany. The Secretary of State said that Kohl found it a very difficult question to address. Baker agreed. Kohl tended to take the line that we need not worry: Germany's home was in the West. We needed a framework approach. Bush said he hated to see us all so gloomy on the issue but what was happening was mind-boggling. The Secretary of State said that German membership of NATO was crucial. We should face a very fragile situation if that was not the case. Even the Russians appeared to attach importance to the kind of stability which NATO provided. Bush said he did not detect much isolationist sentiment in the USA. There was some very minimal pressure to bring back all US troops, but the real danger came from a general sense of euphoria that everything was going swimmingly and that any words of caution were out of step with reality.

The Secretary of State repeated his concern about the need to keep Germany within NATO in subsequent conversation with Scowcroft and Blackwill. Scowcroft agreed. He doubted whether Kohl wanted to leave NATO but if Gorbachev made the offer of unification in return for neutrality, he would be very tempted. The Secretary of State said that Gorbachev was in no position to make that offer. Blackwill commented that the worst situation would be one in which the two Germanys simply went their own way without any consultation with the respective allies. That would revive all the Soviet nightmares.

5. FCO please advance to PS/No.10.

---

[4] See No. 110.

No. 110

Sir A. Acland (Washington) to FCO[1]

No. 235 Telegraphic [WRL 020/1]

Confidential   WASHINGTON, *30 January 1990, 2.05 a.m.*

Secretary of State's Visit to Washington: Meeting with Baker

Summary

1. On 29 January the Secretary of State had a 20-minute private meeting with Baker, followed by lunch at which there was discussion of Germany, Eastern Europe (including COCOM, EBRD, and CSCE), EC/US, Hong Kong and CITES, Vietnamese boat people, Middle East, Southern Africa, Argentina. This telegram deals with Germany. Other subjects dealt with in my six IFTs.[2]

Detail

2. On German reunification, Baker said he would tell Shevardnadze at their meeting now arranged for 8/9 February that the Four Power forum was not appropriate for talks about the whole of Germany. But it was important to find a suitable framework. The Germans hoped to manage reunification bilaterally, but this was not on. Reunification was an issue which would determine the future of NATO. He hoped there would be further discussion of this among Political Directors.

3. The Secretary of State gave an account of his impressions following his visit to the GDR. Modrow seemed to be a tired man whose sights were fixed on getting to the elections. The Secretary of State said that unification was virtually inevitable, it should nevertheless take place following free elections in the GDR and FRG, and a period of transition. He and Baker assented to Bartholomew's (Under Secretary of State) view that this year's elections in Germany would, in effect, constitute a referendum on reunification. The Secretary of State said that three main complications needed to be addressed:

(i) NATO: would a united Germany (or the western part of it) remain in NATO? This was of crucial importance for European security:

(ii) EC aspects:

(iii) the attitude of the Soviet Union and the need to work out a framework to manage change. The need for a framework should not be interpreted as exercising a negative influence on the process.

4. Baker agreed that reunification needed to be carefully managed. His Berlin speech had articulated clear conditions (or, rather, circumstances) in which reunification should take place.[3] The only one which the FRG had since probed was continued German membership of NATO. He said Genscher did not rule out that a reunified Germany would retain NATO membership, but he could not imagine that NATO troops would be stationed on GDR territory. Baker wondered what assurances NATO might give in this regard. It was important for NATO not

---

[1] Repeated for information Immediate to Paris, Bonn, Rome, Moscow, UKDEL NATO, East Berlin.
[2] Not printed.
[3] See No. 76, note 2.

to be seen to be obstructing reunification which had been NATO policy for the past forty years.

5. The Secretary of State said there might be ways round the problem of stationing troops in Germany, e.g. by looking at earlier proposals. He said he believed the Germans did not want to be pinned down at the moment.

No. 111

Letter from Mr Powell (No. 10) to Mr Wall

[*PREM: Internal Situation in East Germany*]

Secret and Personal   10 DOWNING STREET, *31 January 1990*

[No salutation on this copy]

Germany

The Prime Minister has read with interest the accounts of the Foreign Secretary's discussions in Washington on German reunification, as well as on the new American proposal for reductions in US stationed forces in Europe (but has not yet seen the account of Sir Patrick Wright's separate discussions with American officials).[1] She looks forward to discussing them with him this afternoon. You may like, before then, to have a brief indication of what is in her mind.

The Prime Minister finds the overall picture very worrying. Events are moving faster than ever. We now have Gorbachev's statement recognising that reunification will take place.[2] There is Genscher's statement that in a united Germany today's GDR should not become a part of NATO.[3] Graf Lambsdorff said at dinner at the German embassy last night that he could not see how a united Germany could be a part of NATO (although he did not say this in his talk with the Prime Minister earlier in the day). Against this background there is bound to be increasing speculation here about the future of our troops in Germany: and there will be added urgency for the work on a possible new defence posture commissioned after Saturday's meeting. Against this background of growing uncertainty in Western Europe and continuing turmoil to the East, the Prime Minister thinks she ought to send a substantial message to the President setting out her views, following the Foreign Secretary's return. Such a message could draw quite heavily on the conclusions of Saturday's meeting at Chequers.[4] She will want to discuss this with the Foreign Secretary this afternoon and also raise the question of whether she herself should not go to see the President in the fairly near future.

[1] See No. 112, note 3. The US proposal was discussed in Cabinet on 1 February: see No. 114.

[2] Made at a press conference on 30 January, during Herr Modrow's visit to Moscow.

[3] In a major speech at Tutzing on 31 January (No. 123, note 4), Herr Genscher addressed the question of how a united Germany and NATO membership might be reconciled. He proposed that, while a united Germany would be a member of NATO, 'there would be no extension of NATO territory to the east'. The former GDR would remain outside NATO's military structures and no NATO forces would be stationed there. Meanwhile, both NATO and the Warsaw Pact would 'have to define their role increasingly in political terms' and would eventually come together in a new security system under the CSCE process.

[4] See No. 108, note 2.

She thinks this would convey a good political signal, as well as adding urgency to the official-level talks.

C.D. POWELL

No. 112

Minute from Mr Weston to Mr Wall

[*WRL 020/1*]

Secret   FCO, *31 January 1990*

Follow-up Work on East-West and Germany[1]

1. The Secretary of State may wish to have a brief note on where matters now stand, before his bilateral with the Prime Minister this afternoon. I have discussed what follows with the PUS this morning.

2. Following an office meeting which I chaired yesterday we have in hand:

(*a*) Mr Goulden (at present abroad on business) is working out a schema for the 'Political and Strategic Assessment' of the effect of recent developments (Eastern Europe and the Bush initiative) on NATO strategy. This meets the remit in Charles Powell's letters of 28 and 29 January.[2] I will discuss this with him further on his return and submit about how we move this forward with the Americans and subsequently the French. If a small team is needed, I envisage this being Broomfield/Goulden, plus Mottram, though I will chair any inter-departmental oversight in London.

(*b*) 'German Reunification and how a united Germany could be accommodated within NATO.' I have asked Security Policy Department and WED to work up a paper offering options and the way forward for a unified Germany remaining within NATO with a special regime applying to the *Länder* of the former GDR. Judging from my own contacts with my German counterpart and yesterday's discussion at the WEU Reinforced Council, the omens for finding a way through on this basis seem reasonable.

(*c*) The PUS's Washington Tel No 240 and the UK/US ultra confidential channel on Germany.[3] We shall prepare a draft telegram of instructions as a basis for Andrew Wood to talk to Zoellick, which will be submitted to Ministers. It will cover a Four point agenda:

---

[1] i.e. following the meeting at Chequers on 27 January.

[2] Not found.

[3] In this telegram Sir P. Wright reported a meeting at the British Embassy on the evening of 29 January between himself and Mr Wood on the one hand, and Mr Blackwill and Mr Zoellick on the other (PREM: Internal Situation in East Germany). After a wide-ranging discussion of German issues the participants agreed to establish a confidential high-level channel of communications between the US and the UK. This idea seems to have originated from a suggestion made in Sir A. Acland's telegram No. 84 of 11 January (No. 98, note 2), and had already been the subject of discussion between senior US and British officials. It has not been possible to establish the relationship, if any, between these developments and the Prime Ministerial initiative recorded in Zelikow and Rice, p. 173: 'A few days earlier Thatcher had urged President Bush to set up a discreet channel for bilateral U.S.-U.K. discussions on developments in Central Europe. Hurd had raised the matter and the channel was now being opened, with the British embassy on one side and Zoellick and Blackwill on the other.'

(i) Germany/NATO (the British ideas as at (*b*) above);

(ii) GDR/EC: an explanation of the negotiating stages to permit absorption of the GDR;

(iii) Four Power rights/the Russian dimension. This may *inter alia* tackle the question whether the time is now ripe to propose that the Four Powers plus two (Germanys) should become the effective forum;

(iv) CSCE—wider framework for any agreements for Germany, relevance of any CFE follow-on, assurances and guarantees.

3. We shall need to keep a particular eye on how discussion of these matters is harmonised as between individual allies and other restricted fora. The logic of Chequers was that we need to be in constant close touch with the Americans, the French and the Germans themselves; as well as, in a different way, with the Russians. The special confidentiality of the channel with Zoellick must obviously be respected but I do not see this as giving the Americans an absolute right of priority or veto.

4. I shall be submitting separately a game plan for our up-coming contacts with the FRG, as requested by the Secretary of State on our departure from Chequers.

P.J. WESTON

P.S. Special caveat: copy addressees on no account to mention the Zoellick channel outside the FCO or to other Americans.

No. 113

Letter from Mr Powell (No. 10) to Mr Wall

[*PREM: Internal Situation in East Germany*]

Secret and Personal   10 DOWNING STREET, *31 January 1990*

[No salutation on this copy]

German Reunification

The Foreign Secretary reported this evening to the Prime Minister on his visit to Washington and his discussions with the President and Secretary Baker on German reunification and its implications. He had put it to the Americans that there were problems in four areas: how a united Germany would fit into NATO, the relationship of the former GDR to the European Community, the CSCE aspect and borders, and Four-Power rights. All these would require complex negotiations and there must be adequate time for them. The Americans had welcomed the idea of consultations with the United Kingdom on these points, but had insisted that they must be restricted to a very small circle of people in Washington. This was bound to be a constraint.

The Prime Minister commented that we appeared to have taken our thinking further than the Americans. We should prepare some papers for discussion with them. She thought it would be helpful if she herself were to send a message to the President, which would provide a framework of ideas for handling all these issues. There was much material in the record of the discussion at Chequers on 27

January. The Foreign Secretary agreed that this would be useful. He would put work in hand. It might be better to delay despatch of a message until after his own visit to Germany next week.

I am copying this letter to Simon Webb (Ministry of Defence).

CHARLES POWELL

No. 114

Extracts from Conclusions of a Meeting of the Cabinet held at 10 Downing Street on 1 February 1990 at 9.30 a.m. [1]

[CC (90)4]

Secret

Foreign Affairs: Visit to Washington by the Foreign and Commonwealth Secretary

3. *The Foreign and Commonwealth Secretary* said that he had visited Washington on 29 and 30 January, where he had had talks with the President, Mr George Bush, the Vice-President, Mr Dan Quayle, the Secretary of State, Mr James Baker, and General Brent Scowcroft, Assistant to the President for National Security Affairs. It had been useful that he and the Secretary of State for Defence had been in Washington at the same time. The principal issue for discussion had been the announcement, about which the British Government had been informed in advance, in President Bush's State of the Union message on 30 January proposing mutual reductions in American and Soviet forces stationed in Europe to 195,000 troops in the central zone and 225,000 in Europe as a whole. When the President's special representatives[2] had discussed this matter with the Prime Minister in London on 29 January, the Prime Minister had said that the figures for United States force levels should constitute a floor level and should not be followed by further reductions. The Prime Minister had also urged that the proposals should be fully integrated into the negotiations on conventional force reductions in Europe (CFE) and that in future the level of United States forces should not be linked directly to the level of Soviet forces. It was important that the United States should retain a significant presence in Europe irrespective of any changes in Soviet troop levels in Eastern Europe. During his visit to Washington he had detected strong pressure within Congress to take advantage of the so-called peace dividend and

---

[1] Present at this meeting were: Mrs Thatcher, Sir G. Howe, Lord Mackay (Lord Chancellor), Mr Hurd, Mr Major, Mr D. Waddington (Secretary of State for the Home Department), Mr Walker, Mr N. Fowler (Secretary of State for Employment), Mr King, Mr Ridley, Mr K. Baker (Chancellor of the Duchy of Lancaster), Mr K. Clarke (Secretary of State for Health), Mr J. MacGregor (Secretary of State for Education and Science), Mr M. Rifkind (Secretary of State for Scotland), Mr C. Parkinson (Secretary of State for Transport), Mr J. Wakeham (Secretary of State for Energy), Lord Belstead (Lord Privy Seal), Mr A. Newton (Secretary of State for Social Security), Mr C. Patten (Secretary of State for the Environment), Mr P. Brooke (Secretary of State for Northern Ireland), Mr J. Gummer (Minister of Agriculture, Fisheries and Food), Mr N. Lamont (Chief Secretary, Treasury) and Mr M. Howard (Secretary of State for Employment).

[2] Mr Eagleburger and Mr Gates had been despatched secretly to explain President Bush's planned troop cuts to West European leaders: see Zelikow and Rice, p. 171.

that since the threat that justified the presence of United States forces in Europe had diminished, United States forces should be withdrawn and defence spending cut. The more responsible members of Congress were resisting these arguments, as indeed was Secretary of State Baker. The British Government had rightly supported President Bush's announcement in public while advancing in private the arguments which the Prime Minister had put forward. His main impression from his visit to Washington was that American policy was formulated by a small, tightly-knit group of political figures and officials in the White House and State Department. One consequence of this secrecy was that surprisingly little forward thinking had been done on constructing a policy framework for the North Atlantic Treaty Organisation (NATO) over the next few years. His suggestion that the British and American Governments should consult urgently to work out such a framework had been warmly welcomed . . .

German Democratic Republic

The Foreign and Commonwealth Secretary said that events in the German Democratic Republic were moving quickly. The date for free elections had now been brought forward. In return the opposition parties had moved into a Grand Coalition with Prime Minister Modrow's government. The Social Democratic Party was currently in the strongest position. Meanwhile in Moscow, President Gorbachev had changed his position from outright opposition to German reunification to stating that no one was placing the principle of German reunification in doubt. Within West Germany the political parties were preparing for the elections in December. They were concerned not to be outflanked on the issue of German reunification, especially by the extreme right wing Republikaner party. Within the Alliance, the United Kingdom was well placed to set the broad policy framework for the months ahead. The United Kingdom had supported the principle of self-determination for Germany for many years. The key issue now was to ensure that any changes took place in a context of stability and peace. The principal issue for the future would be the role of any united Germany within the North Atlantic Alliance and the European Community (EC). It was clear that East Germany could not simply become a member of the EC while it remained a command economy. The United Kingdom was alone among all the Allies in being a member of all the four major international fora where these issues would need to be discussed: the EC, NATO, the Four Powers and the Conference on Security and Co-operation in Europe. Bilateral discussions were already under way with the United States, France and Germany in parallel with existing contacts with the Soviet Union at all levels.

No. 115

Sir C. Mallaby (Bonn) to Mr Hurd[1]

No. 121 Telegraphic [WRL 020/1]

Confidential   BONN, *1 February 1990, 3.45 p.m.*

Personal for Private Secretary, PS/PUS, Weston, Head/WED

British Position on the German Question

Summary

1. British position seen as the most negative of the Four Powers. Recommendations for your speech here on 6 February.

Detail

2. *Bild* newspaper (tabloid, circulation 4.3 million) comments today that only one person—the Prime Minister—is now determined to do everything possible to fight German unity. Reports of Lambsdorff's talk with the Prime Minister attribute a cautious approach to her.[2] There are comments contrasting Gorbachev's latest remarks on German unity with the British position. Although the German press has repeatedly commented that France is reluctant about German unity (I shall comment separately on Paris telno misc 31),[3] the criticism of Britain is much more in volume and much sharper.

3. I believe that our policy should be to work hard with the USA and France to influence the manner and speed of movement towards German unity and above all to get right the repercussions for security in Europe and for the Community. If we are seen as opponents of German unity, we shall have much less influence, because the Federal Government and public opinion will be disinclined to listen to us and Kohl would face domestic political costs if he was seen to do so.

4. Your speech here on 6 February is the major opportunity for projecting an image which can help restore our influence. If you can make some new suggestions, it will be clear that the British are looking forward positively.

5. I suggest that the following material might be worked into the speech:

(*a*) German unity is up to the Germans. That is what self-determination means. If you decide for unity, we shall respect that, as we have always said.

---

[1] Repeated for information Priority to Paris, Washington, UKDEL NATO; Routine to Moscow, BMG Berlin.

[2] See No. 111. According to Mr Powell's record of her meeting with Count Lambsdorff, 'The Prime Minister said that what worried her most about the present situation was that no-one was sitting down and looking systematically at the consequences for NATO of the rapid developments in the Soviet Union and Eastern Europe and of the prospect of German unification. She was seriously worried that, without this, there was a risk that NATO would break up. Her aim was to secure a transition period before German unification was realised, which would last long enough to enable the very difficult issues concerning NATO, the European Community and Four-Power rights to be sorted out.' Letter from Mr Powell to Mr Wall, 30 January (DZN 061/40).

[3] In this telegram to Bonn of 31 January Sir E. Fergusson reported a conversation with the Secretary-General of the French Foreign Ministry. M. Scheer, who had 'expressed disquiet about what he described as the current campaign against France being whipped up in the West German press' which must, he thought, 'be more vociferous than any current criticism of the United Kingdom'. Sir E. Fergusson asked whether Sir C. Mallaby's reading of the West German press bore this out: 'Having invested so much in the Franco-German relationship the French are inevitably sensitive to public German criticism' (WRL 020/1).

(*b*) The Germans, if they choose unity, will need time to bring the Federal Republic and the GDR together. Despite the many similarities, the fundamentally different institutions would have to be replaced by joint ones. The legal systems are completely different. So are the economic systems. As if that were not enough, look at the example of totally different social security systems. The need for the Germans to think through those changes and reach decisions and implement new arrangements means that there will be a period of time between a decision for German unity and completion of unity. You will need arrangements for an orderly transition. It will be up to you whether this should be covered in the proposed treaty between the two Germanies about a contractual community.

(*c*) The necessary transition period will give time for international discussion of the international framework that would accompany German unity. There are important questions, notably concerning security and the continued need for NATO and concerning the European Community. Hans-Dietrich Genscher rightly said last week that we need more not less security in the Europe of tomorrow.

(*d*) My vision is that, at the end of an orderly transition, German unity, if the Germans choose it, and a new stable architecture in Europe and a much more far reaching version of CSCE should all come about together. I think that would accord with the title of Hans-Dietrich Genscher's important speech last week: 'on German unity in the European framework'.[4]

6. The reference to the proposed inner German treaty in (*b*) is designed to avoid the impression that we are proposing an alternative to that treaty. I think it better not to put a number of years on the concept of transition, since the Federal Government has not decided on this point and we should not precipitate it. If there was a breakdown in the GDR or a sudden call for immediate unity, before or after the elections there, the need for an orderly transition would be no less, although its achievement would be far harder. Genscher's speech yesterday, mentioned above, is being reported separately.

7. It is a widespread conviction here that Gorbachev could not possibly agree to the GDR becoming part of the military structure of NATO and many are convinced that GDR membership of NATO in any form is out. There is also a strong consensus for the FRG remaining in NATO. I suggest that your best tactic on this is not to state clearly that the GDR must be in NATO on the same basis as the FRG but to use words which can accommodate something less than that.

[4] See No. 111, note 3.

No. 116

Submission from Mr Synnott to Mr Weston, with Minute by Mr Weston

[*WRL 020/1*]

Confidential and Personal   FCO, *1 February 1990*

The German Question: German Views about Britain

1. The Secretary of State's visit to Bonn on 6 February will be an important opportunity to attempt to set the record straight about Britain's position over the

German Question and to repair some of the damage which has been caused as a result of the German perception that Britain is the most reluctant of the Four Powers (including the Soviet Union) to contemplate the prospect of German reunification. In a separate submission to the Private Secretary[1] I have suggested a number of ways in which the speech could be made rather warmer and hence, it is to be hoped, more effective for this purpose.

2. I fear, however, that whatever the Secretary of State may say on 6 February, it will not have sufficient impact to improve our capacity to influence the Germans in handling the transition to reunification, which I believe to be already under way and which will be given further impetus by the elections on 18 March. I expect that the Secretary of State's meeting with Chancellor Kohl on 6 February may be rather sticky. My reasons for these singularly unconstructive observations are as follows.

3. There is plenty of evidence that the Germans have noted with some satisfaction the positive formulations used recently by Mr Waldegrave and the Secretary of State (e.g. in Bonn on 17 January and at the East Berlin press conference on 24 January respectively). But it is widely believed in Germany, in the press and at the very highest level there, that the Prime Minister has radically different views on the subject. Well-placed contacts in the Chancellor's Office have said, in terms, that the views of British Ministers other than the Prime Minister are of little significance in the present circumstances. They have told us that the transcript of the Prime Minister's interview to the Wall Street Journal has been translated in its entirety and has caused '*unheimlich viel Weh*' (enormously great pain) in the Chancellor's Office.[2] (I attach a highlighted copy of the transcript.[3] Page 8: A reunified Germany unbalances. Page 9: What is the unit which is entitled to self-determination? Page 10: Kohl has not formally agreed to the Oder-Neisse line. Page 11: Nationalism has not died in Germany. Page 15: The British text for political cooperation was filched by the Germans. Part B, page 3: Examples of *uncommunautaire* practice in Germany. Page 5: 'Thank goodness we can, because we were able to override Germany.')

4. This mood will be enhanced by the attached piece of knocking copy filed on 31 January by the German Press Agency correspondent in London.[3] It may be expected to hit the German press widely over the next few days (just before the Secretary of State's arrival in Bonn). Today's mass-circulation *Bild Zeitung* states that Mrs Thatcher will do everything possible to fight German unity (although another more weighty paper suggests that Gorbachev's new course is prompting London to 'wake up to reality'). These are not just recent or isolated examples. The perception in Bonn is quite clear.

5. Meanwhile, there is currently a risk of engaging in megaphone diplomacy with the Germans on the conundrum of reunification and NATO. Genscher's delphic remarks about not extending NATO to the Oder-Neisse line have evidently caused a stir in No 10.[4] Fortunately, these remarks are now being most helpfully clarified by the Germans and in a speech yesterday by Genscher himself. But we seem to be perilously close to sending public 'warning signals' to the Germans on this issue.

6. What can be done? As I have suggested in a separate submission, I hope that we can now turn the necessity of acceptance of the principle of reunification into a

---

[1] Not found.
[2] See No. 108, note 4.
[3] Not printed.
[4] No. 111, note 3.

virtue. First, I think we should accept that the Germans *are* capable of being influenced favourably about the external aspects of reunification (the recent positive glosses on the NATO issue demonstrate this); and second, that a confrontational approach in the context of an election year will encourage the Germans to close ranks and will therefore be counter-productive. We *already* have some good ideas (possibly more advanced than those of the US and France). We should share them with the Germans, soon.

7. I believe that our ability to influence the Germans favourably will only be improved by means of a change in German perceptions of our underlying attitudes and that this would require a positive intervention by the Prime Minister personally. Given the Prime Minister's evident strength of feeling, as demonstrated by the *Wall Street Journal* interview, I am reluctant to suggest precisely how this might be done (and I am under no illusions about the difficulty). One possibility would be for the Prime Minister publicly to associate herself with the Secretary of State's speech next week. Another might be a warm and forthcoming personal message to Chancellor Kohl (which also might usefully be published); or a visit to Bonn having the same purpose. Any such message or visit could also counsel prudence and help get across our very legitimate concerns about the security of Europe in the context of reunification. But it would be essential that we projected the appearance of warm and sincere support for the prospect of reunification if that is what the German people decide upon.

8. Without wishing to sound apocalyptic, I fear that alternatives to this sort of approach are likely, in this election year, to be pretty bad for our interests. At best, our views will be ignored by the Germans (although we may still be able to exert influence through the US and France). At worst they will promote nationalism in the FRG; help the Republikaner surmount the 5% barrier next December; and provide anti-NATO material for the mercurial Lafontaine, the SPD's probable Chancellor-candidate—the very outcomes we wish to avoid.

9. The attached list outlines the existing opportunities for dialogue with the Germans.[5] The next meeting at Head of Government level is not until the Königswinter Conference and Summit on 29 and 30 March. This is, I suggest, too late for the purposes described above (and is after the GDR elections), not least because all the contacts before this will be coloured by German doubts about our position.

10. Meanwhile an oral question on Germany is down for answer by the Prime Minister on 6 February, when the Secretary of State is in Bonn.

H.N.H. SYNNOTT

Minute from Mr Weston to Mr Wall

Confidential and Personal   FCO, *2 February 1990*

Private Secretary
I warned the Secretary of State last night that this was coming. The Dep[artmen]t. are right to bring this matter squarely to Ministerial attention. It cannot be in British interest for German perceptions to be as described in § 3 & 4 above.

---

[5] See Enclosure in this document.

I hope that fence-mending can begin well before Königswinter and the Summit. I shall discuss ways and means with Sir C. Mallaby over the weekend. At the very least it would be good if the Secretary of State were able to secure (*a*) a personal message from the PM to Kohl which he could deliver in Bonn on 6 Feb (*b*) the PM's public endorsement of his speech that day and (*c*) an upbeat reference to Anglo/German relations in the PM's answer to a PQ. Even better would be an offer by the PM to spend a couple of hours with Kohl in advance of the Königswinter/Cambridge summit, so that the latter occasion can be devoted to realising its full potential not just damage limitation. But I recognise that this may be asking a lot.

P.J. WESTON

ENCLOSURE IN NO. 116

FORTHCOMING OPPORTUNITIES FOR DIALOGUE WITH THE GERMANS

Prime Minister and/or Secretary of State
February
> 1: Secretary of State to host working dinner for Count Lambsdorff (FDP Chairman)
> 2: Secretary of State to have talks with Herr Momper (Governing Mayor Berlin)
> 6: Secretary of State to address Konrad Adenauer Foundation, call on Kohl and Genscher

March
> 29-30: Anglo-German Summit
> 29-31: Königswinter Conference

FCO Ministers
February
> 1: Mr Maude to host dinner for Herr Momper
> 2: Mr Waldegrave to have talks with Herr Momper
> 19: Mr Waldegrave to have talks with Herr Wilz (*Bundestag* Defence Committee)

March 29-31: Königswinter Conference. Mr Maude to attend

FCO Officials
February
> 4-5: Mr Weston to FRG for talks with Dr Kastrup
> 9: PUS to have talks with Herr Sudhoff (PUS equivalent)
> 12: Mr Tait and delegation to Bonn for East-West talks
> 28: Contacts with Dr Kastrup

Ministry of Defence
February
> 3-4: Mr King to *Wehrkunde* Conference
> 7-9: Lord Arran (PUSS Armed Forces) to FRG
> 21-23: Herr Stoltenberg (FRG Defence Minister) to UK

March 12-13: Mr Hamilton (Minister Armed Forces) to Bonn

Other Opportunities
June
    North Atlantic Council and preceding contacts
Still to be arranged:
    Other contacts by Mr Weston with Dr Kastrup and others

No. 117

Sir A. Acland (Washington) to Mr Hurd

No. 276 Telegraphic [PREM: Internal Situation in East Germany]

Secret   WASHINGTON, *2 February 1990, 5 p.m.*

Personal for Ambassadors,[1] Cabinet Office for Powell, No. 10.

Bilateral Discussion of German Issues

Summary
1. The clear US message is that speed is essential if we are to avoid a free fall to German unity. I recommend an early presentation to the Americans of possible practical steps to stabilise transition, including: endorsement of the (former) GDR as a demilitarised zone while the (former) FRG would remain in NATO: quadripartite discussion of how to give NATO more political content: exploitation of the Berlin Four mechanism: and consideration of how eventually to integrate the (former) GDR into the Community. We need to address the questions of which Germans to talk to, what we should tell the Americans of our discussions with the French, the future of the Quadripartite mechanism in this context, and how to bring in other NATO partners.

Detail
2. You will by now have had time to reflect on the restricted talks the PUS held here on 29 January.[2] At the risk of covering well-trodden ground, it might be useful to set out some of the parameters, as seen from Washington, for the next step in our discussions with the Americans.

3. Two clear messages came over on 29 January—that the Americans believe events will move even faster than we have so far expected, and towards German unification: and, secondly, that we need to get a grip now if we are to exert an influence. I believe this US sense of urgency to have been heightened because the East German elections have been brought forward to 18 March, because Genscher is already arguing that the outcome of this alone would be the trigger for the two states to take decisions on the relationship between them, and also because the future of Germany will be one of the subjects to be looked at by Baker when he goes to Moscow on 8 February. This meeting will form an essential introduction to the Ottawa Open Skies meeting at which the Americans hope a number of wider issues will be considered. Much of the wider change is contingent on what happens next in Germany.

---

[1] i.e. in Bonn, Paris, Washington and UKDEL NATO. See also Nos. 125-6, 151-2.
[2] See No. 112, note 3.

4. The Americans still feel in no better contact than us with the Germans on the three major issues which arise from the possibility of German unification: a united Germany's relationship with NATO, with the war-time allies, and with the Community. These particular issues, which we need to address in our bilateral talks, are also central to the wider agenda: preserving acceptance of the NATO military structure and adequate force levels in a changing East/West situation, giving fresh political content to the Alliance, the further development of the EC and the relative weight for the future of the CSCE process. The latter issues will need to be discussed with a wider range of Americans and Europeans than are privy to UK/US exchanges on Germany. They too are subject to perhaps increasing time constraints. The difficulty in controlling this mix seems all the greater, viewed from Washington, because the domestic and intra-German agenda is predominant for Bonn in an electoral year, raising the fear that the Germans will not see the problems of a free fall towards unity and could thereby compromise the wider East/West agenda. The Americans believe that unless they are able to seize the initiative, they risk becoming by-standers in a potentially dangerous situation. The obvious way for them to get a better lever on the Germans is to persuade the latter that they want actively to help manage the transition to a united Germany in the common interest.

5. I am uncertain as to whether we see matters in quite so urgent a light as the President's advisers. If we do not accept the analysis presented by Zoellick and Blackwill on 29 January, we should of course make that clear as soon as possible. But assuming our ideas are not too far apart, I recommend very early action with Zoellick. I think it most desirable to get some thoughts in before Baker's talks in Moscow. We are now in apparent general agreement with the Americans on the terms on which unity should be achieved, though our views on the timescale may be different. If we do not act soon, we may be overtaken by events.

6. A presentation by us to the Americans might include:

(*a*) The most obvious way for us now to ensure continued effective West German membership of NATO would be to accept that the territory of the GDR would, in a united Germany, be kept free of non-German NATO forces. Reference to a demarcation on the basis of *Länder* might presumably help. Two alliances in one country cannot be the longer term answer. The Germans themselves would presumably have to retain the right to station some of their own forces in the area, if only for the purposes of maintaining law and order. On the assumption that we could agree some such approach with the Americans, and then the French, there would be advantage in talking to the Germans before agreeing the details on an Alliance basis. It would be for consideration whether or not we should suggest that the Baker/Shevardnadze session in Moscow be used to sound out the Russians in advance.[3] A transition period for Soviet troops to remain in the GDR could be built into this sort of framework, the more easily because the prevailing assumption is that the Russians will have to leave some time in the foreseeable future anyway. If we were able to agree such an approach with the Germans, and to make it clear publicly what we had done, that would presumably help persuade German public opinion that the Western Allies were on their side.

(*b*) Assuming we were able to agree on this basic approach with the Germans— and what they themselves have said lends credence to that belief—the Quad

---

[3] Mrs Thatcher noted: 'What are the ideas?'

might then usefully discuss what flesh to put on the bones of the proposal that the Alliance should take on more political content. There is plenty of ambiguity to be resolved here over the relationship between this idea and the future of CSCE (to which the Germans seem to attach particular importance) as well as the EC. We shall also need to agree with the Americans, as well as with our other Allies, on a military justification for NATO in the changing circumstances of a uniting Germany and, presumably, a more democratic Eastern Europe. This complex of questions need not be handled on the restricted bilateral net suggested on 29 January, but the development of our policies would have to be tied in to that context.

(*c*) We might try to agree with the Americans on how to discuss with the Germans and the Russians how best to fit in a unification process with the interests and rights of the four Berlin Powers. The Germans would have to be brought to see this mechanism as helpful in assuring the safe birth of a new Germany and as a means of getting the Russians on board. We have had indications that the Americans might be tempted to talk to Shevardnadze on 8 February about the possibilities of a Four plus Two mechanism. It would seem prudent to make sure that Berlin issues, like direct elections, which would fall naturally into place following a general settlement, did not get out in front of the wider process. Nor should it be complicated with Soviet demands for a peace conference.

(*d*) We, alone or in conjunction with others, will need, perhaps after discussion with the Germans of the above three points, to explore with the Germans the question of how best to integrate the former GDR territories into the Community framework, once unification has been endorsed by the electorate. A British initiative here could perhaps prove useful in Bonn, though we would presumably wish to sound out the Germans informally before acting in Brussels. It would obviously be essential for the West Germans to be persuaded of the practical need for time for any such process. The more we were able to think over the details of where and how the GDR *Länder* had to adjust, the more convincing and practical our presentation would be and the better placed we should be to counter any assumption in German (or American) minds that our object was to delay the inevitable rather than to help all of us adjust to change.

7. We shall presumably need to talk to both Genscher and Kohl. Genscher is visiting Washington today, 2 February. The American view of the best channels to work through in Bonn may presumably be affected by this visit, but I believe they would welcome any advice we may have. We should also let the Americans know of our discussions with the French[4] and perhaps consider at some stage turning the present bilateral exercise into a three cornered discussion. The Quadripartite mechanism will become the natural one to use when and if we have managed to agree with the Germans on the basic thrust of our approach.[5]

---

[4] Mrs Thatcher noted: 'That would *NOT* please Mitterrand.'
[5] Mrs Thatcher minuted on this telegram: 'The essential thing is to agree with Gorbachev/ Shevardnadze. *Then* we can try to persuade Germany.'

No. 118

Sir E. Fergusson (Paris) to Mr Hurd[1]

No. 139 Telegraphic [WRL 020/1]

Confidential   PARIS, *2 February 1990, 6.56 p.m.*

Call on Dumas: Developments in Europe

Summary
1. Dumas believes that the FRG government have made reunification their absolute priority. He is strongly in favour of closer Anglo-French cooperation. He repeats his conviction that European integration must be accelerated, but points to the need to respond to positive developments in Eastern European countries. He finds US policy unclear. Important for the British and French to decide on a floor for arms reductions.

Detail
2. I called on Dumas this afternoon to ask for his views on recent developments in Europe. He was alone. He said that events in East Germany and the reaction of the FRG Government to them had convinced him that, more than ever, it was vital to advance quickly towards a reinforcement of the structure of the European Community. The FRG Government were now making reunification with East Germany their overriding priority. He feared that, if neutrality was the price to be exacted for reunification, the FRG Government would be ready to pay it. Similarly, if the FRG Government had to choose between reunification and the continued development of the EC, they would choose the former. For these reasons it was vital for Britain and France to persuade the FRG Government to look seriously at the possible consequences of their actions. I said that Dumas must be aware that going full tilt towards the strengthening of the Community raised difficult political issues for the UK. We needed to examine the question whether reinforcing the structure of the EC was in fact the best way of ensuring stability in Central Europe. Indeed it was because the answers to such questions were so important that France and the UK needed to discuss them with as much frankness as possible.

3. Dumas agreed that more than ever it was important for the British and the French to maintain a detailed exchange of views and to seek to increase their bilateral cooperation. President Mitterrand had been very pleased with his conversation with the Prime Minister on 20 January: such exchanges should take place on a regular basis so that we could discuss the common problems facing both countries. I told him of the forthcoming meeting on 4 February at *Wehrkunde*[2] between the Secretary of State for Defence and M Chevenement: Dumas welcomed it warmly. I underlined the extent of the progress in Anglo-French relations in cooperation on defence matters in recent years: the frequency and depth of regular contact that now existed was very important. Dumas agreed. He particularly welcomed the forthcoming opportunities he would have to see you and

---

[1] Repeated for information Priority to EC Posts, Moscow, Washington, UKDEL NATO; information to BMG Berlin.
[2] The International Conference on Security Policy, held annually in Munich since 1962.

added that, given the constant diary difficulties which Ministers face, he was concerned to use every opportunity in the margins of multilateral meetings to stay in touch with you.

4. At an EC Ambassadors' lunch on 1 February, Dumas enlarged on some of the above points. He said that we could either let the post-war Europe decompose into pre-First World War nationalism or we could build on the existing level of European construction which, though strong, was fragile (he referred here to the altercation with the FRG over Schengen).[3] We needed first to finish the work required to complete existing decisions taken by the community. He would then be ready, provided that everyone was ready, to consider more far-reaching questions such as political union. There were, however, more immediate problems. He cited the case of Hungary, which had already moved significantly towards democratic pluralism and now wanted to come closer to the EC. We could not offer them integration, but must look for some new type of association on an *à la carte* basis. We could not leave Hungary, and other countries like it, without a response. Another option was to see what could be done within the CSCE framework. He was firmly against proposals which would extend the European Commission's competence.

5. Asked about the GDR, Dumas said that the GDR Government had not yet asked for EC membership: we did not yet know what they might demand after the March elections. There were both legal and political problems. The legal issue was not a problem for the FRG, but the rest of us needed to be very clear of [*sic*] the political consequences of anything we decided. We should accept that reunification would happen, but it must take place in a way which would give reassurance to all those whom it would affect. Dumas accepted, when I raised the point, that we should not move so precipitously that Gorbachev's position would be affected, but added that Gorbachev's attitude had changed significantly since Mitterrand's meeting with him in Kiev, as his remarks during Modrow's visit to Moscow showed. All the same, Dumas did not think that underlying Russian attitudes had changed.

6. On the Alliance, Dumas said that the crumbling of the Warsaw Pact need not necessarily lead to the disappearance of NATO, but there were consequences which needed to be considered. We needed to think carefully about the future link between Europe and the US. An American presence in Europe remained desirable and the Americans themselves wished to stay. It seemed that the Russians wished them to stay too. So long as the Soviet Union remained the dominant military power on the European continent, the US must remain as a balancing factor. On the other hand, he found US policy unclear. The Americans persistently played their tune in both the European and the Soviet register: it was hard to know which they favoured. At times they preferred to deal direct with the Soviet Union and were reluctant to allow the Europeans to put constraints on the bilateral super-power relationship. The same seemed to apply to their resistance to Soviet participation in the EBRD. In these circumstances the Europeans needed to harmonize their own position better. This afternoon Dumas told me that he broadly agreed with you on the importance of strengthening EC/US links. I mentioned your discussion with Baker in Washington. Dumas also thought that it was wise to avoid a formal treaty.

[3] The Schengen Agreement was signed by France, Germany and the Benelux countries on 14 June 1985. The Convention Implementing the Schengen Agreement was signed on 19 June 1990, although it did not come into effect until 1995.

7. Asked at the EC lunch about arms control, Dumas said that we needed to be clear about what threshold of security we ought to maintain. Progress over arms control focussed attention on both the British and French deterrent forces. How should they be included in arms control and what was the right level for deterrent forces? There should be a floor, but US and Soviet reductions had a long way to go before that point was reached.

8. Resident clerk please pass to Gozney, Private Office.[4]

[4] Mrs Thatcher minuted on her copy of this telegram: 'They are now playing back to us some of our views about Germany. The problems will *not* be overcome by strengthening the E.C. Germany's ambitions would then become the *dominant* and *active* factor' (PREM: Internal Situation in East Germany).

No. 119

Letter from Mr Hurd to the Prime Minister

[*PREM: Internal Situation in East Germany*]

FCO, *2 February 1990*[1]

Dear Prime Minister,

We are sending Charles what I propose to say in my speech at Bonn next Tuesday. I think it is on the lines of our recent discussions, and that to say less about unification at this stage would weaken our influence in the transition – you will have seen how the idea of transition has caught on.

If you agree I w[oul]d like to have a short *tête à tête* with Kohl, giving him a message from you—to the effect that you think it crucially important from all points of view that the CDU sh[oul]d win in the autumn, will do whatever you can to help, and that he sh[oul]d let you know at any time about this. Is this about right, and is there anything you w[oul]d like me to add?

Yours,
Douglas

[1] Dated in error '2.i.90.'.

No. 120

Minute from Mr Synnott to Mr Ratford

[*WRL 020/6*]

Confidential   FCO, *2 February 1990*

Call by Ministerial Direktor of the Ministry for Inner German Relations

1. I found Dr Dobiey's conversation with us yesterday both revealing and depressing.

2. It was revealing, in particular, that he said that the draft of a treaty between the FRG and the GDR which specified a goal of complete unity already existed

and had been submitted to the Federal Chancellor's Office.[1] (Sudhoff told Sir C. Mallaby recently that he had not yet seen any draft of a treaty. Bonn telno 103.)[2] While Dobiey confirmed that there was no question of concluding any such treaty until elections had occurred in the GDR, he made absolutely no reference to the question of consultations with the Four Powers.

3. Dobiey's concentration on the micro-economic level of cooperation (tarmac at border crossings; despatch of first-aid parcels etc), and his inability to answer repeated questions about the nature of the various economic, social, political etc measures which might have to be in place before unification was finalised, was tedious but also revealing in its way. One must conclude that if serious work on these issues is being carried out in the Federal Government, Dobiey's Ministry is not part of it (he did not strike me as being a good enough actor to dissemble on this point). In other words, we got nowhere in our effort to try to establish a minimum timescale in which the internal processes of reunification might occur.

4. I nonetheless formed the impression that that minimum timescale could in practice be quite short. Dobiey did not exclude the possibility that the five former *Länder* in the GDR could be in place again before the local elections on 6 May.

As regards parliamentary contacts (a crucial element for the development of 'confederative structures'), Dobiey said that the pace of these would be determined by the parliaments themselves and posed the rhetorical question as to what the FRG could do if, in accordance with Article 23 of the Basic Law, 'other parts of Germany' were to declare that they acceded to the Basic Law (in which case, presumably, the Basic Law would apply there).[3] He indicated that contacts were already proceeding apace and suggested that Federal legislation could be made to apply in the GDR very quickly, even if aspects of GDR practice did not conform to it: grace periods could be applied. Dobiey stressed repeatedly that the FRG's first and overriding priority was to stabilise the GDR, both to halt emigration by offering light at the end of the tunnel and to stop the country falling apart.

5. It is perhaps not surprising that, given the responsibilities of his Ministry, Dobiey should concentrate on the purely Inner German aspects of the question. But given the only too well-known British sensitivities about the question, and the seniority of Dobiey's personal position, I find it remarkable that he should not once have mentioned the external aspects or even have attempted to reassure us that the process of stabilising the GDR, and hence the transitional period, would take some considerable time.[4]

H.N.H. SYNNOTT

[1] Probably the draft of 18 January printed in *Deutsche Einheit*, No. 139. It did not speak of unity as such, but of a 'treaty community' (*Vertragsgemeinschaft*), to be achieved through the deepening of cooperation and the establishment of common institutions, that would further develop the special relations between the two states and thus contribute to overcoming the division of Germany and of Europe.

[2] This was a parenthetical comment by Sir C. Mallaby in telegram No. 103 of 29 January reporting a briefing of the three Western Ambassadors by Herr Seiters on recent developments in the GDR and Herr Modrow's forthcoming visit to Bonn on 13 February (WRL 020/1).

[3] Article 23 of the Basic Law of the Federal Republic of 1949 read: 'For the time being, this Basic Law shall apply in the territory of the *Länder* Baden, Bavaria, Bremen, Greater Berlin, Hamburg, Hesse, Lower Saxony, North Rhine-Westphalia, Rhineland-Palatinate, Schleswig-Holstein, Württemberg-Baden and Württemberg-Hohenzollern. It shall be put into force for other parts of Germany on their accession.'

[4] Mr Ratford minuted to Mr Synnott on 2 February: 'I agree, particularly about the speed at which this is happening, and may continue.'

No. 121

Letter from Mr Powell (No. 10) to Mr Wall

[*PREM: Internal Situation in East Germany*]

Strictly Personal   10 DOWNING STREET, *4 February 1990*

Dear Stephen,

The Prime Minister has seen the personal letter from the Foreign Secretary about the message which he proposes to give Chancellor Kohl.[1] She is content with what he proposes to say, but would like him also to underline the importance of agreeing the main steps on the way to unification with Britain and the United States, France and the Soviet Union. She would also like the Foreign Secretary to emphasise the crucial importance of Germany remaining in NATO: she thinks Chancellor Kohl's robust stand on this is absolutely right.

Yours sincerely,
C.D. POWELL

[1] No. 119.

No. 122

Sir C. Mallaby (Bonn) to Mr Hurd[1]

No. 134 Telegraphic [*WRL 020/1*]

Confidential   BONN, *5 February 1990, 9.56 a.m.*

Your Visit to Bonn 6 February

Summary

1. FRG Government and public wholly preoccupied by unification. Strong sense of speed of events and of fragility of situation in GDR and public opinion here. Less euphoria and growing anxiety about problems ahead. Kohl not (not) at present in a dominant position. Government finding it difficult to manage simultaneously the foreign policy and security implications, the economic and inner-German aspects and the party political side.

Detail

2. The German question overshadows everything else. The fragility of the situation in the GDR is becoming widely recognised. There is talk of a threat of economic collapse. In the Federal Government there is much uncertainty:

—Will the authority of the GDR state survive to 18 March and will the situation after that be any more stable?

—Can economic measures be taken before and after 18 March, with a scale and speed that would stem emigration and steady the GDR? Can an even greater wave of emigration be avoided then? Is economic and monetary union of the two German states going to be necessary before state unity (my letter of 1

[1] Repeated for information Priority to Washington, Paris, BMG Berlin, East Berlin.

February to Ratford)?[2]

—How can German unity be reconciled with membership of NATO? How best to squash the call for neutrality from Modrow? (My telno 133 about the *Wehrkunde* conference).[3]

—How can the Federal coalition parties gain political advantage from the handling of this complex and fragile situation?

3. It is dawning on public opinion that the costs of bailing out the GDR will be enormous. This could become a major issue here before the Federal elections in December. That could rebound against the coalition parties, helping the *Republikaner* and the SPD.

4. Kohl is probably feeling the need to reassert his leadership. I do not exclude another major pronouncement from him on unification—possibly the economic aspects—designed *inter alia* to influence the elections in the GDR where the parties of the centre right look ill-organised and the SPD well placed. There is the strange prospect that the GDR Government after 18 March could be led by the East German SPD, which means steered by the Federal German opposition. Here, the SPD has drawn level with the CDU in the latest opinion poll and Lafontaine's convincing win in the Saarland elections means that Kohl almost certainly faces this canny populist as his opponent in the December Federal elections.

---

[2] In this letter Sir C. Mallaby suggested that there might be 'some advantages for us in decoupling of economic from state unity in Germany. First, it adds another stage into Kohl's Ten Point programme, and can thus gain some time. Second, it would accelerate economic change in the GDR and would provide the least bad prospect of giving people there the feeling that things are really happening on the economic front, whatever the accompanying discomforts. That might reduce pressure in the GDR for early state unity. Third, it would raise in much more acute form the need for massive resource transfers from the FRG to the GDR . . . All this might inject some sobriety into Federal German attitudes to unity and that in turn might militate for some steadiness of pace. The result might be that state unity would be delayed or less pressed for; and that would delay the conundrum about unity and NATO, among other difficult issues' (WRL 020/1).

[3] This telegram of 5 February reported 'clear signs of SPD unsoundness on a united Germany's relationship to NATO' (WRL 020/1).

No. 123

Sir C. Mallaby (Bonn) to Mr Hurd[1]

No. 137 Telegraphic [WRL 020/1]

Confidential   BONN, *5 February 1990, 4.44 p.m.*

*FRG Policy on the German Question: German Political Director
gives read out on Genscher's Talks with Baker*

Summary

1. Kastrup says that the situation in the GDR is now so near collapse that the Federal Government is embarking immediately on economic and monetary union without waiting for GDR elections. After 18 March, outline of a unification treaty will be drawn up with the GDR government with aim of presenting this to the

---

[1] Repeated for information Immediate to Washington, Paris, East Berlin, BMG Berlin; Priority to Moscow, UKDEL NATO.

CSCE summit. Kastrup claims that Baker is on board for this. Describes Genscher's other ideas for the CSCE summit. Takes strong and negative line on exercise of 4 power rights.

Detail

2. John Weston spent a day in Bonn following the *Wehrkunde* Conference in Munich.[2] Over lunch, his German opposite number, Dieter Kastrup, gave a briefing on instructions concerning the evolution of the Federal Government's policy on the German question, which had formed the major theme of Genscher's talks with Secretary Baker on 2 February.

3. Kastrup said that the situation in the GDR was exceptionally fragile. Only the consensus of the opposition parties held the country together. In talks with the Minister President of Baden-Württemberg on Friday, Modrow had told Späth that he could not exclude collapse and chaos within two weeks. The Soviet Union was not in a position to help. The GDR was entirely dependent upon the FRG. He asked for immediate help.

4. Kastrup said that the Federal Government had concluded that the development of a 'treaty community' (*Vertragsgemeinschaft*) after 18 March was too slow.[3] The term had been dropped from the Government's vocabulary. Instead Federal Government policy was now in two phases: up to 18 March and thereafter. In cabinet on Wednesday the Government would confirm the existence of a number of cabinet committees and sub-committees to deal with different aspects of the unification process. These had started work today (Kastrup will chair the first meeting of the foreign policy and security committee this afternoon).

5. Kastrup said that up to 18 March, the committees would be concerned with conceptual thinking and immediate help. The latter included devising the first steps towards economic and monetary union which would not wait until after an election. The Federal Government would put precise proposals to Modrow during his visit to Bonn on 13 February. The second phase would deal with, as he put it, 'the demand of the elected Government of the GDR to proceed towards unification' and its modalities. There would be negotiations soon after 18 March between the two on a treaty on German unity with the aim of presenting the basic elements at the CSCE summit. By then he expected the two governments would be acting in agreement on unity.

6. The Federal Government would be ready, throughout this process, to consult in an orderly way with the three Allies. The Federal Government worked on the assumption that formal consultation with the fourth power (i.e. Soviet Union) would be done by the still existing Government of the GDR. The Federal Government would reserve the right to talk to the Russians bilaterally as no doubt would the Western Allies. The Federal Government did not feel that the Bonn Group was an adequate mechanism for Western consultation in current conditions and that it should be at Political Director level.

[2] In a 'lengthy conversation' that morning (*Deutsche Einheit*, No. 162), Mr Weston had sounded Herr Hartmann of the Federal Chancellery as to the attitude of the FRG Government towards the idea that a conference of the Four Powers together with the two German states might accompany the unification process. Herr Hartmann had given his personal opinion that, while the Four Powers must be involved in a final resolution of the German question since that also included the problem of Berlin, the current process of *rapprochement* between the two German states must take place solely on the basis of their right to self-determination. He had informed Herr Kastrup briefly of the content of the conversation; the latter had affirmed that he would make the same point when he met Mr Weston later that day.

[3] See No. 120, note 1.

7. Kastrup continued that the Federal Government was 'adamant' that Four-Power discussions on Germany would not be acceptable. The Four Powers could not be seen to act over the heads of the German people to decide their fate. Genscher would say this to the Secretary of State tomorrow. The Federal Government did not think that it would be appropriate to have a formal peace treaty confirming German unity. 'Other ways and means' would have to be found, quite possibly the CSCE process.

8. On security aspects, Kastrup said that Baker had agreed with Genscher's conceptual approach as outlined in the latter's recent speech at Tutzing (my telno 126)[4] *viz* a special status for the GDR with no extension of the NATO area beyond the existing limits. Baker had explicitly agreed to the holding of a CSCE summit subject to his familiar three conditions with which the Federal Government were happy. On the third (this year's summit should be regarded as preparation for 1992) Genscher had said that he did not accept the terminology of preparation, but agreed with the idea of agreeing mandates for the 1992 summit. These in his view should cover security structures in Europe and the development of Mitterrand's idea of a European confederation. Genscher had told Baker that the Federal Government's contribution could be a statement on Germany's eastern border. This could take the form of any (or all) of the following: statement by the two governments in the framework of a treaty on unity, statement by both parliaments, or a statement alongside or within the framework of the CSCE summit.

9. In subsequent discussion, Kastrup made the following additional points. He confirmed that the draft treaty (para 5 above) would set out the structures of the transitional phase to unity which it would foreshadow and to which it would commit the two states. It would require ratification. Actual unification could come about either by accession of the eastern *Länder* or by a constitutional conference (Articles 23 or 146 of the Federal Constitution).[5] It was too early to decide.

10. In answer to John Weston's suggestion that the Four Powers might play their role via invitation from the two Germanys to consult (i.e. in effect the Four plus Two), Kastrup said that the Federal Government would be 'very reluctant' to contemplate a formal role for the Four Powers in the process of unification, even in such a manner, but would not rule it out completely. In a second run later over this ground, Kastrup seemed mollified at the thought of the German states taking the initiative and did not argue with the proposition that Four-Power endorsement could have its uses to Germany. But he remained very reserved on this.

11. Refusing to elaborate, Kastrup volunteered towards the end of discussion that there would be 'another important event' between now and the Open Skies meeting in Ottawa. (Comment: this could be a further major statement by Kohl (my telno 134)).[6]

Comment

12. The Federal Government now regard preventing the collapse of the GDR, which they think virtually imminent, as the top priority. Far reaching discussions, especially on the economic front, cannot wait for the GDR elections. It is Federal Government policy to proceed immediately to the integration of the two economies via economic and monetary union, even without a treaty basis. A conversation with

---

[4] Telegram No. 126 of 1 February; further detail in No. 127 of the same date (WRL 020/1). See also No. 111, note 3).

[5] For Article 23 see No. 120, note 3. Article 146 read: 'This Basic Law shall become invalid on the day when a constitution adopted in a free decision by the German people comes into force.'

[6] No. 122.

Hartmann (Chancellery) earlier in the day[7] suggested that while the idea of a treaty community had now been dropped, 'confederative structures' such as joint government and parliamentary bodies would still play a role in the process to unity.

13. Genscher is also proceeding full blast on the external front, evidently aiming to get the outline of a unification treaty into the international arena before the end of the year. Kastrup gave the impression that the Americans were on board for this as well as for the CSCE summit and presentation of German plans at it. It is not clear from Kastrup's description whether the proposed treaty would deal at all with security related aspects which he did not mention. This obviously needs probing: extreme German sensitivity to Four Power talks on German affairs came through clearly in this conversation and at the preceding one with Hartmann. The Federal Government accept the exercise of Four Power rights in connection with the final peace settlement. They are willing to consult the 3 Western Allies over matters governed by the Relations Convention but do not accept that 4 Power rights in relation to Germany as a whole should be exercised in connection with the process of self-determination which is for Germans alone. The Federal Government should be left under no illusion that, where necessary, the Four Powers will exercise their rights and responsibilities in the process towards unification. Equally we should make it clear that we are aware of German sensitivities, would consult and would be careful over public presentation.[8]

---

[7] See note 2.

[8] Mr Powell minuted on Mrs Thatcher's copy of this telegram: 'This *is it:* the Germans are going *full tilt* for reunification without waiting for *anyone*' (PREM: Internal Situation in East Germany).

No. 124

Sir A. Acland (Washington) to Mr Hurd[1]

No. 295 Telegraphic [PREM: Internal Situation in East Germany]

Confidential   WASHINGTON, *5 February 1990, 5.30 p.m.*

Genscher's Visit to Washington: 2 February

Summary

1. Genscher's visit further confirms US views that unification is on the fast track. Genscher repeats his formula for a unified Germany in NATO but argues that after March 18 the principal forum for handling international implications should be CSCE. Baker emphasises need for intermediate steps and other consultative fora, but agrees not to surface proposals publicly before the GDR elections. Genscher promotes ideas on US/EC similar to our own.

Detail

2. Genscher paid one of his characteristically rapid and semi-private visits to Washington on the evening of 2 February, confined on this occasion to a talk with Baker, preparatory to Baker's meetings with Shevardnadze on 7/8 February. Press coverage has been brief and officials have told us that Genscher sprang no surprises. But he clearly used the opportunity to promote his own thinking on the

---

[1] Repeated for information Immediate to Cabinet Office, Bonn, Paris, UKDEL NATO, Moscow, MODUK.

future role of NATO and the CSCE, on the lines of his earlier speech at Tutzing (Bonn telno 127).[2]

3. We spoke to Dobbins (principal DAS, European Bureau) before and after the visit. Dobbins said that beforehand, there was still some uncertainty within the administration as to whether unification was on a slow track (defined here as stages leading from treaty, to confederation to federation over a 2-3 year timescale) or the rapid conflation of these processes during the course of this year. Genscher's remarks had reinforced other indications that matters were now moving towards the fast track which the coalition leadership had previously been seeking to avoid.

4. On specifics, Dobbins said that although Genscher was concerned to indicate his reliability on the NATO issue, he was also clearly thinking that once 'unification negotiations' began with the GDR after 18 March, the CSCE framework would immediately become the main forum for discussing the international implications and for moving ahead in a stable way. In reply Baker had stressed that these developments could not be handled so simply or broadly and that other intermediate steps and consultative processes would also have to be involved. Genscher had evidently conceded that other fora should have a role to play, but was anxious that nothing should be said about them publicly until after 18 March for fear of counterproductive political repercussions in the FRG in the run-up to the election.

5. Genscher's concerns about consultative machinery were particularly acute in the Berlin Four Power context. That forum, he said, would simply not work. Baker had then floated the idea of widening this into a 'Four plus Two' grouping. Genscher expressed interest and said that he would think about it. But he repeated that it was essential that nothing should be said until after the GDR elections. (Dobbins said that Baker was now expected to cast a fly over Shevardnadze in this regard, if only to the effect that the Four-Power forum will not be acceptable to the Germans and that some other way will need to be found to handle these issues.)

6. Immediately after the meeting Genscher announced to a hastily assembled press conference that he and Baker were in 'full agreement' that reunification would not involve the extension of NATO to the east. Dobbins said that Baker had not in fact blessed Genscher's particular formula, even though it was the best available at present. The Administration had made its position clear in December with its four principles, and was now cautious about being too specific, lest it be interpreted by the German opposition as an imperial dictat or upset the Russians before Baker's talk with Shevardnadze.

7. Dobbins added that Genscher had also spoken in support of closer US/EC relations, very much along the same lines as those which you had outlined during your visit last week.

8. The German Ambassador is giving an EC briefing on the visit later today. I shall report further if there is anything to add.

---

[2] See No. 111, note 3.

No. 125

Sir E. Fergusson (Paris) to Mr Hurd[1]

No. 142 Telegraphic [*PREM: Internal Situation in East Germany*]

Secret   PARIS, *5 February 1990, 5.43 p.m.*

Personal for Ambassadors, Cabinet Office for Powell No 10

Washington Telno 276: Discussion of German Issues[2]

Summary
1. The French will wish to be involved in discussions. They are worried about German priorities. They too have a sense of urgency. Their thinking is likely to be close to ours on the principle of maintaining a strong Western Alliance (though with some specific differences), on Four Power responsibilities and on the development of the CSCE process: and (despite differences over EC integration) in opposing early accession of the GDR to the EC.
2. Need to keep discussions with Americans and French in parallel and coordinated, involving French at earliest possible stage. The French might accept early trilateral discussion. Your meeting with Dumas on 15 February an important opportunity to agree on the way forward.

Detail
3. You will know from recent direct contacts with the French and from reporting from here that the French are just as concerned as we or the Americans about the possible consequences of the German reunification process, if uncontrolled. They will wish to be fully involved in discussions between the major Allies. When I saw Dumas on 2 February he showed clearly that, given the difficulty of frank discussions with the Germans, some alternative to the Quadripartite forum was required.[3] This reinforced the case for closer Anglo-French bilateral contact. I judge, though with less than total confidence, that Dumas would accept a trilateral exercise with ourselves and the Americans, despite the danger of leakage, so long as this did not become formalised or carry too much of the burden. The French feel that their present bilateral contact with the Germans is less than satisfactory and worry at the way in which the Germans are giving priority to reunification over everything else (cf Dumas's remarks to me, para 2 of my telno 139).[3] Yet they will not stand in the way of a determined German drive towards reunification because they are more defeatist than we are about the chances of controlling the process.
4. The French, at least at senior official level, also share the US feeling of urgency. Dufourcq told the Minister on 2 February that he feared that we would be faced on or soon after 18 March with a clear expression of the German will for unity, and that unless the three Western Allies got to grips collectively with the issues soon, they would be overwhelmed by events.

---

[1] Repeated for information Immediate to Bonn, UKDEL NATO, Washington, Moscow, Cabinet Office.
[2] No. 117.
[3] No. 118.

5. In trying to predict how the French will react to the kind of proposals discussed in TUR, we need to be careful about coordination in the French machine. Mitterrand can make decisions, and voice opinions, which do not necessarily reflect the advice of his most senior advisers (some of whom can also be unaware of what their President has said privately to other leaders). Even Dumas is not in perfect contact with his own people in the *Quai*. The French Ministry of Defence tend to evolve their own line of thinking. The key players below Mitterrand are likely to be Dumas, Bianco and Vedrine (Bianco today has welcomed the chance of a meeting with Sir Robin Butler). Dufourcq, who will participate in meetings of Political Directors, also has influence with Dumas.

6. The French continue to hold to the principle of a strong alliance and a continued US presence in Europe, surprisingly strongly on the latter. They are worried about the future role of a united Germany within NATO. They are dismayed at the German willingness to talk and without thoroughly thinking this question through. I believe they will give serious consideration to the ideas sketched out in para 6(*a*) of TUR. Beyond that, they will continue to have doubts about strengthening the political role of NATO, especially while that concept lacks clarity. They accept, and have contributed to, a professional NATO approach to arms control, but they will need a good deal of persuading if NATO's role is to extend further. Whatever importance they attach to preserving the link with the United States, their instinct will be to look first for a more purely European way forward.

7. The French are strong on the need to maintain Four Power rights and responsibilities, though they are aware that there will be severe limits to Four Power leverage on the Germanies. They talk in general terms about the CSCE providing a framework, but they have so far been unspecific (Mitterrand's European confederation idea is particularly and deliberately vague): and they have shown a marked distaste for allowing others, through the CSCE, to detract from Four-Power responsibilities. When Momper, in talks in Paris on 1 February, proposed the idea of a CSCE sub-committee of the Four Powers, the two Germanies and perhaps Poland, the French side was quick to point out the impracticalities. They also spoke against the idea that the 35 might have a supervisory role over a German settlement, or do anything more than bless a settlement reached by other means.

8. The French, as you know, differ from us in their enthusiasm for accelerated EC integration as a means of locking the Germans into their European commitment. We must also be careful how we bring the French into close-ally discussions of the EC aspects of the German question. The French are keenly aware that there are some most important longer-term institutional issues relating to the Community's internal political balance which could be affected by short-term decisions on EC/GDR. They would take it badly if, for instance, we showed that we had had prior discussions with the Americans on EC/GDR relations. In this area at least, I hope that we could have a bilateral word with the French before it is raised on a trilateral basis. Védrine's visit to London on 7 February provides an early opportunity.

9. More generally, I see a need to proceed so far as possible in parallel with our discussions with the US and France at every stage, so that the one does not get out of line with the other. Your forthcoming meetings with Dumas will provide opportunities, especially that on 15 February when I hope you will be able to go deep into the substance of the issues and to endorse a timeframe and methods for

addressing them with the US and the Germans, separately or together. Seen from here, a trilateral discussion before long could be helpful.

10. FCO please advance to PUS, Weston (Political Director), Goulden and Kerr.

No. 126

Sir C. Mallaby (Bonn) to Mr Hurd[1]

No. 139 Telegraphic [PREM: Internal Situation in East Germany]

Secret   BONN, *5 February 1990, 6.13 p.m.*

Personal for Ambassadors

Washington Telno 276: German Issues[2]

1. I have reported in separate telegrams the increased feeling of fragility and rapid change on the German question.

2. On a number of the matters discussed in TUR the Federal Government has not yet made up its mind. If we move fast, the Western Allies can have real influence.

3. I support the idea of a move by the three Allies and the FRG about NATO (paragraph 6(*a*) of TUR). The feeling in the Federal Government is that while a united Germany should be in NATO, some special military status will be needed for the GDR. There are various ideas about what status, but the most common one appears to be that only German forces should be stationed in the GDR. I think that the idea of a transition period for Soviet troops to remain in the GDR ought to be saleable here. The aim, I take it, would be to make it easier for the Russians to be seen to agree to continued permanent stationing of American (and other) forces in West Germany.

4. West German resistance to meetings of the Four Powers remains strong. (My telno 137.)[3] I would not exclude the Germans eventually agreeing to a meeting of the Four Powers with the two Germanies. But it would be preferable not to include this element, which is so unpalatable to them, in any early package of Western proposals.

5. I would also favour a British move on the relationship between the GDR and the EC. The Germans have decided to integrate the two economies straight away (my telno 137). German economic and monetary union means that negotiations in Brussels on what in effect, will be a transitional phase to full membership by the eastern part of the united Germany will almost certainly need to begin soon. The UK could gain some kudos here by recognising this early on and helping fashion the appropriate procedures. This could also have for us the helpful byproduct of putting us in a good position to ensure that the ensuing playing field was level and that all Community firms enjoyed equal access to the GDR market.

---

[1] Repeated for information Immediate to Washington, UKDEL NATO, Paris, Moscow.
[2] No. 117.
[3] No. 123.

No. 127

Sir C. Mallaby (Bonn) to Mr Hurd[1]

No. 140 Telegraphic [WRL 020/1]

Confidential   BONN, *5 February 1990, 6.32 p.m.*

Personal for PS, PS/Mr Waldegrave, PS/PUS, Weston, Ratford, Head/WED.

A Sense of Coming Crisis in Germany?

1. My telegram No. 134 of this morning described, on the eve of your visit to Bonn, the greater feeling of fragility and rapid change on the German question that has formed here in recent days.[2] This telegram adds some more speculative points, to show the direction in which things might go.

2. The Federal Government is now mounting a major and long term economic rescue operation without waiting for the GDR elections. No-one in Bonn yet knows precisely what this involves, though it is clear that a large *de facto* transfer of sovereignty from the GDR to the FRG is likely to take place with economic and monetary union. Separate GDR institutions of government would continue to exist but would presumably execute policies formulated either in the joint confederative bodies, when these exist, or in the FRG. (The *Bundesbank* would resist having its powers put into commission.)

3. The aim is that early measures (Kohl hopes to have precise proposals to put to Modrow on 13 February) should have the effect of stabilising the GDR political scene in the short term and slowing down emigration to the FRG. The combination of money and visible political support might conceivably do the trick. But the task is so big (people here are only just beginning to realise how big and how difficult) and the route so uncharted that I foresee a number of possible developments:

—Even when reconstruction gets underway, people in the GDR may still be tempted to migrate rather than live through rising prices, probably falling standards of living—at least early on—and economic dislocation. Those who lose their jobs will tramp across. Even if social benefits here for resettlers are reduced, as seems likely, the rate of migration could continue to be high enough to have significant political repercussions in the FRG.

—The costs of reconstruction will become controversial. Even if West German firms provide most of the investment resources, the GDR is going to be like one vast region demanding a large scale regional policy. Striking the balance between GDR needs and FRG taxpayers pressure not to go wild with the public purse will not be easy.

—Continued emigration and/or the cost of unification could become such critical issues that the question might arise here of forming a grand coalition government consisting of CDU/CSU, FDP and SPD, to deal with the emergency. That might affect the date of the Federal elections, which might be delayed by agreement among the parties or just possibly brought forward as a prelude to creation of a grand coalition. A government in Bonn which included

---

[1] Repeated for information Immediate to Washington, Paris, UKDEL NATO, East Berlin, BMG Berlin.
[2] No. 122.

the SPD might be better able to deal with a government led by the East German SPD, if that is what emerges from the elections on 18 March.

4. Another speculative question, which has not yet surfaced in debate, is whether, were government to collapse completely in the GDR, the Federal Government would need to engineer an emergency coalition there by pressuring the embryo political parties. Such a government in the GDR would be a total satellite of the Federal Government. This last resort would add to the case for a grand coalition in Bonn.

5. If economic integration can be pulled off successfully on a rapid timetable, this is probably in our interests. It would consume a good deal of German energy, but it would also help stabilise the German political scene, allowing for a decoupling of the timescale for the realisation of economic unity from that for state unity, thus possibly enabling security and other issues to be tackled in a more measured way.

No. 128

Minute from Mr Gozney to Mr Synnott

[*WRL 020/1*]

Confidential and Personal   FCO, *6 February 1990*

Secretary of State's Talk with Dumas in Brussels

In the margins of the Foreign Affairs Council in Brussels on 5 February, and at M. Dumas' request, M. Dumas and the Secretary of State met for 5 or 10 minutes. I was the only other person present.

M. Dumas asked how the Secretary of State saw the latest developments in German unification, and their consequences.

The Secretary of State gave M. Dumas a copy of his speech for Bonn on 6 February. When he had drafted it, a week earlier, it had seemed quite adventurous, but no longer. He saw four areas of policy in which the German question needed to be considered. Only France and Britain were active in all four:

(*a*) NATO needed to reconcile continued German membership of the Alliance with legitimate Soviet anxieties. Politicians in the GDR, and some in the FRG, had been suggesting, or at least hinting at, neutrality as a consequence of unification. Their statements now seemed better and he had been encouraged recently by talks with Lambsdorff of the FDP and Momper, the SPD's governing Mayor of Berlin.

(*b*) In the Community we could not accept that the FRG would suddenly introduce 16 million new people. He thought that M. Delors was not yet focussing on the mechanics of the transition period of the GDR assimilating itself into the Community. M. Dumas asked who would meet the cost of the extra 16 million. If the FRG was so keen to have them in the Community, then the FRG would have to pay. He asked about British intentions towards reinforcement, i.e. further integration, of the Community. It was very important for Britain and France to understand each other on this point. Somehow the rest of the Community needed to attach the FRG firmly to the EC. The UK had a problem with the proposal of the others; did we have any alternative ideas? The

Secretary of State thought that there might be scope at the Dublin Summit for a declaration, directed to the Eastern Europeans, but also including a statement of what the Community stood for (and what not).

(*c*) The Secretary of State said that the third area of policy was that covering the Four Powers. M. Dumas said this was very difficult because the Germans were hyper-sensitive, and he had little to suggest. Perhaps the Four Powers could say that there was an issue here which was a relic of World War II and which needed to be 'liquidated', with the Germans' help.

(*d*) The fourth area was that of frontiers and the Helsinki Agreement. M. Dumas said this was an especially important area for the Poles, who were looking again to the Russians for reassurance. But the CSCE forum of 35 states might not be the right place to seek to fix the Oder Neisse border, because an exercise in that forum might also amount to recognition of the Baltic States' incorporation in the Soviet Union.

M. Dumas undertook to let the Secretary of State know of any new French statement on the German question; President Mitterrand was toying with the idea. M. Dumas thought that there was a period of about two months during which discussion would be useful, and when the results might influence events. Afterwards it would be too late.

R.H.T. GOZNEY

No. 129

Mr Hurd to Sir C. Mallaby (Bonn)[1]

No. 85 Telegraphic [WRL 020/1]

Confidential   FCO, *6 February 1990*

From Private Secretary

Secretary of State's call on Herr Genscher: German Unification

Summary

1. Genscher anxious about instability in GDR. Reiterates continued FRG commitment to NATO and European Community and to strengthening the CSCE. Accepts need for discussion of implications for NATO and the EC of German unification but does not favour too much planning in a vacuum, given dynamics of the situation and need to await outcome of GDR elections.

Detail

2. The Secretary of State had a 50 minute meeting with Genscher this afternoon. The principal topic was German unification. The Secretary of State asked whether the GDR would get through to the elections on 18 March. Genscher hoped so. It would not have been possible for them to last until 6 May. The decision to bring forward the elections had been the right one, though he had had doubts about it. Any stability in the GDR was not the result of the authority of the state or individual politicians but solely down to the reasonable behaviour of the people. The situation was very unstable and would become more so (a point on which

---

[1] Repeated for information Priority to Washington, Moscow, UKDEL NATO, Warsaw, East Berlin, BMG Berlin, Paris.

Genscher several times repeated his anxiety). The best test of stability would be the figure for departures. If public opinion in the GDR was disappointing [*sic*: ?disappointed], the figure would increase. There were exaggerated expectations but the new government could not bring an early substantial change to the way of life of its citizens. All it could offer was a new beginning. That was why the FRG needed to offer the GDR the political perspective of unity and the economic perspective of substantial help. Currency was the key: good money for good work. The prospect of unity was difficult but the GDR could not be treated like a foreign country. Its problems would be easier to solve if the people stayed there rather than migrated to the FRG. In this context Genscher commended Gorbachev's recent comments on unification which had been made in order to give hope to Germans in the GDR.

3. The Secretary of State said that we understood the dynamic facing the Germans but there were several areas where the Allies and partners needed to get into discussion, namely over NATO, Community membership, Four Power issues and the CSCE. What was the right timing for these discussions? They had to be tackled at some time—obviously showing sensitivity to the election process. The previous day in Brussels Genscher had spoken about private discussions with France and Britain.

4. Genscher said a number of issues (social, health, investment, monetary, commercial infrastructure) could all be handled below what he called the threshold of the Alliance and the Four Powers. The question was how all this was going to take place in relation to unification which was not a decision for the FRG alone but also for the GDR. He did not know how the democratic leadership of the GDR would define their decisions after the election. He thought they would want unity in the near future to help solve their difficult internal problems. In the meantime, the FRG could speak only for itself. The German Government wanted neither to extend nor to leave NATO. They wanted the two alliances to become integral parts of all-European structures. His own conversation the previous day with the Polish Foreign Minister had been revealing. The Pole had agreed with Genscher that the neutralisation of Germany would be wrong. If that had been the message coming from the British, French or some other NATO Foreign Minister that would have been understandable. Coming from the Poles it had special importance. The Federal German Government often said it did not want to isolate itself and it stood by that. They would promote the integration of the European Community and, in parallel, the development of the CSCE process. We would all live to see of what enormous importance the CSCE process was both substantially and to help save the face of the Soviet Union. The CSCE summit, devoted to the future of Europe, would be an important vehicle for helping the Soviet Union to come to terms with the erosion of the Warsaw Pact. Genscher added that when he talked about not wanting to extend NATO that applied to other states beside the GDR. The Russians must have some assurance that if, for example, the Polish Government left the Warsaw Pact one day, they would not join NATO the next.

5. The Secretary of State said that clearly there would need to be a NATO discussion about doctrine and posture but Genscher seemed to be saying that the discussion could not usefully begin yet. On the other hand, military commanders hated uncertainty. Genscher said he saw no reason why the military consequences of the reduced threat in Europe should not be discussed straight away. But the future political framework was subject to a dynamic process and we should not work on the basis of blueprints. Did that mean, the Secretary of State asked, letting

the position develop? Genscher assented, but added that we needed a certain number of fixed points. One of them was the EC. Another was NATO. The third was the CSCE process, which Germany wanted to promote. One could not be separated from the other.

6. The Secretary of State asked how Genscher assessed the Soviet position. They had moved on unification. How did they now stand on the presence of their troops in the GDR and US troops in the FRG? Was it still their ambition to see US troops withdraw from Germany or did they see them as part of the new order?

7. Genscher said that to answer the question one needed to understand the basis of the US and Soviet presence. In part, it was the consequence of World War II. But the Soviet Union was also geographically a part of Europe. They were there whether we liked it or not. In the case of the Americans we had created two instruments which included them in the European process: NATO and the CSCE Final Act. The Warsaw Pact meant that the Soviet Union could link to itself countries who were in the Russian front garden. For the US, the Alliance afforded them the opportunity to be present in Europe. Setting aside the questions of rights acquired as a result of World War II (arguments which did not impress anyone very much), the Western Alliance had a different quality from the Warsaw Pact as far as European stability was concerned. For that reason the Americans would continue to be present in Europe—and that would not be against the will of the Russians. Malta had shown the way the Soviet Union was moving. At the same time, Russia attached importance to keeping its forces in the GDR for psychological reasons but not necessarily at present levels. This question of the number of Soviet troops in the GDR did not necessarily have to do with German unity or GDR membership of the Warsaw Pact. But Genscher did now know what the position of the new GDR government would be.

8. The Secretary of State commented that the people of the GDR or a united Germany would probably want to have Soviet troops out. Genscher said that different countries were taking different positions. The Hungarians and the Czechs wanted the Russians out. The Poles wanted Russian numbers reduced: the Poles knew they were touching on a raw nerve. Discussion of these issues was too static in what was a dynamic situation. Quite soon a number of questions would present themselves in a different way. Of one point he was quite sure: the Germans should not be given a status which took them out of Europe. Genscher did not believe that what Modrow said about German neutrality reflected his master's voice. He could not imagine the Russians wanting a Germany outside European structures. That was the importance of the CSCE. It offered a partnership and a means of showing the Soviet Union that we did not want to shift the balance of power. Genscher then repeated his concern about the internal situation in the GDR. The Russians would not mobilise their forces. Nor could one say that the answer lay with Four-Power responsibilities. The most urgent task was to avoid chaos in the GDR. He agreed with the Secretary of State's comment that this was not a matter of sending in the troops or police to keep order but of persuading people to keep their suitcases in their rooms. That in turn meant practical help. It also meant making moves towards economic and monetary unity between the FRG and the GDR. That could not happen before the elections, but even talking about it had a positive effect. Productivity in the GDR had declined by at least 5 per cent. People in the GDR were doing more talking than working.

9. The Secretary of State said he had tried to show his understanding of these problems in his speech in Bonn that day. He was sure Genscher would keep us in

the picture hour by hour. We must begin to think about these questions even if we could not yet take discussions forward. He referred again to the EC aspects of the problem and the need to consider how to handle Russian pressure for Four-Power talks. Genscher referred to Baker's visit to Moscow. The real task was to open up perspectives which would appeal to the peaceful millions in Europe. We should do what we could to preserve stability.

No. 130

Letter from Mr Powell (No. 10) to Mr Wall

[*WRL 020/1*]

Secret and Personal   10 DOWNING STREET, *6 February 1990*

Dear Stephen,

German Issues

The Prime Minister has been following the telegrams about German reunification very closely. She has been, as you would expect, most concerned by the way in which the Germans are constantly forging ahead without any proper consultation with their Allies. She herself believes we *ought* to have a Four Power meeting, despite German sensitivities: but she recognises that the Americans and French are probably unlikely to agree to this. She would not object to a meeting of the Four Powers plus the two Germanies, but it would no doubt take some time to negotiate that. She has commented that, in the circumstances, a tripartite discussion with the French and Americans as proposed in Paris telegram number 142 would be very helpful and is urgent.[1] Among the matters it would consider are those mentioned in Bonn telegram number 139, namely a united Germany's relationship to NATO and the military status of the former GDR, as well as the handling of the GDR's relationship with the EC.[2] She thinks we ought to make an early proposal for such a meeting at ministerial level and would like the Foreign Secretary to consider this. It would still enable us to pursue the idea of a meeting with the Four plus the two Germanies subsequently.

I am copying this letter to Simon Webb (Ministry of Defence) and to Sir Robin Butler.

Yours sincerely,
C.D. POWELL

[1] No. 125.
[2] No. 126.

No. 131

Speech by Mr Hurd to the Konrad Adenauer Foundation[1]

BONN, *6 February 1990*

For the countries of eastern Europe, the phase of smashing statues and hunting secret policemen is almost over. They are engaged now in something more

[1] Extracts printed in the *Daily Telegraph*, 7 February 1990.

difficult, namely the building of free political institutions—and something more difficult still, the building of market economies. [. . .][2]

Since the future is unsettled, though no longer massively threatening, it would clearly be foolish to suppose that our defence and security problems have in some way been solved and that we need no longer to think seriously about them.

All history warns us against such empty optimism. We need now, in Europe and in the Atlantic Alliance, to undertake a rapid and rigorous review. We need to establish which of our present policies we need to retain on the grounds that they will be as important for our future as they have been for our past.

Then we need to identify those policies which can and should change in order to ensure that flexibility which will be needed for our future success.

As regards the European Community, I believe that it would be sensible to think in terms of keeping steady its present basic institutions and broadly the present membership, at least for the next three years.

We have a massive workload which will test those members of those institutions to the utmost, without adding the complication of a further major round of accession negotiations. We have to complete the last great reform agreed by the Community in the Single European Act, and thus open up to our peoples the practical realisation of a citizen's Europe.

We have to create and then constantly enrich the right framework for our relationships with the newly democratic countries of eastern Europe.

The British Government believes that this is best done on the basis of individually tailored association agreements, flexibly drafted, so that their content can increase as the country concerned travels further towards the kind of market economy which makes our association more fruitful and worth while. [. . .]

We need to continue and intensify the discussion within the Community about the best route towards economic and monetary union. [. . .]

The Treaty of Rome is a charter for economic liberalism, and so is the Single European Act. The 1992 drive for a genuine Single Market has wholehearted support in Britain. [. . .]

As regards Nato, how do we distinguish between what must be permanent and what can be adapted to new circumstances?

Adaptation includes a radical, but orderly, process of disarmament negotiations. President Bush's proposals have contributed to that. [. . .] I would regard the following as necessary continuing attributes to Nato—its present membership; the US strategic commitment; the presence of significant stationed forces, including US, Canadian and British on the continent of Europe; a sensible mix of nuclear and conventional forces; an integrated command. [. . .]

As far as one can see into the future, Nato offers us the promise of stability in a world which will certainly remain turbulent to the east and to the south of our part of Europe. [. . .]

Together with the European Community, Nato offers its European members the guarantee that its members will not in future revert to conflicting, and therefore self-defeating, national policies in the fields of defence and foreign policy. [. . .]

I also agree with the concept of a fuller political role for Nato and believe that this could be reconciled without too much difficulty with the growing importance of political co-operation within the Community of Twelve. [. . .]

---

[2] Ellipses in original.

It is in the context of these themes that Germany's friends and allies consider the prospect of German unification.

We in Britain do this in a spirit of constructive friendship. We have accepted, and indeed advocated, the right of self-determination by the German people for many years. We still do.

It is inconceivable to us that of all the people in Europe, only the German people should be denied that right. That is our commitment and our conviction.

The amazing success of the Federal Republic of Germany, not just in developing its economy but in founding and maintaining the institutions of a stable democracy, has naturally enough acted as a stimulus.

It is not surprising that so many East Germans have already voted with their feet or that others might feel inclined, once they have the chance, to vote in the ballot box for a united Germany. That is a matter for them.

We, with the other friends and allies of Germany, will work with full energy and goodwill to fit their decision into the framework of a stable and harmonious Europe.

If this path is to be trodden, the first need is obviously an undisputed expression of the wish of the peoples of the FRG and the GDR: an act of self-determination.

I recently visited the GDR and realised how fragile is its stability as it seeks to move towards free elections on March 18.

It seems to me highly desirable for the stability of Europe that these elections should take place in a fair and orderly way, under a process which gives equal access to all contenders and which is sustained as widely as possible by the emerging political groups and parties within the country.

I pay tribute to the courageous men and women in the GDR who risked their freedom to bring democracy to their fellow countrymen. I also pay tribute to all those in the Federal Republic without whose political and economic support the cause of freedom could so easily have foundered.

For all the uncertainties, the prospect before you is a bright one and we in Britain share your excitement as the Berlin Wall comes down and the old, divisive order is swept away.

In the next stage, a number of highly practical problems would arise in which, as the Federal Chancellor has often, pointed out, Germany's friends and neighbours would be intimately involved.

The conclusions of the European Council at Strasbourg last December, endorsed the following week by the Nato Council, set out the context, and we stand clearly by these words:

We seek the strengthening of the state of peace in Europe in which the German people will regain its unity through free self-determination.

This process should take place peacefully and democratically, in full respect of the relevant agreements and treaties and of all the principles defined by the Helsinki Final Act, in a context of dialogue and East-West co-operation. It also has to be placed in the perspective of European integration.

In the perspective of integration in the European Community, for example, there obviously could be no place for a command economy.

The concepts under which the GDR economy is at present run, and in particular its total dependence on subsidies and state aids, would need to be radically changed. So a period of transition would be required.

As regards Nato, it seems to me that none of us has yet begun to think with any rigour of the consequences for the Alliance of German unification, if that was the Germans' choice.

When I wrote these words a few days ago, they were true. But since then a number of interesting and constructive suggestions have been made.

If there is truth in what I have sketched above as the essential elements of Nato, then among those elements German membership will continue to be a crucial element in the security of us all.

We must together find some way of reconciling German membership of Nato with the persisting anxieties of the Soviet Union, however unrealistic we may believe these anxieties to be in view of the proven record of Nato as a defensive alliance and the proven democratic record of the Federal Republic.

These anxieties also, of course, cover the question of the eastern frontiers of Germany. I welcome the growing recognition here in the Federal Republic of the need to use our imagination and energy in devising the best answer to this particular aspect of the problem. We shall be glad to join in this work.

These considerations are part of the reality of the situation. I believe that reasonable periods of transition would enable us to find tenable answers to the questions which will be posed if a decision in principle is taken by the inhabitants of the FRG and GDR.

The Germans, for their part, would need time to think through and resolve the many questions involved in amalgamating the two countries.

Certainly the friends and allies of Germany would have no wish to obstruct the process, and have every sympathy with the underlying aspiration.

Equally, it would not be in the interests of the German people to achieve unification in circumstances which aroused anxieties or sent nerves jangling throughout Europe. Such reconciliation would be a test of statesmanship, but not a test which should be beyond our wits to pass.

I can readily envisage that, at the end of an orderly transition, German unity and a new stable architecture in Europe should come about together.

No. 132

Mr Eyers (East Berlin) to Mr Hurd[1]

No. 109 Telegraphic [WRE 014/1]

Confidential   EAST BERLIN, *7 February 1990, 9.25 a.m.*

Bonn Telno 137 to FCO: The GDR—Internal Situation[2]

Summary
1. Could the GDR collapse into chaos within the next two weeks? Introduction of the DM could stave it off, but then the West Germans would run the country.

---

[1] Repeated for information Priority to Bonn, BMG Berlin; Routine to Paris, Moscow, Washington, UKDEL NATO, UKREP Brussels, Actor, CICC(G); Saving to East European Posts, UKDEL Strasbourg, BRIXMIS, Peking.
[2] No. 123.

Detail

2. I propose at the end of this week to set the scene for Modrow's visit to Bonn on 13 February but it seems desirable to analyse now the political and economic realities underlying Modrow's assertion (para 3 of TUR) that he could not exclude collapse within 2 weeks.

3. Under the pressure exerted by West German parties and the 18 March election deadline, political formations which stand a chance of attracting substantial support are beginning to take shape. The SPD, which enjoys not only West German assistance but also the prestige of association with people like Brandt, Schmidt, Vogel, Rau, and Bahr, continues to look likely to emerge as the strongest party on 18 March. It is attracting former members of the SED—the change of name to PDS is not preventing disintegration and Modrow has distanced himself from his party. A centre right grouping (Alliance for Germany) based on the CDU (East) and Democratic Awakening (DA) has been established under pressure from the Western CDU. Kohl (notwithstanding the vote at the Round Table on 5 February against West German politicians participating in the GDR election) intends to speak at their rallies. And FDP has been formed in the liberal interest, because the LDPD (chairman Gerlach is acting Head of State) is compromised by past association with the SED. Its members appear to be transferring in large numbers to the FDP. Thus prospects of the voters being offered a choice of credible political forces on 18 March are improving. In this sense the country is no nearer to collapse than it was at the beginning of the year.

4. The economic story is altogether different. Although the exodus has lost the visible drama of the autumn trains and treks through Czechoslovakia and Hungary, the loss each day of about 2,000 young people (mostly now under 30) is disastrous. Industrial production is falling. Wild-cat strikes are increasing and the social services [*sic*] mild winter has relieved Modrow of the need to call on the West Germans to provide emergency power supplies, but in all other respects the economy is deteriorating fast. There is moreover a crisis of disappointed expectations. There have been repeated promises of massive West German assistance, but apart from emergency help for the medical services, virtually nothing has happened on the ground. Modrow and his deputy, Frau Luft (on whom he relies for economic advice) seem to have decided that only the dramatic signal of [a] West German rescue operation will stop the exodus and provide some prospect of staving off disintegration. The need for such a signal which would have immediate impact may have impelled Modrow to paint a bleaker picture of prospects to Späth (and Kohl in Davos) than the situation objectively warrants, but not much.[3]

5. At the meeting of the Round Table on 5 February Frau Luft (who has hitherto stood for minority share holding for 'foreign' partners in joint ventures, public ownership of heavy industry and preserving the value of GDR mark savings) out-lined the advantages of immediate introduction of the DM as legal tender. She said that the Government was not planning a currency reform in the sense of devaluing savings, but the GDR was unable to stick to this plan on the basis of its own financial resources. Early agreement with the Federal Republic on a currency union was needed. Introducing the DM as legal tender would have the advantages of eliminating shortages, improving travel possibilities and forcing enterprises to work under the permanent pressure of the world market. There would also be

---

[3] The World Economic Forum meets annually in Davos in late January.

disadvantages which could not be foreseen precisely. Productivity and wages would not necessarily rise. Nor would the exodus necessarily slow down. But introduction of the DM would definitely involve the closure of many factories and unemployment. Savings would be threatened. Real estate and other assets would have to be revalued. The *Bundesbank* would determine currency policy, the GDR would surrender its sovereignty in this area. Frau Luft said that the political implications and social consequences would be so great that this issue should be decided by a referendum. Meanwhile the *Bundesbank* should support GDR industry by financing partial convertibility of the GDR mark at 1:1 or 1:2. The Federal Government for its part should make an immediate gift of between DM10b and DM15b and agree to economic union.

6. In the light of these remarks and of Modrow's position (as reported in TUR) I conclude that he and Frau Luft have abandoned their attempt to stabilise the economy by introducing their own reform, supported by West Germany. Instead they are asking the Federal Government, the *Bundesbank* and West German industrialists to come to their rescue at once. The only measure which could presumably be introduced very quickly, providing a political and economic signal that unification is just around the corner, is the substitution of the DM for the (East) mark. Modrow's visit on 13 February could be well timed for an announcement.

Comment

7. In the course of my initial call on 5 February on State Secretary Bertele, Head of the FRG Permanent Representation, he said that he had recommended some time ago introduction of the DM as the only measure that would give people a perspective for the future and slow down the exodus (fuller account by teleletter to FCO, Bonn and BMG).[4] The longer this step was delayed, the greater the cost would be. That he was prepared to talk frankly about it (my staff who have close contacts with his mission had not previously heard of this recommendation) suggests that this move may now be imminent. It is not for me to comment on the implications for West Germany. Here it would involve rough justice, as Bertele recognised, especially to small savers. It would place the GDR administrative machine at the disposal of West German authorities who would then be running the country. Unification would have begun.

---

[4] Not printed.

No. 133

Letter from Mr Wall to Mr Powell (No. 10)

[*WRL 020/1*]

Secret and Personal   FCO, *7 February 1990*

Dear Charles,

Foreign Secretary's Call on Chancellor Kohl: 6 February

Thank you for your letter of 4 February.[1] The Foreign Secretary had an hour and 10 minutes with Chancellor Kohl in Bonn yesterday, with only an interpreter present.

The Foreign Secretary said that the Prime Minister had asked him to say that she very much agreed with what Chancellor Kohl had said about NATO. Continued German membership was crucial. On the party front, the Prime Minister also regarded the success of the CDU as crucial. She hoped Chancellor Kohl would let her know if there was any way in which we could help.

Chancellor Kohl said he was grateful. He had nothing personal against the Prime Minister, but was not happy at the state of our official relations. He cited the Prime Minister's *Wall Street Journal* interview.[2] He had known the Prime Minister for 15 years. How could he be accused of nationalism? He then went on to give a long account of his family history, his credentials as an internationalist and his views on the German question. He dwelt on the risks of disintegration in the GDR and the continuing catastrophic flow of emigrants to the West. This was on very much the same lines as Herr Genscher's conversation with the Foreign Secretary earlier in the afternoon (see telegram enclosed).[3] Chancellor Kohl said that the Federal Government had to respond to the deteriorating situation in the GDR. The cabinet would agree on 7 February on proposals for discussion of an economic and monetary union with the GDR designed to make the GDR currency stable.

The Foreign Secretary said that he too would speak frankly. The Prime Minister's anxiety was based on a realistic acknowledgement of Germany's great economic strength and the fear that other German leaders at some point in the future might use that strength to establish a new hegemony. The Prime Minister of course understood that events had moved fast. She was therefore concentrating on those areas where unification would require a transitional period. She had mentioned areas of which the Chancellor himself had spoken.

The Foreign Secretary mentioned Kohl's 10-point plan to which the Chancellor had earlier alluded. The surprise involved had been disconcerting. The fewer such surprises the better. Chancellor Kohl said he took the point (though in any competition with the Prime Minister on Alliance consultation he would win). The speech had been made in very difficult circumstances when Krenz was in office, and Kohl had had to speak to Gorbachev (to whom he talked quite often on the

---

[1] No. 121.
[2] See No. 108, note 4.
[3] No. 129.

telephone) about Krenz's inadequacy. He had not even felt able to consult his coalition partners. He emphasised his wish to work closely with us.

Chancellor Kohl said that, as he had told the Japanese Prime Minister, the 1990s were going to be the decade of Europe. He referred to a visit he had once made to Britain where, with a couple of hours to spare, he had been to see Churchill's grave. Later, he had had a long talk with the Prime Minister about Churchill at which he had said: 'The difference between you and me, Margaret, is that you are Churchill before the Zurich speech and I am Churchill after it.' It was preposterous to suppose that Europe could be made without Britain. He spoke appreciatively of his last meeting with Sir C. Mallaby but said that he also needed a political point of contact. He suggested that this might be the Foreign Secretary. The Foreign Secretary said, at the end of the meeting, that he would be happy to come for a quiet talk at any time it could be useful.[4]

Chancellor Kohl went into something of a ramble about the issue of a peace treaty. He was not prepared to have a conference of all the people who had ever declared war on Germany between 1939 and 1945—people like the Uruguayans who had come in 1944 and would no doubt be seeking reparations (which Germany had already made in large measure). At the right time there should be a meeting of the Four Powers and the Poles formally to establish the peace.

On the internal political scene, Chancellor Kohl said that the CDU should be in a strong position at the elections with the economy buoyant and unemployment less serious than the figures implied, because of the black market. He hoped they were past the worst with the farmers, though cereal growers were still indignant. The coal miners were a difficulty because his predecessors had neglected the necessary decisions on run-down. Law and order was a real problem with the kind of people who were tempted to vote for the Republicans. There were lots of Italian, Chinese and other foreign restaurants in his own *Land* (Rhineland-Palatinate). With them came drug money, protection money and other things which the Germans were not used to and of which their police had no experience. That was why he had proposed a European FBI. But Mitterrand had effectively squashed the idea. Europe had to get its act together on policing. The real uncertainty in the FRG election was the unification issue. He did not know how this might affect what would otherwise be a strong CDU position.

We understand that Chancellor Kohl may be visiting Moscow very soon and, though he did not mention it himself, I understand he will be going to Camp David at the end of the month. It seems likely that, if he follows normal form, he will have a meeting with President Mitterrand at about the same time. The Foreign Secretary thinks that the Prime Minister might want to consider your saying to Teltschik later this week that she would welcome a chance to talk to Kohl before they meet in Cambridge at the end of March.

The Foreign Secretary has seen on his return from Bonn your letter of 6 February.[5] It is pretty clear from his visit that Genscher and Kohl are not now pushing but pulling. They are genuinely anxious about the possible collapse of the GDR into chaos and the emigration which would follow. They think of little else. They will go for a currency union and maximum FRG party involvement in the GDR election campaign to shore things up until 18 March. After that (and only after that) will they discuss the four transitions (NATO, EC, Four Power,

---

[4] Mr Powell minuted on his copy of this letter: 'I don't think this is very satisfactory. You are in charge and Kohl must deal with you.' Mrs Thatcher minuted: '*No*'.

[5] No. 130.

frontiers/CSCE) with us all. They hope (and the SPD so far agree) to keep the NATO issue out of the FRG election campaign. Their public utterances on NATO are now better, ditto on frontiers. There is no disposition to alarm the Russians. They have not turned their minds to the EC complications.

The Americans believe we are being unduly alarmist. The French sympathise with our worries but Dumas, in conversation with Mr Hurd on Monday, had no answer to these except one we can't accept, namely more EC institutional integration.

The Foreign Secretary will seek opportunities at Ottawa next week to discuss with Baker and Dumas the Prime Minister's first subject (NATO and the military status of the former GDR in a united Germany). We also have a Quad Meeting of Foreign Ministers on 13 February which will be important. On 15 February, he will discuss with Dumas her second subject, i.e. EC. The Foreign Secretary is commissioning papers with our own ideas on both and will send these to the Prime Minister.[6]

Yours,
J.S. WALL

[6] Mr Powell minuted on his copy of this letter: 'Prime Minister. *Not at all satisfactory or reassuring*. We are just *told* to *leave it all* to the *Germans*, even whether there should be a *peace* treaty. I do *not* think you can *accept that the Foreign Secretary* can be an alternative political contact for Kohl, in place of you.' Mrs Thatcher minuted: 'F[oreign and] C[ommonwealth] S[ecretary] *can't* be an alternative contact' (PREM: Anglo-German Relations).

No. 134

Letter from Mr Powell (No. 10) to Mr Wall

[*WRL 020/1*]

Secret and Personal   10 DOWNING STREET, *8 February 1990*

Dear Mr Wall,

Germany

The Prime Minister and the Foreign Secretary had a further talk this evening about German reunification. The Prime Minister stressed the very great importance which she attached to organising collective discussion of the implications of reunification. She thought the most practicable form was probably the Berlin Four plus the two Germanies. She knew that the West German Government were not keen on this. But we should try to secure American and French acquiescence and then press them hard. The ideal would be to have some sort of initial meeting in the margins of the Open Skies Conference in Ottawa. Failing that she thought we should at least try to have a tripartite meeting with the French and Americans. The Foreign Secretary emphasised the difficulties of securing American acquiescence: the whole emphasis of American policy was to help get Chancellor Kohl re-elected. The Prime Minister said that we must find a way of avoiding the unification becoming a *fait accompli*, before we had worked out the implications.

The Foreign Secretary said that he would be letting the Prime Minister have tomorrow a paper on the implications of German unification for NATO.[1] The Prime Minister said that she would look at this on Sunday and we would telegraph any comments to the Foreign Secretary in Ottawa.

The Prime Minister said that she hoped we were also getting on with work on the implications of reunification for the European Community. We must avoid the situation in which the EC as a whole took on massive new financial obligations, or there was a substantial increase in the United Kingdom's net contribution.

Looking to the longer term, the Prime Minister and the Foreign Secretary saw the CSCE as a potential framework within which to dilute German influence in Europe. No single West European country was big enough to balance Germany and we would in the long run need to rely on Russian influence to do so. But this was a distant prospect.

The Prime Minister commented that she was in principle ready to meet Chancellor Kohl in the next few weeks, either in Bonn or London, but doubted whether he would relish a meeting in the light of his comments to the Foreign Secretary. Her priority remained to organise a collective discussion of the Berlin Four with the two Germanies.

Yours sincerely,
Elizabeth Lambert
pp CHARLES POWELL

Dictated by Mr. Powell and signed in his absence.

[1] No. 139.

No. 135

Minute from Mr Synnott to Mr Ramsden

[*WRL 020/1/90*]

FCO, *8 February 1990*

Secretary of State's Speech: German Reactions

1. The Minister Counsellor at the FRG Embassy telephoned me today, ostensibly with thanks for a copy of the Secretary of State's speech, which I had sent him.[1] He offered his opinion on it 'as a friend'.

2. Klaiber said that, while it contained some positive aspects, he had frankly been disappointed by it and had hoped for something more, especially since it had been trailed as a development of the British position. Second, he said, he was surprised that the important German Question had been addressed at the end of the speech when it was surely a subject in the forefront of everyone's minds.

3. I responded appropriately, commenting that such a speech had to be designed for a wider audience than the country in which it was delivered and on the desirability that the German Question should be put in a broad perspective.

[1] No. 131.

4. Bonn telno 156 records other comment about the speech and, particularly, about the Prime Minister's statement in the House of Commons.[2]

H.N.H. SYNNOTT

[2] On 6 February Mrs Thatcher had stated, *inter alia*, 'I agree with my hon. Friend [Mr Michael Latham MP] that the German people are likely to vote for unification. I agree with him, too, that it is a matter not only for the German people but for other countries which will be seriously affected by it. Germany has also entered into obligations under the NATO Alliance—we must consider its effect on that—the Helsinki accord which 35 nations signed, and the four-power agreement on Berlin. We must agree these things. It seems that a lengthy transition period is needed so that they can all be properly worked out and so that the unification of Germany gives rise not to more worries but to greater security. We must keep up the level of our defence, both conventional and nuclear, and not make changes until they are agreed with NATO or through the CFE talks.' *Parl. Debs., 5th ser., H. of C.*, vol. 166, cols. 757-8. Telegram No. 156 of 8 February reported negative comment on the Prime Minister's statement in the tabloid *Bild*, while *Die Welt* had 'argue[d] that the extent to which the UK as a whole is behind the game is revealed by the positive evaluation in the British press of the Secretary of State's speech in Bonn' (WRL 020/1). In a minute of 9 February, Sir P. Wright recorded a conversation in which he had told Dr Sudhoff, his German opposite number, that 'we had been rather disappointed to note the somewhat downbeat coverage which the Secretary of State's speech at the Konrad Adenauer Stiftung had received from the German press. I said that I knew that there was an impression in Germany that the British were taking an obstructive and blocking position on the question of unification, and that the Foreign Secretary had gone out of his way to correct that misapprehension in his speech . . . I nevertheless read out to him verbatim the passage saying that we were following these events "in a spirit of constructive friendship"; and that we had "accepted, and indeed advocated, the right of self-determination by the German people", and that we still did' (WRL 020/1). See also No. 144, note 1.

No. 136

Minute from Mr Powell (No. 10) to Mrs Thatcher

[*PREM: Internal Situation in East Germany*]

Secret and Personal   10 DOWNING STREET, *9 February 1990*

Germany: Meeting with Herr Teltschik

I spent this morning in Bonn talking to Herr Teltschik about German unification.

There is a heady *atmosphere* in Bonn. Great events are in the air, and for the first time in 45 years Germany is out in front. For the Germans, this is the breakthrough. After decades of sober and cautious diplomacy, and adjusting themselves to fit in with decisions taken by others, they are in the driving seat and Toad is at the wheel.[1] The exhilaration is unmistakeable. This time they are going to take the decisions and others can tag along. The Allies must of course be involved but not allowed to call the tune. The Germans' moment has come: they are going to settle their destiny.[2]

The other point that strikes you is how much unification is a *party political issue*. Kohl feels he has pulled off a masterstroke by putting himself at the head of the movement for unification. It's not so much that he's grabbed the leadership from the opposition but from Genscher and the FDP. There is a lot of crowing

[1] The reference is to Kenneth Grahame's *The Wind in the Willows* (1908).
[2] Mrs Thatcher noted: '*Nationalism*, n'est-ce pas?'

about how Kohl outflanked Genscher with his 10-points. Having taken the lead, Kohl is now under enormous pressure to keep it, by constantly pressing ahead with unification and avoiding any hold-up or delay. The politics of it mean that he cannot falter or stop if he is going to win his election in December.

These two reasons do much to explain—but not justify—Kohl's annoyance with our approach, which is perceived as one of trying to hold back a tidal wave which Kohl believes will catapult him to be first Chancellor of a newly united Germany, which will in turn be a global power.[3]

I set out to explain to Teltschik *why the gathering pace of unification worried us*. There were deep-seated and entirely natural fears in Britain and no doubt other European countries about the consequences of a united Germany. First that it might lead us once again to conflict and destruction. This was not of course an immediate worry, but an unease about the future, based on our experience twice this century. Second there was concern about the economic might of a united Germany and how it could come to dominate Europe. Third—and more urgent— there was a strong feeling that the Germans were being egotistical and putting their interest in unification ahead of the wider interest shared by all of us in stability and security in Europe. While we recognised that German unification was legitimate and unstoppable, we wanted it to be an orderly process. That meant consultation about the consequences of unification for NATO, the EC, Four-Power rights and the Helsinki process: and proceeding on the basis of agreed positions.

I continued that we had all played our part in defending Germany for the last forty years: we could not and would not be sidelined now. Instead of trying to evade proper consultation, either in the (western) quadripartite framework or with the Four Powers, Germany should be using these institutions to the full. How the rest of us viewed Germany once it was united, would be much affected by the manner in which unification came about. It would be a great mistake to believe that Britain (or indeed the other Allies) were just obstacles which Germany could navigate around. If they were not prepared to consult collectively with us, then we would have to talk to the others, including the Russians, without the Germans. It would be a great pity if we had to put aside the co-operative tradition of the last 40 years and return to the balance of power diplomacy of an earlier age.

I concluded that, as a friend, I saw a real risk that Germany was developing tunnel vision about unification, and losing sight of its wider interests and obligations. This should be a moment of hope and of triumph for the West as a whole. It would be a tragedy if it turned into a parting of the ways. No-one wanted that: but if the Germans did not show more sensitivity and consideration, there was a real risk that this would be the direction in which we would move.

Teltschik's reply can be broken down into a number of points:

—we were wrong to believe that the Federal Republic was pushing recklessly ahead. They were simply reacting to an *ever-worsening crisis in East Germany*. We seemed to have no idea of how dramatic the crisis there was. Total economic and political collapse could come at any minute. Modrow and his government could take decisions, but they operated in a vacuum and had no idea whether their decisions would be carried out. Industry was crumbling. The armed forces were just signing off and going home. The police force was beginning to disintegrate. Herr Pöhl had just been to East Berlin and was appalled at the state of the East German economy: it could collapse completely

---

[3] Mrs Thatcher noted: 'Nationalism with a *vengeance*.'

at any moment. In the meantime the exodus was continuing, indeed gathering pace. The main purpose of Kohl's visit to Moscow would be to convince Gorbachev of the gravity of the situation. (Comment: whether or not this is exaggerated, there is no doubt that the Germans have convinced themselves of it, and it has become the justification for their policies.)

—the Germans would much prefer to move forward step by step, as set out in Kohl's ten points. But events were constantly moving ahead of them. Three days ago, a currency union had just been one of several options to be studied: forty-eight hours later it was a firm proposal adopted by the German Cabinet.[4] Implementing it would be horrendously expensive; no government in its senses would welcome added expenditure on that scale in an election year. But there was no alternative. Within a week, Herr Pöhl would be running the East German economy.

—More generally, no-one had any idea what would happen after the election of 18 March in the GDR. It was perfectly possible that the new Parliament would meet and, rather than elect a government, simply vote to join the FRG immediately under Article 23 of the FRG constitution. The German government would be unable to refuse. Alternatively, the GDR Parliament might propose the establishment of a constituent Assembly to adopt a new constitution for Germany as a whole, with elections throughout a united Germany early next year. No-one could control what might happen. It was difficult to consult in a situation of incipient crisis. The Federal Government was fully occupied with preparing to cope with the imminent breakdown of the GDR.

—Kohl was not averse to a *meeting of the Four-Powers plus the two Germanies*. But it should not be held yet. Involving the Russians now would simply give them leverage and encourage them to try to thwart unification or impose unacceptable conditions—e.g. neutralisation—of Germany. The very speed of developments was keeping the Russians off balance and this was an advantage.

—there was another reason to avoid such a meeting now: it would seem to many people as an attempt by the Four Powers to interfere with the exercise of Germany's right to self-determination. If we persisted, people might become anti the West.

—but he agreed on the need to avoid mistrust. The Quadripartite meetings of Foreign Ministers and Political Directors were intended to achieve this. He did not rule out other formats: for instance we should all keep in touch bilaterally, and advisers to the four Heads of Government could meet. On the question of involving the Russians, much would depend on the outcome of Kohl's meeting with Gorbachev. He would report the Prime Minister's strong views on the need for an early meeting of the Four plus the two Germanies to Chancellor Kohl, but he was dubious whether he would agree to any meeting before the elections in the GDR.

We then dealt with a number of *separate aspects*.

Teltschik said that the Germans simply did not know what to expect from the *meeting with Gorbachev*. The Chancellor regarded it as probably the most important meeting he had ever attended. But there were conflicting signals on the Russian side. Some were taking a hard line, saying that if the Germans went ahead with elections to the *Bundestag* from Berlin, the Russians would start to interfere

---

[4] Mrs Thatcher noted: '*No* study of its implications or the possible effect on others.'

with the access routes to Berlin. Others were suggesting that Gorbachev would set out, or at least hint at, the price that Germany would have to pay for unification, in terms of its future status. A neutral Germany might be suggested: but a more subtle approach, and one which caused real problems on the German side, would be to propose the removal of all nuclear weapons. This would certainly be exploited by Genscher. But Teltschik's own view [was] that Gorbachev would not be very specific: rather he would try to use the meeting—which had been requested by the Germans—to win time.

On the question of the relationship of a *united Germany to NATO*, Teltschik said there was no reason at all to doubt Kohl's determination to keep Germany in NATO. He had been the first to reject neutralisation. But Russian interests would have to be handled very carefully. It must not appear that they had lost the war 45 years after it had ended. It might be necessary to accept the continued presence of Soviet troops in the former GDR, at least for a transitional period, for instance until implementation of reductions agreed in the CFE negotiations was complete. Thereafter it would not be feasible to have no troops in the former GDR. There might have to be limits on the number or the nature of the German or other forces permitted there. One possibility would be to have multi-national forces.

I asked how Teltschik saw the role of the *Helsinki process* in all this. We were disturbed by some of Genscher's references to it, which seemed to imply that it could somehow replace NATO. Teltschik said that Kohl at least did not see the CSCE as a substitute for NATO. But it might be useful to create CSCE institutions which would serve the security interests of Europe as a whole, for instance a body to monitor and verify force reductions.

Teltschik was uncomfortable when pressed on the presence of *nuclear weapons* in a united Germany. It seemed most unlikely that the Congress would ever vote funds for the modernisation of LANCE.[5] If that was the case, then Kohl would much prefer a decision not to go ahead with FOTL[4] to be taken this year, so the issue could not be used against him in the election campaign. It was clear that, deprived of the lead in German unification, Genscher was determined to make disarmament the major theme of the election campaign. I reminded him that the NATO Summit had deliberately postponed this issue to the far side of the German elections. But it was clear that Teltschik was saying that the Germans would nonetheless revive it this year. Personally he hoped there could be agreement to keep other American nuclear weapons in Germany. But he did not want to mislead! If the Russians made this a major issue, he doubted whether any German government could resist, especially if it was made the price of unification. This is a most worrying signal.

Teltschik volunteered that he assumed we would be reducing *British Forces in Germany*. I did not pursue this.

It was impossible to get any clear answer as to how the Germans envisage completing the international formalities surrounding unification. Teltschik was clear that there should not be a *peace Treaty* as such: it would be humiliating to Germany. Equally he did not seem to regard the proposed CSCE Summit as the right forum, fearing that the Russians intended to use it to confirm the inner-German border. He seemed rather to be thinking of some sort of meeting and agreement between the Four Powers and Germany, which would formalise the

[5] See No. 1, note 6.

decease of Four Power rights. The Oder-Neisse line as Germany's eastern frontier was not in question.

Finally, Teltschik seemed to have given no thought at all to the *EC aspects* (but then he generally does not deal with the EC). He assumed there would be some sort of transitional arrangement with the EC following German unification.

We touched briefly on a number of other points:

(1) *CFE.* Teltschik seemed to think that the UK might be difficult about concluding an agreement this year. I disabused him of this. It was clear that EAGLEBURGER and GATES had given Kohl a graphic account of their meeting with you, but had not tried to pin down Kohl on American nuclear weapons in Germany (so much for their promises).[6]

(2) *EFA.*[7] Teltschik thinks that the Germans will agree to the project going into the development phase. It would simply be too expensive to cancel.

(3) *South Africa.* Kohl has just sent a friendly and encouraging message to De Klerk.

I *concluded* by stressing once more the need for consultation. You would be willing to see Kohl earlier than the planned Anglo-German summit at the end of March if he would find that useful. But the Germans could not expect us to moderate our insistence on proper consultation, to ensure that the consequences of unification were dealt with in an orderly manner. Teltschik said that the Germans wanted to co-operate and he would report your views to the Chancellor. But with events moving so fast, it was very difficult to reach conclusions on issues such as the relationship of a united Germany to NATO and the EC. I pointed out that we thought these issues should take precedence: we needed to know what was intended on NATO, Helsinki, Four Power rights and the EC before we went any further on unification. But I don't think the point is registering: unification is the only subject which matters. How that is handled will determine the electoral fortunes of all the principal players and the external aspects are a distraction.[8]

C.D. POWELL

[6] See No. 114, note 2.

[7] The European Fighter Aircraft project was begun by the UK, France, West Germany, Italy and Spain in 1983. France withdrew in 1985. The Eurofighter (now named the Typhoon) went into production in 1998 and began to enter into service in European air forces in 2003.

[8] Mrs Thatcher minuted: 'We are right once again and Kohl *resents* that his tactics have been rumbled.'

No. 137

Memorandum by the Policy Planning Staff[1]

[*RS 021/216*]

Confidential   FCO, *February 1990*

FORMATION OF A SIX POWER FORUM

Introduction

1. The Americans have proposed to the Russians and the Germans that the Four Powers should be expanded to include the two Germanies. The Prime Minister has made the same proposal to the [*sic*] Medvedev.[2] If the Russians react favourably how should we proceed?

The Four Powers

2. The Four Power grouping reflected reality in 1945. During the course of the last 45 years it has lost much of its relevance and is no longer an appropriate forum for negotiations on Germany. It would be contrary to our policy on self-determination if the future of Germany was to be decided by a forum from which the Germans are excluded. The Germans are adamant that the Four should not discuss Germany as a whole both because to do so could provoke a serious nationalist reaction in the FRG, and because it gives the Russians a greater *droit de regard* over developments than we would wish. It is extremely unlikely that we will overcome German reluctance and equally unlikely that the Americans would agree to use the Four Powers in this way in the face of German opposition.

3. Nevertheless we do need to find a way of bringing the Soviet Union into the process. The Soviet Union will have to be party to a final settlement (which will fix German's borders for good) and it will have to be involved in returning Berlin to German sovereignty. Its 375,000 troops in East Germany have to be removed. Most importantly of all we need to reassure the Soviet Union that their security interests will be taken into account and to ensure that developments in Germany do not unseat Mr Gorbachev. We therefore need to find some forum in which we can involve the Soviet Union and allow it to let off steam.

CSCE

4. One option would be to put the German question on the CSCE agenda. This would have the advantage of bringing in the Poles, the Czechoslovaks, the Dutch,

---

[1] Sent under a covering minute by Mr Cooper to Mr Wall on 9 February, which stated: 'It recommends that we aim for a six power meeting as soon as possible after the GDR elections in March. As this subject is likely to come up at Ottawa the Secretary of State might like to discuss it with Mr Weston and Mr Goulden en-route. There has not been time to clear it with all the relevant departments.'

[2] In her conversation with Mr Medvedev on the evening of 7 February, Mrs Thatcher had expressed her concern 'that developments in Germany were taking place piecemeal . . . We had to devise a framework within which the other countries concerned could discuss the implications for European's [*sic*] security and stability. It was not right for leading politicians just to sit and watch things happen, they must exercise their leadership. She had no fixed idea as to the right forum in which to discuss these matters. One suggestion was it should be the Four Powers together with the two Germanies. She could agree to that. Indeed she was less averse than some others to discussion in the Four Power framework alone. Whatever it was, we had to find a way to sort out the issues posed by unification rapidly.' Letter from Mr Powell to Mr Wall, 7 February (WRL 020/1).

the Belgians and others concerned as well as the Germans themselves. But the forum is too large for a serious negotiation on such a sensitive issue. Nor would we want to make resolution of the German question subject to a Cypriot veto (the CSCE works by consensus).

Six Powers

5. The enlargement of the Four Power Group to include the two Germanies might provide a solution. There is already a historical precedent. In 1959 the Geneva Foreign Ministers' conference was enlarged to include the two Germanies as 'advisers' (we insisted that their status be limited and that they sit at a side table: the Russians were in favour of full participation by the two Germanies).[3]

6. The *advantages* of a six power forum would be:

—The Germans could not object that they were being excluded from discussion of their own future.

—It could discuss the future of Germany (rather than just Berlin) and thereby offer reassurance to the Soviet Union.

—It would give us a handle on the unification process.

—It would ensure that we were consulted at every stage of the process (e.g. on a bilateral GDR/FRG treaty committing the two sides to union). The German Government would not be able to pick us off with bilateral deals (they may feel that if they can square the Americans and Russians they don't need to worry about us and the French).

—In the short term it might help shore up the Modrow government and in the longer term give a focus to a democratically elected GDR government. (After unification it would presumably become a five power group.)

—It might form the kernel of a European security council, including the UK, in the longer term. It would bring in both the European great powers (the Soviet Union and Germany) and would help tie the US to Europe.

7. Its *disadvantages* would be:

—It might give the Soviet Union a veto over the terms of German unification, e.g. membership of NATO (but they have a sort of veto on Berlin etc anyway). This could be overcome by good preparation on the Western side. We would outnumber the Russians five to one.

—It excludes the Poles, Czechoslovaks and other interested parties. Western allies (Netherlands etc) might make a fuss (although they recognise the legal rights of the Four Powers).

—It might undermine Four Power rights. But as explained above these are limited in practice if not in theory to Berlin.

How would such a system work in practice?

8. If the Soviet reaction to Baker's proposal in Moscow is favourable we could pursue the idea at Ottawa at the Secretary of State's meeting with major Western allies and subsequently with the Russians. If there is agreement we should aim for a first meeting *immediately after the GDR elections*. If the meeting is put off until after the Secretary of State's visit to Moscow in April we run the risk of being overtaken by events. We need to get a handle on developments as soon as there is an elected government in the GDR.

9. The first weeks could either be a summit or at Foreign Ministerial level. It would be a major media event and it might be better to hold it in some city other

---

[3] The so-called 'Katzentisch'—an arrangement regarded as humiliating by the FRG Government which still had resonance in 1989-90: see Elbe and Kiessler, pp. 85-6 (where, however, the Geneva Conference is misdated to 1954).

than Berlin for historical reasons (to keep it away from the Allied *Kommandatura*). The meeting would need to be thoroughly prepared. Ground rules and the agenda should be agreed in advance.

10. Subsequent meetings could be held at Foreign Ministerial and Political Director level at say two monthly intervals. The initial meetings would presumably consist of a fairly general discussion, allowing the two Germanies to explain what they were doing and permitting the Russians to let off steam. We would want the meetings to remain as informal as possible to avoid procedural questions. As the group progressed more formality might be necessary, if for example we decided it was the appropriate body to negotiate a final peace settlement. Decision making would presumably have to be by consensus.

11. Close *Western consultation* would be essential. The Germans have claimed that the Bonn Group is too low level for current requirements. This could be reinforced by regular Western meetings at Ambassadorial level in Bonn and more regular meetings of Western Political Directors.

12. We would also need to consider the six power group's *relation to the CSCE*. It might make its existence more palatable to other European countries if it were seen as a sub-group of the CSCE. Any eventual settlement it reached could be presented to the CSCE for ratification. But renegotiation would have to be excluded (we would have a useful precedent in the inclusion of the 23 mandate on the Vienna Concluding Document without renegotiation).[4] We would need to make a decision on the relationship prior to the CSCE Summit.

13. We would need to make it clear that the six did *not* replace the *Four Powers*. The latter should continue in existence, if only for discussion of Berlin matters.

[4] This document marked the conclusion of the meeting of CSCE states at Vienna from 4 November 1986 to 19 January 1989, in accordance with the provisions of the Helsinki Final Act of 1975. Its provisions relating to religious freedom were of particular importance. The text is available at http://www.osce.org/documents/mcs/1989/01/16059_en.pdf.

No. 138

Letter from Mr Wall to Mr Powell (No. 10)

[PREM: Internal Situation in East Germany]

Confidential   FCO, *9 February 1990*

Dear Charles,

Germany and NATO
I enclose the paper which the Foreign Secretary promised the Prime Minister[1] on how a united Germany could be accommodated within NATO.[2]

[1] See No. 134. In a minute of 8 February to Mr Ricketts recording a discussion between Mr Hurd and FCO officials of this paper on 7 February, Mr Wall wrote: 'Since I dictated the above, the Secretary of State has spoken to the Prime Minister. He has described the outline of our paper to her and said that, if it is approved, he will use it as a basis for discussion with the French, American and Germans in Ottawa. He would also use Ottawa as an opportunity to take preliminary soundings on the idea of a Four + 2 Summit' (WRL 020/1).

We think, from recent discussions with the Americans, French and Germans, that option (*b*) in the paper could be an acceptable basis for agreement. Option (*b*) provides for a united Germany to remain a full member of NATO, including of the integrated military structure, but NATO would voluntarily forswear the deployment of non-German forces on the territory of the former GDR, except in time of war.

If the Prime Minister and the Defence Secretary are content with the broad thrust of this paper, the Foreign Secretary proposes to speak to it during his discussions with the American, French and German Foreign Ministers in Ottawa on 11-13 February.

I am copying this letter to Simon Webb (MOD) and Sonia Phippard (Cabinet Office).

Yours,
J.S. WALL

² No. 139.

No. 139

FCO Paper

[*PREM: Internal Situation in East Germany*]

Confidential   FCO, *9 February 1990*

GERMANY AND NATO

1. For the purposes of this paper we assume:
—that the two German States will unite to form a new Federal Germany;
—that there will be a transitional period between the decision to unite and effective unification;
—that the process will begin soon.
Objectives
2. The key British objectives are:
—the retention of NATO, with an integrated military organisation;
—that Germany remain within NATO;
—a continued US military presence in Europe;
—arrangements to achieve these objectives which give an adequate sense of security to other European countries, including Germany's neighbours and in particular the Soviet Union.
Options
3. There are three main options for continued German membership of NATO.
(*a*) *A unified Germany in NATO, remaining a full member of the Integrated Military Structure*
A unified Germany would be a member of NATO, and the North Atlantic Treaty would apply to the whole of its territory. Its forces would form part of the integrated military structure. The Western front line would move to the Oder-Neisse. NATO collectively would become responsible for the defence of what is now the GDR. The present strategy of forward defence at the Inner-

German border would be obsolete, as would much of the infrastructure created to implement it. US, British and other stationed forces would need to be deployed on the territory of the former GDR if collective defence was to be implemented. The *Bundeswehr* and the East German Armed Forces would be merged under one command.

Advantages

—This option could, if accepted by all the key countries in Europe, provide a lasting solution to the German problem. It is the only solution that provides for the complete unification of Germany.

—It would strengthen NATO by the incorporation of additional population and territory.

Disadvantages

—The most humiliating and threatening outcome for the Soviet Union, since the front line in any future conflict would be moved closer to Soviet territory.

—The movement of NATO's front line Eastwards and the potential size of the new *Bundeswehr* could provoke nervousness on the part of other East European countries and a consequent disinclination on their part to loosen the Warsaw Pact.

—It would be expensive, since NATO would have to invest in new infrastructure to implement the new strategy that would be required to defend former GDR territory.

(*b*) *Germany would remain a member of NATO, but NATO would voluntarily forswear the deployment of non-German forces on the territory of the former GDR*

The North Atlantic Treaty would cover all German territory: we would therefore have a collective obligation to defend any part of Germany against aggression. The Integrated Military Structure, including US and British stationed forces, would continue to operate in the Western part of Germany. But in respect of the territory of the former GDR, NATO (or Germany alone) would undertake:

—that stationed Western forces would not be deployed or exercise there in peace-time.

—that the number of German troops deployed there would be subject to a numerical ceiling, and would not be part of the Integrated Military Structure.

—that there would be a transitional period permitting the orderly withdrawal of Soviet forces. This could be generous, though public opinion in East Germany might turn against them. The Soviet Union might have the right to retain a permanent inspection mission to assure themselves that the restrictions were being observed.

4. This approach separates the territorial from the functional aspects. There are precedents for such self-imposed restrictions: Norway does not permit the deployment of non-Norwegian troops to Finmark in peace-time.

5. The commitment to defend the territory of the former GDR would be fulfilled by mobile defence based initially on German forces stationed in the territory, reinforced in time of crisis by NATO units from the Western part of Germany and national territories.

6. The declaration giving effect to these new arrangements would need to be discussed in advance with the Soviet Union. But it would remain a unilateral undertaking which could be rescinded if necessary in response to aggressive moves against any part of Germany.

Advantages

—It would not involve an Eastward movement of NATO's military front line, so would be more acceptable to Gorbachev.

—US, British and other stationed forces could stay in the Western part of Germany (at reduced levels).

—It anchors Germany in the Alliance in a way which may (unlike (*a*)) be acceptable to the Soviet Union.

Disadvantages

—The need for special arrangements for defending the territory of the former GDR, involving the *Bundeswehr* operating outside the Integrated Military structure. Could be a source of concern to e.g. Poland.

—Continuing vestigial division of German territory, even though these arrangements would have been accepted by Germany and other NATO Allies.

(*c*) *Germany would remain a member of the North Atlantic Council but would withdraw from the integrated military structure*

All stationed forces would leave Germany. The German armed forces would be subject to CFE constraints but would not be part of a multinational command. There would be no joint exercises and no NATO nuclear weapons on German soil.

Advantages

—As in (*a*) and (*b*) Soviet forces would leave the GDR (but they probably will anyway).

—Savings from withdrawal of BAOR. Treats all of Germany equally.

—More reassuring to the Soviet Union in the short term.

Disadvantages

—Almost as bad as German neutrality. We would still have a commitment to defend Germany but no direct means of doing so.

—The Integrated Military Structure would cease to have any substance.

—US forces would be withdrawn. Some could remain elsewhere in Europe (UK or Italy), but the great majority would return to the US,

—Germany would not be firmly embedded in the West.

7. One further option mentioned in Germany is that the former territory of the GDR would be excluded from the coverage of the NATO treaty, as well as from the integrated structure. This has, from the Western point of view, crippling disadvantages:

—it leaves the Germans with sole responsibility for the defence of their most vulnerable *Länder*;

—it involves different degrees of security for different Germans—with Berlin, as capital, enjoying less protection than it does under today's arrangements;

—it could be the first step to option (*c*) or neutrality for the whole of Germany.

Soviet Attitude

8. Four power rights will continue to apply until a final settlement is reached. These include the right for the Russians (like the Western Allies) to station forces in Germany by virtue of their original occupation rights. Transitional rights to station some forces in the GDR may make the outcome more tolerable to the Soviet Union. We do not yet know the Soviet Union's bottom line. Option (*a*) would mark the total defeat of 40 years of Russian policy. Option (*c*) has long term drawbacks for them (risk of Germans going it alone). We need to convince the Russians that it is better in the long run to have Germany fully within a multilateral

framework rather than 'a wanderer between the worlds'. Option (*b*) achieves this without allowing NATO forces up to the Oder-Neisse line.

Conclusion

9. Of the three options considered above, only the first two would adequately meet the objectives set out in paragraph 2. Option (*a*) would be a good outcome for NATO but hard for the Russians to swallow and not what the government of the FRG have in mind. Option (*b*) would also represent a satisfactory outcome for NATO and would be significantly less threatening for the Russians. It would tie the Germans firmly into NATO, avoid any Soviet *droit de regard* over Germany and any sense that a special regime had been imposed on the GDR *Länder* from outside.

10. Discussion of future security options for Germany is already underway, much of it in public. We therefore need to move quickly to channel debate in the direction of our preferred outcome. Specifically, we should hold very early discussions with the US, France and Germany with the aim of consolidating support for (*b*). All three are already working on these lines.

No. 140

Letter from Mr Powell (No. 10) to Mr Wall

[*WRL 020/1*]

Confidential   10 DOWNING STREET, *10 February 1990*

Dear Stephen,

Germany and NATO

The Prime Minister has now been able to consider the Foreign Secretary's note on how a united Germany could be accommodated within NATO, sent under cover of your letter of 9 February.[1]

The Prime Minister agrees that the second option identified in the note—Germany to remain a member of NATO, but NATO to forswear the deployment of non-German forces in the former GDR—is the only feasible one of the three. She notes that the Americans and Germans are anyway already discussing it with the Russians, so we do not have much choice. It is not without disadvantages. In addition to those which you point out, it would encourage the Russians to press for demilitarisation of the former FRG: and it would place the probable capital of a united Germany in an area where NATO would not be militarily present. But the Prime Minister agrees that the Foreign Secretary should support this option in discussion with his colleagues in Ottawa.

The Prime Minister has three substantive comments on option B:

—It must be absolutely clear that under this option, significant US forces and nuclear weapons would remain in that part of a united Germany that was formerly the FRG. This option must not be an excuse either for the Germans to try to secure removal of nuclear weapons from their territory or for the Americans to renege on the 'floor' of 195,000 US forces in the central zone. The Prime Minister would wish the Foreign Secretary to make this point very

---

[1] Nos. 138 and 139.

strongly.

—We must show some consideration for Mr Gorbachev's position. That depends in part on what he wants, and we shall no doubt have a better idea of this when Baker and Genscher debrief on their talks in Moscow. But the Prime Minister feels that we should be ready to envisage a substantial transitional period during which some numbers of Soviet forces would be allowed to remain in the former GDR, or at least along its eastern border. We should not be pressing for Soviet troops to be precipitately removed in a way which might undermine Mr Gorbachev's position. To put it bluntly, we have to bear in mind—although not say—that we might one day need the Soviet Union as a counter-balance to a united Germany.

—The Prime Minister thinks it unsatisfactory to have individual governments going off separately to Moscow to discuss the question of how to accommodate a united Germany within NATO. We should agree a position among the Western Four, and then discuss it in the Berlin Four plus the two Germanys forum. She considers a meeting in this forum more urgent that ever. She hopes that the Foreign Secretary will try very hard to secure an agreement on it in Ottawa.

Even with option B, there will be significant implications for NATO's force structure and strategy. The Foreign Secretary will want to take account of the comments by the Defence Secretary.

I am copying this letter to Simon Webb (Ministry of Defence) and Sonia Phippard (Cabinet Office).

Yours sincerely,
Patricia A. Parkin
pp. CHARLES POWELL

No. 141

Mr Fall (Ottawa) to FCO[1]

No. 111 Telegraphic [*WRL 020/1*]

Secret   OTTAWA, *12 February 1990, 8.00 a.m.*

Following from PS/FCO for Powell (No 10).

I am sending separately a record of the Four Power Ministerial discussion this evening.[2] The Secretary of State would also be grateful if you could give the Prime Minister the following note from him:

Begins.

On the assumption that German unification is likely, our main objectives (apart from negotiating the transition on EC matters) are:

—to secure German membership of NATO and avert German neutrality:
—to secure the continuance of Canadian and US troops in Europe:
—to secure unification on terms reasonably acceptable to Gorbachev.

---

[1] Mr Hurd was attending the Open Skies Conference at Ottawa.
[2] Ottawa telegram No. 113 of 12 February (WRL 020/1). Not printed.

These are closer to attainment than a fortnight ago. The US, France and the FRG all come broadly to the conclusions contained in my paper on German membership of NATO after unification.[3] All concur in the idea that [*sic*: ?of] a meeting of the Four plus Two— the Germans and Americans both believe it should take place after the 18 March elections in the GDR. The question of date, place and the relationship with the decision of principle on unification remain to be considered, as does the question of nuclear weapons. I shall be having more discussions with Baker, Dumas and Genscher on Tuesday morning.

One anxious question is whether the GDR will reach 18 March. Genscher continues to give intensely gloomy accounts, probably, in part, because he wants to prove that the FRG is being pulled inevitably into measures such as currency union.

Ends.

[3] No. 139.

No. 142

Miss Neville-Jones (Bonn) to FCO

No. 181 Telegraphic [WRL 020/1]

Restricted   BONN, *13 February 1990, 2.58 p.m.*

Following Personal for Head of WED

German Unification: FRG View of the UK Position

Summary

1. Prime Minister's reservations now causing growing resentment. Genscher's call on 14 February a chance to show our good will.

Detail

2. The Prime Minister's attitude to German unification is now attracting widespread criticism in the FRG press. Since the beginning of February the country's major tabloid (*Bild*) has been running a sustained campaign. The tone is deplorable. But damage is being done.

3. At the political level too there is open displeasure:

(*a*) Today's *Frankfurter Allgemeine* and *General Anzeiger* both suggest that Kohl's decision to brief Mitterrand (on 15 February) personally on his Moscow trip but not the Prime Minister is a deliberate snub.

(*b*) Speaking on television on 11 February about the need for the FRG to discuss unification with the Four Powers, Kohl referred to 'our Soviet partners, our American friends, our French friends and Great Britain'.

(*c*) Hennig, Parliamentary State Secretary in the Ministry for Inner-German Relations, was quoted in the *Osnabrücker Zeitung* of 12 February (translation by fax)[1] in sharply critical vein: 'anyone who is genuinely interested in a friendly relationship with Great Britain cannot but shake their heads over the Prime Minister's remarks'. He is normally well disposed to the UK: his constituency (Gütersloh) includes a major RAF station.

[1] Enclosure in No. 144.

(*d*) the evidence of CSU concern described in Munich telno 2 to Bonn.[2]

4. Genscher's call on the Prime Minister provides a good opportunity to supply a corrective.[3]

[2] Not printed.
[3] See No. 147.

No. 143

Mr Fall (Ottawa) to FCO

No. 124 Telegraphic [PREM: Anglo-German Relations]

Confidential   OTTAWA, *13 February 1990, 2.59 p.m.*

From PS/FCO for Powell, No 10.

1. The Secretary of State would be grateful if you could pass the following note from him to the Prime Minister.

Begins

I had a long talk yesterday with Shevardnadze, who was in a melancholy and fatalistic mood. He is gloomy about German unification but accepts that it is going to happen. He also thinks that a united Germany will ask for the withdrawal of Soviet troops and clearly thinks this too will have to happen. In that case he foresees the disappearance of the Warsaw Pact and argues half-heartedly that NATO too should be dissolved but he went on to argue that a united Germany could become a threat to its neighbours if Kohl and Genscher, whom he trusted, were replaced by something like the Republicans. I said all the more reason to bind the Germans in by having them as part of NATO, with American troops on German soil. He seemed to half accept this.

We are this morning, after our Quad breakfast, close to agreement on meetings of Four plus Two, to begin soon after 18 March with preparatory exchanges before then. Shevardnadze agreed last night to put this to Moscow and we await that reply. This would be a big step forward, achieved by a firm front among the Americans, French and ourselves. Quite apart from its own importance, it should be an effective rebuttal of the charge that we have been pushed to the margin of events.

Genscher will talk to you at length about the emotions of the Germans at coming together after so long a division, about their irreversible commitment to democracy and to Europe, and their rejection of neutrality. He will stress that the swift pace of events has been dictated by the collapse of the GDR, which is certainly occurring though not as fast as he says. He is too clever to share the indignation shown by Kohl and the German press about our recent public statements. Indeed he continually thanks me for our understanding. But our influence in the new Four plus Two process will certainly in part depend on our willingness to sound welcoming and constructive, while continuing to restate in public and private what we believe to be the essentials of European security.

Ends.

No. 144

Minute from Mr Synnott to Mr Ratford

[*WRL 020/1*]

Unclassified   FCO, *13 February 1990*

German Question: Prime Minister's Remarks at Torquay[1]

1. Ministers and others may wish to be aware of an official Federal German Government reaction to the Prime Minister's perceived position on German unification. This is set out in the attached text of an interview by the Parliamentary State Secretary in the Inner German Ministry, published yesterday. It represents the plainest and toughest speaking by a senior German of which I am aware so far and contrasts with the more understanding approach of Dr Sudhoff (the PUS's opposite) on 9 February.[2]

2. Bonn telno 172 reports further negative and hostile reporting in yesterday's German press. *Bild Zeitung* has continued the campaign today.[3]

3. Bonn telno 178 records reaction in the CSU in relation to the role of the Conservative Party in the European Conservative Group.[4]

H.N.H. SYNNOTT

---

[1] In answering questions after her speech to the Young Conservative Conference in Torquay on 10 February, Mrs Thatcher had declared that, according to the Helsinki Agreement of 1975, 'no boundaries would be changed, except by agreement. So, if any boundaries are to be changed this requires massive consultation between us and we are hoping to have a Helsinki Conference towards the end of this year. All of this means that the changes which are taking place now in Germany and the way in which they go towards unification, must be done in conjunction with those other obligations to which we are all signed-up. And what we are saying is that there are great changes and we must have time for transition, to see that those changes take place against a background of security and stability and it is up to politicians to value that security and stability sufficiently to see that, happen what may, we retain it' (full text available at http://www.margaretthatcher.org/speeches/display document.asp?docid=108011). See also No. 182, note 1.

[2] In his conversation with Dr Sudhoff on 9 February (No. 135, note 2), Sir P. Wright had continued: 'I said that I also knew, speaking entirely personally, that there was an impression in Germany that the Prime Minister took a very cautious and reluctant view on German unification. It was probably true to say that she took a more cautious view than many of us; Dr Sudhoff interrupted to say that he found this entirely understandable, and thought that any difference of emphasis was probably generational. He could quite understand, as a German, why the older generation in this country should regard German unification with some suspicion. He wanted nevertheless to give me an absolute assurance that all Germans, with their recollections of what had happened twice in this century, were absolutely determined that Germany should never again make the mistakes it had in the past.'

[3] Of 12 February: not printed.

[4] This telegram repeated telegram No. 2 from Munich to Bonn, in which Mr Blake-Pauley (Consul-General Munich) reported concern in the Bavarian CSU about the Prime Minister's attitude to German unification. Blake-Pauley observed: 'Mrs Thatcher had no greater body of admirers than the CSU. Her political approach and the manner in which she had pulled round the British economy had been an inspiration for all Conservatives in the FRG and the European Community generally. There was a danger that much of this support and admiration would be irretrievably lost over the one issue of her approach to the unification issue.' Mr Ratford minuted on 15 February: 'We can only hope that Genscher's talk yesterday [No. 147] will break this very disturbing downward spiral' (WRL 020/1).

ENCLOSURE IN NO. 144

Fax from British Embassy, Bonn

BONN, *12 February 1990, 6.07 p.m.*

Following is full text of the interview given by Parliamentary Secretary of State in the Inner German Ministry, Dr. Ottfried Hennig, to the *Osnabrücker Zeitung.*

Q. Dr. Hennig, the British Prime Minister, Mrs Thatcher, has recommended caution in relation to unification of the two German states, and has made it a precondition that all 35 signatory states of CSCE approve this union. Would you say that these reservations are justified?

A. Anyone who is genuinely interested in a friendly relationship with Great Britain cannot but shake their heads over the Prime Minister's remarks. In these historic hours for Germany and for Europe as a whole we expect from our British friends unconditional sticking to agreements and natural solidarity, not petty nagging. What Mrs Thatcher has to say is completely incomprehensible and unfounded.

Q. As to sticking to agreements, is it the German Treaty you have in mind?

A. Yes. According to the German Treaty, concluded in 1954, a reunited Germany is our common goal. The Prime Minister would be well advised to reread this agreement which is still in force unaltered. If she did, she could learn from it any time that a Government which questions reunification does not act in accordance with the Treaty.

Q. What about Mrs Thatcher's request for approval of German unity by the CSCE. Is there any basis for it?

A. The right of self-determination for the German people does in no way depend on the approval of all CSCE member states. The British Government especially has always been very particular about Germany's legal position. There have been many perfectly clear statements over the years, for example in the House of Commons or by British Ambassadors in Bonn. At the moment when Helmut Kohl is successfully managing international policy and is about to pass into history as the Chancellor who brought about German unity Mrs Thatcher should not stab him in the back.

CHAPTER III

14 February – 30 November 1990

No. 145

Mr Fall (Ottawa) to FCO[1]

No. 127 Telegraphic [*PREM: Internal situation in East Germany*]

Secret   OTTAWA, *14 February 1990, 12.01 a.m.*

From Private Secretary

Meeting of Four Foreign Ministers: 13 February

Summary

1. Agreement on procedure for setting up a meeting of the Four plus Two. Emotional speech by Genscher thanking his allies for support over German unification. Agreement in principle on German proposal on Berlin elections but nothing to be said to the Russians for the moment.

Detail

2. The four Foreign Ministers met for breakfast this morning.[2] The main topic was follow-up to yesterday's discussions with Shevardnadze on establishment of a meeting of the Four plus Two (or as the Germans would prefer it, the Two plus Four). Baker reported that he had talked to Shevardnadze who, while still hankering after something else, had agreed that this approach seemed inevitable. He had consulted Gorbachev overnight and we awaited the Soviet response.

3. Much of the ensuing discussion was a mixture of substance and procedure. The main points were:

(*a*) It was agreed that, if the Russians were on board, we should aim for a statement by the Six later today. There would be no substantive meeting of the Six in Ottawa but they should be willing to meet for a photograph when the statement was issued. Genscher was adamant that there could be no collective discussion with Fischer: the GDR Government now had no legitimacy and Kohl had insisted that Modrow be accompanied on his visit to Bonn by representatives of the Roundtable.

(*b*) The first meeting at Foreign Minister level should take place after the 18 March elections. It was agreed that all the meetings would be in Germany, some possibly in the West, some in the East. Genscher was keen that the statement

---

[1] Repeated for information Immediate to Paris, Bonn, Washington, UKDEL NATO.

[2] i.e. 13 February.

should say that the Germans would host the meetings but Dumas, the Secretary of State and Baker resisted this. The Secretary of State said that, in practice, the meetings would be hosted by the Germans but it was important from the Soviet point of view, and to some extent from ours, that the meeting of the Six should not just appear to rubber stamp something already agreed between the two Germanies.

(*c*) Exchanges between Political Directors in preparation for a meeting after 18 March could start straightaway. The four Political Directors would anyway discuss how to handle these contacts. Genscher was once again adamant that there should be no collective meeting of the Six involving the Political Director or equivalent from the present GDR Government.

4. Election of members of the *Bundestag* from Berlin. Genscher asked for the views of his allies. Baker said the Americans had no problem on the substance of the proposal but he wondered if it was right to raise it with the Russians until the process of the Four plus Two had got underway. This would be just one more jab in the Russian eye, which would not be wise. The Secretary of State and Dumas agreed. Genscher said he was happy with that. If everybody was agreed in principle, then there was no need to raise the matter with the Russians now. He clearly thought that, with the demise of an independent GDR, the issue would quite quickly become academic.

5. Genscher then made a rather emotional statement. His colleagues could understand how everything that was happening in Germany was deeply moving for the Germans and for himself. He wanted to express his gratitude to his friends and allies for their continuous support. This was appreciated not only by the Government but by ordinary Germans as a whole. Genscher himself was very familiar with the views and feelings cherished by the German people. They had always been part of a community of democratic countries. That was irreversible. He wanted to address himself particularly to his two colleagues who were members of the European Community. What was now happening in Germany should serve to increase their mutual efforts to continue the integration of the Community in all areas and to speed up the process. He also hoped that the Community would find ways and means to develop its relationship with the United States, in keeping with the new situation. He also believed, as he had told Shevardnadze, that there was scope for a closer relationship between the EC and the Soviet Union. Genscher said that he had not willingly left the GDR as a young man but had been forced to do so. His colleagues could imagine what it meant to him to visit his home town of Halle later in the week to tell the people there of the exciting developments. Once again he wanted to express his heartfelt gratitude to his allies. They would find in the Germans friends, partners and allies on whom they could rely.

6. The Secretary of State said we could all make the effort of imagination to understand Genscher's feelings. We would all do our best to be friendly and constructive as his vision became a reality. Dumas (whose father was shot by the Germans) said rather ruefully that Genscher would appreciate what was in everyone's minds with all the history that lay behind them. All this was a matter of past relationships as well as of the future. We were turning a new corner and needed strong links in the future.

7. Baker said he appreciated Genscher's remarks about the strengthened ties between the EC and the US. These ties would play a larger role in a changed Europe. He had been moved when Genscher had called him last November and

when the German switchboard operator putting through the call had said 'God bless America and all you have done for Germany'. These were historic times. If the Soviet Union agreed to the Two plus Four mechanism they had discussed that morning, that too would be a small part of history,

8. The Secretary of State said he was sorry to drag matters back to the pedestrian but it was important that we should all bear in mind that, with the NATO Council in June, preceded by a meeting of the four Foreign Ministers at Chevening, followed by the European Council and the Economic Summit, we needed to think through the opportunities that would be open to us to manage the process of change. All the others agreed, Dumas emphasising the need for flexibility.

9. Baker stressed that, in preparing for the CSCE Summit, it was very important that the NATO Council should be able to bring some influence to bear. These matters must be shaped within the NATO Council and not completely apart from it. NATO would become less of a military and much more of a political alliance. It was the Alliance which tied the United States to Europe and it was vital not to lose that political combination. So the special group preparing for the CSCE must report to the NATO Council or NATO would be diminished. The Secretary of State agreed. Dumas said that we needed a broad discussion on the future of NATO. Baker, with considerable emphasis, said that as long as Europe wanted the US to be coupled with the continent and to have the benefits of the nuclear umbrella, there must be clear political linkage. He had suggested more political contacts with the Community. NATO was another forum. One way or another the links must be maintained.

10. The Secretary of State asked for his colleagues' views on Shevardnadze's idea of a meeting of the 35 at Foreign Minister level before the Summit. Genscher said it would be useful. The Russians needed it as the Warsaw Pact eroded. We might all need something to keep Europe together. In the face of the danger of balkanisation, we needed something more than NATO and the EC. The Secretary of State said he could not very easily see a meeting of Foreign Ministers taking place on the sort of timescale Shevardnadze seemed to envisage. Baker asked what such a meeting would do. Genscher said that it was not a matter of principle whether such a meeting took place, i.e. meaning that we should not oppose it.

No. 146

Mr Hurd to Sir A. Acland (Washington)[1]

No. 315 Telegraphic [RS 021/1]

Secret   FCO, *14 February 1990, 1 p.m.*

My tel no 262: Bilateral Discussion on German Issues[2]

1. As foreshadowed in TUR, Weston had further talks with Zoellick and Seitz in the margins of the Ottawa Open Skies Conference on 11-13 February. Much of the discussion and related contacts in the corridors centered on the efforts (now successful) to get the Four plus Two formula launched. But it is worth recording

[1] Repeated for information Immediate to Paris, Bonn, UKDEL NATO, Moscow.
[2] Not found.

that Zoellick had formed the impression from their own bilateral contacts with the Russians that the latter were increasingly beginning to realise at a rational level the importance of NATO in relation to a united Germany. The main Russian problem, he thought, was how to find face-saving devices for coping with this recognition *vis-à-vis* Soviet public opinion. Hence among other things the importance of the Four plus Two framework giving the Russians an involved status: and the salience of the issue of Soviet troop presence in the GDR. Zoellick was impressed by the degree to which Soviet interlocutors saw a problem of Russian nationalism if the German question was not handled adroitly. He also seemed to be forming the view that there might be some kind of trade off between Soviet security concerns *vis-à-vis* German unity and the German capacity to aid the Soviet Union economically.

2. Against the background of recent evidence that the French might be open-minded about a discreet UK-French-American trilateral to discuss the German question (confirmed by the French political director privately at Ottawa) Weston asked Zoellick and Seitz for an American reaction to this idea. Both admitted the objective case for such a meeting but Zoellick thought the risks of ructions with the Germans, should it come out, outweighed the advantages and Seitz was only slightly less emphatic on this score.

3. This channel of discussions with the Americans seems likely now to be partly subsumed in the process of multiple bilateralism that preparations for the Four plus Two formula will involve over coming weeks. Zoellick made it clear that he was very ready to continue using Wood as his contact in Washington. In due course we will let you have a list of the major areas for discussion on which official level preparations for the Four plus Two might focus.

No. 147

Letter from Mr Powell (No. 10) to Mr Wall

[*WRL 020/1*]

Confidential   10 DOWNING STREET, *14 February 1990*

Dear Stephen,

Prime Minister's Meeting with the German Foreign Minister
The Prime Minister had an hour's talk this morning with Herr Genscher, who was on his way back from the Open Skies Conference in Ottawa. Herr Genscher was accompanied by the German Ambassador and by his Private Secretary. The Foreign Secretary was also present.

The discussion was robust but basically good-humoured, and a positive line was agreed for the press at the end. You will be receiving separately a transcript of the remarks made by the Foreign Secretary and Herr Genscher outside No. 10.[1]

The Prime Minister began by congratulating Herr Genscher and the Foreign Secretary on the agreement reached in Ottawa to establish a framework for meetings of the Berlin Four and the two Germanies. But before getting into that, she wanted to tell Herr Genscher how strongly Poland's Prime Minister felt about

[1] Not printed.

the need for a Treaty to confirm the Polish/German border.[2] Herr Genscher indicated that he was aware of Mr. Mazowiecki's concerns, but gave the impression that he did not take them very seriously. There was no doubt about the substance of the German position on borders. Any problems could be sorted out in the CSCE framework. The Prime Minister said that Mr. Mazowiecki had been quite clear that there must be a Treaty. She thought he was justified in demanding this. Poland did not want to be side-lined and the border must be put beyond legal dispute. Herr Genscher said that Germany did not want to have to sign a Peace Treaty with everyone. They would clarify their position on the border and find a way to convince the Polish Government. He repeated that there was no difficulty on the substance. The Prime Minister said she could not see why, in that case, there was any difficulty about having a Treaty.

Discussion then turned to the subject of German unification. The Prime Minister said that it was very important that Germany should understand the anxieties of others about unification. She tended to speak up more openly than others. But she could assure Herr Genscher that the anxieties she expressed were widely shared in Europe. Her basic concern was that the German government seemed entirely pre-occupied with German unification and had not given sufficient attention to consultation with Germany's allies about its wider consequences. As a result the rest of us were feeling ignored or excluded, and problems were being dealt with piecemeal. We had played our full part in preserving Europe's and Germany's security for over 40 years. We had kept to our commitment under the Brussels Treaty to keep substantial forces in Germany, even though it might have suited our interests better to organise our defence differently. She was determined that German unification should not have the effect of undermining the stability and security which Europe enjoyed. Had the Germans been ready to accept from the beginning that the consequences of unification should be discussed in the Four Power Forum, there need have been no problem. As it was, we were simply told that such vital matters as the future of NATO would be settled in due course. We understood the emotion which unification generated in Germany: the Germans, for their part, should show more sensitivity to the no less genuine emotions of others. The agreement now reached to establish a forum of the Berlin Four plus the two Germanies was an important step forward. But it was a pity it had taken so long.

Herr Genscher said that he needed no convincing of the importance of dealing with the consequences of unification. He had dealt with these aspects fully in three recent speeches. The problem lay rather with the pace of events and that stemmed basically from the collapse of East Germany. It was possible that the situation could be held until the elections on 18 March. But people would expect the process of unification to start immediately thereafter: and if it did not they would simply unite Germany de facto creating chaos. Herr Genscher continued that some people used to think that a divided Germany was in itself a contribution to stability. He had never accepted that: it was certainly not true now. To all intents and purposes, the GDR no longer existed as a state. Under these pressures, the FRG simply had to move forward. The Prime Minister interjected that Herr Genscher was constantly stressing the priority which had to be given to unification. But it was important that the wider issues should be sorted out before unification took place. By his own admission, unification could happen shortly after the elections on 18 March. In that case, it was urgent to get down to resolving the issues such as

---

[2] Mrs Thatcher had met Mr Mazowiecki on 12 February.

borders and the implications for NATO without any delay. It was not as though there were many options to be considered. We all accepted unification. But we felt hurt that our interests were simply being put on one side.

The Prime Minister continued that neutrality could not be an option for a united Germany. It was also vital that the United States should keep substantial forces and nuclear weapons in Germany. Herr Genscher interjected that there was no disagreement on these two points. Not even the East European countries wanted a neutral Germany. The Prime Minister said the main question was what should happen to Soviet forces in the GDR. In her view, they should be able to stay there, at least for a transitional period. Herr Genscher said there was no problem over this either. He had told President Gorbachev and Mr. Shevardnadze that if they wanted to keep Soviet troops on GDR soil, that was perfectly acceptable to the FRG. Soviet security interests had to be taken into account. At the same time it was clear that the Warsaw Pact was disintegrating. This was one reason why the Soviet Union attached so much importance to a CSCE summit, as an alternative means of providing security. The Prime Minister commented that such a summit should reaffirm existing borders all over Europe. Herr Genscher said that the principles of the existing Helsinki Final Act could be made legally binding.

The Prime Minister said that she was glad that she and Herr Genscher could talk frankly without causing any resentment. She hoped that she had made clear to him why she felt strongly about the way in which unification was being handled. It was this to which she objected, not to unification itself. Herr Genscher said that he hoped that he had persuaded the Prime Minister that Germany did not want anything to happen behind the backs of the Four Powers. They must be involved in the talks between the two Germanies from the beginning. The procedure which had been agreed in Ottawa was a good one. For his part, he wanted to say to the Prime Minister that it was important that the FRG's allies should not give the impression that they had reservations about unification. While the leaders of the three main political parties in the FRG were determined that Germany should remain in NATO and that American forces should stay, there were others on the extreme right and left who favoured neutrality. If the impression gained ground that the allies were putting obstacles in the way of unification, that would only strengthen extremists. He hoped, therefore, that the Prime Minister would take every opportunity to make clear that she favoured German unification. People in Germany must believe that they had the support of the allies. The Prime Minister said that she had no difficulty in giving such support, provided that German Ministers took every opportunity to make clear that they recognised the need to deal with the consequences of unification now, in full consultation with the allies. Until recently they constantly emphasised unification and neglected to talk about the consequences. These ought to be addressed now and if possible resolved before the elections were held in East Germany. Otherwise unification might just come about and no decisions would have been taken on, for instance, the position of Soviet forces in East Germany or Germany's role in NATO. She was worried that people were doing things for political reasons without working out the wider consequences. Herr Genscher said that there was no need to be alarmed about Germany's intentions on this. The Prime Minister responded that she would not be alarmed provided we got the wider framework sorted out. This could not be done by German unification alone. Nor without it, said Herr Genscher. The Prime Minister concluded that she was now much happier that a structure had been agreed in Ottawa.

Herr Genscher said that he had been struck when in Moscow by how Gorbachev, during his meetings with his German visitors, appeared to have no other preoccupation except the matter in hand. Shevardnadze, by comparison, appeared deeply preoccupied with some of the developments at the Central Committee Plenum, particularly the criticism of Soviet foreign policy.

Herr Genscher also referred to his own remarks in Ottawa on the importance of establishing better relations between the European Community and the United States. This would be absolutely fundamental to the future.

Herr Genscher said that he would be addressing political meetings in East Germany later this week. His impression was that the SED would receive between 5 and 10 per cent of the votes in the elections on 18 March, mostly from party members who feared losing their jobs. The Social Democrats would do very well: the GDR had formerly been a stronghold of social democracy. He thought that the Liberals would also do well, perhaps better than in the FRG. The unknown was the likely performance of the various Conservative groupings. There were very few catholics in East Germany and it was catholics who made up the bulk of the CDU's support in the Federal Republic. He thought the most likely outcome would be an all-party government excluding the SED.

There was then a brief discussion of what should be said to the press. The Prime Minister said that we should welcome the agreement reached in Ottawa on a framework of the Berlin Four and the two Germanies to discuss the wider consequences of unification. It should be clearly stated that the United Kingdom supported unification in accordance with its previous undertakings. At the same time, it would be made clear that the German government agreed that unification must take place within a framework which guaranteed the continued stability and sure defence of Europe, and would be ready to consult fully to ensure this.

I am sending a copy of this letter to Simon Webb (Ministry of Defence) and to Sonia Phippard (Cabinet Office).

Yours sincerely,
C.D. POWELL

No. 148

Letter from Mr Powell (No. 10) to Mr Wall

[WRL 020/1]

Confidential   10 DOWNING STREET, *15 February 1990*

Dear Stephen,

German Reunification

The Prime Minister and Foreign Secretary had a talk this morning about recent developments over German unification.

The Prime Minister said that the decision to establish a framework of the Berlin Four and the two Germanies to discuss the consequences of unification for NATO and European security was a considerable success. We should make sure that work started straight away at official level in this forum.

The Prime Minister continued that it was now very important to make similar arrangements to handle the EC aspects of German unification. The Commission had been slow to start on this. The Community should be looking urgently at the financial and other implications of absorbing East Germany into the Community, with the aim of ensuring, so far as possible, that the additional financial burden was borne by the Federal Republic. We should have a significant number of allies for this approach. She hoped that the Foreign Secretary would raise the matter at the forthcoming Foreign Affairs Council. We should also liaise closely with the Secretary-General of the Commission.

The Foreign Secretary reported that Mr. Haughey was considering holding an informal meeting of EC Heads of Government shortly after the East German elections in March, to talk about the implications of unification. The Prime Minister commented that this would be too late. The preparatory work should be in hand now.

I am copying this letter to John Gieve (HM Treasury), Neil Thornton (Department of Trade and Industry), Michael Harrison (MAFF) and Sonia Phippard (Cabinet Office).

Yours sincerely,
C.D. POWELL

No. 149

Letter from Sir C. Mallaby (Bonn) to Mr Weston[1]

[*WRL 020/1*]

Confidential   BONN, *16 February 1990*

Dear John,

Germany: Four plus Two and All That

1. This letter comments on some of the matters which, as seen from here, need consideration following agreement at Ottawa on the Four plus Two negotiating format. The subject of the GDR and the EC is covered in separate correspondence.

2. I start with a key point. Of the Western Three, the Americans have incomparably the most influence here at present. The French, because of the Franco-German special relationship, have a good bit. We can exert influence effectively if we first convince both or at least one of these, and only then the matter is put to the Germans.

3. One of our key tasks in the spring and summer will be to try to keep progress on the inner German track from racing ahead of progress on the international track of Four plus Two. I shall continue to press the Germans on their intentions in this regard, as I did with Seiters on 14 February (my telegram no 189).[2] There are factors which might possibly make the inner German track go less breathtakingly

---

[1] Copied to HM Ambassadors in Moscow, UKDEL NATO, Washington, Paris, UKREP Brussels, East Berlin, Warsaw, Minister, BMG Berlin; Air Marshal Sir R. Palin.

[2] This telegram recorded a briefing by Herr Seiters of the three Western Ambassadors on Herr Modrow's visit to Bonn on 13 February and the current intentions and views of the Federal Government (also recorded in *Deutsche Einheit*, No. 183). Herr Seiters stated that their intention was that 'progress between the two Germanies towards unity and in the 2 plus 4 forum on the external aspects should march in parallel. I asked whether that meant that the two should reach their conclusion at the same time. Seiters and Sudhoff said that was the Federal Government's aim' (WRL 020/1).

fast. One is that the Federal Government will need to take more account of the views of an elected GDR Government than it does of Modrow. Another is that the costs to the Federal Republic of restarting the East German economy are a growing political issue here. Another is that the Federal SPD are taking a distinctly cautious line on use of the rapid route to unity via Article 23 of the Basic Law. That suggests that the SPD (East), likely to be the biggest element in the GDR government after 18 March, may come under fraternal pressure not to opt for Article 23.

4. We must nevertheless be prepared for the internal track to continue to move very fast. The three Western Allies should be thinking what leverage they have to bring the Germans to work hard for the right solutions on the external side, so that speed is kept broadly similar on the two tracks. At least two of the actions that the Allies will need to undertake in the process of German unification could be relevant: the lifting of our rights in relation to Germany as a whole and the termination of our functions and rights in Berlin. On Berlin, much the more visible and concrete factor, the Allies might say to the Germans, privately and soon, that they are keen to lift their reservations on the Federal Basic Law, and thus allow Berlin to become part of a united Germany at the same time as the GDR. But the Allies would add that they would want to be sure beforehand that agreement was going to be reached on the security arrangements to accompany German unity. I realise that the Americans in their present mood may not look at this kind of manoeuvre, but I believe we should try the idea on them, arguing the case about parallel movement along the two tracks. After Berlin had become part of united Germany, there would need to be a transition period, during which Allied functions would be handed over to German authorities in Berlin. Another way of linking the need for Allied rights to be lifted in Berlin to our interest in satisfactory security arrangements in Europe would be to ask the Federal Government to undertake that the internal and external tracks concerning German unity would move approximately in parallel and reach conclusions simultaneously, in return for our agreement to lift our reservations on the Federal Basic Law. The trouble with this is that it relies on the Federal Government, if it gave such an undertaking, being able to uphold it. Theoretically they might have the power to delay somewhat the implementation of a GDR decision to accede to the FRG, but politically—e.g. if emigration was still high—they could well be in great difficulty.

5. As regards Allied rights in relation to Germany as a whole, we should keep them in being until the final moment when a package of agreements and arrangements in Europe, including German unity, takes full effect. The German wish that we should lift those rights gives us a locus throughout the process and a bit of leverage. But unification of the two Germanies can go a very long way in practice without our lifting those rights and under Article 23 of the Federal Basic Law it is arguable (my telegram no 160)³ that even *de jure* unification might be

---

³ In this telegram of 8 February Sir C. Mallaby reported that 'The possibility of unification via the half-forgotten Article 23 has gained momentum over the last week, partly because the SPD have been taking a close look at it.' Mallaby commented that the relationship between Article 23 and Allied rights was not straightforward: 'As seen from here the Allies could not object on legal grounds to unification being achieved through Article 23 and the extent to which they could delay it is doubtful. But reserved rights in respect of reunification and a peace settlement (Article 2 of the Relations Convention) entitle the Allies to be fully consulted . . . particularly on issues such as borders and security. As necessary we must insist on the exercise of these rights, though we should bear in mind the requirements for the Allies in turn to consult the Federal Republic on their exercise (Article 7(4) of the Relations Convention) and not to interpret the rights under Article 2 as allowing

possible. There is therefore a risk that we could be left, after unification, with rights and responsibilities that had little meaning and were a problem in our relations with a united Germany.

6. In the Four plus Two discussions, Germany's frontiers should not be a problem in substance. But the procedure for involving Poland in the final legal fixing of the Oder Neisse frontier presents difficulties. The Poles will need certainty before German unification that the frontier is final, which presumably means before the Four plus Two meetings are completed. Yet it is the signature of the united Germany that is needed on the legal instrument finally fixing the frontier. And the Federal Government has problems in giving a definitive undertaking before the Federal elections on 2 December. Presumably the answer to this riddle will be on the lines that the Four plus Two will make a declaration, coordinated or even jointly made with Poland, to the effect that there will be a legal fixing of the frontier immediately Germany is united. The idea of dealing with this problem by making the Helsinki obligations legally binding would I imagine take too long to satisfy the Poles.

7. On the key conundrum about ensuring security in Europe, the Federal Government, I think, has a firm position that:

(*a*) United Germany will not be neutral.

(*b*) United Germany will be in NATO.

(*c*) NATO's military arrangements will not be extended East of the inner German border.

(*d*) American forces in reduced numbers will remain in West Germany; European too, though I think Federal firmness on this could be less resistant to public and/or Soviet pressure during the coming negotiations,

(*e*) There will be some German forces in the old GDR, not assigned to NATO.

8. The Federal Government has no firm position yet on:

(i) What limit should be set on German forces in East Germany.

(ii) Whether Soviet forces should stay in East Germany and, if so, how many and how long.

(iii) The continued presence of American nuclear weapons in West Germany.

9. On (iii), our impression is that the Germans have not done much thinking yet. The Federal Government intend that some American and other nuclear weapons should stay, the types and numbers being determined inter alia by arms control. They know that the Americans will insist that US forces remaining here have nuclear protection. If the Russians were to try to make de-nuclearisation of West Germany a condition of their agreement to a deal on security overall, the Federal Government would fear that the majority of its own public opinion would support the Soviet proposal. The Americans would have to put all possible pressure, with us, on the Federal Government.

10. There is a general expectation here that a limit will be set on the German national (not NATO) forces in East Germany, but no idea what limit. As regards Soviet forces there, I think the FRG will want a transition period of a finite number of years for their running down. The manpower reduction in Central Europe, now agreed in principle, means that the Soviet presence in the GDR must go down to 195,000 at the very most. Such a reduction, Federal officials calculate, would take three years at least. After that, the Germans would want a reduction to a symbolic

them to derogate from their undertakings to the FRG in the Bonn/Paris Conventions (letters of 26 May 1952/23 October 1954). In Article 7(2) of the Relations Convention we undertook to "co-operate to achieve . . . their common aim of a re-unified Germany . . . "' (WRL 020/1).

level, several thousand troops or less, over several more years. The Soviet forces remaining permanently would be so few as to be militarily insignificant; their stated function would be verification of the limit on German forces in East Germany, liaison and other sorts of motherhood.

11. If the lasting presence of several thousand Soviet troops is not enough for the Russians, the present German government might just live with that, but would very much want some element of time limitation, such as reconsideration after a finite period. As of now, the possibility that significant numbers of Soviet forces might stay beyond a handful of years in East Germany has not been addressed in public by the government and there has been no serious debate about it. I hope greatly that we can avoid it. Quite apart from our interest in reducing the Soviet threat, the continued presence of Soviet forces would increase the likelihood of public opposition in Germany in due course to all stationed forces. One pitfall to watch in the negotiations is that the Russians might argue that their forces remaining even for a time in the GDR must be on the same legal basis as before, i.e. that their rights and responsibilities in relation to Germany should to this extent remain. The Legal Advisers may wish to comment.

12. Some people in the FMOD and the US Embassy here are thinking that the three garrisons in the Western Sectors in Berlin might remain, in reduced number, during the run-down of Soviet forces in the GDR. The US Embassy seem to think that we might retain enough of Berlin's present status to provide the legal basis for the remaining garrisons. But that would imply the continuation of an element of the occupation regime; even if that were possible legally, I doubt that it would be acceptable politically to the Germans. The other possible way to provide a legal basis for the garrisons to remain would be to include this element in one of the various agreements to be negotiated in connection with German unity. This approach would incidentally be compatible with the idea about lifting our Berlin rights discussed in paragraph 4 above. On the substance, there would be political advantage in acceding to a German request to retain the garrisons, as well as the element of security advantage. Michael Burton will wish to comment.

Yours ever,

C.L.G. Mallaby

No. 150

Extract from Conclusions of a Meeting of the Cabinet held at 10 Downing Street on 22 February 1990 at 10.00 a.m.[1]

[CC(90)7]

East and West Germany

3. . . .[2] *The Foreign and Commonwealth Secretary* said that the United Kingdom had played a major part in creating the framework for dealing with the problems posed by German unification. The United Kingdom's forthright stand

---

[1] For attendance at this meeting see No. 114.

[2] A statement by Mr King on the disagreement between Herr Genscher and Herr Stoltenberg on defence arrangements for the territory of the GDR in a unified Germany (No. 154, note 6) is here omitted.

had sometimes been criticised, but the mechanism of the two Germanies plus the Four Powers (2+4), which had been agreed in the series of Ministerial meetings during the Open Skies Conference in Ottawa, was now taking shape. The United States Administration had also come forward with the helpful proposal that the North Atlantic Treaty Organisation (NATO) should have a wide-ranging discussion on the implications of German unification. This would be a useful way of involving the smaller NATO member states without cutting across the 2+4 framework. In addition, there would be an informal European Council meeting at the end of April, although it might be difficult to do all the necessary preparatory work on European Community aspects in the time available. There had been an acrimonious debate within the Commission about the handling of German unification, in which the Vice-President of the Commission, Herr Bangemann, had established his own working group, but an Inner Group had now been set up to oversee the work. In order to secure the United Kingdom's basic objectives in this process, it was essential to continue to make clear that the British Government accepted the principle of unification.

In discussion, it was pointed out that while the United Kingdom could justifiably take credit for its contribution towards establishing the present policy framework for handling German unification, the West German media were determined to portray the British attitude as negative, even though in many instances Ministers were describing the problems and implications in similar terms to those used by Chancellor Kohl and Herr Genscher. The West German Government had been opposed to efforts to create a framework for German unification, and was still strongly resisting the idea of a Peace Treaty. There was considerable support in many European countries for the way in which the Prime Minister and other Ministers had emphasised the need for German unification to be accomplished within a framework of security and stability. It was important to take proper account of Poland's legitimate concerns. The situation in East Germany continued to cause concern. The West German Government had proposed a plan for converting savings held in East Germany into West German Deutschmarks to be phased over a five year period. It now seemed increasingly likely that the East German Social Democratic Party (SPD) would emerge from the elections on 18 March as the strongest party. In that case, they might form an alliance with their opposite numbers in West Germany on the issues relating to unification, thus putting Chancellor Kohl in an intensely difficult position. It was not improbable that the SPD would obtain a majority in the elections scheduled for West Germany in December 1990, thus bringing about a fundamental change in German attitudes with important implications for Allied policy.

The Cabinet—

Took note.

No. 151

Sir C. Mallaby (Bonn) to Mr Hurd[1]

No. 228 Telegraphic [WRL 020/1]

Confidential   BONN, *22 February 1990, 12.08 p.m.*

Personal for Ambassadors.

Britain's Influence in Germany

1. Britain's public standing in Germany is at its lowest for years. That applies not only in Bonn but in other cities, as my visits this week to Stuttgart (with Mr Walker) and Munich (with Mrs Chalker) have shown. Politicians and media are bitterly criticising Britain and the Prime Minister personally, and that includes those on the right of centre who have admired Britain's achievements in the eighties. The reason is our perceived attitude to German unification. From November to January we were thought to be reticent on unification and, when we did say anything, to be keen to stress delay. We are compared unfavourably with France and especially the USA and now with the Soviet Union.

2. When a strongly negative impression takes root, it is hard to shift it. Your speech here on 6 February[2] was an example. Most of the German press saw in it movement in our position but not enough to bring us up with the other players. The Prime Minister's remarks in speeches since then are seen as evidence that she, though evidently not you, is still against unification and will do all she can to cause delay. Because we are so mistrusted, the parts of Mrs Thatcher's statements which concern the necessary framework for German unity get all the attention here and are seen as attempts to set conditions and to warn the world against the Germans.

3. This matters because it destroys our influence here. Your efforts to strike up an effective relationship with Genscher, which he appreciates, can bear full fruit only if our public standing is recovered. It will not be easy. But a public statement by you

   (*a*) reiterating at some length that we support self determination and the spread of democracy in Europe and

   (*b*) demonstrating that we have new and constructive ideas for the international context of German unity

should help a lot. MIFT[3] contains suggestions for (*b*). Some may be ahead of the policy making process. But our policies will cut ice only if we recover our

---

[1] Repeated for information Immediate to Paris, Washington, UKDEL NATO.

[2] No. 131.

[3] In telegram No. 229 of 22 February, Sir C. Mallaby proposed a number of 'elements for the second part of an early statement, following a warm welcome for the spread of democracy in Europe and a declaration of unreserved support for German self-determination and of keenness to contribute in Two plus Four'. Among the proposals under the first heading, 'Security in Europe', were that Britain should welcome the Federal Government's position that Germany should be a member of NATO and that NATO structures need not be extended to East Germany; and could propose much greater integration of Allied armed forces in Western Europe, including the possibility of international corps comprising divisions from different countries. Under the second heading, 'GDR and EC', the statement could express the hope that British firms would invest in the former GDR and 'cooperate, as partners and suppliers, with West German firms engaged in developing East Germany', and that Britain would cooperate in helping to bring East Germany into

standing, so I hope that such a statement would reach as far forward as possible. If elements simply must be deleted, I hope that they will be replaced by other new suggestions. My point is that an early statement demonstrating flexibility and goodwill should help us to play our role to the full in this time of major change.

the EC, subject to appropriate transitional arrangements. Under 'Frontiers', the statement could express willingness to help in bringing about a agreement that would reconcile the German wish for a united Germany to have the external frontiers of today's FRG and GDR, and Poland's desire for a binding guarantee of her western frontier. Under the final heading, 'Allied Rights', the statement could stress the UK's willingness to adapt its rights in Berlin to the wishes of the city's inhabitants and to 'move with the times, however fast they go' (WRL 020/1).

No. 152

Sir A. Acland (Washington) to FCO[1]

No. 447 Telegraphic [WRL 020/1]

Confidential   WASHINGTON, *23 February 1990, 6.15 p.m.*

Personal for Ambassadors.
Madrid for Private Secretary to the Secretary of State.[2]

Germany/East-West Relations

1. As requested (telecon Wall/Wood)[3] we have sent the text of your speech in the Commons on 22 February to senior officials in both State Department and the National Security Council, who have undertaken to draw it to the attention of Baker and the President before their talks with Chancellor Kohl at Camp David this weekend.[4]

2. I would expect your statement to provide clear confirmation to the Americans that we share the same basic objectives, particularly as regards the security framework for German unification and the importance of ensuring that Germany remains a full member of NATO, inside the integrated military structure, with a

---

[1] Repeated to Immediate Madrid; information Immediate Paris, Bonn, UKDEL NATO.
[2] Mr Hurd was attending a bilateral UK-Spanish meeting in Madrid.
[3] Not found.
[4] *Parl. Debs., 5th ser., H. of C.*, vol. 167, cols. 1087-96. In his speech Mr Hurd described the outcome of the Ottawa discussions and welcomed the prospect of German unification. He went on:

Before the Ottawa meeting, we felt that the external aspects were not always adequately heeded as the West German Government grappled with the rush of events in the GDR. Until last week we lacked a framework for discussing the external aspects of German unification. We were not alone in our concern as others were worried that we seemed to be in a scramble towards unification without the framework for handling the external aspects, including membership of NATO by a united Germany, the implications of that for the territory of what would be the former GDR because of the Soviet troops there, the status of Berlin and the final settlement of borders, as well as the implications of unification for the EC.

Our message was not one of obstruction, but that we risked muddle and instability if the issues were not addressed in some orderly way. Many felt those anxieties and told us about them and we were probably foremost in spelling them out. Because of that, a notion grew up, particularly in parts of the German press, that we were in some way going back on our traditional support for the principle of unification. I hope that that notion has now been dispelled to the comfort of us all.

continuing US troop presence, and nuclear weapons, on ex-FRG soil. An undertaking by Chancellor Kohl to work for such an outcome is the principal American goal at Camp David (my telno 446).[5] But I would also expect the speech to provide the Administration with welcome confirmation that we are developing a broadly similar approach, designed to increase the prospects of achieving the outcome we all want. The expressions of support for the positions taken so far by the FRG Government, for the broader process of self-determination and democratisation in Europe and for developing the political role of the CSCE (while preserving the Western security core of the Alliance) will all resonate well here. (My telno 446 contains further comment on tactical aspects, notably on 2 + 4.)

3. There is the further question of Britain's influence in Germany itself. This aspect is mainly for others and important points have already been made by Sir C. Mallaby (Bonn telnos 228/229)[6] and Sir M. Alexander (UKDEL NATO telno 080).[7] I would add only that the Bush Administration is similarly concerned that our public standing in Germany continues to be low and will welcome evidence that we are taking steps to bring about an improvement. As I have said on several occasions before, the Americans would rather work with Britain than with anyone else in charting the way ahead at this crucial juncture. But they will feel able to do so only so long as we are seen to be central to the European debate and regarded by our European partners as having a powerful influence on the way forward.

[5] No. 154.
[6] No. 151.
[7] In this telegram of 22 February Sir M. Alexander commented that 'the perception of my colleagues here is similar to that of Sir C. Mallaby. This inevitably tends to diminish our ability to guide discussion and to influence e.g. the Americans. . . . Whether a single statement can repair our public standing in this area must be a little doubtful. But it would, plainly, help—particularly (perhaps only) if it can be seen as heralding a genuine and sustained change of tone and policy' (WRL 020/1).

No. 153

Letter from Mr Powell (No. 10) to Mr Wall

[*WRL 020/1*]

Secret   10 DOWNING STREET, *23 February 1990*

Dear Stephen,

German Unification: The Wider Consequences

The Prime Minister and the Foreign Secretary had a talk this afternoon about initiatives which the United Kingdom might take on the future architecture of Europe, in the wake of German unification.

The Foreign Secretary said we must not appear to be a brake on everything. Rather we should come forward with some positive ideas of our own. We had been successful in securing a proper forum for discussion of the consequences of unification. But we needed to look beyond that. He thought the most promising area would be to work up a plan for strengthening and expanding the CSCE framework. In essence, the purpose would be to add support for democracy and a market economy to the existing purposes of the Helsinki Agreement, and possibly to give it some additional machinery, for instance for monitoring arms control agreements. We might also examine to what extent the Council of Europe could be brought into a closer relationship with the CSCE framework. He would have some ideas worked up, with the aim of providing material for the speech which the Prime Minister would give at the Königswinter Dinner at the end of March. The Prime Minister indicated she would be very ready to consider any ideas.

The Foreign Secretary continued that we needed to follow a similar approach in regard to the European Community, and try to get ahead of the curve by putting forward some ideas of our own about the Community's future. The Prime Minister recalled that we had in fact taken successful initiatives in the Community, for instance with the Single Market, and reform of the CAP and the Community's budget. We could not commit ourselves to Stages 2 and 3 of Delors:[1] nor was it feasible to join the ERM for now. More generally she was not prepared to lead the United Kingdom into a European federation. The Foreign Secretary agreed this should in no way be the Government's aim. Nor did he see much future in meeting [*sic*: ?making] our initiatives in the economic and monetary field, although there was a need to give more substance to our ideas on what might follow Delors Stage 1. One area which might be worth exploring was that of giving more substance to Delors' principle of subsidiarity. It was likely that in the course of the year we would be confronted with agreement by others to hold an IGC on reform of the Community's institutions. It would be no good putting forward ideas at this which had no chance of attracting support. Although he would not wish to see the Commission given any additional power, it was not realistic to aim to reduce those which it had already.

The Prime Minister suggested that one answer might lie in trying to shift the focus of activity from development of the Community to building a wider European association, embracing EFTA and the Eastern European countries, and in the long term the Soviet Union. There was a link here with the Foreign Secretary's proposal for strengthening the CSCE framework. She was also struck by President Mitterrand's success in proposing institutions which extended beyond the Community, for instance EUREKA[2] and the European Development Bank. She wondered whether we could not come up with something similar in a different field. Generally speaking she would not want to see anything proposed which led to a more rigid and restrictive Europe: her interest was in seeing a Europe of opportunity and greater openness.

The Foreign Secretary said he would reflect further on the discussion and let the Prime Minister have some suggestions.

Yours sincerely,
C.D. POWELL

---

[1] See No. 29, note 1.

[2] EUREKA, created as an inter-governmental initiative in 1985, aims to enhance European competitiveness by supporting research and development in businesses, research centres and universities.

No. 154

Sir A. Acland (Washington) to FCO[1]

No. 446 Telegraphic [WRL 020/1][2]

Secret   WASHINGTON, *24 February 1990, 12.45 a.m.*

Madrid, for Private Secretary to the Secretary of State.[3]

Your Telno. 350[4] *and Telecon Wood/Weston of 22 February:*[5] *Germany/NATO*

Summary
1. Americans concerned by Kohl statement.[6] President plans thorough discussion at Camp David with particular stress on a public declaration by Kohl that a united Germany would be a full member of NATO and its integrated military structure. US fears of a slippery slope during the German electoral year. Reluctance to engage the 2 + 4 mechanism until the Western position is firm.
Detail
2. I spoke to the President on 22 February. I said we were worried by Kohl's statement which had serious implications for the strategy and defence posture of the Alliance. The President agreed that these were just the sort of matters that needed to be thought and talked through. His meeting with Kohl at Camp David on 24/25 February would provide an opportunity for serious discussion.
3. The Minister[7] has spoken to Blackwill and Seitz, and the Counsellor Pol/Mil[8] to Dobbins, Seitz's principal deputy. Both the NSC and the State Department have the text of paras. 1, 3, 4 and 5 of your telegram under reference. They will be considering how best to get across these points to the Germans. Those concerned have made it plain they share our concern both as to the substance of the present German position and the way it was arrived at. The President is briefed to raise the matter with Kohl and to urge him against any arrangements which might imply the 'bifurcation' of security for a united Germany. Seitz remarked to the Minister, however, that 'you could never tell what parts of the briefing the President would use'.
4. Blackwill told Wood on 23 February the President had three principal goals:
(*a*) To get Kohl to agree that a united Germany would be a full member of

---

[1] Repeated for information Immediate to Paris, Bonn, Moscow, UKDEL NATO, Madrid.
[2] Note that this telegram postdates Washington telegram No. 447 (No. 153) despite its lower number.
[3] See No. 152, note 2.
[4] Not found.
[5] Not found.
[6] Since the beginning of February there had been disagreement between Herr Genscher and Herr Stoltenberg over the military status of the former GDR in a united Germany. While Herr Genscher stuck to his 'Tutzing' formula (No. 111, note 3), Herr Stoltenberg wanted NATO jurisdiction to cover the whole of Germany. Herr Kohl resolved the dispute by coming down on the side of his Foreign Minister, ordering the two Ministers to issue a joint declaration, released on 19 February, which, while confirming that Germany would be a member of NATO, also stated that no NATO forces, including those of the *Bundeswehr*, would be stationed on the territory of the former GDR.
[7] Mr A. Wood.
[8] Mr Tebbit.

NATO and a participant in its integrated military structure, and to state that publicly at the joint press conference on 25 February.

(*b*) To get Kohl to agree on the necessity of the continued presence of US troops on German soil—a point it would be as well for him to make in public too, though a private assurance was perhaps more likely.

(*c*) To get Kohl, lastly, to agree to the continued necessity for the stationing of US nuclear weapons on German soil. Blackwill did not think it likely that Kohl would say this in public at present.[9]

5. Blackwill said it was for question whether making our points to the Chancellor in the form which we had outlined would help achieve these basic goals. His own view was that it might be better to make them to Teltschik. Kohl was notoriously hard to pin down. Wood commented that if the Chancellor were prepared to make point (*a*) above clearly in public, that ought to provide the answer as to whether or not the North Atlantic Treaty would apply to the whole of the future Germany or only to the territory of the former FRG. What especially worried us was the possibility of a damaging dynamic being set up during a German electoral period. Blackwill said he very much agreed. The Americans had noted increasing talk in Germany, especially in the newspapers, of the possibility of a 'French solution' whereby Germany would withdraw from the integrated military structure while remaining a member of the Alliance. Such withdrawal might or might not be accompanied by a request that foreign forces leave Germany. The risk of things moving in this direction was already present and might well increase. If something like that happened it would spell the effective end of NATO. It would be extremely revealing whether or not Kohl was prepared on Sunday to make the public statement the Americans planned to put to him that day.

6. Blackwill said we too would probably have noticed Kohl seemed more willing to talk of the unacceptability of German neutrality than of the necessity of German membership of NATO. It would be difficult in practice to envisage a situation whereby Germany was not a member of the integrated military structure, yet US troops remained for long in Germany. In any case the Americans wanted to persuade Kohl that undue ingenuity in approaching the question of NATO membership of a united Germany would lead to the end of the US troop commitment. He expressed considerable fears of the possibility of the election campaign leading Germans further and further down this dangerous road.

7. Wood suggested to Blackwill the Germans might be putting more faith in the possibility of an eventual CSCE security structure for Europe than present facts would justify. Blackwill said he thought it was fine for the Russians to talk in these terms if that was a way of their disguising acceptance on their part of continued German membership of NATO. With such continued German membership, CSCE could have a useful security aspect. Wood suggested the way to get the debate on a more practical and less distracting plane was to accelerate work on present realities in preparation for the CSCE summit later this year. Blackwill said that he personally thought such work might have the opposite effect, and could encourage illusions as to the long term security viability of the CSCE. We should repeat as often as possible in public that the CSCE process had its use and its promise but

---

[9] Herr Kohl confirmed the first two points in his joint press conference with President Bush on 25 February: Washington telegram No. 460, 26 February (DZN 061/40).

did not and could not provide a substitute for NATO in protecting our security in the real world.

8. Blackwill said he was the more convinced of this because, firstly, the Russians tended to throw CSCE into the pot with everything else, including the 2 + 4 mechanism, and secondly, because of the US assessment of the Soviet position on German unity. The Americans would be interested in the views of HM Ambassador Moscow. His experts told him (a line also put over to Tebbit by Dobbins and lying behind what Seitz told Wood on 22 February) that the Soviet position on German membership of NATO became vaguer the higher up the Soviet echelons one went. It was natural for people like Adamishin to say that membership of NATO for a united Germany was not acceptable. Shevardnadze was vaguer, and Gorbachev even more so. Their style was to put off hard decisions. Wood wondered whether the Soviet objective in playing for time was not to draw us on to dangerous terrain during the course of the German elections. Blackwill said he thought this was not their objective, though he acknowledged events might play that way. Germany was obviously a sticky issue for the Soviet leadership internally as well as externally. They knew that if everyone stood firm they would have no choice but to accept it. In the meantime, if we pushed them too far they would probably feel bound to say no, making a necessary retreat later more difficult. This was where the 2 + 4 mechanism held dangers. If we pushed matters too fast we risked a nightmare situation whereby following a 2 + 4 meeting in Germany, Shevardnadze appeared before the television cameras and pronounced NATO membership of a united Germany unacceptable. That would send a flash fire across the German electoral scene. It was the US assessment that the Russians at present wanted to put the day of reckoning off. Gorbachev had told both Baker and Kohl he was thinking about this question and would be holding a seminar or seminars about it. He had not said 'no'.

9. Blackwill (and Dobbins earlier, Seitz being less clear) said the Americans believed it would be unwise to start 2+4 meetings, even at political director level, until a NATO position was firm and Kohl and Genscher were properly tied down. We ought to address this matter through NATO as well as more restricted western fora before going on to 2 + 4. He did not necessarily think the Russians were at present in a great hurry. He noted they had not yet spoken to the Americans in the terms used by Adamishin to Sir P. Cradock (Moscow telno. 289—not to all).[10] He added that President Bush had not yet come to any conclusion as to what the right pace should be for the 2 + 4 mechanism. This weekend's talks would clearly play an important part in influencing the President's thinking. He would, Blackwill believed, want to talk with the Prime Minister before coming to any conclusion.

Comment

10. It is clear from these discussions that there is a consensus among the main players here on the need to pin down the Germans over external aspects of unification, so as to bind Germany firmly in the Western camp, notably over security arrangements. We share this objective, though we may perhaps have a different tactical approach. It is key to the US position that a number of major present uncertainties need to be pinned down more firmly in the West before engagement at 2 + 4. The crucial question among these is how to secure a

---

[10] This telegram of 21 February reported Mr Adamishin's 'robust and somewhat histrionic presentation of Soviet views on Germany. He suggested in particular that a meeting of the Six should be held before the East German elections. Otherwise we would find ourselves simply rubber-stamping whatever decisions the two Germanies reached among themselves' (WRG 020/1).

continuing German commitment to NATO and its integrated military structure. If that commitment is less than rock solid, as people here now fear may be (or become) the case, Soviet acceptance of the otherwise inevitable will become less probable. Whatever the arguments as to long term Soviet interests, the temptation offered to Soviet meddling by any German wavering on this issue during what may be a troubled German electoral year would, as seen from here, be too much for the Russians to resist. The Americans fear that if in these circumstances we proceeded too soon to 2 + 4, we could all too easily find the Germans being prised loose from the NATO structure, with all the harm that would imply to US (and British) national interests.

No. 155

Letter from Mr Powell (No. 10) to Mr Wall

[*PREM: Internal Situation in East Germany*]

Secret and Personal   10 DOWNING STREET, *24 February 1990*

Dear Stephen,

Prime Minister's Talk with President Bush

The Prime Minister had a forty-five minute telephone conversation with President Bush at lunchtime today, the call being initiated by her.

The material in this letter is very sensitive and should be given only a very limited distribution.

President Bush said he was glad the Prime Minister had telephoned. He had been anxious to talk to her before his meeting with Chancellor Kohl. The Prime Minister said she had seen a number of leading European political figures recently, including Andreotti, Genscher, Stoltenberg, Mazowiecki and Giscard d'Estaing. She had detected a number of worries which the non-German among them shared. They accepted that German unification was going to happen. But they were worried about the speed of it and at Germany's reluctance to consult about the consequences. The decision at Ottawa to establish a Four plus Two framework had allayed some of these fears. There was now an opportunity for real consultation. Some European Governments like Poland, Italy and the Netherlands feared being left out. We needed to reassure them that they would be consulted. The first point she wanted to make to the President was that we should not wait to start work in the Four plus Two framework until after the East German elections: we should be starting now at official level. She hoped that the President would put this to Chancellor Kohl. It would also be helpful if he would press Chancellor Kohl on the need for a Treaty to guarantee Poland's border. The Poles were very exercised about this and feared that the Germans would try to wriggle out of having a Treaty. She had promised Mazowiecki support.

The Prime Minister continued it was also very important to sort out the relationship of a unified Germany to NATO. Chancellor Kohl had been very good in his insistence that Germany should stay in NATO, with United States troops remaining. The problem lay with the treatment of the GDR. If all Soviet forces were forced to leave, this would be difficult for Gorbachev. It seemed best to allow some Soviet forces to stay for a transitional period at least, without any terminal date. It was important not to make Gorbachev feel isolated, otherwise that could affect his domestic position.

The Prime Minister continued that she was most grateful to the President for proposing that there should also be discussions about unification in NATO. This was very desirable. But, looking to the future, we should also need a broader political framework in which to discuss Europe's security, and this must include the Soviet Union as well as the United States. The best course would be to strengthen and build on the CSCE framework. Not only would this help avoid Soviet isolation, it would help balance German dominance in Europe. One had to remember that Germany was surrounded by countries, most of which it had attacked or occupied in the course of this century. Of course, Germany today was very different: but other countries would become alarmed if there was not some sort of counter-balance. In practical terms—and looking well into the future—only the Soviet Union could provide balance in the political equation. She therefore thought we should try to give more substance to the Helsinki framework, by building in a commitment to democracy and a market economy, and use it as a wider political framework for Europe.

The Prime Minister said there would also be significant problems for the European Community arising from German unification. The Community would have to absorb a country equivalent in terms of population to Belgium, Denmark and Ireland combined. The Germans would have to meet the main costs of absorbing the GDR, otherwise the Community as a whole would not have the resources necessary to help Poland, Hungary and Czechoslovakia. There would be a lot of working out to do.

The Prime Minister added that there was one final point of concern and that was the political aspect. It seemed likely that the Social Democrats would do well in the GDR elections. That could have implications for the future political balance within a unified Germany. She would be very worried by the prospect of a Socialist Germany and others shared this concern.

President Bush said the Prime Minister's remarks were very helpful, timely and interesting, against the background of his forthcoming talk with Chancellor Kohl. He agreed that we had to take unification as a fact. He would be seeking from Chancellor Kohl a clear commitment to NATO membership for a unified Germany. So far, Kohl seemed to be saying all the right things, but he would want to get it from the horse's mouth and in the clearest and most specific terms, including the continued integration of German forces into NATO and the retention of American troops in the FRG. The Prime Minister interjected that Chancellor Kohl had been admirably firm on this. The problem arose rather over future defence arrangements for East Germany. Stoltenberg had put forward some proposals but had been slapped down by Genscher.[1] President Bush said Genscher appeared to want the demilitarisation of the GDR. He was not at all sure that was a good idea. The Prime Minister said that it would not necessarily suit Mr Gorbachev either. He would want to be able to keep some forces in the GDR: that was probably the only way of persuading him that a united Germany should be in NATO.

President Bush continued that President Havel had recently been in Washington and had started by proposing that all stationed forces in Europe, American and Russian alike, should be withdrawn. He had explained to Havel that the position of

[1] See No. 154, note 6.

US and Soviet forces was very different: the Russians had imposed themselves while the Americans were there because they were wanted. By the time he had left Washington, Havel seemed to accept this distinction. The Polish Prime Minister, on the other hand, seemed to want Soviet forces to remain in Poland. He doubted whether that would really be very popular with the Polish people, despite their worries about Germany. Had the Prime Minister discussed this with Mr Mazowiecki? The Prime Minister confirmed that Mr Mazowiecki had wanted to retain Soviet troops, and had pointed out that they would be needed anyway to provide logistical support for Soviet forces in the GDR. He had been very fearful of a united Germany and saw the Soviet Union as a balancing factor. President Bush said that, nonetheless, he was uneasy about this. It would be a hard position to sell in the United States.

The President said that Chancellor Kohl would be coming to Camp David without Herr Genscher or the German Ambassador, and he was looking forward to a very frank talk, particularly on the political aspects of all this. The United States had a lot at stake in the success of Chancellor Kohl in the forthcoming elections. The Prime Minister agreed that we did not want a Socialist Germany. Chancellor Kohl was a politician to his finger tips and he had no doubt thought out all these problems. The risk was that, if the Social Democrats did well in the GDR elections, and unification came rapidly, then Kohl could find himself losing the election in a unified Germany. Genscher would not be so worried, since he had been in coalition with the SPD before. President Bush said that what he heard about Herr Lafontaine made him anxious, although General Walters had assured him there was no need to worry. He seemed a flamboyant fellow who might lead Germany off in the wrong direction. The Prime Minister agreed that he seemed to be a buccaneer type. She found it hard to judge how serious a threat he posed to Chancellor Kohl. Kohl would presumably go into the election as the man who brought about unification: but that might not be enough.

President Bush said that he was wondering what subjects ought to be discussed in the Four plus Two group. He did not want to give the Russians a forum in which they could exploit Germany's domestic divisions, in order to force a looser association between Germany and NATO. He thought the focus should be on working out the details of giving up Four Power rights and responsibilities for Berlin and for Germany as a whole. But the group should also be a chance to satisfy the Soviet wish to be fully involved, and the place to settle the question of NATO membership. The Prime Minister said that the group would certainly need to range more widely than just Berlin alone. It must deal with the big issues.

President Bush said that surely everyone was agreed that the Polish borders were permanent and inviolable. This was guaranteed by the Helsinki Accord. The Prime Minister pointed out that Helsinki was not a treaty. The Poles were determined to have a legally binding instrument. The President asked whether the Prime Minister had told Mazowiecki that we all regarded Poland's border as a settled issue. The Prime Minister confirmed that she had. The trouble was that Chancellor Kohl would not openly say this. Poland's anxiety was increased by the speed with which we were moving towards unification of Germany. She hoped the President would raise the Polish problem with Chancellor Kohl.

President Bush asked whether the Prime Minister had recently discussed these issues with President Mitterrand. What was his view? The Prime Minister said that, in private, he was just as fearful as anyone else. He had told her that, if we were not careful, Germany would win in peace what she had failed to achieve in war.

She thought President Mitterrand would be adamant on the need for a treaty to regulate Poland's border. He was also talking about a broader European confederation, although he did not seem to have thought out the details. In her view, this could best be done by updating and strengthening the CSCE framework. She urged the President not to underestimate the concern in Europe at the prospect of German dominance. It was enhanced by the speed with which they were pressing for unification. It all created great uncertainty. She knew that people in the United States were worried about Japan. Just imagine if Japan were in the middle of a continent.

The Prime Minister continued that she had talked to President Mitterrand about closer Anglo-French relations, particularly in the defence sphere. He had been receptive and officials were now involved in discussions. The President said that he had some feeling that Mitterrand would be less helpful over the aspect of keeping Germany in NATO. The Prime Minister said that Mitterrand would probably argue that the military implications for NATO of unification were not a matter for him. He was more likely to focus on the political and European Community aspects. But he would be solid on retaining US forces in Europe. The Prime Minister added that we would need to begin to think about the size of our own forces in Germany. This was regulated by the Brussels Treaty of 1955.[2]

The President said that the United States would remain firm on the presence of its forces and nuclear weapons in Europe. He would work with the Prime Minister on the CSCE idea. But, for him, NATO was fundamental, indeed more important than ever. Not everyone in the United States agreed, but he was sure of it. The Prime Minister said she was aware of the battle which the President was having to fight in the United States. It worried her that there were people who were so blinkered that they did not realise NATO's value, and she was immensely grateful for the President's firm stand which was fully echoed by the United Kingdom. President Bush said the trick question put by journalists was: who is the enemy now? His reply was that the enemy was apathy and unpredictability. The Prime Minister said her reply would be that you never knew where a threat might come from. In her years as Prime Minister there had been the Soviet invasion of Afghanistan, the Iran/Iraq war, the invasion of the Falklands. The Middle East was full of ballistic missiles and chemical weapons, and there was the awful prospect of more countries obtaining nuclear weapons. By the time you could see who your enemy was, it would be too late to prepare. She was committed to strong defence.

President Bush interjected that he was increasingly concerned about the chemical plant at Rabta in Libya.[3] The intelligence was very worrying and people had not been made aware of the danger because of the sensitivity of the intelligence. He intended to raise the matter with Chancellor Kohl. The Germans still seemed to have an input. The Prime Minister said she fully shared the President's concerns.

The President concluded that he and the Prime Minister were very close on the key questions. He would telephone her to fill her in after Chancellor Kohl had left. He wondered whether it might not be a good idea for him, the Prime Minister and

---

[2] The Brussels Treaty of 1948 was revised and expanded in October 1954 to include the FRG, which became a member of NATO in May 1955.

[3] The Rabta facility for the manufacture of chemical warfare agents was constructed in 1984-88 with the help of experts from the West German chemical industry. The FRG Government publicly acknowledged its purpose in February 1989, but US-West German relations remained strained over the issue.

President Mitterrand to get together for a discussion. He thought this could be presented in such a way that the Germany did not feel excluded. It could be a useful triumvirate at some point. The Prime Minister said that she would be ready to take part in such a meeting. She made a point in keeping in close touch with President Mitterrand.

The President said that he was concerned about Gorbachev's position in the Soviet Union. He had slightly changed the American position so that they no longer spoke only about support for perestroika but of their desire to see Gorbachev succeed. He certainly faced terrible problems, with the economy in even worse shape than we had all thought. The Prime Minister said that Gorbachev had shown great tactical skill. She would be seeing him in June. The President asked whether Gorbachev had sought food aid from the United Kingdom. It was clearly a very sensitive subject for him. He had not made any direct approach to the United States. But Havel had said that the Russians were desperate for food. The Prime Minister said we had received no direct request. She would make some enquiries.

The Prime Minister congratulated the President on the success of the Drugs Summit in Colombia. The President said that he would very much like to talk to the Prime Minister about these issues.

The Prime Minister said that she would be going to the Aspen Institute in early August. The President said they must get together, but he hoped to see the Prime Minister well before then. He would ring her after Kohl's visit.

I am copying this letter to Simon Webb (Ministry of Defence) and to Sir Robin Butler.

Yours sincerely,
C.D. POWELL

No. 156

Sir R. Braithwaite (Moscow) to FCO[1]

No. 321 Telegraphic [*WRL 020/1*]

Confidential   MOSCOW, *26 February 1990, 10.30 a.m.*

Madrid for Secretary of State's Party.[2]

Washington Telno 446 to FCO: Soviet Views on Germany[3]
1. We have reported the views of a wide range of Soviet opinion formers and officials over recent weeks. Sir P. Cradock's visit has brought our knowledge up to date.[4] The picture is pretty clear. It boils down to the following.
Unification
2. There is no doubt among responsible Russians that German unification is going to take place. Since the autumn, Gorbachev himself has been very careful

---

[1] Repeated for information Immediate to Paris, Bonn, Madrid, UKDEL NATO, Washington.
[2] See No. 152, note 2.
[3] No. 154.
[4] See No. 154, note 10.

never to rule out unification as the likely result of historical change. With Modrow's visit to Moscow on 29-30 January he publicly recognised that history had now taken control. Those lower down the official hierarchy have been slower to recognise the inevitable. In mid-December Deputy Minister Adamishin, who habitually exaggerates for negotiating effect, was still arguing that the Four Powers could in some way shape or even prevent unification if they stuck together. But last week he admitted to Sir Percy that the Soviet Union had very few levers indeed with which to influence the process at all. Some of the academic institutions have long foreseen this outcome. And Soviet television, in its extensive and on the whole objective coverage of politics in both Germanies, speaks as if unification is a foregone and not very distant conclusion.

3. But even if they now seem ready to surrender to the inevitable, the Russians still hope that they can somehow influence the manner in which unification takes place, and the external environment in which a united Germany would be placed. They hope that the Government of the GDR will retain enough credibility after the 18 March election to carry at least some negotiating weight with the Federal Government. They hope that, once that election is over, the practical difficulties of combining the financial, economic, and social systems of both Germanies will act as a natural brake on the process. They hope that this will give them more time to secure binding assurances from the Germans and their Western Allies over frontiers and future security arrangements.

4. They know they cannot achieve these aims on their own. Hence their desire for an early meeting of the Two plus Four, even if only at expert level, before the 18 March election tilts the negotiating balance even more decisively against the East Germans and themselves. But even if they secured such a meeting, their position would be weakened by their lack of a clear and convincing conception of post-unification Europe to set against the Western idea of a liberal and democratic Germany anchored in NATO and the European Community.

Frontiers

5. The Russians' most immediate and concrete requirement is for a binding legal instrument to settle Germany's post-war frontiers and beyond doubt. It is not only that they fear that Germany's actual frontiers with Poland on the Oder-Neisse line might be brought into question. Beyond that, as Adamishin told Sir Percy, they fear a revival of German claims to the former German territories they hold themselves: East Prussia, Königsberg and elsewhere. This may seem fantastic to us, and in their cooler moments it probably seems fantastic to them. But it is a real underlying fear.

6. Though they talk as if these matters could be settled through the CSCE process, what the Russians would really like is the formal certainty of a peace treaty. They have barely begun to think how a peace conference would be organised, when it would be held, nor who might participate (The Brazilians, who joined the Allied coalition when victory was certain? The Albanians?).

Security Arrangements.

7. Intellectually, the more sophisticated Russians can understand and even accept the Western argument that German adventurism can best be prevented, and the mistakes of Versailles and 1939 avoided, if united Germany remains in NATO. But in practice even the coolest of them cannot—yet—swallow the proposition that the Soviet Union should give up the fruits of victory and the defensive glacis in Eastern Europe, in exchange for an arrangement whereby Soviet security would in effect be guaranteed by German membership of a Western alliance set up forty

years ago to oppose them. Hence the firmness with which at present they reject the idea.

8. Hence also the talk of a 'new European security system' building on the conventional arms negotiations and the CSCE process, and the concept of the 'common European house'. According to Adamishin, this would give new content to the traditional concepts of 'neutrality' and 'security'. I do not know what he means. I suspect that the Russians have no plan, but simply hope that the process of multi-lateral negotiation will slow things down and—in some unforeseeable way—cast up opportunities they can exploit.

9. Meanwhile all of our interlocutors claim that the Russians are not really afraid of German expansionism or aggression. Though this is hard to reconcile with their obvious agitation, I believe it to be true. As one of Gorbachev's closest advisers has told us, the Russians will be able to sort out the Germans as long as they retain their nuclear weapon. No doubt this is why the Russians seem increasingly reconciled to the doctrine of minimum deterrence.

10. The Russians' biggest practical headache in the short term is the substantial force they still maintain in East Germany. For the time being they believe these troops can remain there on the basis of victors' rights and the Four Power agreements. They hope that the Vienna negotiations and the CSCE process generally will provide a respectable cover for their reduction and eventual withdrawal. One close adviser to Gorbachev thinks the troops may be home in two or three years. But though our interlocutors are uneasily aware that even this timetable could collapse under the headlong pressure of the Germans to unify, there is no sign that they have yet given thought to the terms on which Soviet troops might remain in East Germany, at least perhaps for a transitional period as is now being suggested in the West.

Domestic Politics

11. All our interlocutors tell us that the German issue still arouses great popular emotion, and remains a domestic hot potato. There is no reason to doubt them. Ligachev made an attempt to exploit this popular sentiment in the recent plenum. Gorbachev found it necessary to respond to it in his press interview last week. Gorbachev's German policy would doubtless figure in the indictment against him if he fell. Popular emotions probably act as a brake on the evolution of Soviet policy. But I do not have the impression that they are in any way decisive. If Gorbachev can manage the disengagement of Soviet troops from the DDR and Eastern Europe without incident, and without too obvious an affront to Soviet prestige, the people will acquiesce. They have more pressing problems at home.

Conclusions

12. It follows from the foregoing that I agree with much of the US assessment in Washington telno 446. Gorbachev has been very careful in public and in private not to close off options. Even on the most difficult question of all—German membership of NATO—he has been most circumspect. Unlike some more junior Soviet officials, he knows that there is not much he can do about it unaided.

13. But that does not mean that he feels the need at this stage openly to accept the Western line. Given the uncertainties of current German politics, he can reasonably hope to secure useful limitations on united Germany's participation in Western security: Genscher and Stoltenberg have already shown the way. He may conclude that, on this issue at least, time is not necessarily against him. I would therefore expect Soviet officials to continue for a while to say, as Adamishin did to

Sir Percy, that German membership of NATO is unacceptable to the Soviet Union: and to play on German doubts as best they can meanwhile.

14. The Russians would like to be involved in early talks either bilaterally or multilaterally. They have three objectives: to secure acceptable agreements if they can: to exploit Western disarray where it exists: and to be seen—by their own public at least—to be participating as equals in the reorganisation of central Europe. They do not want to appear to be acquiescing in a diktat concocted amongst the Western Allies.

15. As seen from here, however, the immediate task for all four Western Allies is to agree on their objective (Germany in NATO and binding legal guarantees for Germany's frontiers), on the means of achieving it (procedures for phasing out Four Power rights and special transitional arrangements for former GDR territory and for the Soviet troops there): and on procedures (timetable and agenda for Four plus Two meetings: Polish participation: other 'peace conference'-like means of settling the frontiers) and so on.

16. I believe that the Russians can in time be brought to acquiesce in our main objective. They have little choice if the Allies play their hand properly. There is much to be said for delaying the Four plus Two talks while we sort ourselves out, as the Americans suggest. But even this will not eliminate the risk of the Russians attempting to preempt the outcome by strong public statements intended to affect German domestic politics. They are already moving that way (see statements of 24 February reported in my telegram no 322).[5] So the first priority for the West is to stop the Germans wobbling. Though the BBC news this morning was not very encouraging about Camp David, the Americans are still the best placed to do this.

17. This does not mean that we should not be talking to the Russians meanwhile. On the contrary, we need to keep them engaged and to know how their thinking is developing. And there are concrete issues to discuss—such as Soviet ideas on Four Power rights and transitional arrangements for their forces, on the nature of a conference on frontiers, and on the shape of a future European security system. We can pursue these without prejudice to the central issue of Germany in NATO. Early guidance to our thinking will be useful, of course. So will instructions that enable me to insist on appointments with senior officials, and Gorbachev's personal advisers, which are not always easy to come by.

18. FCO please advance immediate to Charles Powell and Sir P. Cradock, No 10 Downing Street.

[5] This telegram of 26 February reported statements by the Soviet Foreign Ministry and Mr Shevardnadze rejecting the idea that a united Germany should be a member of NATO (WRL 020/1).

No. 157

Minute from Mr Wall to Mr Weston

[*WRL 020/1*]

Confidential   FCO, *26 February 1990*

Britain's Influence in Germany

The Secretary of State saw Bonn telnos 228/9.[1]

He thought that most of the points made by Sir C. Mallaby had been covered in his speech in the House of Commons.[2] He believes that the line established in that speech and in the *Die Welt* interview[3] will remain the base for us between now and 18 March. We should work out and put to No 10 a new line for thereafter.

The Secretary of State agrees that we should pursue the idea in paragraph *a*(iv) of Bonn telno 229, i.e. of greater international integration of Allied armed forces in Western Europe. He thinks the idea of an international corps should be pursued. He would be grateful for advice.

The Secretary of State also agreed with the idea in *b*(i) that we should encourage British firms to cooperate as partners and suppliers with West German firms engaged in developing East Germany.

J.S. WALL

[1] No. 151 and note 3.
[2] No. 152, note 4.
[3] Not found.

No. 158

Letter from Mr Powell (No. 10) to Mr Wall

[*WRL 020/1*]

Confidential   10 DOWNING STREET, *27 February 1990*

Dear Stephen,

EC/Germany

The Prime Minister has noted press reports that Herr Genscher has challenged a comment attributed to her, namely that the former GDR could not automatically become a member of the European Community following unification of Germany. I think this is a matter of semantics. The Prime Minister's point was that there would have to be detailed negotiations, covering such matters as derogations and transitional periods, and that GDR membership could not take place (as Tommy Cooper used to say) 'just like that'. You might like to make sure that Herr Genscher understands this.[1]

Yours sincerely,
CHARLES POWELL

[1] This message was conveyed in FCO telegram No. 136 to Bonn of 1 March (WRL 020/1).

No. 159

Mr Hurd to HM Representatives Overseas

Guidance No. 11 Telegraphic [*WRL 020/1*]

Restricted   FCO, *28 February 1990, 2 p.m.*

German Unification

Introduction

1. Events have moved rapidly over the last three months. The unification of Germany now seems virtually certain.

Line to Take (Unclassified)

2. We have long supported the principle of German unity. This is something for the German people to decide, in the first instance. But there are important external aspects, as Chancellor Kohl has pointed out. The Four Powers (UK/US/France/USSR) together with the two German states (the Six) will pursue these further. We envisage close consultations within the EC and NATO.

Additional Points (Unclassified—Unattributable)

3. *Will a Unified Germany be in NATO?*

—Western countries, including the FRG, believe that a united Germany must remain in NATO. A neutral Germany would not contribute to stability or security in Europe.

—But no interest in exploiting the situation to the Soviet Union's disadvantage. Aim is to find a durable solution which takes account of others' legitimate concerns.

—Will be exploring in future talks (including in the Six) how such concerns can be met. Likely to include special arrangements for territory of former GDR.

4. *Will GDR Become Part of EC?*

—Now seems almost certain that the territory of the GDR will become part of the Community following German unification (i.e. not as a separate member state).

—Adaptation of present GDR law and practice to Community rules will call for detailed negotiation and will no doubt involve derogations and transitional periods. But do not overestimate scale of problem. GDR population 5 per cent of EC's, GDP 15 per cent of FRG's, and GDR already has special EC status. Commission currently reviewing whole subject. Community discussions expected in spring.

5. *Position of German Borders (Especially GDR/Polish Border)?*

—Genscher has said that a united Germany will be the present FRG, GDR, and Berlin. We agree. We have told the Poles that we share their view that there should be a formal treaty instrument.

—Chancellor Kohl has also said that Germans do not wish to link the question of unification with changes to existing borders.

—Clearly important that this issue should be settled definitively.

6. *Position of Berlin?*

—Western protecting powers and Soviet Union will need to discuss with the Germans how the Four Power regime in Berlin should be wound up. This will be a matter for discussion among the Six.

7. *Risk of Fourth Reich?*

—No. FRG has changed fundamentally since Nazi period. Forty years of well-established liberal democracy. A close friend, partner and ally.

8. *Right of Others to Have a Say?*

— Internal aspects of unification are primarily a matter for the Germans themselves. We have always supported their right of self-determination.

—Four Powers have rights and responsibilities relating to Berlin and Germany as a whole. But the establishment of the Group of Six is not meant to exclude others. Relevant issues will need to be discussed also in, e.g., NATO and EC. Will also be taking account of concerns of others, e.g. Poles.

9. *Role of CSCE?*

—Formal approval of unification by all 35 CSCE states is not (not) required. But the Six are likely to make a presentation at summit this autumn.

10. *Future of Soviet Forces in GDR?*

—Yet to be agreed. But we could imagine a transitional period when some forces remained in what is now the GDR, even after unification. We have no wish to cause instability through sudden change.

11. *UK Opposed to German Unification?*

—No. we have been committed to it for well over 40 years. We have been anxious to see that security implications and other external aspects are properly considered. This is now provided for. We shall be working hard to take the process forward.

Background (Restricted—may be drawn on with trusted contacts)

12. The UK, US, France and FRG are committed by the 1955 Bonn/Paris Conventions to work for their common aim of a 'reunified Germany enjoying a liberal-democratic constitution, like that of the Federal Republic, and integrated within the European Community (of states)'. Until recently, any suggestion of German unification was firmly opposed by the Russians. As recently as October 1988, for example, Gorbachev described attempts to raise the 'so-called German question' as unpredictable and even dangerous.

13. The mass exodus of GDR citizens into the FRG last autumn put the German question back on the agenda. The turning point, which led directly to the opening of the Berlin Wall on 9 November, was Gorbachev's visit to the GDR in October when he made plain that he would not support Honecker's wish to suppress opposition. 344,000 GDR citizens left in 1989, and over 100,000 have left so far this year. Virtually none have returned. Under the FRG's Basic Law, all Germans are entitled to come and live in the Federal Republic. The FRG believes that the only way of stopping the outflow is by giving GDR citizens the hope that their economic situation will improve soon.

14. HMG's view was set out in the Secretary of State's speeches to the Konrad Adenauer Foundation in Bonn on 6 February and to the House of Commons on 22 February (VS Nos 09/90 and 017/90).[1]

15. There have also been intensive discussions in Ottawa on 12/13 February at the Open Skies Conference. It was agreed that the two German states and the Four Powers would meet at Foreign Minister level to discuss external aspects of German unification, including the issues of security. This configuration avoids creating the impression that the Four Powers are deciding the future of Germany over the

[1] Nos. 131 and 152, note 4.

Germans' heads, while enabling the Four to discharge their Four Power rights and responsibilities. (Briefly, these include reunification and a peace settlement, Berlin, borders, and stationing of forces.)

16. Foreign Ministers will not meet until after the GDR's elections (the FRG do not wish to confer extra status on the present GDR Government). But bilateral ministerial meetings and meetings of officials may take place sooner.

17. The GDR Prime Minister, Modrow, with some Soviet support, has called for German neutrality. All major parties in the FRG have rejected this. The Poles have told us that they find the prospect of German neutrality worrying, and would rather see a unified Germany staying in NATO where its partners can act as a restraining influence.

18. The Russians still do not accept the idea of a unified Germany being in NATO. One of the main Western objectives in the Four plus Two talks will be to convince them that this poses no risk. Although the Western position has not been formally agreed, Western countries have separately suggested to the Russians that the whole of Germany might be within the NATO area, but no NATO forces would be based in the territory of the present GDR.

19. Successful incorporation of the GDR's territory into the EC following unification would require economic reform, and the creation of a climate in which outsiders can invest with confidence. The GDR is at present plainly incapable of fulfilling EC obligations, and the pace at which the ex-GDR adjusts to Community law and practice, and the Community accepts goods from the present GDR as Community-produced, will need to be the subject of negotiations. The Commission has set up a group of Commissioners to review specific areas. The subject will no doubt be discussed at the informal EC summit in April, for which the Commission are preparing a paper.

20. Since there has been no final peace settlement with Germany, the question of borders has yet to be settled. Four Power rights and responsibilities relate to Germany within its 1937 borders. Some right wing politicians in the FRG still favour pressing territorial claims. Kohl has avoided taking a firm position on this in public: he cannot afford to lose many votes to the extreme right-wing parties in the FRG's elections this December. But we do not believe that this masks any real intention to reopen the issue.

21. There are already signs that some countries (Poland, Italy, Netherlands, Denmark) are sensitive to any implication that the Four plus Two framework excludes other allies from addressing their own legitimate concerns. We shall be considering how we can satisfy them, without so broadening the core group that talks get completely bogged down. NATO will have a particular role in this.

No. 160

Minute from Mr Eyers (East Berlin) to Mr Munro

[*WRE 014/1*]

Confidential   EAST BERLIN, *28 February 1990*

Call on Herr Modrow, Wednesday 28 February

1. I paid a courtesy call on Herr Modrow on 28 February. He gave me over fifty minutes. After welcoming me and wishing me success in my job, he spoke of the situation in the GDR since November, at the present time and in the future.

2. Looking back, he said that developments had not gone quite as expected in November, and there had been times of great strain, but the situation had steadied once the Round Table had joined the Government. It had taken time. There had been a moment when people had too often wanted to put a spoke in the Government wheel, while being unready to offer alternatives or take any responsibility. That period was now over and the members of the Round Table were now sharing full responsibility as they ought. He would ask me not to pass on the comment to them, but he thought they were grateful for the opportunity to learn the ropes, and to get a feeling for the workings of Government for a couple of months before some of them took over. Relations within the Government were ones of mutual respect, though there were substantial differences of background and approach. It was not easy, given that there were 13 parties represented, but a good deal of solid work was being done to clear the decks for the election and the period thereafter.

3. The present was marked by the run up to the election. For the moment things were relatively on an even keel (though that could change). The electoral scene was composed of five groups: the Alliance with links to the CDU; the SPD; the Liberals; church groups; and the PSD [*sic*: ?PDS] and its friends. The first three were distinguished by their being in receipt of Federal German support, to the extent that they were hardly distinguishable from the corresponding Federal German parties. That said, he noted that in the more sober mood now gripping the country, apart from those attending the SPD congress, Federal German politicians visiting the GDR were finding that they were drawing now very much smaller crowds than in the past.

4. Looking forward, he thought it impossible to say how the elections would go. People had become much more reticent and careful after the first flush of enthusiasm had faded. It seemed likely, however, that the SPD would do better than most. He was worried that the more cautious attitude that had set in might be reflected in a low turn-out on 18 March. That would be a bad thing.

5. I asked Herr Modrow how he saw the timing of unification and in particular how the internal and external aspects should be tied up. He answered that no-one could accuse him of having acted in a way calculated to put obstacles in the way of unification. His concept '*Deutschland einig Vaterland*' showed otherwise. But he was convinced that the process should be a careful one, each step being thought out. The trouble was that the Federal authorities did not wish to adopt this approach. The Federal Chancellor's treatment of his Government when they went to Bonn had been surprising. It was not a good augury. It had not gone down well in the GDR and had contributed to the much more sober mood that now existed. It

was evidently too much marked by electoral considerations rather than the responsible long-term thinking which was called for. The reasons were evident enough, but he thought that it might prove that Herr Kohl's policies benefitted the SPD rather than his own Party.

6. It seemed to him possible to think in terms of currency and economic union by the autumn. There were three aspects which needed to be tied together: currency union, unification of the two economies, which would involve a lot of new legislation, and a social net to compensate for the impact of the changes. The trouble was that the currency union issue had been pulled forward and the process was not at a kilter. It was because the process would take time that a solidarity contribution had been necessary. In his haste the Chancellor was moreover missing a number of important political elements. One of these was the value to Western Europe of the GDR's importance to the Soviet Union as a supplier and market. Business people realised the importance of this factor but there was no sign that the politicians did so. It was of great importance for us all to give the Soviet Union a helping hand in the interests of stability and the GDR was singularly well placed to act as a channel for this.

7. Against that background, Herr Modrow said that he wished to ask for British help, not in preventing the present movement towards unification, which was inevitable, but in controlling it in the interest of stability in Europe. It was of great importance that there should be time to think through the relationships, not only between the two Germanies but between whatever emerged and the European Community. (He mentioned in this context, though without any great emphasis, his suggestion for a militarily neutral German state.) I said that the UK's view was that whether and how the two German states were united was the business of the Germans alone. But if they decided that they did wish to unite, the interests of their neighbours and others concerned must be consulted and taken into account. It was for this reason that we were uneasy before Ottawa and relieved that agreement was obtained after discussions between the Four and the Two. We thought it particularly important that a united Germany should be bedded into the European Community and equally important that Germany should be bedded into NATO though we could contemplate arrangements which would allow Soviet troops to remain for a while in what was now the territory of the GDR.

8. After some Private Secretary had beaten a few times on the door to indicate that the next caller was waiting, I made to go. Herr Modrow insisted, however, on repeating his message that he looked to us to steady the pace of the discussion of the external aspects of German unity; and asked that his personal good wishes be passed to the Secretary of State and the Prime Minister.

P.H.C. EYERS

No. 161

Minute from Mr Weston to Mr Wall

[*WRL 020/1*]

Confidential   FCO, *28 February 1990*

Berlin Four

1. I chaired a meeting at 1 Carlton Gardens today of my counterparts from the United States, France and Germany. Both Bob Zoellick and Ray Seitz attended for the Americans. A full record will issue separately.[1]

2. On the question of an early meeting of the Four plus Two at Political Director level, both my French colleague and I argued in favour, Kastrup declared an open mind and the Americans, initially at least, remained hesitant. After we had talked it through at some length and re-assured the doubters, both as to substance and procedure, the mood seemed to become more favourable. It was left that Kastrup would reflect further and give us a response within twenty-four hours and the Americans would then deliver their verdict in the light of the German decision. With luck, we may still get consensus on this. Kastrup incidentally will be seeing both Adamishin and, separately, his East German counterpart, within the next few days.

3. On Polish borders too, the German attitude (or at least Genscher's) was encouraging. Kastrup said that Genscher found the Polish approach very attractive. He thought they could live with the idea of some contingency consideration of a Polish draft treaty quite soon on the basis that this would not be signed or ratified until after the achievement of German unity. He also spoke of joint or identical resolutions by the *Bundestag* and by the new East German Parliament after 18 March expressing the required sentiments on the Polish border question.

4. On modalities of a unified Germany within NATO, Kastrup was pushed quite hard by all three of us. In particular, I took him through all the questions set out in our own paper on the defence of a unified Germany and all of us urged him to accept that these were matters for joint determination.[2] We had an interesting discussion about the military defence of Berlin. Zoellick argued strongly that the presence of allied garrisons there together with German troops after German unity would be consistent with recent German Government pronouncements because Berlin [was] not part of the GDR; and that it was difficult otherwise to see how the future capital of a united Germany could be defended, given the residual presence in the former GDR of large numbers of Soviet troops. On all these questions, Kastrup pleaded no position pending further consultations in Bonn, but took careful note.

5. On other German-related points, the Americans will provide and circulate a Legal Adviser's paper on possibilities for a final peace settlement; we agreed to set up a working group of the 3 Allies and the Berlin *Senat* to take stock on Four Power rights in Berlin and to identify priorities; on direct elections, it looks as if we shall have to fall in with a consensus that the Germans be allowed to introduce their proposal to the *Bundestag* on 5 March, but the French, Americans and I

[1] Not printed.
[2] No. 139.

attached importance to not bouncing the Russians; and we agreed on the broad relationship between the Four plus Two and the CSCE Summit, as well as the modalities for briefing NATO.

6. All in all quite a productive day. I was struck throughout by the extent to which the Americans (particularly Zoellick) seemed to be going out of their way to defer to German sensitivities, and are anxious that we should not let the Russians in through the Four plus Two door until there is a clear Allied position on the agenda to be discussed there. Kastrup clearly valued this cover.

7. Zoellick drew attention to the likely presence in Namibia on 21 March of our four Foreign Ministers (and indeed Shevardnadze).[3] He thought this would probably be an opportunity too good to miss.

P.J. WESTON

[3] At a ceremony to mark Namibia's independence from South Africa.

No. 162

Letter from Mr Powell (No. 10) to Mr Wall

[WRL 020/1]

Secret and Personal   10 DOWNING STREET, *1 March 1990*

Dear Stephen,

Germany

The Prime Minister and the Foreign Secretary took stock this evening of developments over Germany. Their assessment was that our views and policies are gaining ground: but a great deal of work remains to be done.

They agreed that Chancellor Kohl's visit to Camp David had gone quite well, in the sense that he had re-affirmed Germany's commitment to NATO and had been put under some pressure on the issue of the Polish border. But there appeared to have been little discussion of future security arrangements for East Germany: and generally the Americans were a bit too easily pleased with rather vague commitments by the Germans.

Looking ahead, the Prime Minister and the Foreign Secretary identified the following tasks:

—we needed to work out in greater detail our own ideas on security arrangements for East Germany. It made no sense for the FRG to take over the GDR and make no plans for its defence (which seemed to be Genscher's position). Once we had a clear view, we should put it forward in the Four plus Two group;

—we needed to give thought to the EC Heads of Government meeting on 28 April, in particular how we could avoid a bounce on an IGC or institutional questions. One way would be to insist that COREPER and the Council should draw up and agree an annotated agenda in advance. This should be pursued by the Foreign Secretary next week. The key decision which we should seek at the 28 April meeting would be to establish a clear framework for negotiations on the GDR's absorption into the EC;

—we also needed to give careful thought to the Anglo-German Summit at the end of March and particularly to the handling of the press conference. It might be worthwhile trying to agree in advance on the line which the Prime Minister and Chancellor Kohl would use on unification and its consequences at the press conference (on the model of the agreed line on SNF at the Frankfurt Summit). It would also be helpful to have Herr Teltschik over to No. 10 to prepare the Summit (although he would probably find it difficult to leave Bonn around the time of the GDR elections);

—the Foreign Secretary would let the Prime Minister have as soon as possible some further thoughts on how the CSCE framework might be developed.

Yours sincerely,
CHARLES POWELL

No. 163

Mr Hurd to Sir M. Alexander (UKDEL NATO)[1]

No. 54 Telegraphic [WRL 020/1]

Confidential   FCO, *6 March 1990, 7.30 p.m.*

Kohl's Appearance at NAC: 8 March

1. You should seek an opportunity to speak during this session. Unless the occasion turns out to be wholly platitudinous, you should aim to make one point of substance, though without appearing to lead the pack.

2. The main points of your intervention, approved by Ministers, should be as follows:

(i) HMG welcome the arrangements now set up to ensure consultation among allies about the external aspects of German unification. Kohl's presence eloquently symbolises the importance which his Government attaches to this.

(ii) We warmly welcome his clear affirmation that Germany, when united, will remain in NATO and his firm repudiation of demilitarisation in the former GDR.

(iii) British Ministers remain determined that British forces should play their part, along with German and other Allied forces, in the defence of German territory under Article V of the Treaty. We look forward to discussing the appropriate arrangements—in terms of logistical facilities, positioning of ammunition, and (in the event of crisis) forward deployment—which will enable us to fulfil this role in a way which contributes to the overall security of Germany.

3. We do not believe that you need to spell out in your intervention our support for German unification. But if others speaking ahead of you play this point up, you have discretion to include a passage on the following lines:

—Successive British Governments have always supported the principle of German unification, to be brought about as a result of the freely expressed choices of the peoples of the two Germanies. We are very glad that the years of painful division for Germany are coming to an end.

---

[1] Repeated Priority to Bonn, Washington, Paris, East Berlin.

No. 164

Mr Hurd to Sir C. Mallaby (Bonn)[1]

No. 167 Telegraphic [*WRL 020/1*]

Confidential   FCO, *7 March 1990, 6.25 p.m.*

Prime Minister's Message to Chancellor Kohl: Telecon Budd/Keefe

1. Grateful if you could deliver the following message from the Prime Minister to Chancellor Kohl as soon as possible. Text has already been faxed to you. There is no signed original.

Begins

Dear Helmut

It was very good of you to let me know so quickly about your Government's decision on the border between Germany and Poland.[2] I have been following the matter closely and very much agree that the border should be entirely secure and guaranteed by treaty. I therefore welcome your intention that the two German Governments and Parliaments should issue formal declarations about this as soon as possible after the elections in the GDR, and this should be followed by a treaty soon after unification.

These are most statesmanlike steps. They will help dispel the previous uncertainty and will be greatly beneficial.

Warm regards,

Margaret

Ends

[1] Repeated for information Immediate to Paris, Washington, East Berlin, BMG Berlin.
[2] On 2 March the *Bundestag* made a declaration that Germany had no claims on Polish territory, and Herr Kohl agreed to joint *Bundestag* and *Volkskammer* declarations on the inviolability of the German-Polish frontier after the GDR elections.

No. 165

Minute from Mr Weston to Mr Wall

[*WRL 020/1*]

Confidential   FCO, *7 March 1990*

Germany: Two plus Four

1. My steering group had a run over the ground this afternoon in preparation for the meeting in Paris on 13 March of the Berlin Four, to be followed by a meeting in Bonn on 14 March of the Two plus Four, both at the Political Director level.

2. The Germans, who see themselves as having made a concession in agreeing to this meeting before the GDR elections, propose that the 14 March meeting should concentrate on settling organisational questions about the future working of the Two plus Four forum and wish to avoid serious substantive discussion in the absence of legitimate GDR representation. Annexed to this minute is a list of

organisational points and the line I propose to take when we seek to agree an Allied view on 13 March.[1] I think it is desirable that the location of meetings should rotate, though not a ditch to die in. But if the whole series is to take place on German soil, the case for rotation of Chairmanship is reinforced, to prevent the impression that the whole affair is one prolonged German benefit match.

3. As for the first Ministerial Two plus Four, the assumption is that this should certainly take place within a month of the GDR elections. This would point to the need to prepare the ground beforehand among the four Western Foreign Ministers (as well as by Political Directors at Two plus Four). The presence of the four Foreign Ministers concerned in Namibia on 21 March is an obvious opportunity. The recent news that Shevardnadze will also personally attend the Namibia event means that something very close to a Ministerial Two plus Four would also be achievable should time permit.

4. We need to agree in Paris on 13 March the list of legitimate agenda items for discussion in the Two plus Four forum, as well as the likely items the Russians will suggest and the line we should take on these. It now becomes increasingly important for the three Allies to begin to put pressure on the Germans to agree the essential elements for a united Germany in NATO, especially security arrangements for East Germany. We cannot effectively fend off Soviet marauding tactics until we have an agreed position among the four Western Allies. Moreover that position needs to be Alliance-proofed in wider NATO consultations. The extra NATO Foreign Ministers' meeting Wörner is seeking in April, and (at the very latest) the Turnberry Ministerial in early June, should aim to set the elements of this position in concrete, thus minimising the risk of further erosion as the German elections approach.

5. The unspoken fear in all this is that Kohl may already have sold the pass to Gorbachev in Moscow, and that he has intimated as much already to President Bush at Camp David.[2] This would explain why Kohl came down so quickly with Genscher against Stoltenberg over no *Bundeswehr* in East Germany and why President Bush apparently failed to press Kohl on this, despite having given the Prime Minister the impression he would do so.[3] The only way to try to flush this out is by advancing our own positive ideas for united Germany in NATO among the Four, on the basis of the two papers we sent to the Prime Minister on 2 March. I doubt if we will have time to get into this in great depth on 13 March.

6. Once the Two plus Four forum gets into its stride, we must expect considerable press attention. The Russians may indeed seek publicity for the meetings and their own policy approach, and we shall need to think how best to counter this. But for 14 March it should be possible to hold the public line that we are clearing the ground on organisational and procedural questions so as to ensure that the Two plus Four is up and running for serious substantive work as soon as the GDR elections are over.

[1] Not printed.

[2] Herr Kohl visited Moscow on 10-11 February. He told President Gorbachev that, while a united Germany must remain in NATO, he could accept the restriction of NATO forces to the territory of the former FRG and that Soviet troops could remain in the former GDR. In a joint press conference on 25 February, at the end of their Camp David meeting, Herr Kohl and President Bush declared their shared belief that Germany should remain a full member of NATO, including its military structure, with a 'special military status' for the territory of the former GDR.

[3] See No. 154, note 6, and No. 155.

7. Further internal work in the FCO should now in my view concentrate with some urgency on the legal implications of German unity: in particular how to handle the Allied reservation on Berlin over Article 23 of the Basic Law, and a more detailed account of the major components of a package approach to a peace settlement (as distinct from a general peace treaty).

P.J. WESTON

No. 166

Teleletter from Mr Budd (Bonn) to Mr Synnott[1]

[*WRL 020/1*]

Confidential   BONN, *12 March 1990, 9.55 a.m.*

FRG/Polish Western Border

1. I discussed with Bitterlich of the Federal Chancellery on 9 March the background to the recent controversy here, and the likely way forward.[2]

2. He told me (please protect) that the officials responsible for foreign affairs in the Chancellery had been horrified by the statement by the Government spokesman linking reparations and the German minority in Poland to the frontier issue (our telno 266)[3] which had sparked off this episode. For once, 'even Teltschik' had not been to blame (an allusion to Teltschik's recent forays into controversy over inner-German relations: e.g. his much criticised claim that the key to German unity now lies in Bonn). The problem had been that Kohl had found the foreign policy considerations less weighty than those flowing from the internal dynamics of centre-right politics. Kohl's long-standing party intimates had argued in advance that the grassroots needed reassurance on the questions of reparations and the treatment of the German minority in Poland, and remained—to Bitterlich's astonishment—convinced that in overall terms the operation had been well worthwhile.

3. Bitterlich gave me a blow by blow account of the coalition negotiation which led up to the adoption of the text in our telno 286[4] (He admitted, incidentally, its various imperfections, but argued that in the circumstances it was the best that could be achieved.) The most interesting point was that Genscher had at no point pressed the merits of the Mazowiecki plan (i.e. the case for negotiating and

---

[1] Copied to Heads of Political Sections Paris, Warsaw, Moscow; Head of EED, FCO.

[2] The *Bundestag's* declaration of 2 March regarding Polish territory (No. 164, note 2) had been qualified immediately afterwards by a spokesman of the Federal Government, as reported in Bonn telegram No. 266 (note 3 below).

[3] This telegram of 2 March reported a statement in which journalists were told that in Herr Kohl's view the proposed declaration by the *Bundestag* should *inter alia* make clear that the Polish declaration of 1953 relinquishing reparations claims against Germany remained valid; and that the rights of the German community in Poland should be guaranteed by treaty (WRL 020/1).

[4] This telegram of 6 March reported the text of the coalition resolution to be voted on by the *Bundestag* on 8 March. Its purpose was 'to reaffirm the inviolability of Poland's borders as an indispensable basis for peaceful coexistence in Europe in accordance with the principles of the CSCE Final Act and with regard to German unity' (WRL 020/1). The *Bundestag* passed the motion 'after a heated debate' (Bonn telegram No. 299 of 8 March, *ibid.*).

initialling a Polish/German treaty in advance of German unity):[5] the sole focus of discussion had been the proposed declarations by the two German parliaments. Equally, however, he had given no undertaking to abandon his earlier support for it. Bitterlich (whose last job was in Genscher's private office) said that his own assumption, like ours, was that provided there was continuing Polish dissatisfaction with the position now reached Genscher would at some point resume his advocacy of the Mazowiecki plan.

4. Reverting to his orthodox role as a defender of Kohl's position, Bitterlich made these points:

(*a*) The Prime Minister's message[6] had given Kohl much pleasure (on the morning of 9 March the Government spokesman told the press that Kohl had received positive messages from the Prime Minister and Bush, the former starting with '*Lieber Helmut*'):

(*b*) The Chancellery were however much concerned by the disapproval evident in Paris, and worried especially that the French might start to argue that the Polish/German border should be internationally guaranteed. If a 'guarantee' meant the same protection that all other European borders would have after the CSCE summit, well and good. But any more specific idea would be taken seriously amiss by the FRG:

(*c*) The Federal Government remained firmly opposed to the FRG doing anything further at the governmental level to compensate Poles who had done forced labour in Germany during the last war. There was however a possibility that there might be a kindly official eye for one idea now being considered: the establishment of a foundation, funded by major FRG companies, designed solely for the purpose of meeting such claims.

COLIN BUDD

---

[5] This proposal was contained in letters sent by Mr Mazowiecki to Presidents Bush, Gorbachev, and Mitterrand and Mrs Thatcher on 21 February.
[6] No. 164.

No. 167

Mr Hurd to Sir C. Mallaby (Bonn)[1]

No. 177 Telegraphic [*WRL 020/1*]

Confidential   FCO, *12 March 1990, 9.20 p.m.*

From Private Secretary

Secretary of State's Visit to Bonn: Call on Foreign Minister Genscher
Summary

1. Genscher in forthcoming mood. Envisages interim period while Soviet troops still in former GDR in which Articles 5 and 6 of NATO Treaty would not apply. Believes only German forces would be *Bundesgrenzschutz* (border police).

---

[1] Repeated for information Immediate to Washington, Paris, other NATO Posts, Moscow, East European Posts.

Genscher clear that all meetings of the Two plus Four should be in Germany with the first meeting at Ministerial level in April. Accepts need for good preparation among the four Western Allies with a Political Directors meeting before each Two plus Four meeting. Happy to accept a meeting of the Two plus Four with the Poles but not in Warsaw.

2. Libya. Described Libyan suggestion that Rabta could be dismantled if Germans pay. See separate tel not to all.[2]

3. Bazoft. Agrees to appeal for clemency to Iraqi President and Foreign Minister (separate tel not to all).[3]

Detail

4. Genscher said opinion in the GDR election campaign was shifting. The FDP had made a bad mistake by not having the same name in the GDR as in the FRG. The SPD was still in front but it would not get more than 50 per cent of the vote. The best outcome would be a broad coalition of all three main parties. Later, over lunch, Genscher described the extraordinary and moving enthusiasm of the crowds he was addressing in the GDR. But their enthusiasm was for West German politicians. They were completely apathetic about their own people.

5. Genscher said he was very grateful for the Prime Minister's message on the Polish border.[4] At the Four Power meeting in Ottawa he had said how important it was for the meetings of the Two plus Four to take place in Germany. We should stick to that. The Polish Government would want to participate at some point. (Much of the subsequent discussion centred on how to handle this issue and the Polish invitation to a meeting in Warsaw.) Genscher said that the Polish Prime Minister and Foreign Minister had reacted positively to the *Bundestag* resolution. Only Jaruzelski had complained that there was no specific mention of the Oder/Neisse. The Poles had subsequently made clear that they wanted negotiations on an agreement in advance of unification. The agreement would be initialled at this stage but would only be signed and ratified by an all-German government and parliament. Dumas had telephoned him on Saturday about the Polish invitation to a Two plus Four meeting in Warsaw. He (Genscher) could not agree to that. We should stick to meetings in Germany. Otherwise we would lay ourselves open to demands to meet in Moscow. As regards the form an eventual agreement with Poland might take, normally one would expect such an agreement to be bilateral. He acknowledged that the Russians were suggesting signature by the Four or the 35. The 35 came too close to a peace treaty. The Four would be better. But his understanding had always been that the Four would give a more general blessing to a treaty and then indicate that their own powers had lapsed. He did not know if the Four would guarantee the border.

6. The Secretary of State said the important thing was to establish a clear Western position on the future of Soviet troops in the former GDR and on the defence of the former GDR. Would Articles 5 and 6 apply?[5] We thought they would have to but that there would not be NATO forces stationed there. If,

---

[2] Not printed. See No. 155, note 3.

[3] Not printed. Farzad Bazoft was an Iranian-born journalist working for the *Observer* in Iraq. He was convicted of espionage on 10 March and executed on 15 March.

[4] No. 164.

[5] Article 5 of the North Atlantic Treaty reads, in part: 'The Parties agree that an armed attack against one or more of them in Europe or North America shall be considered an attack against them all'. Article 6 defines the territories and armed forces against which an attack under Article 5 will be deemed to have occurred.'

following the Genscher/Stoltenberg discussions, the *Bundeswehr* were not to be stationed in the former GDR, what troops and in what uniform would be there?[6] It would of course be a mistake to link these questions with those of the US or British presence in the west. Brandt had suggested symmetry between the Soviet presence and the American presence. We did not accept that.

7. Genscher agreed. Either the Soviets could remain for a number of years or their presence could be tolerated until a certain stage of development was reached. Genscher thought the Russians would move sooner than any of us expected on this issue. They would not immediately accept a total withdrawal of their troops: they needed a face-saver. And they would talk about all the problems they would face over e.g. having no barracks in the USSR. As the GDR economy improved (which it would do—quickly), they would also notice the disparity over standards of living. They would want to be paid in some form. Genscher was convinced in the end the Russians would accept Germany's presence in NATO. The Secretary of State said that the Russians were claiming that this issue was vital to Gorbachev's survival. He thought they were building themselves a tough negotiating hand.

8. Reverting to the question of the German military presence in the former GDR, the Secretary of State said that one could envisage various scenarios in which troops could be needed, e.g. trouble perhaps arising from the presence of the Soviet garrison. Genscher said that the German constitution absolutely ruled out the use of military force for domestic disputes. It was conceivable to use the border police (*Bundesgrenzschutz*) but they would have to be real police, not military in disguise. The issue would have to be discussed with the GDR government who would themselves probably propose something on these lines. But these forces would not be former members of the GDR army in police uniform. They would have to be genuine police, though including police in barracks.

9. The Secretary of State asked whether Articles 5 and 6 would apply. Genscher said that they would in the last analysis. The real question was what to do in the period when the Russians were still present. Whatever the situation, we had to bear in mind that the cards were all stacked in favour of the West: the Russian presence in the GDR would be restricted, the GDR would not be part of the Warsaw Pact, the Russians would be out of Czechoslovakia. The Secretary of State said that if, by any mischance Gorbachev were overthrown by the generals, Germany would nonetheless face 250,000 Soviet troops on her territory. Genscher said that, thanks to CFE etc, the numbers would be a maximum of 175,000. He accepted that there would need to be a separate stationing treaty with regulations covering what should happen in the event of violations. It was possible (and Genscher emphasised that he was thinking aloud) to make provision for Articles 5 and 6 to apply once Soviet troops were withdrawn or in the event of the regulations governing the Soviet troops being violated, i.e. there could be a trigger. But this should be a matter of negotiation by the Alliance, not a Soviet/German issue. He did not want to give the Russians leverage by putting too many ideas on the table. He expected the Russians to say that the *Bundeswehr* was anyway too numerous. Once the Soviets reduced their troop levels under CFE, there would be a disparity and Germany would no doubt have to make reductions. This too was a matter for the Vienna negotiating table. It was in the interests of the Alliance that Germany should not be seen as a special case. In parallel with the Two plus Four talks, we should develop

[6] See No. 154, note 6.

our approach to the Vienna negotiations. The Secretary of State agreed with this approach. The West was in a strong position,

10. The Secretary of State and Genscher agreed that the Russians were very worried about the use of Article 23 but Genscher said that they should be reassured. Even Article 23 could only come in at the end of a procedure which would settle the external aspects of German unity. He had made this public in the *Bundestag* debate last week and had also made clear that once unity was achieved, the relevant parts of the preamble as well as Articles 23 and 146 would be deleted from the Basic Law.

11. Genscher said that in discussions with the GDR Government he had made clear that issues of substance could only be discussed once the freely-elected Government was in power. It had been agreed that all the meetings should be on German territory. He agreed with the Secretary of State that we must properly prepare for the Ministerial Two plus Four talks. This should be done by Political Directors. He thought the first meeting at Ministerial level would take place some time in April.

12. In further discussion of the possibility of a meeting of the Two plus Four in Warsaw, Genscher said this would be very bad for German public opinion. If the Poles wanted a guarantee of their borders by the Four he could live with that. He later told the Secretary of State again that Warsaw would be very difficult. The Secretary of State urged him to say as positively as he could that the Poles would be welcome at the Two plus Four talks at the relevant moment, leaving until later the question of venue.

13. The Secretary of State asked Genscher how he thought we could deal with the Russians' legal hold over the Article 23 process in respect of Berlin. Genscher said it was the FRG's clear intention to settle all the external aspects before unification was finalised. He agreed with the Secretary of State that it would be sensible to offer to discuss how to wind up the occupation regime but we should not allow the Russians to filibuster. The aim should be to present the CSCE summit with the results of the Two plus Four discussions.

14. Over lunch there was some discussion of the EC aspects of unification. The Secretary of State said that we envisaged short transition periods. It would require a major effort to bring the GDR up to Community standards and we were asking a lot of the FRG. What was Genscher's view on the impact of GEMU?[7]

15. Genscher said that EC questions were not the most difficult. The most difficult were problems like property and pension rights. With the present rate of exodus from the GDR, there was no alternative to GEMU. The creation of a single currency was the best way of exerting pressure for market conditions. The private banks in the FRG, who were as cautious as they came, supported this process. Genscher agreed with the Secretary of State that it would be very difficult to keep all these issues on a stable footing during the long FRG electoral campaign. He personally hoped that domestic issues would displace external issues at the top of the agenda. He did not regard the border question as being the real problem though Kohl might see things differently. It was very important that the German public should not see the Two plus Four process as Germany being trampled on. Hence the importance of the talks being held in Germany.

[7] German Economic and Monetary Union, under discussion within the FRG Government since early February

16. Genscher said he attached a lot of importance to investment in the GDR by other EC member states. It was politically necessary for the whole Community to be seen to be involved, and that the FRG should not have an unfair advantage.

No. 168

Mr Hurd to Sir C. Mallaby (Bonn)[1]
No. 180 Telegraphic [*WRL 020/1*]

Confidential   FCO, *12 March 1990, 10.05 p.m.*

From Private Secretary

Secretary of State's Visit to Bonn: Call on Chancellor Kohl

Summary

1. Kohl gives his version of events on Polish border but regards the issue as less significant than Germany's place in NATO which he sees as central to FRG election campaign. Unlike Genscher, does not give a clear view on application of Articles 5 and 6 of NATO Treaty. Grateful for Prime Minister's support on *Bundestag* resolution on Polish border. Prepared to see Polish Government involved in Four plus Two talks at relevant moment but thinks a meeting in Warsaw would be too sensitive politically for the Germans. Thinks the CDU have caught up in the eastern German election campaign. Sees best outcome as one in which no party has absolute majority.

Detail

2. The Secretary of State spent nearly an hour with Kohl in Bonn this afternoon. Kohl said he had no special feel for the outcome of the GDR election campaign. He thought that the CDU had caught up with the others. The SED [*sic*: SPD?] had made ground earlier on but he implied that their earlier links with the SED and the willingness to accept up to 30 per cent of former SED members was now telling against them. Kohl described the enormous audiences he was getting for his speeches in the GDR. The substantive problems there remained. The Communist leadership had deliberately taken a long time to establish an electoral law. Economic reforms had not started. The security police were still threatening people ('we'll still be here even after the elections'), and the exodus from the GDR was continuing unabated: 132,000 since 1 January, i.e. half a million by the summer at current rates. Hence the importance on [*sic*] currency/economic union. Kohl's original intention had been to proceed at a much slower pace. In the British press he was accused of hotting things up but the opposite was true. He envisaged three sets of elections in the GDR this year: the elections on 18 March, regional elections in May (which could lead to the re-establishment of the old *Länder*) and elections in the *Länder* themselves. Elections in the Federal Republic would go ahead in December. There might be all-German elections next year but he would want international agreements to be in place before then. He hoped the Two plus Four process would be concluded by the end of the year, i.e. prior to the proposed CSCE meeting and to the FRG elections.

---

[1] Repeated for information Immediate to Washington, Paris, Moscow, other NATO Posts, East European Posts.

3. Kohl said that membership of NATO was crucial and not to be bargained, i.e. he would not be tempted down the path of leaving NATO as the price of German unity, though there were forces at work in the opposite direction. It was in this context that he was against unification taking place under Article 146. Article 146 was bad (1) because it would involve a debate which could last up to 18 months while a new constitution was discussed. One of the lessons of 1948 had been not to repeat the mistakes of the Weimar constitution: (2) under Article 146 the constituent assembly could change a number of things by simple majority, e.g. destroying the social market economy: (3) the NATO and other treaties could be re-negotiated. Lafontaine wanted to leave NATO. Article 146 for him would be an elegant way of achieving that. There were some people who claimed that Article 23 was an Anschluss. It was not. The GDR would have to submit a request under Article 23 and there would have to be agreement on a transition. A number of issues would have to be resolved which would take many years. Property rights were completely different for example.

4. Kohl said he was grateful to the Prime Minister for her message on the Polish border issue. He looked for close cooperation with us in the Two plus Four framework. Of course we would have to talk to the Soviet Union about NATO but he repeated that there was not a price to be paid for German membership. The aim was that Germany should be a completely normal country within NATO with the sole and long-established exception of being a non-nuclear state. Of course Soviet troops would not leave the GDR overnight (he mentioned a 5 year transition) and for a transitional period the *Bundeswehr* would have no presence in the GDR. These were issues to be discussed. The Russians were playing the cards they had in their hand but he believed that in the end the Russians would want Germany to be a member of NATO—albeit for not very friendly reasons.

5. The Secretary of State said we understood what Kohl was trying to achieve. What he had said about NATO was crucial. We imagined it would be a big issue in the Federal campaign. In a British newspaper article that day Brandt had said that there should be a symmetrical withdrawal of Soviet troops from East Germany and American troops from West Germany. That was a false symmetry.

6. Kohl agreed. When he had become Chancellor in 1981 people thought he would be a bird of passage. But he had beaten off the opposition. He had taken them on over INF stationing and won. The SPD alliance with the SED in the GDR was pulling the SPD down the path towards neutrality. Brandt's comments tended in the same direction. He recognised that NATO would change but that was quite different from what Brandt was saying. Kohl was confident he would win the battle. He would only be defeated if the SPD, FDP and the Greens came together. He was working to keep the present Coalition together. He thought a majority in the coalition supported the Article 23 route. He did not think the FDP would be looking for a new partner, but they did want some more leeway.

7. Kohl said that getting the resolution he had secured on the Polish border in the *Bundestag* had been something of a triumph. One had to remember that there were strong feelings on both sides of the border. Terrible things had been done by Germans in Poland. But the displacement to Poland of people of German origin was also a wound that continued to irritate. Both sides needed a gesture. Germany had already paid large reparations to Poland and he did not want that whole issue re-opened in a peace treaty. The Poles were still talking in large figures. It should be possible to reach an agreement provided the whole issue was not magnified. He

himself would be 60 in a few days time. He would rather stand down than be misunderstood by his friends.

8. The Secretary of State said we were satisfied with the way the decision had come out. The Poles had got reasonable satisfaction on substance but wanted something on procedure to show they were not to be presented with a *fait accompli*. On the wider issues, of course Soviet troops would remain in the GDR for a time. But if there were not troops from the *Bundeswehr* there who would defend the former territory of the GDR if things went wrong? Kohl agreed that the issue had to be discussed. We needed an interim solution. Gorbachev would have about 200,000 troops there (which would, however, be a reduction from present levels). We should not move too speedily. Much of the basis of conflict would have been reduced. NATO itself was much more than a military alliance. His own life-long support for it had been based on a concept of bringing together people in states with the same basic ideas and order: the Western community of values. It was that that needed protection against attack. He had set out his position clearly in NATO the previous week.

9. Reverting to the question of the Two plus Four discussions, Kohl said he had had a telephone call from Jaruzelski last week urging the need to avoid a new Yalta. Kohl accepted that but if the Two plus Four talks were held in Warsaw that would create a psychological situation which would have devastating effects. The German public accepted the reality of a settlement with the Poles but they could not be expected to be jubilant about it. He had accepted that the Poles should be at the table for the Four plus Two meeting for the relevant discussions but to have that discussion in Warsaw would be very difficult for him politically. He was not suggesting that the Poles must come to Bonn or Berlin but why could they not meet in Dresden or Frankfurt or Leipzig? Those psychological factors apart, once a meeting was held in Warsaw then the Russians could demand a meeting in Moscow. He wanted to keep these issues under control so that he could fight the main battle which was not about the Oder/Neisse line but about Germany's place in NATO.

10. Kohl said that the newly united Germany would have a very different power axis from the Germany of 1983. The capital of a united Germany had not been decided but the real centre would, as with the FRG now, be in the south or south-west. Modern power lay not in coal but in the computer. Prussia would not be the centre of power that it had been. The situation would be no different from now when German prosperity lay in the provinces like Hesse, Baden-Württemberg, Bavaria and Rheinland-Palatinate. Fears about the developments of a united Germany ran unfounded. Whoever believed Poincaré was a good adviser was wrong.[2] Poincaré was dead.

---

[2] The French statesman Raymond Poincaré had been an outspoken advocate of punitive treatment of Germany during and after the First World War, and had encouraged separatism in the Rhineland.

No. 169

Sir C. Mallaby (Bonn) to Mr Hurd[1]

No. 315 Telegraphic [WRG 026/10]

BONN, *13 March 1990, 2.29 p.m.*

Secretary of State's Visit to Bonn on 12 March: German Media

Summary

1. Extensive German media coverage. Most reports concentrate on your remarks on the Polish border question, Germany's position in NATO and the need for an 'orderly process' towards unification.

Detail

2. Virtually all leading German newspapers give front-page coverage to your visit here yesterday, reporting your remarks to the press conference held in the Embassy after your meetings with Genscher and Kohl. Most focus attention on your statement that a treaty on the question of the German-Polish border should be put in place as soon as is practicable and that the Poles should be present when their borders are discussed. Both the *Süddeutsche Zeitung* (independent) and the *Frankfurter Rundschau* (left of centre) interpret this as in line with President Mitterrand's recent proposals. Your welcome of Bonn's stated readiness to conclude a border treaty is reported with satisfaction, as are your remarks on the need for an 'orderly process' as regards both the border question and the constitutional procedures necessary to achieve unification.

3. In two reports, *Handelsblatt* (liberal) draws attention to your statement that the eventual absorption of the present GDR into the EC will require a very tough series of discussions involving derogations for the GDR from certain aspects of Community law and at the same time protection for other member states, with particular reference to agriculture, fisheries and the structural funds. The relationship between a united Germany and NATO is described as HMG's primary concern.

4. The electronic media also played up the importance of the visit. Your calls on Kohl and Genscher and your Embassy press conference (at which 9 television teams were present) were covered in all the national news bulletins. The first national channel (ARD) carried your statement that HMG's main concern is the future of the North Atlantic Alliance, and noted your stress on the importance for the security of Europe of continued German membership of NATO. A linked commentary suggested that the British aim was no longer to 'put the brakes on unification' but instead to speed matters up within an orderly process.

5. The extent and warmth of media coverage were in marked contrast to the cooler reception the media gave you when you were last here.

6. We shall report further on any editorial comment arising from your off-the-record briefing to senior editors.

---

[1] Repeated for information Priority to UKDEL NATO, Washington, Paris, Warsaw, Moscow, BM Berlin, East Berlin, CICC(G), UKREP Brussels.

No. 170

Letter from Mr Hurd to Mrs Thatcher

[*PREM: Internal Situation in East Germany*]

Personal and Confidential   FCO, *13 March 1990*

Dear Prime Minister,

Bonn, March 12

You will have seen the telegrams on substance.[1] Kohl was much more relaxed than at my last meeting, and grateful for your message.[2] He twice asked me to tell you that he would never trade German membership of NATO for German unification. Germany wanted no special status; she must be part of NATO and the EC. He had a tussle on his hands on NATO with the SPD. So far from speeding up German unification, he was trying to get a grip on it to slow it down.

I tried to pin down both Kohl and Genscher on the security issues, which seem to me the most important. Kohl mentioned five years as the possible time limit for stationing Soviet troops in East Germany. He would not be drawn on Articles 5 and 6 of the Treaty or on the defence of East Germany, beyond questioning whether there was an enemy any longer to defend it against.[3] Genscher is thinking in terms of police stationed in barracks, and possibly the triggering of Articles 5 and 6 if something untoward occurred. Otherwise Articles 5 and 6 would apply once the Soviet troops were out.

The people who still make Kohl bristle are the Poles. He was very defensive about the events of last week, and refused to contemplate a meeting of the Six in Warsaw. On the other hand, Genscher has already conceded the alternative put forward by the Poles in Paris, namely that they should attend any meeting at which their frontiers were discussed. We must build on that and move towards a Treaty as rapidly as possible, though the first step will be the declarations of the two free German Parliaments endorsing the present frontiers. Kohl, in almost elegiac mood, said at nearly 60 he was past political ambition, and willing to stand down rather than be misunderstood by his friends. The Germans believe (rightly I think) that, in stiffening their stance on German neutrality, the Russians are building up a tactical negotiating position. But all depends on the flow of German opinion. The Russians may not concede the point until after the FRG elections, in case a SPD Government eases their problems. Brandt (an antique figurehead now) was equivocal on this point. That timing would upset the Kohl-Genscher plan, which is to present the results of the Six-power process, including NATO membership, to a CSCE Summit before the FRG elections.

The strong emphasis from Kohl and Genscher now is on the need to agree these external aspects before unification occurs—'no surprises for our friends'. The German editors whom I met, and the British press corps, still feel that the pressures from the East, in particular continuing high emigration, may force a faster pace. For example, if East German prices rose towards West German levels but salaries

---

[1] Nos. 167 and 168.

[2] See No. 133 for the Kohl-Hurd meeting of 6 February. Mrs Thatcher's message to Herr Kohl is printed as No. 164.

3 See No. 167, note 5

stayed at a fraction of the West German level, then emigration might reach levels which would compel instant unification.

Yours,

DOUGLAS HURD

No. 171

Letter from Sir A. Acland (Washington) to Mr Weston[1]

[*WRL 020/1*]

Confidential and Personal WASHINGTON, *14 March 1990*

Dear John,

US Attitudes to British Policy on Germany and Europe

I was away from Washington for 9 days from the end of February on a speaking tour in the Midwest and then a long week-end of skiing. On my return, I read accounts by Andrew Wood and Kevin Tebbit of conversations they had recently had with Blackwill and Dobbins, and brought myself up-to-date with both press cuttings and other reports of contact between the Embassy and various parts of the Administration. I was worried by what seemed to me to be the unjustified nature of the perception here, both in the Administration and in the media, about British attitudes towards Germany and Europe. Indeed my initial, reactions both on substance and on personalities were very similar to those you expressed recently to Andrew Wood.

A useful analysis by Kevin Tebbit of the substance of our policies, as compared with those of the United States, Germany and France showed, as I had expected, that while there are shades of difference and emphasis in a number of areas, we are not very far apart from the Americans on the main points of substance. In a fast moving situation and with different geo-political interests, it is not surprising that there are some differences of emphasis and tactics between us and I expect that, as negotiations continue and further developments take place, we will all modify our positions and tactics to some extent, while holding on to the essentials which we share (a unified Germany's membership of NATO within its military structure, treaty assurances about the Polish border and so on).

I thought that it would be worth having a frank talk with someone at the top of the State Department about all this. Baker, who always has a hideous schedule, was not immediately available (but I hope to see him at a social function at my house this week) so I went to see Eagleburger. I am not sure that he is always central to the details of the problems surrounding German unification, but he is in touch with all the main players and is a good interpreter of mood.

I began by speaking much on the lines of paragraph one of this letter, adding that if it was a question of perception rather than of substance, it was important to get those critical of British policy to focus on what our policies actually were. If they were found to be not out of line, this might gradually deal with the problem of perception. I also said that it was not helpful to either US or British interests for

---

[1] Copied to HM Representatives in Paris, Bonn, Moscow, NATO (Strictly Personal).

people to go around saying that Anglo German relations were at an all time low, since this merely exacerbated the problem.

Eagleburger said that in some parts of the US Administration, there was a perception, fuelled by some of the Prime Minister's public and private statements, that we remained unenthusiastic about German reunification and would like to slow it down. This perception certainly existed in the European Bureau, who were having to deal with day-to-day issues and problems. But it did not exist much on the 7th floor of the State Department, and certainly not with him and only to a limited degree with Baker. As far as he was aware, there were no major differences between us and the Americans on substance. We were more enthusiastic about an early meeting of the 2 plus 4, and there was some worry in the Bureau that we and the French would form an alliance to the detriment of the Americans and Germans. But equally there was anxiety that the French and the Russians might get together to the disadvantage of others. Eagleburger admitted that the German position was, of course, always central to American thinking. I did not mention particular names myself but Eagleburger commented that Dobbins, whom he described as being very clever and knowing Germany very well from his time as Minister in the US Embassy there, attached special importance to the German aspect.

Turning to the White House, Eagleburger said categorically, and on more than one occasion, that there was no problem as regards the President. He retained a very high regard for the Prime Minister, although he had been struck by the vigour of her expression from time to time about Japanese and German national characteristics. Eagleburger, who is himself a great admirer of the Prime Minister, said that he knew that she tends to say what is at the top of her mind, and does so partly to test her opinions against others and to see if there are good arguments against them. Nor, said Eagleburger, was there any problem with Scowcroft. He commented that Blackwill was better than Dobbins on the German issue but not really important, although he had some influence with the President (it might be salutary for Blackwill to hear this assessment of him!).

Eagleburger said that inevitably the Bureau, who had to deal with the immediate day to day problems, sometimes grew frustrated if agreement was difficult to reach, and inevitably tended to take a short term view. Eagleburger himself believed that one of the most important issues for the next few years would be the continued US presence in Europe. He intended to make a speech about this before too long. On an issue like that, he had absolutely no doubt that the United Kingdom, under Mrs Thatcher, would be the most important and staunch ally. The French would not necessarily be supportive, nor perhaps would the Germans. Eagleburger was, in general, very critical of the way in which Kohl and, to some extent, Genscher, failed to take account of the sensitivities of neighbouring and other countries.

I asked Eagleburger what he thought could be done about the perceptions. He said that it would of course help if the Prime Minister could sometimes say some nice things in public about Kohl and Germany. I told him that relations were excellent between the Secretary of State and Genscher, that the Prime Minister and Kohl would be meeting before too long and that she did indeed send the Chancellor encouraging messages from time to time—for example on his handling of the *Bundestag* debate on the Polish frontier. We concluded by agreeing essentially that all those involved in German issues at the State Department and other parts of the Administration, as well as journalists, should constantly be encouraged to concentrate on the substance of our policy, rather than on some people's perceptions of it.

I would not claim that this talk with Eagleburger will bring about any rapid change of attitude. Nor would I place too much reliance on his characterisation of attitudes in the NSC, where the urge to help Kohl and the mistrust of Soviet motives in 2 plus 4 could continue to make harmonisation of positions difficult. But I do not think that it will have done any harm to have had this frank exchange with him. He urged, as he usually does, that his confidences about people and policies be very strictly respected; and I should be grateful if he is not quoted in any way.

Yours ever,
ANTONY ACLAND

No. 172

Extract from Conclusions of a Meeting of the Cabinet held at 10 Downing Street on 15 March 1990 at 10.30 a.m.[1]

[*CC(90)10*]

German Unification

3. *The Foreign and Commonwealth Secretary* said that the first meeting of officials of the two Germanies and the Four Powers (the 2+4) had taken place on 14 March. There had been useful agreement on the procedural arrangements, and the key issues for further discussion had been identified. The process would now gather speed. A meeting at Ministerial level was likely to take place in April. By then his own visit to Moscow would have taken place, so that he would have had an opportunity to probe the position of the Soviet Government. The recent flurry of activity over the issue of Poland's borders with Germany had now settled down. It had been agreed that representatives of the Polish Government would be invited to an early meeting of the 2+4 in order to discuss the border question. Hence, the Polish Government, with the support of the British and French Governments, had achieved their basic aims over substance and procedure. The German Government had been obliged to accept that there would have to be a Treaty with Poland confirming the Oder-Neisse line. He had had useful discussions in Bonn on 12 March with the West German Chancellor, Dr Helmut Kohl, and his Foreign Minister, Herr Hans Dietrich Genscher, and had also met Herr Willy Brandt. Anglo-German relations were on an even keel. It was noticeable that German Ministers were now making statements about the need to proceed in an orderly fashion over unification of a kind which British Ministers had been making for the previous two months. Chancellor Kohl was much more relaxed than in the past. Although polling in the West German elections would not take place until December, the election campaign was effectively under way. An increasingly important issue in the elections would be whether Germany should continue to be a full member of the North Atlantic Treaty Organisation. Chancellor Kohl continued to take a firm line, though Herr Genscher's position was less solid. By contrast, the

[1] For attendance at this meeting see No. 114.

position of the Social Democratic Party was much more equivocal. This underlined the importance for the Alliance of a victory for Chancellor Kohl in December.

The Cabinet—

Took note.

No. 173

Mr Eyers (East Berlin) to Mr Hurd[1]

No. 197 Telegraphic [WRE 014/1]

Confidential   EAST BERLIN, *15 March 1990, 4.15 p.m.*

The GDR on the Eve of Elections (on 18 March) to the Volkskammer (Parliament)

Summary

1. A fair campaign, heavily influenced by West Germany, to be followed by free and fair elections. A centre right/centre left grand coalition the likely outcome. Thereafter the tempo of negotiations on unification would speed up. If the PDS do well enough to hold up formation of an anti-Communist coalition the exodus could resume, leading to considerable confusion, even chaos. This is a possible, but unlikely outcome. After 18 March the German question can be addressed.

Detail

2. Fifty years after Hitler broke the Munich Agreement by invading Czechoslovakia, setting the conditions for the outbreak of war, Germans in (East Berlin and) the GDR go to the polls. The poll will take place six months after the Hungarians precipitated the East German revolution by opening their border with Austria.

3. The last elections in this part of Germany in which the voters had a choice between alternative policies, were held under Nazi (1933) and Communist (1946) auspices. On the evidence of those polls and of the 1990 campaign, the reservoir of support for the centre right is somewhat greater than for the centre left. There has been one issue: the timing and modalities of unification. The centre right CDU-backed Alliance for Germany favour the fastest possible route: accession to the FRG via Article 23 of [the] Basic Law. The SPD are also in favour of early unification, but on the basis of a new all-German constitution. The PDS (successor to the Communist SED) and assorted left wing groups which have been wooing the 'angst . . .' vote quite successfully, want to slow things down. It seems likely, however that the majority still favour early unification. Kohl attracted more than twice as many people (around 250,000) to his final election rally on 14 March) in Leipzig than Willy Brandt. Alliance support for Article 23, and Kohl's offer, as Federal Chancellor, of currency union, also suggests a strong showing for the Alliance, although the Schnur affair (my telnos 193 and 194)[2] could trim their support. The situation of Genscher (possibly the most popular and certainly most

---

[1] Repeated for information Priority to Bonn, BM Berlin, Paris, Moscow, Washington, UKDEL NATO, UKREP Brussels, UKDEL Strasbourg, UKDEL Vienna, UKMIS New York, Actor, BRIXMIS, East European posts, Peking

[2] Not printed. Wolfgang Schnur, Chairman of Democratic Awakening, had been forced to resign shortly before the election, having been revealed as a long-standing Stasi informer.

trusted of all West German politicians here) compared with the weakness of the liberals suggests that people will vote for big parties that can get things done or slow things down.

4. The typical PDS voter would be a youngish, under-employed (in future, unemployable) female office worker or sociologist worried about free kindergartens. Modrow and Gysi (the only two significant GDR personalities in the campaign with the possible exception of SPD leader Böhme) have indicated that they expect to be in opposition next week. But if the PDS polls well enough to bid for a place in the new Government or holds up formation of an anti Communist coalition there is likely to be a further mass exodus and something approaching chaos. Fortunately the likely outcome is a grand coalition between the alliance and the SPD. In the final stages of the campaign, the Alliance, the SPD, and their West German backers have largely refrained from attacks on each other.

5. The external aspects of unification have hardly featured in the campaign, reflecting a conscious decision by the West Germans and all East German political formations. On the contrary, the Hungarians and Gorbachev personally have been praised for making free and fair elections possible. The FRG's permanent representation here have confirmed that Kohl and Genscher did not want the '2+4' talks to discuss substance before 18 March because they could have forced external aspects of unification on to the election agenda.

6. There are many foreign observers here. They have seen a campaign that was fair in the circumstances. The only area of controversy has been West German involvement, an issue for the PDS which has no Western support. The first results are expected on Sunday evening but the lack of a data base (of previous results) and the numerous (24) parties will make it more difficult than in West Germany to predict the final result quickly.

7. On 19 March the pace of events will pick-up. If there are difficulties over coalition building, the population will put pressure on their newly elected parliamentarians by voting with their feet again. There could be attempts, by Saxony and Thuringia for example, to join the FRG via Article 23 at once. If on the other hand, a grand coalition can be formed quickly, negotiations on currency union will forge ahead, allowing political unification and the external aspects to be dealt with at a more measured pace. This outcome would also allow for orderly preparation of local elections to be held on 6 May.

8. The elections on 18 March will not answer the German question but they will permit it to be addressed.

No. 174

Mr Hurd to Sir A. Acland (Washington)[1]

No. 482 Telegraphic [*WRL 400/1*]

Confidential   FCO, *16 March 1990, 4.03 p.m.*

My Tel No 190 to Bonn.[2]

Two plus Four Talks: A Peace Settlement

1. Discussion in the Two plus Four talks on 14 March failed to agree on whether the question of a peace settlement should be placed on the agenda for future talks. The four Western Allies had indeed agreed on 13 March that the question should form part of the first agenda item: borders and a general peace settlement. But at the Two plus Four the Germans who were in the chair appeared to resile by dropping the second half of this item, and received American support. We should be grateful if you would go over the ground again with Zoellick and/or Seitz in order to explain why we believe that the subject needs to be addressed and Allied views clarified.

2. First, some more background in amplification of our reporting telegrams. On 14 March, Kastrup's only reference to this question was under the fourth agenda item in terms of Four Power rights and responsibilities and 'successor arrangements'. When asked to explain what this meant, he suggested replacing the last two words by 'their termination' and agreed that this might be taken to encompass all aspects of a final settlement. In the ensuing discussion Adamishin drew a distinction, which in our view was justified, between (*a*) the termination as such of our Four Power rights and responsibilities and (*b*) arrangements amounting to a general peace settlement which would draw a line under all the wartime and post-war arrangements arising from the conquest of Germany in 1945. Kastrup, however, was adamant in opposition to terminology relating to a peace settlement or even a peaceful settlement (we assume that the phrase was too close to 'peace treaty' for the Germans' liking). But he said he could contemplate a formulation such as 'the possibility of a final settlement'. This, as the French pointed out, could imply that no form of final settlement was needed. The French preferred specific reference to a peace settlement. For our part, we did not wish to expose internal differences on the part of the Western Allies and acted through notes to the chairman. But Kastrup would not be moved and, somewhat to our surprise, was supported throughout by Zoellick. The matter was therefore left unresolved.

3. Grateful if you could tell the Americans that we think that this is an issue which needs to be addressed squarely among the Western Four and talked through since it will otherwise be a bone of contention, not only between Germany and the Russians, but of wider significance. As the Russians have obliquely pointed out in the Soviet Foreign Ministry's statement (Moscow tel no 425),[3] the issue features in

---

[1] Repeated for information Immediate to Paris, Bonn, Moscow, East Berlin.

[2] This telegram of 16 March reported a 'businesslike first meeting of the Two plus Four' (WRL 020/1).

[3] This telegram of 14 March reported the Soviet Foreign Ministry's statement on Germany of 13 March, which stated *inter alia*: 'One must recall that the Potsdam Agreement unambiguously proceeds from the premise that the restoration of German statehood should proceed in an orderly

a treaty between the four Western Powers as well as being covered in the Potsdam Agreement. It cannot therefore be evaded. Article 7 of the 1954 Convention on Relations between the three Western Allies and the FRG states that 'an essential aim of their common policy is a peace settlement for the whole of Germany, freely negotiated between Germany and her former enemies, which should lay the foundation for a lasting peace . . . The final determination of the boundaries of Germany must await such settlement'. This phraseology clearly goes beyond Four Power involvement.

4. In pointing this out to the Americans (whose paper on this subject promised on 28 February is still awaited, incidentally) you should stress that we do not have fixed and rigid views about the arrangements which might eventually be deemed to amount to a settlement. It certainly need not imply a single overall peace treaty in the traditional sense. We would share many of the German reservations about a peace treaty, not least because it might involve any or all of the 57 belligerents and because it could greatly complicate the handling of claims and reparations. This in turn could lead to a very lengthy process and uncertainty, and hence risk instability.

5. Our preliminary view is that a settlement could be brought about through a framework comprising several different elements and involving a variety of participants. The key elements would include borders, relations between the Three Powers and Germany, relations between the USSR and Germany (terminating USSR/GDR agreements), Berlin, and relations between the Four Powers and Germany. Other elements, perhaps not of such primary importance, would include aviation, the question of existing treaties, reparations, debts and claims. (An illustrative note by Legal Advisers—not for handing over—follows by bag.)[4] All this might involve a number of treaty or other instruments being drawn up as part of a settlement, with the settlement as a whole coming into force when all states concerned had ratified the instruments. On that day the Four Powers might issue a declaration finally terminating the rights and responsibilities assumed in 1945.

6. At this stage we would regard this as illustrative only. It could be susceptible to much flexibility and variation. But the main point of substance, which we hope that the Americans would recognise is that an overall settlement of some sort is needed. On terminology, this concept is described in current treaties in terms of a peace settlement. Clarity points to continuing to use this term. But this may not be essential. We could live with the term settlement.

7. We need to develop a common approach to all this among the Western Four if the Russians are not to have a field day at our expense. The Germans ought to be persuadable that it is in their broad interest too and that this is indeed the best way of outflanking talk of a general peace treaty. But the Americans must engage in the substance. So far Zoellick's performance has been disappointing. He seems to have an exaggerated attachment to the tactics of the moment in any given meeting, and to protecting what he conceives to be German interest (quoting Genscher almost more than Kastrup does). But there is not much sign that he has taken any advice within the State Department on the hard core of the subject matter, and Seitz in his presence remains very quiet.

democratic framework, that the procedure and conditions for unification should be decided on the basis of agreement among all interested parties, and principally the Four Powers. This fundamental provision was also recorded in West Germany's treaties with the three Western powers and the treaty of the German Democratic Republic with the Soviet Union' (WRL 020/1).

[4] Not printed.

No. 175

Sir C. Mallaby (Bonn) to Mr Hurd[1]

No. 337 Telegraphic [*WRL 400/1*]

Confidential   BONN, *16 March 1990, 6.16 p.m.*

FCO Personal for Synnott, Head WED
Washington Personal for Wood

Two plus Four: Legal Aspects

Summary

1. Recommendation that US and UK Legal Advisers meet to discuss legal aspects soon.

Detail

2. I noted John Weston's comment to Zoellick after the Two plus Four meeting that consensus between the Western Four on the question of the nature of any final German settlement would have to be re-established urgently (para 14 of your telno 190).[2] The impression given by the US Embassy here is that US legal thinking is not at present well focussed and is driven excessively by a desire to put as little as possible in formal instruments, thus avoiding submission to Congress. This impression was confirmed during discussions last weekend between Hill (my Legal Adviser) and Propp (of State Department Legal Advisers, in Bonn on a private visit). Propp said that a paper on legal aspects of a settlement was being prepared by the State Department Legal Advisers, primarily by Koblitz (former Legal Adviser, US Mission Berlin). Propp said that Berlin aspects were being thoroughly considered (because that reflected the expertise of the US Legal Advisers concerned) but they had not got far with Germany as a whole (borders, reparations, the Bonn/Paris Conventions etc).

3. You may already be considering the possibility of US/UK legal discussions. I recommend that these be pursued. I am willing to spare Hill for travel to London or Washington if appropriate.

---

[1] Repeated for information Immediate to Washington.
[2] See No. 174, note 2.

No. 176

Letter from Mr Powell (No. 10) to Mr Gozney

[*WRE 014/1*]

10 DOWNING STREET, *18 March 1990*

Dear Richard,

Elections in the GDR; Possible Statement by the Prime Minister

I have consulted the Prime Minister about the proposed Statement on the East German elections. She agrees that it would be right to issue one, subject to the outcome being broadly in line with expectations. I attach a version which she has approved and which we would propose to use, unless you let me know to the contrary by 0930 on 19 March.[1]

Yours sincerely,
CHARLES POWELL

ENCLOSURE IN NO. 176

The free and democratic elections which took place yesterday mark a new beginning for the people of East Germany and a further step in the spread of democracy through central and Eastern Europe. We look forward to the establishment of a democratic government in East Germany and shall want to work with it.

It is now for the people of East Germany to decide through their elected representatives when they wish to seek unification.

In anticipation of their views we are already considering the external consequences of unification within the Four plus Two talks and with our allies and partners in NATO and the European Community. I am also looking forward to discussing all these matters with Chancellor Kohl during the Anglo-German Summit in Cambridge and London in 10 days' time.

It is a great day for East Germany and for Europe, and we all send the people of East Germany our warm congratulations and good wishes for the future.[2]

---

[1] East Berlin telegram No. 201 of 19 March reported a 'convincing victory [on 18 March] for CDU-led Alliance for Germany engineered by Chancellor Kohl. But, short of an absolute majority, they will seek coalition partners. The SPD the unexpected losers. PDS (successors to Communist SED) in third place will remain a significant opposition force. This result sets the scene for currency union and unification' (WRE 014/1). In mid-April the SPD and FDP joined a grand coalition under the leadership of CDU Chairman Lothar de Maizière.

[2] Mrs Thatcher also sent personal messages of congratulation on 19 March to Herr de Maizière and Chancellor Kohl.

No. 177

Sir C. Mallaby (Bonn) to FCO[1]

No. 349 Telegraphic [*WRL 020/1*]

Confidential UK Comms Only　　　　　　　BONN, *20 March 1990, 6.20 p.m.*

MODSH pass to CICC Germany
Windhoek for Secretary of State's party.[2]

German Unification: The Prospects Following the GDR Election

Summary

1. Dramatic success for Kohl. Presence of CDU-led coalitions in Bonn and East Berlin should facilitate inner German negotiations on transformation of the

---

[1] Repeated for information Immediate to Windhoek; information Priority to Moscow, Paris, Washington, UKDEL NATO, UKREP Brussels, East Berlin, BM Berlin, CICC Germany; information Routine to other NATO Posts, East European Posts; information Saving to Vienna.

[2] Mr Hurd was attending the celebration of Namibian independence from South Africa.

economic system in the GDR, to be followed by monetary union. Kohl in a better position to influence timing of state unification under Article 23 of the Federal constitution. His statements since the GDR elections designed to reassure other countries that unity will come only after agreement in 2 plus 4. GDR election result could be helpful regarding question of Germany in NATO.

Detail

2. The GDR election result is seen in the Federal Republic as a clear democratic decision for early monetary union and German unity.

3. The Federal Government devoutly hope that the rate of migration from the GDR (144,000 so far this year) will now diminish. It is not certain. German monetary union will make things worse in the GDR before they get better.

4. There is a widespread view that the GDR election result makes rapid unification even more likely. It is true that negotiation between two coalitions led by the CDU should be much easier than if the SPD had been the dominant party in the GDR Government. The more so since the Federal CDU has enormous influence over the East German CDU. So agreement on the introduction of the legislative framework for economic transformation in the GDR should be facilitated, and the prospect of German monetary union within months is stronger. Seiters told the US and French Ambassadors and me today that, although a two-thirds majority was required in the *Volkskammer* for some economic legislation, the East German SPD was hardly likely to oppose measures that had obviously been endorsed by the election and were supported by the Federal SPD. The Federal Government, Seiters said, aimed at GEMU this summer, perhaps on 1 July.

5. On state unity, as distinct from economic and monetary, the election result need not mean acceleration. Kohl is now in a position greatly to influence the timing of a move by the GDR to join the Federal Republic under Article 23 of the Basic Law, which is now the expected route. He has been at pains, since the election, to reassure other countries (my telegrams 342 and 344),[3] stressing *inter alia* that unification would come only after completion of work in the 2 plus 4 forum. Seiters made the same point to the three Ambassadors today. He said that, even if there was an early move in the *Volkskammer* to vote for accession to the FRG under Article 23, the procedures to give effect to that, in the *Bundestag* and elsewhere, would delay state unity. He could not see it before 1991. Even Egon Bahr, on the left of the SPD, told me on 19 March that state unity must depend on agreement on international aspects.

6. Seiters also made these points to the three Ambassadors:

(1) The strong showing of the PDS in the election in East Berlin showed that large numbers of GDR officials were still pro-Communist. That might greatly hamper the effectiveness of the democratic Government for some time.

(2) It would be important for the inner German negotiations on economic fusion to show visible progress before the East German municipal elections on 6 May. Otherwise the CDU result could be much less good than this time.

(3) The Federal Government planned to reduce the special advantages enjoyed by migrants from the GDR on 1 July. It was thought premature to do this before monetary union, since the DMark would be a major factor in bringing down the rate of migration.

(4) Genscher was disappointed at the result achieved by the Liberals in the

---

[3] Bonn telegram No. 342 of 19 March reported Herr Kohl's comments on television the previous evening (WRE 014/1). Telegram No. 344 of 19 March reported his speech to the opening session of the CSCE Bonn conference on 19 March (WRG 022/2).

GDR. They had made many mistakes, including the failure until today to adopt the title FDP.

7. Other likely effects of the GDR election results include:

(*a*) The SPD is very badly placed to urge changes in the Federal constitution before it is applied to a united Germany. The prospect is now that the changes will be few (notably the deletion of articles which if retained after unity might imply that there were other parts of Germany beyond the FRG and GDR).

(*b*) The GDR Government will be more susceptible to pressure from Bonn to acquiesce in united Germany's membership of NATO than an East German coalition led by the SPD would have been. To this extent, the surprise election result strengthens our hand regarding the hardest aspect of the 2 plus 4 talks.

(*c*) The confidence of West German and foreign investors in the economic future of East Germany should be increased by the CDU victory, and the prospects of rapid investment should be improved.

8. The CDU/CSU, as of now, looks well placed for the Federal elections on 2 December and for all-German elections which on present form are foreseen in late 1991. Lafontaine, who yesterday agreed (my telno 347)[4] to be SPD Chancellor candidate in the Federal elections, takes over just after a major setback for his party instead of the expected victory in the GDR. His ability to anticipate and exploit the popular mood is famous. Lafontaine has said that Kohl cannot fulfil the promises he made in the East German election campaign, and will make the most of any apparent failure to do so. As Egon Bahr admitted to me on 19 March, Lafontaine must decide whether to exploit popular fears in West Germany about the costs of unity and thus risk seeming half-hearted about unification, which itself is very popular. To get this balance right in the Federal election campaign will be hard enough. and an appearance of half-heartedness could do major harm to the SPD in East Germany and prejudice their chances of the real prize—to beat the CDU in all-German elections and establish a structural majority in united Germany.

[4] Not printed.

No. 178

Mr Wallis (Windhoek) to FCO[1]

No. 190 Telegraphic [*JSN 026/2*]

Confidential   WINDHOEK, *21 March 1990*

From Private Secretary.

Namibian Independence: Secretary of State's Meeting with Jim Baker
Summary

1. Baker rescues the Secretary of State from chaos and Arafat. Briefs Secretary of State on his three hour meeting with Shevardnadze. Latter very exercised about Germany.

[1] Repeated for information Priority to Washington, Moscow, Cape Town Embassy, NATO Posts.

Detail

2. Last night's independence celebrations were pretty fair chaos. The Secretary of State was rescued from the melee by one of Baker's party who found him a seat next to Baker in the stadium. By going into a huddle, the Secretary of State and Baker were able to avoid a triumphal progress by Arafat. Jesse Jackson, who was also with Baker, was instructed to keep lookout until Arafat was safely past, while Baker kept his face firmly turned away muttering 'if I have to shake hands, Jesse, it will set back the peace process by four years'.

3. In the odd gaps between the speeches and fireworks, Baker told the Secretary of State that he had had three hours with Shevardnadze in Windhoek. He had found Shevardnadze very exercised about Germany. He did not distrust the present leadership but who would be running the country in six years time?

4. The Secretary of State told Baker that the Romanian Foreign Minister had said that at the recent Warsaw Pact summit four countries had spoken in favour of German membership of NATO and that Shevardnadze had spoken against, but without apparent conviction. Baker said that he had not got the same impression. Shevardnadze had appeared to mean everything he said and Baker had been unable to make much impression on him.

5. The Secretary of State said that German membership of NATO was crucial. He was worried that the Russians would drag out the Two plus Four discussions so that they got entangled in the Federal German election campaign. The Russians might well hope that the SPD would win, thus giving them a new hand to play next year. We must keep up the momentum of the Two plus Four discussions.

6. Baker said that he was at a loss to know why the French were so difficult about keeping NATO Allies informed about the Two plus Four talks. The Secretary of State said he had tackled Dumas about this in Muscat, but without getting a satisfactory answer. Baker talked about reporting back to NATO after his next discussions with Shevardnadze but did not mention the date.

7. At this point Genscher appeared a row or two behind the Secretary of State and Baker, waving his arms and calling out 'the Coalition as before'. Baker commented to the Secretary of State that while the FDP would be in the GDR coalition, they would not of course have a decisive voice.

FCO please pass to PS/No 10.

No. 179

Sir C. Mallaby (Bonn) to Mr Hurd

No. 375 Telegraphic [*WRG 020/3*]

Confidential   BONN, *23 March 1990, 3.15 p.m.*

British-German Summit 30 March

Summary

1. Teltschik sees marked improvement in British-German relations, caused notably by Prime Minister's two recent messages to Kohl. Teltschik welcomes suggestion of a pre-agreed line on unification for the Prime Minister and the Federal Chancellor to take at the press conference after the Summit. German

comments on our draft early next week. All Kohl's main points for talks with the Prime Minister concern unification. Same applies to his speech in Cambridge.[1]

Detail

2. I called on Teltschik today, and began by saying that I thought that there had been a marked improvement in British-German understanding in recent weeks and in the public perception of it in the FRG. Teltschik agreed warmly. He said that the Prime Minister's messages to Kohl about the Oder/Neisse frontier and then the GDR election result had been brilliantly effective in improving relations.

3. I gave Teltschik the draft enclosed with Charles Powell's letter of 18 March of a line on German unification for the Prime Minister and the Chancellor to use at their joint press conference on 30 March.[2] I reminded Teltschik of the success of the joint press conference in Frankfurt in February 1989, where a joint line on SNF had been prepared beforehand. Teltschik welcomed the idea of a joint line on unification. His only initial comment was that the fifth paragraph—about CSCE—was very general, and could be built up to say more about future development of CSCE, for instance through institutionalisation. I said that institutionalisation was an idea which was not always popular in London. But British and German ideas about the future of CSCE coincided in important other respects, such as the need to introduce principles about the rule of law, democratic elections and the free market. I thought that strengthening of the CSCE language in the proposed joint press line should be possible and could mention these fields of future CSCE development. Teltschik said that he would give me on 26 March a first reaction to the draft line and Hartmann, his deputy, would be ready to discuss it fully with Powell in London on 27 March. The Germans would propose further language on CSCE.

4. I said that we might have some suggestions between now and the Summit about matters in the field of British-German relations which might be mentioned at the press conference. Teltschik expressed interest. I await instructions.

5. I said that I thought that the Prime Minister would wish, in her talks with Kohl on 30 March, to go over the major aspects of unification and Two plus Four, notably the critical question of Germany's arrangements within NATO. I thought that she might ask whether the Chancellor was confident that he could control the speed of progress towards German unity so that it did not get ahead of progress in Two plus Four. Teltschik agreed that the questions concerning NATO were the hardest of the Two plus Four talks. See MIFT[3] for subsequent discussion of this. He said that the Federal Chancellor was absolutely confident that he could maintain synchronisation between the German-German track and the Two plus Four track of unification. He said that de Maizière, in presenting the policies of the new coalition in East Germany, would make a declaration of intent that unity should be effected through Article 23 of the Federal Constitution. But de Maizière had agreed with Kohl that a move by the GDR under Article 23 should be made only after agreement was sure in the Two plus Four process. Teltschik said that Kohl, in the talks with the Prime Minister, would wish to describe his view of how the process of unification would now develop and his vision of the timetable. He would want particularly to describe the economic reforms that the Federal Government would now seek in negotiations with the new government in the GDR

---

[1] The annual Königswinter Conference was to take place at St Catharine's College Cambridge on 29 March.

[2] Not printed.

[3] No. 180.

and his intentions regarding German monetary union. He would wish to review the main agenda subjects for Two plus Four.

6. I said that I thought that the main themes of the Prime Minister's speech on 29 March in Cambridge would be Germany, especially the crucial importance of NATO membership, and the future development of CSCE. Teltschik said that Kohl would talk about German unification—the GDR election, the next stages especially German monetary union, the relationship between the German-German and Two plus Four tracks towards unification, the Oder/Neisse frontier and his determination that Germany should remain embedded in NATO and the EC. His speech would also include brief sections on CSCE and on the EC focusing on EMU and mentioning his goal of political union in one general phrase. Another section of the speech would bring out the British contribution to Germany's interests over the years, with stress on Berlin and British forces Germany.

7. See MIFT.

No. 180

Sir C. Mallaby (Bonn) to Mr Hurd[1]

No. 376 Telegraphic [WRG 020/3]

Confidential   BONN, *23 March 1990, 5.03 p.m.*

MIPT (only to FCO): Teltschik on German Unification and NATO[2]
Summary

1. Teltschik believes that Soviet Union will agree to German membership of NATO, but not easily. Urges us to keep stressing publicly that Germany should remain in NATO. Foresees very difficult negotiations with Soviet Union in 2 plus 4 about other security matters, especially nuclear weapons in Germany. Latter point could pose great difficulties for Federal Government. Teltschik thinks *Bundeswehr* should be stationed in East Germany after Soviet forces go. Wants to hive off questions of limits on *Bundeswehr* and further reductions in US forces in Germany for a further CFE negotiation. Urges early discussion of a mandate for this in NATO.

Detail

2. When I saw Teltschik today in preparation for next week's British-German Summit, I said that the NATO aspects would be the most important and difficult element in the 2 plus 4 negotiations. In our view, the NATO guarantee should be extended to East Germany from the time of unification. Sufficient military capability must be identified in order to make the guarantee credible. Transitional arrangements were needed in the sense that the Soviet withdrawal from East Germany would require some time. But it would be dangerous to postpone until after that the decisions on how to maintain the security of East Germany, as some people in Bonn seemed to be suggesting.

3. Teltschik said that he thought the Soviet Union would eventually accept German membership of NATO. Gorbachev seemed still to be thinking about it.

---

[1] Repeated for information Priority to Washington, Paris, UKDEL NATO, East Berlin, BM Berlin, Moscow, MODUK; information Routine to UKDEL Vienna.
[2] No. 179.

But according to the Soviet Ambassador here, Kvitsinsky, the Soviet military were increasingly opposed to Germany being in NATO. Teltschik said that Allied unity was essential on the matter, and he hoped that we would continue to stress publicly that Germany must remain in NATO. I took the opportunity to say that agreement on the 2 plus 4 subjects especially the security aspects, would be needed among the four Western participants before we got into substance with the Russians. Teltschik emphatically agreed.

4. He continued that the Soviet Union would probably try in 2 plus 4 to insist on limits on the *Bundeswehr* and on deep cuts in American forces in Germany beyond those already foreseen, as well as cuts in other stationed forces. The Russians would press, above all, for the removal of nuclear weapons from Germany. Things would become very tough for the Federal Government if the Russians tried to make agreement to their position on any of these matters a condition of German unity. Teltschik said that, if there was an all-out Soviet push for the removal of nuclear weapons from Germany, the Federal Government would have great difficulty in standing up to the Russians, since public opinion in both German states would see attraction in the Soviet position. He implied that this issue could prejudice the otherwise good prospects of the CDU in the Federal elections in December. Teltschik said that the question of nuclear weapons in Germany might need to be taken up by Bush at his summit with Gorbachev in June.

5. I said that I had been puzzled by the Genscher/Stoltenberg statement that the *Bundeswehr*, even units not assigned to NATO, would not be stationed in East Germany.[3] Without that, how could a NATO guarantee be made credible? Teltschik agreed that the *Bundeswehr* must in due course be stationed in East Germany. But he doubted that this would be possible while Soviet forces were still there. It must be clearly agreed in 2 plus 4 that the *Bundeswehr* would later be stationed in East Germany, but it could be agreed that certain types of weapons would be present only in West Germany and that the bulk of *Bundeswehr* would be in West Germany. Teltschik thought that the question of *Bundeswehr* in East Germany was less important to the Russians than the question of nuclear weapons in Germany.

6. Teltschik said that 2 plus 4 must agree on a timetable for Soviet withdrawal from East Germany. But the Federal Government would not be willing in that forum to agree to limits on the *Bundeswehr* or further reductions in US forces in Germany. These matters should be remitted to a second CFE conference. In order to gain 2 plus 4 agreement to this approach, a mandate for a future CFE negotiation would be needed quickly. Federal officials were working on ideas. Early discussion in NATO was desirable.

7. Teltschik said that there were many indications of major Soviet interest in economic cooperation with united Germany. The Federal Government was thinking how to derive leverage from this in 2 plus 4.

Comment

8. Teltschik's remarks are further evidence that German thinking on the security aspects of 2 plus 4 is not well advanced. There have been signs that some of the players in the Federal Government are tempted by a solution that would leave the question of military resources to uphold a NATO guarantee of East Germany for decision between unification and the completion of Soviet withdrawal from East Germany. There is still no remotely convincing answer to the question how a

[3] See No. 154, note 6.

NATO guarantee of East Germany could be made credible during the period from unification until completion of Soviet withdrawal.

9. Teltschik did not mention SNF negotiations. But I do not (not) attach importance to this omission. There are other indications here that the Germans are preparing a proposal to accelerate the opening of SNF negotiations (my telno 359).[4]

[4] This telegram of 21 March reported that Herr Dreher, Head of the Foreign Ministry's NATO Department, had told Mr Budd that 'the FRG would press for NATO to start preparing its position for SNF negotiations in the run-up to the Nuclear Planning Group (NPG) in early May. This would put the West in a better position in the 2 plus 4 to deflect Soviet proposals to limit nuclear forces in or around Germany' (DZW 083/1/90).

No. 181

Sir C. Mallaby (Bonn) to Mr Hurd[1]

No. 388 Telegraphic [*WRG 020/3*]

Confidential   BONN, *26 March 1990, 5.03 p.m.*

Poland's Western Border

Summary
1. Teltschik expresses officially Kohl's shock and astonishment at Prime Minister's reply to *Der Spiegel* on Oder Neisse frontier. Federal spokesman describes quotation attributed to Kohl by the Prime Minister as inaccurate. Recommendation on best way of drawing a line under this episode.

Detail
2. Teltschik asked me to call today, to receive comments on two subjects. The first was the Prime Minister's reply to *Der Spiegel* about the Oder Neisse frontier.[2] The second (reported separately)[3] was the preparations for the joint press conference of the Prime Minister and the Chancellor on 30 March. Hartmann (who calls on Powell on 27 March) was present.

3. On Oder Neisse, Teltschik said he wished to say officially that the Federal Chancellor was shocked and astonished at the Prime Minister's replies to *Der Spiegel*. Teltschik made 3 points in explanation of Kohl's reaction:

(*a*) The Federal Chancellor had never refused to recognise the Oder Neisse frontier. The only question had been when that frontier should be formally and definitively recognised. The Chancellor had said in the conversation at Strasbourg that the frontier could be formally recognised only by a united Germany.

(*b*) Informal discussions at European councils were confidential. Kohl was surprised that the Prime Minister had quoted a remark allegedly made at one.

[1] Repeated for information Immediate to Warsaw, Paris, Washington, UKREP Brussels.
[2] A lengthy interview with Mrs Thatcher was published in the German magazine *Der Spiegel* on 26 March. After discussing the need for a treaty between a united Germany and Poland to guarantee the Polish-German frontier, Mrs Thatcher declared: 'You know what happened with previous assurances: they were overturned by the German courts, and I heard Helmut say: "No, I guarantee nothing, I do not recognise the current frontier." I heard it myself, in Strasbourg [at the European Council on 8 December] after the dinner' (editor's translation).
[3] Not printed.

(*c*) Kohl was surprised at the Prime Minister's interpretation of the position of the German courts. The Federal Constitutional Court in 1975 had upheld the Warsaw treaty and had said, in line with the position of the UK and the other Allies, that the final legal fixing of the frontier should occur in a peace settlement for Germany.

4. Teltschik continued that this episode had affected the climate between London and Bonn. It was a most unhappy development. The questioning of the Chancellor's position would undermine his so far successful attempts to combat the *Republikaner*, whose entry into the *Bundestag* next December would hardly please the Allies.

5. I said that I would report Teltschik's remarks. The Oder Neisse frontier was a matter of widespread interest, on which others as well as Britain had clear views. Teltschik acknowledged that France was one of those others. I said that, as the Prime Minister's recent message to Kohl had shown, HMG were glad that it had now been agreed that there should be a treaty to fix the Oder Neisse frontier finally.

6. The Federal spokesman, Klein, this afternoon told a press conference that the Chancellor considered himself to have been quoted inaccurately by the Prime Minister. He had been reported as saying after dinner at Strasbourg during the last European Council that 'I will not guarantee, I will not accept the present borders'. This reflected neither the letter nor the spirit of what he had actually said. The Chancellor also moreover regarded as 'unfounded and unusual' what the Prime Minister had said about the role of the German courts.

7. Klein then gave the press (see MIFT)[4] the Federal Chancellor's own version of what Kohl had said at Strasbourg, and commented also on the attitude of the Federal Constitutional Court.

Comment

8. I recommend that we should now seek to draw a line under this exchange. Since it relates to an episode some months back, the best way of doing so might be to tell the media simply that the Prime Minister's view of the situation now reached in relation to Poland's western border is summed up in her message to Kohl of 7 March (your telno 167).[5]

[4] Not printed.
[5] No. 164.

No. 182

Letter from Mr Wall to Mr Powell (No. 10)

[*PREM: Internal Situation in East Germany*]

Confidential   FCO, *26 March 1990*

Dear Charles,

German Unification: Treaties

Thank you for your letter of 20 February about the German-Polish borders and the question of a general Peace Treaty.[1]

[1] On 19 February Mr Wall wrote to Mr Powell correcting a statement made by Mrs Thatcher to Young Conservatives in Torquay, according to which German unification could not come about

Chancellor Kohl's agreement on 6 March, subsequently endorsed by the *Bundestag*, that there should be a Treaty on borders between Poland and a united Germany gives the Poles most of what they say they want—a bilateral treaty, to be ratified after unification. The first round of the Two plus Four negotiations will have helped to ensure that the Germans stick to this. We played a large part in securing agreement that the Poles should be involved in any discussion of their borders.

Mr Mazowiecki's letter to the Prime Minister of 21 February also suggests that the FRG has in the past stated that the borders could only be settled by a 'treaty of peace'. He says that Poland would be prepared to take part in work on such a treaty. But he does not insist upon a Peace Treaty, and indeed refers in the same paragraph to a 'peace settlement', as if he makes no distinction between the two.

The Foreign Secretary believes that there is in fact an important distinction. There are three main difficulties with a Peace Treaty, if by that we mean a single, legally binding instrument settling all matters outstanding after the war. First, it might need to include all the States involved in the war (in which there were 57 belligerents). This would greatly complicate negotiations, drawing out the uncertainty surrounding unification and increasing the risk of precipitate action by the Germans. Second—and more important in terms of getting what we want—the process of drawing up a Peace Treaty with so many states would reduce the influence and significance of the Four Powers, making it more difficult for us to use the leverage that our remaining Four Power rights and responsibilities give us. Third, the US and FRG strongly oppose a Peace Treaty.

Fortunately, a peace settlement does not need to take the form of a general Peace Treaty. It need not be a single instrument. It could instead consist of a series of agreements which would allow each of a wide range of topics to be dealt with by those directly involved, using legally binding instruments where necessary but avoiding them where not.

Further work is being done on this, with the help of Legal Advisers, within the FCO as part of the Two plus Four process. In addition to the legal guarantees of this settlement, the CSCE framework could provide political endorsements. We see no reason to doubt that this would satisfy the Poles, provided their bilateral treaty with the Germans were in the bag. This bilateral treaty could in turn be 'underwritten' by the Four Powers when they relinquish their status; we are giving more thought to just how this could best be done.

without approval from all 35 CSCE participants since, according to the Helsinki Final Act, national boundaries could not be changed without agreement (see No. 144, note 1). Mr Wall quoted the address by the then Prime Minister, Mr Wilson, to the Helsinki Conference in July 1975 stating that the Final Act was neither a treaty nor a peace settlement, and did not in any way affect Four Power rights and responsibilities relating to Berlin and Germany as a whole. Mr Wall concluded that, while a CSCE summit might give its blessing to the disappearance of the inner-German border as a result of German unity, there was no legal or political requirement for it to do so: 'The Final Act is not legally binding' (WRL 020/1). In his letter of 20 February Mr Powell replied that Mrs Thatcher had not referred to approval, but only to 'massive consultation' with the CSCE signatories. He continued: ' Your letter does, however, lead one to wonder why we attached so much importance to securing, in the Strasbourg Communiqué, a reference to unification taking place in full respect of relevant treaties and agreements and of all the principles defined in the Helsinki Final Act. The letter also leads to the conclusion that the Poles are absolutely right to seek a proper Peace Treaty to regulate the eastern border of Germany: and raises the question whether we are right to connive in German attempts to avoid a more general Peace Treaty to terminate the Second World War and regulate its results more generally. The Prime Minister would like further advice on these points, and suggests that the correspondence should also be seen by the Law Officers' (WRL 020/1).

I am copying this letter and your own to Juliet Wheldon in the Legal Secretariat to the Law Officers.

Yours,
J.S. WALL

No. 183

Sir A. Acland (Washington) to Mr Hurd[1]

No. 721 Telegraphic [WRL 020/1]

Confidential   WASHINGTON, *27 March 1990, 6.50 p.m.*

My Telegram No. 662: 2+4 Talks: The Security Issues[2]

Summary

1. Americans agree about the need to deepen coordination among the Western Four on security issues. No responses to our questions on specific aspects as yet. Concerns about the French attitude heightened by report of Mitterrand's 25 March television interview. Further evidence of possible early shift on SNF in order to pre-empt pressures for denuclearisation. Our points generally well taken. A further round with Zoellick due on 2 April.

Detail

2. Wood saw Zoellick on 27 March, primarily to underline the need to come to an early understanding among the Western Four on the handling of the security aspects of unification—tactically and as far as possible, substantively—against the risk of Soviet pressure and German vulnerability to it. He went through the points in Weston's letter of 16 March, making it clear that we were not seeking to provide prescriptions on these fundamental questions but to provide preliminary views on the ground that had to be covered and on which we should aim to arrive at common positions as soon as possible.

3. Zoellick said that he heartily endorsed the need to get the Western act together, and sooner rather than later. This had been brought home to him forcefully by the remarks reported to have been made by Mitterrand in his television interview on 25 March in which the French President seemed to be contemplating a new-look NATO after German unification in which the Russians would pull their troops out of East Germany in return for the withdrawal of NATO forces from West German soil. This was hardly helpful. French policy seemed at present to veer around three conflicting elements: EC integration: a European balance of power including a Franco-Russian axis: and continuing American

---

[1] Repeated for information Immediate to Paris, Bonn, Moscow, East Berlin.

[2] This telegram of 21 March reported a meeting between Mr A. Wood and Mr Blackwill on 20 March. The latter 'thought the British and American approaches were very close'. He said that 'the guiding principle for the Americans was to avoid a situation where the Germans appeared to be singled out by other powers for special, arguably second-class, treatment'. Mr Wood agreed that, while 'there were, of course, legal and security issues to be addressed', he 'saw no reason why we should wish, in doing so, to put Germany in an inferior or subordinate position'. Mr Blackwill suggested that 'it would be very desirable to achieve a common UK/US view before Genscher came to Washington on 4 April'. It was agreed that Mr Wood would seek an interview with Mr Zoellick, preferably that week (WRL 020/1).

involvement in Europe without defining how this was supposed to be achieved. Perhaps the British could work on them.

4. Wood said that we had no fixed ideas on how consultation among the Western Four might be arranged, but the process ought to have started in earnest before the next 2 + 4 meeting. Bilateral discussions between us and, separately, with the Germans were obviously important. In that context we hoped that it might be possible to get together with Zoellick and Blackwill on the evening of 9 April in Washington in the Ambassador's residence. Zoellick agreed: Seitz should be involved too. It was possible, but no more, that he and Seitz would be in Europe on or around 9 April, in which case it would make more sense to transfer the meetings to Brussels from Washington. Wood said it might also be desirable to set up a 1 + 3 sub-group at a later stage to consider certain technical aspects.

5. Zoellick said that it would be important to preserve flexibility and ensure that the Germans were fully involved at every stage. It was also vital that active consultations took place in the Alliance at every stage – and that the arrangements were not overly formalistic in ways which could upset the French (as Wörner seemed in danger of doing).

6. Zoellick added that he was working on less orthodox ways of promoting sensible views in Germany as well. He wanted American Embassies in Europe to work with local socialist parties in order to counter left-wing SPD influence and educate them about the value of NATO and of a continuing US role in Europe. Similarly it would be important to educate the new GDR Government, as a future participant in 2 + 4, on the virtues of NATO membership as against neutrality. He hoped we would consider similar action.

7. As regards substance, Zoellick made two preliminary points:

(*a*) Applicability of Articles 5 and 6: he said that it would be most important for the NATO Treaty area and security guarantee to cover all the territory of a united Germany from the outset. Otherwise it could lead only to trouble and instability in the longer run. He hoped that it would be possible to take a firm stand on the issue.

(*b*) Denuclearisation: he confirmed that an active process of consideration was currently under way within the Administration on whether and how best to modify NATO's current SNF posture and stance on SNF negotiations, in order to prevent denuclearisation and preserve key capabilities, notably TASM. The handling of Congress over FOTL also came into the picture. He was well aware of our request for separate bilateral consultations on these aspects and thought that the administration would wish to clarify its own thinking a little further before discussing the matter with us. But the timescale was nevertheless pretty short: he envisaged an exchange of views by the time of the President's meeting with the Prime Minister in Bermuda and thought that a new SNF policy would need to be agreed by the key players before the NPG meeting in early May. He did not expect a US position to be put to Shevardnadze during the 4-6 April talks.

8. The discussion was cut off after 45 minutes when Zoellick was summoned by Baker. He suggested that we continue early next week, a meeting since arranged for 2 April.

No. 184

Sir C. Mallaby (Bonn) to Mr Hurd[1]

No. 406 Telegraphic [WRG 020/1]

Confidential   BONN, *28 March 1990, 3.14 p.m.*

UK/FRG Summit 30 March: Scene Setter

Summary

1. Coalition strongly placed at home. Marking time briefly on actual steps towards unification, pending formation of GDR Government. Uncomfortable awareness that prospect of a larger Germany still causes anxiety abroad. Franco-German relations going badly. German attempts to reassure others.

2. On unification, consciousness of need to synchronise internal and external tracks. This may in due course be difficult. This Summit well timed to influence German thinking for 2 plus 4. Key issues for discussion are the security aspects of unification, both transitionally and in the longer term, and German monetary union and its implications.

Detail

3. The latest opinion poll gives the Coalition parties a substantial lead over the opposition. They are more popular than at any time since the *Bundestag* elections of 1987. The Greens and *Republikaner* have fallen back since unification became the big issue. The economy continues to boom and migrants from East Germany are just recently down (since the GDR election about half the rate of over 2,000 a day before then). The balance between the parties is:

CDU/CSU   45 per cent (37 a year ago)
FDP   9 per cent (7)
SPD   36 per cent (40)
Greens   5 per cent (9)
*Republikane*r 2 per cent (4).

4. The CDU may now retain their precarious hold on Lower Saxony in the *Land* election there on 13 May and thus keep control of the *Bundesrat* (the FRG's upper house). In the run up to the Federal elections in December Kohl will however be challenged by Lafontaine to demonstrate that he can keep his promises to the GDR voters to bring prosperity quickly and his pledge to FRG voters that taxes will not be increased.

5. There is a lull in the actual steps towards unification while a coalition is constructed in the GDR. As the collective adrenalin level has moderated, the magnitude and complexity of the issues that have to be resolved has become more widely known. Some Government supporters will still justify Kohl's handling of the Polish border on domestic grounds. But most know it was a mistake which revived mistrust of Germany abroad and among other things upset relations with France. This has made the Federal Government and many politicians more careful in their statements about the external aspects of unification and has led them to say repeatedly that state unity will come only after agreement is reached in 2 plus 4.

---

[1] Repeated for information Priority to MODUK; information Routine to Moscow, Paris, Washington, BM Berlin, East Berlin, UKDEL NATO, UKREP Brussels, CICC Germany; information Saving other NATO and East European Posts.

Kohl's visit to the EC (UKREP telno 930)[2] and Genscher's to WEU at Strasbourg, both on 23 March, had this purpose of reassurance. In giving new emphasis to European political union, perhaps via another IGC, Kohl has sought to pacify Mitterrand by parading European colours, while still refusing to start the IGC on EMU before his December elections.

6. The Federal Government now has a reasonably clear view of the broad sequence of events on the road to unification (my telno 399).[3] The chosen constitutional method is accession of the GDR to the FRG under Article 23 of the Federal constitution. Kohl and Genscher claim that they can control the timing of this by using their influence over the GDR coalition and delaying the implementing legislation in the *Bundestag* until agreement is sure in 2 plus 4. But if in due course inability to settle the security (or other) aspects of 2 plus 4 threatened to delay unification, there would be a real danger of the Germans wanting to concede too much to the Soviet Union. It is now urgent to agree the Western position on crucial issues so that the 4 plus 2 process can get into substance once there is a GDR Government. The British/German Summit is well timed to influence German thinking. Despite recent difficulties between us, I think Kohl will want to consolidate areas of agreement. The press conference gives an opportunity to highlight these in public.

7. Important issues at the Summit will be:

(*a*) Security issues in 2 plus 4. It will be important to press Kohl to be clear about the extension of NATO Articles 5 and 6 to East Germany and the military assets to make that credible while the Russians are withdrawing. There is some evidence (my telno 396)[4] that Kohl may recognise that German ground troops of some kind must be present in East Germany even during a transition period. But I do not exclude that people here could be tempted, if 2 plus 4 was difficult on this aspect, to postpone all questions concerning the security of the GDR, except Soviet withdrawal, for a subsequent negotiation. That would create serious uncertainty about future European security.

(*b*) European defence and security in the longer term. There are important differences between Kohl's and Stoltenberg's goals on the one hand and Genscher's on the other. Kohl means it when he says that he wants a united Germany permanently in NATO and the integrated military structure and accepts the continuing need for nuclear weapons on German soil. But there is an incipient tendency in Bonn to argue that some of the key issues that the Soviet Union is likely to raise in 2 plus 4, notably nuclear weapons on German soil and the future size of German armed forces, can only be settled in other fora—SNF negotiations or a second round of CFE—where Germany will not be 'singularised'. Kohl is apprehensive about how hard the Russians will press, especially on nuclear weapons (my telno 375).[5] Genscher makes it increasingly clear (my telno 397)[6] that NATO with its present form and functions will only

---

[2] In this telegram of 23 March Sir D. Hannay reported: 'His message throughout was that a united Germany belonged in a united Europe' (WRL 020/1).

[3] Not found.

[4] This telegram of 27 March reported FMOD's belief that the East German armed forces (NVA) would have to 'remain in being to form the basis of a German defence force for the former GDR in a united Germany'. Herr Kohl was said to have spoken in support of this view (WRG 020/3).

[5] No. 179.

[6] This telegram of 27 March reported a speech to the WEA Assembly in Luxembourg on 23 March in which Herr Genscher 'developed further his thinking on the need for alliances to become more political and in due course to be replaced by a pan-European security system' (DZN 061/40).

be needed for a transitional phase of unspecified duration until the military pacts can be absorbed into a new cooperative European security order.

(*c*) German Economic and Monetary Union. Kohl has committed the FRG to an exchange rate of 1 DM to 1 East Mark for current flows and small savers. Debate rages over the right rate for other funds and there is a good deal of confusion about the timing and nature of the economic reforms which must accompany monetary union, the target date for which is 1 July. I suggest that Haussmann should be probed on the relationship between monetary and economic union, on medium and longer term economic prospects for the GDR and on his Department's views (which differ in important respects from those of the *Auswärtiges Amt*) on East German absorption into the Community. I suggest that Waigel should be asked about the effects of unification on the DM. Haussmann and Waigel could be asked about possible overheating of the FRG economy as GDR consumption is pumped up and about consequential prospects for inflation and interest rates.

(*d*) Berlin. There is increasing talk in Berlin, across party lines, of Allied garrisons staying there on a new contractual basis as long as Soviet forces are in East Germany. Provided the Germans want this and are prepared to say so publicly, there are obvious attractions. Neither Kohl nor Genscher seems to have focussed on this idea.

8. Other issues for this summit are:

(*a*) Financial services. The Federal Government have said that they want their European partners to participate in developing the GDR. They have also agreed that East Germany should if possible adopt EC-compatible legislation from the start. This has implications for the FRG in instances where it is out of line with EC obligations. Federal Chancellery and Finance Ministry officials have recently been cooperative in making bilateral progress on two EC dossiers which, if unblocked, would increase British chances of providing financial services in a united Germany. These are life insurance and the rules for non-bank financial institutions. The summit provides the opportunity for ministers to endorse the efforts to break the log jam in a way which commits the Germans to follow through in Brussels (my telno 395).[7]

(*b*) Promotion of the English language in the GDR. English can now displace Russian as the first foreign language in East Germany. I hope we can announce at the summit the start of a British Council programme on this. It would be much welcomed here.

(*c*) For use at the press conference, the briefing for the Summit will also list subjects where bilateral cooperation is currently successful. These cover scientific and academic research, the fight against drug trafficking and cooperation over military exercises.

9. Please advance to PSs to Chancellor of the Exchequer and Secretaries of State at DTI and MOD.

---

[7] This telegram of 27 March reported a meeting between officials of the DTI and the Federal Ministry of Finance that agreed a text supporting the European Commission's programme for completing the internal market in insurance. This text was to be agreed formally by the respective Ministers (Mr Ridley and Herr Waigel) at their meeting on 30 March and then to be endorsed by Mrs Thatcher and Herr Kohl (WRG 020/1).

No. 185

Mr Hurd to Sir A. Acland (Washington)[1]

No. 575 Telegraphic [WRL 020/1]

Confidential   FCO, *29 March 1990*

Your Telno 721 (not to UKDELs): Two plus Four Talks[2]

1. If time allows in Wood's meeting with Zoellick on 2 April, the following additional topics might usefully be aired:

(*a*) De-brief on Weston's discussions with Adamishin (Moscow telno 546).[3]

(*b*) De-brief on the discussions in Paris on 28 March (FCO telno 201 to Paris and Paris telno 369 now repeated to UKDEL Vienna).[4]

(*c*) De-brief on Anglo-German Summit (records will follow, if possible by fax).

(*d*) We would entirely endorse the point made by Zoellick in paragraph 7 of TUR, that the NATO Treaty including articles 5 and 6 should cover the whole of united Germany (Dufourcq indicated to Synnott that this might be too much to expect from the Germans but we have taken a number of recent opportunities, including the recent pol/mils with the French in London to stiffen French spines; and now see also (*c*) above).

(*e*) On de-nuclearisation we were relieved to hear that Baker will not be putting a new US position to Shevardnadze before consultations with key Allies. We remain keen to have a full bilateral discussion of all this with the Americans as soon as they are ready.

(*f*) Does the US share the French perception of a Soviet intention to link Soviet agreement to progress on CFE to satisfaction on the question of the 'status of Germany'? (Paris telno 369) If true, we think it should be resisted and the Russians should if necessary be isolated and shown to be responsible for holding up unnecessarily the CFE treaty. Any suggestion that there should be, for example, ceilings on forces in Europe, other than those of the US and Soviet Union, would be for consideration in the context of the follow up to the CFE negotiations, whose principal purpose, in our view, should be to establish the military security framework (in terms of force levels in Central Europe) within which unification will take place. We are of course conscious of the risks that German public opinion might be adversely influenced by any such Soviet negotiating ploy: such is the task we face collectively.

[1] Repeated for information Immediate Paris, Bonn, Moscow, East Berlin, UKDEL Vienna, UKDEL NATO.

[2] No. 183.

[3] This telegram of 29 March summarised the discussion between Mr Weston and Mr Adamishin as follows: 'No new ideas from the Soviet side. Adamishin argued for a peace treaty and against German membership of NATO and unification under Article 23. He showed interest in our ideas of a settlement and that the Two plus Four could work as a steering group. Adamishin raised Berlin elections to the *Bundestag*' (WRL 020/1).

[4] FCO telegram No. 201 to Paris of 28 March reported part of the discussion between Mr Hurd and M. Dumas in Paris on the same day. The two Ministers agreed that it was important to keep up the pace of the Two plus Four negotiations and to maintain pressure on the Russians (WRF 020/8). Paris telegram No. 369 of 29 March recorded discussions of Berlin-related issues and the wider aspects of the Two plus Four negotiations between Mr Synnott and MM. Dufourcq and Gauer (WRL 020/1).

(*g*) We look forward to the legal talks on 3 April (separate telegram on arrangements and participants).[5]

(*h*) Further indications of American thinking on the future of Allied garrisons in Berlin, for a transitional period covering the continuing presence of Soviet forces in eastern Germany, would help our own deliberations, which are advancing. Our current thinking is that:

(i) A clear German request would be a prerequisite.

(ii) It would be desirable that the Germans should indeed make such a request.

(iii) A *Bundeswehr* presence would be highly desirable (though not perhaps essential).

(iv) The structure of Allied presence should be militarily sound, with adequate provision for training.

(v) The Germans should pay (although not necessarily as much as at present).

(vi) Special arrangements could be made for Soviet presence, including, e.g., honour guards at war memorials.

2. The French wish to raise relatively minor and technical Berlin points in the Two plus Four, which is in our view unwelcome. It risks causing the Allies to be blamed for lack of progress on areas of importance to Berliners. And it offers the Russians unnecessary leverage. Dufourcq implied that Dumas had personally taken decisions on this. Anything the Americans can do to help, before the next Three plus One meeting, would be helpful.

---

[5] FCO telegram No. 568 to Washington, 29 March. Not printed.

No. 186

Sir A Acland (Washington) to Mr Hurd[1]

No. 773 Telegraphic [*WRL 020/1*]

Confidential   WASHINGTON, *2 April 1990, 11.52 p.m.*

My Telegram Number 721 and Your Telegram 575: 2+4 Talks[2]

Summary
1. Zoellick repeated on 2 April we should agree a point of view on security issues among the Western Four while taking care not to get across work in NATO. Germany should be covered by articles 5 and 6 from the beginning and should not be singularised. We had to sort out what fell to CFE I and what to CFE II. The President would want to talk about nuclear issues at Bermuda.

Detail
2. The Minister had a further talk with Zoellick on 2 April. Seitz was also present.

---

[1] Repeated for information Priority to Paris, Bonn, UKDEL NATO, Moscow, East Berlin, UKDEL Vienna.

[2] Nos. 183 and 185.

3. Zoellick said our points had been useful in focussing American minds. He repeated that he very much accepted the basic idea that we should agree a point of view on security issues among the Western four as practicable. The existing 1 + 3 mechanism provided the natural focus. We had also to take full account of the need to coordinate with NATO and existing groups, including in NATO, which were already grappling with some of the questions we had raised. Bilateral discussion would also be important, especially the President's meeting with the Prime Minister on 13 April.

4. Zoellick had three basic points to make:

(*a*) We should avoid getting into a situation of unstable disequilibrium, particularly over the application of Articles 5 and 6. Either the GDR should be in or out. Kohl's position seemed to be firmer than Genscher's. The American view was that the GDR should be covered from the beginning. Ambivalent transitional arrangements would be risky. It was very difficult to see how they would work in practice. We could be more open about how transitional arrangements would operate, given the presence of Soviet troops, but our aim should be that once the transitional period was complete, Germany would be treated as a totally normal state able to put its military forces where it liked, including in the former GDR.

(*b*) Germany should not be treated as a special case.

(*c*) The 2 + 4 should not necessarily be the prime forum treating all the security issues we had raised. This was partly a matter of keeping the alliance together and making sure that all the sixteen were kept properly in the picture. It also made better tactical sense *vis-à-vis* the Russians. CFE and eventual SNF talks had an important role to play.

5. Wood asked whether the Americans shared the French perception of a Soviet intention to link Soviet agreement to progress on CFE to satisfaction on the question on the status of Germany. Zoellick said the Americans had not had such indications. He thought the Russians were eager for progress on CFE not least because of the current pressures on their military dispositions outside the Soviet Union. But of course he realised they also wanted to get the *Bundeswehr* capped. The natural place to treat such questions was in CFE. He remarked that he had heard we might believe a new mandate had to be negotiated for a CFE II. He had doubts as to whether this would be the right approach, partly because of the time it would take and partly because it would immediately raise the question of what would have to be included. He hoped we would not go down this route. Wood said he did not think we had taken any firm position on this. Seitz remarked it would be important not to let the agenda for this year become unmanageable. The President had tied the achievement of CFE to holding a CSCE summit. He would want to discuss the question of what fell to CFE I and what to CFE II with the Prime Minister at Bermuda.

6. The President would also want to talk about the nuclear issue. We were all moving towards an acceptance of the inevitability of SNF talks. He repeated that the Americans had no intention of making any moves before 13 April: they wanted to go over the issues thoroughly with the Prime Minister. We had to be careful to fit the tactics to the German electoral campaign. TASM was not a vote winner. Teltschik had remarked that the German public would be happy to throw off nuclear weapons altogether. There was a dilemma between letting sleeping dogs lie and trying to pre-empt unravelling.

7. Zoellick speculated that we might be able to make progress with the Russians by taking them up on the fears they had expressed about the possible actions of a German government in five or more years time. He wondered whether it was really in the Soviet interests for example to press for a special military status for the GDR which might have as its result the growth of German military forces outside NATO. It would also be counter productive over the longer term to put special limits on the *Bundeswehr* which did not fit into a general European scheme. Treating Germany as a special case now could do long term harm to Soviet interests. Perhaps we could use this factor to sensitize them on short term issues.

8. Wood gave Zoellick and Seitz full accounts of Weston's discussions with Adamishin and the Paris talks ((*b*) of your telegram under reference). They look forward to further discussion with Weston, either here or in Brussels if debriefing the Alliance on the Baker/Shevardnadze talks fell out that way.

No. 187

Minute from Sir C. Mallaby (Bonn) to Mr Budd

[*WRG 020/1*]

Confidential   BONN, *2 April 1990*

Chancellor Kohl

1. I had a long conversation with Kohl, sitting next to him at dinner in Cambridge on 29 March.[1] As usual, much of what he said was expansive reminiscence or historical disquisition. This note records some more specific points from that conversation and several shorter ones that I had with Kohl in the margins of the Anglo-German summit on 30 March.

2. Kohl told me firmly that articles 5 and 6 of the North Atlantic Treaty should apply to East Germany from the moment of German unity. This position, of course, is more definite than the one put to the Secretary of State by Genscher on 30 March. I tried several times to get Kohl to talk about the military resources which would make a guarantee of East Germany's security credible. Kohl waved his arm dismissively and said that this question was a secondary one to which a reasonable answer would be found. Several of Kohl's close advisers, including Information Minister Klein, have told me that the Chancellor would not be averse to finding a way round the Genscher/Stoltenberg statement of 18 February which said that the *Bundeswehr* would not be stationed in East Germany after unity.[2]

3. Kohl told me that he would not agree to the negotiating or initialling of a German-Polish treaty about the Oder Neisse frontier before unity. He had moved considerably on this subject and would not make this further major concession (I recorded last week what Teltschik told me about the Chancellor's retaining room for manoeuvre with regard to the terms of a *Bundestag* and *Volkskammer* resolution).[3] I asked Kohl whether his impression was that Poland was still

---

[1] At the Königswinter Conference: see No. 179, note 1.
[2] In fact of 19 February: see No. 154, note 6.
[3] No. 181.

insisting on prior negotiation and initialling of a treaty. Kohl said brusquely that he did not know and did not care; his position was clear.

4. After talking at length about the weaknesses of the Soviet economy, Kohl said that the Soviet interest in close economic relations with united Germany was a major lever in getting Soviet agreement to satisfactory security arrangements concerning Germany after unity. It was clear that he set great store by this aspect.

5. We had a talk about the question of the future German capital. Kohl said that press reports that he had declared for Berlin were inaccurate. He personally would prefer Berlin. But the matter must be decided by an all-German parliament. He thought that Berlin's cards were losing strength. The people of the GDR seemed to see Berlin as a symbol of the SED regime. They might not be for Bonn but they were against Berlin. (Kohl's remarks were compatible with the growing consensus in Bonn that the government and ministries will remain there for some years after unity, although Berlin may become the formal capital and the Federal President's main seat.)

6. Much of my discussion with Kohl was about German domestic politics. He confirmed the press reports that his relations with the Federal President are currently poor. It is clear that he resents Weizsäcker's strictures about the Federal Government's pressure for early German unity and about the party political motivation of aspects of the Chancellor's policy on unification. Kohl told me that the Federal President should be elected for a longer period but without the possibility of a second period in office. It would, he said gravely, become clear that Weizsäcker's ten years in office were more than he could carry through successfully.

7. I put to Kohl the widespread view that the up and coming generation of politicians in the SPD (Lafontaine, Momper, Engholm *et al*) contained more talent than the same generation in the CDU. He agreed that that was widely believed but in fact, he said, the CDU was strongly placed. The stars of the future were Schäuble and probably Rühe. Seiters might not be a potential Chancellor but he would be outstanding in any position at the second level. I asked about Frau Süssmuth. Kohl looked doubtful, and went off into a disquisition about how she owed her position as *Bundestag* President to him. But he then said that if she did well as Minister President of Lower Saxony—a position he was sure she would obtain—she might prove to be a future national leader. Kohl himself mentioned Späth, rather to my surprise. The trouble with Späth was that he was too diffuse, trying to do everything at once and not achieving a great deal in anything. It was clear, however, from the way Kohl spoke that while he would not like Späth to succeed him, he could not rule it out.

C.L.G. MALLABY

No. 188

Mr Hurd to Sir R. Braithwaite (Moscow)[1]

No. 553 Telegraphic [*WRG 020/1*]

Confidential   FCO, *4 April 1990, 12.57(?) p.m.*

Anglo-German Summit: Message to Gorbachev

1. Please convey the following message to Gorbachev about the Prime Minister's meeting with Kohl on 30 March.[2] There will be no signed original.

Begins:

Dear Mr President,

When we spoke on the telephone, I promised to let you have a note of my talk with Chancellor Kohl on 30 March. Charles Powell did give an immediate briefing to a member of your Embassy staff, and I hope you will have had an account of this.

Chancellor Kohl and I spent the greater part of our meeting in discussion of German unification. My impression is that he hopes and expects to bring about economic and monetary union this summer, but that his timetable for full unification is rather more extended. He clearly envisages that unification will take place under the Article 23 procedure. He is quite categoric that the external consequences have to be settled in advance: he hopes this can be done by the end of this year.

We both agreed that a united Germany should be a member of NATO. This is the clear wish of the German people: and membership of NATO offers a framework within which to meet their defence needs. We also agreed that there should be arrangements by which Soviet troops would remain in the GDR for a transitional period, perhaps in the form of a treaty, if that was what was wanted. We noted particularly the importance for the Soviet Union of maintaining existing trading arrangements with the GDR.

On the question of Germany's eastern border with Poland, Chancellor Kohl confirmed the Federal German Government's intention that the definitive nature of the Oder-Neisse border should be embodied in a legally-binding treaty immediately after unification. I believe this assurance should be very satisfactory to Poland.

Chancellor Kohl described the enormous task which lay ahead in rehabilitating the East German economy, and how the Federal Republic proposes to finance this. We also discussed the arrangements which would be necessary to incorporate the GDR into the European Community.

I gave Chancellor Kohl a brief account of our telephone conversation on 26 March on Lithuania.[3] We agreed that the situation was complex and sensitive and could only be resolved by dialogue and discussion: and that nothing should be done to add to the difficulties.

---

[1] Repeated for information Immediate to Bonn, Paris, East Berlin, Washington, UKDEL NATO.

[2] The German record of this meeting is printed in *Deutsche Einheit*, No. 238.

[3] Lithuania had declared itself independent from the Soviet Union on 11 March; Mr Gorbachev had threatened a blockade of Lithuania, which he ultimately imposed on 17 April.

We also touched on a number of other regional problems including the situation in southern Africa.

I was glad that we were able to talk the other day, and hope we can remain in close touch.

With every good wish,
Yours sincerely,
Margaret Thatcher

Ends

No. 189

Letter from Mr Wood (Legal Advisers) to Mr Hill (Bonn)

[*WRL 020/1*]

Confidential   FCO, *5 April 1990*

Dear Jeremy,

German Unification: Legal Talks with US Officials

1. I should record some of the main points to emerge from our talks with State Department Legal Advisers on 3 April. In general, it was clear that US thinking on the legal aspects of German unification was along similar lines to our own, although by no means so far advanced. It remains to be seen to what extent the views of the State Department lawyers feature in eventual policy decisions. It was particularly discouraging to learn that the long promised legal paper will not in fact prove particularly illuminating. As the lawyers said to us both at the meeting and privately the paper had been hijacked and their input had been essentially damage limitation.

2. The State Department team consisted of Michael Young (Deputy Legal Adviser), Don Koblitz (Office of the Legal Advisor) and Pierre Shostal (Hilary Synnott's opposite number, dealing with central Europe). On our side in addition to you and me there were Hilary Synnott, Denis Keefe and Hugh Salvesen.

3. London was the first stop for the US team, who were going on to Paris, Bonn and Berlin. It will be interesting to see what their impressions are at the end of this tour.

4. I enclose a copy of the agenda which we proposed to the Americans, and which formed the basis of our discussions.[1] (Their own suggested agenda covered the same ground, though in much less detail.) Although we had virtually a full day of talks there was not in fact time to discuss items B. 6, 7, 9 and 10.

5. I shall not attempt to record all the discussion, much of which consisted of us explaining our thinking to the Americans. The following are the more significant points to emerge on their side.

6. They made it clear at the outset that the discussions were exploratory and without commitment, and on this basis could be very frank. We said the same went

---

[1] Not found.

for us, but we stressed the need to have clear positions in the near future. At the end of the discussion, we considered how to take forward discussions at the detailed legal level among the three Western Allies and the three Western Allies plus the FRG. One idea that was floated was that there should be a sub-group of the Political Directors to consider the kind of agenda we had discussed in some detail.

7. On *the form and timing of a settlement*, the US side made it clear that, while they would prefer to avoid instruments which required the advice and consent of the Senate (i.e. treaties within the meaning of the US Constitution), they accepted that this might well not be possible, given the substance of the settlement. They shared our assessment that the most likely form for a settlement was a series of agreements, Declarations, exchanges of Letters etc.

8. We discussed whether there would be any time gap between State unification and the final settlement. On our side, we pointed out that since only a united Germany could be a party to the instruments in question (e.g. the Germany-Poland Border Treaty) it seemed to follow that unification must precede the settlement. Whether the intervening period was very short (a matter of hours or days) or significant (weeks or months) would depend in large part on German internal processes. The texts could be negotiated in advance of unification and enter into force virtually immediately thereafter. On the US side, Koblitz suggested the possibility that the Four Powers could renounce their rights and responsibilities subject to specified agreements being ratified by the united Germany.

9. On *borders*, I would only record the concern expressed by the US lawyers about the use of the word 'guarantee' in relation in particular to Poland's western frontier. Michael Young said that as lawyers we had to ensure that the term was not used without a full understanding of its implications. It should be avoided unless there was a deliberate policy intention to undertake some specific obligations for the future.

10. On the question of *the identity of a united Germany*, which is particularly important in relation to treaty obligations, we suggested that a possible approach would be that there was continuity between pre-War Germany and a united Germany as well as between the FRG and a united Germany (i.e. they were the same international person), whereas there would be a succession of States between the GDR and a united Germany (i.e. the GDR is a different international person from the pre-War Germany and the united Germany). Such a view would be consistent with the two German States' own view of their identity, and would moreover be highly convenient from a policy point of view since it would ensure that, in general, FRG treaties continued for a united Germany while GDR treaties, particularly those of a highly political nature, terminated. In this connection, the US side sought to distinguish between a united Germany which came about through Article 23 of the Basic Law and one that came about under Article 146. In their view, if unification took place under Article 23 the continuity between the FRG and a united Germany would be clear. It would be less clear if unification took place under Article 146. On our side, we expressed the view that even if unification took place under 146 there would be continuity between the FRG and a united Germany. It was noted that among the reasons why the Soviet Union insisted upon 146 was that they might wish to argue that the united Germany was a new State. The US side agreed that continuity would be possible under 146, but pointed out that this would depend very much upon what a united Germany itself said about its identity.

11. On *Berlin issues*, we raised the question whether some action was needed to ensure Allied control over the *Senat's* current activities (in particular, Momper's Seven Point Plan), and suggested the possibility of a BK/L.[2] The US side said they were concerned about Allied lack of influence on the *Senat's* activities, but thought that to use an instrument such as a BK/L might appear anachronistic. The Ministers in Berlin should be instructed to meet Momper to stress the need for full consultation with the Allies at all stages, in order to avoid prejudicing important positions prior to the settlement. They could, perhaps, leave a speaking note. We emphasised the need for some such action to be taken swiftly.

12. On the assumption that forces of the Three Powers would continue to be stationed in Berlin for some time after the settlement, the Americans suggested that the Status of Forces Agreements which apply in the FRG (i.e. principally the Supplementary Agreement to the NATO SOFA)[3] could apply *mutatis mutandis* in Berlin. This could be done by a simple exchange of Letters. We pointed out that there might also be a need for further agreements on specific Berlin matters. It was noted that, in addition to questions of the status of forces, many practical issues e.g. relating to property, would need to be sorted out. The American side stressed the need to ensure continued access to Berlin for so long as Allied troops remained there. This would need to be on a completely new basis once Four Power rights were gone. One element might be a provision in any agreement about the continued presence of Soviet troops in the territory of the GDR to the effect that these troops would not interfere with Allied access to Berlin.

13. There was some discussion as to whether a formal agreement would be needed to confer the right for Allied troops to be stationed in Berlin. While stationing of forces does not require a formal treaty basis but can be agreed informally, for political reasons (both in Germany and in the US) it might well be necessary to have an agreement with a united Germany on stationing.

14. On *reparations, debts and claims*, the US side said that they had identified five main areas of interest to them:

—private claims against the GDR amounting to 78 million dollars plus interest;
—US Government claims against Germany arising out of the First World War: one billion dollars without interest;
—an unknown amount of private and governmental claims arising out of the Second World War;
—Jewish claims. An organisation in New York was raising claims on behalf of Jews worldwide against the GDR. These amounted so far to 100 million dollars;
—outstanding bonds which had been in part settled by the London Debt Agreement. The GDR part of these bonds remained outstanding;
—29 billion dollars of debts owed by US Allies from the First World War. These debts had been linked by the Allies at the time to reparations.

15. The US Government had as yet taken no position on these claims and debts and would not necessarily see a need to address them in the Two plus Four. But at the very least it would want to avoid its position being prejudiced.

---

[2] Berlin *Kommandatura* Letters usually contained instructions or directives to the Governing Mayor, or conveyed Allied decisions. They were binding on the local Berlin authorities.
[3] Agreement of 19 June 1951 between the Parties to the North Atlantic Treaty regarding the Status of their Forces (SOFA); Agreement of 3 August 1959 to Supplement the Agreement between the Parties to the North Atlantic Treaty regarding the Status of their Forces with respect to Foreign Forces Stationed in the Federal Republic of Germany (SA).

16. All in all, I think this proved to be a very useful occasion and, so far as it went, a reassuring one. US thinking, so far as it goes, on the legal aspects of a settlement seems reasonably close to our own, and Michael Young in particular seemed to adopt a very sensible approach and be very open to reasoned discussion. The US side seemed genuinely pleased with the day, and went away saying that they had learned a great deal!

Yours ever,
M.C. WOOD

No. 190

Minute from Mr Cooper (Policy Planning Staff) to Mr Weston[1]

[*WRL 020/9*]

Confidential   FCO, *6 April 1990*

The Soviet Veto in the Two plus Four Talks

1. At your meeting on 4 April I argued briefly that the Soviet Union has little or no leverage in the Two plus Four talks and that in the end it would have to accept more or less whatever the Four or the Five could agree on. This minute is an attempt to explain the thought more fully.

2. If the Soviet Union does not like what is going on in the Two plus Four talks there are two things it could do:

(i) it could make difficulties about withdrawing its troops from the GDR

(ii) it could refuse to dissolve the Four Power arrangements and return full sovereignty to a united Germany.

3. The first of these is an unattractive option for the Soviet Union. In military terms it would make little sense to leave a high quality army isolated since Poland is a less than reliable ally these days—some distance from their main line of defence. The Soviet army in Germany would be seen increasingly as an army of occupation and would attract hostile reaction from the local population. It might be

---

[1] Mr Cooper sent a copy of this minute to Mr Gozney with a note: 'You might like to glance on your way to Moscow' (see No. 191). Mr Gozney replied on 17 April: 'The Secretary of State has seen your minute of 6 April to PS/Mr Weston which he thought contained sound minuting.' Mr Cox minuted to Mr Salvesen on 20 April: 'Not clear whether S of S has seen subsequent critical minuting.' In a minute of 9 April Mr Greenstock agreed with Mr Cooper's description of the real degree of Soviet leverage but was less convinced by his conclusions: 'It is precisely the German perception of the Soviet capacity to introduce difficulties into the talks which will give the Soviet line strength. The Russians are not bad players of this kind of hand.' A minute by Mr Lever of 11 April agreed that 'The fact that the Soviet Union cannot, at the end of the day, prevent German unification from taking place without Soviet consent to its conditions, does not mean that the Soviet Union is without diplomatic leverage, or that its actions are "essentially bluff" . . . convincing the Germans to hang tough as recommended in paragraph 8 of your minute is likely to be far more fraught an enterprise than you acknowledge. Moreover the Russians have other international negotiating cards which they could play.' If, on the other hand, Soviet positions showed signs of evolving in ways acceptable to the West, 'then it will surely be in our interests to seek to accommodate them in ways compatible with our own security. In such circumstances the "sod off" approach may not be the most prudent.' Mr Synnott minuted: 'I commented orally in a similar vein on 6 April'.

prone to defections and it would be expensive since under these circumstances the Germans would surely not support it in any way. If they wished the Germans could make difficulties about supplying it as well. In extremis the Russians could use force. But they could not be certain they would succeed. And the consequences for Perestroika would be catastrophic.

4. Refusing to return sovereignty to the Germans would also be unpopular in Germany particularly if the other three powers made clear that only the Soviet Union was standing in the way. Since it would leave the Polish border question unresolved it would hardly help Soviet relations with Poland either. Meanwhile this action would do nothing to prevent German unification since whatever the Soviet Union said, GEMU, the Article 23 procedure and incorporation of the GDR into the European Community would go ahead anyway. And if the Soviet Union was uncooperative in this way there would be no need for the Germans to cooperate in terms of honouring existing contracts with the Soviet Union.

5. Although the Soviet Union can do little it can say a lot. It can threaten to withhold its consent to German unification without e.g.

—a neutral Germany

—withdrawal of all foreign forces from Germany

—a de-nuclearised Germany

—agreements in the economic field

But the point of the brief analysis above is that these threats are essentially bluff. In practice, unless it is prepared to take very drastic steps indeed, the Soviet Union cannot prevent German unification.

6. Thus the Soviet Union will only be able to obtain concessions to the extent to which:

(*a*) we, or the Germans, allow ourselves to be bamboozled

(*b*) its proposals attract popular support in Germany (as de-nuclearisation might well)

(*c*) we are prepared to make cosmetic concessions to save Soviet face.

7. The last is highly desirable since, for longer term reasons, we do not want to send the Russians away hurt and resentful. As I suggested at Mr Weston's meeting the broad shape of the deal will probably be a Western (i.e. FRG) economic price for the Soviet Union coming along quietly on security issues.

8. The policy implications of this are that

(i) we should not take the Soviet bluff in the Two plus Four too seriously; and we should make sure that the Soviets are aware that we will not be taken in.

(ii) we should convince our western partners, in particular the Germans, of the strength of the Western position.

(iii) we should handle German opinion very carefully indeed.

The only real weapon the Russians have is the possibility that they can convince German public opinion to accept denuclearisation etc as the price of Soviet consent.

R.F. COOPER

No. 191

Sir R. Braithwaite (Moscow) to FCO[1]

No. 667 Telegraphic [WRL 020/1]

Confidential   MOSCOW, *11 April 1990, 7.04 a.m.*

Part one of two.[2]

From Private Secretary.

Secretary of State's Meeting with President Gorbachev

Summary

1. An hour and a half with Gorbachev devoted mainly to Germany, Lithuania and bilateral relations. Gorbachev in expansive mood. He did not strike the Secretary of State as a man under pressure, though Lithuania was obviously the dominant issue on his mind.[3] Although he sought to give reassurance, there was a hint of steel as well.

2. On Germany, Gorbachev said the subject would not be treated in isolation. He doubted whether the Supreme Soviet would agree to Germany being part of NATO. Instead of Germany in NATO, he wanted some broad and unspecified pan-European security structure. He said he was under pressure from the military and others to slow things down in Vienna so that the Soviet Union did not bear the brunt of the sacrifices.

3. On Lithuania, Gorbachev repeated much of the message we had already had from Shevardnadze (Moscow telno 663).[4] He sought to portray the Lithuanians as extremists and himself as a man who was working within the constitution for a peaceful settlement. He came through as genuinely wanting to play it long and peacefully but equally determined not to let the Lithuanians get away with what he described as extremism and anarchy. He said he was under pressure to impose president's rule. While he did not refer to the use of force, he did not explicitly rule it out. Warm remarks on Anglo/Soviet relations and greetings to the Prime Minister.

Detail

4. The Secretary of State had an hour and a half with Gorbachev this afternoon. Gorbachev was in expansive mood and at the end of the meeting commented that it had been a long time since he had spoken so freely with a Western visitor. Gorbachev had come from what he claimed was a 4-hour meeting with a thousand members of the Young Communist League. He had obviously handled hundreds of questions and the adrenalin was still flowing. The entire conversation was peppered with jokes and heavy-handed humour at the expense of Zamyatin, who looked uncomfortable.

---

[1] Repeated for information Immediate to UKDEL NATO, other NATO Posts, East Berlin, BM Berlin, Warsaw, UKDEL Vienna.
[2] Second part not printed.
[3] See No. 188, note 3.
[4] Of 11 April (ESB 027/6). Not printed.

5. Gorbachev said that relations with the UK had improved in a way which made it possible to seek and find opportunities for further progress. The Soviet Ambassador in London was busy enough but the British Ambassador was even more active. Such was the trust and confidence between the two Governments that he and the Foreign Secretary need not waste time on diplomatic ploys and procedures. Without such mutual trust and personal contacts, it was impossible to see eye-to-eye. Our relations had been conducted in a well considered manner, even if explanations were necessary from time to time. He thought that changes in Europe and the wider world were by and large developing in a rational rather than an anarchic way even if problems like the German one forced us to stop and think from time to time.

6. Gorbachev said he was grateful for the letter the Prime Minister had sent him after the Anglo/German summit.[5] She had done as she had undertaken to do when they had spoken on the telephone. After reading the letter and listening to statements by the Prime Minister and Mr Hurd, he thought that the British and Soviet positions were very close indeed.

7. The Secretary of State said that we would not find ourselves in 100% agreement. We should look at the problem from the point of view of the stability of Europe as a whole. It would be better to have this big power, Germany, in NATO than loose, untied and perhaps with US troops having gone home. It would be better to have Germany within the Alliance, albeit an Alliance with less weapons, lower troop numbers and a more political role. NATO provided a good anchor and framework for a united Germany, but we recognised the importance of doing nothing to prejudice Soviet interests and dignity. We also needed to work for a good settlement on Soviet troops in East Germany.

8. Gorbachev said President Bush had tried to persuade him of the same case, saying that a united Germany in NATO would make very little difference from the present arrangements. Gorbachev responded that in that case a united Germany might as well be in the Warsaw Pact—an answer which had perplexed Bush. This matter must be resolved in a way which prevented misunderstanding and the erosion of the capital which had been built up by our joint efforts. He wanted to create even more valuable capital for the future and the issue of security arrangements was part of that. If we were talking about a common dialogue about a new Europe stretching from the Atlantic to the Urals that was one way of dealing with the German issue. Of course, there would have to be a transition before new security arrangements came into force but we could accelerate the pace and synchronise it with finding a solution to the problem of the two Germanies. It was clear that we approached unification from different positions. If no new perspective was established and the West was looking at the problem from only one perspective, i.e. that a united Germany should be in NATO, that would be a very serious matter. It was very unlikely that the Supreme Soviet would agree to such an approach. Already, he was beginning to get signals from political, military and diplomatic circles to the effect that the Soviet Union should not rush the Vienna process. If a united Germany was going to be incorporated into NATO, why accelerate the process of reducing Soviet armed forces? That could upset the balance of security, which would be unacceptable to the Soviet Union. Those who were allies in great events should behave responsibly and avoid generating concern within Soviet society. Some people were not taking a responsible approach. For its

[5] No. 188.

part, the Soviet Union would be constructive and responsible. These were very difficult issues but not insurmountable ones if handled with care and caution.

9. The Secretary of State said that our countries were engaged together in three major efforts: the 2 + 4, the CFE and the CSCE, including the proposed Summit at the end of the year. Gorbachev agreed with this description, which he called correct and constructive. The Secretary of State continued that the Americans and British would not go to a CFE summit unless and until there was agreement at Vienna. He noted President Gorbachev's concern that unification should be linked with progress on other areas: what he had called synchronisation. Gorbachev said that it seemed to him that the United States, the Soviet Union's partner and even friend, had its own concerns to pursue. They were worried about the creation of a wider, more cohesive Europe involving the Soviet Union and were apprehensive about the development of a European power. We should not allow the Americans to be on the sidelines. Their interests must be taken into account. The US might therefore want to slow down these developments. We should do all we could to eliminate these American concerns (this was said with apparent seriousness but may have been partly tongue in cheek). Shevardnadze was just back from Washington (where he had had the red carpet treatment). There were two very difficult outstanding issues with the US, namely ALCMs and SLCMs. Unless these two problems were resolved satisfactorily; the whole treaty would be invalid. The floodgates would open wide to circumvention and the question would arise as to why anyone should do away with their heavy missiles. Now that a date for the Summit had been set, Gorbachev thought that would provide an impetus towards finding a solution. He thought European developments would impinge on all this. Some of the Young Communist League delegates to whom he had spoken had urged him to push the Americans harder to stop nuclear testing altogether. That would indeed have a positive impact but of course there was more of a problem with the British and French on that score than with the Americans. (Shevardnadze interjected that perhaps all tests should be conducted in Nevada from now on.)

No. 192

Minute from Mr Weston to Mr Wall

[*WRL 020/1*]

Secret   FCO, *11 April 1990*

Meeting of the One plus Three in Brussels on 10 April
1. Accompanied by Mr Synnott and Mr Powell I attended a meeting of the Political Directors of the Berlin Four in Brussels yesterday. The United States was represented by Zoellick and Seitz. Discussion, which centred on Two plus Four issues, is being fully reported by telegram in the usual way.

2. We compared notes on our respective recent contacts with the Russians, including my own visit to Moscow in late March, the Baker/Shevardnadze meeting and Kastrup's latest six hours of discussion with the Soviet Foreign Ministry the previous day. Our general sense was that the Soviet compass needle on German matters is still veering uncertainly, but that there is some evidence of evolution in their thinking. Kastrup, for example, reported that Bondarenko had told him on 9

April that a united Germany in NATO was 'not totally unacceptable' to the Russians. There is also evidence that they have moved from insistence on a general peace treaty toward the more flexible concept of a legal settlement. Kastrup's judgement was that the Russians will eventually swallow the NATO pill provided it is coated with sufficient sweeteners about cooperative security structures stemming from the CSCE and combined with appropriate assurances about how legitimate Soviet security concerns could be accommodated in a follow-on to CFE.

3. On procedure for the next Two plus Four meetings we agreed to explore 24 April for the next meeting at official level; and 5 May as a possible date for the first Two plus Four Ministerial. If the latter were feasible, the Americans may be thinking of a NAC on 3 May for Baker to brief the Allies between his two meetings with Shevardnadze, in the margins of which one could envisage a meeting of the Four Western Foreign Ministers to concert before the Two plus Four Ministerial. But this timing is tight, and depends critically on mobilising the new GDR Government and on Soviet availability (Genscher will meet the new GDR Foreign Minister next week).[1] The Germans argued strongly that the Poles should not be invited either to the next official Two plus Four or to the first Ministerial, since there would not have been time for the FRG to pursue bilateral contacts with the new GDR Government and in tandem with them to talk to the Poles. We agreed that any such delay in Polish involvement needed to be explained carefully to the Poles and a firm plan to invite them decided on soon. On agenda we agreed to add 'forms of a settlement' to the existing four agenda items, but that the other Soviet suggestions should be resisted.

4. On politico-military issues I advanced again the case for a clear private understanding among the Western Four over Germany/NATO, so that we could confidently fend off Soviet inroads in the Two plus Four. I suggested that this could probably not be taken much further than the following for the time being: united Germany a full member of the Alliance, the North Atlantic Treaty to apply, Allied stationed forces within an integrated military command albeit at lower levels, a sensible mix of nuclear/conventional weapons, and transitional arrangements for East Germany. Kastrup wriggled slightly but there was a general sense that these commanded broad support, provided the implications were not pushed too far at this stage. Zoellick itemised possible questions the Russians might raise (size of the *Bundeswehr*, NBC assurances, nuclear weapons in Germany, status of the Soviet troop presence, military status of the GDR, Germany/NATO membership). Each of these, he argued, could be met procedurally by showing that it was for decision/action either by Germany herself or in fora such as NATO, CFE or SNF negotiations; but this need not preclude discussion in the Two plus Four in order to convince the Russians of that, or where the point was less easily assigned elsewhere e.g. Soviet troop presence.

5. On the nature of a final settlement, Kastrup applauded the minimalist US paper as a basis for further discussion. Dufourcq and I were more reserved, and I tried hard but unsuccessfully to secure the early formation of a One plus Three legal advisers group to take work forward. While not ruling this out later, it was agreed meanwhile to circulate to each other written comments on the US paper. This provides the UK with an opportunity to try to focus the others on the substantive elements we think a settlement might involve.

[1] Herr Meckel.

6. I asked others what they thought the first Ministerial Two plus Four meeting should do. The American view was:

(*a*) approve the substantive agenda;

(*b*) discuss whether in political terms any other potential items needed to be addressed;

(*c*) decide on the nature of Polish involvement;

(*d*) have a first discussion in substance on borders and the form of settlement (but not in Zoellick's view on politico-military issues at this first Ministerial).

7. All this is fine, as far as it goes. But I came away from this meeting with a strong sense of very close US/FRG bilateral coordination and a wish on their part to keep One plus Three discussion within closely defined parameters rather than to use it for a full and frank exchange of views. The Americans, as Sir A. Acland has pointed out, are seeing things through the German prism. And the Germans are moving to the beat of their own drum. Indeed having created the Two plus Four mechanism with something of a political splash, we may all now be drifting toward a minimalist interpretation of its actual role. The 'steering group' concept, of identifying relevant pieces of work and notionally assigning them to the appropriate quarter, has something to be said for it, not least in allaying concern on the part of those who resent being apparently excluded. But the Two plus Four framework must also provide added value on its own account, and as the Secretary of State has himself observed, it may not improve with keeping.

P.J. WESTON

No. 193

Minute from Mr Synnott to Mr Wood (Legal Advisers)

[*WRL 020/1*]

Confidential   FCO, *11 April 1990*

US Paper on Options for a Settlement on Germany

1. As you will see from the record of the 1+3 Meeting on 10 April, the Americans did not in the event suggest a meeting of Legal Advisers.[1] The Germans spoke warmly of the American paper, particularly commending its 'minimalist' approach. Mr Zoellick, incidentally, revealed that, while the first draft had been prepared by State Department lawyers, he had personally edited it.

2. In view of your very useful commentary on the paper,[2] together with our combined perception that the Americans and French might not be very well informed about the legal ramifications surrounding unification, Mr Weston suggested a meeting of legal experts with a view to establishing between ourselves what these ramifications might be in order most effectively to decide how to deal with them. The others, however, did not favour this, with the Germans and Americans particularly feeling that it would be premature. It was agreed instead, at

---

[1] See No. 192.

[2] Final version printed as Annex to No. 195.

French suggestion, that we should all offer written comments on the American paper as soon as possible.

3. I should be grateful if you would take this on in the first instance (Mr Weston will wish to be consulted about the final version). I suggest that we use this as an opportunity to set out our own views, albeit in a preliminary way, about what issues need ultimately to be tackled and how. In other words, I think that our commentary should be a mixture of legal and political considerations, identifying the more appropriate options and not dwelling on others (for instance the 1+3 are all agreed that a global 'Peace Treaty' should not be pursued). I should be glad to discuss further if you wish.

4. Incidentally, we mentioned that the American paper did not touch on such issues as aviation and stationing of forces, which we regarded as involving Four Power rights and responsibilities (as do claims, which were not mentioned at all). Mr Seitz contested this view, except insofar as they relate to Berlin, but said that they would look at the matter again. It seems to me that Mr Seitz is entirely misguided on this point (cf Berlin Declaration)[3] and that our commentary would be a good way to put them right. I suggest that we should also touch lightly on the Four Power relationship to claims and repatriations.

H.N.H. SYNNOTT

[3] The 'Declaration regarding the defeat of Germany and the assumption of supreme authority with respect to Germany by the Governments of the United States of America, the Union of Soviet Socialist Republics, the United Kingdom and the Provisional Government of the French Republic' of 5 June 1945.

No. 194

Submission from Mr Synnott to Mr Weston

[*WRL 020/1*]

Confidential   FCO, *20 April 1990*

Legal Aspects of German Unification: UK Comments

1. I *submit* a paper containing our thoughts on the legal aspects of unification which incorporates a commentary on the American 'draft preparatory paper' which was given to us on 9 April.[1] This is covered by a draft letter from yourself to your three opposite numbers.[2]

[1] No. 195.

[2] Mr Weston wrote on 23 April to M Dufourcq, Mr Seitz and Herr Kastrup:
As agreed at our meeting on 10 April, I am sending you our comments on the US 'draft preparatory paper' on German unification and a settlement. In addition to commenting specifically on the US draft, we address in some detail the question of form and timing of the settlement (i.e. the broad elements of a package, and how they inter-relate), and also those issues of substance that are likely to arise. In our view, such issues might usefully be discussed by the Western Four as soon as possible, in preparation for the possibility of the issues being discussed (or raised by the Soviet Union) in the Two plus Four. Our comments are intended to assist such discussion.

2. The paper itself, which is largely the work of Mr Wood, has gone through several versions and incorporates comments from Chancery Bonn, Mr Hill in Bonn, and myself. My own involvement has related primarily to the presentation of the paper and the desirability of not dwelling on issues which are known to be unpalatable to the Germans unless there is a good reason to do so.

3. You will see from the telegrams that the Federal German administration is creaking under the strain of dealing with GEMU: many important and sensitive issues have evidently not been sufficiently thought through. I see every possibility that a similar situation could arise over legal issues if German laissez-faire attitudes were allowed to prevail: but in this case Allied rights and responsibilities would be more directly at stake. I therefore remain of the view that we should not be coy about focussing others' attention on these issues and that a meeting of 1+3 legal advisers, under the auspices of the Political Directors, would be desirable soon.

4. As regards timing, I suggest that our contribution should issue as soon as possible before the next 2+4 meeting. This is best achieved by using the confidential fax to the three Posts concerned.

H.N.H. Synnott

No. 195

Draft Paper

[*WRL 020/1*]

Confidential   FCO, *20 April 1990*

German Unification and a Settlement: Legal Aspects
UK Comments

1. There is already broad agreement among the Western Four that a settlement should take the form of a series of instruments dealing with different subjects and involving different parties. It is important that the Western Four should have common positions on all other major aspects of an overall settlement, both political and legal, in advance of discussion within the Two-plus-Four. This is necessary for two reasons. First, the Western Four need to have a common view on what is legitimate for discussion within the Two-plus-Four, and to have so far as possible common positions on such matters for discussion with the Russians. The greater the degree of agreement among the Western Four, the less the opportunity the Russians will have to make mischief. Second, there are other matters that arise in the context of unification and a settlement which need to be settled between the Three Western Powers and Germany.

2. Some general and more detailed comments on the US 'Draft Preparatory Paper' are included in the Annex to the present paper.

3. The legal issues which should be discussed among the Western Four fall into two broad headings.

A. The form and timing of the settlement.

B. Particular substantive questions, including territorial questions; Berlin; Three

Power/Germany matters; NATO and WEU Treaty commitments, and force stationing; USSR/Germany matters; reparations, debts and claims; possible interests of other States.

In addition, there is the question of the legal identity of a united Germany (continuity with the FRG, a successor to the GDR), on which it would be helpful to exchange views among the Western Four. The Soviet Union is likely to assert that the united Germany is a new State: this may lie behind its position on the Article 23 route to unification. This question, which is particularly relevant to treaty rights and obligations, is discussed below at paragraphs 17 to 20.

A. *The Form and Timing of a Settlement*

4. There is broad agreement among the Western Four that the settlement could take the form of a series of instruments dealing with different subjects and involving different parties (e.g. declarations, treaties, exchanges of letters). It is agreed that, for both legal and political reasons, it is best to avoid a settlement in the form of a peace treaty in the classical sense.

5. The *timing* of the settlement in relation to the state unification of Germany needs careful thought. There are many possibilities. But as the united Germany would presumably have to be a party to various instruments (e.g. a treaty with Poland), the completion of the settlement (as distinct from its negotiation) would have to *follow* state unification. The interval could be very short, or a matter of weeks or even months, depending largely on internal procedures in the various countries involved.

6. Unification and a settlement could involve the following three broad elements:

(*a*) *The unification of Germany* with 'a liberal-democratic constitution, like that of the Federal Republic'. If the Basic Law becomes the constitution of a united Germany appropriate changes will be needed to make it clear that Germany consists of the territory of the FRG, GDR and Berlin, no more and no less, and has no territorial claims.

(*b*) *A series of instruments* of various kinds involving different parties and dealing with particular issues. These could, for example, *include*:

(i) A Germany/Poland treaty (as already envisaged by the FRG and GDR Governments).

(ii) An exchange of letters or agreements on certain Three Power/Germany matters (e.g. on terminating the Relations Convention and the Settlement Convention).

(iii) Various instruments concerning Berlin matters.

(iv) Exchanges of letters with Germany terminating Allied responsibility for Three Power and Four Power legislation.

(v) Letters from the Four Powers to the Secretary General of the United Nations for circulation in the General Assembly and the Security Council concerning Germany's membership of United Nations and disposing of the earlier letters from the Four Powers (UN Docs. S/10952-5).

(*c*) *A final instrument or instruments* coming into effect when other elements of the settlement package have come into effect. Such an instrument or instruments could include the following points:

(i) Recognition that Germany is henceforward a sovereign independent State.

(ii) Statement that the borders of Germany, as described (e.g. by reference to a statement by the Government of a united Germany), are no longer provisional.

(iii) Termination of 'the rights and responsibilities of the Four Powers and the corresponding, related quadripartite agreements, decisions and practices' [the language of the Quadripartite Declaration of 9 November 1972 on UN membership of the two German States].[1]

7. In connection with point (c)(iii) above it could be made clear during the negotiations that among the agreements, decisions and practices no longer in force are the Declaration of Berlin of 5 June 1945, the London Protocol on the Zones of Occupation, the Agreement on Control Machinery in Germany, the Protocol of the Proceedings of the Berlin (Potsdam) Conference, the Quadripartite Agreement of 3 September 1971 and the Quadripartite Declaration of 9 November 1972.

B. *Particular Substantive Questions to be discussed among the Western Four*

8. The following list of questions is not comprehensive. Some of the questions fall outside the scope of the Two-plus-Four. But, for the reasons given, it is highly desirable that each of them be considered in some depth by the Western Four.

I *Territorial Questions*

9. It needs to be clear that a united Germany consists of the present territory of the FRG, GDR and Berlin, no more and no less, and that Germany has no territorial claims. The principal elements of a settlement as regards territorial questions might be:

(a) Appropriate provisions in the German constitution.

(b) A Germany/Poland treaty.

(c) A statement by the Government of the united Germany describing the borders of Germany and stating that Germany has no territorial claims.

(d) A Four Power statement that the borders of Germany, as described, are no longer provisional.

II *Berlin*

10. Many detailed points will need to be considered among the Western Four in connection with the termination of original rights and responsibilities relating to Berlin.[2] These include the lifting of Allied reservations in respect of the Basic Law and the Berlin Constitution; the future status of Allied legislation; property questions; aviation, including future Berlin air traffic control. The Western Four may also need to consider points that may arise prior to the termination of original rights (e.g. if there is a significant interval between unification and such termination), and they may also need to discuss possible transitional arrangements for the period following termination of original rights.

III *Three Power/Germany Matters*

11. A number of Three Power/Germany agreements, including the Relations Convention and the Settlement Convention, will need to be examined in order to decide which provisions are to be terminated and which, if any, need to be replaced.

---

[1] Parentheses in original

[2] For discussion of these issues see Series III, Volume VI, *Berlin in the Cold War 1948-1990,* Nos. 461-89.

IV *USSR/Germany Matters*

12. In particular the Conventions on relations between the GDR and the Soviet Union, the Warsaw Pact, and arrangements for stationing forces, need to be reviewed.

V *NATO/WEU/Stationing*

13. In political terms these matters are clearly among the most important areas, and will have to be discussed among the Western Four so that they have a common position when the Russians try to raise them. Discussion among the Western Four would also be useful to facilitate consideration within NATO, WEU etc. In legal terms it will be necessary to consider the position of a united Germany in respect of the North Atlantic Treaty and the modified Brussels Treaty (WEU) and its Protocols. The rights of the six Western Sending States to station forces in the Federal Republic under the Presence of Foreign Forces Convention will also require review.

VI *A United Germany's Treaty Rights and Obligations*

14. This is closely related to the question of a united Germany's legal identity: see paragraphs 17 to 20 below.

VII *Reparations, Debts and Claims*

15. This needs to be reviewed and the issues identified in the light of treaty provisions such as Chapter Six of the Settlement Convention and Article 25 of the London Debt Agreement (which concern also the interests of a number of other States). Among other things we need to decide how to respond if and when approached by other States and by individuals.

VIII *Possible interests of other States*

16. Such States will have a particular interest in other matters such as significant multilateral treaties, stationing (in particular the six Western Sending States) and borders (the States bordering a united Germany).

The Legal Identity of a United Germany

17. An understanding among the Western Four on the question of the legal identity of a united Germany should facilitate consideration of a united Germany's treaty rights and obligations. It may also be necessary to counter any Soviet assertion that a united Germany is a new State (cf. their opposition to the Article 23 route).

18. Given the uncertain rules of international law in this field, such an understanding will not lead to an automatic solution to all treaty questions. Consideration could be given to a statement on this matter to be issued by the Government of a united Germany.

19. A possible basis for an understanding among the Western Four, which would be consistent with positions held hitherto, would be as follows:

(*a*) There is legal continuity between pre-war Germany and the Federal Republic of Germany, and between the Federal Republic of Germany and a reunited Germany (i.e. there is a form of continuing legal personality).

(*b*) The GDR has claimed to be a new State in Germany (i.e. a successor State to pre-war Germany), and on this basis a re-united Germany would be a successor State to the GDR (i.e. a re-united Germany and the GDR will be different international legal persons).

(*c*) There is legal continuity between the re-united Germany and pre-war Germany, which has continued in being since 1945 (i.e. they are the same international legal person).

20. While the above understanding is clearly compatible with unification under Article 23 of the Basic Law, it is not incompatible with unification under Article 146.

ANNEX

Comments on the US Draft Paper[3]

1. The US draft paper seems to be based on the view that there is an exhaustive list of distinct Four Power rights i.e. with regard to a peace settlement (Issue I); with regard to Germany's borders (Issue II); with regard to Germany's unification (Issue III); and with regard to Berlin (Issue IV). Yet Four Power rights and responsibilities relating to Berlin and to Germany as a whole are a bundle of inter-related rights and responsibilities, whose precise scope has nowhere been defined. In any event, in addition to the points mentioned in the US paper there are other Four Power rights and responsibilities, including those relating to the stationing of armed forces in Germany and to aviation. The difference of view between the Three Powers on the one hand and the FRG on the other concerning the nature of Allied stationing rights—whether they are original or purely contractual—need not prevent consideration of these matters among the Western Four. Four Power rights in relation to aviation are reflected *inter alia* in Chapter Twelve of the Settlement Convention.

2. To separate rights relating to unification from rights relating to a settlement may risk giving too much emphasis to the former. Thus, as regards Issue III in the US paper, it is doubtful whether there will be any need expressly and separately to terminate, still less exercise, a Four Power 'right with regard to Germany's unification'. In this area the 'exercise' of the right could simply involve non-interference with the process of unification.

3. The options under Issue I (a settlement for Germany) seem to deal essentially with the question of 'peace'. But the settlement, even in the narrow sense of matters of Four Power concern, embraces all the issues that still have to be settled following the War, and thus includes territorial questions, Berlin, reparations etc, and the termination of Four Power rights and responsibilities.

More detailed comments

4. The final paragraph before the heading 'Issue I' is misleading. At least in the view of the Three Powers, Allied rights and responsibilities remain original rights that are reflected in wartime and post-war agreements and in later agreements between the Four and the German States; they cannot be said to 'derive from' such agreements.

5. A number of the options in the US draft paper refer to 'the Two-plus-Four participants' agreeing on something. It is not clear whether it is intended that the two German States should be a party to the instruments in question, or whether

---

[3] Not printed.

these references should (as we believe they should) refer to a united Germany and the Four.

6. In options V to VII under Issue II there is a reference to 'the devolution of Four Power rights and responsibilities'. It is likely that Four Power rights and responsibilities will terminate rather than 'devolve' upon any other person.

7. As regards Issue IV (Berlin), it is not necessary to repeal all Allied legislation in order to end the city's occupation status (though this could be done if the German side so wished). If some Allied legislation is not repealed, action may be needed to ensure that it can be repealed by the appropriate German legislation.

8. The idea that Berlin's occupation status could be preserved for the period in which Soviet troops remain in the territory of the former GDR is interesting but difficult to envisage in legal terms. Four Power rights and responsibilities relating to Berlin are an integral part of Four Power rights and responsibilities relating to Germany as a whole, and if the latter are terminated the former are likely to be something quite different from what they are now.

No. 196

Mr Hurd to Sir C. Mallaby (Bonn)[1]

No. 323 Telegraphic [WRL 020/12]

Confidential   FCO, *6 May 1990, 12 p.m.*

Two plus Four Ministerial: Bonn 5 May

Summary

1. Serious and conciliatory atmosphere. Agenda and pace of further meetings agreed. Poles to be invited to the next Ministerial but one in Paris. Soviet Union attempts to limit German sovereignty after unity by means of a transitional period during which Four Power rights would be extended pending satisfaction of 'external aspects'. See 2 IFTs.[2]

Detail

2. Foreign Ministers of the two Germanys, France, the Soviet Union, the United States and the United Kingdom met in Bonn today for the first Ministerial discussion at 2+4, to discuss the external aspects of German unity in accordance with the Ottawa mandate. Detailed records of discussion follow by separate telegrams.

3. The substantive agenda for the 2+4 process was agreed. It consists of four items: borders, politico/military issues bearing in mind approaches for suitable security structures in Europe, Berlin, and final settlement under international law and termination of the Four Power rights and responsibilities. The Ministerial series will continue with the next meeting in East Berlin in June, followed by Paris

---

[1] Repeated for information to Desk by 7.05 a.m. Moscow, 7.07 a.m. Paris, East Berlin, UKDEL NATO, Warsaw, 7.14 a.m. Washington; information Priority to UKMIS New York, other CSCE Posts.

[2] Telegram No. 324 reported Herr Genscher's public summing up of the day's proceedings at a press conference; telegram No. 325 reported discussion at the morning session of the plenary meeting (DZN 061/40).

in July (to which Poland will be invited) and Moscow in early September. At this rhythm, the UK would chair the final meeting of the first round of Ministerials in London around November. To prepare these Ministerials, Political Directors were instructed to intensify the frequency of their own meetings in the months ahead.

4. In substance the day's discussions showed what I called at the press conference afterwards 'a serious and conciliatory approach' on all sides. There was agreement that the process of German unity should be achieved in an orderly way and without delay: that Four Power rights and responsibilities should be terminated by means of an appropriate settlement: and that an expanded and intensified CSCE process had an important part to play in the wider context.

5. The main interest in the day's proceedings lay in Shevardnadze's contribution to the morning's first exchange of views on the substance. This revealed the Soviet preoccupation that even though they recognise that German state unity would occur in the near future (no expressed worries about Article 23), the external aspects should not be concluded in the same rapid time-frame: and that Four Power rights should not be terminated until after a transitional period (possibly of some years) during which a package of potential controversial issues had been sewn up in the final settlement (including borders, military forces, the military status of Germany etc). This approach of course implies a continuing limitation on the sovereignty of a united Germany by the perpetuation of Four Power rights. To underpin this thesis Shevardnadze advanced the notion of the 2 + 4 as a kind of coordinating group to ensure that the resolution of external aspects of German unity went hand in hand with progress on wider European security issues, arms control, CSBMs, CSCE etc. The rather stilted addition to the second agenda item in paragraph 3 above reflects attempts to give Shevardnadze some minor recognition on this 'synchronisation' concern, without conceding anything of principle from the Western angle.

6. The Soviet reservations on a united Germany in NATO also came through clearly but without rancour. Shevardnadze asserted that Soviet political opinion was irreconcilably opposed and spoke of concerns about the dangerous implications for Soviet security interests. But he also showed that he was alive to the fact that NATO itself was adjusting and moving with the times, and his presentation seemed to leave open a number of conceptual escape routes.

7. All in all, a non-confrontational and businesslike occasion, so far as it went. But the underlying Soviet approach is at odds with that of the other five on how much lies within the competence of the 2 + 4 as such. Their wish to spin out the process is designed to minimise the extent to which German unity can be seen whether at home or abroad as a diplomatic defeat for the Soviet Union, in circumstances where they hold few winning cards. There is likely to be some hard slogging ahead before we can be sure that in Secretary Baker's words it has been a game from which only winners (and no losers) emerge at the end of the day.

8. See 2 IFTs.[2]

No. 197

Mr Hurd to Sir A. Acland (Washington)[1]

No. 791 Telegraphic [WRL 020/12]

Confidential   FCO, *9 May 1990, 4.07 p.m.*

Two plus Four: Reactions to the Soviet Position

1. Please take an early opportunity to seek American reactions to the position laid out by Shevardnadze in Bonn on 5 May.[2] HM Ambassador in Paris might like to do likewise with the French.[3] HM Ambassadors in Bonn and The Hague should also draw on the following in their continuing contacts with German and Dutch officials (I intend to have a further word with van den Broek on the telephone).

2. I agreed with Jim Baker in Bonn that we ought to treat Shevardnadze's approach with great reserve. Since then there have been signs that Genscher is rather seduced by the Soviet proposal to separate internal from external aspects, so that German unity can take place sooner while hard questions about Germany's politico-military status risk being put off for a transitional period during which the Russians retain leverage through Quadripartite Rights (QRRs). Van den Broek (my tel no 66 to The Hague)[4] was particularly concerned by Genscher's demeanour in Brussels on 7 May, where I gather Genscher sounded positive toward Soviet thinking and implied that others in Two plus Four had tended to agree with him.

3. Since then Kohl has come out with a helpful statement (Bonn tel no 588)[5] making clear that he does not accept the Soviet approach. It will be important to consolidate NATO unity around Kohl on this, particularly as we move toward the major NATO meetings over the next two months.

4. I therefore hope our respective officials can keep in touch as we approach the next One plus Three and Two plus Four at official level on 22/23 May, bearing in mind that Meckel wants the Two plus Four Ministerial in Berlin in June to concentrate on the politico-military issues. We also need to ensure that the NAC (whom John Weston and Kastrup briefed on 7 May) has another opportunity to air wider Alliance views before the Two plus Four process is again engaged.

5. On the substance we have the following preliminary reactions.

---

[1] Repeated Immediate to Paris, Bonn, UKDEL NATO, The Hague; information Priority to Moscow, East Berlin, BM Berlin.

[2] See No. 196, para. 5.

[3] In telegram No. 545 of 10 May, Sir E. Fergusson reported a conversation with M. Dana, M. Dufourcq's assistant in the Two plus Four negotiations. M. Dana's analysis was 'virtually identical to our own'. He was 'unaware of any wobbling by Genscher on this issue' and 'did not believe that the German Government would be prepared to accept special limitations on their sovereignty after unification'. Although the Soviet position was weak, 'we should not expect them to concede overnight. A process of negotiation was necessary to enable the Soviets to save face' (WRL 020/11).

[4] This telegram of 8 May reported a telephone conversation between the Dutch Foreign Minister and Mr Hurd in which Mr van den Broek expressed surprise at Herr Genscher's apparent willingness to accept the Soviet desire to decouple the internal and external aspects of German unification (DZN 061/40).

[5] This telegram of 8 May reported a statement by Herr Kohl at a meeting of the CDU/CSU parliamentary party, in which he came out 'squarely against Shevardnadze's decoupling proposal, stressing his continuing commitment to the aim of settling the internal and external aspects of unity at the same time' (WRL 020/12).

6. The Shevardnadze approach certainly poses something of a challenge, but the Alliance should avoid getting rattled by it. The underlying Soviet negotiating hand is relatively weak and they know it. At the end of the day Germany will unite and Germany will still be in NATO. The only theoretical leverage the Soviet Union has is the Soviet troop presence in East Germany and their new found enthusiasm for QRRs. The former are little practical use to them, and could well become an albatross. The latter would also be of doubtful real value, particularly if retained in isolation because the three Western Powers decided to waive their own residual rights (as legally they are mostly free to do) at or very soon after the moment of unity. Whatever Genscher may say now, it is not obvious that a Soviet attempt to limit German sovereignty after unity and to retain a major Soviet hand in German affairs on the basis of occupation rights can contribute to stability and avoid resentment in united Germany, not to speak of neighbouring East European states. The East German Foreign Minister's attitude in Bonn was eloquent on this.

7. Germany's status in NATO will be decided by Germany and the rest of the Alliance, not in the Two plus Four whatever the Russians may say. The Turnberry meeting and the London Summit will be very important in this context and we should all work hard to achieve a position that will stick.[6] No doubt President Bush will be impressing this on Kohl when the latter visits Washington on 17 May. My own instinct is that we should camp on the few key propositions (united Germany in NATO, North Atlantic Treaty to apply, US and other stationed forces within an integrated military structure, sensible mix of nuclear and conventional forces, special transitional arrangements for East Germany) which since the Anglo-German summit now seem largely common ground and have not been contradicted even by Genscher. To push beyond that on the detail (exercises, forward basing, precise status of article 5 and 6, peacetime contingency plans, etc) may be more than Bonn circuits will bear at this stage (Bonn tel no 586, para 3)[7] especially with elections looming.

8. In any case the Soviet position toward Germany in NATO seems to be still evolving, despite Shevardnadze's 'negative attitude' in Bonn. It is significant that his ideas about a transitional period for the retention of occupation rights were explained in a private talk with Genscher rather than set out in the 2+4 session itself. Nowhere in his lengthy statement did he say that Germany's membership of NATO as such was a matter for decision as part of the final settlement during the transitional period. Given his references to difficulties with Soviet public opinion, it is interesting that the Soviet press since then (*Izvestia* 7 May) seems to be softening up its readers to expect that Germany will remain in NATO (with East European support) but that her association with the Warsaw Pact will fall away. All this suggests the need for continuing Alliance firmness with the Russians on the central principles, while maximising the scope for dignified escape routes through emphasis on arms control perspectives, strengthening the CSCE and the changing nature of the Alliance itself.

9. On the Soviet demand for a transitional period we could respond by inviting the Russians to take their individual concerns one by one, and to demonstrate why any special arrangements after German unity would be essential. On the question

---

[6] The NATO Ministerial Council was to meet at Turnberry on 7-8 June; the North Atlantic Council was to meet in London on 5-6 July.

[7] This telegram of 8 May reported divided opinion on the implications of the Soviet decoupling proposal, with Herr Genscher showing signs of readiness to accept it as the price for achieving unification without delay, and Herr Teltschik taking a more critical line (DZN 061/40).

of the Soviet troop presence in East Germany we have already signalled a willingness to consider a generous transition of up to five years, if that is necessary to allow the Soviet garrison to bow out with dignity. The basis for their continued presence during such a transition would need to be agreed. We would no doubt wish to argue that this would best be done by a new bilateral agreement between united Germany and the Soviet Union, rather than by the Russians trying to rely on 'original rights' (in the absence of any support from the other three powers). Even the Soviet-GDR Relations Treaty of 1955 states that Soviet forces 'shall temporarily remain in the GDR with the consent of its government'. It is of course this latter proviso (consent) that falsifies any supposed analogy with Western stationed forces elsewhere in Germany.

10. A related issue would be the military status of Berlin. It is possible that the future united German government would see value in a continuing foreign troop presence in Berlin so long as Soviet forces remain in East Germany, but we cannot bank on that. Moreover any such initiative would need to come from the Germans themselves. If Western forces were to be retained there this would be on the basis of new bilateral agreements with united Germany rather than by running on QRRs (though the question of who paid would be important). Any such remaining Western force presence in Berlin might be withdrawn when Soviet troops finally left East Germany, thus providing an element of face-saving quid pro quo without calling in question the role of Western stationed forces elsewhere in Germany. If the Russians also wished to discuss a continuing role for military liaison missions (replacing BRIXMIS and SOXMIS) or their proposed risk reduction centre in Berlin (provided it was open to all CSCE 35) we might also be prepared to look at these.

11. But our overall line should be that none of these individual matters requires the systematic prolongation of QRRs for a significant transitional period. There would be no basis for this once unity had taken place and borders were settled. None of this need hold up the final settlement under international law, of which the essential components would be borders, Berlin, the achievement of unity itself, certain subordinate elements like military liaison missions and aviation, coupled with a final act to terminate Four Power rights and responsibilities. There is a good deal of related business to be put to bed among the One plus Three (e.g. review of Bonn and Paris Conventions) but there should be ways of ensuring that, even if not completed in detail, this need not hold up the final settlement itself. Nor of course by definition would it be of any direct concern to the Russians.

No. 198

Minute from Mr Butcher to Mr Synnott

[*WRL 020/9*]

Confidential   FCO, *14 May 1990*

Two plus Four Ministerial: Soviet Views

1. On 14 May Ivanov (Minister-Counsellor, Soviet Embassy) accompanied by Second Secretary Chancery, Chashnikov, called on Mr Weston at his own request to discuss the last Two plus Four Ministerial meeting in Bonn.

2. Ivanov expressed satisfaction that work was under way and noted that the Soviet side was optimistic. He expressed appreciation for what he interpreted as British sensitivity toward Soviet interests, including what he represented as willingness to come to 'favourable arrangements' for a transitional period of extended Four-Power rights after German state unity.

3. Nevertheless there were also 'difficulties' in the three Western powers' approach to the Two plus Four process. The Three seemed to wish to pass individual questions to other fora for substantive treatment on a piecemeal basis (e.g. borders to Poland and German bilaterally) whereas the Soviet side regarded all questions as organically linked and preferred a package approach.

4. Mr Weston recalled the Secretary of State's description of the Bonn Ministerial as serious and conciliatory. But the implied UK commitment (in Ivanov's remarks) to the USSR's position on a transitional period was overstated. Although we had publicly indicated a willingness to discuss transitional arrangements for the continued presence of Soviet troops on the territory of the former GDR, this did not mean acceptance of Shevardnadze's concept of a general transitional period covering other external aspects and defined by the systematic extension of Four Power rights. The Soviet proposal in effect amounted to a limitation on German sovereignty after state unity. This was likely to be counterproductive and go down badly with the German people.

5. Continuing, Mr Weston said that if the USSR had particular concerns about the external aspects of German unification, these could be discussed seriatim to see in each case what the best practical way of meeting them, where justified, would be. For example, the German-Polish border issue should be settled by bilateral treaty to be brought into force simultaneously with, or soon after, German state unity. CFE was the proper forum for any discussion of future conventional force levels, since the interests of other countries not represented in the Two plus Four would also be involved.

6. Ivanov quoted from a recent statement by the Secretary of State to the effect that the internal and external aspects of German unification should be solved in parallel. Was this not similar to Shevardnadze's view?

7. Mr Weston said that in arguing this the Secretary of State had no doubt intended to convey that, given the rapid onset of state unity, the external aspects had also to be resolved quickly if there was not to be an untidy and uncertain aftermath. It did not mean holding up state unity while other problems were solved in slow time. Shevardnadze's speech also seemed to accept that German state unity could take place in the near future, by means of Article 23 of the FRG Basic Law.

8. Ivanov was keen to underline Shevardnadze's flexibility on the question of a final settlement, although the Soviet side still consider the most important task to be to elaborate a single integral document embracing all elements of the settlement.

9. Mr Weston explained our view of a final settlement consisting of a number of different instruments whether in treaty form or for the Polish-German border or of a more declamatory kind; and perhaps consummated by a Final Act which would ring down the curtain on Four Power rights and responsibilities. It was not yet clear whether we were in fact speaking of a 'single integral document' in the Soviet sense but the difference in our respective approaches need not be all that great.

10. Ivanov raised the subject of a unified Germany's politico-military status, and quoted Falin to the effect that NATO was 'a structure of the past'. Mr Weston

reminded him of a few home truths about the Alliance and the sovereign right of CSCE member states to choose their alliances under Principle No 1 of the Helsinki Act, but went on to reassure him that we remained sensitive of the Soviet Union's security concerns. That was why the elaboration of arms control perspectives, the strengthening of the CFE process and adaptation of the Alliance itself to changing circumstances should be reassuring to Moscow. The German-USSR economic relationship was no doubt also important in this context.

11. Ivanov concluded with the rather solemn observation 'off the record' that the Soviet MFA could be under some pressure, and that Shevardnadze was not bluffing about the difficulties of selling the idea of German membership of NATO in 'certain quarters'.

12. In reply to Mr Weston's query about whether Bondarenko would continue to represent the USSR at Political Director level, rather than Kvitsinsky, Ivanov said this should not be regarded as a downgrading of Soviet representation, and that, with all the personnel changes taking place, no-one should be regarded as a permanent fixture in the Soviet MFA!

J. BUTCHER

No. 199

Sir C. Mallaby (Bonn) to Mr Hurd[1]

No. 634 Telegraphic [WRL 020/20]

Confidential   BONN, *17 May 1990, 5.25 p.m.*

German Unification: The Timetable Accelerates

Summary
1. Federal Government evidently considering state unity before CSCE summit in November. Recommendation that you telephone Genscher.
Detail
2. The intention of Kohl and Genscher, now widely known, to hold all-German instead of merely Federal elections in December is evidently leading to reconsideration of the Government's intentions for earlier stages in the process of unification. Lambsdorff told the House of Commons Foreign Affairs Committee today that the Coalition wanted to hold all-German elections in December, probably on 2 or 9 or 16 December. Early January 1991, which would still be constitutionally possible, was not favoured by Kohl. One precondition was that 2 plus 4 should have reached 'an almost final result'. In conversation, Lambsdorff modified this to say that it might be right to settle in 2 plus 4 for whatever had been agreed. United Germany should be fully sovereign from the start. Lambsdorff said that, if there were all-German elections in December, state unity would have to occur before the CSCE summit in November. The reason was that an electoral law would have to be adopted, constituencies drawn and candidates selected for the election. Lambsdorff made clear that the underlying reason for this rapid timetable

---

[1] Repeated for information Immediate to Washington, Paris, Moscow; information Priority to UKDEL NATO, UKREP Brussels, BM Berlin, East Berlin.

were [*sic*] the need for an all-German Government to be able to control events in the GDR in the very difficult process of unification, notably the economic side, instead of the Federal Government trying to steer them indirectly through the East German Government. Moreover it now seemed that West German industry might not invest much in East Germany so long as the GDR Government was in place.

3. Vogel, chairman of the SPD, told the FAC that unity would be needed on 2 September, to allow the statutory 90 days for preparations for an all-German election on 2 December. But I know that Federal Government lawyers think that the 90 day requirement is not absolute. Lambsdorff told the FAC that the Constitutional Court would be likely to rule in this sense.

4. After Lambsdorff's meeting with the FAC, I took him aside and said that I thought that, if state unity occurred before the full cycle of six 2 plus 4 Ministerial meetings and before the CSCE summit, which was supposed to bless the results of 2 plus 4, Germany could face a very difficult diplomatic atmosphere. This procedure would amount to the decoupling of the external and internal aspects of unification which Shevardnadze had proposed and Kohl had rejected with admirable firmness and with approval of the United Kingdom and the United States among many others. Lambsdorff said he understood this political point very well. The question was whether it would be possible in constitutional and procedural terms to set up the arrangements for state unity and all-German elections before the CSCE summit yet to put them into effect after that summit and in time for elections in December. He would look into this. No decisions had yet been taken by the coalition about the date of state unity.

Comment

5. Kohl and Genscher, when you saw them on 15 May, were still talking about not separating the external and internal aspects of unity.[2] For the Germans to go ahead with unity before the date by which the external aspects are supposed to be settled is likely to cause ill feeling among European countries, which the Russians could exploit in the context of their positions in 2 plus 4. The timing of state unity is likely to be discussed in a meeting of the German Cabinet tomorrow. I suggest that you might telephone Genscher between 1130 and 12 noon your time tomorrow or during his Cabinet meeting from noon to 1500 your time. Genscher will have returned overnight from his current visit with Kohl to Washington. You might say that Lambsdorff seemed to be saying to the FAC that state unity might come while 2 plus 4 was still meeting or at least before the CSCE summit, that this was not what Genscher and Kohl were saying on 15 May and that you assume that the policy of not decoupling stands.

6. FCO advance to Weston, H[ea]d of WED, and Private Secretary.

---

[2] Mr Hurd's meetings with Herr Genscher and Herr Kohl were reported in Bonn telegrams No. 345 and and 347 of 16 May (WRL 020/12) (not printed).

No. 200

Mr Powell (No. 10) to Mr Wall

[*WRL 020/12*]

Confidential   10 DOWNING STREET, *18 May 1990*

Dear Stephen,

German Unification

The Prime Minister and the Foreign Secretary had a word this morning about Bonn telegram No. 634 which reports indications that the Germans may consider speeding up unification so that it happens before the external consequences have been settled in the Two Plus Four process.[1] They agreed that this would be undesirable and that the Foreign Secretary should stress to Genscher at the weekend the importance of allowing the Two Plus Four process to reach an orderly conclusion. It would be very undesirable to have the question of Four-Power rights still unresolved after unification had taken place. We should take early steps to find out whether there had been any discussion of this between Chancellor Kohl and President Bush in Washington.

The Foreign Secretary reported that Herr Genscher would like to pay a further visit to London and see the Prime Minister. The Prime Minister said she would be happy to see him.

Yours sincerely,
C. POWELL

[1] No. 199.

No. 201

Minute from Mr Weston to Mr Wall

[*WRL 020/1*]

Confidential   FCO, *18 May 1990*

Bonn Tel No 634: Paragraph 5: Timing of German Unity[1]

1. Talk of decoupling in this context risks confusion rather than clarity. It was the West who originally by proposing the creation of Two plus Four, created a formal separation between internal and external aspects of German unity. It is of course true that the working aim is to tie up loose ends on the external side in the Two plus Four broadly in parallel with the approach to state unity, so that there is not a messy aftermath. This may not be completely achievable (e.g. it may not be possible to bring a Polish-German border treaty into force until some time after day 1 of German state unity). This does not matter, provided there is a political

[1] No. 199.

understanding among all concerned about how any leftovers will be disposed of after state unity. It may not even matter if the Russians are in a minority of one in disagreeing about certain external aspects as day 1 of German unity approaches (though it is in their interests as much as ours that this should not be so).

2. What we do need to avoid is conceding the Soviet position that QRRs should be run on systematically for a significant period after day 1 of state unity. I therefore think Lambsdorff was right in his modified view that by day 1 of German state unity we should 'settle in Two plus Four for whatever had been agreed'. And to ensure our clear backing for German sovereignty from the start, the three Western Allies may need to say (if the Russians are by then still holding out) that for them QRRs have exhausted their purpose and have thus been discarded.

3. I see no urgent need for the telephone call to Genscher.[2]

P.J. WESTON

[2] Mr Hurd minuted: 'The point is surely that the Russians have one awkward card in their hand, namely their QRR, and too quick a timetable gives that card nuisance value—or, if it is ignored, gives them a major grievance (de Michelis, Sir C. Mallaby and the PM at one on this!). Mr Weston minuted on 22 May: 'WED: I explained to the S/S, after we gave evidence today in the House, that the Russians do not perhaps—at the end of the day—have a veto.'

No. 202

Mr Hurd to Sir C. Mallaby (Bonn)[1]

No. 359 Telegraphic [DZN 061/109]

Confidential   FCO, *23 May 1990, 1.50 p.m.*

MIPT: German Unification: Meeting of the Western Four: US/USSR[2]

Summary

1. Report on Baker's discussions on Germany in Moscow. Gorbachev takes a tough line on Germany and NATO. Suggests Soviet Union may want to join NATO. Kvitsinsky insists agreement must be reached in Two plus Four before all-German Government formed. Agreement on need not to make concessions to Russians at this stage.

[1] Repeated to Immediate Moscow, Paris, East Berlin, BM Berlin, UKDEL NATO, Warsaw, Washington; information Priority to UKMIS New York, UKREP Brussels, Tokyo, other CSCE Posts.
[2] Telegram No. 358 of 23 May reported on the meeting of the four Western Political Directors in Bonn on 22 May, in advance of the official-level Two plus Four meeting that took place later the same day. There had been differences among the Western Four over the sequence of unification, settlement and renunciation of Four-Power rights and responsibilities, with the US and FRG wishing all elements to happen simultaneously, while the French envisaged unification and the formation of an all-German government before a settlement was signed. It was agreed that Mr Zoellick would circulate a paper on the sequence and that the legal experts of the Western Four would meet in Paris on 31 May to 'flesh out the French paper by beginning to put the key element[s] of a settlement in juridical form' (DZN 061/109).

Detail

2. Zoellick reported on Baker's discussion of the German question with Gorbachev, Shevardnadze and Kvitsinsky in Moscow.

3. Baker had outlined nine areas where the West was ready to meet Soviet concerns on Germany:

(*a*) Willingness to agree to a follow on to CFE I which should address the reduction of forces in a central region.

(*b*) Negotiations on SNF should be brought forward.

(*c*) A German assurance on nuclear, biological and chemical weapons.

(*d*) No NATO forces would be stationed in the GDR for a transitional period.

(*e*) Soviet forces could remain in the GDR for a transitional period.

(*f*) There would be a review of NATO strategy.

(*g*) The question of German borders would be settled.

(*h*) Concrete proposals for strengthening the CSCE and ensuring a significant role for the Soviet Union in Europe.

(*i*) The satisfactory handling of economic ties between Germany and the Soviet Union.

4. Gorbachev had been tough on Germany and NATO. A change in the existing balance would threaten stability. If Germany went ahead and became a member of NATO the Soviet Union would have to consider walking out of negotiations, and rethinking its military doctrine. The West should not take advantage of the Soviet Union at this time. If we trusted Germany why did it need to be a member of NATO? What if Germany left NATO and became non aligned like France (*sic*)?[3] Perhaps the Soviet Union would ask to join NATO itself (Baker believed the Russians might be serious about this). Gorbachev emphasised the connection between German unification and building up the CSCE.

5. Shevardnadze had said the West must take account of Soviet interests. The Two plus Four should decide how the *Bundeswehr* would be limited in CFE I.

6. Kvitsinsky had insisted that agreement must be reached in the Two plus Four before a unified German Parliament and a unified Government took office. We could then decide when to terminate Four Power rights. There would be no need for a long delay. In contrast to Shevardnadze, he said the Two plus Four should agree a ceiling for the *Bundeswehr* to be inserted into CFE 2.

7. The Americans had the impression that the Russians wanted to accelerate economic reform and were anxious to secure access to Western capital markets. They had referred several times to a sum of dollars 20 billion being needed while price reform took place.

8. Zoellick said he believed the Russians were digging in on hardline positions. We should engage them in negotiation but not make concessions at this stage. We might be able to agree to a crisis management centre in the CSCE, but we should not give way on this—nor economic issues—too soon. In particular the FRG should be cautious about providing the financial means for the Russians to prolong their military presence in the GDR.

9. Weston suggested it might be necessary to clear our minds about how far, at the end of the day, it would be possible for the Western Three on their own account to lay aside a large part of their rights and responsibilities if despite imminent German unity on wholly satisfactory terms the Russians remained

---

[3] In 1966 France withdrew from NATO's integrated military structure while remaining a member of NATO.

obdurate in seeking to perpetuate limitations on German sovereignty. Zoellick said the US had also been considering whether we could at the end of the day go ahead without the Russians. But Weston emphasised and all agreed that this would be very much a second best outcome. The aim must remain to bring the Russians to an agreement on external aspects in parallel to the approach to German unity, if at all possible.

No. 203

Mr Hurd to HM Representatives Overseas

Guidance No. 31 Telegraphic [RS 021/1]

Restricted   FCO, *23 May 1990, 6 p.m.*

German Unification

Introduction

1. Unification is moving swiftly. The 2+4 talks on external aspects have begun in earnest.

Line to Take (Unclassified)

2.—Glad 2+4 process underway. Constructive and conciliatory Ministerial meeting on 5 May agreed agenda for future work and pattern of future meetings.

—Much to do. Can now see way to completing work on external aspects in harmony with internal unification process.

Additional Points (Unclassified)

3. *Shevardnadze Proposal to Decouple Internal and External Aspects?*

—We agree with Chancellor Kohl. Would be undesirable (see para 14 below), to decouple internal and external aspects of unification. Aim to complete in the same timeframe. Significant that Soviet Union now accepts that unification will and should proceed.

4. *Will a Unified Germany be in NATO?*

—Western countries, including the FRG, believe that a united Germany must be in NATO. So do East European members of the Warsaw Pact. A neutral or non-aligned Germany would not contribute to stability or security in Europe.

—Principle I of Helsinki Final Act sets out the right of every country to decide whether or not to be a member of a military alliance.

—But no interest in exploiting the situation to the Soviet Union's disadvantage. Aim is to find a durable solution which takes account of others' legitimate concerns.

—We are considering bilaterally (and in the 2+4) how such concerns can be met. Likely to include special transitional arrangements for territory of former GDR.

—Soviet Union must recognise that other developments in Europe (strengthened CSCE, progress on arms control, NATO changing) are helping to meet its legitimate concerns.

5. *Incorporation of GDR in EC?*

—Want to see GDR integrated into EC as fully, quickly, smoothly and transparently as possible. Have endorsed Commission's framework for this process. Look to them and FRG/GDR to keep Council fully in picture.

—Basically, see EC *acquis* in all areas applying to ex-GDR territory from unification. But some temporary derogations may be needed where EC standards cannot be met at once (e.g. environment).

—Important that measures taken under German economic and monetary union before political union are aligned with EC law.

6. *German Borders (Especially Border with Poland)?*

—Clearly important that this issue should be settled definitively.

—Welcome agreement among Poland, GDR and FRG that Poland's western border (Oder-Neisse line) should be enshrined in a treaty. Poland invited to 2 + 4 Ministerial in Paris in July, when borders will be on agenda. Poles will also attend the official level meeting which will prepare for this.

7. *Position of Berlin?*

—Western protecting powers and Soviet Union will need to discuss with the Germans how the Four Power regime in Berlin might best be wound up. Agreed that this will be on the 2+4 agenda.

8. *Risk of Fourth Reich?*

—No. FRG has changed fundamentally since Nazi period. Forty years of well established liberal democracy. A close partner and ally.

9. *Right of Others to Have a Say?*

—Internal aspects of unification are primarily a matter for the Germans themselves. We have always supported their right of self-determination on a democratic basis.

—Four Powers have rights and responsibilities relating to Berlin and Germany as a whole. But the establishment of the 2+4 framework is not meant to exclude others or intrude upon decisions for other fora. Relevant issues are discussed in e.g. NATO and EC.

10. *Role of CSCE?*

—Outcome of 2+4 should be laid before CSCE summit.

11. *Future of Soviet Forces in GDR?*

—Yet to be agreed. Primarily a matter between the FRG and Soviet Union but FRG, as NATO member, have indicated their intention to consult closely with allies. But it is envisaged that there might be a transitional period when some Soviet forces remained temporarily in what is now the GDR, after unification. We have no wish to cause instability through sudden change.

Background (Restricted—may be drawn on with trusted contacts)

12. The first 2+4 Ministerial took place in Bonn on 5 May, preceded by preparation at Political Director level. Future meetings are planned for East Berlin in June, Paris in July (when the Poles will attend), Moscow in September and then Washington and London. Political Directors also met on 22 May and will meet again on 9 June and, probably, 4 July.

13. The agenda agreed for future talks is:

—Borders

—Politico-military issues, bearing in mind approaches for suitable security structures in Europe

—Berlin

—Final settlement under international law and termination of the Four Power rights and responsibilities

14. The main development in Bonn on 5 May was Shevardnadze's proposal that the internal aspects of unification (which could be settled quickly by the Germans)

and the external aspects (which should be subject to a transition period during which 4 power rights would be continued) should be de-coupled. The Germans have since firmly rejected this proposal. It would prolong the Soviet locus in German affairs: continue singularisation of Germany by limiting her sovereignty after unity: and create false parallelism between the presence of Allied and Soviet forces in Germany. The issue was not raised at the 2+4 official level meeting on 22 May.

15. The Russians also aim to secure an outcome which restricts the freedom of German action such as limits on the *Bundeswehr*, united Germany not (not) in NATO integrated structure etc.

16. The Ministerial meeting in June is likely to focus on structure of a final settlement including ending of provisional nature of borders, Berlin and termination of Quadripartite Rights and Responsibilities. Politico-military issues are also likely to be aired. But the Western Four are determined that the 2+4 should not (not) take decisions on issues which are the responsibility of other fora, e.g. CSCE, CFE, SNF and NATO. There may be some cross reference to these. But 2+4 should act as no more than a 'post-box'.

17. Russian concerns might be met by referring to developments in these other fora and to acts of German self-determination such as over NBC weapons.

18. Internally unification is moving swiftly. The FRG/GDR State Treaty providing for economic, monetary and social union was initialled on 18 May and has passed to the two German parliaments for ratification. Target date for GEMU itself is 2 July. The signs are that the GDR may move towards state unity with the FRG by the turn of the year with Kohl now going for all-German elections in December or January, dropping the FRG elections scheduled for 2 December.

19. The Western Four are taking care to keep NATO and EC partners fully briefed both multilaterally and individually. The Dutch and Italians have been particularly sensitive.

20. For further background see paragraphs 12-21 of Guidance telno 11 of 28 February.[1]

[1] No. 159.

No. 204

Mr Burton (BM Berlin) to Mr Hurd[1]

No. 34 Telegraphic [WRL 020/12]

Confidential   WEST BERLIN, *25 May 1990, 8 a.m.*

From Ambassador

German Unification: The Rising Political Temperature in the FRG

Summary
1. Coalition accelerating towards state unity. SPD advocate slower approach, and strongly oppose an all-German election as early as December/January. With

[1] Repeated for information Routine to Bonn, Moscow, East Berlin, Paris, Washington, MODUK, UKREP Brussels, UKDEL OECD, UKDEL NATO, Warsaw, The Hague, Dublin, CICC (Germany); and for information Saving to Vienna, Rome, Brussels, Luxembourg.

much at stake, both government and opposition are taking risks. Growing realisation of magnitude of task of effecting economic unity and risk of major economic crisis in GDR. Anxiety breeding bitter controversy in politics. Worries increased by awareness of pressures on Gorbachev.

Detail

2. The current *Spiegel* cover shows Kohl firmly in control of a car zooming along towards German unity, with an alarmed de Maizière playing with a toy steering wheel beside him. The caption reads: 'Kohl's intoxication with power.'

3. That is a widespread view. There is growing unease about the speed of events and the uncertainties ahead. To the existing popular apprehension about the costs of unification (Bonn telno 615) has been added fear that economic transformation in the GDR may mean economic chaos there, and perhaps still higher costs.[2]

4. Kohl however remains intent on going as fast as possible. His reasons include his conviction that the GDR will need to be under competent West German management as soon as possible, in order to manage the total economic transformation. Delay, he thinks, would mean even greater costs. He is also worried that Gorbachev's position is weakening and that getting Soviet acquiescence in Western intentions regarding unification could be even harder with a successor in the Kremlin.

5. The Federal coalition also have party political interests in speed. They fear that Federal elections in December/January, with a prospect of all-German ones a few months later, could produce a freak result. So they want all-German elections in December/January instead. The date is still being discussed. A few people are toying with complicated ideas for concluding state unity after all-German elections. But the general conviction is that it must precede them. The coalition appear to have drawn back, for now at least, from the scenario described by Lambsdorff (Bonn telno 634), whereby state unity would also precede the CSCE summit.[3] Instead they are investigating a different approach. The GDR would introduce an electoral law identical to that of the Federal Republic. Once the Article 23 declaration had taken effect, the two laws could be amalgamated and used as the basis for an all-German election. On this scheme, state unity could take place as little as two weeks before all-German elections, i.e. in November/December.

6. The SPD are bickering among themselves. Some wanted to endorse the state treaty on GEMU. Lafontaine insisted that the party demand improvements to it. Lambsdorff (FDP) also wants supplementary arrangements to improve the state treaty to be negotiated before it comes into force on 1 July. So I think Kohl will seek some. The SPD may thus be spared the odd position of opposing a treaty signed by an SPD Minister on behalf of the GDR. The SPD are united in fury at Kohl's domination of the unity issue, which they portray as an undemocratic attempt to force the pace and run everything himself. Lafontaine, while good at articulating fears about the costs of unity and currently outscoring Kohl 50-39 per cent in the personal popularity polls, is so luke warm about unification that he is

---

[2] Bonn telegram No. 615 of 14 May reported the outcome of the *Land* elections in North Rhine Westphalia and Lower Saxony. Both results represented a 'bad blow for Kohl'. The SPD retained their absolute majority in North Rhine Westphalia and replaced the CDU in Lower Saxony, enabling them to lead the new government and giving them a majority in the Federal second chamber, the *Bundesrat*. 'Concern over the likely costs of unification was the dominant reason' (WRG 011/2).

[3] No. 199.

vulnerable to the accusation of lacking patriotism. To outflank Kohl the SPD will need to demonstrate not only that Kohl's policies are flawed but that they have a better policy. They are a long way from this and their proposed additions to the state treaty cost money.

7. The SPD's opposition to an early all-German election also derives from calculations about their electoral prospects. They think they will do better later when the full costs of unification are more apparent to West German voters and the economic transformation in East Germany has produced more resentment. They want *Bundestag* elections on schedule on 2 December, with the date for all-German elections left open (leading figures in the party have spoken of the second half of 1991). Kohl has an interest in bringing the SPD along with his policies and will see SPD chairman Vogel on 29 May, no doubt to try to secure acquiescence in the state treaty.

8. The political temperature is heightened by the spreading realisation that the task of transforming the GDR economy is enormous and unprecedented and could cause even greater hardship and crisis there than has so far been expected. There is a feeling of vertigo in politics. Anxiety is increased by awareness of the domestic pressures on Gorbachev, which are widely seen as growing rapidly now.

9. I do not expect any of this to deflect Kohl and Genscher from their present course. But it demonstrates that they are playing for high stakes and increases the domestic cost of any apparent setback. For Genscher, a great deal depends on the Russians starting to be flexible. If Shevardnadze showed any flexibility in their meeting on 23 May, Genscher will make the most of it to show that his policies are bringing progress. The other great question is how bad things will really get in the GDR after GEMU. If they were very bad, I would not exclude a further move to bring state unity forward.

No. 205

Mr Hurd to Sir C. Mallaby (Bonn)[1]

No. 368 Telegraphic, Parts 1 and 2 [WRL 020/13]

Confidential   FCO, *29 May 1990, 10.05 a.m.*

From Private Secretary.

Secretary of State's Meeting with Genscher: 28 May

Summary
1. Genscher gives account of latest meeting with Shevardnadze. Believes Russians are coming to terms with German membership of NATO and that their desire for CSCE summit this year gives the West leverage. Genscher says Russians are looking for financial help but this has not been discussed with the Russians in detail. Describes Soviet concern at troop levels in central zone. Denies that any German proposal has been put to the Russians on manpower limits in the enlarged central zone but thinks this is the key area in which a negotiation should take place as part of CFE1. The Secretary of State stresses need for consideration of

---

[1] Repeated for information Immediate to NATO Posts, Moscow, Warsaw, BM Berlin.

substance, tactics and timing. Genscher agrees to discussion at Copenhagen on 5 June.

Detail

2. Genscher flew to Oxfordshire on 28 May for just over an hour's talk with the Secretary of State. The purpose was to brief the Secretary of State on his talks with Shevardnadze. He had found Shevardnadze in good shape, less anxious than when they had met just before the first Ministerial Meeting of the 2+4. Shevardnadze had shown himself very interested in relations between a united Germany and the Soviet Union. The Russians were anxious to preserve agreements reached with the GDR, e.g. the 1989 declaration, and to work through the consequences of the economic relationship, e.g. the fact that energy supplies from the Soviet Union to the GDR would start to be paid for the [*sic*: ?in] Deutschmarks rather than Rouble currency units. Genscher clearly thought that the Russians were more relaxed than hitherto about GEMU, though Shevardnadze had raised one particular concern, namely the need for a guarantee of the protection of Russian monuments and cemeteries. The Russians had been surprised by things that had happened in Hungary and Czechoslovakia (though Shevardnadze did not specify). Genscher said he had subsequently heard from the Americans about action against Soviet monuments in Bulgaria. Shevardnadze had also seemed to want compensation paid for the return of properties which had been confiscated by the Russians in the GDR after WW2. Genscher had not given him much joy on this.

3. On the speed of German unification and the relationship between the internal and external aspects, Shevardnadze had noted German problems over the internal aspects and had surmised that it might possible to solve the external aspects sooner. He had appeared satisfied with what the FRG proposed in respect of Polish borders. Genscher had explained that the united Germany would make clear that it had no claim to the territory of any European country. Shevardnadze had explained Russia's proposals for deepening the CSCE, along the lines of Shevardnadze's recent letter and Genscher had indicated that there was a great deal with which Germany could go along.

4. Genscher said that Shevardnadze's requirements on the Alliance were less clear. He said that the Soviet Union wanted a guarantee that there would be no military activities either by the Germans or third parties conducted from German soil. It had become clearer during the conversation that Shevardnadze was referring to aggressive action. Genscher had reiterated that it was Germany's right, laid down in the Helsinki agreement, to choose its own alliance. If it would help the Russians, he was prepared to see the 1982 NATO summit declaration on self-defence repeated by all concerned.

5. On German membership of the Alliance, Shevardnadze had put forward four possibilities. The first two he had immediately acknowledged would not be acceptable to the FRG. The options were:

1—both German states to leave their existing alliances.

2—a neutral united Germany.

3—the development of a pan-European security structure.

4—the simultaneous destruction of existing alliances.

He acknowledged that all these were hypothetical and said that the Soviet Union was looking for a way out. He speculated about an agreement between NATO and the Warsaw Pact involving association or cooperation or something similar. All this had confirmed Genscher in his view that the Russians were trying to de-demonise NATO. They perhaps wanted a statement of the kind which the two

Presidents had made at Malta when they had said that they did not see their respective alliances as a threat to each other.

6. In reply Genscher had firmly restated Germany's commitment to membership of NATO, making clear that this position was agreed with the present GDR Government. He had spoken on the issue of Germany as a non-nuclear weapons state and on BW and CW[2] drawing on speaking notes which Baker had used in Moscow. He had confirmed that NATO troops would not be deployed in former GDR territory and had acknowledged that there would be a transitional period for Soviet troops in the GDR but had said that the transitional period should not be linked in any way with the presence of Allied troops in the FRG. He made clear Germany's willingness to see practical cooperation with the Soviet Union and to discuss cooperation in CSCE. These were matters of importance to Shevardnadze. Genscher had explained to Shevardnadze the importance of avoiding the singularisation of Germany. This was the one thing which could lead to the resurgence of the far right, which had otherwise taken a battering. Drawing an analogy with Orwell's Animal Farm, Genscher had said that you could not have a situation in which all animals were equal but one animal was less equal than the others. Shevardnadze had smiled at this and appeared to acknowledge its validity.

7. Quoting from what Shevardnadze had said in public after their meeting, Genscher said that the Soviet Union now appeared to accept that the size of the *Bundeswehr* was something that could only be dealt with in the CFE discussions in Vienna. The issue remained a considerable preoccupation because the Russians feared for their position once they had withdrawn from Hungary and Czechoslovakia, and after a transitional period, (Shevardnadze had mentioned 21 months) from the GDR as well. At several points Shevardnadze had mentioned Soviet interest in the success of the CFE negotiations and the need to achieve success before the CSCE summit. Genscher himself had referred Shevardnadze to the speech which he had made to the *Bundestag*, making clear that he did not want a united Germany to be burdened by any outstanding questions. All issues should be resolved before unification. Shevardnadze had read the speech and Genscher thought he understood that all aspects of unification would have to be concluded before the CSCE summit. Genscher went on to say that he thought the size of the *Bundeswehr* and other Western forces was a legitimate question to be raised in Vienna and he would not be surprised if the Russians raised it sooner or later. If we were ready to discuss these matters within the framework of the mandate, that could make things easier for the Soviet Union. If we wanted the Russians to agree on a united Germany being in NATO, the Russians would need some guarantee of the size of troops on both sides.

8. Genscher then turned to the internal situation in Germany. He was confident that agreement would be reached in the *Bundesrat* and that GEMU would go ahead on 1 July. The draft treaty would be unchanged, though there would be some extra declarations, e.g. on the environment. On the FRG side, they were trying to persuade the East German CDU and the Liberals to get rid of their party property in the GDR, most of which had been acquired by illegal expropriation. The main long-term concern was to ensure that the period between 1 July and unification was not too long. The longer it was, the greater the risk to confidence, in particular to the willingness of investors, both within and outside the country, to invest. Although there were new faces in the GDR, much of the central administration was

---

[2] Biological and Chemical Weapons.

still in the hands of the old guard. It was now more or less decided to go ahead with all German elections in the timescale allowed for under the Basic Law and Constitution. This meant that 13 January would be the latest possible date, though the Chancellor would prefer 16 December. Historically, the Christmas break had often had an important impact on public opinion in election campaigns, though this break had worked to the advantage of the FPD in the past. Genscher had said to Shevardnadze that 1990 was the only year on which something definite would be on offer. The Russians were interested in a CSCE summit. There was no possibility of having one summit in 1990 and another six months later.

9. The Secretary of State said we had four things on the agenda:

1—the question of German unification, where he could see the case for acceleration.

2—the 2+4.

3—CSCE.

4—Vienna.

All had to reach the winning post in 1990. The difficult issue was the Vienna negotiations because the manpower agreement reached in Ottawa did not cover the point of greatest concern to the Soviet Union, namely the size of German and other Allied forces. This would need careful work. We had seen some reports suggesting that each country should be restricted to 400,000 troops in the enlarged central zone. We did [not] know how the French would view that. Nor did we know whether it would be right to make that proposal now or whether to suggest that this was a matter for discussion in the next stage. If we changed our view on the timing of discussion of national forces, we might find ourselves having to make more concessions in order to get an agreement. Genscher questioned whether it would constitute a concession to talk about the central zone when the Russians would be leaving that zone anyway. The Secretary pointed out that the Russians were building up their forces just outside it. The question of the zone and the one of timing were crucial. Genscher said that the issue of timing was also crucial for the Soviet Union. For us, these were matters of security. For the Russians, there was the question of what to do with their soldiers in terms of housing, barracks and jobs. It was also worth bearing in mind that the Russians only had about 400,000 troops in the extended central zone, which included the Baltic District. He hoped that we could consider carefully whether, by including the zone in negotiations, we could help secure progress. He thought it would be important to talk in terms of numbers rather than percentages, so that one had certainty on numbers.

10. Genscher said he did not know whether the Russians would raise this issue in Washington. He doubted whether they would make a proposal but expected them to argue that they had left Hungary and Czechoslovakia and would be leaving the GDR while, on the other hand, nothing had changed in the West. They might imply that, if there was some agreement on this issue, then they would agree to German membership of NATO.

11. The Secretary of State said that the Russians had three cards, none of which was particularly strong. (1) was their occupation rights, but this was not a very strong card if the other wartime Allies had given up their rights. (2) public opinion in Germany, which they would try to influence. (3) the card which the Fourth Republic in France had often played, i.e. if you want us to survive, you must help us. We nonetheless had to take account of these Russian cards, at any rate the last one, and it was clear that Herr Genscher was inclined to think that we should take stock of our position in a positive sense and change our negotiating stance in

Vienna. Genscher said that we should at least consider doing so. He had not gone into any of this with Shevardnadze, making clear that these were not matters for Germany alone. We had to bear in mind that the US proposal on the central zone was already much less attractive to the Russians than it had been when it was first made. Genscher wondered whether reaching an agreement on the central zone rather than the extended cultural zone might be easier because Britain, France and Italy would not be affected. The Secretary of State commented that we had all made clear our willingness to discuss national force strengths in Vienna. The question was when. The people most closely concerned should get together to identify quite clearly our policy and tactics. It was agreed that the meeting at Copenhagen on 5 June would be an opportunity to do so.

12. Summing up, Genscher said that the strategy which had been adopted from the start was the right one, i.e. a united Germany in NATO but not extending NATO troops to East Germany. These three points were not now in dispute. It was a question of how to make them more acceptable to the Soviet Union. Shevardnadze was serious when he had talked of finding a way out. It was also significant that Gorbachev had talked about Germany remaining in NATO but on the French model. Shevardnadze had not said anything like that. What this meant was that both men were feeling for a way through the issue.

13. Genscher said he had spoken to Dumas on the telephone that day, following the Mitterrand/Dumas visit to Moscow. Dumas had said that he expected Gorbachev to start a propaganda offensive on German public opinion. It had not been clear to Dumas exactly what form this would take but that it would happen seemed to him a certainty.

14. The Secretary of State asked when the Coalition would fix an election date. Genscher said that they were governed by the 90-day rule. In terms of the relationship between that date and the 2+4, he hoped to settle the Polish border issue in July in Paris. He also hoped, though he recognised that this was far from being a certainty, that the Soviet Party Convention in July would make matters easier for the Soviet leadership. When the 2+4 met in Moscow in September, he hoped that some progress could be made on CSCE and on our own position in the Vienna talks, if that was of interest to the Russians.

15. Genscher said that the GDR Government was not quite in line over the issue of unification. There was some uncertainty over de Maizière's position, though it was not clear whether this was based on conviction or tactics, the tactics being the need to keep the coalition together until GEMU was ratified. The Chancellor was seeing de Maizière that day. What was certain was that only unification would give the confidence needed for investment.

No. 206

Mr Hurd to Sir C. Mallaby (Bonn)[1]

No. 371 Telegraphic [DZN 061/109]

Confidential FCO, *30 May 1990, 3.26 p.m.*

1 plus 3 Political Directors' Meeting: 5 June: German Unification

1. The agenda for the Ministerial Meeting at Turnberry is set out in a separate telegram.[2] We envisage that the main focus of discussion by Political Directors and by Foreign Ministers should be German unification.

2. Grateful if you would inform appropriate representatives of host Governments of how we, as Chairman of the 1 plus 3 Political Directors' meeting, plan to handle it.

3. The immediate task will be to prepare for the 2 plus 4 official meeting on 9 June and hence the Ministerial Meeting at the end of June (date not yet fixed), although this need not preclude some wider discussion. We suggest the following agenda.

(i) Timing sequence of unification, settlement and termination of QRRs.

(ii) Preparation of a paper on elements of a final settlement for agreement by 2 plus 4 Ministers.

(iii) Preparation of a paper on borders for similar agreement.

(iv) Public presentation of outcome of 2 plus 4 Ministerial.

(v) Further exchanges on pol-mil issues and, if appropriate, Berlin.

4. We offer the following thoughts, which might form a starting discussion on each item.

Timing

5. Discussion in the 1 plus 3 in Bonn on 24 May was inconclusive. The Americans undertook to circulate a paper on the sequence of events (FCO telno 358).[3] Subject to that, and to others' views, we envisage the following possibility:

(*a*) Completion of 2 plus 4 negotiations and agreement therein on the settlement texts.

(*b*) Outcome of 2 plus 4 negotiations laid before the CSCE summit.

(*c*) German state unification, followed by all-German elections and formation of an all-German Government.

(*d*) Amendments made to the basic law and ratification of the settlement package.

(*e*) Ratification and entry into force of Poland/Germany treaty.

(*f*) Entry into force of settlement package and termination of Four Power rights.

6. It follows from the foregoing that any necessary ratification procedures by the 4 Powers would need to have been completed by stage (*f*). While accepting that there may be some German sensitivities over this, we envisage that stage (*f*) should follow stage (*e*), partly for political reasons with regard to the Poles and partly to be able to demonstrate that the 4 Powers have adequately fulfilled their

---

[1] Repeated Immediate to Washington, Paris; information Immediate to Moscow, East Berlin, BM Berlin, UKDEL NATO.

[2] Not printed. The NATO Ministerial Council was to meet at Turnberry on 7-8 June.

[3] See No. 202, note 2.

responsibilities. Presentation in this case would be important, so as to avoid too much of an implication that the bilateral treaty was somehow a requirement determined by the 4 Powers.

7. It seems desirable to decide upon the likely sequence of events at an early stage since the text for a final settlement will be crucially dependent upon it.

Elements of a Final Settlement

8. The French paper circulated in the 1 plus 3 and read out in the 2 plus 4 on 22 May (FCO telno 354)[4] is a useful basis for discussion and will be pursued further at the meeting of legal experts on 31 May. The 1 plus 3 meeting on 22 May envisaged that it should be worked up into a form suitable for agreement by 2 plus 4 Ministers. In keeping with the strategy of locking the Russians into the 2 plus 4 process by making early progress on the least controversial aspects, at this stage we should concentrate on the nature of the 2 plus 4 instruments needed to mark the unity of Germany and the termination of QRRs. Berlin and, particularly, a preambular political declaration (as envisaged in the French draft) might be left till later.

Text on Borders

9. Further work is also called for on Kastrup's 5 principles (para 4 of FCO telno 360),[5] on which the Germans were to circulate something. The Germans may wish to lead on this.

Public Presentation

10. It would be useful to know whether 1 plus 3 Ministers intend to make initial statements for subsequent dissemination, as to a large extent occurred on 5 May. Our own preliminary view is that this risks reducing the time available for negotiation. Are others still of the view that we should concentrate on agreeing texts as in items (ii) and (iii) above? Should there be another joint press conference? (If so, we are likely to be stuck with this procedure throughout.) We shall also need to be able to explain how we have reached a text on borders before there has been any discussion between the 2 plus 4 and Poland: it might be described in terms of procedural preparation for the July Ministerial Meeting.

11. Please see IFT[6] for action by Bonn only.

---

[4] Telegram No. 354 of 23 May reported the discussion of the Final Settlement. An outline of the Final Settlement had been proposed by France. The Soviet Union had accepted this but also wanted pol-mil issues to be covered in the settlement and had continued to argue against German membership of NATO. The Western powers had argued that pol-mil issues were for solution in fora other than the Two plus Four (WRL 020/15). See also No. 202, note 2.

[5] Tel No. 360 of 23 May reported the discussion of borders. The five principles were: (*a*) a treaty should be negotiated between Poland and Germany and submitted to the Two plus Four (*b*) the FRG and GDR should state that a unified Germany would consist of the FRG, GDR and Berlin (*c*) they should state that Germany had no territorial claims against any other country (*d*) they should state that the preamble and Articles 23 and 146 of the German constitution would be amended or deleted (*e*) the Four Powers should take note of these statements. In discussion Mr Weston said that he supported these principles: 'The final point was crucial . . . The Four Powers would in effect take cognisance of the fact that, in consequence of the acts described in Kastrup's other principles, Germany's borders would no longer be provisional' (WRL 020/15).

[6] No. 207.

No. 207

Mr Hurd to Sir C. Mallaby (Bonn)[1]

No. 372 Telegraphic [WRL 020/12]

Confidential   FCO, *30 May 1990, 3.27 p.m.*

MIPT: 1 plus 3 Political Directors' Meeting: 5 June: German Unification[2]

1. We are concerned that sight should not be lost of other points arising from the prospect of German unification which are of particular concern to the four Western Allies. Despite some references at Political Director and Legal Adviser level, the Germans have shown no enthusiasm for pursuing them. We would not wish either to embarrass them or to arouse doubts about our motivation by harping on the subject in a wider forum. Grateful therefore if you would approach the Germans at a suitably senior level (perhaps Kastrup and/or Hartmann) to seek their views and advice on how such issues might best be handled. In doing so, you should stress that we are not trying to cause difficulties, nor are we pursuing this subject with the Americans and French at this stage, although they (particularly the French) may have similar concerns.

2. Our general concern relates to the consequences for certain existing agreements which would either fall away or be affected by conclusion of a settlement. The 1954 Presence of Foreign Forces Convention expires upon a settlement. This Convention, and 'original rights', form the basis on which British and other forces are currently stationed in Germany (other legal instruments such as the stationing of forces agreement relate to modalities rather than the principle of stationing). How should it be arranged that Allied forces should stay on? What ratification procedures for new arrangements would be necessary, and hence what timescale?

3. Similarly, the Convention on Relations and the Settlement Convention will clearly need somehow to be reviewed and, at least, modified. How and when?

4. The issue of claims is almost infinitely complicated and many aspects can no doubt be left over, by prior agreement, for settlement in slower time. But such prior agreement will be necessary. And some cases (e.g. claims by Channel Islanders) represent potentially very awkward domestic political problems about which we are currently receiving enquiries from claimants and MPs. Some of these issues, including the above example, have been left to be resolved in the context of a final settlement. What should we now say in relation to such claims?

5. Many of the foregoing issues are not necessarily politically delicate but nonetheless need resolution and hence some solid groundwork. We are ready to contribute to this. What are German preferences?

---

[1] Repeated for information Immediate to Washington, Paris, Moscow, East Berlin, BM Berlin, UKDEL NATO.
[2] No. 206.

No. 208

Minute from Mr Wood (Legal Advisers) to Mr Synnott

[*WRL 020/10*]

Confidential   FCO, *7 June 1990*

German Unification and a Settlement: Comments on the US Papers Circulated at the Political Directors' Meeting on 5 June

1. The US circulated two papers on 5 June at the meeting of the Political Directors of the Western Four: a paper on Sequencing/Simultaneity; and a draft 'Settlement on Germany'. The following comments are not exhaustive.

Paper on Sequencing/Simultaneity[1]

2. This paper reflects US legal thinking as explained at the Legal Experts' meeting on 31 May.[2] The main question addressed is whether Four Power responsibilities relating to Germany's borders can be fulfilled 'prior to or simultaneous with German unity and prior to the formal ratification by Poland and a united Germany of a new border treaty'. The paper distinguishes legal considerations from political considerations. The conclusion is that it is legally possible to fulfil Four Power responsibilities regarding borders at the same time as unification and before the entry into force of a Poland-Germany border treaty.

3. The German-Poland border treaty is not an essential element of the settlement provided that two preconditions are fulfilled:

(*a*) the necessary changes have been made to the Basic Law;

(*b*) a united Germany is otherwise committed under international law to the Oder-Neisse line e.g. by a declaration by the Government of Germany immediately following unification or by a commitment in the peace settlement agreement itself.

It might be argued that precondition (*a*) is unnecessary, being an internal German matter. But given the long and well-documented history of the Basic Law, and the Federal Constitutional Court's interpretation thereof, without precondition (*a*) it will be difficult to be satisfied that precondition (*b*) has been met.

4. The US legal reasoning is unsound, and they do not appear to be to envisage any preconditions. The paper refers to three post-war documents which reflect Allied responsibility for Germany's borders. To these I would add Article 1 of Chapter One of the Settlement Convention. The paper then states that:

at the time, the Allied powers surely intended to act on their own in establishing Germany's final borders and not make such Allied action contingent on the completion of German acts.

They appear to deduce from this proposition that in 1990 the Four Powers can, unilaterally, determine with binding force the borders of Germany. This is a very dubious proposition.

5. The Declaration of Berlin of 5 June 1945 states that the Four Powers 'will hereafter determine boundaries of Germany or any part thereof'. However, as early

---

[1] Not found.

[2] This informal meeting was held in Paris: minute by Mr Synnott of 1 June (WRL 020/12).

as August 1945 the Potsdam Protocol referred to the final determination of the Western frontier of Poland awaiting 'the peace settlement'. And the Bonn/Paris Conventions of 1952/54 state that the final determination of Germany's boundaries must await a peace settlement, which settlement is to be freely negotiated between a re-united Germany and its former enemies.

6. By their acts in 1945 the Four Powers unilaterally altered Germany's borders by detaching from the Reich all territory outside Germany's frontiers of 31 December 1937. This had the effect that territories incorporated into Germany after that date (e.g. Austria and the Sudetenland) were no longer part of Germany. But the basis for this action was the illegality of the incorporation of those territories into the Reich after 1937. It must be doubtful whether the Four Powers had, even in 1945, the power unilaterally to detach from Germany territories that were lawfully part of Germany. Such action would have been unprecedented, since— except where a conquered State ceases to exist—territorial change following war requires the agreement of all concerned (usually given in a peace treaty). If the Four Powers had purported to detach from Germany territory which was lawfully part of Germany they would have had to have done so on the basis of some special right e.g. acting as the Government of Germany. There were indeed certain agreements between the Western occupation authorities (acting for Germany) and neighbouring states transferring small areas of territory e.g. an agreement between the Commandant of the French zone of occupation and the French Republic transferring part of Germany to France. Then adjustments were minor, and contested by the Germans and such transfers required confirmation in a peace settlement. In any event it seems inconceivable that in 1990 the Four Powers would maintain that their rights and responsibilities extend to the unilateral cession of German territory. Even if they asserted such a right, it is most unlikely to be accepted by Germany.

7. The US paper goes on to suggest that

> one could well argue that, legally, Allied action in establishing Germany's final borders is a precondition for a united Germany concluding bilateral treaties with its neighbours, not vice versa.

There is no merit in this argument. Germany at present cannot conclude a border treaty that will establish a definitive as opposed to a provisional border prior to the settlement, but Germany can be a party to a treaty that, together with the settlement, fixes a definitive border.

8. I agree with the US comment that if there really was some legal imperative for the Germany-Poland border treaty, then new border treaties with a number of Germany's neighbours would be needed (not necessarily all neighbours, as suggested by the Americans, since the borders with Austria, Denmark and Czechoslovakia are those of 31 December 1937).

9. The US paper suggests that 'at a minimum the legal situation' regarding the need for a Poland-Germany border treaty 'is ambiguous', and concludes from this that the necessity or otherwise of a German-Polish treaty is a political question. But if the legal situation really were 'ambiguous' (which in my view it will not be provided the preconditions can be met) then it would be legally necessary to do something about it (unless ambiguity was politically acceptable). The US paper appears to be suggesting that if the legal situation is ambiguous one can, as a policy matter, choose one legal answer rather than the other. This is of course true in one sense, but it does not mean that the legal answer chosen is correct.

10. In discussing the policy considerations the paper suggests that there are disadvantages in requiring either ratification of a Polish-German treaty or revision of the Basic Law prior to a settlement. But their arguments appear to be directed entirely against ratification of a Polish-German treaty. (That, at least, appears to be the meaning of the reference to 'independent action by two Parliaments,' which I take to be a reference to the Parliaments of a united Germany and Poland.)

11. The US paper is full of ambiguities in its use of such words as 'signed', 'concluded', 'at unification' (does this mean immediately before or immediately after?).

12. The US paper does not deal with the possible effects of One plus Three matters on timing/sequencing, which we should not lose sight of.

US draft of a 'Settlement on Germany'[3]

13. This draft instrument appears to be intended to be an international agreement (i.e. a treaty in the international law sense, if not for the purposes of US constitutionally [*sic*] law). But it is in a very curious form. Firstly, it is headed 'A Settlement on Germany', and is referred to as a 'Settlement' on page 2, first paragraph, and page 5, second paragraph, as well as in the testimonium. But it is referred to as a 'Treaty' on page 3, second paragraph, uses the word 'agree' and is stated to 'enter into force'. The form is very unusual for a treaty: the first two pages look more like a resolution, though they include the word 'agree' which suggest a legally binding document. They follow two sections (on borders, and on quadripartite rights) each consist of preambular paragraphs followed by an operative paragraph or paragraphs, which is extremely odd for a treaty. (It looks a little like the Helsinki Final Act, which of course was not intended to be legally binding.)

14. As drafted, the Settlement would be signed by the Two plus Four (i.e. including the two German states) and not by a united Germany, and would come into force 'upon unification'. A footnote suggests that it could be structured to be signed 'at unification'. The intention appears to be that consent to be bound by the treaty will take the form of signature, and that ratification will not be required. It is perfectly acceptable (and indeed quite common) as a matter of international law for consent to be bound by a treaty to be expressed by signature alone, and for there to be no requirement for ratification. It would, however, be very unusual for consent to be expressed by two States and the treaty to come into force for a united State formed out of the two States. It seems doubtful whether this is possible without some action on the part of the united state. Articles 18 and 32 of the Vienna Convention on Succession of States in respect of Treaties (which is not in force) provides that the successor State may 'by making a notification' establish its status as a party to a multilateral treaty which enters into force after the date of the succession of States if a predecessor State was a contracting state (i.e. had indicated its consent to be bound). The important element is the requirement of a notification by the successor State. Of course, provided it were accepted by all concerned (including the Soviet Union) that a united Germany is the same legal person as the FRG then it might follow that the united Germany was bound by the settlement even without the notification. That would presumably be the intention if a draft were adopted along the lines of the American draft. But even then there would be doubts about whether a united Germany was in fact bound in law without some further action.

---

[3] Not printed.

15. I shall not indicate all the difficulties I have with the US draft. They begin, for example, with the first preambular paragraph, which would recognise 'that the States parties have lived in peace since 1945'. Two of the States parties did not exist until 1949, and a number of the States parties have engaged in armed conflicts since 1945. The term 'lived in peace' is presumably not intended to have legal significance; each of the Four Powers terminated the war with Germany, for the purposes of its domestic law at least, at various dates in the 1950s.

16. Other difficulties with page 1 of the US draft are its selective citation of the Purposes of the United Nations, its curious omission from the list of Helsinki Principles of the principle of respect for human rights and fundamental freedoms, including the freedom of thought, conscience, religion or belief; its statement that there is 'right' to change one's frontiers (where Helsinki merely said that frontiers may be changed); and its limitation of the Helsinki commitment to peace to 'the European continent', an ambiguous term.

17. Page 2 contains a number of words whose legal significance is unclear e.g. 'agree to . . . state their intent to address and resolve'; and 'agree to . . . recognise and accept the arrangements . . . '[4]

18. Page 3 likewise contains very unsatisfactory terminology. First, the references to wartime and post-war agreements and decisions, still relevant in connection with Berlin, but surely not something we would wish to emphasise in connection with borders. The reference to the FRG and GDR 'by their sovereign acts' of entering into border treaties, is extraordinary. The whole point about those treaties is that they were entered into by States which did not have sovereignty over the matters in question; hence the border changes were only provisional. The reference to the treaties making the borders 'inviolable' rests upon a misunderstanding of the meaning of inviolability. Borders are inviolable because of the prohibition under international law of the use of force, which is contained in the UN Charter. Border treaties do not make borders inviolable; they merely establish borders. The reference to the existing borders of the FRG and GDR includes the inner German border, and the border around Greater Berlin, which is presumably not intended. The final paragraph on page 3 repeats the error of referring to the 'right' to change frontiers, a concept which would presumably not be popular in Poland.

19. Page 4 would have the six states, or possibly the five, affirm that the borders of Germany, 'consist of' current borders. But all that is necessary is for the Four Powers to state that current borders are no longer provisional. We presumably do not wish to suggest that the borders of Germany can never be changed in the future, by agreement. For the six to state in a treaty that the borders of Germany 'shall consist of' current borders might carry the implication that they were unchangeable, and thus somehow different in quality from any other borders in the world.

20. This point is made more difficult by the statement on page 5 that the settlement 'establishes' the borders of a united Germany. The preambular paragraphs on page 5 seem unnecessary, and might be contentious. On the same page, it is surprising to see it suggested that the Germans should join in declaring dissolved Four Power institutions. The final paragraph on page 5 is an inadequate provision for 'all remaining Allied legislation'.

---

[4] Ellipses in original.

21. Page 6 uses the odd German language put forward in the legal group on 8 May, which they readily abandoned last week. The reference to a united Germany enjoying 'full and complete sovereign rights' is odd, though I see that it occurs in the French paper agreed by the Political Directors. What is meant by 'full' and how is this different from 'complete'? The term 'sovereign rights' is usually employed when something less than sovereignty is involved e.g. sovereign rights over the continental shelf.

22. The above is perhaps sufficient to indicate that the US draft 'Settlement' is a poor basis for work. I therefore very much hope we shall circulate our own draft.

M.C. WOOD

No. 209

Letter from Mr Powell (No. 10) to Mr Wall

[*WRL 020/1*]

Confidential   10 DOWNING STREET, *8 June 1990*

Dear Stephen,

Prime Minister's Meeting with President Gorbachev in the Kremlin
on Friday 8 June[1]

The Prime Minister had a two and a half hour talk with President Gorbachev in the Kremlin this morning. Gorbachev was accompanied only by his assistant, Anatoly Chernyaev. The discussion continued over a working lunch which was attended in addition by Mr Thatcher, Mr Shevardnadze, the Soviet Ambassador in London and HM Ambassador in Moscow.

The Prime Minister commented afterwards that she found Mr. Gorbachev a bit less ebullient than usual, but nonetheless in good form and seemingly well in control of events. Certainly he was very equable and good-humoured throughout. Richard Pollock, who interpreted, thought the mood the best of any of the meetings between the Prime Minister and Gorbachev which he had attended. I would agree with that.

The main interest of the meeting lay in Gorbachev's views on Germany and NATO which are obviously still evolving. At no stage did he say that a united Germany in NATO was unacceptable. He appeared rather to be reaching round for ways to make this more palatable and explicable to his own people. But some of his comments were rather confused and hard to follow. Lithuania did not seem to be at all a high priority for him. He did not raise non-circumvention under the START Treaty, indeed did not dwell on nuclear matters much at all.[2]

This letter contains sensitive material and should be given a very restricted circulation only.

[1] Mrs Thatcher visited the Soviet Union from 7 to 9 June.
[2] The Strategic Arms Reduction Treaty (START), first proposed by President Reagan in June 1982, was eventually signed in July 1991.

Introduction

The meeting started with some banter about Gorbachev's visit to Washington.[3] Gorbachev said that his body was still trying to recover from the effects of the journey and the eleven hour time difference between San Francisco and Moscow. He kept wanting to go to sleep at the wrong time: indeed he had almost dropped off during the Warsaw Pact meeting the previous afternoon.

Gorbachev said one of the reasons he always enjoyed meeting the Prime Minister was that she did not come trailed by a delegation. They could talk more intimately. The Prime Minister said she believed in having only a small staff. Gorbachev said that she was fortunate: in the Soviet Union the policy and the administration functions were combined, which made for a very complex bureaucracy. He was now engaged in trying to take the bureaucratic structure apart: the Prime Minister could probably hear the yelling even in the United Kingdom. Parkinson's Law was no exaggeration.

The Prime Minister congratulated Gorbachev on the success of the US/Soviet Summit in Washington. It had been very extensively and positively reported in the United Kingdom and there had clearly been an excellent rapport between Gorbachev and President Bush. Gorbachev said that he knew the President had telephoned the Prime Minister to give her an account of the meetings. Indeed he seemed to have telephoned everyone, including some of the East Europeans. But there was no harm in that, he was all for everyone having as much information as possible.

Becoming slightly more formal, Gorbachev then said that he was very happy to see the Prime Minister again. He had a feeling that her visit would be productive and successful. The Prime Minister said she was honoured that Gorbachev had taken the time to receive her at such a critical moment in the Soviet Union, when he had many pressing problems with which to deal. Gorbachev said that their meeting had been arranged long before the US/Soviet summit and he had been determined to keep his promise. The only aspect of the visit he could not manage was accompanying the Prime Minister to Kiev. He was genuinely very sorry about that, but hoped she would understand. He could assure her that he would much prefer to go with her to Kiev than be stuck with resolving his problems in Moscow. The Prime Minister said rather starchily that the problems must come first. Gorbachev observed that at least he and the Prime Minister were having a joint press conference for the first time in their six years of meetings: at last she had agreed. The Prime Minister said that she had not realised that she had been an obstacle to this. But she hoped they could both use the press conference to convey a positive and forward-looking view of the future. The task of those at the top was to point the way forward. Gorbachev said the Prime Minister was very experienced in handling the press: he would take his cue from her: together they would manage to give the right impression. The Prime Minister said that Gorbachev had managed the press extremely well in Washington: he could give her a few lessons.

US/Soviet Summit

Gorbachev said he would start by dealing with the US/Soviet summit since the Prime Minister had mentioned it. It had been a most important visit, with many issues discussed and significant agreements reached. There had been a lot of

---

[3] His summit meeting with President Bush had taken place between 30 May and 3 June. At their meeting on 31 May he had made the crucial concession, possibly inadvertently, that a united Germany would be free to decide which alliance it wished to join. See Zelikow and Rice, pp. 275-85.

discussion of disarmament and neither he nor President Bush had failed to remember the Prime Minister's strong views on this subject. He recalled that the Prime Minister had once said that the British and French nuclear deterrents would not be involved in any negotiations, at least until after a START Agreement which reduced the US and Soviet strategic arsenals by 50 per cent. But that was by the way. He believed a treaty would be signed this year. There had also been progress on chemical weapons and nuclear testing. There had been quite a sharp discussion about the future intentions of each party in the nuclear field. On CFE, they had agreed to aim at a treaty this year. The talks had also covered the whole range of bilateral problems. Discussion of a trade agreement had gone right up to the last day. By now he was accustomed to the American style of fighting your corner up to the last minute and had decided to hang in there himself. The Prime Minister was his only unpredictable interlocutor: he never knew what she was going to say next.

The Prime Minister said that she continued to believe passionately in what Gorbachev was trying to achieve in the Soviet Union. People—and particularly journalists—had become blasé about how much had already changed. He would have her full support, both privately and publicly. From their very first meeting, they had always agreed to speak frankly and on the basis of mutual respect, with each entitled to their own views. Generally speaking she was encouraged by the way things were moving. For instance the communiqué from the Warsaw Pact meeting the previous day would have been inconceivable even a year ago. Gorbachev said that he was now looking for some reciprocal move from the NATO summit in London.[4] He had the feeling that NATO was rather lagging behind the Warsaw Pact. The Prime Minister said that she had looked in on the NATO Foreign Ministers meeting in Scotland the previous day, and in fact the views there had been very similar.[4] But we must always keep strong defence: you never knew where the threat would come from next. Gorbachev said the aim must be for NATO and the Warsaw Pact to draw closer to each other. They must make the transition from confrontation to cooperation. We must mould European structures so that they helped us find the common European home. Neither side must be afraid of unorthodox solutions. He would be more specific about this later in their talk.

The Prime Minister said that when she and Gorbachev had first met some years ago, there had been two wholly different ideologies confronting each other. The Communist ideology had been expansionist and it was this that had caused the basic division of Europe and the confrontation between NATO and the Warsaw Pact. Much had changed since then, due in good part to Gorbachev, and several regional problems were well on the way to solution. There was one point on which the two of them had differences in the past: she believed that nuclear weapons were the most effective deterrent to war. We must keep nuclear weapons, including some in Europe. People asked her who the enemy was. The answer was: you never knew where or when a new tyrant might arise. But you had to be sure that whatever enemy might materialise, you had enough forces to make success impossible for him, so that he would never start a war. President Reagan had a vision of the world without nuclear weapons, but President Bush did not share this and he was right.

[4] See No 197, note 6.

Gorbachev suggested that tyrants were pretty sophisticated these days and would understand that no one would actually use a nuclear weapon. The Prime Minister said that apparently sophisticated people sometimes had uncontrolled emotions and might over-step the mark. The fact was that thirteen countries already had a missile capability, which could deliver chemical weapons. The odds must be that several of them would acquire nuclear weapons in the next 20 years. Gorbachev said that his view was rather different. He believed we should move towards a system of joint action to ensure security. If we could put that together, it would be a good start. The Prime Minister replied that, even then, you would need to keep a certain level of weapons, including nuclear weapons. Gorbachev commented that he and the Prime Minister were back on their old argument. The Prime Minister acknowledged this, but said she wanted Gorbachev to be quite clear that we intended to keep our independent nuclear deterrent, and she thought the same applied to France. Gorbachev said that the reference to France made him think the Prime Minister's view-point was rather like the Maginot Line. If there had been a joint security system in Europe between the wars, the Second World War would never have happened.

The Prime Minister said this led her on to the importance of keeping American forces in Europe. Gorbachev said he had discussed this in Washington with President Bush. The President saw NATO as the only way in which United States forces in Europe could be maintained. His reasoning seemed to be that without a unified Germany in NATO, there would be no NATO: without NATO, there would be no United States forces in Europe: and without that, the United States would have no political influence. He quite seriously and realistically understood that point of view. His own point of departure with President Bush—as it always had been with the Prime Minister—was that there could be no security unless it was equal for all. If one side felt disadvantaged there would be no movement forward. But he also accepted there could be no success without co-operation between the United States and the Soviet Union. That had been a constant in his thinking since 1985. He did not want to drive the United States out of Europe: that would be dangerous. But there was a bit of a paradox here. When tension started to rise, everyone was very keen to persuade the United States and the Soviet Union to patch up their differences. But as soon as relations improved, other countries begun [*sic*] to suspect a condominium. He recalled the Prime Minister's expression: 'We can't afford another Reykjavik'.[5] The Prime Minister said that she had been quite right: we could not afford another Reykjavik. But she agreed that we would only make progress if there was cooperation and understanding between the United States and the Soviet Union.

Germany and NATO

The Prime Minister said she would like to be more specific on the subject of Germany and NATO. She recalled her discussion with Gorbachev last September.[6] She had always been rather apprehensive about a unified Germany. So was President Mitterrand. The difference was that she expressed it publicly and Mitterrand did not. She had been aware of Gorbachev's view that there should be a

---

[5] During their summit meeting at Reykjavik on 11-12 October 1986 President Reagan (without consulting his European allies) and Mr Gorbachev had come close to agreement on an INF treaty. The summit had then broken down over Mr Gorbachev's insistence that such a treaty must be linked to the United States' abandonment of its SDI programme, and President Reagan's refusal to accept this demand. See also No. 51, note 4.

[6] No. 26, note 4.

long transitional period before unification to enable all the details to be worked out. She had supported that view publicly and taken a lot of criticism for it. She had not received much support, even from Gorbachev. It had subsequently become clear that Germany would unify quite rapidly under Article 23 of the Federal German Constitution. Now that unification was almost upon us, ordinary people were beginning to express more doubts about it, particularly in the Soviet Union. We could not now stop or even slow down unification. The task was to find some way to make sure that it did not threaten anyone's security.

The Prime Minister continued that she was glad Gorbachev accepted the stabilising role that the United States played in Europe. Germany was just about the only place that American forces could be present in Europe in any significant numbers. And their presence there represented security not just for Europe but also for the Soviet Union. But that meant a unified Germany must be in NATO, otherwise there would be no justification for the presence of US forces. If we took that as the starting point, we could then look at ways to allay Soviet concerns. Various ideas had been put forward, in particular Secretary Baker's nine points.[7] Gorbachev had himself proposed limits on the numbers of German forces and some sort of joint declaration between NATO and the Warsaw Pact. (At this point, Gorbachev asked Chernyaev to go and fetch his briefcase, from which he produced a document.) We could look at that and she would be interested to hear more about the idea. She had set out her own view in her speech to NATO Foreign Ministers the previous day, which would be available to him. One way of strengthening confidence would be to develop the CSCE, making it a forum for regular political consultation between East and West. Mr Shevardnadze had made similar proposals. The history of central Europe was littered with conflicts and difficulties, and there had to be a forum to sort out problems before they became too troublesome. There should be regular meetings and consultations. None of this would obviate the need for continuing defence, which would in turn require us to keep some nuclear weapons in Germany—perhaps fewer than at present, but still some.

Gorbachev said that he would like to take up some of the Prime Minister's points on Germany. What was going to happen was going to happen: he did not dispute that. But they ought to analyse the situation. Europe used to be two armed camps. Now that was changed. The previous day's meeting of the Warsaw Pact had left no doubt about that. Indeed Europe had travelled a long way since 1985, and he was grateful for the Prime Minister's contribution to that. What he had to say on Germany might seem unorthodox or unusual. But ideas which had seemed Utopian only a few years ago were now being realised in practice. If the two of them could join hands in seeking a solution, they would succeed. He was ready to back any option, whoever was the author, which would produce a solution. But it must be an option which did not undermine the progress which had already been made. And no nation must feel that its interests were not being taken into account.

Gorbachev continued that there were a number of processes in train which ought to be combined. First, there was the process of forming a unified Germany. It ought to be a calm and placid process. But Chancellor Kohl was being a bit hasty and subordinating everything to the demands of his election campaign. Kohl was not exactly displaying a high class of politics. He desperately wanted to be father of a unified Germany. De Maizière, whom he had met the previous day,

[7] See No. 202.

represented the same party as Kohl but took a more sober approach. His great concern was that his people should not be hit too hard in economic terms by unification. Opinion polls even in West Germany showed a growing number of people concerned that unification was going too fast. All the same he accepted that unification would be determined mostly by internal reasons in Germany.

Gorbachev continued that we also had to consider the external front. It was premature to say that the Four Powers had given up their rights in Germany. There had first to be a final settlement. Only then would Germany be a fully sovereign state. There was also the issue of Germany in NATO. Chancellor Kohl claimed to speak for a unified Germany on this, and the Prime Minister supported him. But we did not yet have a unified Germany. Once it emerged, we could talk about it. But for now there could only be preliminary discussions, although he had nothing against them. In parallel, we should be looking at a new security structure for Europe. There were several aspects to this. We should change the nature of our respective alliances and make them more political. Germany should confirm its renunciation of nuclear, chemical and biological weapons. She should also agree to limits on the size of her forces. We should change our military strategies—and in this respect, he had high hopes of the NATO summit in July. If nothing tangible came of that, then suspicions would rise. It was in this general context that he had suggested that the two alliances might sign a declaration or agreement signalling a rapprochment between them. The document could record their intention to co-operate and interact. It might set up a body where the military leaders of the two alliances could talk to each other. As it was, he never saw Yazov these days: he always seemed to be travelling. The Prime Minister interjected that she had seen him. Gorbachev said that was just the trouble. But if we were both thinking of permanent bodies in the CSCE framework, then why not have one for the military, where all these matters could be discussed?

Gorbachev continued that he would like to pursue the point in rather greater detail. One aspect was that of limiting German forces. That could perhaps be pursued in a second stage CFE agreement. Another possibility to be explored was the nature of a unified Germany's membership of NATO. What about the French model? Or the Danish or Norwegian model, under which there were no stationed nuclear weapons or bases? Or even the UK model? His point was that there were many different models of NATO membership, and we should look for a form of membership for a united Germany which would reflect the interests of all of us. In the longer term, and once NATO and the Warsaw Pact were reformed, it might be possible for any European state to join either one of them. Perhaps the Soviet Union could join NATO. What he was saying was that we were in a transitional period, and should be discussing how to alleviate the concerns of everyone about the future status of Germany in defence matters. He had promised to put forward some more detailed ideas, and had agreed with President Bush that their two Foreign Ministers would work on this.

The Prime Minister said that she would respond to some of these points. There was no prospect now of slowing down German unification. The escalator would start to move with German economic and monetary union on 1 July. The political parties in East and West Germany would unite in the autumn. We all had to accept that unification would happen in the timetable foreseen by Chancellor Kohl i.e. by the end of the year. The manner in which Germany would unite meant that East Germany would automatically inherit all the obligations and alliances of West Germany, including membership of the European Community and of NATO. She did not see any way in which Germany could be united for one purpose and not for another. NATO's Foreign Ministers had agreed to look at the Alliance's strategy and structure and consider how it could have a more substantial political role. We were also negotiating reductions in conventional forces. All this should help meet Soviet concerns. She did not think the French model of membership of NATO was at all relevant. The worst thing would be to have Germany in NATO but without its forces integrated into the Alliance's military structure.

The Prime Minister continued that she was interested by Gorbachev's idea of a NATO/Warsaw Pact declaration. But at the moment it was just a skeleton. We needed to put some clothes on it. What kind of declaration would it be? If it was a sort of confidence-building measure she would support it. She could also understand an institutionalisation of the present pattern of exchanges and visits. She could agree a declaration which emphasised that both the NATO and the Warsaw Pact were defensive alliances, which would keep the forces and weapons necessary for defence. Gorbachev interjected that his proposal might also involve the setting up of a centre for conflict prevention. The Prime Minister continued that the CSCE could provide the umbrella for all this, as well as being the forum which brought the Soviet Union fully into discussion about the future of Europe. An organisation in which the United States and the Soviet Union were also present would help balance the growing power of Germany. In short, it was no good fighting causes which had already been lost, such as a longer transitional period before unification. We should put all our efforts into increasing confidence between East and West.

Gorbachev said that he could support most of what the Prime Minister had said. By talking things through, he felt they were making progress. They should agree to put their Foreign Ministers to work on these new concepts and try and come up with a coherent formula. Things were becoming steadily clearer. But until discussion of these matters had been completed, Germany could not have full sovereignty. The Prime Minister said that it was not realistic to hold up German unification on these issues. We should be pressing ahead on all fronts: a final settlement between Germany and the Four Powers: a CFE Agreement: strengthening the CSCE: a NATO/Warsaw Pact declaration. Gorbachev said that he wanted to be completely frank with the Prime Minister. If discussion of the external aspects of unification went entirely normally, he was sure that all these treaties and declarations could be signed. But if one side tried to go ahead unilaterally, there could be a very difficult situation. The Soviet Union would feel its security in jeopardy and might have to reconsider the whole concept of a CFE agreement. He thought that all would go well. But there should be no ultimatums. The Prime Minister said she understood this: it was in no one's interest to jeopardise the Soviet Union's security. But we had to be realistic. Certain consequences flowed from German unification, and membership of NATO was one of them. It was no good fighting it. But we must find ways to give the Soviet Union confidence that its security would be assured. She and Mr Gorbachev should put in hand further work on the basis of their discussion. Gorbachev said that he agreed with that . . . [8]

Yours sincerely,
CHARLES POWELL

---

[8] Remaining paragraphs not printed.

No. 210

Draft Paper by the Policy Planning Staff[1]

[*WRL 020/1*]

Confidential   FCO, *15 June 1990*

BINDING GERMANY IN

Introduction

1. The prospect of a unified Germany has made it fashionable to talk of the need to bind Germany into Europe. This paper examines the thinking behind that proposition. Three examples of this argument are:

(*a*) *Giscard d'Estaing* (to the PM):[2] The choice is between establishing alliances to counter-balance Germany and tying the Germans into a framework in which they are compelled to behave. A dispersed Europe could not keep Germany in check. Unless the European Community moves towards federation Europe will be dominated by Germany. The Americans and Japanese will be interested only in the Deutschmark. Trade negotiations will centre on Germany. Within a tighter Europe Britain and France together would be stronger than Germany. If there were a European Central Bank, German influence would still be important but only one among many.

(*b*) *Rocard* (to the PM):[3] Closer European integration would compel the Germans to take account of the interests of others and cooperate with them. There must be European solidarity in face of the political threats which could arise from almost any quarter and the commercial, technological and industrial threat from Japan. There must be a common organisation enabling Europe to act on the same level as the Soviet Union, Japan or China.

(*c*) *Davidson (F*[*inancial*]*T*[*imes*]*)*:[4] What is happening now is that full sovereignty is being returned to Germany. For those who fear this might be destabilizing the solution is to reduce German sovereignty by building up supranational structures in Europe, notably the Community.

2. The idea that following unification Germany might lose its Western orientation has some historical logic: for roughly 150 years until the end of the Second World War, German (or before 1871, Prussian) policy was basically anti-French. It was for this reason that in 1871 the UK generally welcomed the prospect of a strong Germany. For a good deal of this period a key element of German policy was good relations with Russia; and *Mitteleuropa* formed a natural

---

[1] Sent by Mr Cooper to Mr Synnott on 15 June with covering minute: 'This is part of a package which we may put to DUSs later this month. The other papers of this package are one on the changing nature of power and a short note on the interesting parallels between Japan and Germany [not found]. I should be grateful for any comments by Wednesday 20 June.' No subsequent version of this paper has been found; WED minuting of 18-21 June is not printed; comments by Mr Budd are printed as No. 213.

[2] At their meeting on 19 February (PREM: Anglo-French Relations).

[3] At their meeting on 26 March (PREM: France).

[4] Not found.

extension of the German economy. Germany's Western political orientation and Franco German reconciliation are therefore, historically exceptional.

3. The pull of the East will become stronger. Former German territories and people still remain there, and in acquiring the GDR the West Germans will find that they have also acquired a great number of trading and other relations with the Soviet Union and with Central Europe. The idea of a non Western oriented Germany may also be latent in some SPD ideas such as Egon Bahr's plans for a nuclear free zone in central Europe. Finally the thought that the Germans may soon begin throwing their (economic) weight around in an unpleasant fashion cannot be dismissed: in fact it began some while ago.[5] There are thus some general grounds at least for considering seriously the arguments of those who wish to bind Germany in.

4. Those who believe in binding Germany in usually see a more integrated European Community as a way of solving the problems posed by a large Germany. The problems they have in mind may include the following.

(i) The re-emergence of a (real or perceived) German military threat, including the possibility of a nuclear Germany.

 (ii) A major shift in German foreign policy, either to neutrality or to some kind of adventurism in the East, e.g. an attempt to reacquire lost territory by diplomatic means.

(iii) German economic domination of Europe.

The Re-emergence of a German Military Threat

5. In current circumstances the idea that Germany might once again invade either France or Poland is inconceivable. Circumstances can of course change but there is no more reason to fear German aggression than there is to worry about an attack from France or the United States. This is well understood on a conscious level; but sub-consciously the fears of a militaristic Germany remain.

6. One of the factors which has made the idea of a German invasion of France unthinkable is the creation of the European Community. (The other two are democracy and nuclear weapons.) The idea of strengthening the Community is therefore not an unnatural response. This approach probably also echoes the idea, popular among Americans and, during the war, in European resistance movements, that the division of Europe into nation states was the cause of successive European wars (creating a European super state seems at first sight only to transfer the problem to a higher level; but that is perhaps besides the point). Whether or not the idea behind the Schuman plan—that combining the French and German coal and steel industries would make it impossible for the two countries ever to fight each other again—works at its crudest level, is doubtful. After all the United States managed a civil war despite a much higher degree of economic integration. Nevertheless the fact remains that the Community has transformed political relations among European states. Together with the other factors mentioned, it is quite sufficient to render a Western European war unthinkable. It seems unlikely that EMU or 'Political Union' would add much to the achievements of the Community in terms of preventing a German military threat.

---

[5] Footnote in original: 'Helmut Schmidt for example told Peter Jenkins that the UK could no longer be considered a developed country and President Carter that Germany was not the 51st state of the USA.'

A Major Shift in German Foreign/Security Policy

7. A more independent German foreign and security policy is one likely result of unification. In certain circumstances this could be destabilizing, notably if Germany were to leave NATO. It is at least as likely however that NATO will be transformed according to German thinking: this has always been the pattern in the past. Forward defence was adopted in response to German wishes although its military logic was not compelling; Flexible Response was also devised, after much turmoil, in response to German concerns. The INF twin track decision was adopted because of German concerns and German difficulties over implementing it then became a major factor in Alliance politics. We are now about to abandon certain other aspects of NATO (SNF, low flying, exercise) again because of German concerns.

8. Given Germany's geographical position and its contribution to the Alliance, its dominant position (with that of the United States) is not surprising. Unlike the Community the Alliance remains a system of cooperation among sovereign states but there are still some measures that can be taken to make disentangling more difficult (e.g. more multilateral units) or cooperation easier (changing Alliance strategy).

9. Some may see the process of European integration as contributing to making disentangling difficult. Certainly a fully federal Europe which had a single army and a single defence policy would have this effect: there would be no possibility of German security policy going astray since there would be no such thing as German policy. This however is political fantasy. A more realistic question is whether we could design security arrangements that seemed more European. Leaving them might then seem un-European and thus be unattractive politically. The most important of these steps would be to multinationalise NATO forces in a consciously European fashion: so that there was a higher degree of integration among European forces than between European and American forces. Whether this is achievable will be the subject of a separate paper.

German Economic Domination

10. Germany is already the largest single economy in Europe, and the largest exporter in the world. Its relative weight will be increased by the incorporation of the GDR. In Western Europe Germany is the largest trading partner of every country except Ireland, Iceland, Norway and Spain and in each of these it is a close second. In Eastern Europe the FRG is the largest Western trading partner of each of the CMEA countries and the GDR the second largest overall trading partner. The FRG is also the largest foreign investor in all other Western European countries with the exception of the UK. Finally the D Mark has for some time been the key European currency, and the Bundesbank the key European monetary institution.

11. We argue in a separate paper[6] that care should be exercised in using terms such as 'economic domination': markets do not operate on the principles of hegemony that apply in political and military systems. The challenge presented by a military threat is to the system as a whole; an economic challenge such as that presented by Germany or Japan is within the system. Misleading though it may be the term 'economic domination' probably includes some of the following ideas.

—*big market*: the FRG is already the largest export market in Europe of any

[6] Not found.

European countries. The addition of the GDR will increase its size. In the past this might have given the Germans negotiating leverage in trade disputes or on matters such as standards. The EC single market regime should ensure that this is not so.

—*current account surplus*: a current account surplus represents a sort of power since it enables the acquisition of foreign assets. Unification will almost certainly result in a reduced (united) German surplus, since surplus FRG savings which have hitherto been invested abroad will now be invested in the GDR. How long it will take the GDR to catch up to FRG standards is a matter of guess work but twenty years seems a more likely period than ten. If this is right then by the time the GDR has been fully absorbed in the FRG—i.e. by the time it is capitalized to the same level—the changing age structure of both Germanies should have reduced the saving (and current account) surplus.

—*strong currency*: This probably forms a part of the picture of 'German economic domination' though for different reasons from the items mentioned above. Unification will not increase the influence of the DM. On the contrary, it may, by creating inflationary pressures, tend to weaken it. It may be true that through the ERM the Bundesbank has exercised considerable influence on other countries' monetary policies (i.e. it has obliged them to give a higher priority to counter inflationary policy than they would have chosen otherwise). Those who are concerned about this might adopt the French approach of attempting to tie the Bundesbank into a European system of Central Banks. This argument is however nothing to do with the question of unification.

—*Government Financial Power*: Unification will tend to reduce the German government's ability to throw money at problems. It will have enough calls on its resources in the GDR from infrastructure and social security (not to mention possible payments to the Soviet Union) to reduce if anything its ability to buy influence.

The Other Side of the Coin

12. How do the Germans react to this debate? There are some Germans, especially among the older generation of the liberal intelligentsia who themselves urge the policy of binding Germany in. But there are others particularly younger Germans who must resent being treated as a dangerous breed. Chancellor Kohl's views are interesting: in a private conversation (not for quotation) he was asked how he felt about the notion of binding Germany into Europe. His reply was that the people who used this language were the enemies of Germany but he would take his revenge on them by doing precisely what they suggested.

13. Perhaps of all of the member states Germany is the most seriously committed to Europe. The Germans have almost always been at the forefront of any attempts to move the Community towards federation. Although they have occasional problems with the *Länder* their record on implementation is nearly as good as the UK's (and of quite a different order from the other enthusiastic Federalists in Rome). They have not pressed for the location of Community institutions in Germany but have paid an annual bill of Dm 4bn for the Community without much complaint (compare Prussia's attitude to the *Zollverein* when it accepted a disproportionate financial burden in order to persuade the smaller German states to join). For all its ups and downs Germany has been the most consistent and powerful advocate of the Community in both word and deed.

14. The explanation for this is to be found in history and psychology rather than in national interest. (As argued elsewhere interests may be a less relevant concept today.) For much of the last 150 years Germany has been concerned with its own unification, usually like the Community through a process beginning with economic union. The extension of this to Europe is not unnatural, especially after the disasters brought on Germany and Europe by extreme nationalism. But this explanation may be wrong: the alternative view is that having achieved their major objective—unification—the Germans will drop their European commitment, which was no more than a means to this end. We shall see.

15. This brings us back to the basic argument. Rocard told the Prime Minister we should reduce Germany's scope for independent influence by further integration in the Community; the Prime Minister replied that tying ourselves more closely to Germany would have opposite results—we should be even more under her sway. Both are wrong. Were we to return to a 19th century world of independent states, Germany as the biggest and economically strongest state in Europe would exercise preponderant influence. But the Community as it is now already solves that problem. Power is institutionalised—German weight in the Community is precisely 10 votes, the same as ours. As it happens Germany is voted down more often than any of the other large member states. A looser Community would give the Germans more influence but that does not mean that a more integrated Europe would reduce German influence significantly.

16. The question of whether Germany retains its commitment to Europe will be critical. Their willingness to accept less than their due in terms of voting and budgetary arrangements is greatly to our advantage. If the Germans decide to pursue national interest in a narrow or traditional way they aim to make the Community weaker. We would be the losers if the Community were to work itself looser: it would not be dangerous in security terms but our influence would suffer by comparison with Germany's.

Conclusion
17.
1. We do well, unlike the French, to avoid the language of 'binding Germany in'.
2. The possibility of a more European framework for security is at least worth looking at.
3. The Community does provide important safeguards against disproportionate German economic influence. Further integration would not make much difference but a weaker Community would be against our interests.
4. EMU is a separate issue. This could well reduce German influence but it may be doing so at a moment when German monetary influence is in the process of peaking. (German monetary influence has on the whole been for the good.) But one can argue just as well that what matters is not whether monetary policy is German or French but whether it is good or bad.

No. 211

Minute from Sir P. Cradock to Mrs Thatcher

[*PREM: Anglo-German Relations*]

Secret   10 DOWNING STREET, *19 June 1990*

Visit to Bonn

I spent Monday in Bonn seeing a number of junior ministers and senior officials, including Teltschik. The attached telegrams give highlights.[1] To me the most important points were:

GDR

There was confidence that the GDR economy could be turned round fairly quickly: 4 to 5 years was the period generally cited, though some were even more optimistic than that. But in the short term there was concern over (*a*) the impatience of the GDR Parliament, as shown in Sunday's resolution seeking immediate unification; (*b*) the fragility of the present GDR administration and their possible inability to handle the situation after GEMU. This could force an earlier take-over by the FRG and enormously complicate the timetable. Teltschik's view, however, was that the FRG could probably keep events in the GDR under control (he could not be absolutely certain). They were planning for unification in December and thought they could meet that timetable, but it was essential that there should be no delay beyond that date.

Soviet Attitude

It was thought that the Russians would eventually agree to a unified Germany joining NATO. Not yet; perhaps in the early autumn. Words and presentation to sweeten the pill were very important. In this connection a really forthcoming communiqué from the NATO Summit in July was seen as necessary.

Alliance Declaration

Teltschik did not like the idea of an alliance to alliance declaration as proposed by Shevardnadze. He preferred a statement by individual members of NATO to which other CSCE members could subscribe. He spoke of the idea of a non-aggression treaty.

Aid for the Soviet Union

Teltschik said there was now a letter from Kohl, which you will have.[2] He spoke of the need for very large sums, many billions of dollars, which would be too much of a burden for the FRG alone to sustain. Kohl would want to discuss this in Dublin and Houston. One object he admitted would be to buy Soviet acquiescence on politico-military issues, another to preserve Gorbachev and orderly reform. He spoke of the possibility of providing Western advisers who could do something to ensure that the money was properly used. I went over the obvious objections, pointing out that as yet there was no framework at all into which such money could be usefully placed. More advisers would not suffice;

---

[1] Not printed.

[2] This letter of 18 June raised, in advance of the forthcoming meeting of the European Council in Dublin, the possibility of a collective Western effort to provide credit to the Soviet Union, and informed the Prime Minister of a Soviet request for short-term credit from German banks, for which the Federal German Government would act as guarantor (WRL 020/23).

what was needed was something more like a total receivership of the Soviet economy. So far we lacked even the basic commitments in principle to market development. Teltschik accepted this and in the end fell back upon the argument that we must at least show ourselves forthcoming and ready to help. There is of course a great gap between a gesture of this kind and actually providing the aid he originally spoke of. You will need an agreed line on this for Dublin and later.

NATO Strategy

Teltschik stressed the need for some undertaking to cap the German armed forces in order to reassure the Russians. He would prefer this to be done in as positive and early a form as possible, as part of CFE rather than part of CFE 1 (*a*). But in the end he accepted that a prospective statement about future force reductions would probably suffice.

On the nuclear element, he warned of the extreme vulnerability of German public opinion. Faced with a choice between a fully agreed unification settlement and nuclear weapons they would certainly opt for the first. The denuclearisation card had not yet been played, but the Russians could be reserving it for later on in the game. On tactics over SNF, he was very firm that the less said about it at the moment the better. Later on when it came to negotiation he thought it would be safer to seek an overall ceiling for short range nuclear weapons under which the two parties would have freedom to mix. This is our own preference.

Mood in Bonn

I found my interlocutors naturally obsessed with the German question. Sudhoff for example, the PUS equivalent in the German Foreign Ministry, though briefed to cover with me a whole range of non-European issues, spoke exclusively about the GDR and the external aspects of unification. There is a mood of suppressed excitement, emotion and some optimism—the feeling that they are successfully handling the great range of questions flung at them at the beginning of the year as a result of the revolutions in Eastern Europe. Our own standing is good. I was several times warmly thanked for the support we (and other Western allies) are giving over the external aspects of unification.

PERCY CRADOCK

No. 212

Sir C. Mallaby (Bonn) to Mr Hurd

No. 753 Telegraphic [*WRL 020/1*]

BONN, *20 June 1990, 3.57 p.m.*

Prime Minister's Interview with Jimmy Young 18 June:
German Unification

Summary

1. Prime Minister's remarks about German unification on the Jimmy Young Show reported widely in the German media, and noted by many people in politics.

Detail

2. DPA and Reuter stories on the Prime Minister's comments on the Jimmy Young Show on 18 June have been covered prominently in the German press. A number of reports opened with a reference to the uneasiness expressed by the

Prime Minister at the prospect of a unified Germany being the most powerful European country in the economic and political sense, and went on to quote her statement that the history of this century could not be ignored. The *Frankfurter Allgemeine* also quoted her understanding for the fear felt among older people in the UK, but also mentioned (along with other papers) her comment that West Germany was a very good democracy. All reports also quoted the Prime Minister's view that the right approach was to keep Germany firmly in NATO and the European Community. Several papers juxtaposed this with the comment that the Prime Minister expressed strong reservations about any form of European political union which might lead to a loss of sovereignty.

3. The Prime Minister's interview was also reported as the 5th item on the main national news programme by ARD (the first German TV channel) on the evening of 18 June. ARD reported only the comments on unification.

4. A number of German politicians and prominent journalists have mentioned the interview to me and my staff, regretting the expression of uneasiness about unification and the perceived implication that NATO membership's purpose would be to keep Germany reliable.

No. 213

Mr Budd (Bonn) to Mr J.N. Powell (Policy Planning Staff)

[*WRL 020/1*]

Confidential   BONN, *22 June 1990*

Binding Germany In

1. These are in part my comments, rather than the post's as a whole. But for what they are worth . . .[1]

2. As you know, since your draft paper[2] issued the PM has said on the Jimmy Young Show (on 18 June) that she thought the answer to her worry about Germany was 'to keep Germany very firmly in NATO'.[3]

3. I don't share her worry, but even on her analysis that approach seems to me insufficiently subtle. What is needed is a European framework which both gives the Germans one or more larger entities into which residual national ambitions can be sublimated and provides counterweights to German power. The EC, NATO and the CSCE process each have their value in this connection. The main difficulty/challenge is to shape the NATO/CSCE future in such a way as to give life to the visionary side of Harmel while both protecting our interests and maximising the common ground between us and the Germans.

4. Narrowing the focus, my reactions to your para 17 are that:

(*a*) 'binding Germany in' is a stale, negative, uncreative approach. Shades of the sheet anchor to windward. It tends to assume the existence of certain quite artificial bogeys. Why should we necessarily be scared of a strong Germany? In his memorandum of 1907 Eyre Crowe said that 'It cannot for a moment be

---

[1] Ellipsis in original.
[2] No. 210.
[3] No 212.

questioned that the mere existence and healthy activity of a powerful Germany is an undoubted blessing to the world.'[4] So long as Germany's activity is healthy, I think that holds good, provided the wider framework and counterweights are there. Nor is a more active German *Ostpolitik* necessarily a bad thing. Surely it will suit us if German talents are deployed effectively in the task of modernising and civilising Eastern Europe and the Soviet Union? (Cf a remarkable passage in Keynes's *Economic Consequences of the Peace*: 'It is in our interest to hasten the day when German agents and organisers will be in a position to set in train in every Russian village the impulses of ordinary economic motive').[5] *Ostpolitik* doesn't have to mean Rapallo and Molotov-Ribbentrop.[6] Language like 'The pull of the East' creates, I think, more heat than light. Some people are concerned about lingering Bismarckian tendencies (e.g. Skubiszewski: Warsaw telno 346).[7] They (the tendencies!) need to be guarded against. But not by 'binding in'. Nations, like children, are not to be bound against their will: rather they should be seen as lights to be kindled. Our aim should be to develop a vision of the future of Europe which is one that Germans as well as ourselves find appealing.

(*b*) It can't be beyond our wits to build (eventually) a European security framework which protects our interests while still transcending the bloc-to-bloc approach.

(*c*) On the economic side, I agree that the Community is useful. Partly as a stable framework, provided with counterweights. Perhaps also as a means of diluting German nationalism. Many Germans in the 19th century justified the existence of the nation primarily by reference to the logic of economic development; by the same logic, some now argue that the nation has outlived its role. Further integration will in my view tend to dilute nationalism throughout Europe, including Germany (much more likely than the view at the end of your para 14).

5. Some more detailed points:

(*a*) your para 2 is highly compressed, and scares the reader unnecessarily;

(*b*) the thrust of paras 5 and 6 is certainly right. But to argue that democracy is one of the factors which has made the idea of a German invasion of France unthinkable is distinctly odd. Hitler, after all, came to power through the ballot box;

(*c*) the Bonn Embassy speaks with one voice in seeing multinational forces (your para 9) as one important means of salvation;

(*d*) your para 12: the PM's remarks to Jimmy Young have caused much irritation here, not surprisingly;

---

[4] Eyre Crowe, 'Memorandum on the Present State of British Relations with France and Germany', 1 January 1907, *British Documents on the Origins of the War 1998-1914*, Vol. III, *The Testing of the Entente 1904-6* (London: HMSO, 1928), Appendix A, pp. 397-420.

[5] J. M. Keynes, *The Economic Consequences of the Peace* (London: Macmillan, 1919), p. 275.

[6] For the Treaty of Rapallo see No. 25, note 4. The pact between Nazi Germany and the Soviet Union was signed by the Soviet Foreign Minister Vyacheslav Molotov and the German Foreign Minister Joachim von Ribbentrop on 23 August 1939.

[7] This telegram of 30 April was the first of two recording a meeting between Mr Hurd and the Polish Foreign Minister. In handing over the Polish draft of the frontier treaty with Germany, Professor Skubiszewski said that 'History did not repeat itself but there was a Bismarckian tendency in Germany that could reassert itself. He did not want a repetition of the Ribbentrop/Molotov pact in a generation or two. We must take precautions and those precautions implied continued German membership of NATO and the WEU' (WRL 020/14).

(*e*) the first sentence of your para 16 is to my mind absurd: what else can the Germans do? There is no sign anywhere in Germany, East or West, of an alternative approach.

Yours ever,
C.R. BUDD

No. 214

Mr Hurd to Sir M. Alexander (UKDEL NATO)[1]

No. 149 Telegraphic [*WRL 020/12*]

Confidential   FCO, *23 June 1990*

Dublin (for Political Director).[2]

German Unification: Two plus Four Ministerial Meeting, East Berlin 22 June
Summary
1. Time not yet ripe for major breakthrough. New and unacceptable Soviet paper tabled on final settlement, probably with domestic Soviet factors principally in mind. But Shevardnadze careful to talk language of compromise both at Ministerial lunch and to press. Official texts on borders and interim outline of final settlement agreed by Ministers. Ministers directed officials to draw up an agreed list of outstanding problems to be resolved with recommendations as to appropriate fora. This may provide a device for separating political/military issues from the final settlement. London NATO Summit and CSCE Ministerial in margins of UNGA are important benchmarks for Russians of wider political atmosphere.
Detail
2. The second meeting of the Two plus Four Foreign Ministers took place in East Berlin on 22 June. Meckel was in the chair.
3. Without any Soviet prewarning at the Political Directors' meeting on 20 June, Shevardnadze tabled a lengthy paper on elements for a final settlement which expanded upon and fleshed out previous Soviet ideas, incorporating unacceptable pol-mil aspects and more refined proposals for a transitional period between unification and termination of Quadripartite Rights and Responsibilities (QRRs). An earlier public reference to this at the Checkpoint Charlie ceremony and the simultaneous public release of Shevardnadze's explanatory statement risked giving the Russians the high ground and particularly annoyed Baker ('so much for German sovereignty') and Genscher.
4. It became clear over lunch and in other contacts with Shevardnadze that the draft was intended to a great extent for domestic Soviet purposes and was not immutable. Some plain speaking over lunch elicited agreement on a procedural device designed to unblock progress at official level, whereby contentious points

---

[1] Repeated for information Immediate to Bonn, Moscow, Paris, East Berlin, BM Berlin, Washington, Warsaw, and for information Priority to UKMIS New York, UKREP Brussels, Tokyo, Dublin, other CSCE Posts.
[2] Mr Weston was attending a meeting of the European Council.

would be listed together with alternative fora for dealing with them if not appropriate in Two plus Four for further consideration by Ministers at the Paris meeting on 17 July. The Americans emphasised (stepping back somewhat from earlier positions) that it could not be assumed that contentious issues currently on the table would necessarily find any reflection in any document containing a final settlement, let alone form part of the settlement itself. The West responded to Shevardnadze's proposal that officials should meet in continuous session by suggesting that negotiators should be more flexible and have more instructions and thus allow more rapid progress.

5. On the question of transitional periods, the Western emphasis on sovereignty and non-singularisation of Germany was met by a Soviet assertion that the Two plus Four should lay down a framework within which Germany would fit. Thus they repeatedly declined to accept the proposition that the lifting of QRRs should coincide with unification. Instead it was reiterated that the form of a final settlement (still, of course, undecided) should be agreed upon in time for a CSCE summit (which the French announced they would rearrange for November).

6. The handling of the border issue and minimalist language on elements of a final settlement (which had caused such difficulty because of Soviet intransigence on 20 June) were resolved with much help from Baker supplementing Meckel's weak chairmanship. The importance of not appearing to have disposed of the border issue before discussion with the Poles was clearly noted. The agreed language will be sent to the Poles by the East Germans (as hosts) as a possible basis for discussion with them on 4 July at official level. The unanimous welcome to the 2 German parliamentary resolutions and the two Governments' support for them may facilitate resolution of the issue.

7. Thus a little more progress was made than seemed likely at the outset. The Ministerial meeting on 17 July will deal with the Polish aspect of borders and should also consider detailed points of difference on pol-mil and other issues. But the time may still not then be ripe for resolution of the key problems. The next Ministerial beyond that (in Moscow in September) may possibly find the Russians more prepared for moves on their home ground. By then the political climate may be clearer once past the [?C]PSU party congress and the NATO summit, and with CSCE summit and German unity deadlines looming.

8. Despite the Soviet tactics, the atmosphere on 22 June was friendly and workmanlike, as was noted at the subsequent press conference. Working lunches are proving, for this reason, to be a useful instrument.

9. My 3 IFTs[3] report:

(*a*) Discussion of the final settlement.

(*b*) Handling of the border issue.

(*c*) The Soviet text.

[3] Not printed.

No. 215

Sir C. Mallaby (Bonn) to Mr Hurd[1]

No. 847 Telegraphic [WRG 020/7]

Confidential   BONN, *12 July 1990, 7.21 p.m.*

My Telno 837: Kohl's Visit to Moscow[2]

Summary

1. Teltschik expands on description of Kohl's intentions in TUR. Foresees no new move by Kohl on economic help for USSR. Discloses Kohl's view on future manpower limit on *Bundeswehr* but does not expect Kohl to reveal this to Gorbachev.

Detail

2. Teltschik briefed the US and French Ambassadors and me on 12 July about Kohl's intentions in his imminent visit to the Soviet Union. Teltschik said that Kohl felt himself to be in an excellent position for talking to Gorbachev, after the demonstration of Germany's commitment to the West at the Summits of the EC, NATO and G7. Kohl had three purposes in talks with Gorbachev.

3. The first was to conduct 'a mid-term review' of the situation regarding the external aspects of unification. Kohl did not expect a breakthrough in Soviet policy on German membership of NATO or the lifting of QRR. Kohl would set out in detail the points which should interest Gorbachev in NATO's London declaration.[3] Wörner (who had visited Kohl earlier on 12 July) would have gone through the declaration with the Russians beforehand. Kohl would also explain to Gorbachev the results of the EC and G7 summits on the question of economic cooperation with the USSR. He would point to various recent actions by the FRG which were helpful to the USSR, notably the recent guaranteed credit, the provision through the GDR Government of DM 1.25 billion to help pay for Soviet forces in East Germany and the FRG's tolerance of the exchange of 180 million Eastmarks by the Soviet forces in East Germany illegally at the rate of 2 to 1. Kohl would reiterate to Gorbachev Germany's willingness to set a manpower limit on the *Bundeswehr*.

4. Teltschik said that Kohl would not reveal to Gorbachev what limit he foresaw for the *Bundeswehr*, unless, unexpectedly, this was the one step needed to get Gorbachev to declare acceptance of German membership of NATO. Teltschik said

---

[1] Repeated for information Immediate to Moscow; information Routine to East Berlin, BM Berlin, Paris, Washington, UKDEL NATO, UKREP Brussels, MODUK.

[2] This telegram of 11 July reported a conversation between Miss Neville-Jones and Herr Hartmann in which the latter outlined Herr Kohl's goals for his forthcoming visit to Moscow. He would concentrate on two main themes: the context for Germany's membership of NATO and German-Soviet bilateral relations. 'Hartmann was at pains to play down any expectation that Kohl's visit itself would bring big developments' (WRL 020/15).

[3] The declaration issued at the end of the meeting of the North Atlantic Council in London on 5-6 July included *inter alia* a proposal to the members of the Warsaw Pact for 'a joint declaration in which we solemnly state that we are no longer adversaries and reaffirm our intention to refrain from the threat or use of force against the territorial integrity or political independence of any state, or from acting in any other manner inconsistent with the purposes and principles of the United Nations Charter and with the CSCE Final Act'. Full text available at http://www.nato.int/docu/comm/49-95/c900706a.htm.

in confidence that Kohl's intention was that the upper limit on the *Bundeswehr* should be 395,000 including 25,000 navy. The NVA, which had diminished to 93,000, should be disbanded as completely as possible.

5. Teltschik said that Kohl's second purpose in Moscow would be to discuss in specific terms with Gorbachev the idea of a future treaty on German-Soviet relations. The Russians had made clear that this was important to them, not least in the context of 2 plus 4. The German idea was a comprehensive treaty based on the FRG-Soviet Moscow Treaty and the joint declaration issued when Gorbachev visited the FRG in 1989, and bringing in other bilateral agreements. There would be no negotiation at this stage but Kohl hoped to establish the elements for a future treaty.

6. Kohl's third purpose would be to discuss economic cooperation with the Soviet Union. He would describe what moves by the Soviet Union would open the way for new cooperation, in line with the outcome of the EC and G7 summits. There would be no new offers of credit on this occasion. There might be discussion of increased Soviet oil and gas supplies to East Germany, but only in a preliminary way.

Comment

7. Teltschik's expectation evidently is that the visit will be a reasonable success, without a breakthrough. He interprets Gorbachev's invitation to Kohl to visit Stavropol, his home town, as a sign that the Russians will adopt a friendly style and will not declare very negative positions on aspects of 2 plus 4.

No. 216

Mr Eyers (East Berlin) to Mr Hurd[1]

No. 434 Telegraphic [WRE 014/1]

Confidential   EAST BERLIN, *13 July 1990, 9.50 a.m.*

GDR Prospects

Summary

1. Going gets tougher in the GDR as effects of GEMU start to bite. Coalition still holding together but for all practical purposes Government extremely weak. The country should just about pull through to December but earlier collapse of Government and a demand for instant unity cannot be ruled out.

Detail

2. Government and people in the GDR have been taken aback by the rigours of GEMU. The retailing sector which is still largely state owned has failed to cope. Queues for food have actually lengthened. People have been going to Czechoslovakia to shop. GDR produce goes undistributed or unsold and already the majority of goods on offer comes from the Federal Republic: on a visit to a Berlin shop on 10 July, de Maizière was told that only 15% of the stock was of GDR origin.

3. Prices have also risen sharply. Rises were predictable as subsidies ended but large differences in food prices from shop to shop have led to charges of gross

---

[1] Repeated for information Priority to Bonn, BM Berlin, Washington, Paris, UKDEL NATO, UKREP Brussels, DTI.

inefficiency and even abuse. The Government has announced that the state-owned retail chains are to be broken up and sold off by 30 September to put an end to local monopolies. (Comment: an opening for UK retailers. Separate report to DTI).[2]

4. Market forces should soon start to improve things in retailing, but the industrial front looks much more difficult. We have no hard figures for lay-offs and closures. Registered unemployment is 150,000 but is now rising rapidly. Wage negotiations are adding to the problem. The chemical industry has just conceded a 35% wage increase. Negotiations with the metal workers have been deadlocked, perhaps because unlike the chemical hope of survival (rises of 250-300 DM per month have just been announced). Pöhl (in Berlin on 12 July for the first sitting here of the *Bundesbank*) said that private individuals were behaving prudently with their money, on the whole. But the liquidity problems facing many firms were a matter for serious concern.

5. Agriculture, which employs 800 thousand, is also in deep trouble. Chaos in the food processing industry has hit farmers hard (e.g. milk sales slashed). Cooperatives face a liquidity crisis.

6. Many hopes are pinned on retraining (Bonn telno 821).[3] But people on the ground are asking what jobs workers are to be retrained for, and where the money will come from in practice. In-company retraining in bankrupt firms may not achieve much. The existing industrial training set-up, according to press reports, can offer some 60,000 places only, though it is being expanded. At least 460,000 workers are officially expected to go on to short-time working (with public support) in the near future.

7. The unavoidable weakness of the government system at all levels is making it much harder for people and businesses to get off first base. Municipal government is effectively bankrupt. The Mayor of East Berlin has said that 20,000 construction workers may have to be laid off from next week. *Länder* governments have yet to be formed and there is no answer yet to the question of their future financing. Cities and regions cannot get on with vital infrastructure projects and sorting out their local economies because they lack money and authority, and have no say over the industrial assets now vested in the *Treuhandanstalt* (trust agency). Meanwhile the property market is frozen because of the unresolved property question.

8. The central Government was elected to dissolve itself. Its powers over finance and economic matters have gone. Its own revenues are extremely precarious. It depends very largely on a transfer from the FRG (22 bn DM for the second half of 1990 = $7.5 bn). Its tasks now are to hold the country together until unity, negotiate a second state treaty with the FRG and see in the *Länder*. Can it succeed or will the current timetable (*Länder* in October/November, unity in December) be overtaken yet again? There are several possible sources of trouble: internal political, external and economic.

9. The Coalition has been weakened by turmoil among the smaller parties, leaving three cabinet ministers without a party (interior, aid and justice). But the main parties should hang together because no party will want responsibility for bringing the Government down. That said, the second State Treaty may be trickier than the first. Taking on the FRG economic system was daunting but proved

---

[2] Not printed.

[3] Bonn telegram No. 821 of 4 July reported 'satisfaction in the FRG at the smooth introduction of the DMark in the GDR' on 1 July, but noted that the medium-term prospect for the GDR economy remained highly uncertain: 'So far so good. But the difficult times are still to come' (WRG 090/2).

relatively uncontroversial in the GDR. But issues like the property question, electoral arrangements for the GDR, Berlin's position as capital, the future financing of the *Länder*, or the position of women are all matters of exceptional political sensitivity in the GDR—and in the FRG. Negotiating them against the background of impending elections (and party conferences) will not be easy. There is material here for a political crisis, particularly if the SPD in the west digs its heels in once again. But such political problems are more likely to exacerbate a crisis brought on by other factors than to precipitate one in themselves.

10. External considerations are usually seen here as a factor for prudence. All parties here agree that the pace of unity should respect the pace of the 2 + 4 talks. The government expects the talks to conclude on time (but fears the outcome will have the Russians bruised and thus store up trouble for the future). But if Gorbachev fell there would be pressure for an immediate accession under Article 23. His success this week will have relieved the Government.

11. The greatest threat, however, comes from the economy. Many who have their ear to the ground, like the churches, expect a 'hot autumn'. Resentment will be fuelled by the sight of former SED bosses in factories and offices still running things and arranging soft landings for themselves. There are plenty of unattractive examples, whatever the Government may do to try to stop it.

Conclusion

12. With luck, the formation of *Länder* in October/November will unlock the present paralysis of government while imminent unity will unlock the flow of investment. *Länder* elections should help people run off steam. But against that, new problems surface every day. Despite GEMU, the GDR still seems to be writhing in the coils of its own past. Only the West Germans have their arms free to act. Their take-over accelerates daily. The five months to December will seem very long. On balance, I expect the GDR to arrive for unity in December as planned. It is in the GDR's own interest to do so and they should have every support from Bonn. But it would be prudent to allow for a 10-15% risk of the GDR using Article 23 this autumn to pass the buck to the Federal authorities.

No. 217

Miss Neville-Jones (Bonn) to FCO[1]

No. 855 Telegraphic [PREM: Internal Situation in East Germany]

BONN, *16 July 1990, 12.04 p.m.*

UKREP Brussels for PS/Secretary of State[2]

Mr Ridley's Resignation and the Germany Seminar

Summary

1. Extensive media coverage of Mr Ridley's resignation. 'Independent on Sunday' article on Prime Minister's seminar on Germany less fully reported by

---

[1] Repeated to UKREP Brussels; information Immediate to Paris; information Priority to other EC posts.
[2] Mr Hurd was travelling via Brussels to the Two plus Four Ministerial meeting in Paris on 17 July.

press, but prominent on television and radio.[3] Main impression left by editorials is that episode reveals more about UK self-doubt and internal debate over European policy than it does about today's Germany. Public comment by Waigel, Minister of Finance.

Detail

2. In the first serious reports since Mr Ridley's resignation was announced (there are few Sunday papers here), all leading newspapers today carry a factual article on the front page about Mr Ridley's resignation. Several also have closely argued editorials. The Germany seminar memorandum is reported with extracts in several newspapers. *Spiegel* (circulation 980,000) has reproduced roughly ninety per cent of the text. TV and radio news reports yesterday evening had prominent coverage of the seminar story, including film excerpts of your comments 'on the record'. ARD, the first German TV channel, commented that it was most unusual for a friend to hold a seminar to dissect another friend in this manner.

3. Among the leading editorials, the *Frankfurter Allgemeine* claims that Mr Ridley's article reflects the split in the cabinet on European policy, and suggests that there is widespread feeling in the UK that the Prime Minister is still opposed to the predominance of a united Germany in Europe. But the crisis may serve the more European approach favoured by you and the Chancellor of the Exchequer. Your view is clear: the UK's alliance, partnership and friendship with France and Germany lie at the heart of modern British policy.

4. *Die Welt* too emphasises that the crisis over the article reflects the UK's difficulty in adjusting to its current position in the world. The difficulties the UK is now experiencing (e.g. with the economy, unemployment, transport and the environment) are making the British people look around for someone else to blame. There has been some progress over the last few months in the UK's approach towards Europe: whether any of this will now continue remains to be seen.

5. *Handelsblatt* enlarges on the theme that the crisis stems from a loss of self confidence. The UK is beset by problems (quoting the same example as *Die Welt*) and has begun to lose faith in its institutions (Parliament, the courts and the police). It can no longer rely on the US/UK special relationship to boost its ego, and a loss of nerve is not therefore surprising.

6. The *Frankfurter Rundschau* editorial opens with a full quotation of your comment at Ditchley Park,[4] but then quotes extensively from the British press about the mixed feelings in the UK towards the European Community and Germany. It ends with a reference to the alleged continuing use of the derogatory term 'the Fourth Reich' among the inner circles of Whitehall.

7. The *Kölner Stadt Anzeiger* also comments that the article has brought out into the open divisions on European policy, and doubts about German unification. The Prime Minister's seminar is depicted as reflecting her own anxieties. These are shared by the French and Americans, but they have concluded that the best way to

---

[3] Mr Ridley had resigned as Secretary of State for Trade and Industry on 14 July, following the publication of an interview in the *Spectator* in which he had *inter alia* described European Monetary Union as 'a German racket designed to take over the whole of Europe'. The interview had been illustrated with by a cartoon by Nicholas Garland depicting Mr Ridley adding a Hitler moustache to a poster of Herr Kohl. The leaked record of a seminar held by the Prime Minister with a number of historians on 24 March, by Mr Charles Powell, had been published by the *Independent on Sunday* on 15 July. For text and related correspondence see Appendix.

[4] See No. 220.

deal with them is to anchor Germany more firmly into Europe. The UK's policy towards Germany and Europe is internally contradictory.

8. The only Ministerial comment so far has come from Waigel. Addressing the CSU party conference on 14 July, he departed from the prepared text of his concluding speech to denounce the 'insults' of an 'English Minister'.

Comment

9. The appearance in *Spiegel* in extenso of the seminar record may well stimulate further media comment. With Kohl and Genscher still in Moscow it is hard at this stage to gauge the full political reaction.

10. FCO please pass to Number 10.

No. 218

Mr Budd (Bonn) to Mr Hurd[1]

No. 865 Telegraphic [WRL 020/15]

Confidential UK Comms Only   BONN, *17 July 1990, 4.45 p.m.*

MODSH pass to MODUK and CICC Germany

MIPT: German Unification[2]

Summary

1. Commentary on Kohl's ten point agreement with Gorbachev.

Detail

2. Taking the ten points seriatim:

(1) Further confirmation that Germany has no territorial pretensions.

(2) Acceptance by Gorbachev that QRR will end at the time of unification, without any subsequent transition period. No mention of the sequencing problem.

(3) The key point: Soviet acceptance that united Germany will be a member of NATO.

(4) As the Germans wished, the treaty covering the Soviet forces will be a withdrawal treaty, not a stationing treaty. The 3-4 year period is a compromise between the German position (3 years) and the Soviet (4-6 years). We understand that the financial provisions for the Soviet forces in Germany from 1991 onwards will be 'less generous' than the deal for the second half of 1990. But there will be German help in providing accommodation in the Soviet Union for the returning Soviet forces.

(5) This rules out the extension of NATO 'structures' to the former GDR, but only while the Soviet forces remain. As agreed at Turnberry, NATO Articles 5 and 6 will apply to the whole of Germany immediately after unification.

(6) This puts to rest the Genscher/Stoltenberg statement of 19 February, by

---

[1] Repeated for information Immediate to Moscow, UKDEL NATO, East Berlin, BM Berlin, Washington, Paris, UKDEL Vienna, MODUK; information Routine to CICC Germany

[2] In this telegram of 17 July Mr Budd reported the press conference in which Herr Kohl outlined the ten-point agreement reached during his talks with Mr Gorbachev in Moscow and at Stavropol on 14-16 July (WRL 020/15).

explicitly accepting the presence of *Bundeswehr* (territorial) units, albeit not assigned to NATO, in the ex-GDR and in Berlin immediately after unification.[3] The NVA is not mentioned. The Federal Government now has flexibility to decide how much of the NVA to keep as the basis for this territorial defence force (FMOD are planning for no more than 15,000 regular ex-NVA troops out of a force of say 50,000).

(7) A clear statement that the three Western Allies should keep their forces in Berlin as long as Soviet forces remain in the ex-GDR (n.b. not linked to Soviet forces in Berlin). Once the formal German request has been made, the new legal basis, troop numbers, costs, access and training rights will have to be negotiated between the western allies and the Germans.

(8) The most restrictive provision from NATO's point of view: even after Soviet withdrawal, no foreign troops or nuclear weapons to be moved into the ex-GDR. Nothing is said here about details such as pre-positioned logistic stocks or hardened airfields (both could be provided by the *Bundeswehr*), the possibility of other NATO forces exercising in the GDR (questionable) or the future of the military liaison missions. On the latter, there may be case for coordinating with the US and France a request to the Germans that the missions should continue their work while Soviet forces remain in Germany. As for air defence, our understanding is that the *Bundeswehr* intend to fly FRG-based aircraft over the former GDR. The question of the interface between NATO German and Soviet air policing regimes remains to be resolved.

(9) We understand that Teltschik has told Gen Naumann (FMOD) today that the 370,000 figure for the forces of a united Germany is to be understood as including naval forces. The figure to be declared in the CFE context will exclude naval personnel (perhaps some 20,000). Before this clarification, our contacts had assumed that the 370,000 did not (not) cover the navy.

[3] See No. 154, note 6.

No. 219

Mr Hurd to Sir M. Alexander (UKDEL NATO)[1]

No. 173 Telegraphic [*WRL 020/12*]

Confidential   FCO, *18 July 1990, 9.00 a.m.*

Two plus Four Ministerial Meeting, Paris, 17 July

Summary
1. Kohl/Gorbachev agreement at Stavropol transforms the prospect of a satisfactory final settlement before unification.[2] Shevardnadze underlines importance of London NATO Declaration in making German membership of NATO acceptable. Polish border issue resolved satisfactorily. Two plus Four process now enters its closing phase.

[1] Repeated for information Immediate to Bonn, Moscow, Paris, East Berlin, BM Berlin, Washington, Warsaw; information Priority to UKMIS New York, UKREP Brussels, Tokyo, other CSCE Posts.
[2] See No. 218.

Detail

2. The third Ministerial Meeting of the Two plus Four took place in Paris on 17 July. Dumas was in the chair. Skubiszewski—Poland—took part from lunch onwards.

3. The agreement reached on the preceding day by Chancellor Kohl and President Gorbachev has brought about a sea-change in the negotiations and puts us firmly in the end game. Now that the Soviet Union has accepted the essential Western points on pol-mil issues, including the right of a united Germany to make its own decision about Alliance membership, there is a realistic prospect of wrapping the whole process up at the next Ministerial Meeting in Moscow on 12 September. Shevardnadze underlined the importance of the London declaration in making it possible for the Soviet Union to accept a united Germany as a member of NATO.[3]

4. Agreement was reached on the format of the final settlement. The core should be a legally binding agreement on the lifting of Quadripartite Rights and Responsibilities. This should be accompanied by a preamble setting out broad principles and a separate section taking note of agreements reached elsewhere.

5. In a short meeting Political Directors made some progress in refining the list of outstanding problems agreed in East Berlin on 4 July. They will meet again in Bonn on 19 July to continue this process and to begin drafting the final settlement.

6. On borders, the Poles appeared ready to settle for what they could get from this meeting, while the Four Powers were anxious that the Poles should not be the only participant to go away from the meeting empty handed. Skubiszewski put forward the Polish case at length on borders, on economic issues, on trade and on the pol-mil status of a united Germany, at the formal meeting. But he rapidly accepted a package deal agreed at a preceding bilateral meeting with Genscher and with other ministers over lunch.

7. This involved a number of largely cosmetic Polish amendments to the principles on the handling of the border question. The Polish wish for a link between the suspension of QRRs and a border treaty was partially met by formal statements by the FRG and GDR committing a unified Germany to negotiate a border treaty with Poland as soon as possible after unification, leaving wider bilateral relations for a later treaty: and by a statement by the Four Powers to the effect that no external events or circumstances could put the definitive character of the Polish/German border in question. (This statement was intended to deal with historical references to a requirement that a 'peace treaty' should make Germany's borders definitive. It was noted that there was no question of the statement referred to above constituting a Four Power guarantee of Polish borders.)

8. Skubiszewski declared himself entirely content with the outcome at the meeting itself and at the subsequent press conference. There should be no need for further Polish involvement in the Two plus Four process.

9. It was agreed amongst the Western Four that Dufourcq and Kastrup should brief the NAC.

10. My two IFTs report discussion of the final settlement and of Polish borders.[4]

[3] See No. 215, note 3.
[4] Not printed.

No. 220

Mr Hurd to Miss Neville-Jones (Bonn)[1]

No. 456 Telegraphic [WRG 020/10]

Restricted   FCO, *18 July 1990, 2.09 p.m.*

Anglo-German Relations

1. In explaining the Government's policy towards Germany, in the light of Mr Ridley's *Spectator* interview and the *Independent's* publication of a record of the Chequers seminar on 24 March,[2] you should continue to draw on:

(*a*) The Prime Minister's remarks in the House on 12 July,[3] where she drew attention to Mr Ridley's withdrawal of and apology for his comments, and stated that they did not represent the government's or her own views:

(*b*) My remarks at Ditchley on 13 July (FCO telno 458 not to all),[4] where I noted 'our Allies, our partnership and our friendship with Germany and France lie at the heart of modern British foreign policy. Lingering memories from the past do not prevent us from strengthening the practical proofs of that friendship. Irreversible also is the steadily increasing cooperation with the fellow members and institutions of the European Community, of which the Prime Minister spoke after the Dublin Summit. Nothing will now put these processes in doubt':

(*c*) My BBC interview on 15 July (text already telegraphed in the retract series)[5] where I stressed the importance of the Prime Minister's immediate repudiation on behalf of the government:

(*d*) My comments to the press in Brussels on 16 July, where I expressed the view that this was a short-lived affair which would pass and which did not affect the fundamentals of British foreign policy, including friendship with France and Germany and working steadily for the progress of the Community.

2. Mr Ridley's resignation speaks for itself but it is perhaps worth noting that he contested the accuracy of parts of the *Spectator* account of his interview.

3. You should decline to comment on the detail of the Chequers seminar record, an internal and confidential paper. But you may draw on (*c*) and (*d*) above to point out that it was natural for Ministers to have wanted to take a long look, with expert advice, on the lessons of history and geography for German unification and other far-reaching changes in Europe. It was right to tackle any lingering or deep-seated worries or doubts head-on and in effect to clear them away, as this seminar did. Five days later, on 29 March, the Prime Minister made an authoritative statement of British policy towards Germany in her speech to the Cambridge Königswinter conference: she spoke of 'the close Anglo-German relationship at the heart of NATO and of Europe, which is essential to the success of both': recalling the very considerable part that Britain had played over 40 years in creating the conditions in which German unity could be achieved in freedom, for example in Berlin and through BFG. (The Prime Minister also spoke of the two-way process in our

---

[1] Repeated immediate to Paris, Rome, UKREP Brussels, UKDEL NATO, Washington; Priority to other CSCE Posts, Tokyo, Canberra.

[2] See No. 217.

[3] *Parl. Debs., 5th ser., H. of C.*, vol. 176, col. 449.

[4] Not printed.

[5] Not printed.

relations: 'the Federal Republic has always been the staunchest of allies in NATO, and we shall always be grateful for the strong support we received from successive German Governments for our membership of the European Community'.) The Anglo-German summit on 30 March was also highly successful, and our relations with the Federal Republic have continued close and warm. Since the beginning of the year Genscher and I have met, at bilateral and multilateral occasions, some 27 times (the figure for my meetings with Dumas is the same).

4. You might wish to point to some of the findings of a public opinion poll published in the UK press on 15 July. These confirm that a large majority, especially of younger people, are confident about a united Germany's peaceful intentions. Less than a quarter (23 per cent) do not favour a united Germany. A survey of 25 of the top 100 companies quoted on the FT-SE index found not one that thought there was a 'German racket' to dominate the continent.

5. Finally you could note that we have received no representations about the interview or seminar and that Kohl said on 17 July (your telno 863, not to all)[6] that there was no question of Mr Ridley's views being shared by the British Government, that he had not taken them amiss, and that he understood the concerns of those whose entire national existence had been at stake in the fight against Hitler.

---

[6] This telegram of 17 July reported Herr Kohl's answers to questions at a press conference (WRG 302/1).

No. 221

Minute from Mr Weston to Mr Wall

[*WRL 020/10*]

Confidential   FCO, *23 July 1990*

Germany: Two plus Four

1. When he telephoned me today on another matter I asked Ray Seitz what lay behind the recent press articles out of Washington to the effect that the Administration were miffed about insufficient consultation from the Germans before the Kohl/Gorbachev meeting at Stavropol. Seitz said there was indeed some irritation on this score. In particular the Americans had thought it discourteous that they should have to learn from the wire services that Germany intended to request the US to maintain troops in Berlin after unity, and for how long. They were also less than happy with the way in which a special status for East Germany had de facto been established by Kohl's concessions on non-deployment of NATO stationed forces even after Soviet troop withdrawal; and about the continuing uncertainty as to how the German troop ceiling figure should be handled at Vienna. It was true said Seitz that the Germans had put a couple of questions to Scowcroft in the margins of Houston but unfortunately (in the State Department's view) the latter had not really paid too much attention to these at the time, taking the line that whatever suited the Germans would suit the United States too.

2. I said that HMG had over the past months sometimes risked getting itself a bad name by trying to insist that some of these security related questions should be

addressed in One plus Three with the Germans before they were allowed to come to the boil in Two plus Four or with the Russians. We had not got very much support in this from others around the table who had sometimes conveyed the impression that no possible complication was worth addressing in good time beforehand, if it seemed to cast doubt on the over-riding strategic priority of returning sovereignty with unity to the Germans at the earliest possible moment. But that was now water under the bridge. Seitz said he thought this was fair comment.

3. His reactions in this conversation confirm that Baker's sharp first question at the One plus Three breakfast in Paris and defensive sparring with the US media at the press conference did indeed reflect some underlying concern.

P.J. WESTON

No. 222

Letter from Mr Powell (No. 10) to Mr Wall

[*PREM: Anglo-German Relations*]

Confidential   10 DOWNING STREET, *30 July 1990*

Dear Stephen,

Prime Minister's Meeting with the Federal German Foreign Minister
The Prime Minister had an hour's talk with Herr Genscher this morning. He was accompanied by the Federal German Ambassador and by his Private Secretary. The Foreign Secretary was also present.

Terrorism
Herr Genscher began by expressing sincere condolences on the murder of Mr. Ian Gow, M.P.[1] It strengthened his conviction that the western countries should seek a commitment in the Helsinki process to co-operate against terrorism, so we could be sure that the terrorists had no haven anywhere in the 35 CSCE countries. The Prime Minister agreed that this was a good point and should be pursued.

German Unification
The Prime Minister observed that matters were now moving very fast on German unification, but a lot of details remained to be worked out before the CSCE Summit in the autumn. Many of them were matters for Germany herself, but we would of course help in every way we could. It was very important to get the small print right. One matter which would need to be resolved was the legal basis for the continuing presence of Allied forces in Berlin. There would need to be a clearly defined role for such forces, otherwise their morale would be affected. The Foreign Secretary pointed out that Britain had been the first of the Four Powers to say that we would be willing to keep our forces in Berlin.

Herr Genscher said that he was most grateful for the support which the Federal German Republic had received from the United Kingdom during the Two plus Four talks, and particularly for the helpful role played by the Foreign Secretary at

---

[1] Ian Gow, MP for Eastbourne and a close associate of the Prime Minister, was murdered by an IRA car bomb at 8.49 a.m. on 30 July.

the meetings in Berlin and Paris. Shevardnadze had recently telephoned him to say that the Two plus Four ministerial meeting in Moscow should be the last one. This was a clear indication that the Russians wanted to finish discussion of matters of substance, so that the details could be tied up in good time for the CSCE conference. The Prime Minister said that we were very pleased that the Two plus Four process was working so well.

Options for Defence

The Prime Minister said that the Defence Secretary had made known our plans for reductions in our forces over the next five years, and she had sent Chancellor Kohl a message explaining them. We now looked forward to consultation in NATO. Other members of NATO, including of course the FRG, had already announced proposed reductions.

The Prime Minister noted in passing that the Soviet Union was continuing to place very substantial numbers of tanks behind the Urals, and to transfer aircraft from their air force to their naval aviation, as a way of avoiding limitations under the CFE Agreement.

East Germany

Herr Genscher said that All-German elections would take place on 2 December. A compromise had been found on the question of the electoral system. There were a number of practical problems arising from unification to be resolved, in particular the ownership of property in East Germany. All claims would have to be registered before January, and there would be compensation for those required to give up property or land which they were at present occupying. President Gorbachev had referred to the substantial property which the Red Army held in East Germany, and had made clear that the Soviet Union would be seeking compensation for giving up this. All this could be resolved: but until then it was something of an obstacle to economic development. However, he did not wish to be pessimistic: people in East Germany were responding enthusiastically to the opportunities of economic and monetary union with the FRG.

The Prime Minister asked Herr Genscher to confirm that Article 23 of the Federal Germany Constitution would be annulled after unification. Herr Genscher confirmed that this would be the case. It would be made explicit that unification was the end of the story. The Prime Minister recalled that both German states had agreed to sign a Treaty with Poland as soon as possible after unification. Herr Genscher confirmed that this would be done.

Herr Genscher continued that he was sure that the elections on 2 December would produce a positive outcome for the Government. In response to a question from the Prime Minister, he said he thought the SPD would focus their electoral campaign on the social problems of unification. Within the Federal Republic, they would stress the heavy costs of unification: in the East they would claim that the Government was not spending enough. But trying to have it both ways like this would not carry much conviction. Herr Lafontaine had failed to recognise the historic nature of developments since last autumn.

European Community

The Prime Minister said that she was following developments in Europe's financial markets with interest. Italy and Spain, which had high inflation rates, faced a tremendous inflow of money attracted by their high interest rates. They were rightly refusing to reduce the latter because their domestic monetary conditions did not warrant it, but were having to spend considerable sums to keep within their ERM bands. Their experience demonstrated the difficulties of trying to fix exchange rates while disparities between the economies of member states remained so great. In these conditions, a single currency could only be maintained by massive transfers between the better off and the less well off member states. The United Kingdom would join the ERM in order to use the Deutschmark as a sort of gold standard, which would help bear down on inflation. But the whole purpose of this would be lost if there was a single currency and a European Central Bank, whose governing board would be composed of representatives of countries who would not agree that the sole objective was to maintain the value of the currency. In her own view, there was no case for going further than the existing ERM for the foreseeable future. Europe needed time to adjust to the full consequences of the Single Market, and did not need the fresh turmoil which would be caused by attempts to move to a single currency.

The Prime Minister continued that, despite these misgivings, we wanted to avoid a row in the Community. We had therefore agreed to go further than she herself considered strictly necessary or wise, by proposing a common currency and a European Monetary Fund. But this was as far as we could agree to go. A single currency simply did not make sense and would not be accepted by the British Parliament. She was particularly disturbed to see that the Italian Presidency wanted to accelerate the EMU and reach agreement in December. That would be deliberately divisive and unhelpful, when Britain was already making a major effort to avoid a row with its partners. The truth was that those who supported a single currency were not really so much interested in the economic aspects as in creating a federal Europe, which we could not accept. Our proposals represented a major effort to find an acceptable basis for what should follow Stage I.

Herr Genscher, who had found it somewhat difficult to get a word in, said Germany was determined that a European Central Bank would be like the Bundesbank and entirely independent of Governments. There was a chicken and egg situation: the best way to bring other European countries to adopt reasonable economic policies was to force them to submit to the discipline of a single currency and a strong Central Bank. The Prime Minister contested this view: she would have much more confidence in the discipline of the Deutschmark, based on the historic aversion of the German people to inflation, than in a Central Bank where Germany might find itself out-voted. Other countries could follow France's example of using the link with the Deutschmark to force down inflation. There was also the aspect of sovereignty: a national currency and national decision-making on economic and monetary policy were among the most substantial attributes of sovereignty in the modern world. Herr Genscher replied that Germany wanted Britain in whatever monetary arrangements were agreed for Europe. We were needed as a country which followed orthodox economic policies, and played a major role in Europe's economy.

I am copying this letter to John Gieve (HM Treasury), Martin Stanley (Department of Trade and Industry), Simon Webb (Ministry of Defence) and Sonia Phippard (Cabinet Office).

Yours sincerely,
C.D. POWELL

No. 223

Miss Neville-Jones (Bonn) to Mr Hurd[1]

No. 937 Telegraphic [WRL 020/1]

Confidential UK Comms Only   BONN, *3 August 1990, 5.40 p.m.*

MODSH pass to CICC Germany and MODUK

My Telno 930 and East Berlin Telnos 461-463: German Unification[2]
Summary
1. De Maizière's announcement welcomed by Government Coalition. Both SPDs object, and may try to block the change of the election date. Early unification now a strong probability. Plenty of difficulties but no insuperable problems for us. Russian response crucial. If they acquiesce, likely to press hard for German concessions in their bilateral treaties in exchange for acceleration of unification.
Detail
Reactions in Bonn
2. Kohl and Lambsdorff (FDP chairman) have welcomed de Maizière's proposal for 14 October election. The SPD, however, are objecting. Senior party figures are claiming that the move vindicates their warnings about the dire economic consequences of the Federal Government's 'overhasty' policy on unification. Now the government, they claim, are trying to escape the electoral consequences of their mistaken policy by bringing the election forward.
3. De Maizière's announcement comes against a background of comment in the FRG, much stronger in the last forty eight hours, that early accession by the GDR was becoming inevitable because of the rapidly deteriorating economic situation in the GDR, the GDR's Government's inadequate management of it and the consequent escalating cost to the FRG. At one level, therefore, this development therefore comes as no surprise. But its suddenness, and the fact that very few people indeed in Bonn were privy to de Maizière's announcement before it was made (a Government spokesman has said that they had though de Maizière was going to put his ideas to the *Volkskammer* first), means that little thought has been given to the implications of this revised unification timetable. Officials we have contacted were clearly unprepared. Hartmann's (Chancellery) statement to me (and subsequently to the US Ambassador) that 1 October would be the accession date, and de Maizière's actual statement (East Berlin TURs) that accession should be declared at the last *Volkskammer* session before the elections, is an example of the resulting confusion (though the outcome in practice may be much as Hartmann said).

---

[1] Repeated for information Immediate to BM Berlin, East Berlin, Moscow, UKDEL Vienna, Paris, Washington, UKDEL NATO, UKREP Brussels, CICC Germany, MODUK; information Routine to other CSCE Posts; information Saving to HQ JSLO, HMCGs in the FRG.
[2] Bonn telegram No. 930 of 3 August reported that Herr de Maizière would declare that day that the accession of the GDR to the FRG would take place on 1 October. East Berlin telegrams Nos. 461-3 reported that he had proposed, after consultation with Herr Kohl, that all-German elections should take place on 14 October and that the *Volkskammer* should declare accession under Article 23 before the elections, but without specifying 1 October as the date (WRL 020/1).

Next Steps

4. Will the two Governments succeed in bringing forward all-German elections? This is the first question. The assent of the SPD must be obtained and it is not yet clear how they will play their hand. Under the Basic Law the earliest date on which *Bundestag* elections can be held is 45 months after the last ones—i.e. 18 November. A two thirds majority is required for the necessary constitutional amendment. Lafontaine has already said that he will seek to obstruct this 'transparent attempt at manipulation'. This would leave Kohl only with the option of calling for a vote of confidence and, with the help of his coalition, 'losing' it (as happened in 1982). The *Bundestag* would then automatically be dissolved and new elections called. Apart from this being constitutionally pretty dubious and politically a poor start to the process of parliamentary unification, it still would not work without the SPD's support in the *Bundesrat* (where the SPD has a majority) where they can block the ratification of the election and unification treaties. Urgent contacts between the party leaderships seem likely, and there will be further discussions at the *Bundestag* special session called for 8 August.

5. If agreement on advancing the election timetable cannot be obtained, the following scenario would be possible. Using Article 23, the GDR could still accede earlier than planned—which would give the FRG control over the most pressing problem—the East German economy. The all-German election is intrinsically a less urgent matter and could perfectly well take place on its present timetable under the election treaty which has just been agreed i.e. 2 December. In the meantime members of the *Volkskammer* could be co-opted to the *Bundestag* on some *ad hoc* basis to pass necessary legislation. This would be a practical outcome but not one instantly attractive to the German sense of orderliness. The SPD might however see it as offering the advantage of not being held responsible for blocking unification, but also of ensuring that Kohl did not escape the judgement of the electorate on the costs of unification which will show up in the autumn.

Consequences of bringing forward unification or elections

(a) Internal

6. If unification is brought forward, the second state 'unification' treaty scheduled for legislative passage by end September will have to be passed by both parliaments beforehand. Since Federal law will be applied in the GDR earlier than expected, more extensive transitional arrangements than previously planned might be needed. (The same is likely to apply, *mutatis mutandis*, to EC law.) Neither of these two consequences is going to seem difficult if they help secure the prize of greater confidence in the East German economy.

7. If the elections are brought forward as well, the election treaty which has already been the object of a lot of pain, will need further amendment. The constitutional issue will also have to be resolved (paragraph *(a)* above). The SPD and CDU will presumably bring forward their planned 'unification conferences', currently scheduled for the end of September/early October. The battle that has to be won to bring forward the elections is considerably greater than that to bring early unification.

(b) External Aspects

8. From the moment of unification, there will be one German state internationally, 22 signatories to the CFE, no GDR embassies etc. German eyes will be primarily focussed on Soviet reactions to advanced unification. First press reports suggest that the Soviet Union are not happy about something which they say would 'disturb' the process. Genscher already has a meeting planned with

Shevardnadze at a date yet to be decided in August. As seen from here the Soviet main concerns at this stage will be arrangements for Soviet troops on German soil and the future manpower levels of the *Bundeswehr*—both of which they have expected to get tied up before the termination of Four Power rights. Presumably the Germans could well be faced now with renewed pressure from the Russians for the separation of unification and termination of Four Power rights and/or with Soviet exploitation in negotiation of the time pressure under which the Germans are putting themselves. For the Western Allies, one of the other most important issues will be getting suitable arrangements in place and ensuring that a legal vacuum does not arise for the presence of our garrisons in Berlin if Four Power rights are terminated earlier than expected. Informal contacts with German officials suggest that they hope to avoid having to accept less than full sovereignty at the moment of unification, notwithstanding the fact that it is they who are proposing the changes in the timetable.

9. Among the non-Four Power participants in the CSCE, there could, I imagine, be some grumbling about the fact that the presentation of the work of the Two plus Four at the CSCE Summit will, on this revised timetable, be even more an empty exercise than it is already likely to be.

No. 224

Miss Neville-Jones (Bonn) to Mr Hurd[1]

No. 944 Telegraphic [*WRL 020/1*]

Confidential UK Comms Only   BONN, *6 August 1990, 6.13 p.m.*

My Telno 937: German Unification: External Aspects: Legal Matters[2]

Summary

1. Unification in early October (or even before) would require fast work on many legal aspects if Quadripartite Rights and Responsibilities (QRRs) were to be suspended or terminated then. The question emerging now is whether QRRs can or should be suspended/terminated upon early unification.

Detail

2. My TUR gave initial comment on implications for external aspects of de Maizière's announcement (paras 8 and 9). I noted that, if the timetable for unification were accelerated, one of the most important issues for the Western Allies would be getting suitable legal arrangements in place in time. MIFT gives a summary of unfinished legal business as seen from here.[3] The main question posed for the Two plus Four appears to be whether QRRs could still be suspended or terminated upon unification. Otherwise, early unification affects primarily matters to be negotiated outside the Two plus Four. On the Western side, this means One plus Three issues such as new stationing arrangements for Berlin, and on the eastern side, FRG/USSR troop withdrawal and financing arrangements.

---

[1] Repeated for information Immediate to BM Berlin, East Berlin, Moscow, UKDEL Vienna, Paris, Washington, UKDEL NATO, UKREP Brussels, CICC Germany, MODUK; information Routine to other CSCE Posts; information Saving to HQ JSLO, HMCGs in the FRG.

[2] No. 223.

[3] No. 225.

(a) Final Settlement (Two plus Four)

3. It is intended that the text of the settlement document should be agreed in Moscow on 12 September. Signature could take place shortly thereafter. It appears that the Germans and Russians at least will have to ratify, and that the settlement document will therefore be subject to ratification or approval by all. Even with unification in December, there would have been a need to reconcile Germany's desire to be seen to be sovereign from the moment of unification with the legal requirement of ratification or approval of the final settlement which includes the termination of Four Power rights (your telno 474).[4] Hence the UK proposal for suspension of QRRs upon unification and their termination only upon ratification of the final settlement (your telnos 475 and 487).[5]

4. Unification in October or earlier would, however, effectively leave three options. First, QRRs could still be suspended upon unification (and terminated upon ratification). To avoid legal vacuums arising this would require settlement of all, or nearly all, of the Two plus Four and One plus Three issues prior to unification and the creation of new legal bases (e.g. for Berlin stationing) which could enter into force at that time. Secondly, one could still keep to the proposal for separate suspension and termination, but with suspension deferred until the previously intended date (i.e. early December after the CSCE Summit). Thirdly, the idea of suspension could be abandoned. Advancement of unification could mean that a united Germany would ratify the final settlement earlier than previously planned, thus making more sense to keep QRRs fully in force until ratification whereupon they would be terminated. The last two options would leave more time for outstanding legal business to be settled, but the Germans may well still press for the first option, to avoid any gaps between unification and the visible lifting of QRRs. In any event, the Soviet reaction will be crucial.

(b) One plus Three Issues

5. For these issues, early unification does not appear to create new problems of substance, but (if QRRs are to be suspended/terminated upon unification) it considerably squeezes the time available for the creation of new legal arrangements. New arrangements for the troops in Berlin would be the most complex and pressing, although a minimum legal framework could be created by interim arrangements, with details left to be settled later. There will be risks in hasty negotiation and it might be right to make our agreement on the lifting of QRRs on early unification (if that is what the Germans press for) contingent upon being fully satisfied about essential points. I suspect the Russians will do this in relation to their two stationed forces agreements. In general our negotiating hand is likely to be stronger before rather than after unification, and it must therefore lie in our interest to settle as much as possible beforehand.

6. Broadly the same considerations apply to Berlin aviation. A new legal framework could be put in place relatively easily, but it would be important to safeguard our commercial interests. The renewal of the legal basis for stationing in the FRG may not be quite so pressing: the present basis under the Presence of

---

[4] FCO telegrams No. 474 and 475 of 24 July contained a draft text and draft covering letter from Mr Weston to the Political Directors of the Two plus Four, dealing with the proposed suspension of QRRs (DZN 061/109).

[5] FCO telegram No. 487 of 31 July agreed with the German suggestion that a separate declaration on the suspension of QRRs was preferable to the inclusion of suspension in the Final Settlement (WRL 020/12).

Foreign Forces Convention could be regarded as continuing until ratification of the final settlement.

No. 225

Miss Neville-Jones (Bonn) to Mr Hurd[1]

No. 945 Telegraphic [WRL 020/1]

Confidential UK Comms Only   BONN, *6 August 1990, 6.08 p.m.*

MIPT: German Unification: External Aspects: Legal Matters[2]

1. The following is a list, as seen from here, of outstanding legal business:

(*a*) *Final Settlement (Two plus Four)*

The text is due to be settled in Moscow on 12 September. Draft texts should be circulated by 15 August. For comment on signature and ratification see MIPT.

(*b*) *Berlin*

(i) Stationing arrangements. After suspension/termination of QRRs a new legal base will be necessary for the presence of forces, status of forces, finance, property and other matters. An agreement for the presence and status of forces could be fairly straightforward, particularly if the Germans agree that the rules of the SOFA and Supplementary Agreement should apply. Whether unification is in December or earlier, the Germans may press for interim arrangements, with detailed agreements to be drawn up afterwards. This is because a full agreement would on the German side be subject to ratification by a united Germany and could not under German procedures provisionally enter into force pending ratification.

(ii) Aviation. When QRRs are suspended/terminated, a new legal basis will be required for Allied flights to Berlin. New arrangements for air traffic control will also have to be made. Discussions are under way among the Six, with the FRG in the extended Bonn Group, and bilaterally.

(iii) Technical matters. Provisions for Berlin analogous to those in the settlement convention (e.g. waiver of claims) will be required. These are to be covered either in the Settlement Convention Group or in the Berlin Working Group. The principles for dealing with occupation legislation are agreed on the Western side, but the Germans have to decide whether specific provision is needed in any agreement. Early unification may require more extensive transitional provisions for some legislation. Other technical issues on Berlin (e.g. diplomatic representation, railways, waterways) have been discussed in the Berlin working group and are near resolution. Early unification would, however, require intensification of work.

(*c*) *Stationing in the FRG and Other Pol/Mil Matters*

(i) The Presence of Foreign Forces Convention. A new legal basis for Western troops stationed in the FRG will be necessary upon the expiry of the PFFC

---

[1] Repeated for information Immediate to BM Berlin, East Berlin, Moscow, UKDEL Vienna, Paris, Washington, UKDEL NATO, UKREP Brussels, CICC Germany, MODUK; information Routine to other CSCE Posts; information Saving to HQ JSLO, HMCGs in the FRG.

[2] No. 224.

(upon 'conclusion of a German peace settlement'). This is already being discussed among the Western Four.

(ii) Military liaison missions. The present basis will expire upon suspension/termination of QRRs.

(iii) The SOFA and Supplementary Agreement. These are not related to QRRs. The Germans have indicated they wish these to continue for the present with a review in slower time.

(iv) Air Defence Identification Zone (ADIZ). The legal basis for Allied responsibilities in this area is unclear. In part they are said to be based upon QRRs. In any event the ADIZ role will be subject to review.

(*d*) *Other One plus Three Matters*

(i) The Relations Convention. This will be terminated upon suspension/ termination of QRRs. The modalities have yet to be determined but this is straightforward.

(ii) Settlement Convention. Many of the provisions are obsolete. But there are important obligations (e.g. waiver of claims, validity of acts of occupation authorities) which should be taken over by a united Germany. This is being discussed in the Settlement Convention Group (next meeting 17 August). The aim should be to settle all Settlement Convention matters before unification, which would require acceleration of the Group's work.

(iii) Claims. We will shortly hold a meeting with the French and Americans here. The intention is to have discussions with the Germans prior to unification, but probably no legal instrument before then.

(*e*) *Bilateral Matters*

Early unification would require a more urgent review of bilateral UK/FRG and UK/GDR treaties. The FRG's presumption is that the former will extend to GDR territory unless specific modifications are necessary.

(*f*) *Germany/USSR*

The most important agreements to be negotiated prior to unification are those concerning the withdrawal and financing of Soviet troops in the GDR.

No. 226

Mr Hurd to Miss Neville-Jones (Bonn)[1]

No. 504 Immediate Telegraphic [*WRL 020/1*]

Confidential   FCO, *7 August 1990, 7.30 p.m.*

From Private Secretary.

Secretary of State's Conversation with Genscher: German Unification
Summary

1. Genscher explains next steps on German unification. Possibility of unification by mid-September (but not before Moscow meeting of 2+4). Shevardnadze showing understanding of German position. Genscher accepts need for early work on legal status of Allied forces after unification.

---

[1] Repeated for information Immediate to Washington, Paris, Moscow, BM Berlin, East Berlin, UKDEL NATO, Brussels.

Detail

2. Genscher telephoned the Secretary of State this afternoon. He said the deterioration in the economic situation in the GDR had led de Maizière to seek early unification. It would not be possible to have early all German elections because of the SPD attitude. They would take place on 2 December or perhaps a week or two earlier. The *Volkskammer* would meet tomorrow. They might decide on a mid-September date for unification but this would not be before the Moscow meeting of the 2 + 4. Genscher had spoken to Meckel. He and Meckel would go to Vienna within the next few weeks to make clear their commitment on *Bundeswehr* force levels. Genscher himself was due to visit Moscow in August. Genscher had already spoken to Shevardnadze about what was proposed. Word had reached Genscher that the Soviet Union were a bit nervous about acceleration of the timetable. Although Shevardnadze had not said in terms that he agreed with what was now proposed, his tone had been entirely reasonable. This emphasised to Genscher the importance of personal contact.

3. The Secretary of State asked what the accelerated timetable would mean for the earlier proposal that the results of the 2+4 process would be presented to the CSCE Summit in November. This seemed to be a new point for Genscher. He said that Shevardnadze had not raised it. Perhaps the answer would be for Genscher to report to the preparatory meeting of Foreign Ministers on 1-2 October.

4. The Secretary of State said that we needed to do quick work on the legal status of Allied forces after unification. If we were still working on the assumption that Four Power Rights and Responsibilities would come to an end at that point. Genscher agreed. He had already asked one of his State Secretaries to get on with the necessary work. He had also spoken to Dumas about it.

5. See MIFT for brief discussion on Iraq/Kuwait.[2]

---

[2] Not printed. The Iraqi invasion of Kuwait began on the evening of 1 August.

No. 227

Mr Logan (Moscow) to Mr Hurd[1]

No. 1454 Telegraphic [WRL 020/9]

Confidential   MOSCOW, *8 August 1990, 11.39 a.m.*

My Telno 1436 and Bonn Telnos 943-5: Advancing German Unification:
Soviet Reactions[2]

Summary

1. Soviet Foreign Ministry reluctant to be drawn into a statement.

2. Though accelerated unification would be another bitter pill, the Russians know they have no means of preventing it. After the Kohl/Gorbachev agreement

---

[1] Repeated for information Immediate to Bonn, East Berlin; information Priority to BM Berlin, Washington, Paris, UKDEL NATO, UKREP Brussels.
[2] Moscow telegram No. 1436 of 6 August reported Soviet Foreign Ministry comment on de Maizière's call for early elections. Bonn telegram No. 943 of 6 August reported that the SPD had agreed to early unification, but not to early elections (WRL 020/1). Telegrams No. 944 and 945 are printed as Nos. 224 and 225.

last month, the big game is up for them. They are becoming more passive, and concentrating their efforts on the conclusion of the various documents and agreements. They assume the Two plus Four will conclude in Moscow on 12 September.

Detail

3. Having been fobbed off by Yelisariev (my TUR),[3] we called on 7 August on one of his deputies, V.S. Rogozhin. Rogozhin heads the section dealing with external German affairs, and said he had attended all Two plus Four meetings. He said that Bondarenko, in his new (comment: semi-superannuated) capacity as an Ambassador at large would continue to represent the USSR in the Two plus Four until conclusion.

4. Rogozhin said that there had as yet been no formal discussion of de Maizière's announcement between Soviet and German officials. (The FRG Chargé has taken a similar line with us. He said that Genscher had spoken by phone to Shevardnadze, but appeared to know little about their conversation.)

5. Lyne noted that the Foreign Ministry spokesman had reacted to questions about de Maizière'[group illegible], but observed that there had been no formal statement from the Ministry. Was there a Departmental view? Rogozhin confirmed there was no formal position, and took refuge in a 'personal' analysis. De Maizière had made his statement under heavy pressure from Kohl. The latter was perturbed by the GDR economic situation and wished to take direct action. But before unification, there was no legal (or legitimate) basis for Western investment. The Bonn Government's motives were transparent. His analysis of the SPD's tactics tallied with that in Bonn telno 943.[4]

6. Rogozhin said the situation would become clearer after the *Bundestag* and *Volkskammer* sessions. If the GDR decided on early accession to the Federal Republic under Article 23, he asserted that the eastern part of Germany would be left without a fully-employed government for a long period until the elections (arguing that Bonn would not have the full right to govern eastern Germany until the population had been given the chance to vote in elections). De Maizière was trying to defend the social and economic interests of GDR citizens. These were the subject of the second State Treaty. If unification happened before the Treaty was completed, his hand would be immeasurably weakened.

7. Rogozhin took a resigned attitude to the absence of consultation with other interested Governments on the accelerating timetable. Remarkably (in view of past Soviet attitudes) he commented that the mechanics of unification were an internal matter. Asked about the external implications were the *Volkskammer* to vote for accession before the Two plus Four met, he said mildly that the Soviet Union would of course express dissatisfaction, but virtually admitted that they could not apply the brakes. Events had taken over.

8. Rogozhin said that Genscher's visit would be devoted to bilateral issues, especially the conclusion of bilateral agreements. The Russians hoped that the Two plus Four could complete their work in Moscow on 12 September. Baker and Shevardnadze had agreed this to be a common aim when they met in Irkutsk. The Soviet experts had finished their draft texts. These were being translated and would be handed over soon, probably in Moscow.

---

[3] Mr Yelisariev was a former Minister in Bonn; Sir R. Braithwaite had been due to call on him on 7 August.

[4] Note 2 above.

Comment
9. This was a conspicuously passive performance. It was imbued with a pragmatic recognition that inner-German politics and the economic and social distress of East Germany are dictating the pace, and that it is now beyond the capacity of the Soviet Union to have much influence on the timing of unification. Rogozhin said nothing about Four Power rights or CFE. He gave the impression that the Russians will now devote their efforts to negotiating the fine print (e.g. on economic arrangements and Soviet troops, though we did not discuss these in detail) bilaterally with Bonn.

No. 228

Minute from Mr Cox to Mr Synnott

[*WRL 020/12*]

Confidential   FCO, *21 August 1990*

German Unification: 2+4: British Role
1. The state of play on German unification is summarized in the briefing packs we have prepared for Mr Weston and you,[1] but I thought that you might also like to have a short note focussing on the British role over the past three weeks, particularly as it may appear through German eyes.

2. We have been very busy over the last month but there remains much ground to clear before unification. We might have made more progress if the Germans had not given top priority to their bilateral contacts with the Russians. Thus they:
(*a*) declined to arrange a 1+3 meeting of pol-mil specialists at Mr Goulden's level in the week beginning 13 August; and
(*b*) 'waived' the deadline of 15 August for exchange of final settlement texts.

3. Nonetheless progress has been made. I think that all Whitehall Departments now have a clearer idea of the issues and their bottom line. And satisfactory negotiating frameworks are in place for the main outstanding 1+3 issues.

4. I think that the Germans should be fairly happy about the role we have played over this last month. We were prompt to prepare our text for the final settlement and then to combine it with the US text. We also provided early comments on other partners' texts, most of which the Germans agreed with. The Embassy in Bonn has always been in a position to respond quickly to other German proposals or ideas (the French in particular have continued often to lack instructions).

5. However, it is just possible that the cumulative effect of some of our actions may have caused a little irritation in Bonn:
(*a*) The Private Secretary telephoned Genscher's office on 10 August to express surprise about de Maizière's proposal for bringing forward to October all-German elections and unification.
(*b*) Also on 10 August we expressed serious reservations to the Germans about points in their draft declaration, to be annexed to the final settlement text, embodying some of the Stavropol provisions on the future defence position of the ex-GDR; we also warned that the Secretary of State might raise this with Genscher in the margins of the EC and NATO Ministerial meeting (in the event

---
[1] Not printed.

he was unable to do so). We urged the Germans not to give this text to the Russians before further Allied consultation. (The US supported this demarche.)

(*c*) In discussions of the legal basis for the stationing of Allied forces in the FRG and Berlin after unification, Miss Neville-Jones has argued (again with strong US support) in favour of multilateral rather than bilateral agreements and of extension of the Status of Forces Agreement (SOFA) and Supplementary Agreement (SA) to the whole of the united Germany and resisted proposals for revision of the SA 'to alleviate the burdens of troop presence'.

(*d*) The Secretary of State has sent a message to Genscher urging the Germans not to make unrealistic demands in the forthcoming air services negotiations regarding Berlin.

(*e*) We have instructed the Embassies in Bonn and East Berlin to inform the German authorities that we 'share their preference' for unification on 14 October rather than earlier.

(*f*) We have instructed East Berlin and Bonn to tell the Germans that we consider the claims we presented to the GDR in 1977 to be unaffected by a GDR regulation setting a deadline of 13 October for filing of property claims (and aiming at achieving early certainty for the GDR population and for outside investors about who owns what).

N.J. COX

No. 229

Sir C. Mallaby (Bonn) to Mr Hurd[1]

No. 1064 Telegraphic [WRL 020/20]

Restricted   BONN, *24 August 1990, 2.02 p.m.*

East Berlin Telno 507[2]
German Unity on 3 October: FRG Reactions and Implications

Summary

1. Satisfaction and relief in the Federal Republic. Kohl thanks the Allies for their support. Steps in the end game falling into place. Implications for British interests.

Detail

2. The *Volkskammer* decision for unity on 3 October has been widely welcomed here. Editorials round the country have echoed Kohl's phrase in the *Bundestag* on 23 August: 'a day of joy for all Germans'. What has been a long, messy and demoralising period of political infighting over the modalities of unification is now at last coming to an end.

3. In the *Bundestag* Kohl made the following main points:

---

[1] Repeated for information Immediate to Paris, Washington; information Priority to UKDEL NATO, UKREP Brussels, BM Berlin, East Berlin, Moscow.
[2] This telegram of 23 August reported the *Volkskammer's* vote for German unity on 3 October, as well as its decision the previous day to approve the agreement with the FRG governing all-German elections on 2 December (WRL 020/20).

(*a*) There was now finally clarity as to when German unity would be complete. 'Everyone inside and outside Germany can depend on that.'

(*b*) He expressed warm thanks to Germany's Western friends and partners for their support, 'especially the three Allies, who (. . .) for decades have ensured our freedom'.[3] Special mentions for Bush ('who in recent months has shown himself a true friend of the Germans') and Mitterrand ('the fraternal bonds between the German and French peoples would remain at the heart of the foreign policy of a united Germany').

(*c*) Germany was and would remain part of the Western community of values. The London NATO Summit had provided fresh proof of the constructive role of the Alliance in safeguarding and shaping peace with freedom in Europe.

(*d*) Praise was due above all to Adenauer, whose wisdom in the early years of the Republic had laid the foundations for today's success. The dream of unity in which many had lost hope was now becoming reality.

(*e*) The united Germany would serve world peace as an equal partner in a united Europe. She would be fully sovereign. By 1994 all Soviet troops would have left Germany, 50 years after they arrived.

(*f*) The reconstruction of the GDR would take months and years rather than days. At this turning point in German history what was required was a collective national effort of supreme proportions.

4. For the opposition Lafontaine praised Kohl's achievement in winning over Gorbachev at Stavropol, but warned that real national unity—the unifying of the living conditions in east and west—still remained to be won. He stressed the need for the process of unification to be both democratic and European: Germany's neighbours, especially in Eastern Europe, would not understand it if the Germans became preoccupied with themselves. At home there were hard times still to come: the East Germans should be warned that in the change from a command to a social market economy there would be losers as well as winners. Social difficulties in the east could no more be avoided than sacrifices in the west.

5. While various hurdles have still to be surmounted on the way to 3 October, the route at least is now fairly clear. On the external track much depends on the FRG's current negotiations with the Soviet Union (my telno 1065).[4] If they are brought to a conclusion by 12 September, there should be a good chance of agreement then in 2 plus 4 on suspension of QRRs on 3 October as well as on the content of the final settlement.

6. On the internal track one hurdle was cleared today, when the *Bundesrat* approved the agreement with the GDR governing all-German elections on 2 December. That leaves outstanding the Unity Treaty itself, on which intensive negotiations are in train. The planned timetable for this is as follows:
—27 August: signature
—29 August: considered by FRG Cabinet
—30/31 August: *Volkskammer* debate
—5 September: *Bundestag* first reading
—20/21 September: final approval by *Bundestag* and *Bundesrat*.

7. It is helpful to us that unification has been fixed to take place after the meeting of CSCE Foreign Ministers on 1/2 October. It is also good that the Federal

---

[3] Ellipsis in original.
[4] Not found.

Government will be able to get to grips with the problems of the GDR. The paymaster will now be the manager.

8. We now face some hard and rapid negotiating with the Germans on specific matters like future stationing of forces in West Germany and Berlin and also the future of Berlin aviation. We must be sure that the shortage of time before 3 October works to our tactical advantage. It may increase German willingness to postpone some questions until after unity, and that could be helpful in some cases to us. But it may also increase their current readiness to concede points to the Soviet Union with unpalatable implications for us. On this we shall need to remain alert.

No. 230

Mr Hurd to Sir C. Mallaby (Bonn)[1]

No. 557 Telegraphic, Parts 1 and 2 [WRL 020/12]

Confidential   FCO, *25 August 1990, 3.54 p.m.*

German Unification: Stationing and the Status of Forces

1. This telegram contains our current thinking and suggested line to take, subject to your views, on the issues which will be covered at the meeting in Bonn on 29 August, and instructions for Paris to speak to Guelluy in advance. We confirm that Bill Hedley, Head of Secretariat NATO/UK (Policy), MOD, and Michael Wood, Legal Counsellor, will attend the Bonn meeting. They are in touch separately about the administrative arrangements.

A. *Presence of Foreign Forces Convention (PFFC)*[2]

2. At Thursday's 1 + 3 meeting Kastrup was disposed to agree that the PFFC should be extended until after the all German elections with the minimum adjustment. It may therefore be possible to confine discussion to the legal modalities. We do not at present see merit in an attempt to rely on the suggestion by Dobbins (US) at the 1 + 3 that because article 3(1) of the PFFC refers to 'a peace settlement' and the final settlement is not called a peace settlement, no legal adjustments are necessary. This seems a very uncertain legal basis. Even if accepted by all the parties to the PFFC it might well not stand up in the German courts. And it has implications going beyond the PFFC: other treaties refer to the peace settlement. We would also expect the Germans to stand firm against any such interpretation of the PFFC on political grounds since there might otherwise be suggestions that a separate peace settlement is still necessary.

3. In discussion, we suggest you should:

—express the hope that the Germans will indeed agree that the PFFC can be amended, and that this can be done without ratification by the *Bundestag*, if all that is needed is an adjustment to article 3(1) of the PFFC.

---

[1] Repeated Immediate to Paris; and for information Immediate to Washington, Berlin, Moscow, East Berlin; information Priority to UKDEL NATO, Brussels, The Hague, Ottawa, UKDEL Vienna; information Saving to JSLO.

[2] Signed by the USA, UK, France and the FRG in Paris on 23 October 1954.

4. As Kastrup was inadequately briefed on the PFFC, it is possible that the Germans might on 29 August still favour a new agreement. If so, we suggest you draw on the arguments in our 1 + 3 brief on the PFFC.

B. *Stationing in Berlin*

5. You should:

—State our appreciation of the German agreement at the 1 + 3 that Western stationing should be on a multilateral basis.

—Ask the Germans if they would like to suggest a draft stationing text. (This would probably be the best approach, since the Germans are inviting us to stay.)

—Seek further clarification of the conditions under which Western and Soviet forces would be present. Would they all, for instance, have free operational access to the whole of greater Berlin, or just their previous sectors?

—Enquire how the Germans intend symbolically and operationally to differentiate between the forces of their allies and those of the Soviet Union.

C. *Status of Forces (SOFA) and Supplementary Agreement (SA)*

6. Kastrup was unwilling at the 1 + 3 to expand on the 'political reasons' against application of the SOFA/SA to Berlin and the GDR. It may be best to try to merge application to Berlin and to the ex-GDR in negotiation, not least because on the question of Berlin the Germans are to some extent the demandeurs. In putting our case, you should both stress the political and practical reasons why we feel the SOFA/SA should apply to NATO territory, and argue that the Soviets would have no sensible grounds to object. You could make the following points:

—By far the simplest solution to extend SOFA/SA to Berlin and ex-GDR.

—Germany a single legal area. Can't have one rule for soldiers in Düsseldorf and another in Potsdam. It would be as if a diplomat had immunity in Bonn but not in Cologne.

—SOFA covers all NATO countries, even those which allow no foreign troops to be stationed there such as Norway. (This argument should be used with care as it does not apply to the SA.)

—SOFA/SA are extremely complex. Would be very difficult to negotiate something new in a very short space of time. Deal with everything from tank transport and driving licences to accidents to military/civilian vehicles.

—Strong arguments for extending to GDR as well as Berlin. For example, transit to Berlin will not be simple as it was in the past: troops may wish to travel to Berlin via other destinations in eastern Germany. Our troops will need cover in ex-GDR in other circumstances too, e.g. ships' visits to eastern German ports, other visits/exchanges, emergency landings at airports, possible training on eastern German territory, and they must be able to go on private visits to the GDR.

—Hard to see that Soviet Union could have any valid objection to extension. They have agreed to the application of the NATO Treaty itself. Application of the SOFA/SA does not imply stationing and SOFA/SA do not deal with stationing rights, which in the case of Berlin would need to be covered separately. SOFA/SA do not imply extension of NATO structures. SOFA applies to any forces of one party present in territory of another, not just those under a NATO umbrella. SOFA/SA provide technical/legal rules and regulations. Will be in your/Soviet interest too that soldiers are bound by these.

—Why concede more than was agreed at Stavropol? If necessary, you may probe German views on the possibility of applying the provisions of the SOFA/SA in full without extending the agreements themselves. You could also say that if there are particular provisions of the SA which the Germans consider inappropriate to GDR territory we would be ready to consider how these concerns can be met.

7. There should not be any need to discuss amendment of the SOFA/SA in relation to West Germany, as Kastrup made it clear that this issue would not be brought up before all-German elections. But if raised you can draw on the points in our 1 + 3 brief: i.e. we agree with the points Dobbins made on 23 August.

D. *Berlin Issues*

8. Miss Neville-Jones's letter of 17 August to Weston was a most helpful guide.[3] You should be guided by the following line in explaining our views:

(1) Role of the Garrisons.

—We accept that the garrisons will be of great symbolic importance. But they also need to be capable of combat and to have a meaningful military role in conjunction with other allies, including any German forces. Cannot expect garrison to be self sustaining, but will need to train.

We agree it might be useful if you were to produce a draft text for discussion with the Germans.

(2) Length of Stay. We have seen no evidence that anyone is thinking that Allied forces might stay once Soviet forces have left.

—As PM said in her letter to Kohl,[4] would expect to remain while Soviet forces remain in Germany.

(3) Size. We would prefer to avoid giving a clear commitment at this stage. We shall want to move in step with the US and French and take German views into account. And our position might change if there is any serious disagreement over costs.

—We believe size of our garrison should be reduced. No firm views yet: grateful for any German views.

The view in London on armoured elements is that we should prefer you to discuss further with the Americans and French, before raising this subject with the Germans. If raised:

—Are still considering whether we'd like to retain a tank squadron in Berlin. It would need to be able to train.

(4) Command Structure. We believe it will be right to fall in with German wishes on this, which we understand are that they want Allied garrisons to be subject to German coordination. It would be helpful if you could use next week's meeting to probe their views further. If pressed on the UK position:

—Will need to look closely at the details. But willing to consider garrisons being subject to German coordination.

(5) Future of the Commandants.

You should use the meeting to probe German views, and to point out that we shall need a decision shortly. We look forward to your further thoughts as discussed in telecon with Head of WED.

(6) Training. You may tell the US and the French that we too see no difficulty in the Allies sharing some facilities. Indeed it would be useful. In general:

—Clear that, though their role will be of symbolic importance, Allied forces in Berlin will need some military purpose and will therefore need to train.

—what chance of training outside the city?

---

[3] Not printed.

[4] Of 25 July: not printed. German translation in *Deutsche Einheit*, No. 370.

(7) Access. The SOFA/SA are covered in section C above.

—Soviets must be under clear obligation not to interfere with our access. On air traffic:

—Grateful to know your plans for FRG/USSR air agreement: of interest to us because of need for military air access to Berlin garrisons.

(8) Airfields. It seems unlikely that the Germans will accept Allied airfields in Berlin in future. There is no need for RAF Gatow to stay British. And we would be prepared to contemplate shared usage. We might even have to consider giving Gatow up, but would need to see German proposals before saying so.

(9) Costs. MOD are looking at the German argument that distribution of costs should in future reflect the fact that garrisons will no longer be preserving QRRs, but QRR-related costs are minimal and in logic should not be incurred after unification. You could say that:

—Allied forces in Berlin do have a common purpose related to security of the Alliance. But we are responding to a German initiation to stay, which was given in the context of the continued basing of Soviet forces in the ex-GDR.

—We would therefore expect you to pay for much the same items as at present. We agree that we shall probably need bilateral arrangements on costs, though we will of course need to concert very closely with the US and the French.

(10) Funding for Diplomatic Representation in Berlin. You should say:

—Accept in principle need for adjustment here.

—But hope Germans will continue funding in 1991. Transitional period needed for reorganisation.

—Scale of our diplomatic representation in Berlin hard to define while uncertainty persists over Berlin's status as capital/seat of government.

—May not be easy to draw firm line between diplomatic/garrison personnel (e.g. service attaches).

(11) Military Liaison Missions: you could say:

—We see value in having liaison arrangements while Soviet forces remain in Germany. Both for practical reasons and to reflect new climate of East/West co-operation. But certainly do not wish to perpetuate SOXMIS.

—Open to ideas for a trilateral agreement to accomplish this.

—Note that MLMs have had valuable intelligence roles.

Further discussion on intelligence channels of future coverage may be useful.

E. *Issues Relating to Soviet Forces in GDR and Berlin*

9. German text on forces in ex-GDR. After expressing appreciation that our most important concerns have been reflected in the redraft, you should reiterate the arguments against allowing the Russians to dictate that Western forces should not cross the ex-inner border. You should ask the Germans (preferably with US and French support) to consult us closely over stationing/status arrangements for Soviet forces in the GDR and Berlin. It would be right for them to raise in NATO too.

10. Stationing of Soviet forces in Berlin. The Germans seem to us to be making an unnecessary concession in offering the Russians the same stationing conditions as us. But we have no major reasons for objecting, and our main point has already been won in that Kastrup agreed at the 1 + 3 that stationing arrangements for Western Allies in Berlin should be multilateral. We therefore suggest that you register some unhappiness over the symbolism, and make clear that we would expect the 2 sets of agreements to be clearly distinct even if similar in substance, but that you do not press the point.

11. For Paris. Please put the main points to Guelluy in advance of next week's meeting. In conversation with him today, Goulden made the following points, with which Guelluy said he agreed:

—Multilateral stationing in Berlin.

—Bilateral successors to PFFC, but very similar.

—SOFA/SA must apply to power GDR/Berlin.

—Berlin costs: distinction between West and USSR needed. Constraints on Soviet forces in GDR must be matter for consultation.

12. MIFT covers subjects for a possible call on General Naumann.[5]

_____
[5] Not printed.

No. 231

Minute from Mr Wood (Legal Advisers) to Mr Synnott

[*WRL 020/12*]

Confidential   FCO, *28 August 1990*

Between German unification and termination of QRRs.
What has to be done before suspension of QRRs? And what happens in
Berlin if suspension is not attainable?

1. Before the Russians came into line on NATO, we began to consider a 'worst-case scenario'. The attached draft paper (which is very much a first draft, done in some haste)[1] addresses a quite different scenario, alluded to briefly by Mr Kastrup at the One plus Three Political Directors' meeting on 23 August i.e. one in which the suspension of QRRs at the moment of unification is not possible and there is therefore a significant period between German unification and the day on which QRRs cease to have effect. This period will probably last between two and six months, though it is potentially open-ended (e.g. if the Supreme Soviet or Congress fail to approve ratification of the final settlement). Unlike the 'worst-case scenario' there would not be any question of seeking to impose a Western legal view on an obstructive Soviet Union, at least unless and until it was clear that the Soviet Union's ratification was going to be delayed unreasonably.

2. It seems desirable to consider what kind of a 'transitional regime' might apply in Berlin during this interim period. The Germans may well press us to implement far-reaching changes for this period (e.g. ending the *Mantelgesetz* procedure for taking over Federal legislation);[2] and we may well wish to make changes anyway for the sake of good relations with the Berlin authorities and population (see, for example, Mr Lamont's teleletter of 7 June).[3] Moves towards the adoption of a new or revised Constitution applicable to the whole of Berlin may also force our hand.

_____
[1] Not printed.
[2] A *Mantelgesetz* is a law comprising at least one newly enacted law together with a number of amendments to existing law. Each new law and each amendment becomes an article of the *Mantelgesetz*.
[3] In this teleletter, reproduced in Series III, Vol. VI, No. 500, Mr Lamont argued that the termination of Four Power Rights in Berlin should be at same time as, or close to, unification in order to avoid difficulties.

3. There are two broad reasons why it may not be possible to suspend QRRs at the moment of German unification. First, the Russians may simply not agree, for political and/or constitutional reasons. Second, given the very short time-scale we now face (exactly five weeks between now and unification on 3 October) it may just not be possible to put in place everything that needs to be in place if QRRs are to be suspended on 3 October. In the latter case it would be possible to agree to suspension of QRRs at some later date e.g. the date of all-German elections (2 December); the date on which the *Bundestag* meets following all-German elections or the date on which a Federal Chancellor is elected following all-German elections (in either case, probably towards the end of December); or the date on which the last instrument of ratification or acceptance of the final settlement is deposited by the Four Powers (which could be some time in December). This last option could even meet Soviet constitutional obligations to suspension.

4. In order to give an overview of what needs to be done before suspension, and to put this in context, I enclose a checklist[4] of matters of legal interest that arise at various stages i.e. (1) upon unification (3 October); (2) when QRRs cease to have effect (i.e. upon their suspension on 3 October or later, or upon their termination if not preceded by suspension); (3) upon the entry into force of the final settlement. I also list (4) matters which, while it is not essential to deal with them at this stage, it is desirable to do so, both because it is politically important for the Germans to do away with vestiges of the occupation and for the sake of legal certainty (we should not want the Western Allies to be criticised for leaving the legal position messy).

M.C. WOOD

[4] Not printed.

No. 232

Minute from Mr Weston to Mr Wall

[*WRL 020/12*]

Confidential   FCO, *28 August 1990*

German Unification: Two plus Four

1. You asked for an update on where matters now stand, before the Secretary of State speaks to Genscher on the telephone on 30 August.

2. Internally, the Treaty between the two Germanys on unification is due to be signed imminently and submitted to the FRG Cabinet on 29 August, and thereafter to be debated by the *Volkskammer* on 30-31 August and by the *Bundestag* on 5 September. Final approval by the two German Parliaments would be on 20-21 September, setting 3 October as the date for entry into force.

3. The final session (we hope) of the Two plus Four Political Directors will start in Berlin on 4 September and continue for as long as it takes in order to present a completed draft final settlement to Ministers in Moscow on 12 September. Following a meeting I chaired in London on 23 August, texts for this purpose, fully agreed at 1 + 3, have now been circulated on the Two plus Four net. The Russians are tabling their own complete draft. The gaps between the two should be bridgeable in time, though it may be a bit of a rush to get all four language versions

fully produced in final form before the Moscow Ministerial, and one or two square brackets are not to be excluded.

4. As of today it remains uncertain whether the recommendation will be for Ministers to sign, or merely to initial, in Moscow. Signature may well prove the Soviet preference, but with the day of German unity now fixed for 3 October a separate signature ceremony elsewhere, whether on German soil or in the margin at the UN, would also be feasible. Thereafter, ratification procedures would follow in all five states, with entry into force of the final settlement when the fifth ratification was complete. This timetable should also permit the final settlement to be presented to CSCE Ministers (at the New York meeting) the day before German unity takes place.

5. A possible crux of substance at 2 + 4 may be how to deal with the status of QRRs for the period between 3 October (day of unity) and the entry into force of the final settlement (at fifth ratification). One possibility would be to allow QRRs to run on during this period. This may be the Soviet preference (and even, oddly, Genscher's—Cf his conversation with the Secretary of State on 21 August).[1] The disadvantage is that German sovereignty would be seen as 'fettered' for a period following German unity, and could even be held hostage to delaying tactics on Soviet ratification, thus reintroducing the old Soviet idea of a 'transitional period'. The advantage would be a continuing legal basis for the presence of Allied forces in Berlin and Soviet forces in the GDR, thus providing more time to negotiate new legal agreements for this purpose. The alternative (as set out in the Western drafts) would be a declaration suspending QRRs as from the day of German unity until their final termination on the fifth power ratification. This obviates the political difficulty over the perceived limitation on German sovereignty, but puts a premium on ensuring that where necessary other legal agreements are in place before 3 October. The latter course is preferable, but the UK need not hold out for it if all parties, in particular the Germans, can live with the former.

6. In the meantime intensive 1 + 3 talks are proceeding on the final items of Western business:

(*a*) to ensure that the legal basis for the presence of Allied forces stationed in the FRG, at present assured by the 1954 Presence of Foreign Forces Convention, continues to be watertight, both up to and beyond the entry into force of the final settlement,

(*b*) To draw up a new multilateral agreement providing a legal basis for the continued presence of reduced Western garrisons in Berlin after QRR have lapsed.

(*c*) To agree the shape, size, purpose and costs of such forces.

(*d*) To establish with the Germans whether the terms and conditions covering Western forces in Berlin and in East Germany (as they transit to Berlin or where they may find themselves individually for recreational or other purposes) are those defined by the NATO Status of Forces Agreement and the Supplementary Agreement applying its terms specifically to Germany (SOFA and SA).

(*e*) To ensure that the Germans do not concede more bilaterally to the Russians than was implied at Stavropol on the special military status of East Germany during and after the departure of Soviet troops.

7. Items (*d*) and (*e*) could pose problems that need to be taken up with the German Government at a political level. I am asking the Department to let you

---

[1] No record of this conversation has been found.

have a speaking note for the Secretary of State's telephone conversation with Genscher, taking account of any further points which may emerge from Sir Christopher Mallaby's discussions at 1 + 3 at State Secretary level in Bonn on 29-30 August. Since point (*e*) is relevant to the German statement of intent that we envisage would form part of the final settlement texts, it might be a wise precaution to aim for a brief 1 + 3 Ministerial in Moscow on the evening of Tuesday 11 September or over breakfast the following morning, before the 2 + 4 Ministerial begins.

8. We shall submit separately on the question of Ministerial attendance at any German ceremony to mark unity on 3 October.

P.J. WESTON

No. 233

Sir C. Mallaby (Bonn) to Mr Hurd[1]

No. 1096 Telegraphic [WRL 020/12]

Confidential   BONN, *31 August 1990, 7.55 a.m.*

My Telno 1095: German Unification: Status of Forces

Summary

1. Treaty on German unity, as concluded, precludes extension of Status of Forces Agreement (SOFA) and Supplementary Agreement (SA) to Berlin and ex-GDR.

Detail

2. The treaty on unity was initialled by FRG and GDR during last night and is to be signed at 1100 today.

3. I saw Interior Minister Schäuble, who has the lead in the Federal Government on this treaty, early this morning. I recalled our view that extension of the SOFA and SA to the GDR and Berlin should not be precluded by their inclusion in the list annexed to the unity treaty of agreements that would not apply to the GDR. Schäuble said that my representations to his department this week had been reported to him. He was sympathetic to our viewpoint. But the Minister of Foreign Affairs was responsible for the extension of treaties to the GDR. Schäuble had raised my point again in the Federal Government, and the *Auswärtiges Amt* had ruled that the SOFA and SA should not be deleted from the list.

Comment

4. Genscher has evidently judged that he can ride out the objections expressed repeatedly by the US and UK. So he has presented us with a *fait accompli* (as has also happened this week in Kohl's decision further to restrict low flying). Our objective in the stationing negotiations must now be to get as much as possible of the substance of the two agreements applied to Berlin and the old GDR.

---

[1] Repeated for information Immediate to Washington, UKDEL NATO, Paris, BM Berlin, East Berlin, MODUK, Doha; information Routine to CICC(G), HQ JSLO.

No. 234

Mr Eyers (East Berlin) to FCO[1]

No. 536 Telegraphic [WRL 020/12]

Confidential   EAST BERLIN, *7 September 1990, 5 p.m.*

FCO please pass to the Attorney General's Office.

BM Berlin telno 67.[2]

Two plus Four: Completion of Political Directors' Negotiations
From Weston

Summary
1. Signature in Moscow of final settlement on 12 September now clearly in prospect, following progress today. But still no agreement on two pol-mil issues and on the principle of suspension of Four Power rights and responsibilities. These will need discussion by ministers in Moscow. Full text of final settlement otherwise agreed. Final linguistic comparison to take place in Moscow on 11 September. Kastrup to brief North Atlantic Council on 10 September.
Detail
2. Negotiations late into 6 September and on the following day produced a sudden spurt of progress on minor issues, procedures and technicalities, leaving only three major issues of contention, which will almost certainly need to be resolved by ministers personally in Moscow: there is no sign that the Russians envisage changing their position beforehand. These issues are: the Soviet attempt to exclude dual capable weapons from East Germany, their proposal (in addition to the non-stationing provision) to preclude any movement into East Germany by NATO armed forces, and the question of suspension of Four Power rights and responsibilities in the period between unification and their final termination.

3. After strong statements on each of these points by the UK, US and France, Bondarenko (USSR) sought instructions overnight and then reaffirmed his previous position, expressing the view that they would have to be considered by Ministers. He has argued that the two pol-mil issues were an essential part of the Stavropol agreement, which had to be seen as a package. Kastrup (FRG) retorted usefully that, as the only one in the 2 + 4 talks who was personally present at Stavropol, there had been no discussion of these particular issues or agreement in such terms: nor had they been dealt with in the *tête-à-tête*. In the absence of agreement, square bracketed texts were prepared accordingly.

---

[1] Repeated to Tokyo (for Secretary of State's party), Bonn, UKDEL NATO, Paris, Moscow, Washington; information Immediate to UKMIS New York, MODUK, UKREP/Brussels, BM Berlin; information Routine NATO Posts, Warsaw, Prague.

[2] In this telegram, dated 6 September, Mr Weston gave an account of the state of play in the Two plus Four negotiations, in preparation for the Ministerial meeting in Moscow on 12 September (WRL 020/12). In view of the issues that remained unresolved, and the lack of time available, it was possible that full agreement might not be possible by the time Ministers arrived in Moscow. Failing agreement at that point, various fallback positions might have to be considered. However, 'My personal bet is that, at the end of the day, signature in Moscow will be achieved.'

4. On suspension, the Russians could not agree to our proposed declaration as a way of handling the issue, in advance of resolving outstanding points of substance on the final settlement but Bondarenko said he would consider the proposal in due course and did not raise detailed objections to the text of the British draft, or reject it in principle. This suggests that at the end of the day in Moscow, it may provide the way forward.

Issues Resolved

5. After instructions overnight, Bondarenko agreed, with an appropriate show of reluctance, to withdraw Soviet draft articles referring to verification, presentation of the final settlement to CSCE summit, and military liaison missions.

6. The Russians and Germans agreed together that the latest date for the withdrawal of Soviet forces from East Germany and Berlin would be 31 December 1994, and that this should be in the text.

7. The Russians also agreed, with surprising ease, that the Germans should issue a side letter covering claims, Naziism and war memorials.

8. Linguistic comparisons, drawing on advice from FCO experts, proved satisfactory. It was agreed that further technical comparisons of typed-up texts by legal experts will take place in Moscow on 11 September. We have agreed arrangements with the Americans for the technical production of English language texts for signature, if agreement proves possible.

Briefing Allies

9. It was agreed among the 1 + 3 that Kastrup would brief the NAC on the outcome of these negotiations on 10 September (but not volunteer the actual text), following Baker's debrief on the Helsinki summit. I suggest that some Allied airing of views on the issues of dual capable weapons and this Soviet attempt to prevent NATO forces ever crossing the line into East Germany might help stiffen the German spine.

Comment

10. In the end the Political Directors' marathon session this week has largely delivered the goods. The Russians are not on strong ground over the three remaining issues of substance, and should climb down if the Western Four hold firm on 12 September (there has been no direct consultation with Shevardnadze on all this by Soviet officials because of the latter's absence abroad until today). But much will depend on the Germans remaining robust in resisting Soviet attempts to misrepresent what was agreed at Stavropol. We must beware of any tendency by Genscher to trade firmness on the dual-capable systems point for a concession to Moscow on NATO forces never crossing the line into former East Germany, over which there have been signs of vacillation in Bonn.

11. By the end of today's meeting in Berlin, Genscher's private secretary Elbe had already seated himself conspicuously behind the GDR name plate, changing places with an East German colleague.

No. 235

Sir R. Braithwaite (Moscow) to FCO[1]

No. 1694 Telegraphic [WRL 020/12]

Confidential   MOSCOW, *11 September 1990, 3.11 p.m.*

From Weston

Two plus Four in Moscow

Summary

1. All remaining issues settled except crossing the line and suspension. As of 1600 hours local time (and before Secretary of State's arrival) the crossing the line issue looks precarious because of German weakness and apparent American acquiescence.

Detail

2. When the Political Directors met this morning under Kvitsinsky's chairmanship, agreement was reached fairly easily on several outstanding issues. In particular on the dual capable systems point it was agreed to add a sentence in paragraph 3 of article 5, after the reference to the exclusion of nuclear weapon carriers to read: 'this does not apply to conventional weapons systems which may have other capabilities to conventional ones but which in that part of Germany are equipped for a conventional role and designated only for such'.

3. The real difficulties have arisen on how to deal with the Soviet proposal to preclude other NATO forces from ever crossing the line into East Germany e.g. for exercise or manoeuvre purposes. It is clear that, following Ministerial talks between Baker and Shevardnadze in Helsinki, Genscher and Baker in Brussels yesterday and Shevardnadze and Genscher on the telephone, the Germans (including apparently Kohl) are ready to go a long way towards meeting the Soviet requirement. They explain this by saying that the Stavropol agreement was that foreign forces would not be 'moved' into East Germany (in German *verliegt*), and that the Russians can therefore argue with some justice that the non-stationing provision is not enough. According to Zoellick, Baker could also live with an explicit provision in perpetuity that large scale military manoeuvres by NATO should not take place in East Germany.

4. When we broke at 1600 hrs this afternoon the position was that Kastrup had proposed with American acquiescence, and Kvitsinsky had agreed to consider, adding language to article 5 which could preclude any military activities at all east of the line during the transitional period while Soviet troops withdraw and for the period beyond would add that foreign armed forces be neither stationed nor deployed there. The proposal is that the latter expression be interpreted separately by Ministries and explained publicly as meaning that large scale manoeuvres will

---

[1] Repeated for information Immediate to Bonn, Washington, Paris, UKDEL NATO, East Berlin, BM Berlin.

never take place in East Germany (as defined in Stockholm Article 31.1)[2] and that other military activities will not necessarily take place but are not precluded.

5. This is already a long way down the slippery slope, and I shall tell the Secretary of State on arrival that I cannot recommend it to him. The French are also worried. My own preference would be at the most a provision precluding large scale military manoeuvres during the transitional period (explicable simply as deconfliction), and bilateral political assurances only that thereafter the Allies would exercise discretion and pay due regard to Soviet security interests in any activities east of the line. But I very much doubt that this is attainable. Frankly the German heart is not in it. And the Americans are in a fix-it mood.

[2] Article 31.1 of the concluding document of the Stockholm Conference on Confidence- and Security-Building Measures and Disarmament in Europe (CSBMs) (1986) concerned the prior notification of military activities to participating states. Full text available at http://www.fas.org/nuke/control/osce/text/STOCK86E.htm.

No. 236

FCO to Sir R. Braithwaite (Moscow)[1]

No. 1593 Telegraphic [*WRL 020/12*]

Confidential   FCO, *11 September 1990, 8.15 p.m.*

Moscow for Weston and Secretary of State's Party.

Your telno 1694: 2 plus 4 in Moscow[2]

1. It is good that you reached agreement on the point on dual capable systems.

2. We agree with the line you propose to take (your para 5). If, as seems likely, this does not prevail, we would suggest the following fallbacks.

—Firstly: we concede that there will be no military activities east of the line during the transition period. (It would be worth clarifying the meaning of military activities: they should not include transit to and from Berlin, private visits, military exchanges, emergency landings at airports etc.)

—Secondly: if really necessary, we concede also on the arrangements for the period after Soviet forces have left. This concession would clearly be much more serious than the first one, as it concerns the military status of the GDR in perpetuity (see arguments in our telno 610 to Tokyo).[3] In making it, we should try to avoid use of the word 'deployments' (your para 4), a reference to training or manoeuvres would be better, preferably of course with the qualification 'large scale'. Deployment in times of tension would then not be precluded. We could remind the Western Three that Germany, and NATO as a whole, needs to be able to defend all its territory effectively. The commitment not to deploy

[1] Repeated for information Immediate to Bonn, Washington, Paris, UKDEL NATO, East Berlin, BM Berlin.
[2] No. 235.
[3] Telegram No. 610 of 10 September to Tokyo for the Secretary of State's party and to Moscow for Mr Weston and Mr Synnott contained briefing on political/military issues for the One plus Three breakfast meeting and the Two plus Four Ministerial meeting on 12 September (DZN 061/109). For the issues covered see No. 237.

foreign forces into the ex-GDR would be a unilateral one. The Soviet Union/Warsaw Pact is not being required to give an undertaking of this nature. What would happen in times of tension/crisis/war? We would hope never to need to deploy extra forces into the ex-GDR. But Germany/the Alliance should be free to do so.

3. Mr King is aware of the position. He is content to agree if necessary that there should be no military activities in the GDR while Soviet forces remain. Beyond that he would welcome any additional flexibility you can achieve.

No. 237

Sir R. Braithwaite (Moscow) to FCO[1]

No. 1713 Telegraphic [WRL 020/1]

Confidential   MOSCOW, *12 September 1990, 2.57 p.m.*

2+4 Ministerial Meeting, Moscow, 12 September

Summary
1. Final settlement on Germany signed. Texts on polmil aspects adequate. Suspension of Four Power rights and responsibilities due to occur in New York on 1 October. Two plus Four work thus complete.

Detail

2. The Foreign Ministers of Britain, France, the United States, the Soviet Union and the FRG and the Prime Minister of the GDR signed the 'Treaty on the Final Settlement in Respect of Germany' in the October Hotel in the presence of Gorbachev. The Treaty was accompanied by an agreed minute which was also signed. Full texts follow to the Department.

3. Political Directors ironed out most of the remaining problems on 11 September, having arrived at Soviet request a day earlier than planned. The Russians conceded that dual capable weapons should not be excluded from the present GDR and language was found to express this. For the transitional period no foreign military activity is to be allowed in East Germany. But the thorny issue of movement by non-German armed forces into East Germany after Soviet withdrawal had to be resolved personally by Foreign Ministers through a series of bilateral and multilateral sessions. The UK and US argued strongly against accepting arrangements which would extend limitations on East Germany beyond non-stationing and thus constrain Alliance options. With the plenary meeting delayed by an hour, Shevardnadze was finally brought to agree that, although after Soviet withdrawal foreign forces would not be stationed or deployed in East Germany, questions regarding the application of the word 'deployed' would be decided by the Government of Germany. This important qualification is contained in a minute attached to the treaty which was also signed by the six Foreign Ministers. The fact that Germany's rights and obligations flowing from Alliance membership are also unaffected by this treaty is also clearly stated in the treaty.

---

[1] Repeated for information Immediate to Bonn, Paris, Washington, East Berlin, BM Berlin, UKDEL NATO, Warsaw; information Routine to UKREP Brussels, UKMIS New York, other CSCE Posts, Tokyo.

4. The formal plenary itself was quite brief, and consisted mainly of statements by each of the six welcoming the agreement.

5. On suspension of Four Powers rights and responsibilities in period between unification and their final termination on entry into force of the settlement, the Russians took the line that other, bilateral, arrangements had to be settled with the Germans first. But they agreed in principle to consider again the British draft declaration suspending Four Power rights, with a view to it being signed by the six Foreign Ministers on 1 October, two days before unification, in New York before the CSCE preparatory conference. This outcome seems virtually assured.

Comment

6. A range of bilateral issues, mainly about the presence of foreign armed forces on German soil remain to be resolved before unification, in order firmly to eliminate the last vestiges of occupation rights (progress on this is, of course, well advanced in negotiations in Bonn). But signature of the final settlement effectively resolves the Four Power and other 'external' aspects of German unification. On movement of foreign forces into East Germany (crossing the line), the Germans proved very wobbly up to the last moment, but were prevented by the firmness of their three Allies from completely conceding the point to the Russians. Faced, ultimately, with a united position, Shevardnadze settled for a signed document which does not rule out anything *a priori* after Soviet troop withdrawal except stationing as such, and leaves it clear that it is for sovereign Germany to say whether any specific proposal for NATO military activity in East Germany in years to come would constitute deployment or not. This is as much as we could hope for in the highly charged atmosphere today, both in the German and the Russian camp.

No. 238

Letter from Mr Weston to Sir C. Mallaby (Bonn)[1]

[RS 021/1]

Personal and Confidential   FCO, *17 September 1990*

Dear Christopher,

Two plus Four: The End Game

1. The minor squall that blew up following David Gow's *Guardian* article of 7 September[2] and German press comment after the treaty signing on 12 September

---

[1] Copied to H M Representatives at Moscow, Paris and UKDEL NATO, and to Mr Wood, Washington.

[2] Bonn telegram No. 3 to Moscow of 12 September explained that this article, headlined 'Bonn getting too close to Moscow', mostly contained routine reporting, 'interspersed with a few purported direct and indirect quotations from diplomatic, or Western diplomatic, sources, none of them described as British. The point which gave rise to the headline . . . is not attributed at all.' Sir C. Mallaby continued: 'I think Genscher is over-reacting to a superficial, disjointed piece of reporting. He is wrong in apparently deducing that this Embassy has been expressing to journalists fears about German foreign policy. You may wish to tell Genscher that we actually discouraged the line in the report' (WRL 020/1).

prompts me to put on record a few impressions of the last forty-eight hours before signature of this historic treaty.

2. After four consecutive days work in East Berlin from 4 to 7 September the Political Directors parted late on the Friday with an agreement on an enumerated ten article draft treaty subject to a couple of square bracketed passages and accompanied by a Soviet proposal, which had no status, for a further draft article on 'crossing the line'. We had agreed to foregather in Moscow in the early evening of 11 September to vet the final technical cosmetics by legal advisers and treaty experts, leaving it to Ministers to resolve on the morning of 12 September the three main outstanding issues (dual capable systems, crossing the line, suspension of QRRs). Signature was then scheduled to take place at 4 pm the same day. This put the Russians under a pleasing time bind.

3. Less than twenty-four hours after we left Berlin, when Bondarenko had reported to Kvitsinsky and Shevardnadze had returned from the Far East, we heard in our respective capitals that the Russians were proposing instead a further full day of Political Director work in Moscow on 11 September (requiring us to travel to Moscow on 10 September). This transparent attempt to give themselves more room for manoeuvre should in my view have been resisted. But by the time I got Kastrup on the telephone on Sunday 9 September, he had already conceded the point. The Americans being already in Moscow after the Helsinki Summit, we and the French were clearly not in a position to hold out.[3]

4. We duly met in the whited sepulchre of the Octyabrskaya Hotel on the morning of 11 September. A hastily arranged One plus Three for a few minutes beforehand revealed:

(*a*) intense German annoyance about David Gow in the *Guardian* of 7 September, over which they suspected the UK; and,

(*b*) that the FRG delegation had already been holding bilaterals with the Russians in an attempt to sew up a deal on the final points, misrepresenting US views (at least to us) into the bargain.

The Russians for their part had advanced the signature ceremony from 4 p.m. to 12.30 p.m. the next day and confirmed that Gorbachev would attend personally. [Kastrup then also told me that he thought the Russians would return to their earlier attempt to get us to drop the words 'upon German request' from the provision in Article 5 covering the continued troop presence of the three Allies in Berlin, in an attempt further to blur the distinction between the Allied presence and the residual Soviet forces presence. I told Kastrup, having taken the precaution of speaking to Charles Powell over the weekend before leaving London (the Secretary of State being in Japan), that I knew the Prime Minister's Office attached importance to retaining those words. This may be partly the origin of the later German press canard that British firmness stemmed from the views of the Prime Minister. I had not however discussed 'crossing the line' with Charles Powell, because I did not want to risk placing myself under unrealistic restrictions on that issue. In the event the Russians did not return to the charge on the words 'upon German request'.][4]

5. When we broke at 4 pm on 11 September the position was as described in Moscow Tel No 1694.[5] Dual capable systems were already safely in the bag.

---

[3] The Helsinki Summit, to discuss the Iraq-Kuwait war, was held between Presidents Bush and Gorbachev on 5 September.

[4] Parentheses in original.

[5] No. 235.

Suspension of QRR did not look a stopper. The real crux was on 'crossing the line'. The pass had already been virtually sold for the transitional period covering Soviet troop withdrawal, on the basis that paragraph 1 of Article 5 would preclude any military activity there by armed forces of states other than the Soviet Union and Germany. It also looked uncertain whether for the period thereafter we could hold the position with a provision excluding merely large-scale military manoeuvres (as defined by the 1986 Stockholm CSBMs Agreement),[6] which up to then had been Kvitsinsky's professed major preoccupation. Kastrup was arguing for a simple provision against all deployment, coupled with some kind of oral statement; on the grounds that such was the sense of Stavropol: the reference (ill-defined) to manoeuvres appeared to be intended as a compromise. Dufourcq was personally unhappy about this but inhibited by the fact that his Minister was not due to arrive in Moscow until 3.30 a.m. on 12 September. Zoellick's compass was beginning to veer uncertainly.

6. With the Secretary of State's arrival around 5.30 p.m., bilateral Ministerials got under way—Baker/Genscher, Secretary of State/Baker and later Secretary of State/Genscher. The upshot was that we and the Americans (joined by the French) agreed to camp for the rest of the evening on Ministerial instructions to the effect that, if paragraph 1 of Article 5 precluded all military activity during the transitional period, paragraph 3 of Article 5 should go no further than precluding deployment 'with the aim of holding large scale military manoeuvres'. But our scheduled resumption at 8 pm that evening was delayed for a further hour by private German/Russian bilateral activity elsewhere—a performance described as 'tacky' by Zoellick, who was greatly irritated by it.

7. When Kastrup and Kvitsinsky eventually returned after 9 p.m., the former put to us in the margin before resumption his provisional agreement with the Russians on a simple 'no deployment' formula coupled with a four point oral statement by Genscher at the Plenary negotiating session, which the Russians would undertake to listen to in silence. [The Genscher four points were: no large scale military manoeuvres; military activities below that threshold were not specifically excluded but would not necessarily take place, the application of the word 'deployment' would be for sovereign Germany to decide; in doing so, she would exercise reason and responsibility and bear in mind the security interests of all.][7]

8. This triggered sharp open disagreement among the One plus Three on the sidelines of the meeting. The thrust of UK/US/French objections was that the Alliance should not bind itself by treaty with the Soviet Union in a way which would indefinitely foreclose options extending far beyond the foreseeable circumstances and would further limit German sovereignty beyond Stavropol. With 12 billion DM in their kitty and the world expecting signature in little more than twelve hours, we did not need to offer the Russians any more concessions. The German response was that this was all totally unrealistic since peace had broken out in Europe. ('Oh come on! You can't be serious.' was the stock rejoinder.) They also argued that the German word 'verlegt' describing the deal at Stavropol went a good way beyond a mere no stationing agreement. When the formal session resumed I asked Kvitsinsky whether he would confirm that silence by Shevardnadze in the face of an oral statement by Genscher could be interpreted

[6] See No. 235, note 2.
[7] Parentheses in original.

at the very least as the Soviet Union not disagreeing with this statement. Kvitsinsky declined to provide any such assurance.

9. After further skirmishing we broke inconclusively around 10.30 pm. At that point there were at least five alternatives in the air.

(i) Soviet position: no military activity in transitional period, simple 'no deployment' formula thereafter;

(ii) US/UK/French proposal: no military activity for transitional period and 'no deployment with the aim of holding large-scale military manoeuvres' thereafter;

(iii) FRG position: as for the Russians, but with oral statement by Genscher at plenary session on 12 September to which Shevardnadze would make no reply.

(iv) Zoellick fallback mark I: instead of formulation at (ii) above, after 'no deployment' add new sentence in treaty (crafted with the UK) as follows: 'Decisions on whether, and if so what kind of, military activities take place in that part of Germany would be for the sovereign united Germany to make in accordance with provisions of this treaty, the principles reflected in the Preamble and taking account of the security interests of the states party.'

(v) Zoellick fallback mark II: simple 'no deployment' formula in the Treaty plus a letter from Genscher either to the Three Allied Foreign Ministers or to the NATO Secretary-General setting out the Genscher Four Points.

10. At this juncture the Russians decided to put the frighteners on a bit. They sent senior MFA officials round to each delegation (in my case catching me in my bedroom just short of midnight) to state formally on instructions that because of the failure to agree at official level, the plenary session at 10 am the next day at the Octyabrskaya had been postponed, the timing of signature was in question and the press would have to be informed. Instead Mr Shevardnadze wished to see his Ministerial colleagues alone at a working session in the MFA Mansion at Alexander Tolstoy Street next morning at the same hour. This tactic, which in my view was never convincing since the Russians were under the greatest time pressure of all, got Genscher in enough of a lather for him to go off to see Baker at 1.15 in the morning, when the latter had already taken his sleeping pill and final bedtime drink. [With hindsight this gives a subtle extra flavour to the reference in Baker's speeches at the plenary session and the press conference on 12 September about free citizens no longer being threatened by a knock on the door at dead of night!][8]

11. By the following morning, when One plus Three Ministers met at the French Embassy under Dumas's slightly dishevelled chairmanship, further US/FRG work had produced the form of words which was eventually to become the text of the agreed minute annexed to the Treaty. One plus Three Ministers quickly agreed that they did not wish to hold out for the formulation at paragraph 9 (ii) above at the expense of delaying signature in Moscow. But Baker in particular was clear that if the Administration were to carry the treaty successfully on the Hill, something in writing would be necessary about the provisions on military activity in the former GDR after Soviet troop departure; oral assurances would not do. When we broke from the breakfast the preferred solution was an inspired question and answer at the press conference which Shevardnadze would pass to Genscher who would answer in terms of the latest agreed text; this would then be confirmed as a record of the exchange in the press conference by letter from Genscher to his five Two plus Four colleagues or, failing that, to the Three.

---

[8] Parentheses in original.

12. Genscher and Baker went off to see Shevardnadze. The Russians then let it be known that the timetable for the morning's meetings had reverted to the original plan. Two plus Four Ministers had a private session at the Octyabrskaya Hotel prior to the Plenary session there. It was then that Baker stumbled on the notion of an agreed minute, to be annexed to the treaty and signed in addition to it by all six Ministers. Slightly to everyone's surprise this won Shevardnadze's assent. By this time the German delegation were once more in a highly excitable state, Genscher's Private Secretary, Frank Elbe, being particularly disagreeable, and venting all kinds of nonsense about how close 'some people' had come 'to screwing it up'. The formal plenary session and the predictable speeches for the occasion followed without controversy. We broke to allow final preparations of the text for signature. At this point we moved from the sublime to the ridiculous. The German word-processor back-up went on the blink, thus delaying both German and French texts of the agreed minute. The American delegation, despite being 180 strong in Moscow, were apparently unable to produce a typewriter in the hotel that morning. I began to wonder about the wisdom of having conceded to the Americans the final textual work, the UK team having earned much credit throughout the session in Berlin and the early stages in Moscow with our Toshiba lap-top producing running updates of the texts in near real time around the table.

13. Signature duly followed under Gorbachev's benevolent eye. Bondarenko looked ten years younger on the instant. Champagne and congratulations were lavish. The final forty-eight hours were nevertheless instructive. They brought home for me that, with the arrival of German unity, Germany will not be simply the Federal Republic plus, but a different entity. Looking back on the whole process I see something of a thread running through: the early reluctance of the Germans to discuss politico-military issues at One plus Three, the bilateral concessions made at Stavropol (*pace* Bob Blackwill's valedictory at Carnegie,[9] Zoellick sees that as essentially bilateral) the subsequent systematic ambiguity about what had been agreed there on the troop movement question ('verlegt' in German serving variously as 'stationing', 'deployed' and 'moved' depending on the day and the argument), the *fait accompli* over the exclusion of SOFA/SA from application in the former GDR, the acrimony over the crossing the line issue at the last, Genscher's unforthcoming answer at the press conference to the question about Allied forces in Berlin, and the general obtuseness and emotion on the German side faced with the assertion that an important Alliance interest might be at stake.

14. I do not wish to exaggerate all this or to diminish the achievement, for the Germans and indeed for us all, that German unification represents. We have every reason to work within the Alliance as within the Community to maintain and if possible strengthen the underlying strategic Western solidarity. But as we embark

---

[9] Mr Blackwill gave a breakfast address, largely dedicated to the Bush Administration's policy on Germany, at the Carnegie Endowment in Washington on 25 July, shortly before leaving the NSC to take up a professorship at Harvard. Mr Tebbit's report of 1 August noted that 'Blackwill was evidently stung by the allegations after Stavropol that the United States had been marginalised . . . and determined to defend the Administration record—of which of course he has reason to feel proud. The basic policy, he insisted, had been [the] Bush Administration's invention, as was the tactical game-plan for handling the Germans, Russians and neighbouring countries. It had involved the most intensive application of US diplomacy of all time. Anyone who thought that the Administration had been upstaged by Stavropol must have been living on the planet Zarkon' (WRL 020/10/90).

on this renewed challenge from 3 October I already begin to feel as I look at our German partners that:

'You are not the same people who left that station
Or who will arrive at any terminus . . .'[10]

I would be interested in your diagnosis.

Yours ever,
P.J. WESTON

[10] T. S. Eliot, 'The Dry Salvages', *Four Quartets*, Canto III (London, 1944).

No. 239

Mr Hurd to HM Representatives Overseas

Guidance No. 59 Telegraphic [*WRL 020/12*]

Confidential   FCO, *28 September 1990, 3 p.m.*

German Unification

Introduction

1. The Treaty on the Final Settlement with Respect to Germany was signed in Moscow on 12 September. German unification will take place on 3 October.

Line to Take (unclassified)

2. —Pleased with outcome. Met objective to complete work on external aspects of unification in harmony with internal unification process. 2+4 machinery worked well.

—Final settlement a good treaty, as Foreign Secretary said in Moscow. United Germany will be fully sovereign. Quadripartite Rights and Responsibilities (QRRs) will end. Germany's borders will be definitive. Treaty meets both Alliance interests and legitimate security concerns of Soviet Union.

—Look forward to working with united Germany as friend, ally and partner in the new Europe.

Additional Points (unclassified)

3. *Suspension of QRRs*

—QRRs cannot of course formally terminate until Treaty enters into force, i.e. when all parties have ratified. This may take some months. Plan is thus to suspend QRRs with effect from unification, so that Germany is in practice fully sovereign from the outset. A declaration suspending QRRs will be signed by Foreign Ministers of the Four Powers and noted by the two German states in New York on 1 October.

4. *UK ratification?*

—Treaty will be laid before parliament for 21 sitting days (the 'Ponsonby rule'). Procedures should thus be completed before end November.

5. *Integration of GDR into EC?*

—Want to see GDR integrated into EC as fully, quickly, smoothly and transparently as possible. Are considering Commission's proposals. Interim measures were adopted by Foreign Affairs Council on 17 September. Final adoption of the overall package expected by early December.

—In principle EC law will apply in ex-GDR upon unification. But accept that some temporary derogations are needed where EC standards cannot be met at once (e.g. environment).

6. *NATO interests satisfied?*

—Yes. United Germany will be a member of NATO. NATO treaty, including articles 5 and 6, will apply to all German territory. NATO allies kept fully briefed through 2+4 process.

7. *Restrictions on NATO in eastern Germany?*

—Some. No nuclear weapons in ex-GDR. No stationing of, and no military activity by NATO forces as long as Soviet forces are there. No foreign armed forces to be stationed or deployed there once Soviet forces have withdrawn. But application of word 'deployed' for German Government to decide. Dual capable systems intended for conventional use allowed. A satisfactory outcome to cater for legitimate Soviet security concerns.

8. *Berlin?*

—Treaty provides for UK, US and French forces to remain in Berlin, at German request, for as long as Soviet forces are present in eastern Germany, i.e. until end 1994 at latest. Details subject of separate agreement between Germany and sending states.

9. *UK diplomatic representation in Germany?*

—Three UK Missions in Berlin (British Mission Berlin, British Consulate General, British Embassy East Berlin) will merge on 3 October to form a branch of the British Embassy Bonn. Bonn Embassy to remain for foreseeable future. HM Ambassador to be based in Bonn. The staffing arrangements under consideration.

10. *(If required) rumours of British intransigence?*

—Unfounded. UK fully committed to success of these negotiations from outset. Result a success for all. Germans have thanked all participants for their contributions.

Background

11. The 2 + 4 negotiations on the external aspects of German unification ended on 12 September in Moscow with the signature of a 'Treaty on the Final Settlement with Respect to Germany'. The Treaty does not enter into force until the last instrument of ratification has been deposited with the German government. This may take some months. So as to meet the Germans' wish that they should be fully sovereign from unification on 3 October, the Foreign Ministers of the Four Powers will meet in New York on 1 October to sign a declaration suspending Quadripartite Rights and Responsibilities (QRRs) with effect from unification.

12. The Treaty also provides for the following:

(*a*) Borders. The Treaty states that the definitive external borders of Germany will be the external borders of the FRG and GDR. It states that Germany and Poland will confirm their border in a treaty, and that 'the united Germany has no territorial claims whatsoever against other states and shall not assert any in the future'. Germany undertakes in the treaty to ensure that its constitution does not contain any provision incompatible with these principles.

(*b*) United Germany will not manufacture, possess or control any NBC weapons. Rights and obligations arising from the non-proliferation treaty will continue to apply to the united Germany. United Germany will reduce the personnel strength of its armed forces to 370,000 within three to four years.

(*c*) Soviet armed forces will withdraw from the territory of the present GDR and

Berlin by the end of 1994.

(*d*) For the duration of the presence of Soviet forces, French, British and American armed forces will remain stationed in Berlin at German request.

(*e*) The right of the united Germany to belong to alliances, with all the rights and responsibilities arising therefrom, is not affected.

(*f*) QRRs relating to Berlin and Germany as a whole are terminated: as a result, all quadripartite agreements terminate and all Four Power institutions are dissolved. United Germany accordingly has full sovereignty over its internal and external affairs.

13. *(Restricted—may be drawn on with trusted contacts)*

The pol-mil status of the ex-GDR remained to the end the most difficult issue to resolve. The question of the movement of non-German armed forces into eastern Germany after the withdrawal of Soviet forces by the end of 1994 was ultimately settled personally by foreign ministers in a series of bilateral and multilateral meetings. Shevardnadze was eventually persuaded that, although after Soviet withdrawal foreign forces would not be stationed or deployed in East Germany, questions regarding the application of the word 'deployed' were to be decided by the government of Germany. This important qualification was formalised in an agreed minute attached to the Treaty and also signed by the six Foreign Ministers.

14. *(Restricted—may be drawn on with trusted contacts)*

The German press have since sought to ascribe these last minute difficulties to British intransigence. This was not the case. The UK's position was shared by the US and France and the outcome was satisfactory for us.

15. For background on earlier events, see Guidance telno 11 of 28 February and Guidance telno 31 of 23 May.[1]

[1] Nos. 159 and 203.

No. 240

Mr Eyers (East Berlin) to Mr Hurd

[*WRE 014/1*]

Restricted   EAST BERLIN, *2 October 1990*

Summary ... [1]

Farewell to an Unloved Country

Sir,

1. At midnight to-night the German Democratic Republic will cease to exist as a state, and its component parts will become *Länder* of the Federal Republic of Germany. Sir Christopher Mallaby and I are setting out in a joint despatch our views on the nature of the larger Germany that will emerge from this union. In this despatch I sketch the progression of events since my arrival here, as the new order buried the old; explain the internal forces which imposed a pace which took us all by surprise; and suggest what dowry this part of Germany will bring with it to the union.

[1] Not printed.

2. Events in the GDR this year have fallen into three periods. The first, during which the country was governed by a rump of the communist party under Hans Modrow, in association with the Round Table, ended with the general elections of 18 March. The second period led to economic and monetary union on 1 July. The third ends to-night with the absorption into the Federal Republic of five new *Länder* and of East Berlin.

3. When I took up my post at the end of January, two days after your very successful visit, the GDR was in the first of these periods. The revolution driven by the people in the streets and squares was pretty much over. The mood had been changing, and with it the way in which pressure bore on the government. In late 1989, the adrenalin was flowing. The vast demonstrations still required courage of those taking part, and were a source of great pride. The Tiananmen solution was still a possibility. The SED and organs of state were detested, but not yet disregarded—they seemed powerful. But after the opening of the wall in November and Krenz' removal in early December, the mood changed to one of increasing contempt as the corruption of the old leadership, the miserable state of the industrial infrastructure, and—above all—the extent of the ramifications of the state security machine became apparent. As the contempt grew, the calls for reform changed to calls for unity. Regular demonstrations were to continue until the elections in March, but they lost much of their emotion and impact. Pressure on the government arose increasingly from emigration to the Federal Republic.

4. The importance of emigration throughout the year cannot be overstressed. It became the principal motor of events. The consequences for the Federal Government were uncomfortable: expensive accommodation had to be found, and substantial social support paid to those who came across; the popular welcome wore thin as the newcomers put pressure on the labour market; and there was the prospect of a much more severe reaction if the rate of emigration continued to increase. For the GDR the wave of emigration threatened immediate catastrophe: those who went were people whose skills were necessary to keep the factories and public services going. Worse, emigrants often dragged others after them, since life could quickly become intolerable for those left behind. A small town which lost its baker, bus-driver and doctor risked emptying fast. There were times when 15,000 people left the GDR in a week, the equivalent in a month of a substantial town. But neither government could control the flow: the Federal government, even if it had wanted to, was debarred constitutionally; the GDR authorities because only reestablishment of the wall would have had any effect.

5. Herr Modrow had been elected Prime Minister in early November 1989 by the old SED controlled *Volkskammer*. It seems likely that he saw his task initially as preventing bloodshed: containing the huge demonstrations while holding back those in the army and police who thought the revolutionary process could still be reversed by force. He relied heavily during this period on the Round Table which was associated with every important decision of government, and indeed nominated a number of ministers. Its members were representatives of the churches who had played so important a role in the revolutionary events of 1989, and of the various citizens' movements. Similar Round Tables operated at regional and communal level—at one stage there were some two thousand of them—and in some parts of the country provided the only effective local administration. Although self-elected they were widely accepted as having greater legitimacy than the SED structures they worked with or leavened. Without them the provinces would have collapsed into anarchy.

6. Later, as the excitement behind the demonstrations began to subside, and the impact of emigration on the economy threatened to become devastating, Modrow made an attempt to regain a degree of control over events by proposing talks on an economic and monetary union of the two Germanies. This could lead to a loose confederation, and from there, after elections in both states, to the establishment of a unitary constitution. His proposal—a response to ideas put forward by Chancellor Kohl—foresaw however the military neutrality of the two Germanies, by implication withdrawal from NATO and the Warsaw pact, 'on the way to federation'. Modrow had evidently cleared this plan with President Gorbachev. In accepting the principle of union, it went further than any previous proposal put forward by an Eastern European state for many years. But it came too late. Emigration remained very high. The general elections which had been planned for May were brought forward to 18 March.

7. Was there never a moment when the SED tried seriously to restore itself to the position it had held for forty years? I see no sign that it did, once Honecker had gone, and Krenz had ordered the opening of the wall. With the breaching of the wall, the genie was out of the bottle. Only a Tiananmen could have put it back. The leadership of the SED was by then split, and knew that it would have no backing from Moscow. It must have felt growing uncertainty about the reliability of the armed forces. The people had lost their fear. As the corruption of the Politburo, and the extent of the State Security's network of informers became known, the SED lost the support of many of its rank and file members. It lost at the same time a sense of certainty of its own legitimacy, and any serious will to rule.

8. The elections of 18 March were the first in this part of Germany for over sixty years in which neither intimidation, pressure nor electoral fraud played any part. After forty years in power, the SED's successor, the PDS, secured only 16% of the vote. The SPD, although expected to do well, secured only 22%. The clear winners were the conservatives: the CDU and their friends in Democratic Awakening (DA) and DSU, who between them won 48%. The left-wing citizens' groups who had generated the movement which unseated the SED, and played an important role in the Round Tables, received no gratitude; they did very poorly. The CDU, like the Farmers' and Liberal parties, was one of the so-called block parties, which many supposed discredited by their association with the SED in the GDR's parliament. But this played no role. The CDU stood for union with the Federal Republic and the Deutschmark. It was Chancellor Kohl's party. Union and the Deutschmark were what the electorate wanted and they voted accordingly. After the elections, the question was no longer whether unity, or even what sort of unity, but when?

9. The government which emerged in mid-April was a coalition under Lothar de Maizière, dominated by the CDU, but containing an important minority from the SPD, and two Liberal ministers. In its early days, there was idealism and an evident willingness to put party considerations second. The coalition parties, aware that they were elected to pursue the common goal of union, all pointed in the same direction and set to work with a will.

10. De Maizière presented his government's programme on 19 April. It did not foresee a specific date for unity, saying only that unity must come as soon as possible, but the conditions of unity must be as good as necessary. Underlying this formulation was the received view that time was needed to master the many problems associated with changing from a command economy to a market system, and to prepare the people of the GDR for life in the Federal Republic. This mood

changed in June. The grass roots made their feelings felt. I believe that the possibility of advantage for Chancellor Kohl in the Federal general election also began to play a role. In mid-June de Maizière speaking for his party proposed that the elections to be held in the Federal Republic on 2 December should be all-German ones, and that the two Germanies should unite at that time. Elections for the governments of the *Länder* would be brought forward to mid-October. No significant party in the *Volkskammer* opposed the principle of unity or this broad timetable. The devil proved to be in the detail, since whether the elections were held a day before unity, or a day after, and the precise ground rules applied, gave one or another party electoral advantage.

11. The timetable was accordingly sharply debated, until Maizière proposed in August that all-German elections should be brought forward to 14 October. He told me at the time that it was a decision which he had reached reluctantly. It sat uneasily with Germany's commitments to her partners in the 2 + 4 talks and CSCE, but a stocktaking of the economic and financial position of the GDR had shown that the country would have great difficulty in holding together beyond October. That was no doubt true, though considerations of electoral advantage may also have played a role. I have no doubt that, had Gorbachev not given when he did, we should have been faced with the prospect of a dangerous tension between the issues requiring settlement in the 2 + 4 talks and events on the ground, for in handing to the Federal Republic the running of the economy, problems had been created of a magnitude and nature such that only the Federal Republic could solve them.

12. German economic, monetary and social union came into full effect on 1 July with the substitution of the Deutschmark for the Ostmark. The other main elements, on which work had started earlier were the adoption of the laws necessary to establish a market economy and social system (in essence the laws of the Federal Republic); and the privatisation of GDR firms, hitherto 'people's property'. Ownership of some 8,000 people's businesses was vested in an organisation specially set up for the purpose, the *Treuhandanstalt* or trustee agency.

13. The *Volkskammer* put through what should have been years of work in a matter of weeks, and the legal framework was established with extraordinary speed. The mechanical aspects of the introduction of the *Deutschmark* also went very smoothly, and received a warm popular welcome. While the general rate of exchange was 1 to 2 (1 to 3 for foreigners), personal accounts could be exchanged up to a limit corresponding to the average of family savings at the very generous rate of 1 for 1. Families who had saved for an East German Trabant or Wartburg found themselves able to buy a nearly new West German vehicle of a far higher standard, or, if they were wiser, to invest in small businesses of a sort which had not existed in the GDR for nearly 20 years.

14. But if the introduction of the *Deutschmark* had welcome consequences for family savings, the impact on industry was very different. There were several reasons. The real value of the *Ostmark* in terms of commodities exchangeable internationally was much lower than that of the *Deutschmark*. GDR goods were saleable in *Deutschmark*—if at all—at perhaps a quarter of their previous price in East Marks. Wages were however payable in Deutschmark at the earlier rates. Debt was halved in face value, but increased in real value. Customers in Eastern Europe were unable to pay in *Deutschmarks* and stayed away. Such was the demand for goods from West Germany that many shops started to draw most of

their supplies from there, and sales and production of East German goods went into a sharp decline. Many firms were able to pay wages only by borrowing money which they had little immediate prospect of paying back. Unemployment in its various guises has risen from a negligible figure to some two million. Agriculture was as much affected as industry, though it has been stabilised for the moment by very large sales to the Soviet Union supported by the Federal Republic. There seems little doubt that next year 30% of the total workforce will be unemployed or on part-time.

15. All this was not unexpected, but it had been supposed that capital would move in quickly from the Federal Republic and elsewhere and save the day. This has not happened. The *Treuhandanstalt* was not initially up to its task. The calculation of asset values proved extraordinarily difficult, since calculating the return on an investment or putting a value on a product is not the purpose of accounting in a command economy, and accountants and managers trained in the GDR system found it almost impossible to communicate with colleagues trained in a market economy. Above all, until the Treaty of Union enshrined the principle that an investor would be protected, there was no certainty that real estate purchased might not be the subject of claims by owners expropriated many years before. (There is now a provision that such claimants will be compensated by the state.)

16. The last two months to unity have been curiously dispiriting and thankless, and will have earned politicians in the GDR no public respect: the prolonged rows between the CDU and SPD over the electoral law, the terms of the unity treaty, and much else besides, were seen by the public as unappealing squabbles for electoral advantage. Revelations of the past Stasi connections of several of its members discredited the *Volkskammer* as a whole, and cast a dark shadow over several ministers. De Maizière found it necessary moreover to sack the Ministers of the Economy, Finance and Agriculture for incompetence. The sacking of the latter two, who had been nominated by the SPD, led to the final disintegration of the coalition in August. But by then the government had done its work. There were last minute skirmishes over the Treaty of Union, but even the collapse of the coalition could not prevent its adoption by comfortably more than the two thirds majority necessary.

17. This account may give the impression of a tattered, incompetent, even disreputable political establishment. That would be unfair. An abiding impression of the summer has been of the speed and flexibility with which German politicians in both East and West were able to defuse so many burning issues, even after many hard words had been spoken on each side. East German politicians played a full part. De Maizière himself, Frau Bergmann-Pohl as President of the *Volkskammer*, and several other GDR politicians rightly achieved a measure of personal authority and respect. De Maizière's government held the country together and pushed through a legislative programme of daunting size and complexity. The government and *Volkskammer*, despite their inexperience and the strains generated by the prospect of elections in the Federal Republic, transformed the monetary, economic and social systems and hammered out reasonable solutions to a range of acutely sensitive problems: the ownership of property after 40 years of communism, the dissolution of the Stasi and the disposal of its archives, and the creation of the *Länder* to name but a few.

18. The man in the street followed all this with attention but took little interest in the external aspects of unification, and politicians here have not tried to make an

issue of them. Both perhaps realised that the GDR's influence was negligible with the other players in the 2 + 4 talks. The running has been left entirely to the FRG. That said, many feel great concern at the prospect of friction between the German population and the Soviet troops who remain in the GDR in large numbers for another three or four years.

19. So much for the events leading up to the engagement and marriage; what of the dowry? In particular, is the whole apparatus of the old regime really away, or is it just the scorpion's head that has gone, leaving behind in the trousseau a still dangerous body and tail?

20. The Ministry for State Security—the Stasi—was the principal crutch of the SED and it will take East Germans a long time to come to terms with the role it played in society. There were at least 85,000 full time members, and as many again coopted, with over 100,000 reporting to it from time to time. A priest told me that in the small town of 5,000 where he had his parish forty buildings—houses, flats, garages—had been identified as having been in regular use by the Stasi. They operated on a similar scale throughout the GDR. Although they could be heavy-handed with a crowd, the pressures they exercised were generally non-violent. Closing access to decent employment or education were the usual methods of bringing pressure, rather than murder or torture. It sometimes seemed that the collection of information had become an end in itself. Few people had any idea of the full extent of Stasi activity; even within the party many were appalled when they learned of it.

21. As a structure, the Stasi ceased to exist formally in January, when it was disbanded, but it left two particular causes of concern: the men and the records. Some of the men will continue to surface in positions of influence for years to come. There is also concern over stocks of weapons and explosives that are still missing. But the bigger political problem concerns the Stasi's records which cover some 6 million people. The present intention is to keep them to enable victims of the Stasi to be rehabilitated, candidates for high office vetted, and serious evil-doers tracked down, but at the same time to restrict access so that innocent third parties are protected and vendettas avoided.

22. The army and police are not a worry; they are now firmly under Federal control, and their allegiance lay more with the country than with the regime. Few of the military above the rank of major are likely to be taken on by the *Bundeswehr*. The civil service of the GDR will be more of a problem. Firstly, it was enormous, ministries in Berlin being typically two or three times larger than those in Bonn. Tens of thousands will be redundant. Secondly the *Länder* and cities will be obliged to employ large numbers of middle-ranking and junior civil servants from the old era even if the senior ones go. The government commissioner for Neubrandenburg told me in despair that such people were in a position to slow down or frustrate entirely every effort to change things.

23. The judiciary also present a special problem, since many of the GDR's courts were notoriously political, and even those judges who are honest and fair have no knowledge of the laws and legal culture of the Federal Republic. Their inexperience in such fields as contract law will not help the rapid recovery of the economy. And there are far too few of them for a modern law-based society.

24. What political attitudes and culture will East Germany bring to the marriage? How will the East Germans' attitude to authority, to democracy fit into the larger Federal Republic? It seems to me that ordinary people here have taken to democracy like a thirsty duck to water. There is perhaps a less aggressive and

openly disrespectful attitude to authority than one sometimes sees among young people in the Federal Republic, but I see no tendency to accept authority unreasoningly. After nearly sixty years of totalitarian rule, the people of the GDR are thoroughly inoculated against both left and right-wing extremes, although they may have trouble coping with a sudden plunge into such problems of Western society as unemployment, the increase of crime which goes with less control, and larger numbers of foreigners.

25. The negative aspects of the dowry, like the economic problems, should then be manageable. The positive aspects should not be forgotten: an educated population capable of hard work and ready for it, a large area of beautiful, under-settled countryside, a significant addition in coastline, and extensive links to the new markets of Eastern Europe.

26. The GDR has been called the unloved country. The description is not unfair. A certain arrogance towards socialist brother countries left the GDR without close friends in the East. The old leadership's attempts at any cost to secure recognition for the state's separate existence led to contempt and dislike elsewhere. The wall was the abiding image. As the extent of the economic mess has emerged, and the new GDR politicians have shown their inexperience, this contempt has rubbed off from the state to the people, who feel themselves increasingly treated by West Germans especially as second grade. They do not deserve this contempt. In 1953 they were the first of the Eastern European countries to rise against the Soviet yoke. For forty years they did as best they could within a system imposed on them by the presence of very large numbers of Soviet troops, and succeeded for thirty of these years in sustaining an economy which was the most successful in COMECON. Their achievements in sport, literature, theatre and music were of a very high standard. Their breaking of the hold of the SED in 1989 was achieved with courage, yet without bloodshed. And if their politicians have seemed unrealistic and incapable, remember that the realistic and capable were drawn in the past to the SED, the only available outlet for their talents. I have learned to like and respect many of the people I have met in my short stay here.

27. In what mood do the people of the GDR come to unity? As I draft seemingly endless crowds have been moving past, filling the whole of Unter den Linden, going towards the Brandenburg gate and the Reichstag for the ceremony at midnight. There must be several hundred thousand of them, mostly East Berliners. One or two people banter with the police guarding the Embassy, but there is very little noise from the crowd, or open celebration. My impression is one of deep emotion, of contentment mixed with a certain trepidation in the face of the uncertainties ahead. But none of them is looking back.

28. I am sending copies of this despatch to HM Representatives at Bonn, Washington, Paris, Moscow, Vienna, Prague, Warsaw, UKDEL NATO and UKREP Brussels.

I have, etc.,
P.H.C. EYERS

No. 241

Sir C. Mallaby (Bonn) and Mr Eyers (East Berlin) to Mr Hurd

[*WRL 020/20*]

Restricted   BONN/EAST BERLIN, *2 October 1990*

Summary . . . [1]

Sir,

United Germany

1. This despatch gives our joint views from Bonn and East Berlin on the likely nature and aspirations of the united Germany that will be formed tomorrow. A second despatch, from East Berlin, describes the rapid succession of events in the GDR which led to unification.[2]

2. Germany is again in the ascendant. With the scars of 1933-45 still vivid in many memories, this has not surprisingly caused concern in other parts of Europe. Twice bitten, thrice vigilant. Germany's neighbours naturally wonder how far the Germans have really changed since 1945, and whether following unification there will be another shift in the behaviour of a nation that so often has proved volatile. What will sovereign united Germany be like?

How strong will it be?

3. United Germany will not in terms of area be all that large: 138,000 square miles to Britain's 94,000, France's 211,000, and the EC's 871,000. The population will be 79 million, to Britain's 57 and the EC's 325 million. But with low birth rates in east and west Germany, it will on current projections be no larger by 2040 than the 61 million in west Germany today. On the other hand Germany's central location in Europe will give it advantages as divisions across the continent disappear. Speaking last December to his fellow NATO Heads of Government, Lubbers said that the centre of gravity in Europe had moved hundreds of kilometres to the East. He exaggerated, but he had a point.

4. The FRG's GDP may increase in absolute terms by 13% on unification, and as a proportion of the EC total it will rise from 24% to nearly 28%. There will now be an extremely difficult period in east Germany, in social as well as economic affairs. The speed of east Germany's economic development is the major question facing united Germany. There will be a need for very substantial expenditure by the Federal Government. Some estimates point to DM 150 billion in 1991—20 per cent of this year's total FRG public expenditure—and figures approaching that for some years afterwards. Much of this is expected to be raised on the markets—at a time when a worldwide shortage of investment capital is likely to put up interest rates. The Federal Government can afford the bills, though not, as they may now be beginning to admit, without raising taxes. But when one takes into account the other costs of unification—social security payments in east Germany, possibly in excess of DM 60 billion a year in the early stages; Soviet troop withdrawals (DM 13 billion over 4 years); and Allied garrisons in Berlin (we estimate DM 4 to 5 billion over 4 years)—it seems certain that there will be short and possibly medium

---

[1] Not printed.
[2] No. 240.

term strain on public finance. The gentlemanly debate in West Germany about spending priorities will become a battle. Inflation is likely to rise beyond the present west German figure of 3%—which, given special sensitivities in Germany, will be controversial politically.

5. There is a widespread belief that joining the east German to the west German economy will produce an economic miracle in east Germany. Views differ about whether it will take 5, 10 or 15 years. The advantages in this undertaking are west German entrepreneurial and organisational skills, investment resources and know how, and a reasonably well trained east German workforce which ought, after long privation, to have a strong incentive to earn good money. The main difficulties include uncertainty about property ownership in east Germany; inexperienced politicians working through a discredited, ineffective administration; and severe environmental degradation. There will be major unemployment, not only as inefficient businesses are rationalised or closed but also among the enormous civil service—250,000 in East Berlin alone. The awful infrastructure is a big disincentive to investment, but major expenditure on it will be a boost to the east German economy. Half the population draws water from sources polluted by industry and agriculture; nearly all the power stations must in due course be replaced because they pollute appallingly or are based on risky Soviet nuclear technology; and a new start is needed in telecommunications.

6. The problems seem soluble with time and from the start should be partially offset by growth of local businesses, many of them in new service industries. Yet some knowledgeable people worry that, because of attractive investment opportunities elsewhere, primarily in the rest of the Community, the present slow pace of private sector investment in east Germany may not speed up enough; that west Germans will continue to trade into east Germany rather than investing there; and that the west German unions will use the national wage bargaining system to raise wages in east Germany beyond what is sustainable, thus destroying one of the region's competitive advantages.

7. We believe that the economic miracle in east Germany will come. But there is enough in these doubts to suggest that one should not expect it for, say, 5 years at least. When the upswing comes, it may not spread uniformly across east Germany. Patchy infrastructure and environmental degradation, combined with the rigidities of the German labour market as a whole, may leave quite large pockets of persistent unemployment, alongside enclaves of high technology development.

8. OECD projections suggest that the east German economy would have to grow by 8.5% annually to catch west Germany in 15 years. While high rates of growth from the depressed base may be achieved quite soon, a slower rate looks more likely in the longer run. Our guess, and it is no more than that, is that on reasonably favourable assumptions about performance united Germany would by 2020 account for about 30% of EC GNP. It is certainly going to be big in economic terms, but perhaps not all that much bigger than the old FRG would have been on its own. This should not obscure a central fact. Together with its advantages of geography, even its present economic strength will give united Germany potential political weight unique in Europe.

What will United Germany be like?

9. There are still west Germans who are intolerant of non-Germans, and despise them (and many east Germans) for being less industrious and less prosperous. But the west Germans' love affair with overseas tourism has reduced that sort of egotism; and young people are notably internationalist. In west and east German

society as a whole, the lessons of the Nazi era have been absorbed; and in the west there is complete commitment to the Federal Republic's successful system of democracy, decentralised federalism, market economics, social solidarity and the rule of law. The unification of Germany in 1870 was the extension westwards of autocratic, nationalistic, militarist Prussia. The unification in 1990 is the extension eastwards of the democratic, Western, outward-looking Federal Republic. This time united Germany is geographically smaller; and—virtually for the first time in German history—the country has definitive frontiers with which both a vast majority of Germans and the international community are content.

10. There are other important differences from earlier moments of major change in German history. As Kohl is said to be fond of observing privately, his own achievement in unifying Germany benefits by comparison with Bismarck's. Bismarck unified Germany in 1870 by 'blood and iron' or, more accurately, trickery and war; and the empire was declared, on Prussia's defeat of France, in Versailles of all places. Kohl has done it by democracy and the Deutschmark and with international approval. The Weimar Republic was born in Germany's feeling of humiliation in the First World War and in the peace treaty of Versailles. Germany's resentment provided humus for Hitler's rise to power. The FRG, unlike the Weimar Republic, was a genuinely new start. And the new united Germany is an enlargement of the FRG, a respected member of the West, with forty years of political and economic achievement behind it. The Allies' willingness, once the framework of the 2+4 talks had been established, to engage energetically in the process of settling the international framework for unifying the two German states is widely recognised: in contrast to the resentment towards the powers when the Weimar Republic was established.

11. The reaction of the ordinary west German to unification is sober. Some degree of pride, certainly; and among the many older people with relatives in east Germany, much satisfaction. But there has so far been a marked lack of public excitement—no jingoism about unity, and no idealism about the task of developing east Germany; instead a widespread concern in west and east Germany about the economic effects of unity. Many west Germans fear that the successful mould of the old FRG has been cracked, and wonder whether life will still be as comfortable and affluent.

12. The process of unification made clear that, whatever the cosmetic efforts to suggest a merger between equals, the GDR was in fact being swallowed by the FRG. But it will not simply acquire at a stroke all the characteristics of the Federal Republic. Forty years of Communist dictatorship leave many scars. East Germans fear that they may remain second class citizens. Many older people feel that their life's work has been shown to have been in vain, and that it is too late for them to make a contribution. Some knotty problems will have to work themselves through before east Germans can develop the open, self-confident pattern of civic and political culture of west Germany. Nor will the addition of the GDR leave the FRG entirely unchanged. Some intriguing questions remain to be answered. How will the new Protestant majority in the united Germany and its more northern and eastern spread affect its character? Will the attitudes instilled in east Germany by authoritarianism leave united Germany overall with more respect for authority? And will the more provincial—indeed more traditionally German—atmosphere of east Germany vanish in rapid westernisation, or will it leave traces in united Germany? The answers may vary regionally in east Germany, as the new *Länder* there establish their individuality. Given that the west Germans outnumber the east

Germans by four to one and that the east Germans have sought rapid unity precisely because they wanted Western democracy and prosperity, the changes in Germany overall may not be great.

13. In recent years the two main parties in west Germany have been within a few points of each other. One cannot yet say how the incorporation of the GDR will affect this balance. The SPD, which before 1933 was strong in Berlin and southern east Germany, is in disarray. In the GDR's only free election in March 1990 the CDU scored 41% to the SPD's 22%. The CDU looks set to be the biggest party in east (as well as west) Germany in the first general election in united Germany. Incipient prosperity and the growth of a new middle class may further strengthen the CDU and the FDP in east Germany. But many workers who so far have supported the CDU as the party most likely to bring early unity may move to the SPD, which may also benefit from decline of the neo-Communist PDS. Given the fine political balance in west Germany, swings in east Germany could be significant in individual national elections. Grand Coalitions of the CDU and SPD may prove common in the east German *Länder* and could possibly gain greater acceptability in the west. But the high proportion of west German politicians and voters in the new system means that the overall balance of the party political landscape is unlikely to change substantially. As for right-wing extremism, the Republikaner have fallen back in west Germany in 1990 as suddenly as they appeared in 1989. In east Germany a fringe right wing movement may appear. But on present evidence there is no reason to expect right wing extremism to be a significant force in united Germany.

External Orientation

14. The old Federal Republic benefited enormously from membership of NATO. It enjoyed security for forty years, during which freedom and prosperity could flourish; and those factors were important in now bringing unification. Kohl, Genscher and President von Weizsäcker consistently preach the gospel of Western alignment. Asked recently what he expected to be the hallmarks of united Germany's foreign policy, Genscher replied that there would be no change. There would still be a high priority for European unification, and for the need to adapt NATO and east-west relations to take account of the end of the Cold War. Kohl's line is much the same, with the gloss that he often gives pride of place to US/European relations, as expressed through NATO, the CSCE and EC/US cooperation. These remarks can be taken at face value. The SPD agrees that Western orientation should continue.

15. In a speech in May 1989 President Bush, in a remark which caused great satisfaction here, described the United States and the Federal Republic as partners in leadership. Since then the US and FRG have worked in close harmony in the negotiations concerning unification. But it may be increasingly difficult to avoid bilateral friction over important subjects—the future of NATO and of US forces in Germany, German/Soviet cooperation, and the American expectation of a greater German contribution in defence of Western interests outside the NATO area. These matters are discussed below. But two points should be noted here. If the present Gulf crisis turns into a war, American relations with united Germany may start with a bout of recrimination. Secondly, Germany will seek to maintain a fundamentally close relationship with the United States, but the difficulties on the horizon could strain that relationship seriously.

16. We expect great assertiveness in German foreign policy. There were signs of this before unification appeared on the agenda and the Germans displayed

insensitive high handedness over some points in the 2+4 negotiations. With the national question solved and full sovereignty restored, Germany will expect to pursue its own interests without the rather deliberate restraint that was normal until a few years back. At first there may be some residual restraint, out of fear that others would be quick to accuse the Germans of throwing their weight about now that they are unified. But that will pass. German interests will be pursued by peaceful and legitimate methods, but strongly, in the consciousness of German economic and political weight. Genscher talks openly of a greater German role. He and Kohl have reacted cautiously to a recent Soviet ploy of suggesting that Germany should become the sixth permanent member of the UN Security Council. But it will be surprising if Germans do not in due course warm to the idea.

NATO and CSCE

17. The Alliance has usually commanded strong majority support in west German public opinion. That support actually increased in 1990—perhaps because in times of change one clings anew to familiar arrangements. The achievement of the West in the 2+4 negotiations of bringing the Soviet Union to accept united Germany's membership of NATO is a matter of general satisfaction in west Germany. With coalitions led by the CDU/CSU, Germany will not waver for the foreseeable future in holding to Alliance membership.

18. But there may be changes in German public opinion, and altered policies within the Alliance—or even, under an SPD-led government, major changes of policy which could bring Alliance membership into question. The great debate in west Germany in the early eighties about intermediate range nuclear forces confirmed that there is a trend in public opinion, at times a strong one, which opposes nuclear weapons, dislikes foreign forces in Germany and distrusts the American connection. This is significant in the SPD, which already stands for the removal of nuclear weapons from all of Germany. In east Germany the political orthodoxy since the fall of Honecker is pacifist, anti-nuclear and distrustful of NATO. The vast majority there want to get rid of all foreign forces in Germany. Partly this is the influence of the churches, which have become a major force in east German affairs. Partly it reflects the fact that during the past forty years the Soviet forces and the Warsaw pact embodied alien hegemony; east Germans have not realised yet that the Americans and NATO are really different.

19. Part of the price we paid for Soviet acceptance that united Germany would be in NATO was a special military status for east Germany within NATO. The key points, for the evolution of public attitudes to defence in united Germany, are that in east Germany there will be no nuclear weapons and no stationed foreign forces after 1994. If there is tranquillity, without crises, in Europe for some years, and especially if crises elsewhere involving the West are few, more and more people in west Germany may cry 'me too' and call for east Germany's security status to be extended to all Germany. These three factors—anti-nuclear feelings in west Germany, east German antimilitarism and east Germany's special status—could combust in a few years' time, conceivably sooner, in an all-German movement to get rid of nuclear weapons and foreign forces, and to question Alliance membership and indeed the need for the Alliance in a peaceful Europe. At the least the costs of defence—aircraft noise and army exercises as well as budgetary—will be increasingly unpopular in west Germany, and that will add to the difficulties for us in maintaining forces here.

20. Germans see increasing attractions in the further development of the CSCE process. For the left in west Germany and for many people in east Germany, CSCE

holds out the prospect of moving in the direction of a demilitarised Europe. In due course, the idea of CSCE becoming an all-European security system and replacing NATO—already one of the SPD's aims for the future—may well be taken really seriously in Germany. It is also likely that the theme of defence cooperation among west Europeans, in the EC or WEU, will receive increasing attention.

The Wider World

21. The growing assertiveness of German foreign policy will be felt in parts of the wider world, especially those where German industry wants to invest. But the controversial issue under this heading—whether German forces should be deployed in time of crisis outside the NATO area—will paradoxically be one on which Germany's friends may want it to move faster than it wishes.

22. Kohl said recently that if Germany wanted to be number one in Europe, its response to international crises would have to be less muted than currently in the Gulf. Nobody in Germany would dream of the country sending troops abroad save in good international company. To end the long-standing debate about whether the constitution allows military deployment outside the NATO area, there is general agreement that it should be amended after unification, so as to allow explicitly German participation in operations authorised by the UN. That would mean that, for the time being at least, other types of operation were definitely excluded. German public opinion is likely to remain reluctant about deployments beyond the NATO area. That is partly because of distaste for risks and for military entanglement; partly because of the feeling, still present here, that Germans, with their past, should not court accusations of interference. In cases where Israel would not welcome German involvement, Germany will be especially cautious: Israeli accusations that anti-semitism was reappearing would be painful even though unjustified. The outcome of this debate, and the use made in the coming years of any new latitude to deploy forces, will be the main indicator of the willingness of united Germany to take responsibility as well as seeking economic power and political influence.

European Community

23. Unlike NATO, which the FRG joined after its foundation, the EC was influenced from the start by Germany. Along with the special relationship with France bequeathed by Adenauer and de Gaulle, the Community is seen as a fixed and permanent feature of the Federal Republic's foreign policy, and essential to the way forward in Europe. Public support for European Union—undefined—is strong. All the major political parties advocate it. And even without that factor, the hard headed arguments of economic self-interest would continue to ensure a full German commitment to the EC. There is no reason to expect east Germans to question any of this; indeed they see the EC as a means of avoiding a purely west German takeover of east Germany and as a way of escaping from decades of unnatural isolation.

24. Britain has an interest in keeping Germany embedded in a close Western framework. Many Germans, conscious of the past, favour European integration for that reason. The EC, where German interests and active involvement are certain to endure, is an essential part of such a framework. The Federal Republic before unification already had the largest economy in the Community and did not dominate it. It should be possible to devise policies for handling the phenomenon of united Germany in the Community.

25. The division of Germany was a major reason for west German enthusiasm for the European cause. With national identity ruptured, and terribly stained by the

Nazi past, idealism focused on Europe. With German identity restored, will it survive? Or will concentration, perhaps obsessive, on the need to knit united Germany properly together and develop the east German economy distract German attention to such an extent that further integration in—as distinct from maintenance of—the Community assumes a lower priority than hitherto?

26. Germans are aware that they are being watched, above all by the French, for signs of backsliding. Partly with this in mind Genscher has intensified, in the context of German unification, his calls for speed in achieving European Monetary Union. But he also believes that further deepening of the Community now is desirable in its own right and sees EMU as the next major step in building Europe. On the other side of the debate on EMU are the voices of caution—the Bundesbank, the Finance Ministry and the financial and business community— who accept the goal but urge thorough preparation and no haste. Kohl wants to make progress in building Europe, wants to avoid offending France and yet sees the need for caution on EMU. He is likely to maintain the goal but moderate the speed. It is possible that preoccupation with the development of east Germany will tend to strengthen the advocates of caution about EMU, who already have gained ground as the inter-governmental conference approaches, and add to Kohl's scope for blocking undue haste.

27. The overall German attitude to the Community is likely to reflect many of the considerations that apply to EMU. The desire to make progress towards European union will be in tension on many points with the practical arguments. Preoccupation with German affairs may mean that the idealism becomes less potent in this dialectic. But the Germans will want to continue to deepen the Community, while foreseeing after 1992 the possibility of further enlargement.

Russia and Eastern Europe

28. Germany, in the centre of Europe, has sometimes looked east rather than west. Austen Chamberlain, writing as Foreign Secretary to his French colleague in 1927, said that Britain and France were 'engaged in a struggle with Soviet Russia for the soul of Germany'. Then came the Stalin-Hitler pact; but after that Hitler's attack on the Soviet Union. For the past forty years divided Germany has looked both ways: west Germany has been embedded willingly in the West and has derived great benefit thereby; east Germany has been an unwilling satellite of the Soviet Union and has suffered greatly.

29. Germany was Russia's leading trading partner long before the Soviet Revolution. By the early 1970s the FRG had established itself as the most important Western trading partner for each of the CMEA countries. But such trade accounted for only 3.4% of the FRG's total trade before unification, as against 53.3% with the EC. Nonetheless united Germany is particularly well-placed, in its location, the areas of west German technical expertise, the experience of west German companies and the many eastern links inherited from the GDR, to extend greatly its lead in trade with the east. We expect much greater investment and involvement (but not territorial expansion) in eastern Europe and very probably in Russia to be the major new feature of German foreign policy, especially after the development of east Germany has been achieved.

30. Germany's western orientation will thus be supplemented by strong eastern links. There is a strong wish to develop further the new accommodation with Russia. We have recently seen Genscher take particular pains to anticipate, as well as to respond to, Soviet wishes. The Germans are likely to play up even more than recently the progress in and warmth of German-Russian relations. Public

satisfaction at this in Germany may play back into tendencies, foreseen above, to raise new questions about defence.

31. There will also be a drive in Germany to improve relations with the countries of Eastern Europe. This will be seen here as a contribution to uniting Europe—a contribution Germany owes since the breaking of barriers in Europe made German unification possible. We expect a special effort to achieve a full reconciliation with Poland. Germany's final acceptance of the Oder-Neisse frontier looks like a good basis. But in fact there are serious difficulties. Berlin is but 40 miles from Poland and Poles are not popular in east Germany. Will economic progress in east Germany create a new dividing line in Europe on the Oder-Neisse? Will poverty and social crisis east of that line cause massive emigration into Germany and the EC, not only from Poland but also other countries including Russia? Will there be a burst of resentment in Germany against Polish and other refugees? Will Germany and the EC have to erect a visa curtain against the east?

Conclusion

32. The Federal Republic, determined to avoid anything smacking of the Hitler period, sought for decades a low key role on the international stage. Recently there has been more self-assertiveness. The regaining of unity and sovereignty will be felt by many Germans as marking the end of nearly 50 years of post-War penance; they will feel that Germany's democracy and economic strength give it a right to assert its interests and views. The trend to assertiveness will strengthen.

33. Germany can confidently be expected to remain a strong democracy, rooted in the West and the EC as the foundations of its foreign policy. That orientation will probably be supplemented by increasing involvement in eastern Europe and further development of the relationship with Russia. United Germany is happy to begin its life in NATO, and the present coalition, likely to be re-elected in December 1990, will continue to support the Alliance. But, if Europe is tranquil, we must expect increasing public questioning of the need for the burdens of defence and possibly for the Alliance itself. There is no reason to expect reversion to the behaviour which caused two world wars. Our German ally and partner will be much more difficult but not dangerous to deal with. We shall need in particular to watch out for interaction between greater German assertiveness and pressure from German public opinion over defence policy, which could pose serious problems. Across the board united Germany will be a factor of the first importance in our foreign relations. A further despatch from Bonn will discuss the implications for our policies, in multilateral organisations and bilaterally.

34. Copies of this despatch go to the Chancellor of the Exchequer, the Secretaries of State for Defence and for Trade and Industry, and the Secretary to the Cabinet; to HM Representatives in NATO, EC and Eastern European posts, Moscow, Vienna and New York (UKMIS); and to other posts in the Federal Republic.

We are, Sir,
Yours faithfully
C.L.G. Mallaby
P.H.C. Eyers

No. 242

Letter from Sir C. Mallaby (Bonn) to Mr Weston[1]

[*WRG 020/10*]

Confidential and Personal   BONN, *11 October 1990*

Dear John,

German Unification: Perceptions of the UK

1. My telegrams 1271 and 1274[2] reported the positive side of the way in which the UK was viewed here in connection with the events surrounding German unification. The expressions of thanks to us, like the farewell ceremonies for the Allies in Berlin on 2 October, were sincerely meant and therefore gratifying. But there is also a darker side to the story of Britain and unification, which needs to be kept in focus as we tackle the task of building up our relationship with and influence in united Germany.

2. The background you know well enough: the Prime Minister's evident reluctance between November 1989 and February 1990 about German unification; her interview in *Der Spiegel* shortly before the bilateral summit in London in March; the Ridley affair; and the leaking of Charles Powell's account of the Chequers seminar. The cumulative effect of these episodes has been to create a widespread assumption here that the Prime Minister is essentially hostile to unification. This assumption is now strong enough to cause many German observers to react sceptically to any positive statement by Mrs Thatcher in connection with unification; to give exaggerated publicity to negative comments that are attributed to her (for instance the interview on US television on 1 October when she said that Germany must not dominate in the EC); and to see her hand at work (cf the 2+4 end game) on points on which she has not focused at all. Another effect is to undervalue—on the thesis that what the Prime Minister thinks is the only thing that really matters—the significance of supportive remarks about unification by other leading members of the British Government. Britain's helpful

---

[1] Copied to HM Ambassadors: Washington, Paris, UKREP Brussels, UKDEL NATO.

[2] In telegram No. 1271 of 4 October Sir C. Mallaby reported 'a happy but sober mood in the public celebrations of unification in Berlin' and summarised President von Weizsäcker's speech at the official ceremony on 3 October. He continued: 'During the reception following the ceremony, I was approached by Weizsäcker, Rühe, Lambsdorff, Vogel, Lafontaine and about a dozen Cabinet Ministers keen to express thanks for the British role as a protecting power in Berlin and in Two plus Four. The general mood of the politicians was one of great satisfaction. There was also much discussion of tasks ahead in East Germany and a preoccupation that united Germany must show that it would conduct a responsible foreign policy and that it did not wish to be a great power but a part of the EC and an undivided Europe.' Telegram No. 1274 of 4 October reported German media coverage of the celebrations: 'There are many detailed analyses of the role of the Western Allies in Berlin, picking up comments such as that by Willy Brandt—that the Allies long ago came to be regarded as friends rather than occupying forces. The French are described as having led the Federal Republic into the European Community, and the British as having brought them into the NATO Alliance. All 3 Allies are described as having taught the Germans democracy again. The farewell ceremonies involving the Allied commandants in Berlin are detailed and full of warmth and nostalgia' (WRL 020/20).

role in 2+4 itself is also obscured, not least of course because the details are not public.

3. We fared, on a superficial analysis, well enough on 3-4 October. The tributes to the three allies were in some cases shared out equally—e.g. in von Weizsäcker's address to the nation on 3 October. Kohl did the same in his article for the *Frankfurter Allgemeine* of 2/3 October, and both in his television address of 2 October and his speech in the *Bundestag* on 4 October he put us equal with France, albeit behind the US. As reported in my telno 1274,[3] the messages sent by the Queen, the Prime Minister and the Secretary of State were prominently reported by the media, as were the Prime Minister's comments when she received Kohl's message from the German Ambassador. (To the extent that we suffered by comparison with others, it was self-inflicted. German television carried warm filmed messages from Bush and Mitterrand, whereas the Prime Minister had decided not to provide one.)

4. But that relatively favourable picture is confined to the time of unification itself. When over the past year von Weizsäcker, Kohl and Genscher have on various occasions paid tribute to the role played by Germany's three main allies in helping unification, it has been normal for us to get, as it were, the bronze medal. The United States has invariably been awarded the gold, and France—for all Mitterrand's occasionally apparent doubts about unification—the silver. The tone of the references to the UK has usually been civil. But on one occasion—Genscher's press conference in Bonn on 14 September following his return from Moscow—the bronze awarded to us for our 'cooperation' was accompanied by an ironic commentary that was taken to be dismissive. This tone—of implying that Britain is much less important as well as less helpful than the others—has sometimes been implicit in other comments.

5. You may have seen the reference in the *I[nternational]H[erald]T[ribune]* of 3 October to [Ralf] Dahrendorf's comment that Germany now has two special relationships, with Washington and Moscow, 'with Britain and France disappearing somewhere'.[4] That could become largely true before long, but exaggerates the weakness of the French position. While the French image in German eyes is currently not without its problems, France is still very much in the middle of the German radar screen, whereas we are near the edge and in danger of fading further. The Franco-German partnership continues to be trumpeted as the motor in the drive for 'European Union'. Because of that special partnership, the known but largely private doubts of France about unification are not played up. Partly because of the perceived demerits of our own European policy, the cost of highlighting our doubts is not considered great.

6. We do have assets in our relationship with Germany. Our democratic tradition and the Royal Family are greatly admired. We are a major trade and investment partner of Germany. Our role in Berlin over 45 years is seen with gratitude. The Secretary of State has won repeated plaudits from Genscher and from the media here for his overall skill and his positive attitude to German unification. Sir Geoffrey Howe's recent speech in Stuttgart also was widely welcomed.[5] But German attention continues to focus principally on the views of the Prime Minster herself. The suspicion at the heart of her attitude to unification is

---

[3] See note 2.

[4] Not found.

[5] Sir G. Howe visited Stuttgart, Frankfurt and Mannheim between 9 and 11 September. His speech was given to the British Chamber of Commerce in Frankfurt on 10 September (WRG 026/1).

resented by top politicians here. And her rejection of the view, widely held here, that further progress in European integration is the way to prevent any risk of German domination in Europe both baffles many Germans (see for instance Schmidt's article in *The Times* of 2 October) and is itself instrumental in widening the gap between their strategic approach and ours.[6] The result is further to diminish our influence in Germany just at the time when for unavoidable reasons—the end of QRRs and the reduction in our forces here—we have lost some of our special advantages.

7. So we need to do all we can to improve our visibility and standing in this tremendously important country. There is no quick fix. You will have seen the Bonn/East Berlin despatch of 2 October on united Germany.[7] I shall be sending a companion piece on British-German relations in which I shall make recommendations.[8] Against the background I have just described, I very much hope it will be possible to give them priority in the competition for resources and Ministerial time.

Yours ever,
C.L.G. MALLABY

[6] Not found.
[7] No. 241.
[8] No. 244.

No. 243

Letter from Sir C. Mallaby (Bonn) to Mr Weston

[*WRL 020/12*]

Restricted   BONN, *12 October 1990*

Dear John,

Kastrup on German Unification

1. I should report briefly that Dieter Kastrup took me out to lunch on 11 October, in order to say thank you for the British role in 2+4 and the approach to German unification. He began by saying that unification could not have been achieved without the help and the creative contribution of the western allies, including the British. He greatly regretted the press stories in Germany about differences between the British and the Federal Germans during the last 2+4 in Moscow. Those reports had been untrue (*sic*) and gave very regrettably the impression that the British had been less helpful than the other allies. Your personal letter to Kastrup after the Moscow meeting had touched him; he had been very grateful. I said that I was glad that he recognised that the British role in 2+4 had been creative. One example was the idea of suspending QRRs, pending entry into force of the final settlement; that suggestion had started in this Embassy. Kastrup said that he knew this and had made sure that Genscher knew it too.

2. Kastrup said that there were 4 main reasons for the success of 2+4:

—solidarity in the negotiations among the western 4, which had impressed the Russians;

—the creativity of the western 4, notably in NATO's London declaration;

—western willingness to develop CSCE, as a stage on which the Soviet Union could continue to play a wide international role;

—the obligations willingly entered into by Germany on the eastern frontier, nuclear and other weapons of mass destruction and the size of the *Bundeswehr*.

Yours ever,
C.L.G. MALLABY

No. 244

Sir C. Mallaby (Bonn) to Mr Hurd

[*WRG 020/5*]

Restricted   BONN, *30 November 1990*

United Germany: The Implications for British Policies

Summary ... [1]

Sir,

United Germany: The Implications for British Policies

1. The joint despatch from Bonn and East Berlin of 2 October argued that the united Germany would have potential political weight unique in Europe and be a factor of the first importance in our foreign relations.[2] It is essential that we should use to the full our ability to influence Germany on the multilateral and bilateral levels. This despatch suggests how.

Our Assets; and how the Germans see us

2. Britain has important assets in dealing with Germany. Our foreign policy is recognised as serious and global. We are known to have influence in Washington and to have played an active role recently in East-West relations. We are seen as a significant element in European affairs, and Germans want us to participate actively in the Community. The Royal Family is a focus of deep admiration and interest here. Our language is Germany's first foreign language and our culture is sought after. Most of all, the strength and length of our democratic tradition and our political stability are respected, indeed envied. The Germans admire what they see as the essentially 'civilised' quality of British public life, contrasting this with their own failure in the past to transpose their cultural and intellectual achievements into political morality. There are many anglophiles in key positions in German public life. Many Germans—just over 2 million in 1989—have visited the UK.

3. There is a close network of consultation between the two governments, and working relations are natural and easy. We shall remain an important ally of Germany, even when British Forces in western Germany have been approximately halved; we shall also keep a military presence in Berlin for a time. The United Kingdom and Germany are major trading partners: the UK is west Germany's third largest export market, and west Germany our second (12% of our exports in 1989).

---

[1] Not printed.
[2] No. 241.

Over 1000 companies from each country have subsidiaries and other investments in the other. Some £1.5 billion of German investment came into Britain in 1989 alone, making Britain Germany's favourite investment location in Europe.

4. So we are known and liked in Germany. Yet if we are to exert serious influence we also need to be considered important. That is where we have work to do. There has long been a tendency here to underrate Britain's importance to Germany, exemplified by the sobriquet 'The Quiet Alliance' for the bilateral relationship. Although people directly concerned with unification know that we played a constructive role in the 2+4 negotiations, the public impression is that we were reluctant, at least in the early stages last winter, about unification. Our European policy has for some time been the focus of much scepticism. So we have ceased to be at the centre of the German radar screen. And now we have lost our Four Power status and reductions are planned in British Forces Germany. Germany sees its most important partners as the US and France; and its priorities for improving relations are the Soviet Union and Poland. We risk falling back further unless we can demonstrate to the Germans that our policies and assets, bilaterally and in the wider international setting, are important and must be taken seriously.

5. Wherever possible we should seek to make policy with the Germans. This requires that we identify areas of policy where we can make a sustained effort to get alongside them and influence their thinking. Where we can identify interest groups in Germany with whom we share ground—as we do for example with many in industry and banking over our realistic and deregulative approach to specific EC issues—we should exploit that shared ground. Where we cannot agree with the Germans, however, we should seek to show that our ideas enjoy substantial support elsewhere in Europe and/or in Washington.

6. Three areas of policy will be particularly important:

(*a*) the future of the EC;

(*b*) the future of European security;

(*c*) cooperation with eastern Europe and the Soviet Union.

European Community

7. Kohl and Genscher believe that they share with France, the Benelux countries, Italy and Spain an active commitment to the ever closer union foreseen in the EC Treaty. They will continue to see Germany's partnership with France as the motor that should move the Community towards that goal. The Germans know that the British approach is different; that we look at proposals for new steps in the Community on their merits and insist on maintaining a strong role for sovereign states. The widespread view in Germany, however, is that there is a consensus among most members of the EC on the desirability on principle of further major strides in integration, and that Britain will therefore not be able to make its objections stick and in the end will accept major changes. There is thus a tendency to believe that our positions need not be taken too seriously.

8. Despite the differences between us and the Germans on future steps in the Community, we cannot ignore that the EC offers an important means for embedding Germany in the West and ensuring that it acts with others rather than alone. The single step which would most enhance our standing in Germany would be to make our policies in the Community more positive, in presentation and where possible in content. If we could make our overall style sound more constructive, if we could more frequently advance positive ideas of our own, the Germans would take our views much more seriously. Already there are major areas of British-German cooperation. The single market has been an important one: we and they

have been able to forge alliances on specific issues against the more protectionist member states, especially France and Italy. But that vein is being mined out, leaving tricky issues in the single market (tax harmonisation, social policy, frontier controls etc) where we and the Germans may increasingly be at odds. And the major areas to which the Community's efforts are now turning—above all EMU but also institutional development—are ones where we and the Germans have different views.

9. Our hard ECU initiative is an example of the kind of British proposal that is tactically valuable in Germany. It demonstrates our seriousness about monetary cooperation and cuts off the reproach, which otherwise would come, that we are negative about the whole project of EMU. In speeches explaining our proposal, I have received a friendly hearing from bankers and businessmen not directly involved in making policy on EMU. The Federal Government and the Bundesbank, however, do not agree with our proposal because they are happy with the predominant position of the *Deutschmark* and because it is an axiom here that a parallel currency, or split management of currency, can be inflationary.

10. On EMU, we should continue to argue for an approach which builds on experience and takes full account of the need for economic convergence, seeking arguments that will appeal to the private sector here, which is more cautious than the Government. The more the private sector, and its sympathisers in the CDU/CSU and the FDP, become advocates of gradual progress, the harder it is for the Federal Government to rush ahead. We should also continue to cultivate an alliance with the Bundesbank, because it favours proper attention to the difficult substance, rather than the easy European rhetoric, of EMU; though it also accepts the goal of EMU as defined in the Delors Report[3] and, as a condition of this, is wedded to the full independence of a European Central Bank as the instrument of monetary management. If we could display some willingness to move eventually to the overall goal of EMU, should experience meanwhile with increased cooperation on monetary affairs show it to be desirable, our proposals for increased cooperation in the nearer term would carry greater weight in Germany. If we could go further, and propose ways of achieving price stability under EMU, we would be listened to all the more attentively in Germany.

11. In the inter-governmental conference on institutional reform the Germans do not expect a great leap towards European union. But they do want some significant steps, including a number which we oppose. We should put forward our own ideas with full supporting arguments, energetically and conspicuously. We should talk closely to the Germans on that basis—not only the Government but also members of Parliament and representatives of the *Länder* whose interests might be prejudiced by some of the ideas for institutional reform under discussion in the inter-governmental conference. I suggest that we should not engage in a debate with the Germans about sovereignty and the nature of any future European union. Public opinion here feels that European union should involve a much lesser role for sovereign states and is critical of our insistence on their importance. And were the Germans, against present trends, to start insisting on their own sovereign independence of action, they would become harder than now to live with.

12. We may be able to find common ground with the Germans in the debate about widening and deepening of the Community. The problem here is that they suspect that we support further enlargement of the EC in order to frustrate future

---

[3] See No. 29, note 1.

moves towards European union. But we can play on their idealism about Europe, their affinity with Austria and their yearning for reconciliation with Poland and Czechoslovakia—not to speak of the Community's instant enlargement for the sake of east Germany—to make it hard for the Germans to oppose further accessions in the period after 1992. We should recognise however that enlargement will not detach the Germans from the aspiration of European union and could in due course raise more sharply the issue of a Europe proceeding at several speeds.

13. More generally, when the Germans are difficult and assertive in Community affairs, we should look for allies against them, issue by issue, assembling ad hoc coalitions or encouraging others to do so. When it suits us, we should do deals with the Germans, as we did in 1990 over life insurance. When they are pursuing unacceptable policies we should use the powers and disciplines of the Community, notably competition policy and, if necessary, the Court to advance our interests: the way the proposed German lorry tax was hindered.

European Security

14. As argued in the companion despatch, Germany is less certain to remain a keen member of NATO than of the Community. There is a risk of a debate here about the nuclear element in western defence, foreign forces stationed in Germany and indeed the need for the Alliance itself. We should do everything possible now to maximise the chance that public opinion here will continue to support policies that we consider sound.

15. The reforms of the Alliance that are in hand are a major help. Another key lies in the proposal of multi-national forces in the Alliance. If we can banish the concept of stationed or foreign forces in Germany, and talk only of multinational forces consisting of German and other Allies' units, public support for the presence here of the foreign elements should have more chance of lasting. If German generals have a fair and visible share of the command positions, that will help. If the multinational forces are stationed not only in Germany but also some other European countries of the Alliance, that will be even better in this regard.

16. More broadly, the Germans are being pulled in different directions over defence and security issues. The present coalition wants to maintain the Alliance and the American role in the security of Europe. It wants to bring France back towards involvement in Western defence. It sees the need to develop a European identity in the field of security. And it wants to develop CSCE as the broad forum in which the Soviet Union, or Russia, and the countries of central and eastern Europe can find roles on the stage of European security. Genscher wants a European pillar to be developed within the reformed Alliance, not outside it. I think that the idea of developing that pillar by means of making WEU the European pillar of the Alliance has a good chance of securing German support, especially if France could be persuaded to cooperate to some extent. That would then leave scope for progress in cooperation on broader, non-military security matters among the members of the European Community and also for developing CSCE. German interest in this approach could be considerable, since it may be the only way of keeping the American involvement in European security yet building cooperation with the French. If an arrangement of this kind came into being, it should gain popular approval in Germany, and public support for the reformed Alliance should have a greater chance of lasting through the years. The nuclear element in Western defence, especially the presence of nuclear weapons in west Germany, would remain the aspect most likely to become highly controversial.

Cooperation with the Soviet Union and Eastern Europe

17. We should also seek to influence Germany over relations with other parts of the world. This will become increasingly important as Germany's self-assertiveness increases. Cooperation with the Soviet Union and eastern Europe is by far the most important field, for that is the big growth area of Germany's foreign policy. Few things will do more to enhance our stature here than if we can maintain and develop our position as one of the major players in promoting cooperation between the two halves of Europe, especially if we are prepared to work with Germany. Following their bilateral summit in September, Germany and France are formally committed to the pursuit of a joint *Ostpolitik*. That goal, however, is likely to remain elusive: French determination to go it alone in eastern Europe and suspicion of German motives made previous attempts stillborn.

18. There is considerable common ground between Britain and Germany in this area. The vision of growing East/West cooperation in Europe set out in Mrs Thatcher's Aspen speech in August matches in many respects the ideas of Kohl and Genscher.[4] Our aim now, as all concerned seek practical ways of achieving the lofty objectives agreed by the recent CSCE Summit, should be to look for ways of working together with the Germans, or at least of coordinating our policies more closely. At the primary level, this applies to the practical assistance being provided by both countries through Know-How Funds and the like. It applies a fortiori to the development of new and more imaginative ways to help, including the possibility of bringing the Soviet Union into the Western economic system and indeed the Economic Summits. We and the Germans will not always agree, but they will wish to cooperate as far as possible. Although they sometimes give the impression of wanting the field to themselves, they are in fact keenly aware of the impossibility of solving the enormous difficulties in eastern Europe single-handed. They will also wish to share information and assessments with us about the existential crisis of the Soviet Union and other potential hot spots to their east and south-east.

Bilateral Relations

19. We need to build up our bilateral relations with Germany, to maximise our standing and our influence. How can we make a big step forward here, to compensate for the loss of Quadripartite Rights and Responsibilities and the reduced importance of defence, where British-German relations have been especially important? There is no single answer. The opportunity that is thrown up by unification is the opening of east Germany to the outside world. It needs to start now, from scratch, to build contacts with the West. The German government want that to happen, through investment in east Germany and exchanges of every kind. If we can make an impact for Britain in east Germany, that will boost our standing throughout Germany. It will require a concerted effort, but it is worth it because of the importance of influencing Germany. Our reputation in Berlin itself will be an asset in this. Annexed to this despatch is a note of some ways in which we might better use the instruments of our bilateral relations with Germany, especially in relation to east Germany. Some of the important instruments are described below.

20. The admiration of Germans for the Royal Family makes Royal visits here a most effective way of increasing Britain's standing. A State Visit by The Queen, including east Germany, would have tremendous impact. Germans have greatly

---

[4] Mrs Thatcher's speech to the Aspen Institute on 5 August is available at http://www.margaret thatcher.org/speeches/displaydocument.asp?docid=108174.

appreciated the other visits recently by members of the Royal Family and I hope that it will be possible for their frequency to be maintained.

21. We need frequent contact at the highest political levels in order to consult about policy on the biggest issues and where necessary to boost particular aspects of relations; and to demonstrate to others—especially the media—that the relationship is in good order. We might aim to have one summit, at least one informal meeting of Heads of Government and four Foreign Ministers' meetings per year. Your success in establishing a close dialogue with Genscher has not only been valuable in the business transacted but also has been noticed with approval in the German media. Ministerial visits to Germany should include the ex-GDR if possible; that will add to the publicity nationally as well as to our impact in east Germany. We should continue our efforts to cultivate other leading figures in Germany, in government and opposition, focusing especially on new appointments following the Federal elections on 2 December and on the leaders in the new *Länder* administrations in east Germany.

22. We should maintain the excellent network of official level consultations with the German government. In due course we should consider an intensification of bilateral intelligence cooperation, for with the disappearance of the GDR the security threat to the Federal Republic has greatly diminished.

23. I have no doubt that our military presence, reduced after Options for Change, can remain an asset in British-German relations. NATO aspects of this were discussed above. The Army and the RAF have devoted increasing effort in recent years to good relations with the German authorities and communities around them. We should continue that and intensify it where we can. Visits by Royal Navy ships to German ports, always popular, should be encouraged. We shall continue however to face difficulties over training for our Forces here, on which the Federal Government has lately been highhanded. We should negotiate to secure other Army training areas if as expected the Federal authorities insist on our giving up one of our main ones, Soltau-Lüneburg. We shall also need to be firm in negotiations next year to review the Supplementary Agreement about the conditions under which our Forces operate here. But after three decades, some adjustment will be reasonable.

24. We need to build on the widespread respect in Germany for British cultural achievements. There has been a rapid move in east Germany to replace Russian with English as the first foreign language. That is a big opportunity. We should use it to spread information about Britain, as well as our literature, through training teachers of English and providing teaching materials. The British Council will therefore be one of our most important assets in making an impact in east Germany. They are already seizing the opportunity and their plans deserve full support.

25. One promising idea, recently floated by west German academics and so far still in embryo, is for the establishment in Germany of a multi-disciplinary Institute devoted exclusively to British studies. This would be a British equivalent to the highly successful John F Kennedy Institute at the *Freie Universität* in Berlin. To make maximum impact, a British Institute might now most appropriately be sited in east Germany, perhaps at Leipzig. This could also improve the prospect of attracting funds. We and the British Council will be exploring the idea further, with a view to working up a concrete proposal.

26. On the commercial front, there are particular opportunities in east Germany. In due course there will be an economic upsurge there. But even in the near term

the export opportunities created by major infrastructure projects, new consumer demand and the foundation of service industries will be considerable. West German industry, already working at over 90% capacity, cannot meet all the demand. We are working on a programme of trade missions, seminars and other events in east Germany, which we shall use to promote the UK's commercial image as well as our goods and services. British firms which invest now in east Germany will stand to share the profits in the future boom. A number of major British companies are establishing there and others are considering the possibility.

27. We need to step up our information effort in Germany. We already seek maximum publicity for all Anglo-German events, to help enhance our standing. We should continue this and spread it increasingly to the media in east Germany. British television, of higher quality overall than German, is a tool of which I long to make use in this widely anglophone country. Its availability (as in Belgium and the Netherlands) would add to our standing, particularly among opinion formers. This Embassy is encouraging the British companies to review the possibility. We are also working on the Federal Post authorities to reduce the cost of access to the cable system in Germany: there may be scope for using the mechanisms of the European Broadcasting Directive. We should also support efforts to sell World Television News (produced by ITN) and any future BBC World Service TV News to German companies.

28. United Germany may increasingly be able to stake a claim to be the leading scientific research nation in Europe. Our objective should be to participate in that creative drive. We start from a good position. The recent Anglo-German Round Table on Research Policy identified a rich pattern of existing contacts between researchers. Both countries attach great importance to freedom of research and devolution of responsibility for its management, points where the Germans have more in common with us than, for example, with the French. There are also differences between the UK and Germany, such as the greater official funds for research here. Yet there is wide respect for the quality and tradition of British science and for our strengths in such topical fields as environmental research and biotechnology.

29. We can use these assets to even greater effect. We need to reinforce the success of the British Council's bilateral Academic Research Collaboration programme (ARC), extending it as far as we can to non-university research institutes and also to east Germany. We should make a point of coordinating our research strategies with German opposite numbers and actively seeking potential subjects for joint research. We should establish early contact with researchers in the new *Länder*.

30. The environment is one of the biggest issues in German public life. The catastrophic pollution in the former GDR has added to the concern. The German government is at pains not to fall behind public opinion, and some of its initiatives are hasty. The UK's commitment to the preservation of the environment, and the thorough presentation of our policies, have begun to tell in Germany. Nevertheless, the Germans still tend to consider us slow to act; they suspect that our commitment is shaded by the advantages we gain as sea-washed and wind-swept islands. This background is not an easy basis for cooperation with Germany. Yet both countries are seeking genuine solutions to the same environmental problems, and understanding among the main industrialised countries will be necessary if these are to be overcome. There is a good chance that the sheer difficulty and inter-related nature of environmental problems, as well as the economic and budgetary

impact of the countermeasures, will increasingly compel even the German Environment Ministry to take a more measured view. We should work on that assumption and continue to build up contacts with other interested ministries and expert bodies; last year's meeting between the Royal Commission on Environmental Pollution and their German equivalent was a successful example.

Conclusion

31. Germany will play a bigger role in the coming years, across Europe, and more widely. Its importance for us has grown in 1990 and will grow further. We have many common interests with the Germans, and should build on these in order to influence German policies more effectively. The aftermath of German unification is an opportunity to make a greater impact. We should seize it.

32. I am sending copies of this despatch to the Chancellor of the Exchequer, the Secretaries of State for Defence and for Trade and Industry, and the Secretary of the Cabinet; to HM Representatives in NATO, EC and Eastern European countries, Moscow, Vienna and New York (UKMis); and to our posts in the Federal Republic and the Commanders in Chief in Germany.

I am, Sir,
Yours faithfully
C. L .G. MALLABY

ANNEX

INSTRUMENTS FOR THE DEVELOPMENT OF BRITISH-GERMAN RELATIONS

Royal Visits

1. The Duke and Duchess of Gloucester plan to visit Hanover in 1991. The Duke of Kent plans to visit Bavaria. We shall investigate the possibility of resurrecting the visit of the Duke and Duchess of York (postponed due to timing difficulties because of unification).

Ministerial Contacts

2. We shall need to seek early opportunities after the German elections for British Ministers to establish contact with new German opposite numbers. Speeches and seminars can provide a good platform for getting British views across; facilities for publicising them are very good in Germany.

Parliamentary and Party Links

3. There have been frequent visits by Select Committees over the last twelve months. It is not for us to seek to influence such Committees' choice of destination, but we shall where possible try to encourage them while in Germany to visit the east as well. The bilateral Parliamentary Groups have been quiet recently. After the German elections we shall consider some German ideas for re-invigorating these. Party-to-Party links and visits by senior British politicians to German Party Conferences are an essential part of the overall bilateral relationship.

Contacts between officials

4. As well as the frequent meetings between senior FCO and *Auswärtiges Amt* officials on a range of subjects, there are regular contacts between other UK civil servants and their German opposite numbers. These should be stepped up further as Germany takes on an increasingly important role. The Embassy will be on the look-out for opportunities once the new government has been formed.

FCO/*Auswärtiges Amt* exchanges should be continued; we should select candidates in good time. The UK/Germany Civil Service exchange scheme is useful, with a range of short programmes and longer attachments. But the flow is unbalanced, with many more people coming from Germany than from the United Kingdom, largely because of a lack of German speakers on our side. There are funding problems, which the Civil Service College are currently discussing with the Cabinet Office. It is important that these are overcome quickly.

Nuclear Energy

5. Nuclear energy is seen by Germany's environmental activists as public enemy number one. At a less extreme level, public worries about the necessity of nuclear power are much the same in Germany as they are in the UK. Last year's Joint Declaration on the Peaceful Uses of Nuclear Energy provides the framework within which we can address the policy implications, alongside the contacts at a more technical level which are of long standing. The German Government is increasingly of the view that the only way to counter public suspicions is the broadest possible international understanding on standards and implementation. Equally, Germany recognises that nuclear power is not an area where all the eggs should be put in one basket. This is a consideration which helped us to win our latest share of nuclear reprocessing business here, amounting to some 750 million pounds, with a possibility of more in this and related areas from the former GDR. Our strong selling points are the expertise and competence of our nuclear industry, but we shall need to back these with political support.

British Council

6. The British Council have begun to capitalise on the demand for British culture and in particular on the thirst for English Language Training (ELT) in east Germany. Arts events will be given a much higher profile. Plans are being made for an information and library service. The Council are making arrangements to start English Language Training in Berlin next Spring and expand their Berlin operations substantially. They plan to open a centre in Leipzig as soon as possible. A professional survey of the demand for ELT should be ready shortly. Evidence so far indicates that demand for ELT is very high and that the ability of students to pay for it (under the Council's self-financing Direct Teaching of English method) is higher than expected. We should look to the longer term, too: a larger programme than currently planned would reap greater benefit in terms of influence gained. We shall otherwise lose ground to the Americans.

British Broadcasting

7. Because of the difficulties British companies have encountered, they seem to have become apathetic towards the German market except in respect of joint productions. A recent visit to the UK by the Embassy's Information Officer has, we hope, persuaded some of them to dust off their files: more lobbying is needed.

8. In particular, there will be opportunities to exploit in east Germany, where satellite dishes are sprouting in the absence of cable systems. BBC TV Europe should look at this; there may be scope for Sky to re-enter the German market via this back door. The sale of the BBC's English Language teaching programmes there would also be very valuable, and may be worth an FCO subsidy.

9. We should make the best use of the BBC World Service in English and the German Service. The World Service in English has a good audience particularly in east Germany and for its English Language Teaching programmes. The combined World and German Service output from the BBC's German FM transmitter in

Berlin reaches well into the city's hinterland and enjoys the status of a local radio station. We should support the BBC's efforts to maintain these unique facilities.

Information Work

10. The whole range of information work in a Western country will be extended to the new *Länder*. An intensive period of visiting the media will be necessary to establish our presence and to assess which newspapers and television stations matter among the plethora which have recently sprung up. As the range of opinion formers becomes known, we shall extend our distribution of information material. We should make use also of British training schemes, for journalists from east Germany. The BBC External Service have already made a start with journalists from Radio Sachsen. The FCO scholarships scheme could be used to fund participation in the courses for journalists run by e.g. Queen Elizabeth House Oxford and the Thomson Foundation.

Category I Visits

11. We can devote a large proportion of our Category I visits allocation (perhaps 60% of our total of 28) to east Germany, but particular care will be needed, to select the rising stars and shun those tainted by the old regime. Apart from key opinion-formers (who will be hard to catch over the coming year), one target group is senior academics, particularly in the sciences.

FCO Scholarships

12. Plans are now advanced for directing to east Germany much of the 160,000 pounds available in FY 1991/92 for scholarships in Germany. This emphasis should continue for two or three years. Demand is high and we shall need to choose carefully candidates whose approach can be effectively and positively developed by a spell of life and study in Britain. We have bid for an extra 10% for FY 1992/93.

Anglo-German Foundation (AGF)

13. We need to strengthen the AGF by increasing our official funding to at least the level of the FRG contribution (from 175,000 pounds to 250,000 pounds). It will thereby gain in credibility in German eyes and be able to extend its activities in the eastern *Länder*. The AGF-sponsored Anglo-German Young Journalist Prize will be a useful tool.

Regional/Civic Links

14. British towns have 450 town twinnings with west Germany and 4 with east Germany. Although this is an essentially non-governmental activity, the Embassy, the Consulates General and the FCO could give more support to the establishment of links between towns/regions in east Germany and the UK. The holding of the 1991 Königswinter Conference in Dresden (see below) will provide a good opportunity to highlight the longstanding link between Dresden and Coventry. We are also examining the scope for extending existing British/west German twinnings to towns in the new *Länder* already linked with the west German towns concerned. For example Oxford's link with Bonn could be widened to include Bonn's east German partner, Potsdam.

Youth and Educational Exchanges

15. The British Council funded Youth Exchange Centre (YEC) already spends 30% of its resources on visits between Germany and the UK. Our exchanges with west Germany were already more numerous than between the UK and any other country. And the Council and the FCO are confident that there will be resources to extend the YEC's activities into east Germany. The Central Bureau for Educational Visits and Exchanges is also active in Germany, and both British organisations

have good links with their west German opposite numbers. They will need to develop such links in east Germany. The non-governmental *Deutsch-Britischer Jugendaustausch* (German/British Youth Exchange) also has a role to play. There is a case here for some British funding. This would need to be mainly from private sources, but there may also be a need for official funding, at least on an ad hoc basis. The Department of Employment is engaged in setting up the first official trainee exchange, which we hope will take place in early 1991.

Wilton Park

16. We should be able to increase Wilton Park's usefulness as a tool of Anglo-German relations. It played an important role in instilling democratic values in West Germany after the War and might now have a similar role in east Germany. The Director of Wilton Park visited Bonn on 19-20 November to discuss this possibility with the Embassy, *Auswärtiges Amt*, and others. It was agreed that we should aim to invite a total of some 50 east Germans to Wilton Park in 1991. We shall also be seeking with Wilton Park to improve the quality and variety of west German participants (at present there are too many civil servants).

Deutsch-Englische Gesellschaft

17. The Königswinter Conferences continue to be one of the success stories of Anglo-German relations. To mark unification, the DEG will be holding the 1991 Conference, as an exception, in Dresden. They are in the process of setting up branches in the five new *Länder*. They would like more high-profile British speakers, including Ministers, for their speaker tours.

I have, etc.,
C.L.G. MALLABY

APPENDIX

THE PRIME MINISTER'S SEMINAR ON GERMANY, 24 MARCH 1990

No. 1

Minute from Mr Powell (No. 10) to Mrs Thatcher

[*PREM: Internal Situation in East Germany*]

10 DOWNING STREET, *18 March 1990*

Prime Minister

Seminar on Germany

We have the Seminar on Germany next Saturday. I am coming under some pressure from the participants to say what you want to talk about.[1] Basically, it seems to me, you will want to tap the wisdom of each individual participant in his particular area of specialisation: Professor Craig on German history as a whole: Professor Stern on the lessons of the nineteenth century: Hugh Trevor-Roper on the Nazi period: Timothy Garton-Ash on Germany and Central Europe; and George Urban and Norman Stone on the modern-day politics of it.

But I have also tried to define a number of specific questions to which the Seminar might try to provide answers or at least guidance (and any resemblance to Oxford or Cambridge entrance scholarship papers is entirely coincidental!). The principal ones are:

—what does history tell us about the character and behaviour of the German-speaking people of Europe? Are there such things as enduring national characteristics?[2]

—how strong is the drive to unite all the German-speaking peoples, either within the existing borders of Germany or by extending those borders?

—have the Germans changed in the last 40 years,[3] either as a result of some mutation in their national character or because of changes in their external environment? Or are we really dealing with the same old Huns?

—in the light of history, how can we 'satisfy' the Germans? Is there something they want and we can give them, which will neutralise their desire to extend their sway, whether politically or territorially?

—will German national ambitions be subsumed in the internationalist appeal of an European Community as they claim? Can the sense of a German nation be supplanted by the sense of an European nation? Or is this wishful thinking on their—and our—part?

—how deep-rooted is the German mission in Central[4] Europe? Is it part of their instinctive and historic restlessness? Or is it merely a current calculation of economic and political advantage?

—looking back through history, are there traits in Germany's relations with Britain which have been particularly positive and on which we can try to build in future? Are there some particular aspects of the German character or of German national interests to which we can appeal, to make them more cuddly and less abrasive?

—what is the key to German economic success? Is it something deep in their character and

---

[1] Mrs Thatcher noted here: 'I want to use our experience of the past to help us shape the future. But not to be dominated by the past. We have to enlarge our ideas. We have to build a new framework for the future—for defence, for co-operation beyond Europe and try to see how we can bring the Soviet Union to a real western democracy with economic as well as political [?friends ?funds]. We must consider Central Europe—its minorities and how our security could be upset [?for] the Middle East.'

[2] Mrs Thatcher noted here: '[N.B. —we must rid the new Europe incl[uding] Russia of anti-semitism.]'

[3] Mrs Thatcher noted here: 'or 80 or 150'.

[4] Mrs Thatcher noted here: 'and Eastern'.

psyche a natural sense of discipline and order? Or is it 'simply' sound policy?

—what will be the tendency of a united Germany? Despite all protestations to the contrary, will it lurch inevitably and as often in history, towards geographical and territorial dominance? Or will it find satisfaction in the creation of something broader than Germany?

—can we deduce from history how the Germans as a nation will respond to certain sorts of treatment? Is it better psychologically to 'stand up to Germany'? Or do they respond better to a honeyed approach, based on understanding of their needs and an attempt to manipulate them?

—how strongly German do the remaining Germanic minorities in Eastern Europe and the Soviet Union feel? Is an ambition to protect them likely to re-surface as a factor in German policy?

—to what extent do we need to take account of the growing influence of people of Germanic origin in the United States, as a factor affecting American policy towards Europe?

It would be very helpful if you could indicate whether these are broadly the sort of questions which you want to address: and whether you have any others. I will then try to fit them into a framework which I can circulate to participants.

Content to proceed on this basis?[5]

C.D. POWELL

[5] Mrs Thatcher noted here: We must *widen* the discussion to include the future of the USSR (? or of Russia) and whether we pursue spheres of influence or *alliances of democracy* or geographical alliances. We cannot completely disregard history for the various empires and maritime states have girdled the globe. We must therefore consider some of the old *balance of power*. But it seems to me that, while in the past, history was determined largely by the personalities and ambitions of the *rulers* of the people, in future it will be decided much more by the *character* of the people. However, the lesson of the past two years is that neither character nor pride has been ~~stifled~~ suffocated by oppression.'

No. 2

Letter from Mr Powell (No. 10) to Mr Timothy Garton Ash[1]

[*WRL 020/1*]

Private and Confidential   10 DOWNING STREET, *19 March 1990*

[No salutation on this copy]

Meeting at Chequers on 24 March

I promised to try to let you have a rather fuller idea of the matters which the Prime Minister would like to discuss at our meeting at Chequers on 24 March.

Basically the Prime Minister's objective is to use our knowledge and experience of Germany's past to help shape our policy towards Germany and Europe for the future. She will want to tap the wisdom of each individual participant for this. I suggest, therefore, that we should devote the first half of the afternoon to Germany's past and the lessons to be learned from it: and the second half to wider questions about Germany's future role in Europe, and what changes this may require in our diplomacy.

For the *first part* of the discussion, the following are some of the questions which we might consider (although the list is neither comprehensive nor exclusive):

—what does history tell us about the character and behaviour of the Germany-speaking people of Europe? Are there enduring national characteristics?

—have the Germans changed in the last 40 years (or 80 or 150 years), either as a result of some mutation in their national character or because of changes in their external environment?

—what is the key to German economic success? Is it something deep in their character and psyche, a natural sense of discipline and order? Or is it 'simply' sound policy?

—what will be the tendency of a united Germany? Despite all protest[at]ions to the contrary, will it lurch inevitably and as often in history, towards geographical and territorial dominance? Or will it find satisfaction in the creation of something broader than Germany?

—how strong is the drive to unite all the German-speaking peoples, either within the existing borders of Germany or by extending those borders?

—in the light of history, how can we 'satisfy' the Germans? Is there something they want and

[1] Repeated to Mr Hurd, Professor Gordon Craig, Professor Fritz Stern, Lord Dacre (Hugh Trevor-Roper), Mr George Urban and Professor Norman Stone.

we can give them, which will neutralise their drive to extend their sway, whether politically or territorially?

—how strongly German do the remaining Germanic minorities in Eastern Europe and the Soviet Union feel? Is an ambition to protect them likely to re-surface as a factor in German policy?

—will German national ambitions be subsumed in the internationalist appeal of a European Community as they claim? Can the sense of German nationhood be supplanted by the sense of being part of a European nation? Or is this wishful thinking on their—and our—part?

—how deep-rooted is the German mission in Central and Eastern Europe? Is it part of their instinctive and historic restlessness? Or is it merely a current calculation of economic and political advantage?

—can we deduce from history how the Germans as a nation will respond to certain sorts of treatment? Is it better psychologically to 'stand up to Germany'? Or to pursue a friendly approach, based on understanding of their needs and ambitions?

—looking back through history, are there traits in Germany's relations with Britain which have been particularly positive and on which we can try to build in future? Are there some particular aspects of the German character or of German national interests to which we can appeal, to forge a co-operative relationship?

—to what extent do we need to take account of the growing influence of people of Germanic origin in the United States, as a factor affecting American policy towards Europe?

In the *second half* of the discussion, the Prime Minister would like to range more widely and consider some of the broader consequences of German unification. We might look at some of the following questions:

—one might say that in the past, history was determined largely by the personalities and ambitions of the rulers of peoples. In future it may be determined more by the character of the people themselves. What will the implications be, given the resurgence of national feeling in Eastern Europe in particular?

—given worries about the dominant influence which a united Germay might exercise, what sort of framework should we build in Europe, into which a united Germany would fit comfortably (for future economic, political and defence co-operation)? Is the European Community sufficient? Or should we look for something wider?

—to what extent should such a framework provide also for the Soviet Union, as the only power in Europe capable in crude terms of balancing a united Germany?

—is there still a use for some of the concepts familiar from history such as spheres of influence, geographical alliances and balance of power? Or should we be looking at something much broader, for instance an 'alliance for democracy' which would stretch from the Atlantic to the Urals and beyond?

—how are we going to cope with the return of national feeling in Eastern Europe, now that events of recent months have shown that forty years of communist oppression failed to suffocate it?

These are just illustrative questions—and formulated by me rather than by the Prime Minister. But I hope you will find them of some help in preparing your thoughts.

I look forward to seeing you on Saturday.

CHARLES POWELL

No. 3

Letter from Mr Powell (No. 10) to Mr Wall

[*PREM: Internal Situation in East Germany*]

Confidential   10 DOWNING STREET, *25 March 1990*

Dear Stephen,
Seminar on Germany
The Prime Minister held a seminar on Germany at Chequers on Saturday, 24 March. Those present, in addition to the Prime Minister and the Foreign Secretary, were:
Professor Gordon Craig
Professor Fritz Stern

Lord Dacre
Professor Norman Stone
Mr Timothy Garton-Ash
Mr George Urban

I enclose my summary record of the discussion. I also enclose a copy of the list of questions circulated to participants before the meeting.

It would be very embarrassing and gravely damaging to our interests if the contents of so frank a discussion of one of our closest allies were to become known. *I should be grateful if the record could be given only a very limited circulation to Ministers and to senior officials with a need to know.*

I am copying this letter and enclosure to John Gieve (HM Treasury), Simon Webb (Ministry of Defence), Martin Stanley (Department of Trade and Industry), Sonia Phippard (Cabinet Office) and Sir Christopher Mallaby (HM Ambassador, Bonn).

Yours sincerely,
CHARLES POWELL

ENCLOSURE IN NO. 3

SEMINAR ON GERMANY: SUMMARY RECORD

Introduction

The Prime Minister said that Europe had come to the end of the post-war period. Important decisions and choices about its future lay ahead. She herself had a number of crucial meetings in the weeks ahead, with President Bush, President Gorbachev, and Chancellor Kohl, as well as an informal EC Summit. In all of these, German unification would be the main issue. We needed to reach an assessment of what a united Germany would be like. History was a guide, but one could not just extrapolate. We also had to devise a framework for Europe's future, taking account of German unification and the sweeping changes in the Soviet Union and Eastern Europe. It was important to get the balance right between the lessons of the past and the opportunities of the future. She would welcome the wisdom and advice of those present.

Who are the Germans?

We started by talking about the Germans themselves and their characteristics. Like other nations, they had certain characteristics, which you could identify from the past and expect to find in the future. It was easier—and more pertinent to the present discussion—to think of the less happy ones: their insensitivity to the feelings of others (most noticeable in their behaviour over the Polish border), their obsession with themselves, a strong inclination to self-pity, and a longing to be liked. Some even less flattering attributes were also mentioned as an abiding part of the German character: in alphabetical order, angst, aggressiveness, assertiveness, bullying, egotism, inferiority complex, sentimentality.

Two further aspects of the German character were cited as reasons for concern about the future. First, a capacity for excess, to overdo things, to kick over the traces. Second, a tendency to over-estimate their own strengths and capabilities. An example of that, which had influenced much of Germany's subsequent history, was the conviction that their victory over France in 1870 stemmed from deep moral and cultural superiority rather than—as in fact—a modest advance in military technology.

Have the Germans changed?

It was as well to be aware of all these characteristics. But there was a strong school of thought among those present that today's Germans were very different from their predecessors. It was argued that our basic perception of Germans related to a period of German history running from Bismarck until 1945. This was the phase of imperial Germany, characterised by neurotic self-assertiveness, a high birth-rate, a closed economy, a chauvinist culture. It had not been greatly affected by defeat in 1918, which had been regarded in Germany as unfair. German attitudes, German teaching, German historiography all continued virtually unchanged after 1918, together with a sense of Germany's historic mission (which was why the German aristocracy had supported Hitler, even while regarding him as a vulgarian). But 1945 was quite different and marked a sea-change. There was no longer a sense of historic mission, no ambitions for physical conquest, no more militarism. Education and the writing of history had changed. The institutions were different.

Democracy was deeply rooted. There was an innocence of and about the past on the part of the new generation of Germans. We should have no real worries about them.

This view was not accepted by everyone. It still had to be asked how a cultured and cultivated nation had allowed itself to be brain-washed into barbarism. If it had happened once, could it not happen again? Apprehension about Germany did not relate just to the Nazi period, but to the whole post-Bismarckian era, and inevitably caused deep distrust. The way in which the Germans currently used their elbows and threw their weight about in the European Community suggested that a lot had still not changed. While we all admired and indeed envied what the Germans had achieved in the last 45 years, the fact was that their institutions had not yet been seriously tested by adversity such as a major economic calamity. We could not tell how Germans would react in such circumstances. In sum, no-one had serious misgivings about the present leaders or political elite of Germany. But what about ten, fifteen or twenty years from now? Could some of the unhappy characteristics of the past re-emerge with just as destructive consequences?

What will be the consequences of reunification?

We looked more closely at two particular aspects of the future: the consequences of unification and Germany's role in Eastern Europe.

Even those most disposed to look on the bright side admitted to some qualms about what unification would mean for German behaviour in Europe. We could not expect a United Germany to think and act in exactly the same way as the Federal Republic which we had known for the last forty-five years—and this would be true even though a united Germany would almost certainly inherit the FRG's institutions. The Germans would not necessarily think more dangerously, but they would think differently. There was already evident a kind of triumphalism in German thinking and attitudes which would be uncomfortable for the rest of us. Reference was also made to Günter Grass' comment: in the end reunification will get everyone against us, and we all know what happens when people are against us.

Then, too, there were reasons to worry about the effects on the character of a united Germany of bringing in 17 million predominantly Protestant North Germans brought up under a mendacious orthodoxy. How would this alter the basically Catholic Rhineland bias of the post-war FRG, with its political and economic centre of gravity increasingly in the South and West? We could not assume that a united Germany would fit quite so comfortably into Western Europe as the FRG. There would be a growing inclination to resurrect the concept of *Mittel-Europa*, with Germany's role being that of broker between East and West. It was noticeable that Chancellor Kohl now spoke of Germany's partners in East *and* West.

That tendency could be strengthened by the effect of unification on Germany's party system. The vote for the conservative alliance in East Germany could be seen as a vote for quick unification rather than for the values and policies of the West German CDU. There was a strong pacifist, neutralist, anti-nuclear constituency in East Germany, which could have a considerable effect on the views of a united Germany. That effect could be to make a united Germany both less 'western' and less politically stable than the FRG. At worst, the extremes at both ends of the political spectrum could grow in influence, leading to a return to Weimar politics (although no-one argued this with any great conviction).

Will a united Germany aspire to dominate Eastern Europe?

This led on naturally enough to debate about a united Germany's likely role and ambitions in Eastern Europe. It was widely agreed that Chancellor Kohl's handling of the Polish border issue, in particular his reference to the need to protect the German minority in Silesia, had given the wrong signals. Historic fears about Germany's 'mission' in Eastern and Central Europe had been revived. Some of President von Weizsäcker's comments had contributed to this.

But the facts were more reassuring. The German minorities in Eastern Europe were much reduced in number, and the ambition of most of them was to move within the borders of Germany rather than have the borders of Germany come to them. The Germans' own interest lay in keeping the minorities where they were rather than in encouraging their return. They thus had an incentive to give substantial aid to Eastern Europe. There was no evidence that Germany was likely to make territorial claims, at least for the foreseeable future. To the extent that border problems might arise, it would be as a result of comparatively wealthy Germans buying land and property in poorer Poland and Czechoslovakia (bearing in mind that the Polish border would be only 40 minutes drive from the assumed capital of a united Germany).

More widely, it was likely that Germany would indeed dominate Eastern and Central Europe economically. But that did not necessarily equate to subjugation. Nor did it mean that a united Germany would achieve by economic means what Hitler had failed to achieve militarily. There were undoubtedly still some who believed that Germany had a 'civilizing mission' to the East. But the fact was, the pressure for a German economic presence came as much from the East Europeans themselves as from the Germans. They wanted and needed German help and German investment: indeed it was probably the only way to restore and revive Eastern Europe ('There is only one thing worse than being exploited, and that is not being exploited.') It might indeed be ironic that after 1945 Eastern Europe had set out to avoid ever again being dependent on Germany, but after 45 years of Communism was more dependent than ever. But it was nonetheless a fact. The East Europeans might prefer a British or French presence. But neither was prepared to commit adequate resources.

What sort of framework should we build for the future?

Given that a much larger and more powerful Germany would soon be upon us, we had to consider what sort of European framework would be most likely to encourage the benign effects and diminish the adverse consequences.

The East/West aspects roused the greatest concern. There was a tendency on the part of the Germans to take the credit for unification themselves. In fact the real credit should go to the people of Eastern Europe and to Mr. Gorbachev. They were the ones who created the conditions in which unification could happen. Whatever solutions we adopted—whether in relation to Germany or to the current problems in Lithuania—must take account of their interests, and above all of Mr. Gorbachev's position. That would affect in particular the security arrangements made for the territory of the former GDR in a united Germany. We could not just shove the Russian troops out.

To an extent Soviet and East European interests paralleled those of Western Europe. We wanted Germany to be constrained within a security framework which had the best chance of avoiding a resurgence of German militarism. We wanted a continuing American military presence in Europe as a balance to Germany's power. We would want to see limits, preferably self-imposed through a further CFE agreement, on the size of Germany's armed forces. We would want a renewed self-denying ordinance on acquisition by Germany of nuclear and chemical weapons. We would want to involve the Soviet Union institutionally in discussions of Europe's future security through the CSCE, not least because in the long term (and assuming continued development in the direction of democracy) the Soviet Union would be the only European power capable of balancing Germany.

All that would suggest that an accommodation could be found which would enable a united Germany to remain in NATO, with transitional arrangements to permit the Soviet Union to help keep forces in East Germany. It would also favour building up the CSCE (and possibly giving it a directorate based on the Five). The idea that a united Germany might be a member both of NATO and the Warsaw Pact simultaneously was also canvassed, but given short shrift.

But there were real risks that the situation could develop differently. One was that Gorbachev would be manoeuvred into using force in Lithuania or in some analogous situation: or that his failure to do so would lead to his replacement by a much less moderate leadership. That risk was one reason why it was so important to hold on to the existing structure of NATO: the fact that things had gone the West's way for the last year or so did not absolve us from continuing to guard against something worse.

Another and possibly more likely danger was that the Soviet Union would exploit discussion in the Four plus Two group of a united Germany's membership of NATO and the presence of nuclear weapons in Germany, so that they became issues in the West German election campaign. German public opinion was seen as vulnerable on both points, but particularly on the nuclear issue. The worst fear was that NATO could unravel on the election hustings of Germany. The more positive view argued that this danger only underlined the importance of settling the question of a united Germany's membership of NATO as rapidly and decisively as possible.

Looking longer-term, the aim of building up the CSCE seemed sensible to everyone, not least as a way of managing and conciliating disputes between national minorities in Eastern and Central Europe.

The European Community was surprisingly not much mentioned. German behaviour in the EC—'we pay so we must have our way'—was seen by some as the harbinger of Germany's economic dominance over Western Europe. There were differing views over how genuine the Germans were in saying they wanted a more integrated Europe in parallel with unification. Was it just a tactic to reassure others? Or a genuine desire to subsume the latent nationalist drive of a united Germany into something broader? The latter was not wholly convincing, given that the structure of the EC tended to favour German dominance, particularly in the monetary area. Against this, it was pointed out that the more assertive Germany became, the easier it ought to become to construct alliances against Germany on specific issues in the Community.

Conclusions

Where did this leave us? No formal conclusions were drawn. The weight of the evidence and the argument favoured those who were optimistic about life with a united Germany. We were reminded that in 1945 our aim had been a united Germany shorn of its eastern provinces but under democratic and non-communist government, with the states of Eastern Europe free to choose their own governments. We had failed to get that in 1945, but had won it now. Far from being agitated, we ought to be pleased. We were also reminded that Anglo-German antagonism since the fall of Bismarck had been injurious to Europe as a whole and must not be allowed to revive once more. When it came to failings and unhelpful characteristics, the Germans had their share and perhaps more: but in contrast to the past, they were much readier to recognise and admit this themselves.

The overall message was unmistakeable: we should be nice to the Germans. But even the optimists had some unease, not for the present and the immediate future, but for what might lie further down the road than we can yet see.

C.D. POWELL

No. 4

Letter from Mr D. Marsh (Financial Times) to Mrs Thatcher

[*PREM: Internal Situation in East Germany*]

BONN, *16 July 1990*

Dear Prime Minister,

Please allow me to share with you some of my thoughts upon reading Charles Powell's memo on the Germans drawn up after your March meeting at Chequers, The document was published, as you know, both in *The Independent on Sunday* and in *Der Spiegel*.

1. I realise that the document was not written for general release, and was meant to throw a light mainly on the historical rather than purely on the current perspectives relating to Germany. None the less, I feel it offers an imperfect guide to policy-making. In addition, publication in full in Germany's top news magazine, with a circulation of 1 million has, as you can imagine, added to the general cynicism here about Britain's policies towards Germany already kindled by last week's interview in *The Spectator* by Mr Ridley.

2. The prominence given to the Germans' negative traits suggests a somewhat imbalanced and prejudiced view of Germany and the Germans. Despite the memories of two world wars, this may not be the best starting point for policy. Certainly, the stated attributes—Angst etc—are present in 'the German character', if one may use that generalisation, The memo exaggerates the negative qualities however by failing to note that opposite traits do co-exist—assertiveness is accompanied by a certain lack of self-confidence, for instance—and by ignoring completely the 'good' characteristics, Thrift, precision, pride in doing a job well, capacity for hard work, organisational talent—virtues of which you, Prime Minister, are known personally to be very much in favour—are character traits which run through and influence German history, whether during the Third Reich, the post-war recovery, or the present drive to reunification.

3. Some of the observations in the memo about present-day Germany are false, The tendency for Germans to triumph about reunification or 'to take the credit for unification themselves' is in fact not very high. Apart from the revelry over Germany's World Cup victory, there have been no flags out on West German streets.[1] In utterances by ordinary people or by political leaders such as Mr Kohl, it is above all Mr Gorbachev who gets the credit for making unity possible. It is wrong to suggest that the Germans have been unworried about Mr Gorbachev's position vis-a-vis East Germany. Far from proposing any move to 'just shove the Russian troops out', the *Bundeskanzleramt* has been stressing for several months the need, for a three to four-year transition period, for removing the Soviet troops, This was formalised in Mr Kohl's agreement with Mr Gorbachev today.

4. The reference in the Conclusion about British post-war policies on a united Germany is a central point, made belatedly and rather grudgingly. One awkward characteristic which goes unremarked in the memo is the Germans' attachment to legalisms. They remember that Britain and,

---

[1] In the World Cup semi-final at Turin on 4 July 1990, West Germany beat England 4-3 on penalties.

508

the other western powers gave binding support to a united Germany 'with a liberal-democratic constitution, integrated within the European community' in the *Deutschlandvertrag* of 1955. Your government has on occasion acted as if this undertaking was valid only at a time when unification was plainly impossible.

5. I write, in a personal capacity, as a journalist who has recently published a book on Germany.[2] I argue that unification—for which hardly anyone was prepared—will bring pitfalls as well as opportunities, both in Germany and abroad. Since you obviously have a great and growing interest in the subject, I enclose a copy, in the hope that you will have time to read it.

6. I would add that my insight into the paradoxical ways of Germany has been heightened by the fact that my wife is German. We met in Brighton (my home town) in 1971 while she was on a language course very similar to the ones attended by the German students who were attacked in the town recently after the England v. Germany football match. It is disappointing that so much anti-German prejudice persists in England. It would be tragic if, just at the time when barriers are coming down between East and West, such resentment should flare up again.

With best wishes,
David Marsh

[2] David Marsh, *The Germans: Rich, Bothered and Divided* (London: Century, 1989).

No. 5

Letter from Mr Powell (No. 10) to Mr D. Marsh (Financial Times)

[*PREM: Internal Situation in East Germany*]

Personal   10 DOWNING STREET, *24 July 1990*

[No salutation on this copy]

The Prime Minister has asked me to thank you for your letter of 16 July about the document published in the *Independent on Sunday*, and to reply. I know she will be very grateful for your book and will read it during the summer break.

The points in your letter are perfectly fair: and I can understand that, seen in black and white, some of the points in my note do not go down well in Germany. They were not, of course, supposed to be seen. One always faces a dilemma with this sort of occasion; the purpose is to produce a fair summary of the discussion, as any *rapporteur* at a conference or seminar does. One cannot include in the note things which were not said. Equally one does not attempt to produce a verbatim record, recording every point made and attributing it to a speaker. As regards the point in the very last sentence of your letter, I would refer you to the second part of the penultimate paragraph of my note, particularly the sentence: 'We were also reminded that Anglo-German indoctrinism [*sic:* antagonism] since the fall of Bismarck had been injurious to Europe as a whole and must not be allowed to revive once more.'

Personally I share your admiration and affection for Germans, having some modest knowledge of the language and having lived in Germany for a little over three years in the mid-1970s.

CHARLES POWELL

CHRONOLOGY OF EVENTS

1945

5 June | Berlin Declaration of supreme authority in Germany by US, UK and USSR

1948

17 March | Signature of Brussels Treaty establishing Western European Union (WEU)

18-24 June | Soviets impose blockade of Western sectors of Berlin

1949

4 April | Signature of North Atlantic Treaty

8 May | Establishment of Federal Republic of Germany (FRG); adoption of Basic Law

12 May | End of Berlin Blockade

7 October | Establishment of German Democratic Republic (GDR)

1951

April | Foundation of European Coal & Steel Community (ECSC)

1952

10 March | USSR proposes rearmed, neutral Germany

26 May | Signature of Bonn Conventions

1953

17 June | Workers' uprising in GDR

1954

22 August | European Defence Community rejected by French National Assembly

3 October | Signature of Bonn/Paris Conventions (Relations Convention)

1955

5 May | Ratification of Bonn/Paris Conventions: FRG acquires full sovereignty

9 May | FRG joins WEU and NATO

14 May | Formation of Warsaw Pact

1956

24 November | Soviet troops move in to crush Hungarian uprising

1957

25 March | Treaty of Rome establishes European Economic Communities (EEC)

1958

27 November | USSR demands removal of Western forces from Berlin

1959

11 May – 5 Aug | Geneva conference of Foreign Ministers to discuss Berlin and a German peace treaty

1961

13 August | Erection of Berlin Wall

1968

21 August | Warsaw Pact troops move into Czechoslovakia

1969

21 October | Willy Brandt becomes Chancellor of FRG

1970

12 August | Treaty between Soviet Union and FRG

1971

3 September	Quadripartite Agreement on Berlin

1972

21 December	Signature of Basic Treaty between FRG and GDR

1973

18 September	Recognition of GDR and admission of both German states to UN

1975

1 August	Helsinki Final Act

1979

12 December	NATO twin-track decision on missile deployment

1982

4 October	Helmut Kohl becomes Chancellor of FRG

1984

3 May	UK commitment to German self-determination reaffirmed at meeting between Thatcher and Kohl

1985

11 March	Gorbachev elected General Secretary of CPSU

1987

11 June	Margaret Thatcher becomes Prime Minister for a third term
12 June	President Reagan visits West Berlin; challenges Gorbachev to pull down the Wall
7 September	Honecker's state visit to FRG
10 December	INF Treaty between USA and USSR

1989

6 February	Polish Government and Solidarity begin talks on economic and political reform
12 February	Multi-party system introduced in Hungary
20-21 February	British-German summit
9 March	CFE negotiations begin in Vienna
28 April	Kohl announces new security policy for FRG
2 May	Removal of barbed wire from Hungarian-Austrian border
29-30 May	NATO 40th anniversary meeting
3-5 June	Chinese army suppresses demonstrations in Tiananmen Square
5 June	Solidarity wins landslide victory in Poland
12-15 June	Gorbachev visits FRG
26-27 June	European Council meeting, Madrid
7 July	Warsaw Pact states, meeting in Bucharest, revoke Brezhnev Doctrine
24 July	John Major succeeds Geoffrey Howe as Foreign Secretary
1 September	Thatcher/Mitterand meeting at Chequers
10 September	Hungary allows East Germans to cross into Austria
11 September	Foundation of New Forum opposition group in East Berlin
20 September	Speech by Major in Bonn reiterates UK commitment to German self-determination
23 September	Thatcher/Gorbachev meeting in Moscow
30 September	East German migrants occupying FRG embassy in Prague allowed to travel to the West
3-4 October	Riots in Dresden

6-7 October	Gorbachev visits GDR for 40th Anniversary celebrations; major demonstrations in GDR
9 October	First 'Monday demonstration' in Leipzig
18 October	Honecker stands down as chief of SED, succeeded by Krenz
18-24 October	CHOGM meeting in Kuala Lumpur
26 October	Douglas Hurd succeeds John Major as Foreign Secretary
2 November	Egon Krenz visits Moscow
7-8 November	Resignation of Cabinet and Politburo in GDR
9 November	New regulations in GDR permit private travel abroad. Mass crossings from East to West Berlin across the Wall.
10 November	Todor Zhivkov replaced as General Secretary of Bulgarian Communist Party
13 November	Mansion House speech by Mrs Thatcher
15-16 November	Douglas Hurd visits Bonn and Berlin
18 November	EC Heads of Government meeting, Paris
24 November	Thatcher/Bush meeting at Camp David
28 November	Chancellor Kohl announces Ten-Point programme in response to fall of Berlin Wall.
29 November	Baker announces four principles for German reunification at White House press conference
2-3 December	Bush/Gorbachev meeting in Valletta
3 December	Politburo and Central Committee of SED resign in GDR
4 December	NATO Heads of Government meeting in Brussels
5 December	Seiters/Modrow agreement makes two German states a single travel area
5 December	Unsuccessful leadership challenge to Mrs Thatcher by Sir Anthony Meyer
6 December	Resignation of Egon Krenz as head of GDR; Gorbachev/Mitterand meeting in Kiev
8 December	Communiqué of European Council meeting in Strasbourg reaffirms commitment to German self-determination within context of East-West cooperation and European integration.
11 December	Four-Power meeting in *Kommandatura* in Berlin
12 December	US Secretary of State Baker visits FRG and makes speech at Berlin Press Club
14-15 December	North Atlantic Council confirms Strasbourg Declaration
18 December	Shevardnadze meets EC Foreign Ministers in Brussels
19 December	Kohl visits Dresden
20-22 December	Mitterrand visits GDR
22-25 December	Revolution in Romania; execution of Nicolae and Elena Ceauşescu
29 December	Václav Havel elected President of Czechoslovakia

1990

4 January	Mitterrand/Kohl meeting at Latche
9-10 January	Kissinger talks in London with Hurd and Thatcher
20 January	Thatcher/Mitterand meeting in Paris
22-24 January	Hurd visits GDR
28 January	Modrow announces GDR election for 18 March
29-30 January	Hurd holds talks in Washington

31 January	Gorbachev publicly acknowledges German reunification will take place; Genscher makes speech at Tutzing Academy on how to reconcile a united Germany with NATO
2 February	Genscher visits Washington
2 February	President de Klerk of South Africa announces unbanning of ANC
6 February	Douglas Hurd visits Bonn; speech to Konrad Adenauer Foundation
7 February	CPSU votes to end Party monopoly on power in USSR
10-11 February	Kohl/Gorbachev talks in Moscow
11 February	Nelson Mandela released from prison
11-13 February	'Two Plus Four' framework agreed in margins of Open Skies conference in Ottawa
14 February	Thatcher/Genscher meeting in London
25 February	Bush/Kohl meeting at Camp David: they agree a united Germany should remain a full member of NATO
2 March	*Bundestag* declares there are no German claims on Polish territory
11 March	Lithuania declares independence from USSR
12 March	Hurd/Genscher meeting in Bonn
14 March	Two plus Four Political Directors meet in Paris
15 March	Gorbachev elected President of USSR
18 March	GDR elections: victory for CDU
24 March	Chequers Seminar with British and American historians
29-31 March	Königswinter Conference and British-German summit, Cambridge
31 March	'Poll tax' riot, Trafalgar Square
5 April	In GDR freely-elected *Volkskammer* meets for first time
12 April	Soviet admission of responsibility for Katyn massacre in 1940
4 May	President Bush outlines plans for review of NATO strategy
5 May	First Ministerial meeting of Two plus Four, Bonn
15 May	Hurd meets Genscher and Kohl in Bonn
16-19 May	US Secretary of State leads team in Moscow discussions
18 May	FRG-GDR treaty on monetary, economic and social union
22 May	Meeting of Western Political Directors, Bonn
	Meeting of Two plus Four Political Directors, Bonn
30 May-3 June	Gorbachev/Bush meeting in Washington
7 June	Warsaw Pact summit, Moscow
7-8 June	Meeting of NATO Foreign Ministers, Turnberry
8 June	Thatcher/Gorbachev meeting in Moscow
9 June	Meeting of Two plus Four Political Directors, East Berlin
20 June	Meeting of Two plus Four Political Directors, East Berlin
22 June	Second Ministerial Meeting of Two plus Four, East Berlin
1 July	German monetary, economic and social union
2 July	Gorbachev urges CPSU to pursue *Perestroika* or face 'dark times'
5-6 July	NATO summit, London
14 July	Nicholas Ridley resigns as Trade & Industry Secretary after anti-German remarks in the *Spectator*
	Kohl's visit to the Soviet Union; Gorbachev's acceptance of

15-16 July	German membership of NATO
17 July	Third Ministerial Meeting of Two plus Four, Paris
2 August	Iraq invades Kuwait
20 August	Collapse of de Maizière's coalition in GDR
23 August	GDR *Volkskammer* votes for German unity on 3 October
31 August	Unification Treaty between FRG and GDR
12 September	Fourth Ministerial Meeting of Two plus Four: Final Settlement on Germany signed
24 September	GDR withdraws formally from Warsaw Pact
26 September	US announces plans to withdraw 40,000 troops from Europe
3 October	GDR joins FRG
15 October	Gorbachev awarded Nobel Peace Prize
9 November	German-Soviet treaty
14 November	Treaty on German-Polish border
19-21 November	CSCE summit, Paris
19 November	Signature of CFE Treaty
2 December	*Bundestag* elections: victory for Kohl-Genscher coalition
9 December	Solidarity leader Lech Walesa wins landslide victory in Polish Presidential election

1991

15 March	Final Settlement comes into force

INDEX